JESSE LIBERTY'S
from scratch
PROGRAMMING SERIES

Java™ 2

from scratch

Steven Haines

201 West 103rd Street,
Indianapolis, Indiana 46290

Java™ 2 from Scratch

Copyright © 2000 by Que Corporation

International Standard Book Number: 0-7897-2173-2

Library of Congress Catalog Card Number: 99-63669

Printed in the United States of America

First Printing: October, 1999

01 00 99   4 3 2 1

Trademarks

Warning and Disclaimer

Executive Editor
Tracy Dunkelberger

Acquisitions Editor
Michelle Newcomb

Development Editor
Bryan Morgan

Managing Editor
Lisa Wilson

Project Editor
Tonya Simpson

Copy Editor
Margaret Berson

Indexer
Sandy Henselmeier

Proofreader
Benjamin Berg

Technical Editor
Charles Ashbacher

Novice Reviewer
Dallas Releford

Media Developer
Michael Hunter

Interior Design
Sandra Schroeder

Cover Design
Maureen McCarty

Copy Writer
Eric Borgert

Layout Technicians
Ayanna Lacey
Heather Hiatt Miller

Contents at a Glance

Contents

Foreword

Welcome to *Jesse Liberty's Programming From Scratch* series. I created this series because I believe that traditional primers do not meet the needs of every student. A typical introductory computer programming book teaches a series of skills in logical order and then, when you have mastered a topic, the book endeavors to show how the skills might be applied. This approach works very well for many people, but not for everyone.

I've taught programming to over 10,000 students: in small groups, large groups, and through the Internet. Many students have told me that they wish they could just sit down at the computer with an expert and work on a program together. Rather than being taught each skill step by step in a vacuum, they'd like to create a product and learn the necessary skills as they go.

From this idea was born the *Programming From Scratch* series. In each of these books, an industry expert will guide you through the design and implementation of a complex program, starting from scratch and teaching you the necessary skills as you go.

You may want to make a *From Scratch* book the first book you read on a subject, or you may prefer to read a more traditional primer first and then use one of these books as supplemental reading. Either approach can work: Which is better depends on your personal learning style.

All the *From Scratch* series books share a common commitment to showing you the entire development process, from the initial concept through implementation. We do not assume you know anything about programming: *From Scratch* means from the very beginning, with no prior assumptions.

Although I didn't write every book in the series, as series editor I have a powerful sense of personal responsibility for each one. I provide supporting material and a discussion group on my Web site (www.libertyassociates.com), and I encourage you to write to me at jliberty@libertyassociates.com if you have questions or concerns.

Thank you for considering this book.

Jesse Liberty

From Scratch Series Editor

About the Author

Steven Haines is a software engineer at Wonderware Corporation. He champions the Integrated Development Environment and internationalization efforts for a fully distributed COM-based architecture designed to be used by countless companies in the factory automation industry to provide complete factory solutions. Prior to that, he contributed his design skills and development knowledge to Engage Games Online, an Internet video game company, where among other things he developed their first full Java-based multiplayer game.

His publishing experience includes sharing author credits on Sams Publishing's *C++ Unleashed, Sams Teach Yourself C++ in 21 Days*, and *Sams Teach Yourself Java 2 in 21 Days*. He has worked as a technical editor and reviewer for both Macmillan Computer Publishing and Addison Wesley in the areas of Java, C++, game, and Internet communication programming.

His current explorations into Java technologies are into enterprisewide distributed architecture and design through the forthcoming release of the Java 2 SDK, Enterprise Edition and its corresponding components.

Dedication

This book is dedicated to Linda. You are my inspiration, my life, and my love. I know that I will succeed because you believe in me!

Acknowledgments

I would like to acknowledge the person who has supported me in my life and encouraged me to pursue my writing: namely, my mother, Elizabeth Haines. And as always, nothing in my life would be possible without God, thank you!

This book would not be possible without the help of the fine staff at Macmillan Computer Publishing. Specifically, I would like to thank Michelle Newcomb, Holly Allender, and Tracy Dunkelberger for giving me this opportunity. Thank you, Michelle; none of this would have been possible without you! I would also like to thank Bryan Morgan for the insight and assistance he offered while I was writing this book. I would like to thank my technical editor, Charles Ashbacher, for his quick turnarounds and insightful comments. I would like to thank Tonya Simpson and Margaret Berson for their tireless effort to refine this book! Finally, I would like to thank Jesse Liberty both for the contribution he has made to the publishing world as well as his support and trust in me.

I would like to thank my family and friends for their support while I was writing this book: Jessie Labayen (thanks for being my best man!); my wedding party: Mark An, Mario Riley, Alex Blank, and Yong Yong Heru; and my future brother in-laws, Wei Wei and Yong Yong (thanks for taking care of your sister while I was writing!). Thanks to Chris and Danielle Melby (sorry I couldn't help you move and for all the countless invitations I had to turn down). Thanks to Rashesh and Jyoti Mody for giving me opportunities both at Engage and Wonderware (Modys are great people to work for). Thanks to my ex-roommate Matt Torres for putting up with me for a year. Thanks to my friends at Wonderware: Robert Asis, Abhijit Manushree, Trevor Nguyen, and Brian Erickson. Thanks to my lunch group: Julie Lin and Raemonde Olson. Thanks to my Engage friends: Quang Pham, Scott Hartsman, and Gary McKensie. Thanks to the Canon folks: Bob Iwasaki, Saeed Shabazi, Chris Mangiapane, Jay Tadbiri, Kiyoshi Oka, Michael Le, Bao Vu, and Scott Phillips, and thanks to anyone I missed and everyone who has ever believed in me!

Finally, I would like to thank you, the reader, for adding this book to your bookshelf; grab a chair, a computer, a white board or two, and start learning Java!

Introduction

Why This Book?

So you're interested in learning Java? Glancing around you at all the other books on the shelf, you must be asking yourself what distinguishes this book from the plethora of other Java books. What makes one Java book better than another? What types of things should you look for in a programming book?

Let me address both of these questions in turn, and maybe I can help you choose the right Java book for you.

What Makes One Java Book Better Than Another?

Well, several things make one Java book better than another, actually. You must consider the content: Does the book have enough meat in it to allow you to learn the fundamentals of the language? Does it have all the latest buzz words listed on the cover? (Okay, at least make sure that it has some key points that you want to learn.) Does the book teach you or simply regurgitate the Java Developer's Kit documentation?

A good Java book should cover the fundamentals of the Java language: Java syntax, Abstract Window Toolkit (AWT), file I/O, user interaction, applets versus applications, and so on. It should explain the fundamentals of object-oriented design and its tools: objects, encapsulation, inheritance, polymorphism, Unified Modeling Language, Rational Rose. It should also address the latest in Java technology: Swing, Internet communication, 2D graphics libraries, RMI, JDBC, and JavaBeans.

What Types of Things Should You Look for in a Programming Book?

For any programming book, you must consider the approach: Does the book teach you in a way that is easy to learn? Can you sit down, read a chapter in the book, follow along, and then say to yourself, "Okay, I get it!"? You must consider the author's style: Does his writing style keep you interested or put you to sleep (remember, you are going to be with him for 500 pages)?

A good programming book will not only give you all the pertinent information about the subject, but will present it in a manner that will be conducive to learning and will maintain your interest.

I Think We Have a Winner!

Having said all that, I can assure you that I took each point into account when writing this book. This book provides a unique approach to learning a programming language. Most programming books start by teaching you simple skills and then showing you an example, teaching you some more skills and then showing you an example, teaching you... you get the point! After you learn a new topic, you get an example that demonstrates the topic, but is pretty much useless in the real world. This book, however, throws out this concept and builds one sample program throughout the entirety of the book. You will learn all the skills you will need to write Java programs, but you will learn them as you need them. The concept is to teach you Java by showing you how to write a full-blown Java application that you can actually use!

You will go through an entire project from design to implementation to testing and debugging techniques. You will be presented with the latest design methodology that is actually being used by major corporations: the Unified Modeling Language (class diagrams, use cases, sequence diagrams, and so on). When you have an application designed, you will learn how to use Java to realize your vision:

- You will learn the latest in Swing controls and event handling.
- You will learn all about Internet communication and how to programmatically retrieve the data that you need from a Web page.
- You will learn how to persist data to flat files and eventually to a database using JDBC.
- You will learn how to draw on the screen using the Java 2D graphics libraries.
- You will learn how to properly use multiple threads.
- And much more.

Throughout this experience, you will learn the syntax and semantics of the Java programming language, and most importantly, you will learn how to learn more Java on your own.

My Promise

A long time ago in a book far, far away, I was trying to learn Windows programming. I picked up a book that taught me how to write an application using Microsoft Visual Studio (or whatever it was called back then). The only thing I thought after reading that was, "Well, this is neat; I can write *that* application as many times as I want, but what about my own applications?"

When I was approached about this book, that thought leapt right into my mind. Well, I will make you this promise before you start reading: I will not only show you how to write *this* application—I will teach you how to write any Java application you could want. I will help you build a foundation in the Java programming language that you can use in researching new technologies and show you how I approach a new tool set or functionality that I want to add to my applications.

Conventions Used in This Book

The following are some of the unique features in this series.

 An icon in the margin indicates the use of a new term. New terms will appear in the paragraph in *italics*.

 How To Pronounce It—You'll see an icon set in the margin next to a box that contains a technical term and how it should be pronounced. For example, "`cin` is pronounced *see-in*, and `cout` is pronounced *see-out*."

RunIt An icon in the margin indicates code that can be entered, compiled, and run.

EXCURSION

What Is an Excursion?

Excursions are short diversions from the main topic being discussed, and they offer an opportunity to flesh out your understanding of a topic.

With a book of this type, a topic might be discussed in multiple places as a result of when and where we add functionality during application development. To help make this all clear, we've included a Concept Web that provides a graphical representation of how all the programming concepts relate to one another. You'll find it on the inside front cover of this book.

 Notes offer comments and asides about the topic at hand, as well as full explanations of certain concepts.

 Tips provide great shortcuts and hints on how to program in Java more effectively.

 Warnings help you avoid the pitfalls of programming, thus preventing you from making mistakes that will make your life miserable.

In addition, you'll find various typographic conventions throughout this book:

- Commands, variables, and other code appear in text in a special `computer font`.
- In this book, I build on existing listings as we examine code further. When I add new sections to existing code, you'll spot them in **`bold computer font`**.
- Placeholders in syntax descriptions appear in an *`italic computer font`* typeface. This indicates that you will replace the placeholder with the actual filename, parameter, or other element that it represents.

Chapter 1

Java Development Overview

Welcome to Java!

This chapter takes you through a brief overview of the Java language, including all the benefits of the language and the reasons why you would want to use Java. We'll talk a little about Java's history and then get up and running with your first Java application!

Why Java?

Why should you bother to learn Java? You might have heard some of the geeks in your office talking about Java, or maybe you are taking a Java class in school—or maybe you already know what Java is but aren't too sure why you would want to use it. No matter which category you fall in, let me tell you a little about Java.

Java is a truly object-oriented programming language. As such, it is highly suited for modeling the real world and solving real-world problems. It will adapt to the latest design methodologies, and it provides extensibility so that your large projects will be manageable.

Java is platform-independent: The same Java code will work on Microsoft Windows, UNIX, Apple Macintosh, Linux, Amiga, and any future whiz-bang operating system that implements a Java Virtual Machine.

Java can add interactivity to your Web pages: Java applets provide much of the functionality you are probably already familiar with, such as menus, data entry forms, and other user interface components, as well as some of the neat drawings and animated graphics that bless most Web pages.

With increasing CPU speeds, Java is becoming more competitive with platform-specific compilers for building applications.

Java's new Swing libraries rival the components you see in Microsoft Windows operating systems: tree controls, tab controls, list controls, tables, and so on.

Java has an incredible future in the upcoming decade! There is more and more talk about "intelligent devices" that will host a Java Virtual Machine that can run Java programs. These devices, such as smart toasters, smart televisions, and smart houses, will be networked together so that your television can tell your VCR to tell your toaster to start toasting! This is an exciting, evolving field in which Java technology is at the forefront.

Java has existed in its infancy for the past several years, demonstrating conceptual leaps and bounds and accomplishing the unthinkable. As Java evolves and matures, it is more and more apparent that it will become the prevalent development language of the future; learning Java will not only help you develop incredible applets and applications now, but it will prepare you for the future of computer and device programming.

Why Object-Oriented Development?

Let's take a trip back to the early '90s and see how software development worked in a procedural-programming world. In a procedural world, programs ran from top to bottom, branching to different functions and either manipulating global data or passing obscure structures back and forth between functions. Designs revolved around procedures and how to perform tasks. Data was manipulated by these procedures, but as soon as a different type of data was introduced, new procedures had to be created. Clever programmers soon learned how to modify their procedures to handle the new data. Add about four or five new data formats, and these modifications soon became what we in the programming world called hacks.

 A *hack* is something that programmers do to make their code perform functionality it was never designed to do. A hack will generally make some set of functionality work, but is not implemented correctly.

The long-term detriment of a hack is a lack of extensibility and future enhancement. Trying to build upon something that doesn't work right to begin with is a painful feat!

The end result was that projects were delivered late, with bugs, and were very difficult to maintain and extend beyond the intended functionality.

A *bug* is basically an error or problem in a program; *bugs* can be in the design of a project or the implementation. As you mature in your programming career, you will undoubtedly learn to despise and chase these annoying beasts that can disrupt your projects! The old programming rule states that you will spend 20% of your time writing 80% of your code and the other 80% trying to make it work right (fixing *bugs*).

A new approach was needed. When we look at the real world, do we look at data? In a way, however, we see books, we see cars, and we see all kinds of things. When we look at the real world, do we see procedures? Again, perhaps; however, we can think of reading a book and driving a car, but we wouldn't think of reading a car or driving a book. This abstraction is difficult; we have things and separate procedures that act on things. Now, how do we think of things in the real world? As just that: things, or objects. Think of a car and actions that you can perform on the car: You can turn the car on, you can drive the car, and you can fill up the gas tank. A coupling of things and related actions is natural in the real world.

This coupling of objects and their functionality is the basis for object-oriented development. Data (objects) and functionality (procedures) are grouped together such that if you have a car object, you will have its data: make, model, year, gas, speed, and so on, and you will have its methods: drive, fill up gas, accelerate, tune up, and so on, and those will be grouped together. In other words, anywhere your car data goes, your car methods go too.

Furthermore, when you think of a Porsche 911 and you think of a Porsche 944, do you think of these as completely separate objects, the same way you think of a book and a horse as separate objects? No, they are both cars! They both have four wheels, a body, and a steering wheel. They both accelerate, get gas, and are drivable. Do you think that a Porsche engineer created the 911 and then started over from scratch, forgetting everything he learned, and built the 944? No; the point is, if you create a car object, you can create both a Porsche 911 and a Porsche 944 using it as a template.

Benefits

Modeling your development projects after real-world models enhances extensibility (you can build a new car type from an old one) and maintainability (if there is something wrong with your car, you know exactly where to find the actions that operate on it). Object-oriented development, including object-oriented analysis (OOA), object-oriented design (OOD), and object-oriented programming (OOP), is a little more sophisticated and intricate than I have just described, but when you understand the reasons for the coupling of data and methods, the rest is just details.

Java History Lesson

Before we get started talking about the Java programming language, let me give you a short history of the language and the reasons for its inception. Back in 1991, a research group at Sun Microsystems that was part of their Green project was working to develop software to control consumer electronic devices. The goal was to develop a programming language that could be used to control and network "smart" devices, such as televisions, toasters, and even buildings. These devices would all coexist and could communicate with one another.

The first prototype that Sun Microsystems came out with was a device called the Star7—a device, similar to a remote control, that could communicate with other Star7 devices. The initial intent was to use C++ to control the Star7, but as the result of frustration with C++, James Gosling, a member of the Green project, developed a new language, called Oak, to control the Star7. Why Oak, you ask? The title came from a tree that James could see out of his window while developing the language! Sun later replaced the name Oak with Java because they found that Oak was already being used.

Anyway, as a result of Oak, or Java, being designed to run on small appliances, the language had certain inherent benefits to it:

- It had to be small to run on the limited memory of small appliances.
- It had to be efficient and reliable enough to function as a small appliance—we are all used to crashes using computers, but what if your microwave oven changed its power setting and caused your popcorn to catch fire?
- It had to be portable to run on different pieces of hardware.

So what happened to Java after that? To demonstrate the power of the Java programming language, in 1994, the Green project members developed a World Wide Web (WWW) browser completely in Java that could run Java applets, originally called WebRunner, but now known as HotJava. Java came alive however, in 1995 when Netscape licensed the Java programming language and included support for it in its Navigator product. And the rest, as they say, is history!

Java Versions

Sun has issued several releases of the Java language, but there are some significant milestones:

- Java 1.02—This was the initial version of Java that was adopted by Netscape Navigator and Microsoft Internet Explorer.

- Java 1.1.5—This early 1997 release added some improvements to the user interface and event handling.
- Java 1.2—This late 1997 release added significant improvements to the user interface and event handling, including their powerful Swing libraries.

What Is Java 2?

Now that I've shown you the different versions of Java that Sun has released, where does Java 2 fit in? Well, in December 1998, Sun announced the name "Java 2" for what was previously called the Java Developer's Kit (JDK) version 1.2. So just remember that anything that you see that says JDK 1.2 can now be replaced by the name "Java 2 SDK, Standard Edition, version 1.2 (J2SDK)." The latest version of the developer's kit, as of this writing, is 1.2.2.

So How Do I Get Started?

The Java 2 SDK, Standard Edition (version 1.2.1) is available at no charge on the Sun Microsystems World Wide Web page at `http://java.sun.com/products/ jdk/1.2`. Remember to check the Web site from time to time for updates and the latest news from Sun.

Aside from using the Java 2 SDK, you can also use several third-party tools to develop Java programs. Although the SDK provides the absolute standard for "Pure Java" and is always built to the latest standards, it does not include an integrated development environment (IDE) or a graphical debugger. You might find developing Java programs easier using one of the following tools:

- Inprise JBuilder
- Sybase PowerJ
- Symantex Visual Café
- NetBeans Developer
- Oracle JDeveloper

Don't worry, you can use the Java 2 SDK to develop all the applications in this book! All the code will be written to the "100% Pure Java" standard and will not rely, in any way, on any of the tools provided by any of the aforementioned vendors.

"100% Pure Java" is a certification that Sun has created to maintain the portability and integrity of products developed using the Java languages. In the words of Sun, "Some products that use the Java technology may run on some platforms but not others. The 100% Pure Java logo lets potential customers and end users know that the product bearing the logo is portable across all Java-compatible systems."

The 100% Pure Java initiative is important for the following reasons:

- Unites many operating systems with a common development platform, and opens up new markets and opportunities

- Ensures safe network delivery

- Streamlines software development and deployment

- Reduces product development cycles dramatically

See Sun's Web site for more information on the 100% Pure Java certification: http://java.sun.com/100percent.

Applet Versus Application

You might be more familiar with Java in the form of Java applets. Java applets are small applications that run in the context of a Web browser; you might have seen these in the form of drop-down menus, chat applications, and even full-fledged games. Java applets have helped revolutionize the World Wide Web as we know it!

Java, however, does have the capability to create applications: standalone programs that run through the use of an independent Java Virtual Machine, such as the one installed with the Java 2 SDK. These applications can have the same look and feel as the applications you are used to running (for example, Microsoft Word), the only difference being that you have to launch them through the Virtual Machine yourself.

A Java Virtual Machine (JVM) is the runtime environment that runs a Java applet/application. Your Java-enabled Web browsers (such as Microsoft Internet Explorer and Netscape Navigator) include a Java Virtual Machine for applets. One is also included with the Java 2 SDK for your application running outside the context of a browser.

Both applets and applications have their respective benefits and drawbacks. Applets can run in the context of a Web browser, making them accessible from anywhere in the world. Their integration with the Web browser allows them to take a certain amount of control and provide a truly powerful front end and navigator for your Web site. Applets also have the luxury of using their containing Web browser's user interface—a lot of functionality is provided for them. Applet technology is completely a Web technology at this point, but may be extended to smart devices in the future; that has not been clearly determined.

Applets are very powerful, but because of their public accessibility, especially in the context of a Web page, certain limitations are enforced. As a defense against potential malicious applets that may perform such actions as harming or retrieving files from the user's computer, Java has defined some strict security restrictions on applets:

- Applets cannot read or write files from or to a user's computer.
- Applets cannot launch any programs on the user's computer.
- Applets cannot communicate with any Web site other than the ones they are running on.

Applications, however, are not bound by these security restrictions; they can take complete control of the user's computer. Java applications run as would any application on a computer: They can read and write files, they can launch other applications, and they can do anything on a computer that they have privileges to do. The only limitation that Java applications face is that they cannot be embedded in a Web page and run in a browser. Programs can be written to function as both, but there is a problem with compatibility.

Notwithstanding the security restrictions imposed on applets, the substantial difference, in my humble opinion, between applets and applications is in the level of support for the Java SDK. Applet support in popular versions of Netscape Navigator and Microsoft Internet Explorer is limited to the Java SDK version 1.02. (Some of the newer browsers include a higher level of support for Java, but if you want to reach the majority of Internet users, you are only guaranteed support for version 1.02.) In other words, if you want your applet to work for everyone with a Java-enabled Web browser, you must conform to version 1.02 of the Java SDK. That might not sound bad from the offset, but the feature functionality added in the last few years (yes, it has been a few years since 1.02 was released) is substantial! There is no support for the new Swing libraries, the new 2D Graphics API, enhanced sound support, and so on; the list is long! In order to take advantage of the new features of the Java language, you must write Java applications.

The Stock Tracker Application

Before I start showing you what a Java application looks like, let me first describe the application we are going to develop throughout this book. We are going to develop a Java application that you can use to track your stocks. Take a look at Figure 1.1 for a sample screen shot of the Stock Tracker application in action.

An example of the Stock Tracker application in action.

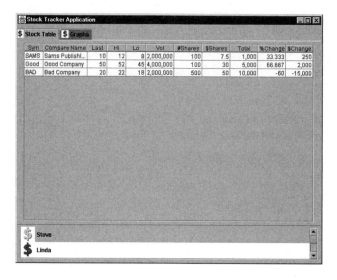

With this application you will be able to maintain multiple stock portfolios. Each portfolio will have a list of stock symbols for that user. The application will allow you to enter as many symbols as you want and an optional purchase price and number of shares that you own. It will display all this information along with the latest stock price and the day's high, low, and volume, and will compute your net gain or loss and percentage change. It will allow you to set up a timer for how often you want to retrieve quotes from the Internet (yes, this thing is going to be live... with a 20-minute delay) and even save historical data that you can plot in the graph tab (see Figure 1.2).

Figure 1.2

An example of the Stock Tracker application's graphing capability.

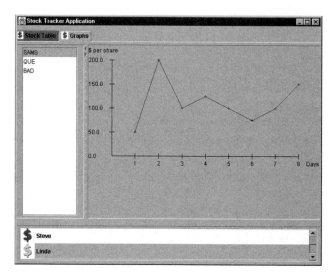

Furthermore, we are going to enhance the application with a little sound support, status updates, and keyboard mnemonics. We'll also discuss ways to persist data to a database and apply the latest in Java technology to the application.

As you can see, this isn't the traditional "Hello World" application! We are going to cover a lot of ground in this book—but don't worry, I will make it as simple and painless as possible.

Getting Up and Running

Before we start, you might want to refer to Appendix A, "Setting Up the Java 2 SDK," for installation instructions for your platform to get everything set up and ready to run.

Let's take a look at two of the files that are installed with the SDK in the `...\jdk1.2.1\bin` folder:

- javac—javac is the command-line compiler for Java programs.
- java—java is the application Virtual Machine that you will use to run your application.

**how tōo
prō nouns′ it**   *Javac* has two popular pronunciations: Java-C (java-cee) and Ja-vac (jaw-vac) as in Jaw and Vacuum.

Before I show you how to use these, let me tell you a little about how Java programs work. Java source files are text files with a `.java` extension written using the Java programming language. The javac compiler compiles the source file into something called *byte-code* and stores it in a `.class` file that matches the names of every class in the source file (note that your source files can contain multiple classes, but more on this later). *Java* is a Java Virtual Machine that knows how to process byte-code and execute your program.

Source files, also called *source code*, are text files that contain programming language statements. These are the files that you, as a programmer, will create.

Byte-code is the semicompiled source code that the Java Virtual Machine interprets to run your programs.

So the steps to build a Java application are as follows:

1. Create a text file containing your source code.
2. Save the file with the filename matching the public Java class implemented in the file and with a `.java` extension (more to come on public classes later).

3. Compile the file using `javac` to make your .class files.

4. Execute `java` with the name of your `main` class as the command-line parameter to run your application.

Now let's try an example!

Your First Java Application

I know that I said that we would be writing one single application throughout the entirety of the book, but what programming language primer would be complete without the inclusion of a "Hello World" example?

 If you are new to programming, you might not be familiar with the "Hello World" example. Back in the late 1970s, Brian W. Kernighan and Dennis M. Ritchie released a book called *The C Programming Language* that is legendary in the programming world. Anyway, the first program that they described in their book and what they noted was that the first program to write is the same for all languages: Print the words "hello, world". And since then, every programming book in the world (okay, there might be a few exceptions) starts out with a program that shows you how to print the words "hello, world" in the language it is describing.

Just so that I don't have to go back on my word, we will modify it a little bit. Our first application will write the words "Stock Tracker Application v1.0" on the screen (you can change it to "hello, world" if you really want to; I won't tell anyone).

Create a text file with your favorite editor (if you are running Windows 9x and don't have one, just use Notepad). Enter the text shown in Listing 1.1 (don't include the line numbers), and save it as `DemoOne.java` (or copy it from the CD in the Chapter 1 folder).

Listing 1.1 `DemoOne.java`

```
1: class DemoOne
2: {
3:     public static void main( String[] arguments )
4:     {
5:         System.out.println( "Stock Tracker Application v1.0" );
6:     }
7: }
```

 Note All the program listings in the book will have line numbers and colons before each line; these are not part of the Java programming language and should be omitted from your programs. They are simply there so that you can refer to specific lines in the programs later on in the discussion.

The next step is to compile this file. This is accomplished by following these steps:

1. Launch a command prompt (in Windows environments select the Start button, then Programs, and select either MS-DOS Prompt or Command Prompt).

2. Navigate to the folder in which you saved your Java source file. For example, if you saved the source file on your C: drive in your `Projects\Java` folder, you would type the following:

```
c:
cd Projects\Java
```

3. Finally, to compile the file, type the following:

```
javac DemoOne.java
```

If you receive an error informing you that the computer cannot find the `javac` file, you have not correctly set up your SDK paths; refer to Appendix A to learn how to resolve this. If you typed it correctly, you will not get any feedback from the compiler, just another prompt. Get a directory of the current folder (at a Windows command prompt, type `dir`), and you will see that the following file has been created:

```
DemoOne.class
```

Now you want to run this thing and see your "Hello, world" or "Stock Tracker Application v1.0."

At the command prompt, type the following command to launch the Java Virtual Machine and load the `DemoOne` class:

```
java DemoOne
```

If everything was successful, you should see the following output:

```
Stock Tracker Application v1.0
```

Now that wasn't so hard, was it? Oh, I should go through the application and let you know what is happening. Here goes:

```
1: class DemoOne
```

In Java programs, `.java` files are compiled into byte-code with a `.class` extension. You can think of `.class` files as the program itself. In this first line, a new class called `DemoOne` is being defined. You can create new classes by using the keyword `class` followed by a name for the class.

Lines 2 and 7, the { } pair, define the body of the `DemoOne` class. Everything that is included between lines 2 and 7 is part of the `DemoOne` class.

```
3:    public static void main( String[] arguments )
```

Line 3 defines a method, or function if you would prefer, that is a member of the DemoOne class called main. main is a very special function in Java, specifically for applications. main is the required entry point that the Java Runtime Engine (JRE), or java.exe, processes when it starts. When you typed

```
java DemoOne
```

you told the Java Runtime Engine to open the class file DemoOne.class and process the main function. Let me break down this function prototype for you a little.

```
public
```

The keyword public is known as an *access modifier*; an access modifier defines what can and cannot see this function (or variable). There are three possible values for access modifiers: public, protected, and private, each having its own restrictions. In this case, we are saying that this function, main, is publicly available to anyone who wants to call it. This is essential for the main function; otherwise, the Java Runtime Engine would not be able to access the function and hence could not launch our application.

The term *keyword* refers to specific words in a programming language that are reserved by the compiler to perform some specific functionality. When we get around to creating our own variables, one restriction on the naming is that we cannot use any of the keywords as variable names.

```
static
```

The static keyword tells the compiler that there is only one method (or variable) to be used for all instances of the class. For example, if you have 100 different copies of the DemoOne class running, there will be only one main function. This functionality will be explained in more detail later when you get a little more Java under your belt, but for now remember that main functions have to be static in a class.

```
void
```

The term void refers to the return type. Functions can return values: for example, integers, floating-point values, characters, strings, and more. If a function does not return any value, it is said to return void. So in this declaration we are saying that the main function does not return a value.

```
main
```

The word main is the name of the function. As I previously mentioned, main is a special function that you must define if you are writing a Java application. It is the entry point into your class that the Java Runtime Engine processes when it starts; it will control the flow of your program.

```
( String[] arguments )
```

Enclosed in parentheses next to the function name is the parameter list that is passed to the function. When you write a function, you can pass any type of data for that function to work with. In this case, the main function accepts an array of `String` objects that represent the command-line arguments the user entered when he launched the application.

 I used several new terms here; let me clarify them a bit for you.

A *string* is a collection of characters, similar to a sentence. The following are some examples of strings:

- "Hello, world"
- "Stock Tracker Application v1.0"
- null—this is the representation of an empty string, or one without any value

An *array* is an ordered collection of some data type and is denoted by the `[ ]` pair. When you define an array, as in this example of strings, you are setting aside enough storage space for a collection of elements. You can access array elements using the same `[ ]` notation and pass it the zero-based index of the data element.

To avoid getting ahead of myself, here is a small example that should clear this up for you.

If the user typed the following command line:

```
Java DemoOne one two three four
```

the command line would have four items sent to it: `one`, `two`, `three`, and `four`. The variable arguments would then contain an array of these four strings. Here is how that would be listed:

```
arguments[0] = "one"
```

```
arguments[1] = "two"
```

```
arguments[2] = "three"
```

```
arguments[3] = "four"
```

Note that the indexes (0, 1, 2, and 3) start at zero and climb up to one minus the total number of elements. This zero indexing is common to many programming languages, like C and C++, and programmers refer to the first element in an array as the "0-th element."

In this first example, the command-line arguments are ignored. Why would you want to send a program command-line arguments? There are many reasons, actually. Command-line arguments can be used to control the behavior of your program. You can define a debug mode for your program where you output more status information as the program is running (to help you find bugs); passing the command-line option -debug may denote this.

Note the minus sign before the word debug. Traditionally programmers have used two different symbols to denote command-line arguments: minus (-) and forward slash (/).

Aside from changing from a retail, or run mode, to a debug mode, command-line arguments can give a program additional information about what tasks to perform. For example, if you wanted to create your Stock Tracker application so that it connected to a specific Web site that you passed to it, you can enter the following:

```
java DemoOne http://www.pcquote.com
```

Then in your main function, you could connect to this Web site without involving the user.

The final popular use for command-line arguments is to automate your program. Several times in the past I wrote programs that provided a nice user interface and great functionality, but I wanted to make the program perform its functionality unattended. By using the command-line arguments, I told the program specifically what I wanted it to do.

Okay, now back to the program. Lines 4 and 6, the { } pair, denote the body of the main function; everything that is written between these braces is part of the main function.

```
5:        System.out.println( "Stock Tracker Application v1.0" );
```

This statement looks a little scary, but don't fret; it is not nearly as intimidating as it looks. Let's break this statement apart a bit.

```
System
```

System is actually a class that the Java language provides for you. This class is the focal point that you will use to access the standard input (keyboard), standard output (monitor), and standard error (usually a monitor unless you have a separate error output defined).

Whenever you have questions about a class, you can always refer to the Java SDK documentation. Here is what the Java 2 SDK documentation has to say about the System class:

"The System class contains several useful class fields and methods. It cannot be instantiated.

"Among the facilities provided by the System class are standard input, standard output, and error output streams; access to externally defined 'properties'; a means of loading files and libraries; and a utility method for quickly copying a portion of an array."

The System class has a collection of public properties, or data members, and a collection of public methods, or functions, that you can access in your program. You access these properties and methods by placing a period (.) after the class name System and then appending to it the method or property name. In this example, we are going to access the System class's out property.

```
out
```

The System class's out property is defined as follows:

```
public static final PrintStream out
```

As with the main function, it is both public, meaning that everyone can access it, and static, meaning that there is only one copy of it for all instances of the System class. The final keyword says that this variable cannot change in value.

As I already mentioned, the out variable represents the standard output device, typically the monitor. Note that the out variable is of type PrintStream.

The PrintSteam class contains a collection of print, println, and write functions that know how to print different types of variables: booleans, ints, floats, and so on; this is how println can print out so many different types of values.

Don't worry if some of these terms I am using are not familiar. I will talk more about the native data types in Java a little later, I promise!

Here is what the Java 2 SDK documentation has to say about the out member variable:

"The 'standard' output stream. This stream is already open and ready to accept output data. Typically this stream corresponds to display output or another output destination specified by the host environment or user."

```
println
```

Okay, finally we are down to the function that actually does all the work for us! `println` has multiple definitions, one for each of the native data types (`int`, `boolean`, `float`, `double`, `String`, and so on). The one that we are concerned with is declared as follows:

```
public void println(String x)
```

This version of the `println` function prints a `String` called "x", which is what you send it, to an output stream.

> Here is what the Java 2 SDK documentation has to say about the `println` member variable:
>
> "Print a `String` and then terminate the line. This method behaves as though it invokes `print(String)` and then `println()`."

You might have noticed that the `PrintStream` class has both `print` and `println` member functions. The only difference here has to do with the line termination. `print` simply prints text out to the screen, whereas `println` prints text to the screen followed by a new line character; this advances the cursor to the next line of the display.

```
"Stock Tracker Application v1.0"
```

Finally we have the text `String` that we are telling `println` to print to the standard output device. The text `String` is enclosed in parentheses and delimited by double quotes (" ").

Note that at the very end, the statement is terminated by a semicolon. This is very important in the Java programming language. All statements are terminated by a semicolon; this is how the Java compiler knows where one statement ends and the next begins.

Online Documentation

Before I close this chapter, I want to point you to the online reference that comes with the Java 2 SDK. Actually, if you download the SDK from the Internet, the documentation is included as a separate download on the same Web page. When you install the SDK, it will create a folder somewhere on your hard drive that is named `jdk1.2.1`. When you install the documentation, it will create a folder called `docs` in this folder and it will have a set of HTML documents (Hypertext Markup

Language), like Internet Web page documents, that contains a complete reference for each class included in the SDK. Using your favorite Web browser (for example, Netscape Navigator or Microsoft Internet Explorer), open the file `index.html` from the `docs` directory. You will see a page similar to Figure 1.3.

Figure 1.3

An example of the online documentation included with the Java 2 SDK.

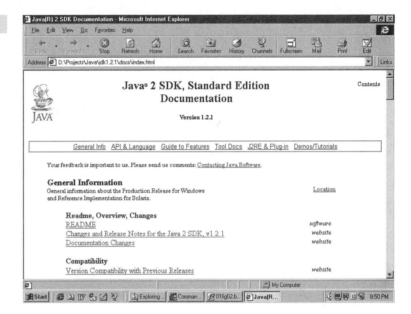

From this page, choose the link *Java 2 Platform API Specification*. This page will allow you to see all the classes and packages specified in the Java 2 SDK (see Figure 1.4 for a sample screen shot). Selecting one of these will give you all the methods and properties available to that class. Figure 1.5 has a sample screen shot of the `System` class that we talked about earlier.

Summary

We have covered a lot of ground in this chapter. We talked about this book and what you can expect to get out of it: a new approach to learning Java through a large and meaningful example. We talked about the benefits of using the Java language both now and in the future; we touched upon the benefits of using an object-oriented approach to developing our application (extensibility and maintainability). We discussed the difference between applets (programs that live in a Web browser) and applications (programs that run the same as any other application on your computer).

Figure 1.4

An example of the online documentation showing the searchable class list.

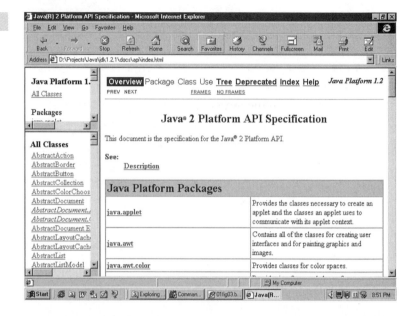

Figure 1.5

An example of the online documentation showing the System class.

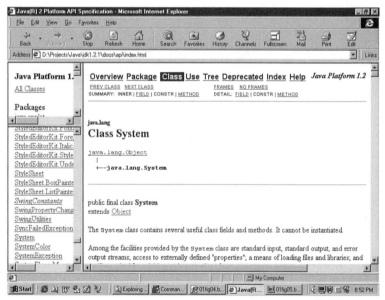

You were also given a brief history lesson in Java from its original inception as a programming language to control small consumer electronic devices to its current use as a platform-independent powerful development language.

We discussed the sample project for this book and all the neat things that you are going to be learning along the way. When we are finished with this book, you will have a fully functional Stock Tracker application that can retrieve stock quotes (20-minute delayed, of course, unless you want to subscribe to a real-time service), manage multiple portfolios, and graph performance information. Furthermore, you are going to learn all the intricacies of using the Swing libraries to develop an impressive user interface!

Finally, you wrote, compiled, and ran your first Java application. Furthermore, you learned a whole lot about how Java works internally from the in-depth discussion of a program as simple as the "Hello, world" example!

Next Steps

So what's next? We are going to start talking about design and the tools we use to design applications. I wanted to let you get your feet wet by writing a sample application before we started talking about design, but whenever you are going to write any major project, you must spend the preparation time designing it properly.

Grab a pad and pencil (maybe a white board or two), and let's get ready for the design phase!

Chapter 2

Design Fundamentals

Now that some of the fundamentals are out of the way, it is time to start on the main focus of this book: the Stock Tracker Application. By building a relatively large project throughout the book, you will learn not only the *syntax* and *semantics* of the Java programming language, but the entire project lifecycle from requirements to design to implementation and testing.

 Syntax, in simple terms, is the proper use of terms and punctuation.

 Semantics is the meaning and purpose of the code.

In this chapter, I hope to show you the benefits of requirements gathering, as well as the importance of a good up-front design. Then, I will show you some of the tools that are used for design and give you some examples that you will begin to apply to this project in the next chapter and that you will be able to apply to your own projects in the future.

When to Spend Time on Design

Some programmers spend an incredible amount of time designing their applications, but others spend no time at all. Which is right?

The answer is: It depends on the project. From my perspective and experience, design should always be performed. The only limiting factor is the amount of time spent on the design; the amount of time is directly related to the size of the project. Now, before you start shouting at me for the "Hello, world" program in the last chapter, I will concede that some programs are too simple to spend time designing. However, it is a good idea to sit down and at least figure out how you are going to write your program before you start writing it.

You might be unclear about what designing an application includes, but to make things simple, design includes figuring out how you are going to solve a problem before solving it. By designing a project, you will learn much more about it than if you were to sit down with an empty text editor and start coding.

Design has three important goals:

- Completeness
- Expandability
- Maintainability

Completeness

First, before you start writing your program, you must be sure that you have made provisions for all the program's requirements. Too often, when writing a program, you forget a feature or two and then when you finally realize it, your program has to be completely rewritten to support them. Take the case of writing a system to handle all the shipping needs for a small company. You sit down and write a program that can handle single items coming in one at a time along a conveyor belt, and you properly update the database to reflect the new quantities. You test this and everything works great. Later you find out that sometimes multiple items come along the conveyor belt together, side by side. Now, all the code you have written handles only single ordered items, not multiple items. You have a choice: You can order all the items (which may not be possible because a man puts all the items on the conveyor belt), or you can rewrite your program to synchronize multiple elements. If you had realized this in the beginning, the change could have been implemented without much difficulty or time, but now that you have everything written, you are either going to have to scrap everything and start over or rewrite all your functions that handle incoming items. So what would you gain by writing a complete design and thinking everything through in this case? Time!

Software engineering includes the concept that the later you catch a bug in the development lifecycle, the more time, and hence money, it takes to fix it. This makes a lot of sense. If you catch a problem when you are designing your project, you can simply change your design and continue—depending on the nature of the change, maybe several days to a week worth of work. Now, if you catch it after you have finished implementing the project, you not only have to modify the design, but potentially rewrite a large amount of your project. This could cause your schedule to slip and could cost a company a great amount of money.

Furthermore, if you find a problem after your project has been deployed and is being used by thousands of people who paid a great deal of money for the software, the repair work could destroy your company!

2

> Good designs and thinking through your project thoroughly will help eliminate many potential problems.

Expandability

Next, let's talk about expandability. I mentioned expandability in the last chapter, but expandability refers to the growth of an application beyond its original functionality after it has been implemented. This is important when you write very large-scale products that are going to be used in creative ways. Getting back to the shipping example, think about what would happen if a slightly larger company were going to use your application with multiple conveyor belts. Say, for example, they had two receiving docks that two trucks could pull up to and deliver merchandise. Now, you did not need to necessarily design in support for multiple conveyor belts, but if you designed the architecture of your shipping project such that it was componentized, you could simply create a new component that could plug right in to your existing architecture and handle the additional workload.

The current trend in the market today is to develop products using some form of component technology. Component technology, such as the Component Object Model (COM) or Common Object Request Broker Architecture (CORBA) , is a specification for creating the equivalent to binary classes. Binary means that the classes are already compiled (not source-code-like classes). The class-like binary files have interfaces that define methods, properties, and events. Methods are like functions, properties are like variables, and events are notifications that the components fire to their containing applications. Conceptually, the benefit to this type of architecture is that individual components can be upgraded and redeployed at runtime. This way, an end user of your product can get a simple one-file binary update that he can update on-the-fly and get new functionality.

Aside from the obvious benefit of only having to update individual components, a side benefit is that if you design your applications in components, the exercise of componentizing all your application's functionality gives you a greater understanding of your project and the problem you are trying to solve. Furthermore, componentizing your application lends itself nicely to distributing your application across various platforms on a network or the Internet.

The bottom line is that designing for future expandability is definitely a huge plus and something that all companies must incorporate if they want their current product to have any kind of shelf life.

Maintainability

Finally, let's talk about maintainability. A good design lends itself well to maintenance. Say, for example, you are having a problem in your shipping program where it is entering data for the wrong product codes. Now if you just wrote your program from start to finish without the forethought of design, you are in for a few weeks of sleepless nights. On the other hand, if you carefully designed your applications such that you had all the product code scanning handled by one component and all the data updating handled by another component, you know exactly where to look. Turn on some debugging in both of the components, and the problem should present itself quickly.

Also, some problems only seem to happen in the field (the end user's site), and trying to get the end user to set up an entire debugging environment is sometimes unreasonable. This is another instance where componentization can help greatly. You can send off both of the questionable components in a debug mode and have the user test those for you.

Requirements

I hope that you now see the benefits of a good design and are ready to get started, but before you can design your project, you must define its requirements.

A *requirement*, simply put, is something that your program must do. Requirements are compiled into a document or documents that define all the functionality of the program (or system). A requirement defines WHAT your program will do, but not HOW it will do it; design addresses HOW your program will implement the requirement. I will talk more about the requirements later in the iterative analysis section.

Design Methodologies

There are several trains of thought when it comes to design methodologies: the classic waterfall method and the new iterative process.

Waterfall Method

In the past, software engineers used a design methodology called the waterfall method. In this method, the software engineering lifecycle had very clear and distinct boundaries. Figure 2.1 shows a graphical representation of the waterfall method.

Figure 2.1

The classic waterfall method.

"Waterfall Model"

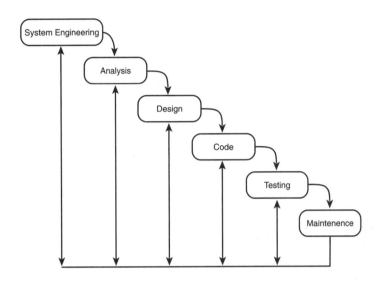

In the waterfall method, you can see distinct boundaries between systems engineering, analysis, design, code, testing, and maintenance. In this methodology, the output of one stage becomes the input for the next stage; for example, the output of analysis becomes the input for design. In this classic approach, the requirements are ALL defined in detail and cast in stone. The customer signs off on the requirements and agrees that the functionality in the requirements document is exactly everything he wants in the final product. The requirements document is then passed on to the designer, who designs the entire system and passes his design document to the implementer. The implementer simply implements the design as specified by the designer. When he is finished with the program, he hands it off to the Quality Assurance (QA) person, who tests the code and then releases it to the customer. This is theoretically a very good model. You and your customer completely agree on exactly what the program will include. The designer designs it, the implementer implements it, and the QA person tests it and ships it off to the customer. Nice, right?

Although theoretically sound, in practice this is a nightmare! We are not perfect and all make mistakes. Consider the case in which a requirement is defined wrong or is not conducive to a smart design. Now, if you catch it in the requirements phase, you are fine, but what happens if you catch it in the design phase or later? Furthermore, when are you most likely to catch it? In the requirements phase? No! You are probably going to catch requirements bugs in the design or implementation phase (when you really start looking at the application). The requirements document has been agreed to by both you and your client and is "cast in stone"; there is no going back. What do you do? Enter the iterative process of software design.

Iterative Process

The iterative process, as its name implies, is iterative, meaning that as you develop software, you go through the entire process repeatedly and try to enhance your understanding of the requirements. The basic concept is that when requirements are defined, a design is started. During the design phase, issues arise that require a modification and enhancement of the requirements. When you have a start on the design, you prototype parts of your project. During this prototyping phase, issues arise that affect the design and possibly even the requirements. This way, the development of a project occurs as it naturally would in practice. To describe the iterative process, here is a sequence of events that occurs throughout the process. Remember that these steps are repeated many times during the course of the development of a project.

1. Conceptualization
2. Analysis
3. Design
4. Implementation
5. Testing
6. Deployment

Note that the names for each of these stages are arbitrary; it is the meaning behind each that is important!

Conceptualization

At the beginning of the project, there is a visionary who is responsible for the project; he or she is the one with the main idea or, if the idea is built by a group of people, this is the one person given the responsibility of ensuring that the project adheres to the vision. This step always occurs in the development of any software project. In this chapter's example, I am the visionary who came up with the idea of a Stock Tracker application to track my stock purchases. Usually the conceptualization is presented in a single sentence or a short paragraph. An example of the vision for this project could be as simple as: "A Java application that can track my family's stock portfolios, get up-to-date information live from the Internet, and allow me to see a graphical representation of my stock's performance." It doesn't have to be difficult; you just need to understand, from a very high level, what it is that you want to accomplish.

Analysis

The analysis phase is the development of the vision into specific requirements. It is the understanding of the problem domain (all facets of the problem including hardware, software, existing networks, and any other factors that relate to the problem).

It involves writing down how the product will be used and how it must perform. There is a set of tools used to help you with these tasks, such as use case analysis and interaction diagrams (sequence diagrams and collaboration diagrams). The final result of the analysis phase includes the following:

- Use cases—Steps showing how the system will be used
- Domain analysis—The definition of the problem domain and the relationships between different domain objects
- Interaction diagrams—The interaction between different objects in the system
- Systems analysis—Hardware analysis documents
- Application analysis document—The customer's requirements specific to this project
- Operational constraint report—Defines performance constraints
- Cost and planning document—Scheduling, milestones, and costs

You might have noticed that I referred to the project as a *problem*; this wasn't a mistake, just some terminology. We refer to our project as a *problem* that we are trying to solve, which makes sense in many circumstances (implementing a new system to replace one that is already in place, but has limited functionality), and lends itself well even to a new project that has something it is trying to accomplish. Furthermore, you might have noticed the term *problem domain*; this refers to all aspects of the problem that you need to consider when deriving a solution. So from now on, if I talk about solving a problem or understanding the problem domain, just realize that I am referring to the vision or project that you are trying to implement.

As you can see, a lot of items are produced in a full-scale large project analysis; my goal here was not to confuse you, but to give you an idea about how much work can be done in the analysis phase. In this example, we are going to look at some of the more common analysis techniques: use cases and sequence diagrams. Even for a relatively small application, you want to understand how the application will be used and how different objects will interact with each another.

Design

Analysis focuses on understanding the problem, whereas design focuses on how to solve the problem. Design is the process of taking the requirements and generating a solution that can be developed in software.

The result of the design process is a design document. A design document defines three key points for your solution: the static class design, the dynamic class design, and the architectural mechanism design. The static class design defines the classes, their methods, and properties. The dynamic class design defines the interactivity between classes. The architectural mechanism design defines such properties of your system as object persistence and how the system will be distributed.

There are several different techniques you can use when performing the design phase of a project, but for this chapter's needs, it will be fairly simple. We will take the use cases and sequence diagrams and determine how to implement them in Java.

Implementation

When you have a design in place and understand how you are going to solve the problem, it's time to actually do the work; that is where the implementation stage comes in. This is the phase in which you will start writing Java code to prototype your designs and actually implement your solution.

Notice that I mentioned prototypes in the implementation phase; this is one of the areas that is different between the waterfall model and the iterative model. In the waterfall model, prototypes are created in the analysis and design phases, and the implementation phase is not started until the design is finalized. In the iterative model, the implementation phase can include prototyping, as when you start creating your prototypes, it will feed right back into the design and analysis.

Testing

After you have implemented something, you need to spend time testing and debugging it. The testing phase is very important to any software project because the integrity of the software must be maintained. In the waterfall model, testing is put off to the end such that the quality assurance department is forced to test the entire project in its complete state. Now the iterative approach allows for formal testing at every stage of the development process.

Deployment

When you have a releasable product, you can deploy it. Note that this may not be the final version of the software! You heard me right; you are releasing software that is not finished! Who would ever do that?

Okay, depending on the product, some may require that all the functionality exists in the product released to the end user, but usually this is considered the minimum set of functionality that will satisfy the user's needs. In some circumstances, companies will release products that establish a baseline of functionality that the user can work with to make it to the market in a timely manner, but they know perfectly well that they are going to enhance the product. Furthermore, most companies will tentatively plan the functionality of different versions of their software out over several years. I say tentatively because this is iterative; the feedback you receive from your customers will help you develop the functionality for the next version of your software!

2

Summary of Design Methodologies

So what have you learned about the iterative model of development?

You learned that you define your problem and problem domain. You analyze your problem, trying to determine what exactly you are going to try to solve, which may affect your understanding of the problem and cause you to redefine the problem. Next, you create a design for how you are going to solve the problem. During the design phase, you may uncover things that you didn't account for in your analysis or things that will enhance your analysis and potentially your understanding of the problem. When you have a good start on a design, you start prototyping your design (note, these prototypes may or may not be thrown out—some may make it to the final product). During this implementation phase, you may uncover facets of the design that have to change (and possibly analysis and problem understanding). When you have a set of code written, it is time to test it. The testing phase may cause alterations to the implementation, design, analysis, and problem understanding. Finally you deploy the product. When customers have your product in their hands, their feedback will help you define the functionality they like and dislike and what functionality you should add to future releases. Not only is this applicable to new release features, but may cause you to retest, reimplement, redesign, reanalyze, and (hopefully not) potentially change your understanding of the problem.

If I put this summary at the beginning of the chapter, I would have probably gotten some blank stares at the page, but I hope that after reading through the last few pages this is starting to make sense. There are many references on object-oriented design and the iterative model of software development. Take a look at your bookstore for books written by Grady Booch, Ivar Jacobson, and Jim Rumbaugh; they are among the pioneers of the iterative model and the modeling language that lends itself well to this type of development: the Unified Modeling Language, or UML.

Use Cases

Earlier, in the analysis and design discussions, I talked briefly about use cases, but now I want to spend some time showing you more specifically what use cases are, what they accomplish, what they look like, and how to use them in your own designs. To emphasize the importance of use cases, consider the fact that use cases drive the analysis, the design, the implementation, and the testing phase, and they aid in helping you identify your classes.

What Is a Use Case?

A use case, put simply, is a high-level definition of how a software product is going to be used. Usually you will sit down with a domain expert (a person who is an expert in the area you are developing software for) and discuss the potential ways that the software can be used. He will help you identify the actors, or people, that interact with your software (or entire system if you are responsible for more).

I used a few new terms in the preceding description. here are some formal definitions for you to refer to:

- Use case—A description of how the system will be used
- Domain expert—A person who has experience in the area you are creating the project for
- Actor—Any person or system that interacts with the system you are developing

What Do Use Cases Accomplish?

Why should you implement use cases? What is their benefit?

Not only are use cases a great place to start your analysis, they also provide you with a better understanding of your product. Think about designing an application without knowing how users are going to use it. This used to happen a lot in software development. People developed software without thinking about how it was going to be used, and they occasionally overlooked something and had to redesign after the product was implemented.

Use cases help you with your analysis and design. What about the other phases of the iterative model?

The testing phase is greatly aided by use cases. They give the quality assurance department concrete test cases that must work (because the software was written specifically to implement the use cases). It is a great starting point for testers!

How Do I Implement Use Cases?

The first step to using use cases is to identify the actors; note that actors can be people or can be other systems that interact with your system.

Let's consider the Stock Tracker as an example. In this project there will be users who tell the application what stock symbols to retrieve information about, what time intervals to check for stock quotes, and even request an instant stock quote lookup. The user is definitely an actor. Are there any other actors? Actually, yes there are. Consider the Internet site that the application is getting its stock information from. It will request a page from a Web server, which will either give you the page, give you an error, or time out. The server, therefore, becomes an actor in your system.

That is enough for now. You could continue searching for more actors and you might find some, but for the initial analysis, just consider the obvious ones.

2

The next step is to determine the first use cases. In this step you start to think about how the actors are going to interact with the system. In a large system, this can become very complex and cumbersome, but it is essential to the project.

Let's get back to the example. What kinds of things can the user do to the system?

- The user adds a new stock symbol.
- The user adds a new profile.
- The user requests a stock quote check.
- The user deletes a stock symbol.
- The user requests a three-month graph of a stock's performance.

These are but a few of the use cases to consider in the analysis of the system. As you can see, the use cases can get detailed, but they spell out pretty clearly what the system must do when it is complete.

How to Derive Use Cases

Some use cases will be obvious; in our example, determining that a user must be able to add a new stock symbol to a stock tracking application is pretty brain-dead, but others may be more difficult to derive. To help you with this, ask yourself the following questions, which can give you more insight into use cases:

- Why is the actor using the system?
- What type of response does the actor expect from each action?
- What must the actor do to use the system?
- What happened to cause the actor to use the system?
- What information must the actor give the system?
- What information does the actor want from the system?

These are a handful of questions that you should consider when deriving your use cases.

What Do Use Cases Look Like?

Before I close out this discussion on use cases, I want to show you what a typical use case will look like (yes, there is a standard form). A use case is composed of the following information:

- Use case—Sentence or two describing the use case itself.
- Scenario—Specific set of circumstances that define the different actions that can occur during this use case; this may include several different scenarios for one use case.

- Preconditions—What must be true for the scenario to begin.
- Triggers—What causes the scenario to begin.
- Description—A detailed description of each scenario, describing what actions the actors take, what results or changes are caused by the system, what information is provided to the actors, how scenarios end, a logical layout of the flow of the scenario, and what causes the scenario to end.
- Post Conditions—What must be true when the scenario is complete.

So for our example of a user adding a new stock symbol, the use case may look like this:

Use Case:

User adds a new stock symbol.

Scenario:

The user successfully adds a new stock symbol to track in his portfolio.

Preconditions:

1. The user has launched the Stock Tracker application.
2. The user has selected his portfolio.

Triggers:

The user clicks in an empty row in the table.

Description:

The user clicks on the symbol column of an empty row in the stock table and enters a symbol. The program instantly fetches the pricing information from the Internet and updates the display.

Post Conditions:

The stock table displays the new stock symbol and it is added to the user's portfolio.

Now you can see that for this use case, we are assuming that the Stock Tracker application is running and that the user has selected his portfolio. The use case begins when the user clicks in the symbol column of an empty row and types in a ticker symbol. The use case includes retrieving data from the Internet and updating the display (creating a new row). One more thing to note is that when the use case is complete, the user's portfolio has been updated, so that must also be included! There, I told you this stuff wasn't that hard. It is just a formal way of doing something that is natural.

A use case can also be displayed in a graphical form, referred to as a use case diagram. Figure 2.2 shows a simple use case diagram for our use case of a user adding a new stock symbol.

Figure 2.2

A very simplistic use case diagram.

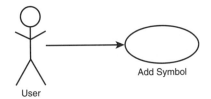

As you can see, there is not much to learn from this type of use case diagram. The only time use case diagrams get a little more interesting is when one use case has some kind of relationship with another use case. For example, say there is a use case that checks the current portfolio for the symbol you are trying to add before adding it. This relationship between the two use cases can be represented graphically. There are two types of relationships that can exist between use cases: <<uses>> and <<extends>>. <<uses>> proclaims that one use case includes the behavior of the other use case. In other words, it is impossible to add a new stock symbol until you have checked to see if it is already there. <<extends>> is a bit unclear and not really used much in practice—it refers to an inheritance type relationship (I'll talk more about inheritance later), but because of the confusion in the industry about the distinction between <<uses>> and <<extends>>, it is rarely used. See Figure 2.3 for an example of the <<uses>> relationship.

Figure 2.3

A use case diagram demonstrating a <<uses>> relationship.

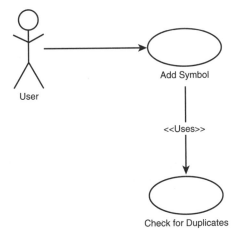

Class Diagrams

After you have gone through your preliminary use cases, it is a good time to start identifying classes and objects. Now the distinction between classes and objects is an important one during design. An object has three characteristics: state, behavior, and identity. An object's *state* represents one of the possible conditions that it can exist in; states are represented by a set of properties, for example, a car can be running or stopped. It also describes what types of relationships the object can have with other objects. The behavior represents how the object will respond to requests from other objects; behaviors are represented by a set of operations (methods). Finally, an object's identity simply provides a unique way of identifying this object: for example, a name.

An *object* is made up of three characteristics:

- State
- Behavior
- Identity

A class, on the other hand, is an abstraction of an object. Classes are a description of a group of objects with common attributes (attributes), common operations (behaviors), common relationships with other objects, and common semantics. In other words, a class is a template for building objects. An object is an item, or instance, of the class.

The goal in deriving class diagrams is to identify the classes in your system (or project). Use cases are a great place to start identifying classes. There is no fixed method to identifying classes. As a matter of fact, Grady Booch, one of the originators of this methodology, once said, "This is hard!" Another thing to remember is that when you are finding classes, you are still working under the iterative design, so these classes will be refined as the project matures.

Okay, now that you have a little bit of an idea about what classes are, let's forego any more theory about classes and look at our use case and see if we can identify some!

First, take the user: Is he a class? He interacts with the system, but he is not a piece of software that we can control, so he must not be a class. Next, let's look at how the user interacts with the system: He clicks in an empty cell in the table. Can the table be a class? This question is subjective; it may or may not be depending on your interpretation of the system. I am going to call it a class.

Let's describe the table. Its properties include all the current stock symbols and user settings it received from the portfolio and all the stock pricing information it received from the Internet.

What kind of relationships does it have? Well, it has to interact with the user to get input, it has to interact with the profiles to get stock symbols, and it has to interact with the Internet to get stock quotes.

How does it respond to other objects' requests? What kind of actions could other objects ask the table to do? When the application is closing, the portfolio could ask the table for the current stock symbols, and the stock history object (that will feed data to the graph later) could ask it for the current prices. The main user interface could ask it to update its stock prices.

Finally, what about its identity? Should we name it Bob? Okay, let's call it `StockTable` (I know, not too original, but a little more descriptive than Bob!).

Now let's make a class diagram from this class. Class diagrams are pretty easy; you just draw a vertical rectangle divided into three sections. The top section is the name of the class, the middle section is a collection of the class's properties, and the bottom section is a collection of the class's methods. See Figure 2.4 for a sample class diagram for the `StockTable` class.

Figure 2.4

A sample class diagram.

 Note

You might notice that next to each property of the class and next to half of the methods there is a little lock. This is the notation that Rational Rose uses to denote that a property or method is private (or not accessible to objects or classes outside of the class). In all cases, properties should be private. (You don't want anyone changing the values of your properties without you knowing and verifying that the values are valid—this is known as encapsulation or data hiding. We'll talk more about that later.) In this case, three methods are private: `GetStockQuoteFromInternet()`, `GetNewStockSymbol()`, and `LoadStockSymbolFromProfile()`. These methods represent methods that the class will call internally to get information for the table—they are not accessible to external classes.

`UpdatePrices()`, `GetStockSymbols()`, and `GetPrices()` however, are public and accessible from external classes. The user interface may call `UpdatePrices()` to tell the table to get information from the Internet, the profile manager may call `GetStockSymbols()` to get all the updated stock symbols, and the historian may call `GetPrices()` to get the price to record for later use.

The methods that are public in a class are sometimes referred to as the class's *public interface*. A *public interface* represents all functions that anyone can call in your class (this is how other classes control or use your class).

Interaction Diagrams

So you have your use case written and you have your class diagrams built; now what do you do with them? You should do at least one more thing before writing code. Figure out who needs to be involved and who has what responsibilities. One method of describing the interaction of classes is to use interaction diagrams. Interaction diagrams show a graphical representation of a scenario. There are two types of interaction diagrams: sequence diagrams and collaboration diagrams.

Sequence diagrams show object interactions organized by time, and *collaboration diagrams* show object interactions organized by an object's connections and links to other objects. Typically, collaboration diagrams are used when a visual representation of the relative locations of objects is important, for example when laying out a plant design. Sequence diagrams are used pretty much everywhere else. Sequence diagrams and collaboration diagrams are almost completely interchangeable, so when you know one, you don't really need to learn the other. I decided to show you sequence diagrams simply because throughout my years of experience, sequence diagrams are the most common.

Sequence Diagrams

As I said earlier, sequence diagrams represent object interaction based on time. Therefore, you must figure out what happens in what order. Sequence diagrams are fairly self-explanatory, so take a look at Figure 2.5 (don't worry, there will be an explanation at the end).

There are column headers that represent the actor (User) and all the classes that the actor is going to interact with (StockTable, InternetManager, and ProfileManager). Each action is ordered and numbered such that the order can be easily extracted. Time increases as you read down the diagram, so you may not always see numbered sequence diagrams. The order is implied simply by the order actions are listed in. As you can see, arrows can point both ways, showing that interaction can occur in both directions.

Let me walk you through this sequence diagram:

1. The user clicks on a cell in an empty row in the table.
2. The StockTable makes the cell editable.
3. The user types in a stock symbol.

Figure 2.5

A sample sequence diagram.

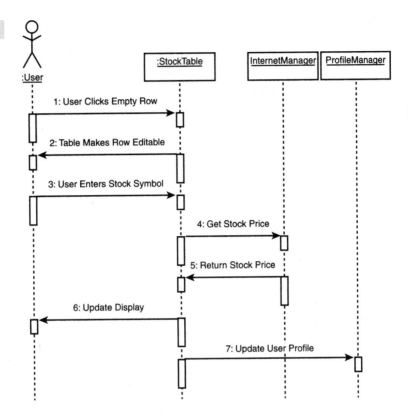

4. The StockTable asks the InternetManager to look up the stock price on the Internet.

5. The InternetManager returns the stock price to the StockTable.

6. The StockTable updates its display. Note that this could either be an arrow back to the user (as it is), or it could be an arrow back to itself, showing that it is affecting itself—either would be fine.

7. The StockTable tells the ProfileManager to update the user profile to reflect the new stock symbol.

Now, you might be asking yourself some questions about some of the details. For example, how does the InternetManager get the latest stock price and how does the ProfileManager update the user profile? These questions would be answered in the use cases and the sequence diagrams for those specific questions. In the InternetManager question, the sequence diagram probably would not even include the request from the StockTable; it would simply show how it gets its information from the Internet. After all, it doesn't care who calls its GetStockPrice() function!

One point to note is that we have not included error conditions in our sequence diagram. This means that you will want to either spell out the conditions in your explanation of the sequence diagram or generate separate sequence diagrams depicting error conditions. An error in this context could be an invalid stock symbol or a bad Internet connection—in any case, you will want to specify how these conditions are addressed.

User Interface Design

Understanding the system design is important, but there is another important design decision, the user interface. Chapter 4, "User Interface Design with AWT," and Chapter 5, "User Interface Design with Swing" delve into the design of a user interface in Java, but there are two things to think about in general user interface design. These key components are usability (screen layout, intuitiveness, and so on) and understanding your user.

The usability of your application has been very involved in the past, but the good news is that it is getting easier now! I don't know how long you have been using computers, but you may recall that back in the 1980s we had a plethora of complicated word processors. One of the major players back then was WordPerfect. People who knew how to use WordPerfect well could do almost anything with it and do it quickly, but because of its cryptic keyboard commands the average person could not figure out how to type his own name! Now this type of user interface could be considered good or bad depending on who you talked to. The question of intuitiveness was very difficult to determine.

What is intuitive to someone who has very limited exposure to computers? That, my friend, is a very difficult question. Something is only intuitive to someone when they have some point of reference to compare it to something they understand. This is the reason we kept seeing computer speakerphones that looked like regular speakerphones and an audio rack that looks like a stereo system. That can definitely be considered intuitive, but is it usable? To the novice user, yes, but to the expert user, probably not. What to do?

Well, now that more and more users are becoming familiar with computers and using them more commonly in their everyday lives, you can start to assume some user interface guidelines. This is one area that Microsoft has excelled in. All the interfaces for all its applications have a similar look and feel. You might argue whether or not the Find command should be in an Edit menu, but you know that it is there—and it will be there in all Microsoft applications and all applications that have a Windows 9x logo! Microsoft has even released a book of software design guidelines, *The Windows Interface Guidelines for Software Design*, that explains its standards in detail. So the bottom line is that if your users are not familiar with your user interface and have to learn it, they can take what they learn and apply it to a horde of other software. Standards, standards, standards: That is the name of the game!

Finally, you must understand your user when designing your user interface. Think about who you are marketing your software to. Who will be using it? What role will they take using your software? Is your software going to play a key role in their profession, or is it going to be something that they occasionally use simply to accomplish a set task?

If a user is using your software as a key part of their job—for example, consider an accountant using an accounting software package—he will want a user interface laced with a lot of features and shortcuts to accomplish his tasks faster. He will spend the time to learn your software and learn it well! Your job is to create the user interface in such a way that he can accomplish his job quickly and accurately—he won't want to be slowed down by involved wizards and features accessible only from menus.

Now consider the other side of the equation. Consider the same accountant using say, a stock tracking application. He has an interest in the stock market, but it is not his livelihood. He may check his stocks in the morning when he gets in and in the afternoon when the market closes. Is he going to spend the time to learn a cryptic user interface? Does he want any advanced "power user" features? I would say no! He wants a simple user interface that he can easily navigate to accomplish his task. He does not want to spend time learning your user interface, so it should be intuitive; I would venture to say that if your interface is too difficult, he would probably choose a different package—there go the royalties! This is the type of user who would appreciate a big button that launches a wizard that guides him through adding a new stock symbol.

The bottom line here is: Know your user! When you are writing software, you don't always know who is going to use your software, but you should have a very good idea! Think about the stock tracker software. Is the previous user I described typical of who will use the software? Do you think that a stockbroker would use it? I think our user interface is going to have to be simple and easy to use, without a lot of "power user" features.

The term *power user* refers to an expert user who has a great amount of knowledge in either the domain of your software or in software in general. This type of person is going to understand almost everything and want additional cryptic features.

Summary

You can pat yourself on the back; you have learned a lot in this chapter! You learned a lot about analysis and design. You learned why they are important in a software project: to enhance completeness, expandability, and maintainability, as well as to help you meet your deadlines. You learned the steps you have to perform in each. Furthermore, you have learned how to organize your thoughts into use cases, how to develop classes from them, and finally how to display them in sequence diagrams. You have now been exposed to all the popular professional analysis and design methods and should have a good theoretical understanding of them.

This is a good place to point out that all the diagrams I have shown in the chapter have been made using Rational Rose, a software package written by Rational Software that is used specifically to develop models of the Unified Modeling Language components. Furthermore, Rational Rose allows you to do far more than simply draw diagrams; it allows you to organize your classes, your relationships, and your entire project. It is a great tool, but a little complicated to learn. If you are interested in learning more about UML and Rational Rose, you can get more information and download a trial version from Rational Software's Web site at http://www.rational.com.

What's Next?

Now that you have these tools under your belt, the next step is to do something meaningful with them. In the next chapter, you are going to take what you have learned here and apply it to the design of the stock tracker application. Don't worry, we will cover a great amount of design work, but I will try not to overwhelm you with too many details.

Chapter 3

Designing the Stock Tracker Application

By now, your head is filled with all the tools you need to do some serious work! I know that the last chapter was a bit deep, but I tried to give you enough information to understand everything without confusing you too much. If you didn't quite get everything, don't fret; the answers are coming! Before you could go through the design of an entire application, you needed to understand the terminology and get your feet a little wet in all areas. I could have tried to explain all this as it came up, but that would have probably been more confusing; in addition, now you have a decent reference on iterative design that you can refer back to later.

In this chapter, we are going to design the Stock Tracker application itself, so you will be able to apply all that you learned in the last chapter. We'll start out defining the vision, and then move into the analysis through high-level use cases. Next, you will see if you can identify the major classes and touch a little on their interdependencies. Throughout the rest of the book, you will refer to these class diagrams and build sequence diagrams to expand on the functionality you are implementing in the chapter at hand.

 Note   All the figures in this chapter are created using Rational Rose. You can obtain a trial version at http://www.rational.com.

Let's get started!

The Vision

Every project has a visionary, a person with a great idea; this is the person who is responsible for ensuring that the vision is adhered to throughout the life of the project. When you are writing your own small programs, you are the visionary, but be sure to go through this exercise anyway. Too often when developing software, we forget, or should I say embellish upon, the initial concept and end up with something that was not quite our initial intention. By simply writing down, in a concise manner, what you are trying to accomplish, and occasionally referring to it throughout the project, you can ensure that you maintain the integrity of the vision.

I already mentioned that we want to write a stock tracker application, but what are the key features that we need in it to call it complete? Here are the major features that I envision when I think of a stock tracker application:

- Tracks stock symbols for all major markets
- Allows the user to enter the number of shares owned and price paid per share or none
- Maintains multiple profiles (such as for me, my wife, and so on)
- Retrieves current information from the Internet at a selected time interval or on demand
- Has the capability to retrieve historical stock quotes from the Internet
- Provides a graphical representation of a stock's performance
- Persists current stock information for later retrieval
- Displays a total or summary of all stock positions
- Supports data exchange in the form of comma-separated variable (CSV) files (import and export)

 The term *CSV*, or *comma-separated variable*, file refers to a universal file format understandable by spreadsheet programs. If you can import and export CSV files, your program will be able to exchange data with virtually any other spreadsheet or database program (a nice feature to have). One word of caution: Although the name "comma-separated" sounds as if the separators are commas, they are not always; it is dependent on the platform—more on that later.

That is quite a list, and a little too much to keep referring to. Let's see if we can come up with a short paragraph that encapsulates all these features:

A stock-tracking application for all major stock markets that maintains multiple user profiles, user purchase information, and computes a summary of user positions. The application is linked to an Internet stock server. Extended capability includes timer-based or on-demand quote updates, the retrieval of historical stock quotes, and CSV import and export.

There it is: everything that we are going to do in this book, in two short sentences. We'll develop this idea further and see what we can come up with.

Brainstorming

In the last chapter, I introduced the concept of a "use case." Writing use cases does not seem that difficult, and it is not. One problem you can encounter, though, is where to start. Let's break it down into three key areas that you want to think about when creating use cases: key features, startup, and shutdown.

I usually start with key features, but after I finish them, I pay particular attention to startup and shutdown. They always seem to give you a whole lot of information that you might otherwise overlook: persistence, startup order of events, and shutdown order of events. Typically, I will uncover a horde of other use cases when I think about all that I have to do when loading the application.

What are the main features of the application?

- Stock tracking—Adding a new stock symbol to a portfolio, deleting a stock symbol from a portfolio
- Computing summary—Computing the user's total dollar and percentage gain or loss
- Internet access—Downloading quotes from the Internet
- Historical information—Retrieving historical information from the Internet, persisting historical information
- HTML parsing—Retrieving stock quotes from a raw HTML page
- Timer mechanism—Updating quotes on a specific interval
- Portfolio management—Adding a portfolio, deleting a portfolio, persisting portfolios
- Graphing—Graphing stock information at variable time intervals (one week, one month, three months, and so on)
- CSV—Importing and exporting

 HTML refers to *Hypertext Markup Language*, or the markup language used on Web pages. Basically it is a markup language that enables you to format text (bold, italic, and so on), create controls (buttons, text fields, and so on), and process forms. It enables you to do most of the simple things that you see on Web pages right now. I will talk more about HTML in depth in Chapter 9, "Implementing the Stock Quote Retriever," when I get to downloading a Web page from the Internet and extracting information from it.

Now, what does the application have to do on startup?

- Open the file with portfolios
- Add an entry for each portfolio
- Load the stock symbols for each portfolio
- Attempt to connect to the Internet and retrieve the latest stock prices

Finally, what does the application have to do on shutdown?

- Check for any changes to a portfolio and prompt the user to save
- Save the latest stock prices retrieved
- Persist historical information (if it is enabled)
- Close any active Internet connections

This list is by no means exhaustive, but it is a very good start! Now let's write up some use cases for these features.

Developing Use Cases

Before we write formal use cases that include scenarios, preconditions, triggers, descriptions, and post conditions, let's just write the use cases themselves. I'll elaborate more in the next section. I'll go through each of the categories in the last section in order.

Main Features

The following sections represent the list of use cases defined by topic.

Stock Tracking

What should the application be able to do regarding stock tracking?

1. Add a new stock symbol to a portfolio.
2. Delete a stock symbol from a portfolio.
3. Enable historical tracking for a stock symbol.

Computing Summary

What is the responsibility of the Summary component?

1. Calculate the total dollar gain/loss from a portfolio's stocks.
2. Calculate the total percentage gain/loss from a portfolio's stocks.

Internet Access

What does the application need to do with the Internet?

1. Download a Web page for a stock symbol from the Internet.
2. Retrieve the stock price information from the Web page.

Historical Information

What type of features should the application include regarding the Historical Information?

1. Download a stock quote for a time other than today.
2. Download a range of stock quotes.
3. Save historical information to a data file.
4. Load historical information from a data file.

HTML Parsing

The HTML Parsing category will be responsible for taking an HTML page and retrieving information from it.

1. Retrieve stock prices from an HTML page.

Timer Mechanism

The Timer will be responsible for initiating a download request at a specific time interval.

1. Set a timer to retrieve stock quotes at a specific interval.
2. Retrieve stock quotes at the set interval.

Portfolio Management

The Portfolio Manager will be responsible for managing all interactions with the portfolios.

1. Add a portfolio.
2. Delete a portfolio.
3. Save a portfolio.
4. Load a portfolio.

Graphing

The Graphing component will be responsible for graphing a stock's performance on a given scale.

1. Set graphing time scale.
2. Graph stock performance points.

When we refer to the units in a graph collectively, we refer to them as a *scale*. A scale can be, for example, 0 to 100 or 57.1 to 62.5; it is all relative to the data points you want to plot. See Figure 3.1 for an example of a scale.

Figure 3.1

Price scale and time scale example.

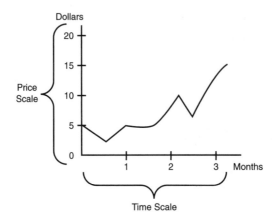

CSV Data Exchange

What type of data do you want to be able to import and export in CSV format? The main benefit for this type of activity is going to occur with historical data and entire portfolios.

1. Import historical data from a CSV file.
2. Export historical data to a CSV file.
3. Import a portfolio from a CSV file.
4. Export a portfolio to a CSV file.

Startup

What activities does the application need to perform during startup?

1. Load all portfolios.
2. Update the user interface portfolio list box.
3. Get stock quotes for portfolios.

I trimmed this down a bit—I'm going for clarity and conciseness in this part of the exercise.

Shutdown

Finally, what happens when the application shuts down?

1. Save portfolios.

2. Save current stock prices.

3. Save historical information.

4. Close active Internet connections.

Refining Use Cases

There you have it: an initial collection of use cases. Now let's build "real" use cases from them and determine what each use case entails from preconditions and triggers to a detailed description and the post conditions.

Main Features

The following sections list the use cases defined by topic.

Stock Tracking

The stock-tracking-related use cases are defined in the following sections.

Use Case #1: Add a New Stock Symbol to a Portfolio

Use Case:

Add a new stock symbol to a portfolio.

Scenario(s):

1. The user successfully adds a new stock symbol to track in his portfolio.

2. The user fails to add the new stock symbol to his portfolio due to a duplicate entry.

Preconditions:

1. The user has launched the Stock Tracker application.

2. The user has selected his portfolio.

Triggers:

The user clicks in an empty row in the table.

Description:

Scenario 1:

1. The user clicks on the symbol column of an empty row in the stock table.
2. The user enters a stock symbol.
3. The user's portfolio is checked for a duplicate entry.
4. The program instantly fetches the pricing information from the Internet and updates the display.

Scenario 2:

1. The user clicks on the symbol column of an empty row in the stock table.
2. The user enters a stock symbol.
3. The user's portfolio is checked for a duplicate entry.
4. The user already has this stock symbol, so the transaction is denied.

Post Conditions:

The stock table displays the new stock symbol, and it is added to the user's portfolio.

Note This use case has two scenarios, one in which the user is successful and one in which the user is not successful. It is important to add these additional scenarios to your use cases so that you will remember to respond to problems as they occur.

Use Case #2: Delete a Stock Symbol from a Portfolio

Use Case:

Delete a stock symbol from a portfolio.

Scenario(s):

The user successfully removes a stock symbol from his portfolio.

Preconditions:

1. The user has launched the Stock Tracker application.
2. The user has selected his portfolio.

Triggers:

The user selects a stock and chooses Delete from the Edit menu.

Description:

1. The user selects a stock by clicking anywhere on its row.

2. The user chooses Delete from the Edit menu.

3. The stock symbol is deleted from the display table.

4. The stock symbol is removed from the user's portfolio.

Post Conditions:

The user's portfolio no longer contains the deleted stock symbol and the display no longer shows the deleted stock symbol. Historical data is not deleted.

Use Case #3: Enable Historical Tracking for a Stock Symbol

Use Case:

Enable historical tracking for a stock symbol.

Scenario(s):

The user successfully enables historical tracking for a stock symbol.

Preconditions:

1. The user has launched the Stock Tracker application.

2. The user has selected his portfolio.

3. The user has selected a stock row.

Triggers:

1. The user clicks the Historical Tracking check box for the stock's row.

2. The user selects Enable Tracking from the History menu.

Description:

1. The user enables historical tracking using one of the aforementioned triggers.

2. A historical tracking file is created for the stock symbol.

3. The stock table's Historical Tracking check box is updated to reflect the changes.

Post Conditions:

A new historical tracking file is created, the user's profile is updated, and the user interface reflects the changes.

Computing Summary

Here are the use cases related to computing a summary of the user's profile.

Use Case #4: Calculate the Total Dollar Gain/Loss from a Portfolio's Stocks

Use Case:

Calculate the total dollar gain/loss from a portfolio's stocks.

Scenario(s):

The Stock Tracker application computes the total dollar gain/loss from the user's portfolio.

Preconditions:

1. The user has launched the Stock Tracker application.
2. The user has selected his portfolio.

Triggers:

1. The application starts.
2. Any field in the table changes.

Description:

1. One of the aforementioned triggers occurs.
2. For all stocks, the application computes the total price paid for all shares.
3. For all stocks, the application computes the current value of the shares owned.
4. The application computes the difference.
5. The application updates the display.

Post Conditions:

The display shows the total dollar amount gain or loss.

Use Case #5: Calculate the Total Percentage Gain/Loss from a Portfolio's Stocks

Use Case:

Calculate the total percentage gain/loss from a portfolio's stocks.

Scenario(s):

The Stock Tracker application computes the total percentage gain/loss from the user's portfolio.

Preconditions:

1. The user has launched the Stock Tracker application.

2. The user has selected his portfolio.

Triggers:

1. The application starts.

2. Any field in the table changes.

Description:

1. One of the aforementioned triggers occurs.

2. For all stocks, the application computes the total price paid for all shares.

3. For all stocks, the application computes the current value of the shares owned.

4. The application computes the percentage change as follows:

   ```
   ((Total Value - Total Purchase Price)/Total Purchase Price) * 100
   ```

5. The application updates the display.

Post Conditions:

The display shows the total percentage gain or loss.

 Note The previous two use cases are separate although they are almost identical. I did this specifically because two different algorithms are used to compute the values and two separate fields are being updated.

Internet Access

The following sections contain the use cases related to Internet access.

Use Case #6: Download a Web Page for a Stock Symbol from the Internet

Use Case:

Download a Web page for a stock symbol from the Internet.

Scenario(s):

1. The application successfully downloads an HTML page containing a stock's current information from the Internet.

2. The application fails to download an HTML page from the Internet.

Preconditions:

1. The user has launched the Stock Tracker application.

Triggers:

1. The timer requests that a stock quote be downloaded.
2. The user chooses Update Stock Quotes from the Quotes menu.

Description:

Scenario 1:

1. One of the aforementioned triggers occurs.
2. The component downloads the HTML page from the Internet.
3. The component returns the HTML in String form to the calling routine/component.

Scenario 2:

1. One of the aforementioned triggers occurs.
2. Some type of error or timeout occurs.
3. The component returns an error to the calling routine/component.

Post Conditions:

The calling routine/component has a String containing the raw HTML from the Internet.

 Note

In the previous section, we had the following use case:

"Retrieve the stock price information from the Web page."

This was omitted because it is duplicated in the HTML Parsing component, which is logically a better place for its definition.

Historical Information

The following sections describe the use cases that relate to historical data.

Use Case #7: Download a Stock Quote for a Time Other than Today

Use Case:

Download a stock quote for a time other than today.

Scenario(s):

1. The component successfully downloads a historical quote.
2. The component successfully downloads a range of historical quotes.
3. The component fails to download a historical quote.

Preconditions:

1. The user has launched the Stock Tracker application.
2. The user has selected his profile.
3. The user has selected a stock symbol from the table.

Triggers:

1. The user selects Get Historical Quote from the History menu.

Description:

Scenario 1:

1. The user selects Get Historical Quote from the History menu.
2. The application displays a dialog box asking the user for historical options.
3. The user selects a date.
4. The component successfully downloads the historical quote.
5. The component returns the historical information to the caller.

Scenario 2:

1. The user selects Get Historical Quote from the History menu.
2. The application displays a dialog box asking the user for historical options.
3. The user selects a range of dates.
4. The component successfully downloads the historical quotes.
5. The component returns the historical information to the caller.

Scenario 3:

1. The user selects Get Historical Quote from the History menu.
2. The application displays a dialog box asking the user for historical options.
3. Some kind of error or timeout occurs.
4. An error is returned to the caller.

Post Conditions:

The historical information for a stock has been updated, and graphing options are expanded to fit the new information.

> In the previous section, we had the use case:
>
> "Download a range of stock quotes."
>
> This use case was combined into an additional scenario in the previous use case. This combination was made because the two cases were so tightly related and they could be grouped together logically.

Use Case #8: Persist Historical Information to/from a Data File

Use Case:

Persist historical information to/from a data file.

Scenario(s):

1. The user saves historical information to a data file.
2. The user loads historical information from a data file.

Preconditions:

1. The user has launched the Stock Tracker application.

Triggers:

1. Some component has called the save historical information method of this component.
2. Some component has called the load historical information method of this component.

Description:

Scenario 1:

1. The component's save historical information method is invoked.
2. The historical information is saved to a data file in a universal format.

Scenario 2:

1. The component's load historical information method is invoked.
2. The component loads the historical information from a data file.
3. The component returns the historical information to the caller.

Post Conditions:

Scenario 1:

The historical information is saved to a data file.

Scenario 2:

The historical information is returned to the caller.

HTML Parsing

The use cases described in the following sections are related to HTML parsing.

Use Case #9: Retrieve Stock Prices from an HTML Page

Use Case:

Retrieve stock prices from an HTML page.

Scenario(s):

1. Stock quote information is retrieved from an HTML page and returned in a predetermined format.

Preconditions:

1. The user has launched the Stock Tracker application.

Triggers:

1. A component has called this component's decode quote data method.

Description:

1. Some component invokes this component's decode quote data method, passing it HTML code.
2. The component decodes the HTML.
3. The component returns the raw stock information in a predetermined format.

Post Conditions:

The caller received the stock quote information.

Timer Mechanism

The following are use cases related to the timer mechanism.

Use Case #10: Set a Timer to Retrieve Stock Quotes at a Specific Interval

Use Case:

Set a timer to retrieve stock quotes at a specific interval.

Scenario(s):

1. A timer is set that will initiate a retrieval of all supported stock quotes.

Preconditions:

1. The user has launched the Stock Tracker application.

Triggers:

1. The user chooses Timer Options from the Quotes menu.

Description:

1. The user chooses Timer Options from the Quotes menu.
2. A dialog box is displayed showing the user the current stock settings.
3. The user enables stock retrieval on a timer.
4. The user closes the dialog box.

Post Conditions:

The timer is set to the user's preference.

Use Case #11: Retrieve Stock Quotes at the Set Interval

Use Case:

Retrieve stock quotes at the set interval.

Scenario(s):

1. The system updates its stock quotes at the specified timer interval.
2. The system fails to update its stock quotes.

Preconditions:

1. The user has launched the Stock Tracker application.
2. The user has entered one or more stocks into one or more portfolios. (Use Case #1).
3. The user has set a timer interval. (Use Case #11).

Triggers:

1. The timer goes off and starts the update.

Description:

Scenario 1:

1. The timer goes off and starts the update.
2. The component initiates a stock quote retrieval for each stock in each portfolio (excluding duplicates).
3. The component receives the stock quotes and updates the tables.

Scenario 2:

1. The timer goes off and starts the update.
2. The component initiates a stock quote retrieval for each stock in each portfolio (excluding duplicates).
3. An error occurs, such as an invalid Internet connection.
4. The user is notified.

Post Conditions:

The table displays the updated stock quote prices.

Portfolio Management

The following are use cases related to portfolio management.

Use Case #12: Add a Portfolio

Use Case:

Add a portfolio.

Scenario(s):

1. The user creates a new portfolio.

Preconditions:

1. The user has launched the Stock Tracker application.

Triggers:

1. The user chooses Add Portfolio from the Portfolios menu.

Description:

1. The user chooses Add Portfolio from the Portfolios menu.
2. The user is prompted for a name for the new portfolio.
3. A new portfolio file for the portfolio is generated.
4. The portfolio is added to the Portfolio list box.

Post Conditions:

A new portfolio is added to the application.

Use Case #13: Delete a Portfolio

Use Case:

Delete a portfolio.

Scenario(s):

1. The user deletes a portfolio.

Preconditions:

1. The user has launched the Stock Tracker application.
2. The user has created one or more portfolios (Use Case #12).

Triggers:

1. The user chooses Delete Portfolio from the Portfolios menu.

Description:

1. The user chooses Delete Portfolio from the Portfolios menu.
2. The user is prompted for confirmation.
3. The portfolio file is deleted from the active portfolios file.
4. The portfolio is deleted from the Portfolio list box.

Post Conditions:

The desired portfolio is deleted.

Use Case #14: Save a Portfolio

Use Case:

Save a portfolio.

Scenario(s):

1. The user saves his portfolio.

Preconditions:

1. The user has launched the Stock Tracker application.
2. The user has created one or more portfolios (Use Case #12).

Triggers:

1. The user selects a portfolio.
2. The user chooses Save Portfolio from the Portfolios menu.

Description:

1. The user selects a portfolio.
2. The user chooses Save Portfolio from the Portfolios menu.
3. The portfolio file is updated to reflect the current stock symbols in the portfolio.

Post Conditions:

The user's portfolio is saved.

Use Case #15: Load a Portfolio

Use Case:

Load a portfolio.

Scenario(s):

1. The user loads a portfolio from a file.

Preconditions:

1. The user has launched the Stock Tracker application.

Triggers:

1. The user chooses Load Portfolio from the Portfolios menu.

Description:

1. The user chooses Load Portfolio from the Portfolios menu.
2. The user is prompted to select the file to import.
3. The portfolio is loaded from the file.
4. The portfolio is added to the active portfolios file.
5. The Portfolio list box is updated.

Post Conditions:

The new portfolio is in the Portfolio list box.

Graphing

The following sections describe use cases related to graphing.

Use Case #16: Set Graphing Time Scale

Use Case:

Set graphing time scale.

Scenario(s):

1. The user sets a time scale to view stock performance on (for example, three months, six months).

Preconditions:

1. The user has launched the Stock Tracker application.
2. The user has created a portfolio.
3. The user has added one or more stocks to his portfolio.
4. The user has enabled historical tracking.

Triggers:

1. The user chooses Options from the Graph menu.

Description:

1. The user chooses Options from the Graph menu.
2. The user selects the graphing interval.
3. The graphing time scale is set.

Post Conditions:

The graphing time scale is set.

Use Case #17: Graph Stock Performance Points

Use Case:

Graph stock performance points.

Scenario(s):

1. A stock's historical performance is graphed.

Preconditions:

1. The user has launched the Stock Tracker application.
2. The user has created a portfolio.

3. The user has added one or more stocks to his portfolio.

4. The user has enabled historical tracking for a stock.

5. The historical data file has data in it.

Triggers:

1. The user chooses the Graph tab.

2. The user selects a portfolio.

3. The user selects a stock with historical data.

Description:

1. The aforementioned triggers occur.

2. The time interval is retrieved.

3. The available historical data is scaled to the time interval.

4. The historical data points are plotted and connected with lines.

Post Conditions:

The graph displays the stock's historical performance.

CSV

The following use cases are related to Comma-Separated Variable (CSV) files.

Use Case #18: Import Historical Data from a CSV File

Use Case:

Import historical data from a CSV file.

Scenario(s):

1. The user imports historical data from a CSV file.

Preconditions:

1. The user has launched the Stock Tracker application.

2. The user has created a portfolio.

Triggers:

1. The user chooses Import from the History menu.

Description:

1. The user chooses Import from the History menu.

2. The user is prompted for the file to import.

3. The data is retrieved.

4. The data is added to the historical file for that stock symbol.

Post Conditions:

The new historical data is available to the Stock Tracker application.

Use Case #19: Export Historical Data to a CSV File

Use Case:

Export historical data to a CSV file.

Scenario(s):

1. Historical data is exported to a CSV file of the user's choosing.

Preconditions:

1. The user has launched the Stock Tracker application.

2. The user has created a portfolio.

3. The user has added one or more stocks to his portfolio.

4. The user has enabled historical tracking for a stock.

5. The historical data has data in it.

Triggers:

1. The user selects a stock symbol.

2. The user chooses Export from the History menu.

Description:

1. The aforementioned triggers occur.

2. The user is prompted for a file to export the historical data to.

3. The historical data is exported in CSV format to the desired file.

Post Conditions:

A new file is created in CSV format with the historical data for the desired stock symbol.

Use Case #20: Import a Portfolio from a CSV File

Use Case:

Import a portfolio from a CSV file.

Scenario(s):

1. A new portfolio is imported from a CSV file.

2. Portfolio information is imported from a CSV file into an existing portfolio.

Preconditions:

1. The user has launched the Stock Tracker application.

Triggers:

1. The user chooses Import Portfolios from the Portfolios menu.

3

Description:

Scenario 1:

1. The user chooses Import Portfolios from the Portfolios menu.

2. The user is prompted for the file to import from.

3. The user is prompted for a name for the portfolio.

4. The portfolio data is loaded from the file.

5. The data is added to the portfolio.

Scenario 2:

1. The user chooses Import Portfolios from the Portfolios menu.

2. The user is prompted for the file to import from.

3. The user selects the existing portfolio he wants to add the imported data to.

4. The portfolio data is loaded from the file.

5. The data is added to the portfolio.

Post Conditions:

The new portfolio information has been added to the application.

Use Case #21: Export a Portfolio to a CSV File

Use Case:

Export a portfolio to a CSV file.

Scenario(s):

1. The user exports a selected portfolio to a CSV file.

Preconditions:

1. The user has launched the Stock Tracker application.
2. The user has created a portfolio.
3. The user has added one or more stocks to his portfolio.

Triggers:

1. The user selects a portfolio.
2. The user selected Export Portfolio from the Portfolios menu.

Description:

1. The aforementioned triggers occur.
2. The user is prompted for a file to export the portfolio to.
3. The data is written to the CSV file.

Post Conditions:

A new CSV file is created with the information from a selected portfolio.

Startup

The following use cases all occur during the application startup.

Use Case #22: Load All Portfolios

Use Case:

Load all portfolios.

Scenario(s):

1. The application loads all its current portfolios and adds them to the Portfolio list box.

Preconditions:

None.

Triggers:

1. The application is loaded.

Description:

1. The application is loaded.
2. The active portfolio list is iterated through for portfolios.
3. The load portfolio method is called for each portfolio.

Post Conditions:

The Portfolio list box displays all the loaded portfolios.

 Note This use case contains the "Update the user interface portfolio list box" because it is very simple and related to this use case.

Use Case #23: Get Stock Quotes for Portfolios

Use Case:

Get stock quotes for portfolios.

Scenario(s):

1. The application loads all the latest stock quotes for the portfolios.

Preconditions:

1. The application has been started.
2. All portfolios have been loaded.

Triggers:

1. The startup routine instigates this use case.

Description:

1. The application iterates through every portfolio.
2. The application iterates through every stock in the portfolio.
3. The application retrieves the latest stock quotes in HTML from the Internet (Use Case #6).
4. The application decodes the HTML and retrieves the stock quotes from it (Use Case #9).
5. The application updates its controls.

Post Conditions:

The latest stock quotes are available to the user in the stock table.

Shutdown

The following use cases occur during shutdown.

Use Case #24: Save Portfolios
Use Case:

Save portfolios.

Scenario(s):

1. All open portfolios are saved.

Preconditions:

1. The application is running.
2. One or more portfolios have been created.

Triggers:

1. The user closes the application.

Description:

1. The user closes the application.
2. The application iterates through every portfolio.
3. The application calls the portfolio's save method (Use Case #14).

Post Conditions:

All portfolios are saved.

Use Case #25: Save Current Stock Prices
Use Case:

Save current stock prices.

Scenario(s):

1. The last known stock price is saved when the application is closed.

Preconditions:

1. The application is running.
2. One or more portfolios have been created.
3. One or more stock symbols have been added to the portfolio.

Triggers:

1. The user closes the application.

Description:

1. The user closes the application.
2. The application iterates through every portfolio.
3. The application iterates through every stock symbol.
4. The application stores the latest stock quote (and time) in the user's portfolio.

Post Conditions:

The user's portfolio has the latest known stock price so that when the application is subsequently loaded, the last known price is displayed if no Internet connection is available.

Use Case #26: Save Historical Information

Use Case:

Save historical information.

Scenario(s):

1. Historical information is saved for all stocks.

Preconditions:

1. The user has launched the Stock Tracker application.
2. The user has created a portfolio.
3. The user has added one or more stocks to his portfolio.
4. The user has enabled historical tracking for a stock.
5. The historical data has data in it.

Triggers:

1. The application is closed.

Description:

1. The application iterates through every portfolio.
2. The application iterates through every stock symbol.
3. The application checks to see if there is new historical information available.
4. The application saves the historical information (Use Case #8).

Post Conditions:

All historical information for all stocks is saved.

Use Case #27: Close Active Internet Connections

Use Case:

Close active Internet connections.

Scenario(s):

1. All active Internet connections are closed.

Preconditions:

1. The application is running.

Triggers:

1. The application is closed.

Description:

1. The application checks for any active Internet connections.
2. The application closes the Internet connection.

Post Conditions:

All active Internet connections are closed.

Deriving Classes

Reading through the use cases might be a bit boring, but they are necessary when designing an application. Writing out the formal use cases might seem tedious, but look how much we learned about the application by doing it. Think about it: In the formal use cases, we started to define some different data files (portfolios, historical stock quotes, and some kind of main file that has a list of active portfolios). We also started to define what type of components we are going to need (portfolio manager, Internet manager, and so on) and much more.

The formal use cases in the last section served two purposes: They concentrated our focus on the problem domain and they helped us identify classes. This section is involved in identifying candidates for classes in our application.

Brainstorming

There's that word again: brainstorming. If you were to do only one thing in your design, I think brainstorming would be at the top of your list. In other words, you should think about your project before you implement it.

From the use cases in the previous section, what candidates can you see for classes? What kind of components can you see that perform some kind of action that someone else may want? This is the time to start thinking abstractly: Try to generalize the functionality in your use cases to components that perform distinct functionality; categorize functionality into related components and see if that functionality would work well together in a single component.

Take a minute and see what you can come up with. Don't worry if your components do not match what I have: Remember that in this discipline, there is no right answer, just an interpretation of the answer.

I made a quick rundown of the use cases for potential objects that would be needed to complete the use cases. Table 3.1 contains the list, with short descriptions, that I came up with.

Table 3.1   Use Case Classes

Class Name	*Description*
StockData	A class that contains an individual stock's information: Symbol, Purchase Price, Current Price, and so on.
Portfolio	A class that has a name and maintains a collection of StockData items. Also knows how to persist portfolios.
PortfolioManager	A class that maintains a collection of Portfolios and provides a general interface for objects to access and manipulate Portfolios.
InternetManager	A class that manages all access to the Internet: posting to and getting data from the Internet.
HistoricalDataManager	A class that manages all historical data for a stock.
HTMLParser	A class that can decode HTML documents and extract information from them.
Timer	A class that maintains a timer control that can fire events at predefined times (download stock quotes from the Internet).
GraphingManager	A class that manages the graphing parameters and is responsible for scaling and drawing the performance information.
CSVManager	A class that understands how to read and write CSV files, regardless of the information in them.
FileManager	A class that knows how to persist data to a file system.
Application	The class that manages all user interface elements and ties everything together.

Note

You might be questioning the Application class, but regardless of the exact name, I always put something like it in my class list. Basically, it is the component that displays the application onscreen, and it is the glue behind the Graphical User Interface (GUI) elements that binds them to "worker" classes (all the other classes in the list).

how too
prō nouns' it

In the preceding note, I referred to the Graphical User Interface, or GUI; the GUI represents all the graphical elements on the screen (trees, list boxes, buttons, and so on).

The Graphical User Interface is referred to as the GUI, pronounced "Gooey."

The next few sections refine these classes into viable components and develop some rudimentary class diagrams.

StockData

The StockData class is going to have to have properties for every field you want to track, as shown in Table 3.2.

Table 3.2 StockData **Properties**

Property Name	Description
Stock Symbol	The stock's symbol
Company Name	The stock's company name retrieved from the Internet
Last Sale	The last price that the stock sold for
High	The day's high
Low	The day's low
Volume	The day's volume
Number of Shares Owned	The number of shares the user owns of this stock
Price Paid per Share	The price the user paid per share for this stock

The last three fields will be computed on-the-fly, so there is no need to save those:

- Total Dollar Value of Shares
- Percent Change
- Dollar Amount Change

On-the-fly means just what you think it does: at runtime or while running. If a value is computed on-the-fly, it is something that is not recorded because the software will compute its value at runtime.

What other functionality are you going to add to the `StockData` class? Remember that as long as the application works, no design is wrong—some may be better than others in terms of maintainability, scalability, and implementation, but it is your project, so go, be free! I am opting to put the Internet communications inside the `StockData` class—because it is so tightly coupled with the data that it will retrieve from the Internet, it feels like the natural place for it.

We are going to make a change a little later when we get down to the `InternetManager` and `HTMLParser` classes, which I will preview for you here. The `InternetManager` class is important and should be its own class (and the same goes for the `HTMLParser` class), but from the `StockData` class's perspective, all it is concerned with is getting actual stock quotes—it does not care about the Internet or the HTML associated with it. What I am proposing is the creation of a `StockQuoteRetriever` class that will encapsulate the `InternetManager` and `HTMLParser` classes and provide a simple interface to download a stock quote.

So now our `StockData` class is going to have a `StockQuoteRetriever` class in it.

Now let's talk about methods. What methods do we need in our `StockData` class? We need methods to get and set all the attributes, read and write information from a file, and update stock information. Table 3.3 shows the methods for the `StockData` class (with the exception of the `Get` and `Set` methods for each property—that would be too tedious to read, and you will see them when you look at the class diagram).

Table 3.3   `StockData` **Methods**

Method Name	Description
Get/Set	`Get` and `Set` properties
Read	Read stock information from a file
Write	Write stock information to a file
Update	Update stock information from the Internet

Finally, let's put this all together into one easy class diagram, as shown in Figure 3.2.

Figure 3.2

StockData class diagram.

StockData

m_strStockSymbol : String
m_strCompanyName : String
m_fLastSale : Float
m_fHigh : Float
m_fLow : Float
m_fVolume : Float
m_fNumberOfSharesOwned : Float
m_fPricePaidPerShare : Float
m_StockQuoteRetriever : StockQuoteRetriever

GetStockSymbol()
SetStockSymbol()
GetCompanyName()
SetCompanyName()
GetLastSale()
SetLastSale()
GetHigh()
SetHigh()
GetLow()
SetLow()
GetVolume()
SetVolume()
GetNumberOfSharesOwned()
SetNumberOfSharesOwned()
GetPricePaidPerShare()
SetPricePaidPerShare()
Write()
Read()
Update()

EXCURSION

Variable Naming Convention

After looking at Figure 3.2, you might be confused by the variable naming conventions that are used. I will talk more about variable naming conventions at length later, but I wanted to give you a little pertinent information now.

First, the `m_` prefix is a remnant from C++ and dominates the Windows C++ programming world (you don't see it too much in Java) and says simply: This variable is a member variable of this class. This notation will help you greatly in differentiating local variables from class member variables when you are working with variables inside your class methods. I am curious as to why most Java programmers have not adopted this, but it clears up a lot of confusion in variable name resolution, so I will stick to it in this book.

Next, you might be wondering what the `str` and `f` are doing in front of the variable names. Now this too comes from C++ and is known as *Hungarian notation*. The idea is to prepend a short description of the variable type to the variable name. In this case, `str` represents a `String` and `f` represents a float data type. Hungarian notation has the benefit of allowing anyone reading your program to know the exact type of the variables in your program without finding their declaration. Java programmers do not use this often either because it does not work too well with user-defined types (classes), but for simple types (`int`, `float`, `String`, and so on) it is great. I will use it throughout all the code in this book. Table 3.4 lists a set of commonly used Hungarian notation prefixes.

Now before you run off and say that I am corrupting your Java programming mind, here are the common Java conventions for variable naming:

- The first letter of the variable name is lowercase.
- Every successive word in the variable name begins with a capital letter.
- All other letters are lowercase.

So, to name the variable in the "Java" convention, it would look like this:

```
String stockSymbol;
String companyName;
Float lastSale;
StockQuoteRetriever stockQuoteRetriever;
```

Which method is better? It is all up to you! Just pick a convention and stick to it, and you will be fine!

Table 3.4   Hungarian Notation Prefixes

Prefix	Description
b	boolean
by	byte
c	character
d	double
f	float—floating-point number
i, n	int—integer
l	long—long integer
s	short—short integer
str	String

Portfolio

Let's talk about portfolios. All that a portfolio is in this application is a collection of StockData objects. It has a name associated with it, and it provides an interface into the StockData objects for the other classes. So what properties do we need? Table 3.5 lists them.

Table 3.5   Portfolio Properties

Property Name	Description
Name	A name associated with this portfolio
StockData Collection	A collection of StockData objects
m_nNumberOfStockDataObjects	The number of StockData objects in the collection

Next, you must define the interface into the Portfolio class. What methods do you need? You need the standard Get/Set method for the Name property, you need an interface to get individual StockData object information, and you need a way to persist your StockData collection. Table 3.6 shows the methods for the Portfolio class.

Table 3.6 Portfolio Methods

Method Name	Description
GetName()	Retrieves the name of the portfolio
SetName(String)	Sets the name of the portfolio
GetNumberOfStockDataObjects	Retrieves the number of stock data objects in the portfolio
GetStockDataObject(int)	Gets the StockData object at a given index
LoadPortfolio()	Loads the portfolio from disk
SavePortfolio()	Saves the portfolio to disk
UpdateStockPrices()	Updates the stock prices for all the stocks in this portfolio

Figure 3.3 shows the class diagram for the Portfolio class.

Figure 3.3

Portfolio class diagram.

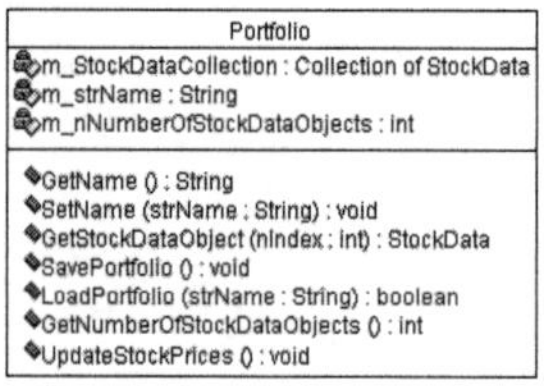

```
                    Portfolio
m_StockDataCollection : Collection of StockData
m_strName : String
m_nNumberOfStockDataObjects : int

GetName () : String
SetName (strName : String) : void
GetStockDataObject (nIndex : int) : StockData
SavePortfolio () : void
LoadPortfolio (strName : String) : boolean
GetNumberOfStockDataObjects () : int
UpdateStockPrices () : void
```

PortfolioManager

The PortfolioManager is simply a collection of Portfolios and may not even be necessary when we get to our implementation. It may suffice to simply have a collection of Portfolios stored in the Application class, but the concept of the PortfolioManager is important. This concept is a simple one, as shown in Table 3.7.

Table 3.7 PortfolioManager Properties

Property Name	Description
Portfolio Collection	Collection of Portfolio Objects
M_nNumberOfPortfolios	The number of Portfolio objects in the collection

The methods are simple as well: we must be able to load all portfolios, save all portfolios, and get a portfolio (see Table 3.8).

Table 3.8   `PortfolioManager` **Methods**

Method Name	Description
`LoadAllPortfolios()`	Loads all the portfolios in the collection
`SaveAllPortfolios()`	Saves all the portfolios in the collection
`GetNumberOfPortfolios()`	Retrieves the number of portfolios in the collection
`GetPortfolio(int)`	Gets a specific portfolio
`UpdatePortfolioStockPrices()`	Updates the stock prices for all stocks in all portfolios in the collection

Finally, Figure 3.4 shows the class diagram for the `PortfolioManager` class.

Figure 3.4

PortfolioManager class diagram.

InternetManager

The `InternetManager` is an important class. It is the class that is going to retrieve all the Internet documents for you! It may be important, and it may take some work to implement, but from the perspective of creating a class diagram and determining how we are going to use it, it is a very simple class.

The class is going to need to maintain some kind of Internet connection (so that it can retrieve multiple objects without reconnecting to the Internet—we'll explore this more when we get to the implementation of the Internet classes) and a single method that retrieves a raw HTML page.

 Note   The Internet class that we write here will be completely reusable in any of your other applications; it simply retrieves a raw HTML page from the uniform resource locator (URL) that you provide.

 A *uniform resource locator*, or URL, is a representation of the access method and location of a resource located on the Internet. Access methods refer to the "scheme," or protocol, of the URL—such as HTTP, HTTPS, FTP, and Gopher. The location is a scheme-specific string. In the context of this application, we are retrieving Web sites from the Internet, so our scheme, or the scheme of the Web, is HTTP.

The scheme-specific string will be the Web address you are used to seeing. Here is an example of the URL for Macmillan Computer Publishing's Web site:

```
http://www.mcp.com
```

All that explanation for just a Web address, huh? URLs are actually pretty interesting creatures that you can learn more about by reading the Request For Comment (RFC) 1738 document, which you can find at `http://info.internet.isi.edu/in-notes/rfc/files/rfc1738.txt`. From time to time in this book when I talk about the Internet, I will refer to these RFC documents. These documents contain all the standards for the Internet and Internet protocols. You might want to peruse them sometime; they are great (although boring) reading.

Now let's define our `InternetManager`. Tables 3.9 and 3.10 show the properties and methods of the `InternetManager` class, respectively.

Table 3.9 `InternetManager` **Properties**

Property Name	Description
InternetConnection	Internet connection object that will maintain a connection to the Internet

Table 3.10 `InternetManager` **Methods**

Method Name	Description
GetHTMLPage(String)	Retrieves the raw HTML page specified by the String passed into the method

Please remember that when you are defining your classes, you are defining the public interfaces (and known contained objects) that you want the class to support; there will definitely be more support functions inside these classes, but the public ones that you want to call are the only ones you really care about at this point. Figure 3.5 shows the class diagram for the `InternetManager` class.

Figure 3.5

InternetManager class diagram.

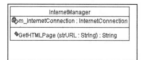

HTMLParser

You have a class that can download raw HTML from the Internet, and now you need to do something with it. The purpose of the HTML parser is to retrieve specific information from an HTML page. Before you can extract data from an HTML page, you first have to understand HTML. I will go into great depth in the Internet chapter, but for now you just need to know that the HTML you are concerned with is composed of text and formatting information that appear as HTML "tags." For example, you can make something bold using the tag combination <B> and </B>, as follows:

```
<B> Bold Title </B>
```

Why is this important right now, you ask? Let me give you a quick little design for how I envision this class working. Because we are only concerned with the actual text and not the formatting information, I envision this class stripping out all the formatting information and building a set of "tokens," or just a set of short character strings. If we are looking for the "Last Sale" price for a stock quote, we strip out all the HTML tags, find the "Last Sale" token, and retrieve the value from the very next token (hopefully!).

To accomplish this, we are going to need to have a method to give the HTMLParser an HTML page to parse as well as methods to retrieve tokens and token information. Tables 3.11 and 3.12 show the properties and methods for the HTMLParser class, respectively.

Table 3.11 HTMLParser **Properties**

Property Name	Description
HTML Page	Stores the text of the HTML page for later parsing—if we want to add any other kind of parsing (extract links or graphic filenames?)
Token Collection	A collection of post-parsed HTML page tokens
Number of Tokens	The number of tokens in the collection

Table 3.12 HTMLParser **Methods**

Method Name	Description
ParsePage(String)	Parses the HTML page contained in the String into tokens
GetNumberOfTokens()	Gets the number of tokens in the collection
GetToken(int)	Retrieves the String token specified by the index integer passed to the method
FindToken(String)	Returns the index of the token that matches the String passed to the method

For a graphic representation of this, see Figure 3.6.

Figure 3.6

*HTMLParser class
diagram.*

StockQuoteRetriever

The StockQuoteRetriever class is now almost trivial! Not really, but the interface is. The class itself must have intimate knowledge of the Web server it is connecting to. It has to

1. Know the URL of the stock server
2. Know the specific format of the HTML (which tokens come when and what labels to search for, like "Last Sale")

But as far as we are concerned, the StockQuoteRetriever contains an InternetManager and an HTMLParser and a method to retrieve the stock information.

Tables 3.13 and 3.14 show the properties and methods for the StockQuoteRetriever class, respectively.

Table 3.13 StockQuoteRetriever **Properties**

Property Name	Description
Internet Manager	An instance of the InternetManager class
HTML Parser	An instance of the HTMLParser class

Table 3.14 StockQuoteRetriever **Methods**

Method Name	Description
GetStockInformation(String)	Returns a StockData object with all the stock information for the symbol passed in the String parameter

For a graphic representation of this, see Figure 3.7.

Figure 3.7

*StockQuoteRetriever
class diagram.*

HistoricalDataManager

The HistoricalDataManager is a rather unique class in this application. The way we want this class to function is that we will give the class a stock symbol and a range of dates, and it will retrieve the historical information for the stock either from disk or from the Internet. This means that it must know how to read and write files, get information from the Internet, and parse HTML. Furthermore, it must maintain a collection of stock information in memory for retrieval.

This description would be a bit overwhelming, but we already have the `InternetManager` class to access the Internet, the `HTMLParser` class to parse HTML, and the `StockData` class to hold stock information. This makes our job very easy! See Tables 3.15 and 3.16 for the properties and methods of the `HistoricalDataManager` class, respectively.

Table 3.15 `HistoricalDataManager` **Properties**

Property Name	Description
StockData Collection	Data structure to hold the historical data for one stock symbol (in StockData format)
Internet Manager	InternetManager class object used to get data from the Internet
HTML Parser	HTMLParser class object used to retrieve historical data from HTML pages

Table 3.16 `HistoricalDataManager` **Methods**

Method Name	Description
Initialize(String,Date,Date)	Initializes the stock symbol for this class. It tells the class to retrieve the stock information for the desired dates, either from disk or from the Internet
GetHistoricalData(Date)	Retrieves the stock information for the specified date (in StockData format)
SaveHistoricalData()	Saves the historical data to disk

See Figure 3.8 for a graphical representation of this class.

Figure 3.8

HistoricalDataManager class diagram.

Timer

The responsibility of the `Timer` class is simply to do some action at a particular time interval. You supply the time interval, say 20 minutes, and you want the timer to tell you when 20 minutes have elapsed. You also want to be able to have the timer inform you after 20 minutes have elapsed, or every 20 minutes (note that 20 minutes is an arbitrary value that will be configured by the user).

In the Timer class, we need to hold the reporting time interval and we need a way to set the timer. Finally, the timer has to have a way to tell you when the time interval is up. See Tables 3.17 and 3.18 for the properties and methods of the Timer class, respectively.

Table 3.17 Timer **Properties**

Property Name	Description
Time Interval	Stores the time interval for the timer
Notify Status	Flag to tell the class whether to notify callers once or every time the timer goes off

Table 3.18 Timer **Methods**

Method Name	Description
StartTimer(Time,Status)	Starts the timer counting down for the specified time. The Status tells it when to report back: once or every time
StopTimer()	Stop the timer

Figure 3.9 shows the Timer class.

Figure 3.9

Timer class diagram.

GraphingManager

The GraphingManager has the unique responsibility of drawing the historical data for a stock in graphical form. It must provide a way to set both the time scale and price scale. The way that I envision this class working is that it will be associated with some kind of graphics object, and we will simply tell it to plot a certain time interval for a given stock symbol. It is then its responsibility to get the historical data (through a HistoricalDataManager object) and plot all the points in the given range. We will let it take care of setting up the price scale (unless we want to force it ourselves), and it will plot all the points for the dates we specify (scaled out to fit the graph).

Therefore, we are going to need this class to contain a `HistoricalDataManager` object, and it is going to need a method to draw the historical data for a stock symbol and time frame. Tables 3.19 and 3.20 show the properties and methods for the `GraphingManager` class.

Table 3.19   `GraphingManager` Properties

Property Name	Description
Historical Manager	Used to retrieve historical data

Table 3.20   `GraphingManager` Methods

Method Name	Description
`Graph(String,Date,Date,Loc)`	Retrieves the historical data for the stock symbol passed in for the specified dates and plots them on the graphics location (`Loc`)
`SetPriceRange(Long,Long)`	Sets the price range for the stock symbol to graph—it will be done automatically if this method is not present

See Figure 3.10 for a graphical representation of the `GraphingManager` class.

Figure 3.10

`GraphingManager` class diagram.

GraphingManager
m_HistoricalDataManager : HistoricalDataManager
Graph() SetPriceRange()

CSVManager

Next is the `CSVManager` class. This class has to know how to import and export data from and to comma-separated variable files. It has to have knowledge of how to do this using both portfolio files as well as historical data files.

Defining an interface for this class shouldn't be too hard. I am defining this more as a utility class, meaning that it does not have properties and does not maintain any state information; you can simply call the methods of a utility class directly, without instantiating the class, and then it will go away. Take a look at Table 3.21 for the methods of the `CSVManager` class.

Table 3.21 **CSVManager Methods**

Method Name	Description
ImportPortfolio(String)	Imports a portfolio from a file specified in the String parameter
ImportHistoricalData(String)	Imports historical data from a file specified by the String parameter
Export(Portfolio,String)	Exports a Portfolio in CSV format to the file specified by the String parameter
Export(HistoricalDataManager,String)	Exports a HistoricalDataManager in CSV format to the file specified by String

See Figure 3.11 for a graphical representation of the CSVManager class.

Figure 3.11

CSVManager class diagram.

FileManager

I have alluded to the FileManager class throughout this chapter through the various load and save methods. This is not a class I think we are going to have to implement; it is another one that is more conceptual than anything. We are going to need some way to save a file to the file system and load a file from the file system. Luckily, Java takes care of all that for us. When we get to reading and writing files, we will use the classes that Java has provided for us.

Application

Now that we have developed an understanding of all the worker classes in our application, we need someone to hold them all together; that is the job of the Application class. The Application class performs two main functions: It is the container and parent for all the controls and it manages the user interface.

The Application class controls the logic of the application by asking various components to perform actions based on the user interface. It is the glue that holds everything together.

When we get to designing the user interface, you will get a better idea about how the application works, but for now let's note the objects that it has to contain. Take a look at Table 3.22 for the various classes that the Application contains.

Table 3.22 `Application` **Properties**

Property Name	Description
Portfolio Manager	An object of type `PortfolioManager` to manage all the portfolios for the application
Timer	An object of type `Timer` to tell the application when to update stock prices
Graphing Manager	A `GraphingManager` object to plot historical data
Historical Data Manager	A `HistoricalDataManager` object to retrieve and maintain historical data

Because of the nature of the class, it does not have any external methods that we can call—it does all the calling. Take a look at Figure 3.12 for a graphical representation of this class.

Figure 3.12

Application class diagram.

Summary

There you have it: You have all the major components for your application! The details about how individual components work are described in the chapters where they are being implemented. What you will do is design some sequence diagrams and implement them when you get there.

You learned a lot in this chapter. You took the design skills developed in the previous chapter and applied them to a full-fledged application. You learned how to model your ideas and how to expand them to fit the design of an application. For the context of this book, you learned about the application you are going to be developing, what elements are required, and the basics for how they work.

By seeing the steps required to design an application at work, you will be able to incorporate them into your own designs and develop a substantial application on your own!

What's Next?

All this design stuff is fun, but when do you get to code? Well, in the next chapter, we are going to take a break from the application overhead and focus on some real Java stuff! Before you can design your user interface in Chapter 5, you need to know what tools are available; if you were building a house and found out that you only had straw to work with, you would need to design your house a little differently than if you had bricks.

Get ready to learn about the various user interface elements available in Java's Abstract Window Toolkit and Swing libraries.

Chapter 4

User Interface Design with AWT

In the last two chapters, we spent some time learning about design methodologies and designed most of the Stock Tracker application. All that information is absolutely essential to building an application, but because you are new to Java, I am sure you are ready to dive back into actual coding!

Before you can build a user interface , you must know what tools are available to build that user interface. For example, it might be exciting to have a scrolling graphical rolodex of phone numbers in a telephony application, but when you find out that you would have to implement that from scratch, a scrollable list box sure looks nice. On the other hand, why use a list box if you have a scrolling graphical rolodex? The point is that you must know what is available to you when you are deciding how your application is going to look.

This chapter takes you through the various user interface elements in the standard Abstract Window Toolkit (AWT). In the next chapter, we will look at the user interface elements available in the new Swing libraries.

This chapter discusses the following AWT user interface elements:

- Labels
- Buttons
- Text fields
- Text areas
- Check boxes
- Choice lists

- Layout managers:
  - Flow layout
  - Grid layout
  - Border layout
  - Card layout
  - Grid bag layout

As you can see, you are going to be busy in this chapter! Let's get started!

Abstract Window Toolkit (AWT)

The Abstract Window Toolkit (AWT) refers to the set of classes provided by Java that enables the creation of a graphical user interface and provides a mechanism to handle user input through the mouse and keyboard. The AWT was the first graphical set of classes for Java (it preceded the SWING classes by several years) and was designed to support applications running under multiple platforms.

Through the unique concept of layout managers, applications developed with Java can adapt to specific platforms and maintain a proper appearance. By specifying relative locations of components, the Java Virtual Machine running the application can resize and rearrange components to appear correctly.

Furthermore, a button might appear differently and in a different size on a UNIX platform than it might on a Windows platform, but that button will look correct for that platform.

The AWT is a very powerful set of user interface classes that is only now being overshadowed by the SWING classes because of their up-to-date set of components; remember that SWING simply enhances the concepts that originated in the AWT.

Labels

A label, as its name implies, is simply a way to present text to the user. Just as you would use a label to identify a file in your file cabinet, you use labels to identify other user interface elements or additionally to provide feedback to your user. Labels are by far the simplest of the AWT components and are accessed through the `Label` class.

When you create a label, you can specify both the text and the alignment of the label: right, left, or center. A label can be constructed as shown in Table 4.1.

Table 4.1 `Label` Constructors

Class Name	Description
`Label()`	Construct an empty label with left alignment
`Label( String )`	Construct a label with the text in the `String` and left alignment
`Label( String, int )`	Construct a label with the text in the `String` and the alignment specified in the `int`: `Label.CENTER`, `Label.RIGHT`, or `Label.LEFT`

This sample snippet constructs a label:

```
Label lblMyLabel = new Label( "Hello, world!" );
```

When a class is created, it is said that the class is *constructed* and its *constructor* is called. A *constructor* is a public method that has the same name as the class and returns no value. A class can have various *constructors* that differ by the parameters that are passed to it. For example, the `Label` class has three different constructors, each of which does something different based on the parameters it receives. A *constructor* that has no parameters passed to it is referred to as the *default constructor*.

The compiler automatically calls the *constructor* when an instance of a class is created.

Listing 4.1 shows the complete code for a Java application that creates three labels and displays them in a frame.

You can either type the code in Listing 4.1 into your favorite text editor (excluding the line numbers of course—they are just there to refer to later) and save it as `Labels.java`, or copy this code from the CD, compile it, and run it. To compile the program, make sure you have the Java 2 JDK properly installed (see Appendix A, "Setting Up the Java 2 SDK") and type

```
javac Labels.java
```

To run it, type

```
java Labels
```

Listing 4.1 `Labels.java`

```
1: // Import the Abstract Window Toolkit (AWT) classes
2: import java.awt.*;
3: import java.awt.event.*;
4:
5:
6: public class Labels extends Frame
7: {
8:
```

continues

Listing 4.1   continued

```
 9:        // Create three labels
10:        Label lblTitle = new Label( "Here are a couple labels:" );
11:        Label lblStockSymbol = new Label( "QUE" );
12:        Label lblStockPrice = new Label( "150.5" );
13:
14:
15:        // Labels class constructor
16:        public Labels()
17:        {
18:            // Set the title of our frame
19:            super( "Labels Example!" );
20:
21:            // Choose the FlowLayout layout manager
22:            setLayout( new FlowLayout() );
23:
24:            // Add our labels
25:            add( lblTitle );
26:            add( lblStockSymbol );
27:            add( lblStockPrice );
28:
29:            // Set our size
30:            setSize( 300, 60 );
31:
32:            // Make our class visible
33:            setVisible( true );
34:
35:            // Add a window listener to listen for our window closing
36:            addWindowListener
37:            (
38:                new WindowAdapter()
39:                {
40:                    public void windowClosing( WindowEvent e )
41:                    {
42:                        System.exit( 0 );
43:                    }
44:                }
45:            );
46:        }
47:
48:
49:        // Main entry point into the Labels class
50:        public static void main( String[] args )
51:        {
52:            // Create an instance of our Labels class
53:            Labels LabelsApp = new Labels();
54:        }
55:}
```

Figure 4.1 shows a screenshot of the Labels application.

Figure 4.1

*Labels application
example.*

Now don't get too frightened by a 55-line program that just shows three labels on the screen! It really isn't that difficult, and we'll go through it line by line.

First, you might be wondering what all those slashes (//) are scattered throughout the program; for example, in line 1:

```
1: // Import the Abstract Window Toolkit (AWT) classes
```

The compiler reads the // as a comment delimiter. This means anything that appears after the // to the end of the line is a comment for the programmer's benefit and is ignored by the compiler. You will find that adding comments in your source code to explain what you are doing will greatly benefit you when you read through it. I use comments extensively in my applications, which you will see in this book.

```
2: import java.awt.*;
```

Line 2 imports the AWT classes. The `import` statement imports classes from a package into your program; using the `import` statement with an asterisk (*) imports all public classes from the named package. The AWT classes are in the package `java.awt`, so you can either import individual classes from the AWT, or all the classes as in line 2.

A *package* is a collection of classes and interfaces. *Packages* usually group classes with related functionality together; for example, the `java.awt` class hosts many user interface related classes.

```
3: import java.awt.event.*;
```

Line 3 imports the AWT event classes. We will talk more about events in Chapter 7, "Building the Stock Tracker User Interface," but for now we need to import this package to be able to close the window, so here is your sneak preview! An event can be anything from a button click to a window closing, and Java enables you to listen for events and perform specific activities when they occur.

You might be curious about the difference between lines 2 and 3; they look similar. Line 2 imports all the classes that are in the java.awt package, and line 3 imports all the classes in the java.awt.event package. The java.awt.event package is a subpackage of the java.awt package, but you must explicitly state that you want the java.awt.event package because the import statement does not import subpackages. I use the term *subpackage* loosely because both packages are considered separate packages, but they are closely related.

```
6: public class Labels extends Frame
```

Line 6 defines the public class (the main application class) for the program `Labels`, and derives it from the `Frame` class. The `Frame` class, part of the AWT classes, is a top-level window with a title and a border. A class is derived from another class by using the keyword `extends`. In this case, you want to derive the `Labels` class from the `Frame` class because you are going to want the application to reside in a window on the desktop.

The `extends` keyword creates a subclass of a given class, which is called the *superclass*. A *subclass* is a class that inherits all the methods and properties of its superclass.

So by saying that `Labels` extends `Frame`, what we are saying is that the `Labels` class is a new class, of our own creation, that has all the functionality of the `Frame` class as well as the new functionality we will add to it. Inside the `Labels` class, you can call any of the methods available in the `Frame` class. For example, the `Frame` class has a method called `setTitle` that changes the title of the window. The `setTitle` method is now available to the `Labels` class, so anywhere in the `Labels` class, you can call `setTitle` to change the title.

Figure 4.2 shows the derivation hierarchy for the `Frame` class. As you can see, a `Frame` is a type of `Window`, which is a type of `Container`, which is a type of `Component`, which is a type of `Object`. So the `Frame` class has access to all the functionality of each of the classes it is derived from. Therefore the `Labels` class has all the functionality of the `Frame`, `Window`, `Container`, and `Object` classes.

Not that I am trying to lie to you, but the previous statement is not entirely true: The `Frame` class does not necessarily have access to all the methods and properties of its parent classes. It has access to all the methods and properties of its parent classes that have access modifiers of either public or protected. An access modifier is associated with both methods and properties and can be one of the following: public, private, or protected.

A *public* access modifier states that this method or property is publicly accessible to both internal methods as well as external classes.

A *private* access modifier states that this method or property is not available to any external classes—it is available only to methods within its own class.

A *protected* access modifier states that this method or property is not available to external classes, but is accessible to its subclasses, or classes derived from it.

The `Frame` will inherit all the public methods and properties of each superclass, and external classes will be able to access these methods and properties as well. It will inherit all the protected methods and properties of each superclass, and any external classes will not be able to access these methods and properties!

Figure 4.2

The derivation hierarchy for the Frame *class.*

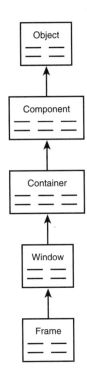

```
7: {
55:}
```

Lines 7 and 55 delimit the body of the Labels class. Furthermore, brackets group statements together and are used to delimit the body of all methods as well as other statements we will encounter later in the book.

```
10:    Label lblTitle = new Label( "Here are three labels:" );
11:    Label lblStockSymbol = new Label( "QUE" );
12:    Label lblStockPrice = new Label( "150.5" );
```

Lines 10–12 create three labels, which denote our fabulous QUE stock at its $150.50 per share stock price! As you can see, these are all initialized in the constructor.

```
16:    public Labels()
```

Line 16 defines the constructor for the Labels class; it is declared public, has the same name as the class itself, and returns no value. Furthermore, because this constructor does not accept any parameters, it is the default constructor for the Labels class.

```
19:        super( "Labels Example!" );
```

Line 19, the first line of the constructor, uses the super keyword. The super key-word, used in a subclass, calls the original method of the superclass. So by using the super keyword in the constructor of the Labels class, you are asking the compiler to call the constructor of the Frame class and pass it the String "Labels Example!". If you refer to the Java 2 SDK documentation for the Frame class constructors, you will see two constructors (see Table 4.2).

Table 4.2 Frame Constructors

Class Name	*Description*
Frame()	Constructs a new instance of Frame that is initially invisible. The title of the Frame is empty.
Frame(String title)	Constructs a new, initially invisible Frame object, with the specified title.

When calling super with the String "Labels Example!", you are calling the Frame constructor and setting the title of the frame to "Labels Example!" Look at Figure 4.1 again and read the title.

```
22:        setLayout( new FlowLayout() );
```

Line 22 does two things: It creates a new FlowLayout class object, and then it calls the Frame class method setLayout. I will spend more time talking about layout man-agers later in this chapter (in the section titled "Layout Managers"). However, to give you a little preview, the FlowLayout class is a layout manager that just starts adding items to the screen one at a time, left to right, until the end of the line, and then continues down the screen. The Frame class' setLayout method sets the layout manager for the frame. So line 22 sets the layout manager of the Labels class to be a FlowLayout.

```
25:        add( lblTitle );
26:        add( lblStockSymbol );
27:        add( lblStockPrice );
```

Lines 25–27 add the previously created labels to the window by calling the Frame class's add method. If you look at the Frame class's documentation, you may notice that there is no mention of the add methods. But if you look further, you will see that the Frame class extends Window, which extends Container. The Container class is the one with all the add methods—five to be exact (see Table 4.3).

Table 4.3   Container Class Add Methods

Class Name	Description
add(Component comp)	Adds the specified component to the end of this container.
add(Component comp, int index)	Adds the specified component to this container at the given position.
add(Component comp, Object constraints)	Adds the specified component to the end of this container. Also notifies the layout manager to add the component to this container's layout using the specified constraints object.
add(Component comp, Object constraints, int index)	Adds the specified component to this container at the given position. Also notifies the layout manager to add the component to this container's layout using the specified constraints object.
add(String name, Component comp)	Adds the specified component to this container. Note that this method is deprecated and add(Component, Object) should be used instead.

The term *deprecated* refers to a class, interface, method, or attribute that is no longer supported. Many of these objects might still be functional, but do not count on them working indefinitely; after something is deprecated there is no guarantee that it will be functional in future releases. When you see that something is deprecated, it usually suggests an alternative replacement that you should try to use instead.

What can you learn from all these methods? If you look back at the documentation for the Label class, you can see that, yes, it is derived from Component. So you know that the Labels class is really a container that holds components such as labels. You can also see that there is an order associated to the components you add to the container. Thus, if you have to have a component in a certain position, you can always place it where you want it. Don't worry about the constraints object yet; we will talk more about that later.

In summary, lines 25–27 add Label instance components to the end of the window object.

```
30:        setSize( 300, 60 );
```

Line 30 calls the Frame class's setSize method, which is inherited from the Component class. The setSize method resizes the window to the specified dimension, which in this case is 300 pixels by 60 pixels; the size is set large enough to see all the labels.

```
33:        setVisible( true );
```

Line 33 calls the Frame class's setVisible method, which is inherited from the Component class as well, and changes the visibility of the component. If you look back to the Frame constructors in Table 3.2, you will notice that Frames are invisible by default, so you must call the setVisible method with a true argument to make the frame visible; in addition, if you pass setVisible a false parameter, it will hide the component.

You might have noticed that the last two methods were derived from the Component class, which is the same class that Label is derived from. Yes, this does mean that you can call these methods on the Label class as well. You can show and hide labels using the setVisible method, and you can resize them using the setSize method. The other components in this chapter are all derived from Component, so these methods are all applicable to them as well!

```
36:         addWindowListener
37:         (
38:             new WindowAdapter()
39:             {
40:                 public void windowClosing( WindowEvent e )
41:                 {
42:                     System.exit( 0 );
43:                 }
44:             }
45:         );
```

Now lines 36–45 are a bit interesting. The Frame class's addWindowListener method is derived from the Window class and is declared as follows:

```
public void addWindowListener(WindowListener l)
```

This method adds the specified window listener to the window to receive window events. If you add an object that implements the WindowListener interface, that object will be notified when one of the seven events listed in Table 4.4 occurs.

Table 4.4 WindowListener Events

Class Name	Description
windowActivated	Invoked when the window becomes the user's active window—when it gains the input focus.
windowClosed	Invoked when a window has been closed through a call to dispose.
windowClosing	Invoked when the user attempts to close the window from the window's system menu.
windowDeactivated	Invoked when the window is no longer the user's active window—when it loses the input focus.

Class Name	Description
windowDeiconified	Invoked when a window is changed from a minimized to a normal state.
windowIconified	Invoked when a window is changed from a normal to a minimized state.
windowOpened	Invoked the first time a window is made visible.

Now the interesting event in this example is the windowClosing event because as soon as the user closes the window, you want to shut down the application. The WindowAdapter class is simply a class that is derived from Object and implements WindowListener. It has method declarations for each of the events in Table 4.4, but they are empty. An easy way to handle one or more of these events is to create a new WindowAdapter and implement the desired methods. Note that we could have easily created a new class that implemented WindowListener ourselves and added that to the window, but we took a shortcut.

So line 38 creates a new WindowAdapter and line 40 adds a handler for the windowClosing event. Line 42 calls the System class's exit method. If you take a look at the documentation for this method, it states that the method terminates the currently running Java Virtual Machine, and effectively shuts the application down. Passing 0 to the exit method indicates normal termination, whereas a nonzero value indicates abnormal termination.

The last bit of business in this discussion, as you might have noticed, is that an instance of WindowEvent is passed to the window events. In our example, we ignore the event and in most cases you will as well, but it does give you several pieces of information: the type of event that occurred (such as windowClosing or windowIconified), the Window that originated the event, and a parameter string to identify the event (which you could use for logging or debugging). If you would like more information about the WindowEvent class, please refer to the Java 2 SDK documentation.

```
50:    public static void main( String[] args )
51:    {
54:    }
```

Line 50 declares the main method, which, as described in Chapter 1, is the main entry point into a Java application class. When you launch your application through the Java Virtual Machine (java executable file), it loads your class and processes your main method. So the code contained within this method is the step-by-step instruction set for what the application will do. Lines 51 and 54 delimit the body of the main method.

```
53:        Labels LabelsApp = new Labels();
```

Finally, line 53 has the only instruction for the `main` method: create a new object of type `Labels`. The creation and initialization of a new class can come in one step or in two:

```
Labels LabelsApp;
LabelsApp = new Labels();
```

Or

```
Labels LabelsApp = new Labels();
```

Either way, this is saying that `LabelsApp` is a variable of type `Labels`, and we are assigning to it a newly allocated object of type `Labels`. Effectively, this creates a new `Labels` object and calls its constructor. From the earlier discussion, you know that the constructor sets the class's title, sets a layout manager, adds a few labels to it, and then creates a `WindowAdapter` to listen for the application to close. Thus, the `Labels` application is born.

There you have it! You have just written your first graphical Java application. The rest of the examples in this section (using AWT) will all be built the exact same way, with the same framework, but will have different components in them.

Try playing with the source code and see what you can do with it. Change the text of the labels. For example, change:

```
11:     Label lblStockSymbol = new Label( "QUE" );
12:     Label lblStockPrice = new Label( "150.5" );
```

To

```
11:     Label lblStockSymbol = new Label( "MCP" );
12:     Label lblStockPrice = new Label( "200" );
```

And recompile and run the application.

Then try changing the size of the frame; for example, change

```
30:         setSize( 300, 60 );
```

To

```
30:         setSize( 500, 60 );
```

Recompile and run the application. Have fun!

Buttons

You are undoubtedly familiar with a standard push button: It has a text label on it, and clicking it causes some action to occur in your program. The AWT supports push buttons through its `Button` class. A `Button` can be constructed in two ways (see Table 4.5).

Table 4.5 **Button** Constructors

Class Name	Description
Button()	Constructs a button with no label
Button(String label)	Constructs a button with the specified label

The Button class is derived directly from Component, so it can be added to any class derived from Container, such as the Frame class.

Most of the methods in the Button class are related to event handling. After all, you're probably going to want to do something when someone clicks your button, but we'll talk more about that in Chapter 6, "Handling Events in Your User Interface." The Button class does provide two methods that allow you to manipulate the button's label: You can set the button's label with the setLabel(String) method and retrieve the button's method with the getLabel() method.

Here is an example of creating a button with the label "My Button":

```
Button myButton;
myButton = new Button( "My Button" );
```

Or

```
Button myButton = new Button( "My Button );
```

Take a look at Listing 4.2 for the complete source code for an application that displays a label and a button.

Type the code from Listing 4.2, excluding line numbers, into your favorite text editor and save it as Buttons.java, or copy it from the CD. Build it as follows:

```
javac Buttons.java
java Buttons
```

The code specific to the Button class is boldface for your convenience and is explained following the source code.

Listing 4.2 **Buttons.java**

```
1:  // Import the Abstract Window Toolkit (AWT) classes
2:  import java.awt.*;
3:  import java.awt.event.*;
4:
5:  public class Buttons extends Frame
6:  {
7:      // Create a label and a button
8:      Label lblTitle = new Label( "Here is a button:" );
9:      Button btnUpdate = new Button( "Update Quotes" );
```

continues

Listing 4.2   continued

```
10:
11:    // Buttons class constructor
12:    public Buttons()
13:    {
14:        // Set the title of our frame
15:        super( "Buttons Example!" );
16:
17:        // Choose the FlowLayout layout manager
18:        setLayout( new FlowLayout() );
19:
20:        // Add our components
21:        add( lblTitle );
22:        add( btnUpdate );
23:
24:        // Set our size
25:        setSize( 300, 60 );
26:
27:        // Make our frame visible
28:        setVisible( true );
29:
30:        // Add a window listener to listen for our window closing
31:        addWindowListener
32:        (
33:            new WindowAdapter()
34:            {
35:                public void windowClosing(WindowEvent e )
36:                {
37:                    System.exit( 0 );
38:                }
39:            }
40:        );
41:    }
42:
43:    // Main entry point into the Buttons class
44:    public static void main( String[] args )
45:    {
46:        // Create an instance of our Buttons class
47:        Buttons ButtonsApp = new Buttons();
48:    }
49: }
```

After that lengthy discussion in the previous section, this Java programming stuff is a piece of cake! With only a few name changes, you only had to change two lines of the code to add a button.

Figure 4.3 shows a screenshot of the Buttons application.

Figure 4.3

*Buttons application
example.*

```
9:     Button btnUpdate = new Button( "Update Quotes" );
```

Line 9 creates a new button called btnUpdate with the label Update Quotes, which could be used to update stock quotes. It uses the second constructor in Table 4.5 to construct the button.

```
22:        add( btnUpdate );
```

Finally, line 22 adds btnUpdate to the Buttons container using the same add method as in the last section.

That is it! We will spend some more time in Chapter 6 talking about how to respond to events when a user clicks a button. However, until then, you know at least how to create a button, modify its properties, and display it on the screen.

Text Fields

A *text field* is a text object that allows the editing of a single line of text. It is similar to an edit box in Windows, and you would see something like it in your Web browser where you enter the URL, or Web address, of the site you would like to connect to.

The Java AWT supports text fields through the TextField class. The TextField class has four constructors, as you can see in Table 4.6.

Table 4.6 TextField **Constructors**

Class Name	Description
TextField()	Constructs a new empty text field
TextField(int columns)	Constructs a new empty text field with the specified number of columns
TextField(String text)	Constructs a new text field initialized with the specified text
TextField(String text, int columns)	Constructs a new text field initialized with the specified text to be displayed, and wide enough to hold the specified number of columns

So, you can create an empty text field or an initialized text field, and you can choose whether or not you want to worry about the number of columns in the text field. A column, in this context, corresponds to the average width of a character in the current platform; this field specifies that the text field should be wide enough to display the number of columns, or number of characters, passed in this parameter.

The TextField class has quite a few methods available for you to use. You might want to peruse the documentation for a complete list, but two that you might be interested in are setText(String) and getText(). Furthermore, if you are interested in creating a password field, where the text field does not echo back the characters the user types in, take a look at setEchoChar(char). With this method you can change the character that is echoed to the display every time the user types a character (for example, change it to an asterisk [*] for a password field).

Here is an example of creating a text field with no text and a text field with "My Text" in it:

```
TextField txtEmpty;
txtEmpty = new TextField();

TextField txtMyText;
TxtMyText = new TextField( "My Text" );
```

Or

```
TextField txtEmpty = new TextField();
TextField txtMyText = new TextField( "My Text" );
```

Take a look at Listing 4.3 for a complete example using the TextField class.

Type the code from Listing 4.3, excluding line numbers, into your favorite text editor and save it as TextFields.java, or copy it from the CD. Build and run it as follows:

```
javac TextFields.java
java TextFields
```

Try experimenting with the text field by clicking in it and typing your name to see how it works!

The code specific to the TextField class is boldface for your convenience and is explained following the source code.

Listing 4.3   `TextFields.java`

```
1:  // Import the Abstract Window Toolkit (AWT) classes
2:  import java.awt.*;
3:  import java.awt.event.*;
4:
5:  public class TextFields extends Frame
6:  {
7:      // Create two label - text field pairs
8:      Label lblSymbol = new Label( "Enter your stock symbol:" );
9:
```

```
10:       // Create a text field with width = 5
11:       TextField txtStockSymbol = new TextField(5);
12:
13:
14:       Label lblQuantity = new Label( "How Many Shares Do You Own?" );
15:
16:       // Create a text field with width = 10 and initial value of "0"
17:       TextField txtNumberOfShares = new TextField( "0", 10 );
18:
19: // TextFields class constructor
20:       public TextFields()
21:       {
22:           // Set the title of our frame
23:           super( "TextFields Example!" );
24:
25:           // Choose the FlowLayout layout manager
26:           setLayout( new FlowLayout() );
27:
28:           // Add our components
29:           add( lblSymbol );
30:           add( txtStockSymbol );
31:           add( lblQuantity );
32:           add( txtNumberOfShares );
33:
34:           // Set our size
35:           setSize( 400, 100 );
36:
37:           // Make ourself visible
38:           setVisible( true );
39:
40:           // Add a window listener to listen for our window closing
41:           addWindowListener
42:           (
43:               new WindowAdapter()
44:               {
45:                   public void windowClosing( WindowEvent e )
46:                   {
47:                       System.exit( 0 );
48:                   }
49:               }
50:           );
51:       }
52:
53:       // Main entry point into the TextFields class
54:       public static void main( String[] args )          .
55:       {
56:           // Create an instance of our class
57:           TextFields TextFieldsApp = new TextFields();
58:       }
59: }
```

Figure 4.4 shows a screenshot of the TextFields application.

Figure 4.4

TextFields application example.

```
11:        TextField txtStockSymbol = new TextField(5);

17:        TextField txtNumberOfShares = new TextField( "0", 10 );
```

Lines 11 and 17 create two text fields, one that shows 5 characters and one that shows 10 characters, respectively. The first text field is empty and the second is initialized to "0".

```
30:        add( txtStockSymbol );

32:        add( txtNumberOfShares );
```

After the text fields are created, they are added to the TextFields class in lines 30 and 32.

Text Areas

A *text area* is similar to a text field, only it can be much larger. You are probably already familiar with text areas in the form of text editors, such as Notepad in Microsoft Windows. Text areas are constructed in Java through the AWT TextArea class. Text areas can be constructed in five different ways (see Table 4.7).

Table 4.7   **TextArea Constructors**

Class Name	Description
TextArea()	Constructs a new text area with both vertical and horizontal scrollbars.
TextArea(int rows, int columns)	Constructs a new empty text area with the specified number of rows and columns and both vertical and horizontal scrollbars.
TextArea(String text)	Constructs a new text area with the specified text and both vertical and horizontal scrollbars.
TextArea(String text, int rows, int columns)	Constructs a new text area with the specified text, with the specified number of rows and columns, and with both vertical and horizontal scrollbars.
TextArea(String text, int rows, int columns, int scrollbars)	Constructs a new text area with the specified text, with the specified number of rows and columns, and with the specified scrollbars. You can pass one of the following constants for the scrollbars parameter: SCROLLBARS_BOTH, SCROLLBARS_VERTICAL_ONLY, SCROLLBARS_HORIZONTAL_ONLY, or SCROLLBARS_NONE. They function exactly as you would think.

You can create text areas either empty or with text, you can specify the size of the text area, and finally you can specify whether or not you want scrollbars.

Here is an example of how to construct three text areas:

```
// Construct an empty text area
TextArea txtMyEmptyTextArea = new TextArea();

// Construct a text area that says "This is my text"
TextArea txtMyInitializedTextArea = new TextArea( "This is my text" );

// Construct a text area with "My Text Area"in 15 rows and 80 columns
// only vertical scrollbars
TextArea txtVertScroll = new TextArea( "My Text Area!", 15, 80,
   SCROLLBARS_VERTICAL_ONLY );
```

A plethora of other methods are available in the `TextArea` class: methods to set and retrieve the number of rows and columns, methods to make the text area editable or read-only, and so forth; please take a look at the Java 2 SDK documentation when you are ready to use this component to its fullest! Two families of methods that you will undoubtedly be interested in are methods to add text to the text area and methods to get text from the text area. These methods are described in Table 4.8.

Table 4.8   `TextArea` **Methods**

Class Name	Description
`append(String str)`	Appends the given text to the end of the text currently in the text area.
`insert(String str, int pos)`	Inserts the given text at the given position in the text area.
`replaceRange(String str, int start, int end)`	Replaces the text between the start and end positions with the text specified by `str`.
`getText()`	Returns the text currently in the text area.

For example, if you had the following in the text area:

```
TextArea text = new TextArea( "My name is Steve, what is yours?" );
```

And you wanted to replace "Steve" with "QUE Reader", you would do it as follows:

```
Text.replaceRange( "QUE Reader", 11, 16);
```

This might take a little explanation. You are replacing the characters between the 11th and 16th characters in text with "QUE Reader". The reason you specify 11 is because the "S" in "Steve" starts at position 11. Now if you are astute, you will notice that the "S" is at position 12—what's up? Well, my friend, all the characters in a text area are indexed —that is, referenced by position—with a zero base, meaning that you start the count from zero. Hence, here is how you know to start at 11:

```
My name is Steve, what is yours?
01234567890123456789012345678901
0         1         2         3
```

So as you can see, it truly is at the 11th position. You should start getting used to this because almost everything in Java is indexed with this zero base—give yourself a little time and you will be talking about the first item on a restaurant menu as the 0th item!

Take a look at Listing 4.4 for a complete example that uses the TextArea class.

Type the code from Listing 4.4, excluding line numbers, into your favorite text editor and save it as TextAreas.java, or copy it from the CD. Build and run it as follows:

```
javac TextAreas.java
java TextAreas
```

Try experimenting with the text area by clicking in it and typing something; try pressing Enter a few times and typing on different lines. It should remind you of a simple text editor (like Notepad if you are using Windows.)

The code specific to the TextArea class is boldface for your convenience and is explained following the source code.

Listing 4.4   TextAreas.java

```
 1:   // Import the Abstract Window Toolkit (AWT) classes
 2:   import java.awt.*;
 3:   import java.awt.event.*;
 4:
 5:
 6:   public class TextAreas extends Frame
 7:   {
 8:       // Create a label
 9:       Label lblDescription   = new Label( "Enter a description:" );
10:
11:       // Create a text area with a width of 80 and a height of 15
12:       TextArea txtDescription = new TextArea( 15, 80 );
13:
14:       // TextAreas class constructor
15:       public TextAreas()
16:       {
17:           // Set the title of our frame
18:           super( "TextAreas Example!" );
19:
20:           // Choose the FlowLayout layout manager
21:           setLayout( new FlowLayout() );
```

```
22:
23:        // Add our components
24:        add( lblDescription );
25:        add( txtDescription );
26:
27:        // Set our size
28:        setSize( 640, 320 );
29:
30:        // Make ourself visible
31:        setVisible( true );
32:
33:        // Add a window listener to listen for our window closing
34:        addWindowListener
35:        (
36:            new WindowAdapter()
37:            {
38:                public void windowClosing( WindowEvent e )
39:                {
40:                    System.exit( 0 );
41:                }
42:            }
43:        );
44:    }
45:
46:    // Main entry point into the TextAreas class
47:    public static void main( String[] args )
48:    {
49:        // Create an instance of our class
50:        TextAreas TextAreasApp = new TextAreas();
51:    }
52: }
```

Figure 4.5 shows a screenshot of the TextAreas application.

Figure 4.5

TextAreas application example.

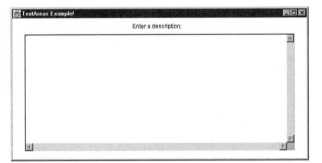

```
12:    TextArea txtDescription = new TextArea( 15, 80 );
```

Line 12 creates an empty text area that has 15 rows and 80 columns using the second constructor in Table 4.7.

```
25:          add( txtDescription );
```

Line 25 adds the text area to the TextAreas frame.

I hope that you are starting to notice how little work you have to do to include these controls in your user interface: Construct them and add them to your frame. There will be plenty of work when you want to do something meaningful with the components, such as take the text the user enters into a text area, spell check it, and send it off as an email to someone.

Check Boxes

A *check box* is a graphical component that can be in one of two states: on or off (or checked or unchecked if you like). Check boxes are great components to use when you want your user to enable or disable something.

The Java AWT classes support check boxes through the class Checkbox. The Checkbox class can be constructed five different ways, as shown in Table 4.9.

Table 4.9   Checkbox **Constructors**

Class Name	Description
Checkbox()	Constructs a check box with no label; initially set to the off state.
Checkbox(String label)	Constructs a check box with the specified label; initially set to the off state.
Checkbox(String label, boolean state)	Constructs a check box with the specified label and state: true = on/checked, false = off/unchecked.
Checkbox(String label, boolean state, CheckboxGroup group)	Constructs a check box with the specified label and state and adds it to the specified CheckboxGroup.
Checkbox(String label, CheckboxGroup group, boolean state)	Constructs a check box with the specified label and state and adds it to the specified CheckboxGroup.

You can create a check box with or without labels and set its initial state, but what is this CheckboxGroup thing? You may be familiar with the concept of a radio button — a group of buttons where one and only button one is selected at a time; the selection of one button in the group deselects all the other buttons. That is precisely what the CheckboxGroup class is for. First you construct a new CheckboxGroup object and then pass it to the constructors of the Checkbox objects you want in the checkbox group. When the user selects a button, the CheckBoxGroup will take care of the logic of selecting the specified button and deselecting the remaining buttons for you.

Here are several examples of how to create some check boxes and a set of radio buttons:

```
// Create an unchecked checkbox
Checkbox cbxTracking = new Checkbox( "Tracking" );

// Create a checked checkbox
Checkbox cbxAdd = new Checkbox( "Add", true );

// Create a group of radio buttons
CheckboxGroup cbg = new CheckboxGroup();
Checkbox cbxOn = new Checkbox( "On", cbg, true );
Checkbox cbxOff = new Checkbox( "Off", false, cbg );
```

You might have noticed that the fourth and fifth constructors look the same, just with the last two arguments reversed. You know what? You're right! There are a couple internal differences in the `Checkbox` component, but they are functionally equivalent for our use.

That is why in the previous example I switched the order of the arguments for `cbxOn` and `cbxOff`; they will function identically.

Two `Checkbox` methods of interest, `getState` and `setState`, are displayed in Table 4.10.

Table 4.10   `Checkbox` **Methods**

Class Name	Description
`getState()`	Gets the state of the check box, returns a `boolean`: true = on/checked, false = off/unchecked.
`setState(boolean state)`	Sets the state of the check box: true = on/checked, false = off/unchecked.

Now take a look at Listing 4.5 for a complete example that creates two check boxes and a set of radio buttons.

Type the code from Listing 4.5, excluding line numbers, into your favorite text editor and save it as `Checkboxes.java`, or copy it from the CD. Build and run it as follows:

```
javac Checkboxes.java
java Checkboxes
```

Try experimenting with the components by selecting and deselecting the check boxes and verifying that the `CheckboxGroup` behaves as I have described it.

The code specific to the `Checkbox` class is boldface for your convenience and is explained following the source code.

Listing 4.5   `Checkboxes.java`

```
1:  // Import the Abstract Window Toolkit (AWT) classes
2:  import java.awt.*;
3:  import java.awt.event.*;
4:
5:  public class Checkboxes extends Frame
6:  {
7:      // Create a label and two checkboxes and a checkbox group
8:      Label lblTitle =
9:          new Label( "Here are some checkboxes:" );
10:     Checkbox cbxHistoricalTracking =
11:         new Checkbox( "Historical Tracking" );
12:     Checkbox cbxAddToPortfolio =
13:         new Checkbox( "Add to Portfolio", true );
14:
15:     // Checkbox groups - radio buttons
16:     CheckboxGroup cbgOrderOption =
17:         new CheckboxGroup();
18:     Checkbox cbxBuy =
19:         new Checkbox( "Buy", cbgOrderOption, true );
20:     Checkbox cbxSell =
21:          new Checkbox( "Sell", cbgOrderOption, false );
22:     Checkbox cbxHold =
23:         new Checkbox( "Hold", cbgOrderOption, false );
24:
25:     // Checkboxes class constructor
26:     public Checkboxes()
27:     {
28:         // Set the title of our frame
29:         super( "Checkboxes Example!" );
30:
31:         // Choose the FlowLayout layout manager
32:         setLayout( new FlowLayout() );
33:
34:         // Add our label
35:         add( lblTitle );
36:
37:         // Add our checkboxes
38:         add( cbxHistoricalTracking );
39:         add( cbxAddToPortfolio );
40:
41:         // Add our radio buttons
42:         add( cbxBuy );
43:         add( cbxSell );
44:         add( cbxHold );
45:
46:         // Set our size
47:         setSize( 300, 120 );
48:
49:         // Make ourself visible
50:         setVisible( true );
51:
```

```
52:          // Add a window listener to listen for our window closing
53:          addWindowListener
54:          (
55:              new WindowAdapter()
56:              {
57:                  public void windowClosing( WindowEvent e )
58:                  {
59:                      System. exit( 0 );
60:                  }
61:              }
62:          );
63:      }
64:
65:      // Main entry point into the Checkboxes class
66:      public static void main( String[] args )
67:      {
68:          // Create an instance of our Labels class
69:          Checkboxes CheckboxesApp = new Checkboxes();
70:      }
71: }
```

Figure 4.6 shows a screenshot of the Checkboxes application.

Figure 4.6

Checkboxes application example.

```
10:     Checkbox cbxHistoricalTracking =
11:         new Checkbox( "Historical Tracking" );
12:     Checkbox cbxAddToPortfolio =
13:         new Checkbox( "Add to Portfolio", true );
```

Lines 10–13 create two check boxes, the first unchecked with the label Historical Tracking, using the second constructor in Table 4.9, and the second checked with the label Add to Portfolio, using the third constructor in Table 4.9.

```
16:     CheckboxGroup cbgOrderOption =
17:         new CheckboxGroup();
18:     Checkbox cbxBuy =
19:         new Checkbox( "Buy", cbgOrderOption, true );
20:     Checkbox cbxSell =
21:         new Checkbox( "Sell", cbgOrderOption, false );
22:     Checkbox cbxHold =
23:         new Checkbox( "Hold", cbgOrderOption, false );
```

Lines 16–23 construct a set of Order Option radio buttons: Buy, Sell, and Hold. In lines 16 and 17, the CheckboxGroup that is going to manage the radio buttons is created. In lines 18–23, the three radio buttons are constructed, each added to the cbgOrderOption CheckboxGroup and with the Buy radio button selected.

```
38:          add( cbxHistoricalTracking );
39:          add( cbxAddToPortfolio );
42:          add( cbxBuy );
43:          add( cbxSell );
44:          add( cbxHold );
```

Lines 38, 39, and 42–44 add each of the check boxes to the Checkboxes frame.
Notice that you do not have to add the CheckboxGroup object to the frame; sending it
as an input parameter to the Checkbox constructors is sufficient.

When we get around to processing events in Chapter 7, we will find that we will typically want to run through our check boxes and determine which ones are selected
before validating a form, for example. That will involve using getState, but more on
that in Chapter 7. Let's get to choice lists!

Choice Lists

You should be familiar with choice lists in their more common name, combo boxes; a
choice list is a drop-down list, or menu, of choices. You would use it when you want
the user to select one and only one selection from a list of items and you are trying
to conserve space.

The Java AWT classes support choice lists through the class Choice. The Choice
class can only be constructed in one way, as shown in Table 4.11.

Table 4.11   Choice Constructor

Class Name	Description
Choice()	Constructs a new empty choice list

You create a choice list as follows:

```
Choice chlistStockSymbols = new Choice();
```

Before you show your choice list, you will most definitely want to add some choices
to it. You have two methods you can use to add elements to a choice list, as shown in
Table 4.12.

Table 4.12   Choice Methods

Class Name	Description
add(String item)	Adds an item to the choice list
insert(String item, int index)	Inserts an item into the choice list at the specified position

You could add a few items to your choice list as follows:

```
chlistStockSymbols.add( "QUE" );
chlistStockSymbols.add( "MCP" );
chlistStockSymbols.add( "GOOD" );
```

And then you could insert an item at the head of the list as follows:

```
ChlistStockSymbols.insert( "SAMS", 0 );
```

Again, you are using a zero-indexed base. To get some real use out of the choice list, the Choice class provides a few methods to help you, as shown in Table 4.13.

Table 4.13   More Choice Methods

Class Name	Description
getItem(int index)	Retrieves the item at the specified position
getItemCount()	Retrieves the number of items in the list
getSelectedIndex()	Retrieves the index of the selected item
getSelectedItem()	Retrieves the selected item (as a String)
remove(int position)	Removes the item at the specified position
remove(String item)	Removes the specified item
select(int position)	Selects the item at the specified position
select(String item)	Selects the specified item

Sorry to give you so much in this class, but without getting to handling events, these methods are pretty important.

Now take a look at Listing 4.6 for a complete example that creates a choice list of stock symbols.

Type the code from Listing 4.6, excluding line numbers, into your favorite text editor and save it as ChoiceLists.java, or copy it from the CD. Build and run it as follows:

RunIt →
```
javac ChoiceLists.java
java ChoiceLists
```

Try experimenting with the choice list by clicking on it and selecting a stock symbol while the application is running.

The code specific to the ChoiceLists class is boldface for your convenience and is explained following the source code.

Listing 4.6   `ChoiceLists.java`

```
1:  // Import the Abstract Window Toolkit (AWT) classes
2:  import java.awt.*;
3:  import java.awt.event.*;
4:
5:  public class ChoiceLists extends Frame
6:  {
7:      // Create a label and a Choice control
8:      Label lblTitle = new Label( "Here is a choice list:" );
9:      Choice chlistStockSymbols = new Choice();
10:
11:     // ChoiceLists class constructor
12:     public ChoiceLists()
13:     {
14:         // Set the title of our frame
15:         super( "ChoiceLists Example!" );
16:
17:         // Choose the FlowLayout layout manager
18:         setLayout( new FlowLayout() );
19:
20:         // Build our choice list
21:         chlistStockSymbols.addItem( "QUE" );
22:         chlistStockSymbols.addItem( "MCP" );
23:         chlistStockSymbols.addItem( "SAMS" );
24:         chlistStockSymbols.addItem( "GOOD" );
25:
26:         // Add our controls
27:         add( lblTitle );
28:         add( chlistStockSymbols );
29:
30:         // Set our size
31:         setSize( 300, 100 );
32:
33:         // Make ourself visible
34:         setVisible( true );
35:
36:         // Add a window listener to listen for our window closing
37:         addWindowListener
38:         (
39:             new WindowAdapter()
40:             {
41:                 public void windowClosing( WindowEvent e )
42:                 {
43:                     System.exit( 0 );
44:                 }
45:             }
46:         );
47:     }
48:
49:     // Main entry point into the ChoiceLists class
50:     public static void main( String[] args )
51:     {
```

```
52:         // Create an instance of our ChoiceLists class
53:         ChoiceLists ChoiceListsApp = new ChoiceLists();
54:     }
55: }
```

Figure 4.7 shows the `ChoiceLists` application after the choice list has been clicked (selected).

Figure 4.7

ChoiceLists application example.

```
9:      Choice chlistStockSymbols = new Choice();
```

Line 9 creates a new choice list named `chlistStockSymbols`.

```
21:         chlistStockSymbols.addItem( "QUE" );
22:         chlistStockSymbols.addItem( "MCP" );
23:         chlistStockSymbols.addItem( "SAMS" );
24:         chlistStockSymbols.addItem( "GOOD" );
```

Lines 21–24 add four stock symbols to the `chlistStockSymbols` choice list.

```
28:         add( chlistStockSymbols );
```

Finally, line 28 adds the choice list to the `ChoiceList` frame.

Layout Managers

Now that you know the basic components that the Java AWT classes support, you need a way to arrange them on the screen so that they are at least aesthetically pleasing! Now don't get me wrong; I think all the examples we have gone through thus far in this chapter have been beautiful, but your users might beg to differ.

To solve this problem, the AWT classes offer the capability to arrange components through what are known as layout managers. As we go through the layout managers, it will quickly hit you that you are going to need to think about your user interfaces in a slightly different way than you are accustomed to.

There are five layout managers:

- Flow layout
- Grid layout
- Border layout
- Card layout
- Grid bag layout

The first three are very easy to use, whereas the last two are more advanced and thus more difficult to implement.

Flow Layout

The first layout manager we are going to talk about is our good friend `FlowLayout`. We have already used the `FlowLayout` layout manager in all the previous examples because it is by far the simplest. As you add components to your frame, it adds them from left to right until it gets to the end of a line, and then it starts again on the next line, just like a word processor.

The `FlowLayout` class supports three constructors, as shown in Table 4.14.

Table 4.14 `FlowLayout` **Constructors**

Class Name	Description
FlowLayout()	Constructs a new `FlowLayout` with centered alignment and the default 5-unit horizontal and vertical gaps.
FlowLayout(int align)	Constructs a new `FlowLayout` with the specified alignment and the default 5-unit horizontal and vertical gaps. Valid alignments are `FlowLayout.CENTER`, `FlowLayout.LEADING`, `FlowLayout.LEFT`, `FlowLayout.RIGHT`, and `FlowLayout.TRAILING`.
FlowLayout(int align, int hgap, int vgap)	Constructs a new `FlowLayout` with the specified alignment and horizontal and vertical gaps.

As you can see, `FlowLayout`s don't give you too much control over the layout of your user interface; you can control the alignment of components and the horizontal and vertical gaps between components.

The alignment options are specified in Table 4.15.

Table 4.15 `FlowLayout` **Alignment Options**

Class Name	Description
CENTER	Each row of components should be centered.
LEADING	Each row of components should be justified to the leading edge of the container's orientation.
LEFT	Each row of components should be left-justified.
RIGHT	Each row of components should be right-justified.
TRAILING	Each row of components should be justified to the trailing edge of the container's orientation.

Enough of this talking, let's code this up and see what it looks like! Take a look at Listing 4.7.

Type the code from Listing 4.7, excluding line numbers, into your favorite text editor and save it as `FlowLayoutExample.java`, or copy it from the CD. Build and run it as follows:

```
javac FlowLayoutExample.java
java FlowLayoutExample
```

The code specific to the `FlowLayout` class is boldface for your convenience and is explained following the source code.

Listing 4.7   `FlowLayoutExample.java`

```
1:  // Import the Abstract Window Toolkit (AWT) classes
2:  import java.awt.*;
3:  import java.awt.event.*;
4:
5:  public class FlowLayoutExample extends Frame
6:  {
7:      // Create our layout manager
8:      FlowLayout layout = new FlowLayout( FlowLayout.CENTER );
9:
10:     // Create four labels
11:     Label lblOne    = new Label( "One" );
12:     Label lblTwo    = new Label( "Two" );
13:     Label lblThree  = new Label( "Three" );
14:     Label lblFour   = new Label( "Four" );
15:     Label lblFive   = new Label( "Five" );
16:     Label lblSix    = new Label( "Six" );
17:
18:     // FlowLayoutExample class constructor
19:     public FlowLayoutExample()
20:     {
21:         // Set the title of our frame
22:         super( "FlowLayout Example!" );
23:
24:         // Choose the FlowLayout layout manager
25:         setLayout( layout );
26:
27:         // Add our labels
28:         add( lblOne );
29:         add( lblTwo );
30:         add( lblThree );
31:         add( lblFour );
32:         add( lblFive );
33:         add( lblSix );
34:
35:         // Set our size
```

continues

Listing 4.7   continued

```
36:            setSize( 200, 100 );
37:
38:            // Make ourself visible
39:            setVisible( true );
40:
41:            // Add a window listener to list for our window closing
42:            addWindowListener
43:            (
44:                new WindowAdapter()
45:                {
46:                    public void windowClosing( WindowEvent e )
47:                    {
48:                        System.exit( 0 );
49:                    }
50:                }
51:            );
52:        }
53:
54:        // Main entry point into the FlowLayoutExample class
55:        public static void main( String[] args )
56:        {
57:            // Create an instance of our FlowLayoutExample class
58:            FlowLayoutExample FlowLayoutApp = new FlowLayoutExample();
59:        }
60: }
```

Figures 4.8, 4.9, and 4.10 show screenshots of the `FlowLayoutExample` application with centered, right-justified, and left-justified alignments, respectively.

Figure 4.8

FlowLayoutExample application example (centered).

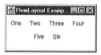

Figure 4.9

FlowLayoutExample application example (right-justified).

Figure 4.10

FlowLayoutExample application example (left-justified).

```
 8:        FlowLayout layout = new FlowLayout( FlowLayout.CENTER );
```

Line 8 creates the flow layout manager for all components to be centered on the display. Figures 4.9 and 4.10 show the layout with `FlowLayout.RIGHT` and `FlowLayout.LEFT` alignments, respectively. To create those examples yourself, use the same Java file and make the following change to line 8:

Right-justified:

```
 8:        FlowLayout layout = new FlowLayout( FlowLayout.RIGHT );
```

Left-justified:

```
 8:        FlowLayout layout = new FlowLayout( FlowLayout.LEFT );
11:        Label lblOne    = new Label( "One" );
12:        Label lblTwo    = new Label( "Two" );
13:        Label lblThree  = new Label( "Three" );
14:        Label lblFour   = new Label( "Four" );
15:        Label lblFive   = new Label( "Five" );
16:        Label lblSix    = new Label( "Six" );
```

Lines 11–16 create six labels that we are going to add to our frame.

```
25:        setLayout( layout );
```

Line 25 sets the new flow layout manager as the layout for the `FlowLayoutExample` class. Note that previously we had done this step inline, like this:

```
setLayout( new FlowLayout( FlowLayout.CENTER );
```

You could have done this in this example as well, but I wanted you to see how to create an actual `FlowLayout` class. You would do this if you wanted to change the layout at some time in the future or if you wanted to use any of the methods to manipulate the behavior of the layout.

```
28:        add( lblOne );
29:        add( lblTwo );
30:        add( lblThree );
31:        add( lblFour );
32:        add( lblFive );
33:        add( lblSix );
```

Lines 28–33 add the six labels to the `FlowLayoutExample` frame.

Grid Layout

Second to the flow layout in ease of use is arguably the grid layout. The `GridLayout` class is a layout manager that lays out a container's components in a rectangular grid with the number of rows and columns that you specify. The container is divided into equal-sized rectangles, and one component is placed in each rectangle.

The Java AWT class `GridLayout` can be constructed in three different ways, as shown in Table 4.16.

Table 4.16 `GridLayout` **Constructors**

Class Name	Description
`GridLayout()`	Constructs a new grid layout with the default values of one column per control in a single row.
`GridLayout(int rows, int cols)`	Constructs a new grid layout with the specified number of rows and columns.
`GridLayout(int rows, int cols, int hgap, int vgap)`	Constructs a new grid layout with the specified number of rows and columns and the specified horizontal and vertical gaps between components.

The `GridLayout` class allows you to specify the number of rows and columns you want to display and specify the horizontal and vertical gaps between components. So construction is simple:

```
// Create a new GridLayout with 2 rows with 3 columns per row
GridLayout layout = new GridLayout( 2, 3 );
```

Or, you can always create the `GridLayout` when you are setting the layout manager:

```
setLayout( new GridLayout( 2, 3 ) );
```

Look at Listing 4.8 for a complete example using the `GridLayout` class. This example uses buttons instead of labels so you can see the complete borders of each component.

Type the code from Listing 4.8, excluding line numbers, into your favorite text editor and save it as `GridLayoutExample.java` or copy it from the CD. Build and run it as follows:

```
javac GridLayoutExample.java
java GridLayoutExample
```

The code specific to the `GridLayout` class is boldface for your convenience and is explained following the source code.

Listing 4.8 `GridLayoutExample.java`

```
1:  // Import the Abstract Window Toolkit (AWT) classes
2:  import java.awt.*;
3:  import java.awt.event.*;
4:
5:  public class GridLayoutExample extends Frame
6:  {
7:      // Create our layout manager
8:      GridLayout layout = new GridLayout( 2, 3 );
```

```
 9:      //GridLayout layout = new GridLayout( 3, 2 );
10:
11:      //  Create six buttons.
12:      Button btnOne    = new Button( "One" );
13:      Button btnTwo    = new Button( "Two" );
14:      Button btnThree  = new Button( "Three" );
15:      Button btnFour   = new Button( "Four" );
16:      Button btnFive   = new Button( "Five" );
17:      Button btnSix    = new Button( "Six" );
18:
19:      // GridLayoutExample class constructor
20:      public GridLayoutExample()
21:      {
22:          // Set the title of our frame
23:          super( "GridLayout Example!" );
24:
25:          // Choose the GridLayout layout manager
26:          setLayout( layout );
27:
28:          // Add our labels
29:          add( btnOne );
30:          add( btnTwo );
31:          add( btnThree );
32:          add( btnFour );
33:          add( btnFive );
34:          add( btnSix );
35:
36:          // Set our size
37:          setSize( 200, 120 );
38:
39:          // Make ourself visible
40:          setVisible( true );
41:
42:          // Add a window listener to listen for our window closing
43:          addWindowListener
44:          (
45:              new WindowAdapter()
46:              {
47:                  public void  windowClosing( WindowEvent e )
48:                  {
49:                      System.exit( 0 );
50:                  }
51:              }
52:          );
53:      }
54:
55:      // Main entry point into the GridLayoutExample class
56:      public static void main( String[] args )
57:      {
58:          // Create an instance of our GridLayoutExample class
59:          GridLayoutExample GridLayoutApp = new GridLayoutExample();
60:      }
61: }
```

4

Figures 4.11 and 4.12 show screenshots of the GridLayoutExample application with two rows and three columns and then three rows and two columns, respectively.

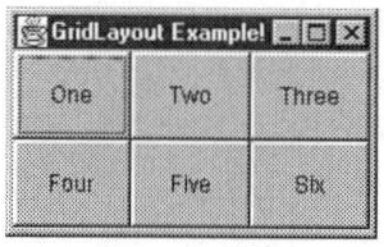

Figure 4.11

GridLayoutExample application example (two rows, three columns).

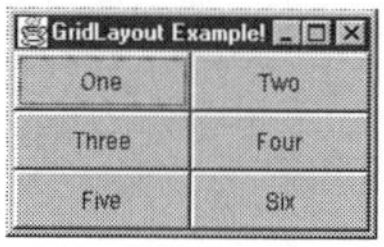

Figure 4.12

GridLayoutExample application example (three rows, two columns).

```
8:      GridLayout layout = new GridLayout( 2, 3 );
9:      //GridLayout layout = new GridLayout( 3, 2 );
```

Line 8 creates a new GridLayout with two rows and three columns. When you are playing with the source code, try commenting out line 8 (use "//") and uncomment line 9 (remove the "//") to see the difference. Figure 4.11 is made from the source code the way it is printed and 4.12 is using line 9 instead of line 8.

```
12:     Button btnOne    = new Button( "One" );
13:     Button btnTwo    = new Button( "Two" );
14:     Button btnThree  = new Button( "Three" );
15:     Button btnFour   = new Button( "Four" );
16:     Button btnFive   = new Button( "Five" );
17:     Button btnSix    = new Button( "Six" );
```

Lines 12–17 create six buttons for you to add to the frame.

```
26:     setLayout( layout );
```

Line 26 sets GridLayout as the layout manager for the frame.

```
29:     add( btnOne );
30:     add( btnTwo );
31:     add( btnThree );
32:     add( btnFour );
33:     add( btnFive );
34:     add( btnSix );
```

Finally, lines 29–34 add the six buttons to the frame.

Border Layout

The border layout starts making this discussion a little more interesting. With this layout manager, components are placed on the container in five distinct regions: north, south, east, west, and center. The border layout manager is accessed through the AWT class BorderLayout, which can be constructed in two ways, as shown in Table 4.17.

Table 4.17 BorderLayout Constructors

Class Name	Description
BorderLayout()	Constructs a new BorderLayout with no gaps between components
BorderLayout(int hgap, int vgap)	Constructs a new BorderLayout with the specified horizontal and vertical gaps

I think these types of constructors should be pretty familiar by now, but here is a quick example to construct a new border layout manager:

```
BorderLayout layout = new BorderLayout();

BorderLayout layoutGaps = new BorderLayout( 5, 5 );
```

Okay, these regions are nice, but how do we specify them? Well, the Container class's add method can accept an optional constraint that specifies the location. See Table 4.18 for the parameters you can send to the add method.

Table 4.18 BorderLayout Add Constraints

Parameter Name	Description
NORTH	North constraint—adds the component to the top of the container.
SOUTH	South constraint—adds the component to the bottom of the container.
EAST	East constraint—adds the component to the right side of the container.
WEST	West constraint—adds the component to the left side of the container.
CENTER	Center constraint—adds the component to the center of the container.

This is how you would add two components to the container:

```
setLayout( new BorderLayout() );
add( new Button( "North" ), BorderLayout.NORTH );
add( new Button( "Center" ), BorderLayout.CENTER );
```

Take a look at Listing 4.9 for a complete example using the BorderLayout class. After you look at the code, take a look at Figure 4.13 for a screen shot showing how all this theoretical discussion is realized on the computer screen.

Type the code from Listing 4.9, excluding line numbers, into your favorite text editor and save it as BorderLayoutExample.java, or copy it from the CD. Build and run it as follows:

```
javac BorderLayoutExample.java
java BorderLayoutExample
```

The code specific to the BorderLayout class has been highlighted for your convenience and will be explained following the source code.

Listing 4.9 BorderLayoutExample.java

```
1:  // Import the Abstract Window Toolkit (AWT) classes
2:  import java.awt.*;
3:  import java.awt.event.*;
4:
5:  public class BorderLayoutExample extends Frame
6:  {
7:      // Create our layout manager
8:      BorderLayout layout = new BorderLayout();
9:      // BorderLayout layout = new BorderLayout( 5, 5 );
10:     //  Create five buttons.
11:     Button btnNorth     = new Button( "North" );
12:     Button btnSouth     = new Button( "South" );
13:     Button btnEast      = new Button( "East" );
14:     Button btnWest      = new Button( "West" );
15:     Button btnCenter    = new Button( "Center" );
16:
17:     // BorderLayoutExample class constructor
18:     public BorderLayoutExample()
19:     {
20:         // Set the title of our frame
21:         super( "BorderLayout Example!" );
22:
23:         // Choose the BorderLayout layout manager
24:         setLayout( layout );
25:
26:         // Add our buttons
27:         add( btnNorth, BorderLayout.NORTH );
28:         add( btnSouth, BorderLayout.SOUTH );
29:         add( btnEast, BorderLayout.EAST );
30:         add( btnWest, BorderLayout.WEST );
31:         add( btnCenter, BorderLayout.CENTER );
32:
33:         // Set our size
34:         setSize( 320, 240 );
35:
36:         // Make ourself visible
37:         setVisible( true );
38:
39:         // Add a window listener to listen for our window closing
40:         addWindowListener
```

```
41:        (
42:            new WindowAdapter()
43:            {
44:                public void windowClosing( WindowEvent e )
45:                {
46:                    System.exit( 0 );
47:                }
48:            }
49:        );
50:    }
51:
52:    // Main entry point into the BorderLayoutExample class
53:    public static void main( String[] args )
54:    {
55:        // Create an instance of our BorderLayoutExample class
56:        BorderLayoutExample BorderLayoutApp = new BorderLayoutExample();
57:    }
58: }
```

Figure 4.13 shows a screen shot of the BorderLayoutExample application.

Figure 4.13

BorderLayoutExample application example.

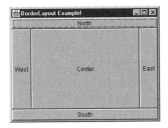

```
8:      BorderLayout layout = new BorderLayout();
9:      // BorderLayout layout = new BorderLayout( 5, 5 );
```

Line 8 creates a new BorderLayout layout manager using the first constructor in Table 4.17. Try commenting out line 8 and uncommenting line 9, and then recompile to see how those horizontal and vertical gaps work. Experiment with different values.

```
11:     Button btnNorth     = new Button( "North" );
12:     Button btnSouth     = new Button( "South" );
13:     Button btnEast      = new Button( "East" );
14:     Button btnWest      = new Button( "West" );
15:     Button btnCenter    = new Button( "Center" );
```

Lines 11–15 create five buttons, each with the name of one of the BorderLayout constraints: North, South, East, West, and Center.

```
24:         setLayout( layout );
```

Line 24 sets the `BorderLayout` as the layout manager for the `BorderLayoutExample` frame.

```
27:          add( btnNorth, BorderLayout.NORTH );
28:          add( btnSouth, BorderLayout.SOUTH );
29:          add( btnEast, BorderLayout.EAST );
30:          add( btnWest, BorderLayout.WEST );
31:          add( btnCenter, BorderLayout.CENTER );
```

Finally, lines 27–31 add the buttons to the `BorderLayoutExample` frame. Note that each one specifies the corresponding location constraint.

Card Layout

The card layout is a layout manager specified by the AWT class `CardLayout`. It is unique in that it treats each component in the container as an individual card. It shows only one card at a time and the order that the components are added to the container is important; the first card added is the first card displayed when the application starts. The layout manager maintains its own ordering of its components and provides a mechanism to either flip through the cards sequentially or show a specific card. Take a look at Table 4.19 to see the `CardLayout` constructors.

Table 4.19 `CardLayout` Constructors

Method Name	Description
CardLayout()	Constructs a new `CardLayout` layout manager with gap sizes of zero
CardLayout(int hgap, int vgap)	Constructs a new `CardLayout` layout manager with the specified horizontal and vertical gaps

To add components to a `CardLayout`, use the `Container`'s `add(String, Component)` method where the `String` specifies an identifier for the card and the `Component` specifies the component to add. When you are ready to show the card, you can call the `CardLayout` class's `first`, `next`, `last`, or `show` methods. See Table 4.20 for the format of these methods.

Table 4.20 `CardLayout` Methods

Method Name	Description
first(Container parent)	Flips to the first card in the container
next(Container parent)	Flips to the next card in the container
last(Container parent)	Flips to the last card in the container
show(Container parent, String name)	Shows the card specified by the name parameter—given when adding the card to the container

The card manager is useful in the context of, say, a Rolodex, where you could store business cards or such. If you were very creative with your cards (by embedding layouts within them—we'll talk more about that later), you could even simulate a Windows wizard-like application through the use of a `CardLayout`.

Take a look at Listing 4.10 for a complete example using the `CardLayout` class. This example is a bit more involved than the previous ones because there is no easy way to show you the functionality of the `CardLayout` itself without the handling action events. We will talk about event handling in greater detail in Chapter 7, but I will give you a preview when we discuss the code.

Type the code from Listing 4.10, excluding line numbers, into your favorite text editor and save it as `CardLayoutExample.java`, or copy it from the CD. Build and run it as follows:

```
javac CardLayoutExample.java
java CardLayoutExample
```

The code specific to the `CardLayout` class is boldface for your convenience and is explained following the source code.

Listing 4.10   `CardLayoutExample.java`

```
1:  // Import the Abstract Window Toolkit (AWT) classes
2:  import java.awt.*;
3:  import java.awt.event.*;
4:
5:  public class CardLayoutExample extends Frame implements ActionListener
6:  {
7:      // Create our layout manager
8:      CardLayout layout = new CardLayout();
9:
10:     // Create four buttons
11:     Button btnOne      = new Button( "One" );
12:     Button btnTwo      = new Button( "Two" );
13:     Button btnThree    = new Button( "Three" );
14:     Button btnFour     = new Button( "Four" );
15:
16:     // CardLayoutExample class constructor
17:     public CardLayoutExample()
18:     {
19:         // Set the title of our frame
20:         super( "CardLayout Example!" );
21:
22:         // Choose the CardLayout layout manager
23:         setLayout( layout );
24:
25:         // Tell our buttons that we will listen to their events
26:         btnOne.addActionListener( this );
```

continues

Listing 4.10 **continued**

```
27:            btnTwo.addActionListener( this );
28:            btnThree.addActionListener( this );
29:            btnFour.addActionListener( this );
30:
31:            // Add our buttons
32:            add( "Card 1", btnOne );
33:            add( "Card 2", btnTwo );
34:            add( "Card 3", btnThree );
35:            add( "Card 4", btnFour );
36:
37:            // Display the first card in the layout
38:            layout.first( this );
39:
40:            // Set our size
41:            setSize( 320, 240 );
42:
43:            // Make ourself visible
44:            setVisible( true );
45:
46:            // Add a window listener to list for our window closing
47:            addWindowListener
48:            (
49:                new WindowAdapter()
50:                {
51:                    public void windowClosing( WindowEvent e )
52:                    {
53:                        System.exit( 0 );
54:                    }
55:                }
56:            );
57:        }
58:
59:    // Respond to the actions we registered in our ActionListener
60:    public void actionPerformed( ActionEvent evt )
61:    {
62:    // Extract the object that generated the event from the event
63:        Object objSource = evt.getSource();
64:
65:        // Now see if that object is one of our buttons
66:        if( objSource == btnOne ||
67:            objSource == btnTwo ||
68:            objSource == btnThree ||
69:            objSource == btnFour )
70:        {
71:            // Advance the layout to the next card
72:            layout.next( this );
73:        }
74:
75:    }
76:
```

```
77:     // Main entry point into the CardLayoutExample class
78:     public static void main( String[] args )
79:     {
80:         // Create an instance of our CardLayoutExample class
81:         CardLayoutExample CardLayoutApp = new CardLayoutExample();
82:     }
83: }
```

Figures 4.14 and 4.15 show screen shots of the `CardLayoutExample` application running. Figure 4.14 shows the application when it starts up, showing the first button, and Figure 4.15 shows the application after button one has been clicked and the application is now displaying button two.

Figure 4.14

CardLayoutExample application example, first screen.

Figure 4.15

CardLayoutExample application example, second screen.

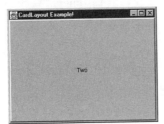

```
5: public class CardLayoutExample extends Frame implements ActionListener
```

Line 5 is quite a class declaration, isn't it? You are already familiar with most of it:

```
public class CardLayoutExample extends Frame
```

This translates to: I want to create the main public class for this Java source file called `CardLayoutExample` that is derived from, or inherits all the methods and functionality from, the `Frame` class. The last part now needs some explanation. `ActionListener` is a special type of class in Java called an interface. An *interface* is nothing more than the abstract declaration of a set of methods that you must implement in your class if you want the functionality of the interface. The `ActionListener` interface is a very simple interface as it has only one method: `actionPerformed`. Take a look at Listing 4.11. It shows the `ActionListener` interface taken directly from the Java source code.

Listing 4.11 `ActionListener.java`

```
1: public interface ActionListener extends EventListener {
2:     /**
3:      * Invoked when an action occurs.
4:      */
5:     public void actionPerformed(ActionEvent e);
6: }
```

From line 1 you can see that an interface is defined in the same manner as a class, but with the keyword: `interface`. The `ActionListener` interface extends the `EventListener` interface, which is the base interface that all event listener interfaces must extend, as shown in Listing 4.12.

Listing 4.12 `EventListener.java`

```
1: /**
2:  * A tagging interface that all event listener interfaces must extend
3:  */
4: public interface EventListener {
5: }
```

The `EventListener` interface is simply a placeholder that has no methods and is used to categorize classes or interfaces as "Event Listeners."

```
5:     public void actionPerformed(ActionEvent e);
```

Line 5 from Listing 4.11, `ActionListener`, shows that your class must define a method called `actionPerformed(ActionEvent e)` if it implements `ActionListener`. The signatures must be exact; you must explicitly define the method as follows:

```
public void actionPerformed(ActionEvent e);
```

In summary of `implements ActionListener`, you must include the `actionPerformed` method in your class. I know what you are saying: Why didn't I just say that in the first place? Anyway, back to the `CardLayoutExample`.

 An `Interface` is a special type of Java class that provides a set of abstract methods that all must be implemented in your class. An abstract method is a method declaration that does not have an implementation associated with it; thus you cannot create an instance of it. When a class supports an interface, it is said that it *implements* an interface, denoted by the Java keyword: `implements`. Although a class can be derived from only one class, it can implement multiple interfaces. This makes sense because implementing an interface is like signing a contract saying that you will implement the methods specified by the interface and there is no limit to the number of methods you can implement.

```
8:     CardLayout layout = new CardLayout();
```

Line 8 creates a new `CardLayout` layout manager using the first constructor in Table 4.19.

```
11:        Button btnOne      = new Button( "One" );
12:        Button btnTwo      = new Button( "Two" );
13:        Button btnThree    = new Button( "Three" );
14:        Button btnFour     = new Button( "Four" );
```

Lines 11–14 create four buttons, labeled One, Two, Three, and Four.

```
23:        setLayout( layout );
```

Line 23 sets the `CardLayoutExample` layout manager to `CardLayout`.

```
26:        btnOne.addActionListener( this );
27:        btnTwo.addActionListener( this );
28:        btnThree.addActionListener( this );
29:        btnFour.addActionListener( this );
```

Lines 26–29 gets back to the `ActionListener` discussion earlier. If you look at the documentation for the `Button` class, you will notice that it has a method called `addActionListener`. This is declared as follows:

```
public void addActionListener(ActionListener l)
```

Its responsibility is to add the specified action listener to receive action events from the button. Then, when the user presses and releases the mouse button over the button, it activates this action event and notifies the `ActionListener` that is listening. So in line 26–29, we are telling each button that the `CardLayoutExample` class is the `ActionListener` that we want it to notify when the user clicks the button.

```
32:        add( "Card 1", btnOne );
33:        add( "Card 2", btnTwo );
34:        add( "Card 3", btnThree );
35:        add( "Card 4", btnFour );
```

Lines 32–35 add each button to the `CardLayoutExample` frame and names them "Card 1", "Card 2", "Card 3", and "Card 4", respectively. These labels are important because if we call for a specific card using the `CardLayout` class's `show` method, we will refer to the card by this label.

```
38:        layout.first( this );
```

Line 38 tells the `CardLayout` layout manager to show the first card added to the container. The `this` parameter passed to the `first()` method represents this instance of the `CardLayoutExample` class. The `this` keyword is used to reference a particular instance of class. You can create multiple instances of the `CardLayoutExample` in your application, just as you can create multiple instances of the `Button` class, and the `this` keyword tells the `first()` method to specifically reference this `CardLayoutExample`.

```
60:     public void actionPerformed( ActionEvent evt )
61:     {
62:     // Extract the object that generated the event from the event
63:         Object objSource = evt.getSource();
64:
65:         // Now see if that object is one of our buttons
66:         if( objSource == btnOne ||
67:             objSource == btnTwo ||
68:             objSource == btnThree ||
69:             objSource == btnFour )
70:         {
71:             // Advance the layout to the next card
72:             layout.next( this );
73:         }
74:
75:     }
```

Lines 60–75 are the implementation of the ActionListener method actionPerformed. The variable passed to the actionPerformed method is of type ActionEvent. An ActionEvent indicates that a component-defined action occurred, such as a button press! Every ActionListener that has been registered with the component is notified when this event occurs. The ActionEvent describes a great deal of information about the event, which we will discuss at length in Chapter 7, but for this example we are concerned with the getSource method.

getSource, which is inherited from the EventObject class, retrieves the object that generated the event. Because we have only registered ourselves as the ActionListener for the four buttons, getSource will return the button that generated the event. Line 63 defines an Object called objSource that will hold the Object that generated the event.

Lines 66–69 compare the object to our buttons by using the logical OR operator (||). This really isn't necessary in this example because if we get an event, we know it is one of our buttons and we are not differentiating between buttons, but it is shown for completeness. When we have verified that it was in fact one of our buttons (surprise!), we tell the CardLayout manager to show the next card in the container.

The logical OR operator isrepresented by two bars (||) and causes the previous comparison to return true if any one of the individual comparisons is true. For example, consider the following comparison:

```
if( state == hungry || food == myfavorite )
{
    Eat();
}
```

This states that I will eat if I am hungry or if the food is my favorite, or both. Contrast this with the logical AND operator, which is represented by two ampersands (&&). It causes a comparison to be true only if both individual comparisons are true. Consider the following:

```
if( state == hungry && food == available )
{
    Eat();
}
```

This comparison states that I will eat only if I am hungry and there is food available. I will not eat if I am hungry and no food is available, nor will I eat if food is available and I am not hungry.

See the difference? Good!

Grid Bag Layout

The grid bag layout is far more advanced than any of the other layout managers we have used thus far. The `GridBagLayout` class is a flexible layout manager that aligns components both vertically and horizontally, without requiring that the components be the same size. It maintains a dynamic grid of cells where components can be placed and where the components can occupy one or more of the cells. The mechanism used to lay out components in a grid is the `GridBayConstraint` class.

The `GridBagConstraint` class specifies several attributes that determine the behavior of a component, as shown in Table 4.21.

Table 4.21 `GridBagConstraints` **Instance Variables**

Variable Name	Description
`gridx, gridy`	Specifies the grid x and y coordinates of the 0-based cell to place the component in. Use `GridBagConstraints.RELATIVE` (default value) to place the component in the container at the next cell following the previous.
`gridwidth, gridheight`	Specifies the number of cells the component should occupy in the grid.
`fill`	When the component's display area (area it is given to show itself) is larger than the control, this variable specifies how it should fill the remaining area. Values: `NONE` (default) = do not adjust the size of the component, `HORIZONTAL` = fill up the width of the area only, `VERTICAL` = fill up the height of the display area only, and `GridBagConstraints.BOTH` = fill up the entire display area.

continues

Table 4.21   continued

Variable Name	Description
ipadx, ipady	Specifies the component's internal padding, or the area outside of the component to count as part of the size of the component.
insets	Specifies the component's external padding, or the minimum amount of space between the component and its display area.
anchor	When the component is smaller than its display area, this variable specifies how it should be drawn in the area: CENTER (default), NORTH, NORTHEAST, EAST, SOUTHEAST, SOUTH, SOUTHWEST, WEST, NORTHWEST.
weightx, weighty	Specifies how to distribute space between components, important when your application is resized. These values specify the widths and heights relative to the other components in the frame. Note that you must specify a weight for at least one component in a row and a column or all components will clump together in the center of the container.

Constructing a GridBagLayout layout manager is simple. There is only one constructor, the default constructor (see Table 4.22).

Table 4.22   GridBagLayout Constructors

Variable Name	Description
GridBagLayout()	Constructs a grid bag layout manager.

After you construct a GridBagLayout layout manager, there are three things you have to do with your components: (1) add them to the container, (2) build a GridBagConstraints object with the configuration you want, and (3) call the GridBagLayout class's setConstraints method.

The setConstraints method appears as follows:

```
public void setConstraints(Component comp, GridBagConstraints constraints)
```

In the preceding line, the comp parameter specifies the component, for example a button or label, to set the constraints for. The constraints parameter specifies the actual constraints for the comp object. I know it looks complicated, but maybe an example would help. Take a look at Listing 4.13.

Type the code from Listing 4.13, excluding line numbers, into your favorite text editor and save it as GridBagLayoutExample.java, or copy it from the CD. Build and run it as follows:

```
javac GridBagLayoutExample.java
java GridBagLayoutExample
```

The code specific to the GridBagLayout class is boldface for your convenience and is explained following the source code. Figure 4.16 shows the GridBagLayoutExample application.

Listing 4.13   `GridBagLayoutExample.java`

```
1:  // Import the Abstract Window Toolkit (AWT) classes
2:  import java.awt.*;
3:  import java.awt.event.*;
4:
5:  public class GridBagLayoutExample extends Frame
6:  {
7:      // Create our layout manager
8:      GridBagLayout layout = new GridBagLayout();
9:      GridBagConstraints constraints = new GridBagConstraints();
10:
11:     // Create ten buttons
12:     Button btnOne     = new Button( "One" );
13:     Button btnTwo     = new Button( "Two" );
14:     Button btnThree   = new Button( "Three" );
15:     Button btnFour    = new Button( "Four" );
16:     Button btnFive    = new Button( "Five" );
17:     Button btnSix     = new Button( "Six" );
18:     Button btnSeven   = new Button( "Seven" );
19:     Button btnEight   = new Button( "Eight" );
20:     Button btnNine    = new Button( "Nine" );
21:     Button btnTen     = new Button( "Ten" );
22:
23:     // GridBagLayoutExample class constructor
24:     public GridBagLayoutExample()
25:     {
26:         // Set the title of our frame
27:         super( "GridBagLayout Example!" );
28:
29:         // Choose the GridBagLayout layout manager
30:         setLayout( layout );
31:
32:         // Fill the entire display area
33:         constraints.fill = GridBagConstraints.BOTH;
34:
35:         // Add the first two buttons
36:         add( btnOne );
37:         add( btnTwo );
```

continues

Listing 4.13   continued

```
38:
39:        // Have the first two buttons occupy one column each
40:        constraints.weightx = 1.0;
41:        layout.setConstraints(btnOne, constraints);
42:        layout.setConstraints(btnTwo, constraints);
43:
44:        // Add the third button
45:        add( btnThree );
46:
47:        // Have the third button take the remainder of the row
48:        constraints.gridwidth = GridBagConstraints.REMAINDER;
49:        layout.setConstraints(btnThree, constraints);
50:
51:        // Add the fourth button
52:        add( btnFour );
53:
54:        // Tell the 4th button to use two grid spaces in height and width
55:        constraints.gridwidth = 2;
56:        constraints.gridheight = 2;
57:        constraints.weighty = 1.0;
58:        layout.setConstraints(btnFour, constraints);
59:
60:        // Add button five
61:        add( btnFive );
62:
63:        // Place button five at the end of the row
64:        constraints.gridwidth = GridBagConstraints.REMAINDER;
65:        layout.setConstraints(btnFive, constraints);
66:
67:        // Reset the vertical weight
68:        constraints.weighty = 0;
69:
70:        // Add button six
71:        add( btnSix );
72:
73:        // Tell it to use the remainder of a new line — all of the line
74:        constraints.gridwidth = GridBagConstraints.REMAINDER;
75:        layout.setConstraints(btnSix, constraints);
76:
77:        // Add buttons seven, eight,  and nine
78:        add( btnSeven );
79:        add( btnEight );
80:        add( btnNine );
81:
82:        // Tell buttons 7, 8, and 9 to use one column for a width and give it a
83:        // heavier y weight so that it will fill the frame
84:        constraints.gridwidth = 1;
85:        constraints.weighty = 2.0;
86:        layout.setConstraints(btnSeven, constraints);
```

```
87:         layout.setConstraints(btnEight, constraints);
88:         layout.setConstraints(btnNine, constraints);
99:
90:         // Add button ten
91:         add( btnTen );
92:
93:         // Tell button ten to use the rest of the line
94:         constraints.gridwidth = GridBagConstraints.REMAINDER;
95:         layout.setConstraints(btnTen, constraints);
96:
97:         // Set our size
98:         setSize( 320, 180 );
99:
100:         // Make ourself visible
101:         setVisible( true );
102:
103:         // Add a window listener to list for our window closing
104:         addWindowListener
105:         (
106:             new WindowAdapter()
107:             {
108:                 public void windowClosing( WindowEvent e )
109:                 {
110:                     System.exit( 0 );
111:                 }
112:             }
113:         );
114:     }
115:
116:     // Main entry point into the GridBagLayoutExample class
117:     public static void main( String[] args )
118:     {
119:         // Create an instance of our GridBagLayoutExample class
120:      GridBagLayoutExample GridBagLayoutApp = new GridBagLayoutExample();
121:     }
122: }
```

Figure 4.16

*GridBagLayoutExample
application example.*

Okay, that was a long program, so let's get to it!

```
8:      GridBagLayout layout = new GridBagLayout();
9:      GridBagConstraints constraints = new GridBagConstraints();
```

Lines 8 and 9 create new GridBagLayout and GridBagConstraints classes, respectively.

```
30:             setLayout( layout );
```

Line 30 sets the new GridBagLayout layout manager to be the frame's layout.

```
33:             constraints.fill = GridBagConstraints.BOTH;
```

Line 33 sets the GridBagLayoutConstraints fill variable to be BOTH, meaning that we want all our buttons to fill up all the display area provided to them.

```
36:             add( btnOne );
37:             add( btnTwo );

40:             constraints.weightx = 1.0;
41:             layout.setConstraints(btnOne, constraints);
42:             layout.setConstraints(btnTwo, constraints);
```

Lines 36 and 37 add the first two buttons to the container. Line 40 sets the GridBagConstraints class's weightx variable to be 1, meaning that the relative weight of this component is 1; we are going to leave this weight the same for all components so that with respect to width, they are all equal.

```
45:             add( btnThree );

48:             constraints.gridwidth = GridBagConstraints.REMAINDER;
49:             layout.setConstraints(btnThree, constraints);
```

Line 45 adds the third button to the container. Note that we are still on the first row. Lines 48 and 49 terminate the row by telling the layout to let this button use the remainder of the row for this button.

```
52:             add( btnFour );

55:             constraints.gridwidth = 2;
56:             constraints.gridheight = 2;
57:             constraints.weighty = 1.0;
58:             layout.setConstraints(btnFour, constraints);
```

Line 52 adds the fourth button to the container. Line 55 gives it a width of two cells, and line 56 gives it a height of two cells. We have to give the button a y-weight, or height weight, value or the layout will not use our grid height. Finally, line 58 sets the constraints for this button.

```
61:             add( btnFive );

64:             constraints.gridwidth = GridBagConstraints.REMAINDER;
65:             layout.setConstraints(btnFive, constraints);

68:             constraints.weighty = 0;
```

Line 61 adds the fifth button to the container. It uses the remainder of the line (which will be two cells), and it retains the same grid height of 2. Finally, line 68 resets the weight of y to 0 so that subsequent lines can set their own values.

 Note
> Notice that we are reusing our `GridBagConstraints` variable. You could easily create a new constraints object for each component, which would be cleaner as you would not have to worry about inheriting a previous component's settings, but it is more work: You must construct a new constraints object for each object, and then you have to set all its variables.
>
> Which way is better? That depends on your application. In this case we are only using buttons that will be very similar, so I opted to reuse one object. However, as soon as your application gets complicated, you will want to create multiple objects or reinitialize the entire object for each use just to be safe!

```
71:         add( btnSix );
```

```
74:         constraints.gridwidth = GridBagConstraints.REMAINDER;
75:         layout.setConstraints(btnSix, constraints);
```

Line 71 adds button six, which is going to take up the entire width of a row. This is because it is the first component in the row and we told it to use the remainder of the row, hence the whole row.

```
78:         add( btnSeven );
79:         add( btnEight );
80:         add( btnNine );
```

```
84:         constraints.gridwidth = 1;
85:         constraints.weighty = 2.0;
86:         layout.setConstraints(btnSeven, constraints);
87:         layout.setConstraints(btnEight, constraints);
88:         layout.setConstraints(btnNine, constraints);
```

Lines 78–80 add three more buttons to the container. Each button has a width of 1 and a y-weight of 2.0. Notice how the buttons initially appear the same height as buttons four and five, whose `gridHeight` was 2 and `weighty` was 1.0. These buttons still have the `gridHeight` of 2 (we never changed that, but without a `weighty` it didn't matter), but their `weighty` is set to 2.0, meaning that they will grow larger faster! Try resizing the application to make it large and see how it looks. Take a look at Figure 4.17 for an example.

Figure 4.17

GridBagLayoutExample application example— large.

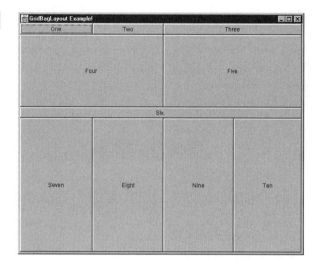

The constraints shown in Table 4.23 were used to create the `GridBagLayoutExample`.

Table 4.23 `GirdBagLayoutExample` **Constraints**

Button	*Constraints*
`btnOne, btnTwo`	`fill = BOTH, weightX = 1`
`btnThree`	`fill = BOTH, weightX = 1, gridwidth = REMAINDER`
`btnFour`	`fill = BOTH, gridwidth = 2, gridheight = 2, weightX = 1, weighty = 1.0`
`btnFive`	`fill = BOTH, gridwidth = REMAINDER, gridheight = 2, weightX = 1, weighty = 1.0`
`btnSix`	`fill = BOTH, gridwidth = REMAINDER, gridheight = 2, weightX = 1, weighty = 0`
`btnSeven, btnEight, btnNine`	`fill = BOTH, gridwidth = 1, gridheight = 2, weightX = 1, weighty = 2.0`
`btnTen`	`fill = BOTH, gridwidth = REMAINDER, gridheight = 2, weightX = 1, weighty = 2.0`

```
91:          add( btnTen );

94:          constraints.gridwidth = GridBagConstraints.REMAINDER;
95:          layout.setConstraints(btnTen, constraints);
```

Line 91 adds the tenth button to the control. It has the same settings as the previous three, but ends the line by setting the width to REMAINDER.

Grid bag layouts are nasty, but when you need a very versatile layout manager for components that could occupy grid cells, this is your monster! Seriously, play around with this some more; change some of the variables in the sample and see how they affect the layout. I would love to show you more grid bag layout examples, but this chapter is getting long and I have a feeling that your eyes are getting heavy! I hope I have stimulated your interest enough to read more and experiment on your own.

Summary

We covered quite a bit in this chapter.

- You wrote your first graphical Java application and through that you learned about all the elements involved:
  - How to create a frame
  - How to set the title of the frame
  - How to set the size of the frame
  - How to add components
  - How to end your Java application when the user closes your window
- You learned about the different Abstract Window Toolkit components:
  - Labels
  - Buttons
  - Text fields
  - Text areas
  - Check boxes (and radio buttons)
  - Choice lists

Next, you learned how to arrange these components on your frame through Java's layout managers: flow layout, grid layout, border layout, card layout, and grid bag layout. Through the card layout example, you were also introduced to the basics of event handling.

Each example was explained in great depth, so you should have a good idea of how some of the internals of Java work. Don't fret; all new concepts and classes will be explained in depth as we get to them, so you can expect to come away from this book with a strong knowledge of Java and how it does its job!

What's Next?

We've covered the Abstract Window Toolkit. Now you know how to create components and use them in your applications, but something is missing. When you look at the commercial applications on the market, they have nice tables, tree controls, list controls, tabs, menus, toolbars, and so on. Although this chapter's application was a neat exercise, the results don't necessarily look that good! In the next chapter, we are going to talk about all the aforementioned "good" user interface elements available to Java through the SWING libraries. So take a little break and prepare yourself for the fun stuff!

Chapter 5

User Interface Design with Swing

In the previous chapter, we spent a lot of time talking about designing a user interface with the Java Abstract Window Toolkit (AWT) and although that was fun, the user interfaces didn't look that good. When you use commercial applications, you are used to seeing trees, lists, tabs, progress bars, tables, and so on, and you undoubtedly will want them in your applications. This is where the Java Foundation Classes (JFC) and Swing come into the picture.

In this chapter, we are going to talk about the Swing user interface elements and how to implement them. We will talk about the following Swing elements:

- Labels
- Text fields
- Text components
    - Text fields
    - Text areas
- Buttons
    - Pushbuttons
    - Radio buttons
    - Check boxes
- Lists
- Tables

- Panes
  - Tabbed panes
  - Scroll panes
  - Split panes

As you can see, we are going to be busy this chapter! Let's get started!

Introduction to JFC and Swing

Before we dive into the Swing components, I want to give you a little background about the Java Foundation Classes and Swing. The Java Foundation Classes, or JFC for short, are collections of classes used to help people build graphical user interfaces. First announced at the 1997 JavaOne Conference, JFC included the features shown in Table 5.1.

Table 5.1   JFC Features

Feature	Description
Swing components	Incorporated all the GUI controls, such as buttons, trees, and tab controls.
Look-and-feel support	Allows any program that uses the Swing components to change the look and feel of the user interface: Windows, Motif, or cross-platform look and feel.
Accessibility API	Supports input and output devices to aid those with disabilities, such as Braille displays.
Java 2D API	Provides advanced support for 2D drawing (special line fills, rotation, scaling) and graphics manipulation (such as applying filters to an image).
Drag-and-drop support	Provides the ability to drag and drop objects to and from a Java application and a native file system application.

The Swing components, look-and-feel support, and accessibility API were all built with the JDK 1.1 and hence were released as a JDK 1.1 extension, called the "Swing Release." The Java 2D API and drag-and-drop support didn't come around until the JDK 1.2 (which became the Java 2 SDK—remember?).

EXCURSION

What Are the Origins of the Name "Swing"?

Swing was the code name of the project that developed the new graphical components, and the name just happened to stick with the classes. It is the unofficial name for the classes, but still referred to as Swing because of the package that you import to use the classes:

`javax.swing`

Structure of a Swing Application

Before we talk about how to implement a Swing application, let me first explain the structure of a Swing application. Let me assure you that using the Swing classes in your applications is a piece of cake, but understanding the workings under the hood is a bit complicated. If you don't get everything in this section, don't worry; I will show you step by step how to use the Swing classes in your applications. After you spend some time using them, this section may be a little more valuable. I don't say this to scare you off, but this section throws a horde of terms and classes at you that may be initially intimidating. Here is a detailed description of the inner workings of the Swing application framework.

Remember the AWT applications in the last chapter that had a Frame object. The Frame object was derived from a Window object that was derived from a Container object. Although we didn't talk about menus, the Frame object could host a menu object. You set the layout manager of the Frame and added all your components to the frame object directly.

Well, the Swing model is considerably more advanced and supports a much richer set of functionality, thus it is considerably more complicated. Figure 5.1 shows a diagram of the structure of a Swing application.

A Swing application, at its highest level, contains a *heavyweight container* (for example, a JFrame that is similar to an AWT Frame); it is responsible for hosting the main window of the application. This heavyweight container contains an object called a root pane that does all its work for it. The root pane enables the Swing classes to support all the robust features that it has, such as tool tips and drag and drop.

The *root pane*, as defined in the Java 2 SDK documentation, is the fundamental component in the container hierarchy. The root pane contains the objects shown in Table 5.2.

Figure 5.1

Structure of a Swing application.

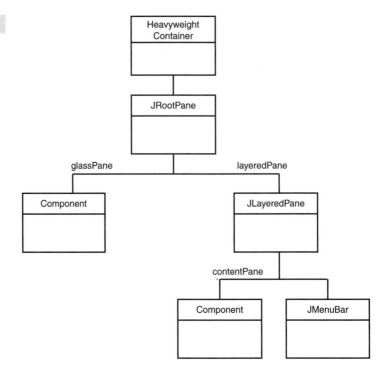

Table 5.2   Root Pane Contents

Component	Description
Content pane	Acts as the parent for all components added to the container
Layered pane	Parent of all children in the root pane and adds the capability to add components at different layers to create a sense of depth to the application
Glass pane	Sits on top of all components in the root pane
Menu bar	Holds a JMenuBar object positioned at the upper edge of the root pane

The *layered pane* manages the *menu bar* and *content pane* and adds depth to the container; components are allowed to overlap each other when needed. The layered pane has an Integer object that specifies the depth of each component in its container: A higher number layer displays above lower number layers. It provides several predefined layers, as shown in Table 5.3 and displayed graphically in Figure 5.2.

Figure 5.2

Layered pane predefined layers.

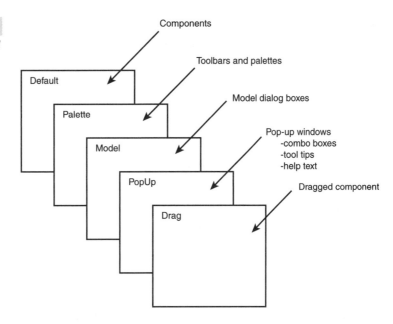

Table 5.3   Layered Pane Predefined Layers

Component	Description
Default	The standard layer where most components go. This is the bottom-most layer.
Palette	Sits over the default layer; useful for floating toolbars and palettes so that they can be positioned over other components.
Modal	Used for modal dialog boxes; modal dialog boxes can appear on top of any toolbars, palettes, or standard components in the container.
Pop-up	The pop-up layer appears above dialogs so that pop-up windows associated with combo boxes, tool tips, and other help text will appear above the components, palettes, or dialogs that generated them.
Drag	When you're dragging a component, reassigning it to the drag layer ensures that it is positioned over other components in the container.

The menu bar is hosted by `JMenuBar` and holds a traditional menu bar at the top of the heavyweight container that pops up menus when selected.

The content pane is a little more interesting. It acts as the parent for all components you add to the container. It maintains a layout manager that you can set, and you can add components directly to it through its `add` method (not the container as you did with AWT). So, to set the layout manager of a heavyweight container, you must obtain the root pane's content pane. This can be accomplished in one of two ways:

```
Component contentPane = getRootPane().getContentPane();
```

Or simply:

```
Component contentPane = getContentPane();
```

As you can see, the heavyweight containers implement a method `getContentPane` that gives you direct access to the content pane. Here is how you would use it:

```
// Set the layout manager
getContentPane().setLayout( new BorderLayout() );

// Add a button to the content pane
getContentPane().add( new Button() );
```

Finally, there is the glass pane. The glass pane is just a `Component` object, but it has the special property that it sits on top of all other components in the root pane. It provides a convenient place to draw above all other components, and it makes it possible to intercept mouse events to facilitate both dragging an object as well as drawing. You can control the visibility of the glass pane by calling its `setVisible` method; initially the glass pane is not visible. If the glass pane is not visible, it acts as if it were not even there.

Now, how is all this depth and component/container manipulation implemented? Through a custom layout manager defined in the `JRootPane` class: `JRootPane.RootLayout`.

This custom layout manager is responsible for the following:

1. If the glass pane is present, it fills the entire viewable area of the root pane.
2. The layered pane fills the entire viewable area of the root pane.
3. The menu bar is positioned at the upper edge of the layered pane.
4. The content pane fills the entire viewable area minus the menu bar.

You have the option of replacing this custom layout manager with your own, but remember that you must support all this functionality yourself, so I would recommend against it. For more information about this layout manager, consult the Java 2 SDK documentation under `JRootPane: JRootPane.RootLayout`.

Setting Up a Swing Application

Let's look at actually using the Swing classes. To use Swing, there are several things you must do:

- Import the Swing libraries
- Set up a heavyweight container
- Set up a lightweight container

- Build your components
- Add your components to the lightweight container

There are many things you have to do to build your user interface, which is the subject of this chapter, and to respond to user events, which is the subject of the next chapter.

Importing the Swing Packages

There are several different Swing packages that you can import into your application, as shown in Table 5.4 (taken from the Java 2 SDK documentation).

Table 5.4   Swing Packages

Package	Description
javax.accessibility	Provides support for assistive technologies
javax.swing	Provides a set of Java components that are designed to work the same on all platforms
javax.swing.border	Provides support for specialized borders to use with Swing components
javax.swing.colorchooser	Support classes and interfaces for the JColorChooser component that prompts a user to select a color
javax.swing.event	Provides event support for Swing components
javax.swing.filechooser	Support classes and interfaces for the JFileChooser component that prompts a user to locate a file on the local file system
javax.swing.plaf	Provides support for Java's pluggable look-and-feel
javax.swing.plaf.basic	User interface elements for the Basic look-and-feel
javax.swing.plaf.metal	User interface elements for the Metal look-and-feel
javax.swing.plaf.multi	User interface for the Multiplexing look-and-feel that allows users to combine different look-and-feel components
javax.swing.table	Provides support for the JTable component
javax.swing.text	Provides support for both editable and non-editable text components
javax.swing.text.html	Provides support for generating HTML editors
javax.swing.text.html.parser	Provides support for HTML parsing
javax.swing.text.rtf	Provides support for generating Rich Text Format (RTF) text editors
javax.swing.tree	Provides support for the JTree component
javax.swing.undo	Provides support for undo and redo options

5

I'm sure you can surmise from perusing this list that Swing is powerful!

You import these packages the same way you imported packages back in the last chapter:

```
import javax.swing.*
import javax.swing.event.*
```

Most of the work you will be doing in this chapter will use only a very small subset of these packages, and most will just be using javax.swing.*.

Setting Up a Heavyweight Container

After you have selected your components (so that you know which packages to import) and imported their required packages, you must set up a heavyweight container; this is the container, similar to the AWT Frame class, that will host the main window of the application. Typically, this will include one of the Swing containers shown in Table 5.5.

Table 5.5   Swing Heavyweight Containers

Container	Description
JFrame	An extended version of the AWT Frame class that supports the Swing components (and much more!) Used as an application window.
JDialog	An extended version of the AWT Dialog class that supports Swing components to create a dialog window. Supports a collection of standard dialogs.
JApplet	An extended version of the AWT Applet class that is used to support Swing components in the context of an applet.
JWindow	A JWindow is a container that can be displayed anywhere on the user's desktop. It does not have the title bar, window-management buttons, or other trimmings associated with a JFrame, but it is still a "first-class citizen" of the user's desktop, and can exist anywhere on it.

In the sample application, you are going to subclass a JFrame. You will use JDialogs as well prompt users for input, but you will not use the JApplet class. The JFrame class, for example, will supply a floating window for you to put all your components on.

You can set up a heavyweight container by deriving your application class from one of the heavyweight containers (JFrame for example), or you can derive your application class from a lightweight container (JPanel for example) and simply create a heavyweight container in your main method and add your lightweight container to it:

```
public class MyFrameClass extends JFrame{}
```

or:

```
public class MyPanelClass extends JPanel
{
    public MyPanelClass()
    {
        // Setup panel
    }

    public static void main( String[] args )
    {
        // Create a JFrame class
        JFrame frame = new JFrame( "My Application" );

        // Create an instance of our class
        MyPanelClass panel = new MyPanelClass();

        // Add our class instance to the JFrame's content pane
        frame.getContentPane().add( panel, BorderLayout.CENTER );

        // Resize the JFrame
        frame.setSize( 640, 480 );

        // Make the JFrame visible
        frame.setVisible( true );

        // Set up a window listener to watch for a window closing
            frame.addWindowListener
        (
            new WindowAdapter()
        {
            public void windowClosing( WindowEvent e )
            {
                System.exit( 0 );
            }
        }
        );
    }
}
```

Setting Up a Lightweight Container

Earlier you learned that each heavyweight container has a content pane that holds its components (through its root pane); actually, the content pane holds lightweight containers that hold components.

A lightweight container is responsible for holding components and potentially providing direct user interface elements. The most common lightweight container is the JPanel class, which doesn't really do more than position the controls, but there are a few others, as shown in Table 5.6.

Table 5.6 Swing Lightweight Containers

Container	Description
JPanel	A generic lightweight container
JScrollPane	A specialized container that manages a viewport, optional vertical and horizontal scrollbars, and optional row and column heading viewports
JSplitPane	Used to divide two (and only two) components, specifying the amount of space given to each component
JTabbedPane	A component that lets the user switch between a group of components by clicking on a tab with a given title and/or icon
JToolbar	A component that displays a set of components, usually buttons, that can be positioned on one of the four sides of a container

You can create a lightweight container either by deriving your application class from it (as shown in the previous section), or by creating an instance of it and use it that way. So, for example, if you derive your application class from a JFrame and want to use a JPanel lightweight container, you could do something like the following:

```
public class MyFrame extends JFrame
{
    // Create an instance of a JPanel
    JPanel panel = new JPanel();

    public MyFrame()
    {
        // Add the JPanel to our JFrame's content pane
        getContentPane.add( panel, BorderLayout.CENTER );

        // Resize ourself
        setSize( 640, 480 );

        // Make ourself initially visible
        setVisible( true );

        // Set up a window listener to watch for a window closing
        addWindowListener
        (
            new WindowAdapter()
            {
                public void windowClosing( WindowEvent e )
                {
                    System.exit( 0 );
                }
            }
        );
    }
```

```
    public static void main( String[] args )
    {
        MyFrame frame = new MyFrame();
    }
}
```

Building User Interfaces Using Components

Building user interfaces using Swing components is the subject of the rest of this chapter, but all these components are similar to use. You use the components based on the constructors, as you did with the AWT components. For example, if you wanted to build an image label with text using the JLabel class (it is a little more advanced than the last chapter, right?), you would do it as follows:

```
ImageIcon icon = new ImageIcon( "icon.gif" );
JLabel label = new JLabel( "My String", icon, JLabel.CENTER );
```

The intricacies of how to construct JLabels will be discussed later in the chapter, but the point is, look at the constructors and create your component according to one of the constructors. We will go through the various constructors for the components in the Swing packages in this chapter, so all will be revealed soon, my friend!

Adding Components to the Lightweight Container

After you have constructed your components, all that is left is to add them to your lightweight container. Because you are using a lightweight container to add your components to and not a heavyweight container, you add them with the familiar add method. You have all the same layout managers at your disposal, and the lightweight containers all have the same add methods inherited from the AWT Container and Component classes.

To add our label to a JPanel-derived container, you could do the following:

```
public class MyApplication extends JPanel
{
    // Create an image icon
    ImageIcon icon = new ImageIcon( "icon.gif" );

    // Create a label with both an image icon as well as a text
    // label
    JLabel label = new JLabel( "My String", icon, JLabel.CENTER );

    public MyApplication()
    {
        // Set the layout manager
        setLayout( new FlowLayout() );

        // Add our label to the JPanel
        add( label );
    }
```

```
public void static main( String[] args )
{
    // Create a JFrame container to hold our application
    JFrame frame = new JFrame( "MyFrame Example" );

    // Create an application object
    MyApplication app = new MyApplication();

    // Add our app to the content pane of the frame
    frame.getContentPane().add( app );

    // Resize, set visibility, and setup a window listener
    ...
}
}
```

As you can see, adding components to a lightweight container is still as simple as using the AWT classes; you just have to get to the content pane before adding anything.

JComponent

Before we talk about individual components, I think it will be helpful for you to learn more about the base class that the Swing components are derived from: JComponent.

First, JComponent is derived from the AWT Container class, so it inherits all the functionality of the AWT Container class, Component class, and Object class, as shown in Figure 5.3.

Figure 5.3

JComponent derivation tree.

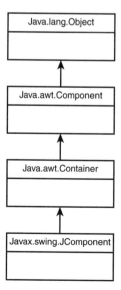

Some of the characteristics of a JComponent are as follows:

- A "pluggable look and feel" that can be set by the programmer or by the user at runtime.
- Components are designed to be combined and extended in order to create custom components.
- Comprehensive keystroke handling that works with nested components.
- Action objects, for single-point control of program actions initiated by multiple components.
- A border property that implicitly defines the component's insets.
- The ability to set the preferred, minimum, and maximum size for a component.
- Tool tips, which are short descriptions that pop up when the cursor lingers over a component.
- Autoscrolling, which is automatic scrolling in a list, table, or tree that occurs when the user is dragging the mouse.
- Simple, easy dialog construction using static methods in the JOptionPane class that let you display information and query the user.
- Slow-motion graphics rendering using debugGraphics so that you can see what is being displayed onscreen and whether or not it is being overwritten.
- Support for accessibility.
- Support for international localization.

Take a look at the Java 2 SDK documentation under JComponent for more detailed information.

I wish we had time to go through this entire class; it is really fascinating. Instead, I would like to point out a few highlights in this list that really make the Swing classes cool: pluggable look and feel, action objects, and tool tips.

First, the pluggable look and feel is something that makes the Swing libraries adaptable to the individual user; instead of being restricted to a single "look and feel," you can select a "look and feel" and plug it into your application! You can make your application look like a Windows application, a Motif application, a Mac application, or use the new Metal look and feel. You simply create standard Swing components and let the user choose his or her preferred appearance. For more information about the pluggable look-and-feel classes, take a look at the Java 2 SDK documentation under javax.swing.plaf.

Next, the concept of an action object makes user interface development a snap; action interface objects provide a single point of control for program actions. For example, a toolbar icon and a menu option can share the same action handler so that when the action object is disabled, both the toolbar icon and the menu option will be disabled; this handles much of the hassle of updating multiple user interface elements.

Finally let's talk about tool tips. If you are not familiar with a tool tip, it is a small text string that appears over a component when you hold the mouse over it for a few seconds and gives some meaningful information about the component. It is particularly helpful for users new to your application who might not necessarily understand your toolbar icons. Remember that however intuitive your interface may seem, someone somewhere won't understand it. Tool tips are very easy to add to components derived from JComponent: JComponent has a setToolTipText method to facilitate the addition of a tool tip to the component. We'll talk more about tool tips later, but I'll start using them in our examples so that you can get used to them before we go into depth about how they work.

Now that you have seen some of the features of the component base class, let's start looking at the components themselves.

Labels

Labels, labels, what is a label? Well, in the last chapter you saw that a label was exactly what you thought it was: a string of characters displayed on the screen. You could put the label next to a component to describe it or simply use it to write a heading for your application. That was then; this is now!

Welcome to the 21st century label! Okay, maybe labels aren't that exciting, but when you look at the feature set of a JLabel, it certainly does not look like a label. A JLabel can display text, an image, or both. Furthermore, it has all the aforementioned JComponent features. JLabel has six constructors, as shown in Table 5.7.

Table 5.7 JLabel **Constructors**

Container	Description
JLabel()	Create a JLabel with no icon and an empty title string.
JLabel(Icon image)	Create a JLabel with the specified image and an empty title string.
JLabel(Icon image, int horizontalAlignment)	Create a JLabel with the specified image, an empty title string, and the specified horizontal alignment. Your alignment options are JLabel.LEFT, JLabel.CENTER, and JLabel.RIGHT.
JLabel(String text)	Create a JLabel with the specified title aligned to the left side of its display area and no image.

Container	Description
JLabel(String text, int horizontalAlignment)	Create a JLabel with the specified title and horizontal alignment and no image.
JLabel(String text, Icon icon, int horizontalAlignment)	Create a JLabel with the specified title, image, and horizontal alignment.

As you can see, you can create labels with text and an image, and you can specify their alignment: left, right, or center. The only thing left to talk about with these constructors is the image icon.

If you look at the definition of the Icon type, you will notice that it is just an interface, not a class. To refresh your memory, an interface is kind of like a contract: If you implement an interface, you must support the set of methods defined in that interface. In this case, there are three methods: getIconHeight, getIconWidth, and paintIcon. The details of these methods are not important to our discussion, but the classes that implement the Icon interface are. Actually, the only one that we are going to be interested in is the ImageIcon class. The ImageIcon has nine constructors, as shown in Table 5.8.

5

Table 5.8 **ImageIcon Constructors**

Container	Description
ImageIcon()	Creates an uninitialized image icon.
ImageIcon(byte[] imageData)	Creates an image icon from an array of bytes that was read from an image file, such as a GIF or JPEG.
ImageIcon(byte[] imageData, String description)	Creates an image icon from an array of bytes that was read from an image file, such as a GIF or JPEG, and provides a textual description of the image.
ImageIcon(java.awt.Image image)	Creates an image icon from an Image object.
ImageIcon(java.awt.Image image, String description)	Creates an image icon from an Image object and provides a textual description of the image.
ImageIcon(String filename)	Creates an image icon from the specified filename. You can specify a filename or path and filename to a support image type, such as GIF or JPEG.
ImageIcon(String filename, String description)	Creates an image icon from the specified filename and provides a textual description of the image icon. You can specify a filename or path and filename to a support image type, such as GIF or JPEG.
ImageIcon(java.net.URL location)	Creates an image icon from the specified URL.
ImageIcon(java.net.URL location, String description)	Creates an image icon from the specified URL and provides a textual description of the image.

I hope I haven't thoroughly confused you! In our examples you are going to use the sixth and/or seventh constructor when building an image icon: You just need to specify a filename from which to build the image. To build an image icon from a file, you could do something like this:

```
ImageIcon image = new ImageIcon( "Icon.gif" );
```

 Note Currently, only two types of image files are supported: JPEG and GIF (.jpg and .gif).

Now that we have that clear, let's get back to the original point: the JLabel class. The following are some examples of how to construct some JLabels:

```
JLabel labelText = new JLabel( "My Text Label" );
JLabel labelCenteredText = new JLabel( "My Centered Text Label",
                                       JLabel.CENTER );
ImageIcon image = new ImageIcon( "icon.gif" );
JLabel labelIcon = new JLabel( image );
JLabel labelCenteredIcon = new JLabel( image, JLabel.CENTER);
JLabel labelTextIcon = new JLabel( "Text", image, JLabel.CENTER);
```

Now that wasn't too difficult. What else can you do with a JLabel? You can do everything you can do to a JComponent: change its color, make it opaque, add tool tips, change its font, and so on, as well as set and retrieve all the information listed in the constructors. Furthermore, you can do a few other neat things such as setting a disabled icon to display when the JLabel is not enabled (setEnabled(false)) by using the setDisabledIcon(Icon) and setting and retrieving the look and feel of the JLabel (setUI and getUI).

Look at the Java 2 SDK documentation under JLabel for more information. We will cover some of the features in the sample application, but the documentation does a pretty good job of explaining the other functionality.

I think you are ready for a full example, so take a look at Listing 5.1.

Type the code from Listing 5.1, excluding line numbers, into your favorite text editor, and save it as JLabelExample.java, or copy it from the CD. Build it as follows:

```
javac JLabelExample.java
java JLabelExample
```

Be sure to copy MoneyIcon.gif from the CD to the same directory in which you are building the JLabelExample.

The code for both the Swing application framework as well as the JLabel class will be explained following the source code.

Listing 5.1   JLabelExample.java

```
 1:  // Import Swing packages
 2:  import javax.swing.*;
 3:  import javax.swing.event.*;
 4:
 5:  // Import AWT packages
 6:  import java.awt.*;
 7:  import java.awt.event.*;
 8:
 9:  public class JLabelExample extends JPanel
10:  {
11:      // Create a JLabel text label
12:      JLabel labelText = new JLabel( "This is a text JLabel",
13:                                     JLabel.CENTER );
14:
15:      // Create an image icon
16:      ImageIcon icon = new ImageIcon( "MoneyIcon.gif" );
17:
18:      // Create a label with the icon
19:      JLabel labelIcon = new JLabel( icon );
20:
21:      // Create a label with both an icon and text
22:      JLabel labelBoth = new JLabel("This is my Icon JLabel",
23:                                    icon, JLabel.CENTER );
24:
25:      // Constructor
26:      public JLabelExample()
27:      {
28:          // Set the layout of our JPanel
29:          setLayout( new GridLayout(3, 1) );
30:
31:          // Change the color of the text label
32:          labelText.setForeground( Color.red );
33:
34:          // Add a tooltip to the text label
35:          labelText.setToolTipText( "This is a JLabel!" );
36:
37:          // Add all of our labels to our JPanel
38:          add( labelText );
39:          add( labelIcon );
40:          add( labelBoth );
41:      }
42:
43:      // Main application entry point into this class
44:      public static void main( String[] args )
45:      {
```

continues

Listing 5.1   continued

```
46:          // Create a JFrame object
47:          JFrame frame = new JFrame( "JLabel Example!" );
48:
49:          // Create a JFrameExample Object
50:          JLabelExample example = new JLabelExample();
51:
52:          // Add our JFrame Example Object to the JFrame
53:     frame.getContentPane().add( example, BorderLayout.CENTER );
54:
55:          // Resize our JFrame
56:          frame.setSize( 300, 180 );
57:
58:          // Make our JFrame visible
59:          frame.setVisible( true );
60:
61:          // Create a window listener to close our application when we
62:          // close our application
63:          frame.addWindowListener
64:          (
65:              new WindowAdapter()
66:             {
67:                 public void windowClosing( WindowEvent e )
68:                 {
69:   System.exit( 0 );
70:                 }
71:             }
72:          );
73:     }
74: }
```

Figure 5.4 shows the JLabelExample application.

Figure 5.4

The JLabelExample *application.*

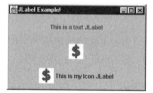

```
2:   import javax.swing.*;
3:   import javax.swing.event.*;
```

The first thing we must do in a Swing application is import the Java Swing packages as shown in lines 2 and 3. The Swing events are not being used yet, but I want you to get in the habit of including them nonetheless—when you start doing real work with these components, you will need them!

```
6:  import java.awt.*;
7:  import java.awt.event.*;
```

If you are using the Swing packages, why do you need the AWT packages as well? If you remember the discussion on JComponent, you will recall that JComponent is derived from java.awt.Container, so you need the AWT packages to use any components derived from JComponent. Furthermore, you need the AWT events for the window adapter in line 65 to watch for a closing window (this was presented in the last chapter, so I am not going to go over it again).

```
9:  public class JLabelExample extends JPanel
```

Line 9 creates the JLabelExample application by extending JPanel, a lightweight container. You may recall from our earlier discussions that you add your lightweight container to the content pane of your heavyweight container, and that is the reason our class is derived from JPanel. We could have derived our class from a heavyweight container and created a lightweight container inside that, but when we get to the next chapter, you will see firsthand the logic behind deriving your classes from a lightweight container. As a sneak preview, if you derive your class from a lightweight container, you can take your entire application (main function and all) and add it to another class's lightweight container or heavyweight container in another application. In the next chapter, we will build a JTable inside a JPanel and see it as an application and then eventually add it to a JTabbedPane that will be added to a JFrame. I will save that for later, but I just wanted to assure you that there is a method to my madness!

```
12:     JLabel labelText = new JLabel( "This is a text JLabel",
13:                                 JLabel.CENTER );
```

Lines 12 and 13 create a centered text label with the title "This is a text JLabel" using the fifth constructor in Table 5.7.

```
16:     ImageIcon icon = new ImageIcon( "MoneyIcon.gif" );
```

Line 16 creates an ImageIcon from the GIF file MoneyIcon.gif using the sixth constructor in Table 5.8.

```
19:     JLabel labelIcon = new JLabel( icon );
```

Line 19 creates a JLabel object from the ImageIcon created in line 16 using the second constructor in Table 5.7.

```
22:     JLabel labelBoth = new JLabel("This is my Icon JLabel",
23:                                 icon, JLabel.CENTER );
```

Lines 22 and 23 create another JLabel object with both a text string as well as the ImageIcon created in line 16. This label is centered.

In the next few lines of the application, I started having a little fun with the text label:

```
32:         labelText.setForeground( Color.red );
```

Line 32 sets the foreground color of the text label created in lines 12 and 13 to red. To change colors of the text of a label, you can use the JLabel's setForeground method, derived from JComponent, that has the following prototype:

```
public void setForeground( Color fg );
```

The Color class enables you to create the color you want based on the RGB values (Red, Green, and Blue) that make the color you want with the option of using an Alpha component, or you can choose one of the predefined colors. The predefined colors are

- Black
- Blue
- Cyan
- Darkgray
- Gray
- Green
- Lightgray
- Magenta
- Orange
- Pink
- Red
- White
- Yellow

The color class can be fun to use, so I encourage you to read up on it more in the Java 2 SDK documentation, but the predefined colors will be more than enough for our sample application.

```
35:         labelText.setToolTipText( "This is a JLabel!" );
```

Line 35 sets the tool tip text for the text label to This is a JLabel!. When you run the application, try holding your mouse over the text label for a few seconds and see how it looks, or take a look at Figure 5.5.

Figure 5.5

*JLabelExample with
tool tip.*

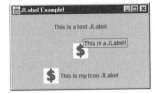

```
38:          add( labelText );
39:          add( labelIcon );
40:          add( labelBoth );
```

Lines 38–40 add each of the labels to the JPanel.

```
47:          JFrame frame = new JFrame( "JLabel Example!" );
```

Line 47 creates a JFrame, our heavyweight container, and gives it the title JLabel
Example!. JFrame has two constructors, as shown in Table 5.9.

Table 5.9   JFrame Constructors

Constructor	Description
JFrame()	Creates a new frame that is initially invisible
JFrame(String title)	Creates a new frame with the specified title that is initially invisible

We used the second constructor so that we could set a title on our frame.

```
50:          JLabelExample example = new JLabelExample();
```

Line 50 creates a new JLabelExample object (our class).

```
53:      frame.getContentPane().add( example, BorderLayout.CENTER );
```

Line 53 gets the content pane from the JFrame using the getContentPane method
and then adds our JPanel-based application class to the center of it. getContentPane
is declared as follows:

```
public Container getContentPane()
```

Internally it gets the frame's root pane, asks it for its content pane, and returns that.
The following code segment is taken directly from JFrame.java:

```
public Container getContentPane() {
    return getRootPane().getContentPane();
}
```

In the preceding segment, getRootPane() returns the JFrame's rootPane member
variable, that is just a JRootPane object.

Next, it asks the content pane to add the JPanel to its collection of components using the standard Container add method you learned in the last chapter.

```
56:         frame.setSize( 300, 180 );
```

Line 56 sets the size of the JFrame to 300×180, enough to display labels.

```
59:         frame.setVisible( true );
```

Finally, line 59 makes the JFrame visible. If you recall from Table 5.9, when a JFrame object is constructed, it is always initially invisible, so this statement is a must if you want to see your application!

The rest of the application should be very familiar: We create a WindowAdapter object that closes the application as soon as the user closes the window. And that is it! Although the underlying architecture behind a Swing application is incredibly involved, it is simple to use.

Text Components

Java text components include both text fields (JTextField) and text areas (JTextArea), similar to the ones you saw in the AWT packages, that are derived from JTextComponent. The JTextComponent class provides all the functionality found in the AWT TextComponent class and offers some additional features that help its derived components adhere to the Swing foundations.

Caret Changes

A caret (the prompt you see in a text field that shows you where the next letter you type will appear) is a pluggable object in Swing text components. You can use the default caret or a custom caret, and you can listen for caret position changes through the CaretListener interface.

Commands

Text components provide a number of commands that can be used to manipulate the component; it is through this mechanism that the component exposes its capabilities.

Key Maps

The JTextComponent class offers the ability to bind various keystrokes to some kind of action. A default key map is provided with the component, but users are encouraged to use key maps.

Model/View Split

The foundation of all the Swing components initially was based on a concept named *model view controller*, or MVC; MVC was a popular user interface paradigm used with SmallTalk (an older object-oriented programming language.) Anyway, the concept was to separate a visual application into three parts: the *model*, the *view*, and the *controller* (see Figure 5.6). The *model* represented the data for the application, the *view* represented the visual representation of the data, and the *controller* accepted input on the view and translated it into changes in the *model*.

Figure 5.6

Model view controller (MVC) paradigm.

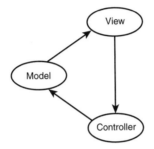

After the first Swing prototype, Sun found that the MVC separation for each component did not work well because of the close relationship between the view and controller and was not very practical when attempting to generate generic controllers. So Sun decided to combine the view and controller into one single user interface object, delegate its user interface appearance to a user interface manager, and maintain a separate model. Figure 5.7 shows a graphical representation of the modified MVC architecture, sometimes called the *Separable Model Design*.

Figure 5.7

Separable model design.

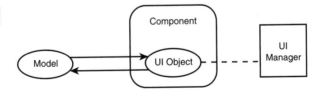

Therefore, each Swing component has a model associated with it that holds its graphical state, its data, or both and it has a user interface manager to display it in the look and feel that the application is running in. JTextComponents support this paradigm using the Document object, which represents the model that maintains the text of the component and monitors changes to the text.

The *separable model design* is an interesting topic that could easily merit a chapter of its own, so I encourage you to read the Java 2 SDK documentation under `JTextComponent` and an article in Sun's *The Swing Connection* archive titled "A Swing Architecture Overview: The Inside Story on JFC Component Design." This article was located at print time at

```
http://java.sun.com/products/jfc/tsc/archive/what_is_arch/
➥swing-arch/swing-arch.html
```

Location Information

Provides the capability to determine the location of text in a particular view.

Undo/Redo Support

Provides support for an edit history mechanism to allow undo and redo operations. Support is provided through the `Document` model.

Thread Safety

The `JTextComponent` class provides a level of support for thread-safe operations. Because of the high level of configurability of the text components, it is possible to circumvent this protection, but the documentation directly notes what methods are safe to call asynchronously.

An application can be made to run in one *thread*, like all the ones we have been writing thus far, or it can be configured to run in *multiple threads*. What is a thread, you ask? Well, having multiple threads means that you can have more than one section of your code running at any particular time. For example, you could let your main thread maintain your user interface by allowing users to click buttons and type in text fields, and you could create a second thread that goes out to the Internet and downloads stock quotes for you.

We will talk about threads in much greater depth later, but suffice it to say that a great deal of overhead is associated with maintaining multiple threads. The main problem you could encounter using multiple threads is having two threads accessing the same member variable at the same time: The first thread sets it to zero, the second thread sets it to one, and then the first thread, thinking it's zero, multiplies it by a variable to make that variable zero. Lo and behold, there is a difficult-to-diagnose bug! Don't worry, we will talk more about this later; I just wanted to give you a preview of things to come.

Another term I used in the last definition was asynchronous. Methods can be of two types: synchronous and asynchronous. *Synchronous* means that you call a method, it performs all its tasks, and it returns to you. You must wait for that method to do all

its work before you can do anything else: You are said to *block* on this call. *Asynchronous* means just the opposite. You call a method, it creates a thread to perform all its tasks, and it returns to you right away. This way you can perform other activities while the asynchronous method goes off and does its thing!

Text Fields

Text fields in Swing are functionally similar to text fields in AWT, with the addition of all the aforementioned JTextComponent enhancements: They support the separable model design, they support key maps, they listen to events through action listeners, and so on.

Aside from the added functionality of the JTextField class, because of its structure, it is very easy to extend the class to create other specialized text components. For example, you no longer have a setEchoChar method to facilitate password fields; you have another class derived from JTextField: JPasswordField.

JTextField has five constructors, shown in Table 5.10.

Table 5.10   JTextField Constructors

Constructor	Description
JTextField()	Constructs a new text field
JTextField(int columns)	Constructs a new empty text field with the specified number of columns
JTextField(String text)	Constructs a new text field with the specified text
JTextField(String text, int columns)	Constructs a new text field with the specified text and number of columns
JTextField(javax.swing.text. Document doc, String text, int columns)	Constructs a new text field with the specified text storage model, text, and number of columns

The following examples show how to construct a JTextField:

```
// Create some standard text fields
JTextField tfEmpty = new JTextField();
JTextField tfTenColumnsEmpty = new JTextField( 10 );
JTextField tfDefaultName = new JTextField( "Linda" );
JTextField tfDefaultName = new JTextField( "Linda", 10 );
```

I will leave the advanced text field example for our sample application later in this section.

What else can you do with a `JTextField`? You can change the background and foreground colors using the following methods:

```
public void setBackground( Color c );
public void setForeground( Color c );
```

You can change the color of the caret (the blinking line on the text component that shows you where your next character will appear) using the following methods:

```
public Color getCaretColor();
public void setCaretColot( Color c );
```

You can change the font using the following methods:

```
public Font getFont( Font f );
public void setFont( Font f );
```

The `Font` class is interesting and can make your input text fields look really good! The `Font` class can be constructed in two ways, as shown in Table 5.11.

Table 5.11 Font Constructors

Constructor	Description
`Font(java.util.Map attributes)`	Creates a new font with the specified attributes.
`Font(String name, int style,`	Creates a new font from the specified name, style, and size. `int size)` The name can be a logical font name (Dialog, DialogInput, Monospaced, Serif, SansSerif, or Symbol) or a font face name, and the style can be PLAIN, ITALIC, BOLD, or both (ITALIC|BOLD).

The latter constructor is the most common and easiest to use, so it's what we will be using in the next example. Speaking of the next example, take a look at Listing 5.2 for an example that demonstrates the following `JTextField` features:

- Different background colors
- Different foreground colors
- Different caret colors (to make foreground color)
- Modified font
- Tool tips (I really like these things!)
- A custom `Document` object that only accepts numeric input

Type the code from Listing 5.2, excluding line numbers, into your favorite text editor and save it as `JTextFieldExample.java`, or copy it from the CD. Build it as follows:

```
javac JTextFieldExample.java
java JTextFieldExample
```

The code specific to the `JTextField` class is boldface for your convenience and is explained following the source code.

Listing 5.2 `JTextFieldExample.java`

```
 1:  // Import Swing packages
 2:  import javax.swing.*;
 3:  import javax.swing.text.*;
 4:  import javax.swing.event.*;
 5:
 6:  // Import AWT packages
 7:  import java.awt.*;
 8:  import java.awt.Toolkit;
 9:  import java.awt.event.*;
10:
11:  public class JTextFieldExample extends JPanel
12:  {
13:      // Create labels for our text fields
14:      JLabel lblName = new JLabel( "Name:", JLabel.RIGHT );
15:      JLabel lblAge  = new JLabel( "Age:", JLabel.RIGHT );
16:
17:      // Create our text fields
18:      JTextField txtName = new JTextField( 40 );
19:  JTextField txtAge = new JTextField(new NumberDocument(),"",10);
20:
21:      // Constructor
22:      public JTextFieldExample()
23:      {
24:          // Create a 2 X 2 grid layout
25:          setLayout( new GridLayout( 2, 2 ) );
26:
27:          // Change the color of the name field
28:          txtName.setBackground( Color.black );
29:          txtName.setForeground( Color.cyan );
30:          txtName.setCaretColor( Color.cyan );
31:
32:          // Change the font of the name field
33:      Font font = new Font( "SansSerif",Font.BOLD¦Font.ITALIC,16);
34:          txtName.setFont( font );
35:
36:          // Add a tool tip
37:          txtName.setToolTipText( "Enter Your Name" );
38:
39:          // Add the name label and field to the JPanel
40:          add( lblName );
41:          add( txtName );
42:
43:          // Change the color of the Age field
44:          txtAge.setBackground( Color.darkGray );
45:          txtAge.setForeground( Color.yellow );
```

continues

Listing 5.2 continued

```
46:            txtAge.setCaretColor( Color.yellow );
47:            txtAge.setFont( font );
48:
49:            // Add a tool tip
50:            txtAge.setToolTipText( "Enter Your Age" );
51:
52:            // Add the age label and field to the JPanel
53:            add( lblAge );
54:            add( txtAge );
55:        }
56:
57:        // Main application entry point into this class
58:        public static void main( String[] args )
59:        {
60:            // Create a JFrame object
61:            JFrame frame = new JFrame( "JTextField Example!" );
62:
63:            // Create a JTextFieldExample Object
64:            JTextFieldExample  example = new JTextFieldExample();
65:
66:            // Add our JTextFieldExample Object to the JFrame
67:            frame.getContentPane().add( example, BorderLayout.CENTER );
68:
69:            // Resize our JFrame
70:            frame.setSize( 240, 80 );
71:
72:            // Make our JFrame visible
73:            frame.setVisible( true );
74:
75:            // Create a window listener to close our application when we
76:            // close our application
77:            frame.addWindowListener
78:            (
79:                new WindowAdapter()
80:                {
81:                    public void windowClosing( WindowEvent e )
82:                    {
83:                        System.exit( 0 );
84:                    }
85:                }
86:            );
87:
88:        }
89:
90:        // Create a Document that only accepts numbers
91:        protected class NumberDocument extends PlainDocument {
92:
93:        public void insertString(int offs, String str, AttributeSet a)
94:                    throws BadLocationException
95:            {
```

```
96:        // Get the characters to insert into the document
97:        char[] strSource = str.toCharArray();
98:
99:        // Create a buffer to copy the results into
100:       char[] strDestination = new char[strSource.length];
101:       int nDestinationIndex = 0;
102:
103:        // Loop through all characters in the source string
104:       for( int i = 0; i < strSource.length; i++ )
105:       {
106:          // See if this character is a digit
107:          if( Character.isDigit( strSource[i] ) )
108:          {
109:              // It is so copy it to the destination buffer
110:          strDestination[nDestinationIndex++] = strSource[i];
111:          }
112:          else
113:          {
114:              // Beep at the user for typing something
115:              // other than a number
116:              java.awt.Toolkit>.getDefaultToolkit().beep();
117:          }
118:       }
129:
120:       // Create a string out of our Destination buffer
121:       String strInsertString =
122:              new String( strDestination, 0, nDestinationIndex );
123:
124:       // Call the PlainDocument insertString method
125:       super.insertString( offs, strInsertString, a );
126:    }
127:  }
128: }
```

Figure 5.8 shows the JTextFieldExample application.

Figure 5.8

JTextFieldExample
application example.

This program creates two label and text field combinations: one to ask the user for his name, and the other to ask the user for his age. The name text field accepts any input, but the age text field will accept only numeric input. Here is a breakdown of what the application is doing line by line.

```
18:    JTextField txtName = new JTextField( 40 );
19:  JTextField txtAge = new JTextField(new NumberDocument(),"",10);
```

Lines 18 and 19 create the two text fields; the first is simply a text field that can accept 40 columns of input, and the second is an empty text field that can accept 10 columns of input all based on the NumberDocument document. The NumberDocument class will be described later, but this is one way to set the document class for the text field to use. The new NumberDocument() statement creates a new instance of the NumberDocument class, and the constructor of the JTextField adds it as its Document object.

```
28:          txtName.setBackground( Color.black );
29:          txtName.setForeground( Color.cyan );
30:          txtName.setCaretColor( Color.cyan );
```

Lines 28–30 set the background, foreground, and caret colors of the name text field, respectively. The text field will have a black background with a cyan foreground and caret.

```
33:     Font font = new Font( "SansSerif",Font.BOLD¦Font.ITALIC,16);
```

Line 33 creates a new font object that is a bold and italic 16-point "SansSerif" font.

```
34:          txtName.setFont( font );
```

Line 34 sets our newly created font to the name text field.

```
37:          txtName.setToolTipText( "Enter Your Name" );
```

Line 37 sets a tool tip for the name text field that reads "Enter Your Name".

```
41:          add( txtName );
```

Finally, line 41 adds the name text field to the application.

```
44:          txtAge.setBackground( Color.darkGray );
45:          txtAge.setForeground( Color.yellow );
46:          txtAge.setCaretColor( Color.yellow );
47:          txtAge.setFont( font );
50:          txtAge.setToolTipText( "Enter Your Age" );
```

Lines 44–47 and 50 set the colors, font, and tool tip for the age text field.

```
54:          add( txtAge );
```

Line 54 adds the age text field to the application.

Now, lines 91–127 create a custom Document object:

```
91:     protected class NumberDocument extends PlainDocument {
```

Line 91 creates a new Document object named NumberDocument that extends the PlainDocument class. The PlainDocument class is a simple document class that is derived from:

```
javax.swing.text.AbstractDocument
```

It is a plain document that maintains no character attributes and acts as a map of the text contained in it. Because we are not concerned with formatting the text and we just want to check the value of each character added to it, it is the perfect choice for this application.

```
93:    public void insertString(int offs, String str, AttributeSet a)
94:                throws BadLocationException
```

Lines 93 and 94 override the `PlainDocument`'s `insertString` method. This method is called every time the user enters a character into the text field or pastes a string into the text field. The method receives the offset into the text field that the insert is occurring at, the string (or character) that is being inserted, and an attribute set for the string. The method throws an exception called `BadLocationException` if an error occurs because the given insert location is not valid in the document.

When errors occur in Java, methods usually throw exceptions. An *exception* itself is a description of an error. When an exception is thrown, program execution stops at the position where the exception is thrown, and the Java runtime engine sends that exception to the method that called this method.

We will talk more about exception handling later, but for now know that it is the mechanism for catching these exceptions. If you do not catch an exception that occurs in your application, the application will *crash*, meaning that it will stop running and an error will be displayed by the Java runtime engine (not a good thing!).

```
97:            char[] strSource = str.toCharArray();
```

Line 97 converts the text string passed into this method to a character array. This is done because later when we check to see if the characters to insert into the document are digits, we will need to use the `Character` method `isDigit`, which accepts a character and not a string.

```
100:           char[] strDestination = new char[strSource.length];
```

Line 100 creates a destination buffer that is the length of the source string. The way this method works is that we are going to step through each character in the source string and copy only the digits from the source string into the destination string. For example, if the following value was in the source string:

```
strSource = "ABC223DEF1";
```

the destination string would contain only the following:

```
strDestination = "2231";
```

```
101:           int nDestinationIndex = 0;
```

Line 101 defines an integer called `nDestinationIndex` that we are going to use in this method to track which character index in the `strDestination` character array we are currently working with. It is initialized to zero so that we start at the beginning.

You might recall that earlier we talked about arrays and indexes, but as a refresher, an array is simply an ordered collection of things. A thing can be an integer, a character, a class, or any atomic unit. Line 100 created an array of characters; that is, an ordered collection of characters.

In the previous example, `strDestination` looked as follows:

```
strDestination[0] = '2';
strDestination[1] = '2';
strDestination[2] = '3';
strDestination[3] = '1';
strDestination[4] = '';
strDestination[5] = '';
strDestination[6] = '';
strDestination[7] = '';
strDestination[8] = '';
strDestination[9] = '';
```

There are 10 elements (from 0 to 9) because when we created the character array, we asked for the length of `strSource`, which had 10 characters. The index starts at zero and continues up to the length of the string minus one (0 to 10 - 1 = 9).

```
104:            for( int i = 0; i < strSource.length; i++ )
```

Line 104 is a special kind of statement called a *for loop*. A looping statement causes a set of statements to repeat either a certain number of times or until some condition is met. Java has several different looping statements, and the `for` loop is the most common looping statement when executing a set of statements for a specified number of times. The format for a `for` loop is as follows:

```
for( initialization; comparison; increment )
{
    statement;
    ...
}
```

`initialization` is an expression that initializes the beginning of the loop. It can be a statement or function call and can include more than one statement, separated by a comma. Typically, `for` loops have what is called a loop control variable (LCV) that you will initialize here. In Line 104, the loop control variable is an integer named `i`. In the initialization section, you can use an existing variable or create a new one as we did in line 104.

```
int i;
for( i=0; ...; ... )
```

or

```
for( int i=0; ...; ... )
```

The *comparison* expression is checked every time the loop completes and if it is true, the statements in the loop will be executed again; it can be a statement or function call. Usually the comparison involves checking the value of the loop control variable. The only requirement of the comparison expression is that it must result in a Boolean value: `true` or `false`. In line 104, we are checking to see if the loop control variable (`i`) is less than the length of `strSource`.

The *increment* expression can be any statement or function call and is executed after the comparison expression evaluates to true. Typically this is used to increment the loop control variable.

The *statement* can be zero or more Java commands; there is no restriction to the type of statements these can be: They can be statements or function calls, including other `for` loops. This section is referred to as the *body* of the `for` loop.

Internally, a `for` loop functions in the following steps:

1. Execute initialization.
2. Test comparison.
3. Exit if comparison is false; otherwise, continue to step 4.
4. Execute statement.
5. Execute increment.
6. Go to step 2.

If you wanted to create a loop that would print the numbers 0 through 4, here is one way to do it:

```
for( int i=0; i<5; i++ )
{
    System.out.println( i );
}
```

These statements create a new integer named `i`, check to see if it is less than 5 (which it is), print the number out to the screen, and then increment `i`.

The operator ++ is known as the *increment operator*. It increments the operand by one unit. So, if we are talking about integers, the ++ operator will increment the operand by 1. The increment operator can appear before the operand or after the operand, but each has a specific meaning. Using the *postfix increment operator* (placing the ++ after the operand) causes the compiler to take the value of the operand and use it before incrementing, and then increment it after it is finished.

The *prefix increment operator* causes the opposite to happen; it increments the operand and then gets its value. Consider the following:

```
1: int i=5;
2:
3: int x = i++;
4: int y = ++i;
```

In this case, x has the value 5 and y has the value 6. Here is what happened:

- In line 3, the compiler said, "Give x the value of i and then increment i."
- In line 4, the compiler said, "Increment i and then give y the value of i."

Furthermore there is an operator called the *decrement operator* (- -) that functions similar to the increment operator only it decrements the operand by one unit. There are both prefix and postfix decrement *operators*:

```
1: int i = 5;
2:
3: int x = i--;
4: int y = --i;
```

In this case, x has the value 5 and y has the value 4. Here is what happened:

- In line 3, the compiler said, "Give x the value of i and then decrement i."
- In line 4, the compiler said, "Decrement i and then give y the value of i."

Back to line 104; it will cause the body of the for loop to execute once for each letter in strSource or for strSource's length number of times.

107:   `if( Character.isDigit( strSource[i] ) )`

Line 107 retrieves the character stored at index i of the character array strSource and calls the Character class's isDigit method. The isDigit method returns true if the character passed to it is between 0 and 9; otherwise, it returns false.

Now, the if statement is a conditional statement of the following form:

```
if( comparison )
{
    true statements;
}
else
{
    false statements;
}
```

The comparison is similar to the for loop condition in that it can be a statement or a function call that evaluates to a Boolean value: true or false. The way that the if statement works is that it executes the comparison, and if it is true it executes the true statements. If it is false, it will execute the false statements. The else clause is optional; you can execute statements only if some comparison is true and do nothing if it is false. The comparison is made only once and the statements executed (true or false) are only executed once, as opposed to a looping statement. The true statements and false statements can be zero or more statements or function calls.

The true statement and false statement bodies can be delimited by braces "{ }" if there are multiple statements, or the braces can be omitted if there is only one statement. For example, you could write the following:

```
if( comparison )
{
    true statement;
    ...
}
else
{
    false statement;
    ...
}
```

Consider the following example:

```
if( 5 > 2 )
{
    System.out.println( "Five is greater than two" );
}
else
{
    System.out.println( "Five is not greater than two" );
}
```

First, the comparison is executed: Is 5 greater than 2? Yes, execute the true statements: Print "Five is greater than two" to the screen. Then, we are finished.

The output of this code is

```
Five is greater than two
```

Line 107 will execute the true statements (lines 108 and 111) if the character at index i of strSource is a digit (0 through 9), or it will execute the false statements (lines 113 to 117) if the character is not a digit.

```
110:            strDestination[nDestinationIndex++] = strSource[i];
```

Therefore, if the if statement in line 107 is true, line 110 executes. Line 110 retrieves the character at index i of strSource, assigns it to index nDestinationIndex of strDestination, and then increments the value of nDestinationIndex (remember our increment discussion from a few pages ago?).

```
116:            java.awt.Toolkit.getDefaultToolkit().beep();
```

If the `if` statement in line 107 is false and the character is not a digit, line 116 executes. Line 116 causes the computer to beep by calling the toolkit method `beep`. What we do is use the `java.awt.Toolkit` class to retrieve the default toolkit and use that default toolkit to execute the `beep` method.

```
121:          String strInsertString =
122:          new String( strDestination, 0, nDestinationIndex );
```

Lines 121 and 122 build a new `String` object from the destination buffer spanning the length of valid digit characters, specified by `nDestinationIndex`.

```
125:          super.insertString( offs, strInsertString, a );
```

Finally, in line 125 we call the `PlainDocument` class's `insertString` method with the modified string that contains only digits.

The way that this method will work is that when the user presses a key in the text field, the `insertString` method is called with the string simply being the character of the key that was pressed. This function checks to see if the key is a digit and if it is, the function passes the digit to the parent `insertString` that will add the character to the display. If the user copies some text to the clipboard and attempts to paste it into the text field, the `insertString` method will be called with the string being the entire text to be pasted on the text field. The `insertString` method then parses through the string and creates a buffer with only the digits in the string and disregards all other characters. Thus if the input were "ABD123DEF45", the buffer would contain "12345". The method then passes this buffer to the parent `insertString` method to be added to the text field.

Text Areas

The `JTextArea` class can display and edit multiple lines of text. It is similar to a `JTextField` except that it supports multiple lines and other functionality related to that, such as line wrapping and the concept of rows (to set and retrieve text in the context of rows).

As with the `JTextField`, you can specify the font for the `JTextArea`, but a limitation of the text area is that it can only support one font for the entire text area. The `JTextField` is similar in Windows lingo to the Notepad application; there is no formatting information and any changes you make to the component affect the entire component and not individual characters.

The JTextArea class can be constructed in six different ways, as shown in Table 5.12.

Table 5.12   JTextArea Constructors

Constructor	Description
JTextArea()	Constructs a new text area
JTextArea(javax.swing.text. Document doc)	Constructs a new text area with the given document model, and defaults for all the other arguments (null, 0, 0)
JTextArea(javax.swing.text. Document doc, String text, int rows, int columns)	Constructs a new text area with the specified number of rows and columns, and the given document model
JTextArea(int rows, int columns)	Constructs a new empty text area with the specified number of rows and columns
JTextArea(String text)	Constructs a new text area with the specified text displayed
JTextArea(String text, int rows, int columns)	Constructs a new text area with the specified text and number of rows and columns

The Document models used in text areas are the same as those used in text fields, like the NumberDocument we created in the last example. Here are some examples for how to construct a JTextArea:

```
// Create an empty text area with no predefined size
JTextArea taEmpty = new JTextArea();

// Create a 10 row X 80 column text area
JTextArea taSized = new JTextArea( 10, 80 );

// Create a 15 row X 60 column text area with text in it
JTextArea taContent = new JTextArea( "This is a text area!", 15, 60 );

// Create a text area using our NumberDocument document model
JTextArea taDoc = new JTextArea( new NumberDocument() );

// Create a text area with everything!
JTextArea taEverything = new JTextArea( new NumberDocument(),
     "This is a text area!",
     10,
     60 );
```

The following are some interesting things you can do with a JTextArea:

- Enable/disable line wrapping—This is done through the use of the setLineWrap method, prototyped as follows:

  ```
  public void setLineWrap( boolean wrap );
  ```

  where a wrap value of true means enable line wrapping and a value of false means disable line wrapping.

- Set word wrapping to wrap words or characters—This is done through the setWrapStyleWord method, prototyped as follows:

```
public void setWrapStyleWord( boolean wrap );
```

where a wrap value of true means wrap words and a value of false means wrap characters; in other words, true will keep entire words together on a line and false will break up words.

The manner in which the JTextArea class handles scrolling is much different than its AWT predecessor TextField. TextArea supported scrolling directly itself, but the JTextArea supports scrolling by implementing the Scrollable interface (actually, the interface is inherited from JTextComponent). Because it implements the Scrollable interface, it can be added to a JScrollPane lightweight container that will manage the scrolling for it.

Because of this tight coupling with JScrollPane, you are going to have to construct a JScrollPane object, which can be constructed in four different ways, shown in Table 5.13.

Table 5.13 **JScrollPane Constructors**

Constructor	Description
JScrollPane()	Create an empty (no viewport view) JScrollPane where both horizontal and vertical scrollbars appear when needed
JScrollPane(java.awt.Component view)	Create a JScrollPane that displays the contents of the specified component, where both horizontal and vertical scrollbars appear whenever the component's contents are larger than the view
JScrollPane(java.awt.Component view, int vsbPolicy, int hsbPolicy)	Create a JScrollPane that displays the view component in a viewport whose view position can be controlled with a pair of scrollbars
JScrollPane(int vsbPolicy, int hsbPolicy)	Create an empty (no viewport view) JScrollPane with specified scrollbar policies

For our example, we are going to construct a JScrollPane using the second constructor, passing it our text area:

```
// Create a new text area
JTextArea taDescription = new JTextArea( "Description", 10, 40 );

// Create a new JScrollPane
JScrollPane scrollPane = new JScrollPane( taDescription );
```

Anyway, let's get to our example. Take a look at Listing 5.3.

Type the code from Listing 5.3, excluding line numbers, into your favorite text editor and save it as `JTextAreaExample.java`, or copy it from the CD. Build it as follows:

```
javac JTextAreaExample.java
java JTextAreaExample
```

The code specific to the `JTextArea` class is boldface for your convenience and is explained following the source code.

Listing 5.3   `JTextAreaExample.java`

```
1:  // Import Swing packages
2:  import javax.swing.*;
3:  import javax.swing.text.*;
4:  import javax.swing.event.*;
5:
6:  // Import AWT packages
7:  import java.awt.*;
8:  import java.awt.Toolkit;
9:  import java.awt.event.*;
10:
11: public class JTextAreaExample extends JPanel
12: {
13:     // Create a label for our text area
14:     JLabel lblTitle = new JLabel( "Enter a description", JLabel.CENTER );
15:
16:     // Create a basic text area
17:     JTextArea taDescription = new JTextArea("Description", 10, 40);
18:
19:     // Create a scroll pane that will hold the text area and support
20:     // scrolling
21:     JScrollPane scrollPane = new JScrollPane( taDescription );
22:
23:     // Constructor
24:     public JTextAreaExample()
25:     {
26:         // Change the color of the name field
27:         taDescription.setBackground( Color.black );
28:         taDescription.setForeground( Color.yellow );
29:         taDescription.setCaretColor( Color.yellow );
30:
31:         // Change the font of the name field
32:         Font font = new Font( "SansSerif", Font.BOLD¦Font.ITALIC, 16 );
33:         taDescription.setFont( font );
34:
35:         // Add a tool tip
36:         taDescription.setToolTipText( "Enter a description" );
37:
```

continues

Listing 5.3   continued

```
38:         // Enable line wrapping
39:         taDescription.setLineWrap( true );
40:
41:         // Tell the component to wrap words (keep words together)
42:         taDescription.setWrapStyleWord( true );
43:
44:         // Add the name label and field to the JPanel
45:         add( lblTitle );
46:         add( scrollPane );
47:
48:     }
49:
50:     // Main application entry point into this class
51:     public static void main( String[] args )
52:     {
53:         // Create a JFrame object
54:         JFrame frame = new JFrame( "JTextArea Example!" );
55:
56:         // Create a JTextAreaExample Object
57:         JTextAreaExample example = new JTextAreaExample();
58:
59:         // Add our JTextAreaExample Object to the JFrame
60:         frame.getContentPane().add( example, BorderLayout.CENTER );
61:
62:         // Resize our JFrame
63:         frame.setSize( 600, 300 );
64:
65:         // Make our JFrame visible
66:         frame.setVisible( true );
67:
68:         // Create a window listener to close our application when we
69:         // close our application
70:         frame.addWindowListener
71:         (
72:             new WindowAdapter()
73:             {
74:                 public void windowClosing( WindowEvent e )
75:                 {
76:                     System.exit( 0 );
77:                 }
78:             }
79:         );
80:     }
81: }
```

Figure 5.9 shows the JTextAreaExample.

Figure 5.9

*JTextAreaExample
application example.*

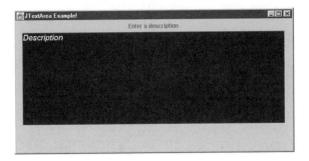

```
17:  JTextArea taDescription = new JTextArea("Description", 10, 40);
```

Line 17 creates our JTextArea with 10 rows and 40 columns. It initially displays the text "Description" in it.

```
21:    JScrollPane scrollPane = new JScrollPane( taDescription );
```

Line 21 creates a new JScrollPane object that holds our JTextArea.

```
27:        taDescription.setBackground( Color.black );
28:        taDescription.setForeground( Color.yellow );
29:        taDescription.setCaretColor( Color.yellow );
33:        taDescription.setFont( font );
36:        taDescription.setToolTipText( "Enter a description" );
```

Lines 27–29, 33, and 36 set the colors, fonts, and tool tips for the JTextArea just as you did in the JtextFieldExample application in the previous section.

```
39:        taDescription.setLineWrap( true );
```

Line 39 turns on the word wrap of the JTextArea.

```
42:        taDescription.setWrapStyleWord( true );
```

Line 42 tells the JTextArea to wrap entire words and not just characters.

```
46:      add( scrollPane );
```

Finally, line 46 adds the JScrollPane to the JPanel. Note that we do not have to add the text area to the JPanel ourselves; it is part of the JScrollPane and adding that to the JPanel is sufficient.

Two more classes that you should look at related to JTextArea are the JTextPane and JEditorPane classes. These are more advanced than the JTextArea in that they provide formatted text with varying fonts. They are interesting, and if you are ever of the mind to write a text editor or a word processor, you should definitely have a look!

Let's move on to buttons.

Buttons

The Java button classes include JButton, JCheckBox, JRadioButton, and JToggleButton. JCheckBox and JRadioButton are both derived from JToggleButton. Figure 5.10 shows the button hierarchy tree.

Figure 5.10

Swing button hierarchy.

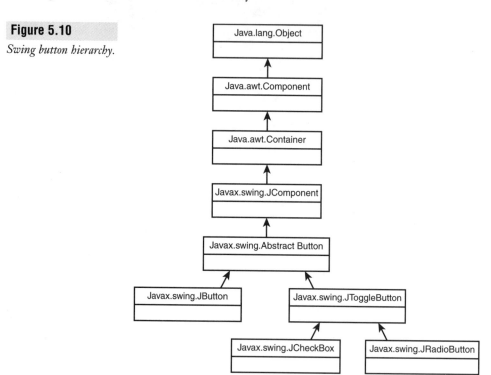

Buttons in Swing have all the benefits of standard buttons as well as the extended features of JComponents, but they also include some interesting icons associated with them. The AbstractButton class has the notion of a button being in one of several states: pressed, not pressed, selected, not selected, and disabled. The default state of an icon, set through setIcon, covers the not pressed and not selected states. The others are set with the following methods: setPressedIcon, setDisabledIcon, and setSelectedIcon. All these states are applicable when we get to individual buttons.

JButton

Pushbuttons are created using the JButton class. They can be in one of three states: pressed, not pressed, or disabled. Take a look at Table 5.14 to see how JButtons are constructed.

Table 5.14   JButton **Constructors**

Constructor	*Description*
JButton()	Creates a button with no set text or icon
JButton(Icon icon)	Creates a button with an icon
JButton(String text)	Creates a button with text
JButton(String text, Icon icon)	Creates a button with initial text and an icon

JButtons can be created with or without text or an icon. If you want to include an icon on your JButton, you can set the default icon through one of the constructors or set it manually using setIcon. If you want to give the user feedback when the button is pressed or disabled, you must set the icons for those states. Here are the prototypes for the icon methods:

```
public void setIcon( Icon defaultIcon );
public void setPressedIcon( Icon pressedIcon );
public void  setDisabledIcon( Icon disabledIcon );
```

JRadioButton

Radio buttons are created using the JRadioButton class. They can be in one of three states: selected, not selected, or disabled. Take a look at Table 5.15 to see how JRadioButtons are constructed.

Table 5.15   JRadioButton **Constructors**

Constructor	*Description*
JRadioButton()	Creates an initially unselected radio button with no set text
JRadioButton(Icon icon)	Creates an initially unselected radio button with the specified image but no text
JRadioButton(Icon icon, boolean selected)	Creates a radio button with the specified image and selection state, but no text
JRadioButton(String text)	Creates an unselected radio button with the specified text
JRadioButton(String text, boolean selected)	Creates a radio button with the specified text and selection state
JRadioButton(String text, Icon icon)	Creates a radio button that has the specified text and image, and that is initially unselected
JRadioButton(String text, Icon icon, boolean selected)	Creates a radio button that has the specified text, image, and selection state

JRadioButtons are special in that an outside class controls their mutually exclusive state. You may recall from the last chapter that a radio button group is a set of buttons in which one and only one can be selected at a time; if one radio button is selected, all the others are unselected.

To facilitate this functionality, the ButtonGroup class is introduced. This class simply maintains the state of all buttons added to it and ensures that only one is selected at any given time. To use the ButtonGroup class for your buttons, you must perform the following steps:

1. Create a new ButtonGroup object.
2. Create all your JRadioButton objects.
3. Call the ButtonGroup object's add method for each radio button in this group.
4. Optionally set the default selection using the ButtonGroup's setSelected method.

As far as painting an icon for these radio buttons, be sure to include the default icon, a selected icon, and an optional disabled icon. Here are the prototypes for the icon functions:

```
public  void setIcon( Icon defaultIcon );
public void setSelectedIcon( Icon selectedIcon );
public void setDisabledIcon( Icon disabledIcon );
```

JCheckBox

Check boxes are created using the JCheckBox class. They can assume the following states: selected, not selected (default), and disabled. Take a look at Table 5.16 to see how to construct a JCheckBox.

Table 5.16 JCheckBox Constructors

Constructor	Description
JCheckBox()	Creates an initially unselected check box button with no text, no icon
JCheckBox(Icon icon)	Creates an initially unselected check box with an icon
JCheckBox(Icon icon, boolean selected)	Creates a check box with an icon and specifies whether it is initially selected
JCheckBox(String text)	Creates an initially unselected check box with text
JCheckBox(String text, boolean selected)	Creates a check box with text and specifies whether it is initially selected
JCheckBox(String text, Icon icon)	Creates an initially unselected check box with the specified text and icon
JCheckBox(String text, Icon icon, boolean selected)	Creates a check box with text and icon, and specifies whether it is initially selected

Because check boxes can be selected or unselected, regardless of other buttons near them, there is no need to use the `ButtonGroup` class. The `ButtonGroup` does operate on `AbstractButton`, so you can add `JButton` and `JCheckBox` to the `ButtonGroup` as well.

When associating icons with `JCheckBox`, be sure to include icons for the following states: selected, unselected (default), and optionally disabled. Here are the prototypes for the icon functions:

```
public void setIcon( Icon defaultIcon );
public void setSelectedIcon( Icon selectedIcon );
public void  setDisabledIcon( Icon disabledIcon );
```

A Button Example

We are going to add check boxes, radio buttons, and pushbuttons to the following sample application. There are one standard check box and two check boxes with icons associated with them. One demonstrates the selected/unselected states and the other one is always disabled. There are three standard radio buttons that demonstrate how to add radio buttons to a button group and select one of them. Finally, there are two pushbuttons that have icons associated with them for both the default and pressed states. Take a look at Listing 5.4 for the full source code.

Type the code from Listing 5.4, excluding line numbers, into your favorite text editor and save it as `ButtonExample.java`, or copy it from the CD. Build it as follows:

RunIt
→

```
javac ButtonExample.java
java ButtonExample
```

The code specific to the buttons is boldface for your convenience and is explained following the source code.

Listing 5.4   `ButtonExample.java`

```
1:  // Import Swing packages
2:  import javax.swing.*;
3:  import javax.swing.event.*;
4:
5:  // Import AWT packages
6:  import java.awt.*;
7:  import java.awt.event.*;
8:
9:  public class ButtonExample extends JPanel
10: {
11:     // Load our icons
12:     ImageIcon iconOKDefault =
13:             new ImageIcon( "iconOKDefault.gif" );
14:     ImageIcon iconOKPressed =
```

continues

Listing 5.4   continued

```
15:                     new ImageIcon( "iconOKPressed.gif" );
16:         ImageIcon iconCancelDefault =
17:                     new ImageIcon( "iconCancelDefault.gif" );
18:         ImageIcon iconCancelPressed =
19:                     new ImageIcon( "iconCancelPressed.gif" );
20:         ImageIcon iconSaveDefault =
21:                     new ImageIcon( "iconSaveDefault.gif" );
22:         ImageIcon iconSaveSelected =
23:                     new ImageIcon( "iconSaveSelected.gif" );
24:         ImageIcon iconBackupDefault =
25:                     new ImageIcon( "iconBackupDefault.gif" );
26:         ImageIcon iconBackupDisabled =
27:                     new ImageIcon( "iconBackupDisabled.gif" );
28:
29:         // Create a couple push buttons
30:         JButton btnOK = new JButton( "OK", iconOKDefault );
31:     JButton btnCancel = new  JButton( "Cancel", iconCancelDefault );
32:
33:         // Create some checkboxes
34:         JCheckBox cbxSaveWork =
35:                 new JCheckBox( "Save Work", iconSaveDefault, true );
36:         JCheckBox cbxMakeBackup =
37:                 new JCheckBox( "Make Backup", iconBackupDefault );
38:         JCheckBox cbxPlain = new JCheckBox( "Plain Checkbox" );
39:
40:         // Create some radio buttons
41:         JRadioButton rbOne = new JRadioButton( "One" );
42:         JRadioButton rbTwo = new JRadioButton( "Two" );
43:         JRadioButton rbThree = new JRadioButton( "Three" );
44:
45:         // Create a ButtonGroup to manage our radio buttons
46:         ButtonGroup bgrpNumbers = new ButtonGroup();
47:
48:         // Constructor
49:         public ButtonExample()
50:         {
51:             // Set the save work selected icon so we can see
52:             // the enabled/disabled states
53:             cbxSaveWork.setSelectedIcon( iconSaveSelected );
54:
55:             // Set the backup disabled icon since we are just
56:             // going to disable it
57:             cbxMakeBackup.setDisabledIcon( iconBackupDisabled );
58:
59:             // Disable the backup checkbox
60:             cbxMakeBackup.setEnabled( false );
61:
62:             // Add our three checkboxes to the JPanel
63:             add( cbxSaveWork );
64:             add( cbxMakeBackup );
```

```
65:            add( cbxPlain );
66:
67:            // Add our radio buttons to the button group
68:            bgrpNumbers.add( rbOne );
69:            bgrpNumbers.add( rbTwo );
70:            bgrpNumbers.add( rbThree );
71:
72:            // Select button two
73:            bgrpNumbers.setSelected( rbTwo.getModel(), true );
74:
75:            // Add our radio buttons to the JPanel
76:            add( rbOne );
77:            add( rbTwo );
78:            add( rbThree );
79:
80:            // Set the pressed icons for the pushbuttons
81:            btnOK.setPressedIcon( iconOKPressed );
82:            btnCancel.setPressedIcon( iconCancelPressed );
83:
84:            // Add our push buttons to the JPanel
85:            add( btnOK );
86:            add( btnCancel );
87:        }
88:
89:    // Main application entry point into this class
90:    public static void main( String[] args )
91:    {
92:            // Create a JFrame object
93:            JFrame frame = new  JFrame( "Button Example!" );
94:
95:            // Create a ButtonExample Object
96:            ButtonExample example = new ButtonExample();
97:
98:            // Add our ButtonExample Object to the JFrame
99:            frame.getContentPane().add( example, BorderLayout.CENTER );
100:
101:            // Resize our JFrame
102:            frame.setSize( 340, 180 );
103:
104:            // Make our JFrame visible
105:            frame.setVisible( true );
106:
107:            // Create a window listener to close our application when we
108:            // close our application
109:            frame.addWindowListener
110:            (
111:                new WindowAdapter()
112:                {
113:                    public void windowClosing( WindowEvent e )
114:                    {
115:                        System.exit( 0 );
```

continues

Listing 5.4 continued

```
116:                    }
117:                }
118:            );
129:    }
120:}
```

Figure 5.11 shows the ButtonExample application.

Figure 5.11

The ButtonExample application example.

```
12:        ImageIcon iconOKDefault =
13:                new ImageIcon( "iconOKDefault.gif" );
14:        ImageIcon iconOKPressed =
15:                new ImageIcon( "iconOKPressed.gif" );
16:        ImageIcon iconCancelDefault =
17:                new ImageIcon( "iconCancelDefault.gif" );
18:        ImageIcon iconCancelPressed =
19:                new ImageIcon( "iconCancelPressed.gif" );
20:        ImageIcon iconSaveDefault =
21:                new ImageIcon( "iconSaveDefault.gif" );
22:        ImageIcon iconSaveSelected =
23:                new ImageIcon( "iconSaveSelected.gif" );
24:        ImageIcon iconBackupDefault =
25:                new ImageIcon( "iconBackupDefault.gif" );
26:        ImageIcon iconBackupDisabled =
27:                new ImageIcon( "iconBackupDisabled.gif" );
```

Lines 12–27 load the icons that will be used in the application. We used this same method of loading icons in the JLabel example, but basically all we are doing is creating ImageIcons from GIF files.

```
30:        JButton btnOK = new JButton( "OK", iconOKDefault );
31:    JButton btnCancel = new JButton( "Cancel", iconCancelDefault );
```

Lines 30 and 31 create our two pushbuttons: OK and Cancel, and set their default, not pressed icons.

```
34:        JCheckBox cbxSaveWork =
35:            new JCheckBox( "Save Work", iconSaveDefault, true );
36:        JCheckBox cbxMakeBackup =
37:            new JCheckBox( "Make Backup", iconBackupDefault );
38:        JCheckBox cbxPlain = new JCheckBox( "Plain Checkbox" );
```

Lines 34–38 create our three check boxes: Save Work and Make Backup contain default icons, and Plain Checkbox is a simple check box. Save Work is checked by default.

```
41:     JRadioButton rbOne = new JRadioButton( "One" );
42:     JRadioButton rbTwo = new JRadioButton( "Two" );
43:     JRadioButton rbThree = new JRadioButton( "Three" );
```

Lines 41–43 create our three radio buttons: One, Two, and Three.

```
46:     ButtonGroup bgrpNumbers = new ButtonGroup();
```

Line 46 creates a `ButtonGroup` named `bgrpNumbers` to manage our radio buttons.

```
53:     cbxSaveWork.setSelectedIcon( iconSaveSelected );
```

Line 53 sets the selected icon for the Save Work check box.

```
57:     cbxMakeBackup.setDisabledIcon( iconBackupDisabled );
```

Line 57 sets the disabled icon for the Make Backup check box.

```
60:     cbxMakeBackup.setEnabled( false );
```

Line 60 disables the Make Backup check box by calling its `setEnabled` method and sending it a `false` argument.

```
63:     add( cbxSaveWork );
64:     add( cbxMakeBackup );
65:     add( cbxPlain );
```

Lines 63–65 add our three check boxes to the `JPanel`.

```
68:     bgrpNumbers.add( rbOne );
69:     bgrpNumbers.add( rbTwo );
70:     bgrpNumbers.add( rbThree );
```

Lines 68–70 add our three radio buttons to the `ButtonGroup` using the `ButtonGroup`'s add method.

```
73:     bgrpNumbers.setSelected( rbTwo.getModel(), true );
```

Line 73 looks a little confusing, but what it is doing is selecting radio button two from the `ButtonGroup`. The `ButtonGroup` class's `setSelected` method has the following prototype:

```
public void setSelected(ButtonModel m, boolean b)
```

The `ButtonModel` specifies which button to modify and the Boolean controls whether the button is selected or not. Recall that in our discussion of the separable model design, we discussed separating the visual representation of a control from its data. The `ButtonModel` is a button's model, or representation of its data. What type of data does a button contain? The relevant information that the button model contains for this example is the button's state.

You can obtain the button's model using the AbstractButton class's getModel method.

```
76:          add( rbOne );
77:          add( rbTwo );
78:          add( rbThree );
```

Lines 76–78 add our three radio buttons to our JPanel.

```
81:          btnOK.setPressedIcon( iconOKPressed );
82:          btnCancel.setPressedIcon( iconCancelPressed );
```

Because we are using icons on our buttons, we are going to want to display a different icon when the button is pressed than when it is sitting idle. Lines 81 and 82 add a pressed icon for our buttons.

```
85:          add( btnOK );
86:          add( btnCancel );
```

Finally, lines 85 and 86 add our pushbuttons to the JPanel.

Lists

Lists provide a visual representation of data elements and allow the selection of one or more of those elements. Lists are represented in Swing by the JList class.

Lists are broken into a handful of elements that we are interested in:

- JList—The JList provides the visual representation of the data in the list.
- ListModel—The ListModel, following the separable model design, holds all the data for the list. It provides the data elements to the JList to be displayed.
- ListCellRenderer—The ListCellRenderer tells the JList how to render (draw on the screen) individual list items.

Of these items, the JList has a default ListModel and ListCellRenderer, but you are free to create your own. As soon as you have meaningful data, you will want to create your own ListModel, and if you want your list to display icons, you will need to create your own ListCellRenderer.

How are JLists constructed? Take a look at Table 5.17.

Table 5.17   JList **Constructors**

Constructor	Description
JList()	Construct a JList with an empty model
JList(ListModel dataModel)	Construct a JList that displays the elements in the specified, non-null model
JList(Object[] listData)	Construct a JList that displays the elements in the specified array
JList(java.util.Vector listData)	Construct a JList that displays the elements in the specified Vector

From these constructors, you can see that you can create lists from either list models, which we will use in the example, an object array, which could be an array of Strings for example, or from a Vector. A Vector is a data structure you can use to store groups of related elements—we will talk more about Vector later.

Anyway, we are going to make use of a ListModel in our example because we want to have complete control over our data. A ListModel is an interface that defines the methods you need to implement in order to be compatible with objects that perform actions on ListModel. In our example, we are going to derive our list model class from AbstractListModel, which is a basic class that provides default implementations of the methods in the ListModel interface. The methods in the ListModel interface are shown in Table 5.18.

Table 5.18   ListModel **Methods**

Method	Description
void addListDataListener (javax.swing.event.ListDataListener l)	Add a listener to the list that's notified each time a change to the data model occurs
Object getElementAt(int index)	Returns the value at the specified index
int getSize()	Returns the length of the list
void removeListDataListener (javax.swing.event.ListDataListener l)	Remove a listener from the list that's notified each time a change to the data model occurs

The two methods we are going to be interested in are getElementAt, which in our case will return a String representation of our item, and getSize, which will return the number of elements in our list.

Our example is a bit contrived, but it shows how to use the JList components without introducing the concept of data structures, which I want to save for Chapter 7. The example is a list of 100 elements of the form "Object n", where n is 0 through 99. I also took the liberty of adding icons to the display, which I will explain during our discussion of the source code. Speaking of source code, take a look at Listing 5.5.

Type the code from Listing 5.5, excluding line numbers, into your favorite text editor and save it as JListExample.java or copy it from the CD. Build it as follows:

```
javac JListExample.java
java JListExample
```

The code specific to the JList class is boldface for your convenience and is explained following the source code.

Listing 5.5   JListExample.java

```
 1:   // Import the libraries this application will use
 2:   import javax.swing.*;
 3:   import javax.swing.table.*;
 4:
 5:   import java.awt.*;
 6:   import java.awt.event.*;
 7:
 8:   // Main application class:  JListExample
 9:   public class JListExample extends JPanel
10:   {
11:       // Create an instance of our list model
12:       MyListModel listModel = new MyListModel();
13:
14:       // Create our JList
15:       JList list = new JList( listModel );
16:
17:       // Create a MyCellRenderer object
18:       MyCellRenderer cellRenderer = new MyCellRenderer();
19:
20:       // Constructor
21:       public JListExample()
22:       {
23:          // Set the JList cell renderer
24:          list.setCellRenderer( cellRenderer );
25:
26:          // Set the width of the JList
27:          list.setFixedCellWidth( 100 );
28:
29:          // Create a scroll pane for our list
30:          JScrollPane scrollPane = new JScrollPane( list );
31:
32:          // Add the scroll pane to the JPanel
33:          add( scrollPane );
34:       }
35:
36:       // Main application entry point into this class
```

```
37:    public static void main( String[] args )
38:    {
39:        // Create a JFrame object
40:        JFrame frame = new JFrame( "JList Example!" );
41:
42:        // Create a JListExample Object
43:        JListExample example = new JListExample();
44:
45:        // Add our JListExample Object to the JFrame
46:        frame.getContentPane().add( example, BorderLayout.CENTER );
47:
48:        // Resize our JFrame
49:        frame.setSize( 180, 180 );
50:
51:        // Make our JFrame visible
52:        frame.setVisible( true );
53:
54:        // Create a window listener to close our application when we
55:        // close our application
56:        frame.addWindowListener
57:        (
58:            new WindowAdapter()
59:            {
60:                public void windowClosing( WindowEvent e )
61:                {
62:                    System.exit( 0 );
63:                }
64:            }
65:        );
66:
67:    }
68:
69:    // MyListModel - Maintains the data for the JList
70:    public class MyListModel extends AbstractListModel
71:    {
72:        // Return the size of the list model (number of
73:        // items in the list)
74:        public int getSize()
75:        {
76:            return 100;
77:        }
78:
79:        // Return the element at position index
80:        public Object getElementAt( int index )
81:        {
82:            return( new String( "Object " + index ) );
83:        }
84:    }
85:
86:    // MyCellRenderer - Tells the JList how to paint each cell
87: class MyCellRenderer extends JLabel implements ListCellRenderer
```

continues

Listing 5.5 continued

```
88:      {
89:  ImageIcon iconRegular = new ImageIcon( "iconSmileySmall.gif" );
90:  ImageIcon iconSelected = new
                        ImageIcon("iconSmileySmallSelected.gif");
91:
92:          public MyCellRenderer()
93:          {
94:              setOpaque(true);
95:          }
96:
97:          public Component getListCellRendererComponent(
98:                          JList list,
99:                          Object value,
100:                         int index,
101:                         boolean isSelected,
102:                         boolean cellHasFocus)
103:         {
104:             // See if this item is selected
105:             if( isSelected )
106:             {
107:                 // Set Colors
108:                 setBackground( Color.blue );
109:                 setForeground( Color.white );
110:
111:                 // Set Icon
112:                 setIcon( iconSelected );
113:             }
114:             else
115:             {
116:                 // Set Colors
117:                 setBackground( Color.white );
118:                 setForeground( Color.black );
129:
120:                 // Set Icon
121:                 setIcon( iconRegular );
122:             }
123:
124:             // Set the text label of the cell
125:             setText(value.toString());
126:
127:             // Return the item we just created — ourself
128:             return this;
129:         }
130:     }
131:}
```

Figure 5.12 shows the JListExample application.

Figure 5.12

*JListExample
application example.*

```
12:     MyListModel listModel = new MyListModel();
```

Line 12 creates a new instance of our list model, which will be described later.

```
15:     JList list = new JList( listModel );
```

Line 15 creates our JList object with our list model created in line 12.

```
18:     MyCellRenderer cellRenderer = new MyCellRenderer();
```

Line 18 creates a new instance of our MyCellRenderer class, which will be described later.

```
24:         list.setCellRenderer( cellRenderer );
```

Line 24 calls the JList class's setCellRenderer method to tell the JList to pass all its list items through the specified list cell renderer before displaying them.

```
27:         list.setFixedCellWidth( 100 );
```

Line 27 sets the width of the JList object by calling the JList class's setFixedCellWidth to define the width of every cell in the list.

```
30:     JScrollPane scrollPane = new JScrollPane( list );
```

The JList class, like the JTextArea class discussed earlier, does not support scrolling natively in its control; it relies on the JScrollPane class to provide its scrolling capabilities for it. List 30 creates a new JScrollPane for the JList.

```
33:     add( scrollPane );
```

Finally, line 33 adds the scroll pane to the JPanel.

```
70:     public class MyListModel extends AbstractListModel
```

Line 70 is the declaration of MyListModel, which as discussed earlier is derived from AbstractListModel. Typically, in this class you would store all your data and supply it to the JList component when it needs it, but in our example we are going to make up the data as it needs it.

```
74:         public int getSize()
75:         {
76:             return 100;
77:         }
```

Lines 74–77 define the `ListModel` method `getSize`, which returns the number of elements in the list. In this case, we are hard-coding the list to contain 100 elements.

```
80:        public Object getElementAt( int index )
81:        {
82:            return( new String( "Object " + index ) );
83:        }
```

Lines 80–83 define the `ListModel` method `getElementAt`, which returns the `Object` for the given index. In our example, we are simply creating a `String` object that gives the `JList` the index back in string form.

```
87: class MyCellRenderer extends JLabel implements ListCellRenderer
```

Line 87 is where some of our work gets interesting. We are creating a new class named `MyCellRenderer` that extends `JLabel` and implements `ListCellRenderer`. The reason we are deriving from `JLabel` is that we can use both icons and text to display in each cell of the `JList`. `ListCellRenderer` is an interface that the `JList` component will use if you call its `setCellRenderer` method and pass it a class that implements this interface. The `ListCellRenderer` is a simple interface that has only one method:

```
Component getListCellRendererComponent(
            JList list,
            Object value,
            int index,
            boolean isSelected,
            boolean cellHasFocus)
```

This method is called every time the `JList` object wants to display a cell in the list component. It sends a reference to itself (`list`), the value stored in the list model (`value`), the index of the cell (`index`), a Boolean telling you if the item is selected in the list component (`isSelected`), and a Boolean telling you if the cell currently has the input focus (`cellHasFocus`). When you're rendering a cell, the important items to consider are the value (in our case a string) and whether or not the item is selected (you are going to have to represent that on the screen.) Read on and let's see how these are handled.

```
89:  ImageIcon iconRegular = new ImageIcon( "iconSmileySmall.gif" );
90:  ImageIcon iconSelected = new
                ImageIcon("iconSmileySmallSelected.gif");
```

Lines 89 and 90 load two icons: one to display when the item is selected and one when the item is not selected.

```
92:        public MyCellRenderer()
93:        {
94:            setOpaque(true);
95:        }
```

Lines 92–95 implement the constructor for the cell renderer. The only thing the constructor does is set the background of the label to be opaque so that the background of the label will show through.

```
97:          public Component getListCellRendererComponent(
98:                              JList list,
99:                              Object value,
100:                             int index,
101:                             boolean isSelected,
102:                             boolean cellHasFocus)
```

Lines 97–102 start the definition of the getListCellRendererComponent method.

```
105:          if( isSelected )
```

The first thing we do in this method is check to see if the item is selected or not.

```
106:          {
107:              // Set Colors
108:              setBackground( Color.blue );
109:              setForeground( Color.white );
110:
111:              // Set Icon
112:              setIcon( iconSelected );
113:          }
```

If the item is selected, we set the background to blue, the foreground to white, and the icon of the JLabel to the selected item icon.

```
114:          else
115:          {
116:              // Set Colors
117:              setBackground( Color.white );
118:              setForeground( Color.black );
129:
120:              // Set Icon
121:              setIcon( iconRegular );
122:          }
```

If the item is not selected, we set the background to white, the foreground to black, and the icon to the regular, unselected icon.

```
125:          setText(value.toString());
```

Regardless of whether the item is selected, we want to display the item's string representation as the text for our label. If we wanted a list of just icons, we could omit this statement.

```
128:          return this;
```

Finally, we return a reference to the component we are working with. This way, every cell in the list component will have a label in it that has both an icon and the name of the item in it. Because this method returns a component, you can return anything derived from the Component class; I will leave this as an exercise for you!

Tables

Tables provide a visual representation of data in a two-dimensional format and are represented in Swing using the JTable class. The structure of a JTable adheres strictly to the separable model design: There is a table model, typically derived from AbstractTableModel, that holds all the data for the table, and there is the actual JTable that is responsible for the visual representation of the table.

Visually, a JTable is composed of a column header and sets of data ordered by rows and columns. The table model is responsible not only for the data in the table, but for the column headers as well. This way, a table model full of data can easily plug into any JTable.

In this section, we are going to talk briefly about JTables, enough so that you understand how to create one. However, in Chapter 7, "Building the Stock Tracker User Interface," we will revisit the JTable class in more detail.

Okay already! How do we construct these things? Table 5.19 displays all seven constructors.

Table 5.19   JTable Constructors

Constructor	Description
JTable()	Constructs a default JTable, which is initialized with a default data model, a default column model, and a default selection model
JTable(int numRows, int numColumns)	Constructs a JTable with numRows and numColumns of empty cells using the DefaultTableModel
JTable(Object[][] rowData, Object[] columnNames)	Constructs a JTable to display the values in the two dimensional array, rowData, with column names, columnNames
JTable(javax.swing.table. TableModel dm)	Constructs a JTable that is initialized with dm as the data model, a default column model, and a default selection model
JTable(javax.swing.table. TableModel dm, javax.swing. table.TableColumnModel cm)	Constructs a JTable that is initialized with dm as the data model, cm as the column model, and a default selection model

Constructor	Description
JTable(javax.swing.table. TableModel dm, javax.swing. table.TableColumnModel cm, ListSelectionModel sm)	Constructs a JTable that is initialized with dm as the data model, cm as the column model, and sm as the selection model
JTable(Vector rowData, Vector columnNames)	Constructs a JTable to display the values in the Vector of Vectors, rowData, with column names, columnNames

You might notice a great deal of support for the DefaultTableModel, but with the latest release of the Swing libraries, custom table models are much easier to work with. Because of this fact, we are just going to create a custom table model from the offset, as you will need to do that when you get to building a meaningful table anyway.

We just going to brush on the functionality of the JTable class in this section, so I urge you to look at the Java 2 SDK documentation for more information. As I said earlier, we will talk more about JTables in Chapter 7, but I could easily spend more than 50 pages just describing tables, so we are going to have to cut our discussion short.

For now you just need to know the following about JTables to create the user interface appearance (without event handling!):

- Tables are composed of cells (rows and columns) that are accessed by integer indices.
- All the data for the table is represented in a TableModel.
- All columns in a table are stored in a class that implements the TableColumnModel interface and individually represented by TableColumn objects.

We are going to create a very simple example of a JTable that follows with the example presented in the Java 2 SDK documentation: a 20-row by 10-column table of integer values that simply has the product of the row number and column number in each cell. Each column has a heading displaying the column number and the table itself is placed inside a JScrollPane to enable scrolling. I will explain everything as we read through the listing. With that said, take a look at Listing 5.6.

Type the code from Listing 5.6, excluding line numbers, into your favorite text editor and save it as JTableExample.java or copy it from the CD. Build it as follows:

```
javac JTableExample.java
java JTableExample
```

The code specific to the JTable class is boldface for your convenience and is explained following the source code.

Listing 5.6 `JTableExample.java`

```
1:  // Import the libraries this application will use
2:  import javax.swing.*;
3:  import javax.swing.table.*;
4:  import java.awt.*;
5:  import java.awt.event.*;
6:
7:  // Main application class:  JTableExample
8:  public class JTableExample extends JPanel
9:  {
10:      // Constructor
11:      public JTableExample()
12:      {
13:          // Create a new Stock Table Model object
14:          MyTableModel myTableModel = new MyTableModel();
15:
16:          // Create a new JTable and associate it with the MyTableModel
17:          JTable numberTable = new JTable( myTableModel );
18:
19:          // Set the size of the table
20:          numberTable.setPreferredScrollableViewportSize(
21:                              new Dimension(600, 200) );
22:
23:          // Set the column widths for the table
24:          TableColumn column = null;
25:
26:          for (int i = 0; i < 4; i++)
27:          {
28:          column = numberTable.getColumnModel().getColumn( i );
29:     column.setPreferredWidth( myTableModel.getColumnWidth( i ) );
30:          }
31:
32:          // Create a scroll pane and add the table to it
33:          JScrollPane scrollPane = new JScrollPane( numberTable );
34:
35:          // Add the scroll pane to our panel
36:          add( scrollPane, BorderLayout.CENTER );
37:      }
38:
39:      // Main application entry point into this class
40:      public static void main( String[] args )
41:      {
42:          // Create a JFrame object
43:          JFrame frame = new JFrame( "JTable Example!" );
44:
45:          // Create a JTableExample Object
46:          JTableExample example = new JTableExample();
47:
48:          // Add our JTableExample Object to the JFrame
49:          frame.getContentPane().add( example,  BorderLayout.CENTER );
50:
51:          // Resize our JFrame
52:          frame.setSize( 640, 260 );
```

```
53:
54:            // Make our JFrame visible
55:            frame.setVisible( true );
56:
57:            // Create a window listener to close our application when we
58:            // close our application
59:            frame.addWindowListener
60:            (
61:                new WindowAdapter()
62:                {
63:                    public void windowClosing( WindowEvent e )
64:                    {
65:                        System.exit( 0 );
66:                    }
67:                }
68:            );
69:
70:    }
71:
72:    // Table Model Class - holds all of our row and column information
73:    class MyTableModel extends AbstractTableModel
74:    {
75:        // Return the number of columns in the table
76:        public int getColumnCount()
77:        {
78:            return 10;
79:        }
80:
81:        // Returns the number of rows in the table
82:        public int getRowCount()
83:        {
84:            return 20;
85:        }
86:
87:        // Return the value for an individual table cell
88:        public Object getValueAt(int row, int col)
89:        {
90:            return new Integer(row*col);
91:        }
92:
93:        // Return the name of the column
94:        public String getColumnName( int col )
95:            {
96:            return new String( Integer.toString( col ) );
97:        }
98:
99:        // Return the width of the column
100:        public int getColumnWidth( int nCol )
101:        {
102:            return 60;
103:        }
104:    }
105:}
```

Figure 5.13 shows the `JTableExample` application.

Figure 5.13

*JTableExample
application example.*

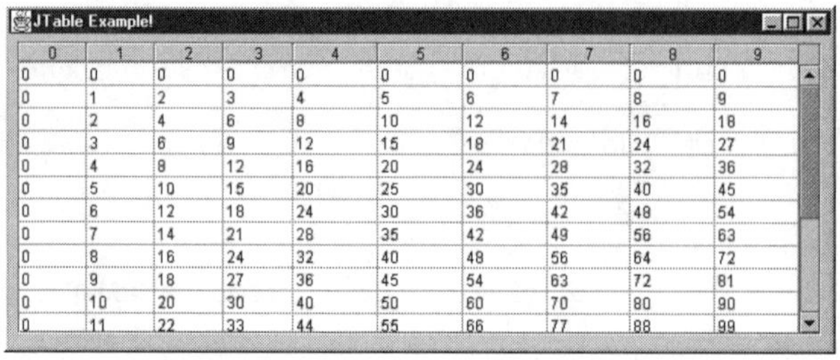

```
14:             MyTableModel myTableModel = new MyTableModel();
```

Let's get started. Line 14 creates an instance of `MyTableModel`, which is our custom `TableModel` that will be discussed later.

```
17:             JTable numberTable = new JTable( myTableModel );
```

Line 17 creates a new `JTable` named `numberTable` that is built from the `MyTableModel` that we built in line 14.

```
20:             numberTable.setPreferredScrollableViewportSize(
21:                             new Dimension(600, 200) );
```

Lines 20 and 21 set the size of the table. The method `setPreferredScrollableViewportSize` is prototyped as follows:

```
public void setPreferredScrollableViewportSize(java.awt.Dimension size)
```

It specifies the preferred size of the viewport for this table. A viewport defines the dimensions of the region of your data that will be visible on the screen at any one time. Figure 5.14 shows the relationship between your data, the viewport, and the screen. Note that the screen does not necessarily have to be completely filled by the viewport. What lines 20 and 21 are saying is that the number table wants a 600×200 viewport of its data represented on the screen at any given time.

```
24:             TableColumn column = null;
```

Line 24 creates a new `TableColumn` object. Remember that a `TableColumn` represents all the attributes of a column in a JTable, such as width, resizeability, and maximum and minimum widths. In the next few lines of code, we are going to be setting the column widths for each column, and this variable will hold simply hold each column that we want to modify.

```
26:             for (int i = 0; i < 4; i++)
27:             {
28:             column = numberTable.getColumnModel().getColumn( i );
29:     column.setPreferredWidth( myTableModel.getColumnWidth( i ) );
30:             }
```

Figure 5.14

Viewport relationships.

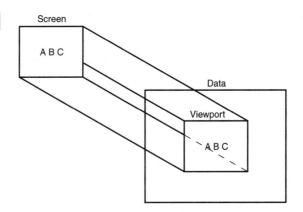

Lines 26–30 are composed of a `for` loop, discussed earlier, that loops through each column in the number table. Remember that rows and columns are ordered and accessed by integer values; that is why we can use a `for` loop control variable as our index.

Each column is stored in a `TableColumnModel`, so to gain access to a `TableColumn`, we need to get the table's `TableColumnModel`. Line 28 gets a column in one step: It asks the number table for its `TableColumnModel` using the `JTable` method `getColumnModel` and then turns around and asks the `TableColumnModel` for its column using `getColumm`. This statement is sometimes referred to as a compound statement: It is composed of two or more simple statements. We could have easily broken this request down to the following simple statements:

```
// Create a TableColumnModel
TableColumnModel columnModel;

// Get the TableColumn Model from the table
columnModel = numberTable.getColumnModel();

// Get the column from the TableColumnModel
column = columnModel.getColumn( i );
```

However, because `getColumnModel` returns a `TableColumnModel`, we chose not to create an instance of it when we needed to call only one of its methods.

Now that we have the `TableColumn` for this column index (remember we are going from 0 to 3), line 29 sets the width of the column by calling the `TableColumn` method `setPreferredWidth`. We added a method to the `MyTableModel` class named `getColumnWidth` that would return the width of each column. This data is, by default, not stored in the model, but because the model knows so much about the data in the table, I felt it was the most educated source to ask for column widths; it could easily ask each data element in that column for its width and return the greatest value for example.

```
33:          JScrollPane scrollPane = new JScrollPane( numberTable );
```

Line 33 creates a new JScrollPane object to hold the number table. As in our discussion on the JTextArea class, the JTable class does not support scrolling directly, so we have to put it in a JScrollPane in order to allow the table to scroll. You will find this true with most Swing components.

```
36:          add( scrollPane, BorderLayout.CENTER );
```

Finally line 36 adds the scroll pane to the JPanel.

```
73:     class MyTableModel extends AbstractTableModel
```

Line 73 creates our table model class; it extends the AbstractTableModel class. Now the AbstractTableModel class is important because it implements the TableModel interface, so I am going to spend a little time on it. First, let's look at the TableModel itself. Take a look at Table 5.20 for the TableModel interface methods.

Table 5.20   TableModel **Methods**

Method	Description
void addTableModelListener (javax.swing.event. TableModelListener l)	Add a listener to the list that's notified each time a change to the data model occurs
Class getColumnClass (int columnIndex)	Returns the lowest common denominator Class in the column
int getColumnCount()	Returns the number of columns managed by the data source object
String getColumnName (int columnIndex)	Returns the name of the column at columnIndex
int getRowCount()	Returns the number of records managed by the data source object
Object getValueAt(int rowIndex, int columnIndex)	Returns an attribute value for the cell at columnIndex and rowIndex
boolean isCellEditable (int rowIndex, int columnIndex)	Returns true if the cell at rowIndex and columnIndex is editable
void removeTableModelListener (javax.swing.event. TableModelListener l)	Remove a listener from the list that's notified each time a change to the data model occurs
void setValueAt(Object aValue, int rowIndex, int columnIndex)	Sets an attribute value for the record in the cell at columnIndex and rowIndex

Now the `AbstractTableModel` model provides default implementations for these methods, so by deriving our table model from the `AbstractTableModel` class, we just need to override the methods specific to our class. We are going to be interested in four of the aforementioned methods: `getColumnCount`, `getRowCount`, `getValueAt`, and `getColumnName` because we are the ones that know about the data in our table. Granted, our table is a bit contrived and doesn't represent any real data, but if we stored our table data in our model, the `getValueAt` method would be very important. Furthermore, we would check our data to compute the number of rows and columns. Let's take a look at our implementations of these methods.

```
76:         public int getColumnCount()
77:         {
78:             return 10;
79:         }
```

Lines 76–79 define our implementation of the `getColumnCount` method. The `JTable` class calls this method to ask how many columns there are in the table.

```
82:         public int getRowCount()
83:         {
84:             return 20;
85:         }
```

Lines 82–85 define our implementation of the `getRowCount` method. The `JTable` class calls this method to ask how many rows there are in the table.

```
88:         public Object getValueAt(int row, int col)
89:         {
90:             return new Integer(row*col);
91:         }
```

Lines 88–91 define our implementation of the `getValueAt` method. The `JTable` class calls this method for every cell in the table when the application starts and whenever there is a change made to the table. In our example, we are simply creating a new `Integer` variable containing the product of the row and column numbers. In a real-world application you would retrieve the actual data from whatever data structure you are using and return that.

```
94:         public String getColumnName( int col )
95:             {
96:             return new String( Integer.toString( col ) );
97:         }
```

Lines 94–97 define our implementation of the `getColumnName` method. In our implementation, we are simply converting the column number to a `String` using the `Integer` class's `toString` method. This method accepts an integer type (`int`) and returns the number in `String` form.

```
100:        public int getColumnWidth( int nCol )
101:        {
102:            return 60;
103:        }
```

Finally, lines 100–103 represent the method that we added to the model to compute the width of each column. In this example, we are simply returning 60, an arbitrary value that looks good on the screen.

Anyway, our table has 10 columns, named "0" through "9", and 20 rows. Each cell has the product of the row number and column number in it. We will have real live data in Chapter 7, so you are just going to have to be patient. I did not want to introduce the data structures in Java that we use to store data yet, so this was the easiest way to make a table with meaningful cells that we didn't have to store ourselves.

Panes

A pane is a component that can hold one or more other components. You have already seen the JScrollPane used several times, in the JTextArea, JList, and JTable examples. There are a few more of interest that I will mention here and let you look them up as you need them:

- Tabbed panes
- Scroll panes
- Split panes

Tabbed Panes

A *tabbed pane* is a component that allows a user to switch between groups of components by clicking on a tab with a given title and/or icon. The JTabbedPane class represents tab panes in Swing. JTabbedPanes are very easy to both construct and use. Table 5.21 shows the constructors for the JTabbedPane class.

Table 5.21   **JTabbedPane Constructors**

Constructor	Description
JTabbedPane()	Creates an empty TabbedPane
JTabbedPane(int tabPlacement)	Creates an empty TabbedPane with the specified tab placement of: TOP, BOTTOM, LEFT, or RIGHT

Adding tabs to a tabbed pane is done through the JTabbedPane class's addTab and insertTab methods. These methods accept a String title, a Component object, an optional icon, and optional tool tip text.

This class is easiest to explain with an example, so take a look at Listing 5.7.

Type the code from Listing 5.7, excluding line numbers, into your favorite text editor and save it as JTabbedPaneExample.java, or copy it from the CD. Build it as follows:

```
javac JTabbedPaneExample.java
java JTabbedPaneExample
```

The code specific to the JTabbedPane class is boldface for your convenience and is explained following the source code.

Listing 5.7   **JTabbedPaneExample.java**

```
1:    // Import the libraries this application will use
2:    import javax.swing.*;
3:    import javax.swing.table.*;
4:
5:    import java.awt.*;
6:    import java.awt.event.*;
7:
8:    // Main application class:  JTabbedPaneExample
9:    public class JTabbedPaneExample extends JPanel
10:   {
11:       // Create a new tabbed pane
12:       JTabbedPane tabbedPane = new JTabbedPane( JTabbedPane.TOP );
13:
14:       // Create an icon for the tabs
15:       ImageIcon icon = new ImageIcon( "iconSmileySmall.gif" );
16:
17:       // Create a couple panels for our tabs
18:       JPanel panelOne = new JPanel( new BorderLayout() );
19:       JPanel panelTwo = new JPanel( new BorderLayout () );
20:
21:       // Create a couple labels to put in our panels
22:       JLabel labelOne = new JLabel( "Tab One" );
23:       JLabel labelTwo = new JLabel( "Tab Two" );
24:
25:       // Constructor
26:       public JTabbedPaneExample()
27:       {
28:          // Tell our labels to center themselves
29:          labelOne.setHorizontalAlignment( JLabel.CENTER );
30:          labelTwo.setHorizontalAlignment( JLabel.CENTER );
31:
32:          // Add our labels to ourpanels
33:          panelOne.add( labelOne );
34:          panelTwo.add( labelTwo );
35:
36:          // Add our panels to our tabbed pane
```

continues

Listing 5.7   continued

```
37:                 tabbedPane.addTab( "Tab One", icon, panelOne,
                                 "This is tab one..."  );
38:         tabbedPane.addTab( "Tab Two", icon, panelTwo,
                             "This is tab two..." );
39:
40:         // Select the first tab
41:         tabbedPane.setSelectedIndex( 0 );
42:
43:         // Set the layout manager of the JPanel so that the
44:         // tab component will fill the entire panel
45:         setLayout( new GridLayout( 1, 1 ) );
46:
47:         // Add our tabbed pane to our JPanel
48:         add( tabbedPane );
49:
50:     }
51:
52:     // Main application entry point into this class
53:     public static void main( String[] args )
54:     {
55:         // Create a JFrame object
56:         JFrame frame = new JFrame( "JTabbedPane Example!" );
57:
58:         // Create a JTabbedPaneExample Object
59:         JTabbedPaneExample example = new JTabbedPaneExample();
60:
61:         // Add our JTabbedPaneExample Object to the JFrame
62:         frame.getContentPane().add( example,  BorderLayout.CENTER );
63:
64:         // Resize our JFrame
65:         frame.setSize( 600, 400 );
66:
67:         // Make our JFrame visible
68:         frame.setVisible( true );
69:
70:         // Create a window listener to close our application when we
71:         // close our application
72:         frame.addWindowListener
73:         (
74:             new WindowAdapter()
75:             {
76:                 public void windowClosing( WindowEvent e )
77:                 {
78:                     System.exit( 0 );
79:                 }
80:             }
81:         );
82:     }
83: }
```

Figure 5.15 shows the JTabbedPaneExample application.

Figure 5.15

JTabbedPaneExample application example.

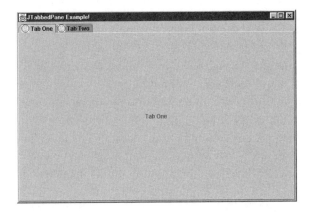

```
12:     JTabbedPane tabbedPane = new JTabbedPane( JTabbedPane.TOP );
```

Line 12 creates a new JTabbedPane object and tells it to put the tabs on the top of the display: Remember you can set them on the TOP, BOTTOM, LEFT, or RIGHT. Try it and see how it looks!

```
15:     ImageIcon icon = new ImageIcon( "iconSmileySmall.gif" );
```

Line 15 creates a new ImageIcon to display next to each tab. It is not necessary, but it looks nice!

```
18:     JPanel panelOne = new JPanel( new BorderLayout() );
19:     JPanel panelTwo = new JPanel( new BorderLayout () );
22:     JLabel labelOne = new JLabel( "Tab One" );
23:     JLabel labelTwo = new JLabel( "Tab Two" );
```

Lines 18 and 19 create two panels and lines 22 and 23 create two labels that will be placed in these panels.

```
29:         labelOne.setHorizontalAlignment( JLabel.CENTER );
30:         labelTwo.setHorizontalAlignment( JLabel.CENTER );
```

Lines 29 and 30 tell the labels to center themselves horizontally.

```
33:         panelOne.add( labelOne );
34:         panelTwo.add( labelTwo );
```

Lines 33 and 34 add our labels to our panels.

```
37:             tabbedPane.addTab( "Tab One", icon, panelOne,
                                   "This is tab one..."  );
38:         tabbedPane.addTab( "Tab Two", icon, panelTwo,
                                   "This is tab two..." );
```

Lines 37 and 38 add our panels to the tabbed pane by creating new tabs using addTab. We give each tab a name, an icon, the panel it is supposed to display in the tab, and a tool tip.

```
41:          tabbedPane.setSelectedIndex( 0 );
```

Line 41 selects the first tab to be initially visible when the application starts. Remember that tabs are indexed starting at zero, so for our example you could send either 0 or 1; 0 means show the first tab and 1 means show the second tab.

```
45:          setLayout( new GridLayout( 1, 1 ) );
```

Line 45 sets the layout of the JPanel to be a grid layout and to contain only one cell. This step is important because if you do not change the layout manager to GridLayout, the default is BorderLayout, and adding a tab control to the center of a BorderLayout has some undesirable effects; namely it is so small you can't see much! Just a word of advice.

```
48:          add( tabbedPane );
```

Finally, line 48 adds the tabbed pane to the JPanel.

See, tabbed panes are a piece of cake now that you are familiar with the Swing way of doing things!

Scroll Panes

Scroll panes are a special type of container that manage a viewport into a component, optional vertical and horizontal scrollbars, and optional row and column headings. The JScrollPane class represents scroll panes in Swing.

You have already used JScrollPane in several examples in this chapter already, so I am not going to give you another example. Take a look back at Listings 5.3, 5.5, and 5.6 to see how we used them with the JTextArea, JList, and JTable classes.

Split Panes

Split panes are used to divide two, and only two components; they can be made to split either vertically or horizontally. The JSplitPane class represents split panes in Swing. Table 5.22 shows how to construct a JSplitPane.

Table 5.22 JSplitPane **Constructors**

Constructor	Description
JSplitPane()	Returns a new JSplitPane configured to arrange the child components side by side horizontally with no continuous layout, using two buttons for the components

Constructor	Description
`JSplitPane(int newOrientation)`	Returns a new `JSplitPane` configured with the specified orientation and no continuous layout
`JSplitPane(int newOrientation, boolean newContinuousLayout)`	Returns a new `JSplitPane` with the specified orientation and redrawing style
`JSplitPane(int newOrientation, boolean newContinuousLayout, java.awt.Component newLeftComponent, java.awt.Component newRightComponent)`	Returns a new `JSplitPane` with the specified orientation and redrawing style, and with the specified components
`JSplitPane(int newOrientation, java.awt.Component newLeftComponent, java.awt.Component newRightComponent)`	Returns a new `JSplitPane` with the specified orientation and with the specified components that does not do continuous redrawing

Although some of these constructors may seem intimidating, let me assure you that using a split pane is simple. The most common constructor used is the last one listed. It accepts the orientation of the split (horizontal or vertical) and the two components to split. Let's take a look at an example. Refer to Listing 5.8.

Type the code from Listing 5.8, excluding line numbers, into your favorite text editor and save it as `JSplitPaneExample.java`, or copy it from the CD. Build it as follows:

```
javac JSplitPaneExample.java
java JSplitPaneExample
```

The code specific to the `JSplitPane` class is boldface for your convenience and is explained following the source code.

Listing 5.8   `JSplitPaneExample.java`

```
1:  // Import the libraries this application will use
2:  import javax.swing.*;
3:  import javax.swing.table.*;
4:
5:  import java.awt.*;
6:  import java.awt.event.*;
7:
8:  // Main application class:  JSplitPaneExample
9:  public class JSplitPaneExample extends JPanel
10: {
11:     // Create a couple panels for our panes
12:     JPanel panelOne = new JPanel( new BorderLayout() );
13:     JPanel panelTwo = new JPanel( new BorderLayout() );
14:
15:     // Create a couple labels to put in our panels
```

continues

Listing 5.8   continued

```
16:     JLabel labelOne = new JLabel( "Pane One" );
17:     JLabel labelTwo = new JLabel( "Pane Two" );
18:
19:     // Create a new split pane
20:     JSplitPane splitPane = new JSplitPane(
21:                         JSplitPane.HORIZONTAL_SPLIT,
22:                         panelOne,
23:                         panelTwo );
24:
25:     // Constructor
26:     public JSplitPaneExample()
27:     {
28:         // Tell our labels to center themselves
29:         labelOne.setHorizontalAlignment( JLabel.CENTER );
30:         labelTwo.setHorizontalAlignment( JLabel.CENTER );
31:
32:         // Add our labels to our panels
33:         panelOne.add( labelOne );
34:         panelTwo.add( labelTwo );
35:
36:         // Set the layout manager of the JPanel so that the
37:         // tab component will fill the entire panel
38:         setLayout( new GridLayout( 1, 1 ) );
39:
40:         // Position the split pane divider
41:         splitPane.setDividerLocation( 200 );
42:
43:         // Add our tabbed pane to our JPanel
44:         add( splitPane );
45:
46:     }
47:
48:     // Main application entry point into this class
49:     public static void main( String[] args )
50:     {
51:         // Create a JFrame object
52:         JFrame frame = new JFrame( "JSplitPane Example!" );
53:
54:         // Create a JSplitPaneExample Object
55:         JSplitPaneExample example = new JSplitPaneExample();
56:
57:         // Add our JSplitPaneExample Object to the JFrame
58:         frame.getContentPane().add( example,  BorderLayout.CENTER );
59:
60:         // Resize our JFrame
61:         frame.setSize( 600, 400 );
62:
63:         // Make our JFrame visible
64:         frame.setVisible( true );
65:
```

```
66:        // Create a window listener to close our application when we
67:        // close our application
68:        frame.addWindowListener
69:        (
70:            new WindowAdapter()
71:            {
72:                public void windowClosing( WindowEvent e )
73:                {
74:                    System.exit( 0 );
75:                }
76:            }
77:        );
78:    }
79: }
```

Figure 5.16 shows the JSplitPaneExample application.

Figure 5.16

JSplitPaneExample application example.

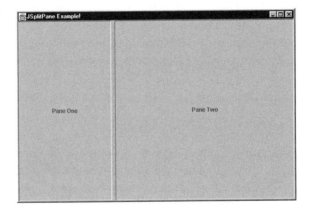

This example is so close to the JTabbedPaneExample example that I am only going to talk about the handful of lines that are directly related to the JSplitPane class.

```
20:    JSplitPane splitPane = new JSplitPane(
21:                        JSplitPane.HORIZONTAL_SPLIT,
22:                        panelOne,
23:                        panelTwo );
```

Lines 20–23 create a new JSplitPane object. The pane is split horizontally, which may or may not make sense to you when you look at Figure 5.16. Table 5.23 shows the two values you can pass in as the first argument to this constructor.

Table 5.23   JSplitPane Split Orientations

Orientation	Description
HORIZONTAL_SPLIT	Horizontal split indicates the components are split along the x axis, that is, the two components will be split one to the left of the other.
VERTICAL_SPLIT	Vertical split indicates the components are split along the y axis, that is, the two components will be split one on top of the other.

The next two parameters are the two panels that we created in lines 12 and 13.

```
41:        splitPane.setDividerLocation( 200 );
```

Line 41 sets the location of the split pane divider to 200 by using the JSplitPane class's setDividerLocation method, which has two prototypes:

```
public void setDividerLocation(double proportionalLocation)
public void setDividerLocation(int location)
```

proportionalLocation is a double-precision floating-point number between 0 and 1.0 specifying a percentage, and location is a relative value to the look-and-feel component.

```
44:        add( splitPane );
```

Finally, line 44adds the split pane to the JPanel.

Summary

In this chapter, we talked about the history and roots of the Java Foundation Classes and Swing, the structure of a JFC application, and how to implement a JFC application. We then turned our attention toward some of the more common Swing components, starting with an introduction to the parent of all Swing components, the JComponent class. You learned how to use the following component classes:

- JLabel
- JTextField
- JTextArea
- JButton
- JRadioButton
- JCheckBox
- JList
- JTable

Next, we took a brief look at a couple of the lightweight containers newly available to JFC applications:

- JTabbedPane
- JScrollPane
- JSplitPane

As you might guess, the JFC classes are very involved and could easily take up an entire book of their own! We touched on a handful of useful ones in this chapter, but there are many more that you will find interesting, so I urge you to dig through the Java 2 SDK documentation: Take a look at JComboBox, JProgressBar, JScrollBar, JSplider, and JTree, just to name a few. We will talk more about JMenu when we get to Chapter 7, so I promise you that you will get a good look at that too!

What's Next?

Now that you know how to construct a good number of the Swing components, you need to start using them effectively. The next chapter discusses responding to user events. Go take a break and meet me back here when you are ready for some more fun stuff!

Chapter 6

Handling Events in Your User Interface

To start with, you are doing well if you survived the last few chapters. They were some pretty deep reading, but I hope you found them enlightening. By now you know how to construct both AWT and Swing user interfaces, and you understand layout managers, various panes, and many of the more popular Java components. More importantly, you now understand how the Java Foundation Classes work and should be very comfortable with the separable model design in which you separate your user interfaces from your data.

Now that you have this beautiful user interface with all these new components, what is the next logical step? By now you have probably started wondering how to react to user interactions—when a user clicks a button, how do you know about that button click? The answer to that question consists of one small word: events.

That is the subject of this chapter: events. We will start with a brief introduction to general event concepts and then cover the types of events that can occur in your application. Next we will talk about how events are supported in the Java Foundation Classes from a theoretical perspective, and finally we will dive into the following event types supported by Java:

- Action events
- Adjustment events
- Focus events
- Item events
- Keyboard events

- Mouse events
- Mouse movement events
- Window events

I will not cover all event types in this chapter, but these are the major generic event types; I will cover more specific event types as they are needed in the following chapters.

What Are Events?

The dictionary defines the term *event* as an occurrence, incident, or significant experience. And, in practical terms, that is what an event in Java is: the occurrence of a user interaction in the user interface. In technical terms, events are notifications made by the Java Runtime Engine, sent to the user interface whenever any element of the user interface is manipulated.

These events can go unnoticed by the user interface, as they have in the last two chapters, or they can be handled by the user interface; the action of handling events is called *event handling*. In your applications, there will be certain events that you will want to handle; for example, if you have a button on the screen, you will want to respond when it is clicked. There are also certain events that you will want to let the Java framework handle; for example, you will ignore most mouse movement events because if you captured them all, you would receive more than you could possibly handle.

Types of Events

What exactly constitutes an event in Java? Luckily for us, Java categorizes its event types. Table 6.1 shows some of these categories of events.

Table 6.1   Event Types

Feature	Description
Action events	Action events indicate that a component defined action occurred, such as a user clicking a button.
Adjustment events	Adjustment events indicate that a component has been adjusted in some way, such as a user moving a scrollbar.
Focus events	Focus events are low-level events that occur when a component gains or loses the keyboard input focus.
Item events	Item events indicate that an item was selected or deselected.
Keyboard events	Keyboard events indicate that a keystroke occurred in some component.

Feature	Description
Mouse events	Mouse events indicate that a mouse action occurred in some component.
Mouse motion events	Mouse motion events indicate that the mouse moved over some component.
Window events	Window events are low-level events that indicate that a window has changed its status.

Table 6.1 describes most of the major event types you will encounter in your standard components. Some of the components will have events specific to them, but this list will give you a good start.

Event Methodology

So how do events and event handlers function in the JFC and Swing? The model for events and event handling in Java is pretty clever and fits nicely with the structure of the rest of the language.

There are three primary components to JFC events:

- A component that generates the event
- An event listener that handles the event
- The event itself

Let's start first with the event listener. An *event listener* is an interface that specifies methods that will be called when an event occurs. Recall our earlier sample programs that closed our application when the window closed. How did we do that?

Here is the code we used to handle a window-closing event:

```
frame.addWindowListener
(
    new WindowAdapter()
    {
        public void windowClosing( WindowEvent e )
        {
            System.exit( 0 );
        }
    }
);
```

This code creates a new class derived from the WindowAdapter class and overrides its windowClosing method, telling it to exit the application when the window closes. It asks the JFrame object to add this WindowAdapter class as the window listener for the frame.

This is a very simple way to implement this event handling, but it cuts a lot of corners and hides a great deal of detail. Let's take this example and break it down to its components.

We were talking about event listeners. In this case, the WindowAdapter class is an abstract class that implements an interface called WindowListener and provides default implementations for its methods; the default implementation is simply a set of empty methods for each method defined in the WindowListener interface. You will typically use the WindowAdapter class when you want to override some of the methods in the WindowListener interface, but not all.

 An *abstract class* is a class that cannot be declared but you can derive a class from it.

We can rewrite our WindowAdapter derived class separately and add it as a WindowListener without taking the shortcut previously shown by doing the following:

```
class MyWindowAdapter extends WindowAdapter
{
    public void windowClosing( WindowEvent e )
    {
        System.exit( 0 );
    }
}
...
MyWindowAdapter myWindowAdapter = new MyWindowAdapter();
frame.addWindowListener( myWindowAdapter );
```

This implementation is much easier to understand and takes the confusion out of the shortcuts you will probably see in most of the source code you encounter in the future.

There we go, we found the event listener. We will talk more about the WindowListener interface a little later, but for now, just know that any class that implements this interface can receive window events.

The next component of a JFC event that I want to talk about is the component that generates the event. In this case it is the JFrame class that generates the event. We tell the JFrame class that we want our class that implements WindowListener to be notified of window events by calling the JFrame class's addWindowListener method. The JFrame class inherits the addWindowListener method from the java.awt.Window class, and it is prototyped as follows:

```
public void addWindowListener(WindowListener l)
```

It accepts any class that implements the WindowListener interface. After calling addWindowListener(), whenever one of the event methods specified by the WindowListener interface occurs, our WindowListener class will be notified.

That brings us to the last component of JFC events: the event itself. When the event occurs, a method in your class that implements the event listener is called, with the event as a parameter sent to it. In the previous example, the `windowClosing` method of your `WindowListener` class is called and the `WindowEvent` is passed to it. The `WindowEvent` tells you what window is closing, so if you have one class that is handling the window events for multiple windows, you will be able to tell who generated this one.

To recap, here are the steps involved in handling JFC events :

1. Identify the interface that represents the events you want to handle.
2. Define a class that implements that interface, or find an abstract class that provides the default implementations for the interface.
3. Add a method (event handler) to that class for the events you are interested in handling.
4. Identify the components that generate the event you want to handle and call the add*EventListener* (where *EventListener* can be `WindowListener`, `ActionListener`, and so on) method specific for that event listener, passing your handler class to it.

And that is it! Simple, huh? Okay, maybe not simple, but you will get the hang of it in no time. Now let's take a look at the different types of event listeners provided by the JFC.

JFC Event Listeners

The number of different event listeners provided by the Java Foundation Classes is overwhelming, but luckily there is a set of standard event listeners that are applicable to most components. Table 6.2 shows a list of these event listeners.

Table 6.2 Standard Event Listeners

Event Listener	Handles
`ActionListener`	Action events
`AdjustmentListener`	Adjustment events
`FocusListener`	Focus events
`ItemListener`	Item events
`KeyListener`	Keyboard events
`MouseListener`	Mouse events
`MouseMotionListener`	Mouse motion events
`WindowListener`	Window events

Most of them have their own abstract classes from which you can derive to get default implementations of the respective event listener interfaces. Take a look at Table 6.3 for a list of these classes.

Table 6.3   Event Listener Abstract Classes

Event Listener	Abstract Class
ActionListener	AbstractAction
AdjustmentListener	none
FocusListener	FocusAdapter
ItemListener	none
KeyListener	KeyAdapter
MouseListener	MouseAdapter
MouseMotionListener	MouseMotionAdapter
WindowListener	WindowAdapter

All event listeners are derived from a tagging interface called EventListener that they must extend in order to be considered event listeners. The EventListener class has no methods or attributes; it is simply used to identify event listeners. Take a look at the Java 2 SDK documentation under EventListener to see the staggering number of event listeners.

The term *tagging interface* refers to an interface that has no methods or attributes and whose sole purpose is to identify objects of that type. By deriving all event listeners from the EventListener interface, we can refer to any event listener at all by simply specifying EventListener. Say, for example, that we had a component that could fire events to 20 different event listeners; it can provide one single add*EventListener* method that accepted an EventListener instead of providing 20 different add*EventListener* methods.

JFC Events

Each of the aforementioned event listeners receives an event object in each of its methods. The number of events is almost as overwhelming as the number of event listeners. Most of the events we are going to be interested in derive from the AWTEvent class. Take a look at Figure 6.1 to see what the event hierarchy looks like.

As you can see from Figure 6.1, the AWTEvent class derives from the EventObject, which derives from the Object class. The types of events generated by the JFC used with the aforementioned event listeners are described in Table 6.4.

Figure 6.1

AWT event hierarchy.

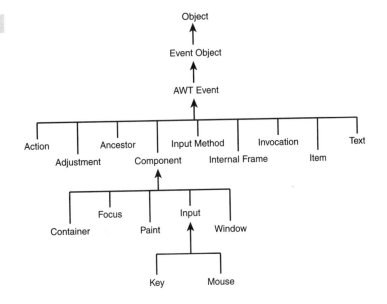

Table 6.4   AWT Derived Events

Event	Listeners
ActionEvent	ActionListener
AdjustmentEvent	AdjustmentListener
FocusEvent	FocusListener
KeyEvent	KeyListener
MouseEvent	MouseListener, MouseMotionListener
WindowEvent	WindowListener
ItemEvent	ItemListener

You can see we are only working with a subset of events, but these will suffice for now. If you are really brave and want to see the top of the tree, take a look at the Java 2 SDK documentation under EventObject and look at the number of different event classes that derive from it—the AWTEvent is only one of them.

The EventObject class has a set of methods that the derived classes can make use of, as shown in Table 6.5.

Table 6.5 **EventObject** **Methods**

Method	Description
Object getSource()	The object on which the event initially occurred
String toString()	Returns a String representation of this EventObject

Furthermore, the AWTEvent class has another set of methods that will help you use the other derived event classes, as shown in Table 6.6.

Table 6.6 **AWTEvent** **Methods**

Method	Description
int getID()	Returns the event type.
String paramString()	Returns a string representing the state of this event.
String toString()	Returns a string representation of this event. Overrides EventObject's toString.

For the rest of the chapter, we will talk in depth about the different events, event listeners, and component methods to add listeners to components.

Action Events

Action events indicate that a component-specific event has occurred, such as the click of a button.

The ActionListener interface listens for action events and is defined in Table 6.7.

Table 6.7 **ActionListener** **Interface**

Return	Method	Description
void	actionPerformed(ActionEvent e)	Invoked when an action occurs

To handle action events, you must create a class that implements ActionListener, and then define the actionPerformed method in that class. The event sent to the actionPerformed method is the ActionEvent event, described in Table 6.8.

Table 6.8 **ActionEvent** **Class**

Return	Method	Description
String	getActionCommand()	Returns the command string associated with this action
int	getModifiers()	Returns the modifier keys held down during this action event
String	paramString()	Returns a parameter string identifying this action event

Combined with the methods provided by the `EventObject` and `AWTEvent` classes, you can obtain the object that caused the event, the event type, the action command, and the state of the modifier keys.

To add an action event listener to a component, you can call the `addActionListener` method of the following Swing components:

- `JButton`
- `JCheckBox`
- `JComboBox`
- `JTextField`
- `JRadioButton`

The `addActionListener` method is defined as follows:

```
public void addActionListener(ActionListener l)
```

Look at an example of the `ActionListener` interface in action, no pun intended, by implementing a message box class. The message box class is a `JFrame` derived class that has two buttons, OK and Cancel, and displays a message string in a `JLabel` in the center of the frame. We will come back to this later in our programs, but for now when you click one of the buttons, the body of the message changes to show you the button you clicked.

Type the code from Listing 6.1, excluding line numbers, into your favorite text editor and save it as `MessageBox.java`, or copy it from the CD. Build it as follows:

```
javac MessageBox.java
java MessageBox
```

The code specific to the `ActionEvent` and `ActionListener` classes is boldface for your convenience and will be explained following the source code.

Listing 6.1 `MessageBox.java`

```
1:  // Import the packages used by this class
2:  import javax.swing.*;
3:  import javax.swing.event.*;
4:
5:  import java.awt.*;
6:  import java.awt.event.*;
7:
8:  // MessageBox Class
9:  public class MessageBox extends JFrame implements ActionListener
10: {
11:     // Message Body
12:     JLabel lblMessage = new JLabel();
```

continues

Listing 6.1   continued

```
13:
14:        // Button panel and buttons
15:        JPanel panelButton = new JPanel( new GridLayout( 1, 2 ) );
16:        JButton btnOK = new JButton( "OK" );
17:        JButton btnCancel = new JButton( "Cancel" );
18:
19:        // Constructor
20:        public MessageBox( String strTitle,  String strMessage )
21:        {
22:            // Set the title of our window
23:            super( strTitle );
24:
25:            // Set the layout manager
26:            getContentPane().setLayout( new BorderLayout() );
27:
28:            // Resize ourself
29:            setSize( new Dimension( 400, 200 ) );
30:
31:
32:            // Set the message
33:            lblMessage.setText( strMessage );
34:
35:            // Center the label on the frame
36:            lblMessage.setHorizontalAlignment( JLabel.CENTER );
37:
38:            // Add the label to the frame
39:            getContentPane().add( lblMessage );
40:
41:
42:            // Build our button panel
43:            panelButton.add( btnOK );
44:            panelButton.add( btnCancel );
45:
46:            // Add our button panel
47:            getContentPane().add( panelButton, BorderLayout.SOUTH );
48:
49:            // Add ourself as an action listener
50:            btnOK.addActionListener( this );
51:            btnCancel.addActionListener( this );
52:
53:
54:            // Listen for window closing
55:            addWindowListener
56:            (
57:                new WindowAdapter()
58:                {
59:                    public void windowClosing( WindowEvent e )
60:                    {
61:                        System.exit( 0 );
62:                    }
63:                }
```

```
64:            );
65:
66:            // Make ourself visible
67:            setVisible( true );
68:        }
69:
70:        // Action Event Handler:  actionPerformed
71:        public void actionPerformed(ActionEvent e)
72:        {
73:            if( e.getSource() == btnOK )
74:            {
75:                    lblMessage.setText( e.getActionCommand() );
76:            }
77:            else if( e.getSource() == btnCancel )
78:            {
79:                    lblMessage.setText( e.getActionCommand() );
80:            }
81:        }
82:
83:        // Main entry point into the application
84:        public static void main( String[] args )
85:        {
86:            MessageBox msgBox =  new MessageBox( "Message Box Text",
87:                                                 "Hello,  world!" );
88:        }
89: }
```

6

Figure 6.2 shows the MessageBox application after you click the OK button.

Figure 6.2

MessageBox example.

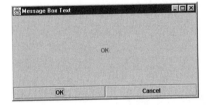

Starting with this example, I am going to scale down the explanations of the source code to only those topics relevant to the concept we are discussing. I do this for two reasons:

1. From the last few chapters, you should already know everything else in the examples. Don't worry, I will mention new topics!

2. I don't want to bore you and force you to read the same thing over and over!

With that said, let's look at the sample.

```
9:  public class MessageBox extends JFrame implements ActionListener
```

Line 9 declares the MessageBox class as extending JFrame and implementing ActionListener. By implementing ActionListener, we can add our MessageBox class as an action listener for components that generate action events, and we are committing to implement the actionPerformed method.

```
50:         btnOK.addActionListener( this );
51:         btnCancel.addActionListener( this );
```

Lines 50 and 51 add our MessageBox class as an action listener for btnOK and btnCancel, respectively. The this variable is a variable maintained within a class and refers to that class. For example, when we make our class visible, we write:

```
setVisible( true );
```

And we could write this using the this variable as follows:

```
this.setVisible( true );
```

The this variable is implied in the former method called and explicitly referenced in the latter method call. When you are telling somebody about your class, you refer to your class using the this variable.

```
71:     public void actionPerformed(ActionEvent e)
```

Line 71 is our declaration of the ActionListener actionPerformed method.

```
72:     {
73:         if( e.getSource() == btnOK )
74:         {
75:                 lblMessage.setText( e.getActionCommand() );
76:         }
77:         else if( e.getSource() == btnCancel )
78:         {
79:                 lblMessage.setText( e.getActionCommand() );
80:         }
81:     }
```

Line 73 calls the ActionEvent method getSource to get the object that generated the event and then compares it to the btnOK object. If the two match, the btnOK button generated the event. Line 75 retrieves the command string associated with this action by calling getActionCommand and sets it as the text of the lblMessage; in this case it is going to set the text to OK.

Line 77 retrieves the object that generated the event in the same manner and compares it to btnCancel. Line 79 retrieves the command string associated with this action, again by calling getActionCommand and sets it as the text of the lblMessage; in this case it is going to set the text to "Cancel".

It's that easy! To find out who generated the event, just call the event method getSource and compare it to your objects. Then you can call any of the ActionEvent methods previously mentioned, as we did with getActionCommand.

Adjustment Events

Adjustment events indicate that a component has been adjusted in some way, such as a user moving a scrollbar. The AdjustmentListener interface listens for adjustment events and is defined in Table 6.9.

Table 6.9 AdjustmentListener **Interface**

Return	Method	Description
void	adjustmentValueChanged(AdjustmentEvent e)	Invoked when the value of the adjustable component has changed

To handle adjustment events, you must create a class that implements AdjustmentListener, and then define the adjustmentValueChanged method in that class. The event sent to the adjustmentValueChanged method is an instance of the AdjustmentEvent event, described in Table 6.10.

6

Table 6.10 AdjustmentEvent **Class**

Return	Method	Description
Adjustable	getAdjustable()	Returns the Adjustable object (an object that implements the Adjustable interface) where this event originated
int	getAdjustmentType()	Returns the type of adjustment which caused the value changed event
int	getValue()	Returns the current value in the adjustment event
String	paramString()	Returns a parameter string identifying this event

This event gives you the additional methods that enable you to get the adjustable object that generated the event and obtain the current value of the object. The getAdjustableType method needs a little clarification: It claims it can return the values shown in Table 6.11.

Table 6.11   Adjustment Types

Type	Description
BLOCK_DECREMENT	The block decrement adjustment type
BLOCK_INCREMENT	The block increment adjustment type
TRACK	The absolute tracking adjustment type
UNIT_DECREMENT	The unit decrement adjustment type
UNIT_INCREMENT	The unit increment adjustment type

Note

The only caveat I have found with the `getAdjustableType` method in the Java 2 SDK version 1.2.1 is that it always returns TRACK. The source code provided by Sun has this comment in the `JScrollBar.java` file:

"Unfortunately there's no way to determine the proper type of the `AdjustmentEvent` as all updates to the model's value are considered equivalent."

Therefore, it hard codes `AdjustmentEvent.TRACK` as the adjustment type.

To add an adjustment event listener to a component, you can call the `addAdjustmentListener` method. The only Swing component that supports this method is `JScrollBar`.

The `addAdjustmentListener` method is defined as follows:

```
public void addAdjustmentListener(AdjustmentListener l)
```

Let's take a look at an example that creates a `JScrollBar` and displays its current value on the screen in a `JLabel`.

Type the code from Listing 6.2, excluding line numbers, into your favorite text editor and save it as `AdjustmentExample.java`, or copy it from the CD. Build it as follows:

```
javac AdjustmentExample.java
java AdjustmentExample
```

The code specific to the `AdjustmentEvent` and `AdjustmentListener` classes is bold-face for your convenience and will be explained following the source code.

Listing 6.2   `AdjustmentExample.java`

```
1:  // Import the packages used by this class
2:  import javax.swing.*;
3:  import javax.swing.event.*;
4:
5:  import java.awt.*;
```

```
6:   import java.awt.event.*;
7:
8:   // AdjustmentExample Class
9:   public class AdjustmentExample extends JPanel
                          implements AdjustmentListener
10:  {
11:      // Create our output labels
12:      JLabel lblValue = new JLabel( "JScrollBar Value" );
13:
14:      // Create a scroll bar
15:   JScrollBar scrollBar = new JScrollBar( JScrollBar.HORIZONTAL );
16:
17:      // Constructor
18:      public AdjustmentExample()
19:      {
20:          // Set the layout manager
21:          setLayout( new BorderLayout() );
22:
23:          // Center the label on the frame
24:          lblValue.setHorizontalAlignment( JLabel.CENTER );
25:
26:          // Add the label to the JPanel
27:          add( lblValue );
28:
29:          // Add the scrollbar
30:          add( scrollBar, BorderLayout.SOUTH );
31:
32:          // Add ourself as an adjustment listener for the scroll bar
33:          scrollBar.addAdjustmentListener( this );
34:      }
35:
36:      // Action Event Handler: adjustmentValueChanged
37:      public void adjustmentValueChanged(AdjustmentEvent e)
38:      {
39:          // See if the event is ours
40:          if( e.getSource() == scrollBar )
41:          {
42:              // Update the value label with the current value of the
43:              // JScrollBar
44:            lblValue.setText( "JScrollBar value: " +  e.getValue() );
45:          }
46:      }
47:
48:      // Main application entry point into this class
49:      public static void main( String[] args )
50:      {
51:          // Create a JFrame object
52:          JFrame frame = new JFrame( "Adjustment Example!" );
53:
54:          // Create an AdjustmentExample Object
55:          AdjustmentExample example = new AdjustmentExample();
```

continues

Listing 6.2 continued

```
56:
57:            // Add our AdjustmentExample Object to the JFrame
58:            frame.getContentPane().add( example, BorderLayout.CENTER );
59:
60:            // Resize our JFrame
61:            frame.setSize( 340, 180 );
62:
63:            // Make our JFrame visible
64:            frame.setVisible( true );
65:
66:            // Create a window listener to close our application when we
67:            // close our application
68:            frame.addWindowListener
69:            (
70:        new WindowAdapter()
71:                {
72:                    public void windowClosing( WindowEvent e )
73:                    {
74:                        System.exit( 0 );
75:                    }
76:                }
77:            );
78:        }
79: }
```

Figure 6.3 shows the AdjustmentExample application after the scrollbar has been adjusted.

Figure 6.3

The AdjustmentExample application.

```
9:   public class AdjustmentExample extends JPanel
                          implements AdjustmentListener
```

Line 9 declares our main public class for this application, AdjustmentExample; it extends JPanel as our Chapter 5 examples did and it implements AdjustmentListener. If we implement AdjustmentListener, any adjustable components we want to listen to will notify us of changes through the adjustmentValueChanged method that we must implement.

```
15:  JScrollBar scrollBar = new JScrollBar( JScrollBar.HORIZONTAL );
```

Line 15 creates a new `JScrollBar` class object. We have not talked about scrollbars yet, so let me give you a brief introduction. A scrollbar itself is either a vertical or horizontal bar with arrows at the ends and an elevator bar somewhere between the two areas. The scrollbar usually represents where you are in the application-specific data at any given point. For example, if you are using Microsoft Word, there is a scrollbar along the right side that shows you where you are in the document. Scrollbars support dragging the elevator bar with the mouse (tracking), clicking on the arrows (unit increment and decrement), and clicking on empty areas of the scrollbar (block increment and decrement).

Swing supports scrollbars through the `JScrollBar` class. It has the constructors shown in Table 6.12.

Table 6.12   `JScrollBar` Constructors

Constructor	Description
`JScrollBar()`	Creates a vertical scrollbar with the following initial values: minimum = 0, maximum = 100, value = 0, extent = 10
`JScrollBar(int orientation)`	Creates a scrollbar with the specified orientation and the following initial values: minimum = 0, maximum = 100, value = 0, extent = 10
`JScrollBar(int orientation, int value, int extent, int min, int max)`	Creates a scrollbar with the specified orientation, value, extent, minimum, and maximum

The five elements of a scrollbar are defined in Table 6.13.

Table 6.13   `JScrollBar` Elements

Element	Description
Orientation	The orientation specifies whether the scrollbar is vertical or horizontal. The possible values for this are HORIZONTAL and VERTICAL.
Value	The value is the current placement of the elevator bar in the scrollbar.
Extent	The extent represents the size of the viewable area.
Minimum Value	This is the value of the scrollbar when the elevator bar is either at the left side, for horizontal scrollbars, or the top, for vertical scrollbars.
Maximum Value	This is the value of the scrollbar when the elevator bar is either at the right side, for horizontal scrollbars, or at the top, for vertical scrollbars.

6

Usually you will use components that have scrolling support provided for them through the JScrollPane class, or you will use the JScrollBar to represent some form of custom data. Look through the Java 2 SDK documentation for more information.

```
33:   scrollBar.addAdjustmentListener( this );
```

Line 33 adds our AdjustmentExample class as an adjustment listener for the scrollbar.

```
37:      public void adjustmentValueChanged(AdjustmentEvent e)
38:      {
39:          // See if the event is ours
40:          if( e.getSource() == scrollBar )
41:          {
42:              // Update the value label with the current value of the
43:              // JScrollBar
44:          lblValue.setText( "JScrollBar value: " + e.getValue() );
45:          }
46:      }
```

Lines 37–46 implement the AdjustmentListener interface adjustmentValueChanged method. Line 40 compares the AdjustmentEvent object, retrieved by calling the AdjustmentEvent getSource method, to our scrollbar. If it is our scrollbar, we update the value label by displaying the current value of the scrollbar. The current value of the scrollbar is obtained by calling the AdjustmentEvent class's getValue method (described in Table 6.10). You can always retrieve this value directly from the JScrollBar by calling its getValue method, but I wanted to show you how to use the AdjustmentEvent class in this example.

Focus Events

Focus events are low-level events that occur when a component gains or loses the keyboard input focus. The FocusListener interface listens for focus events and is defined in Table 6.14.

Table 6.14 FocusListener **Interface**

Return	Method	Description
void	focusGained(FocusEvent e)	Invoked when a component gains the keyboard focus
void	focusLost(FocusEvent e)	Invoked when a component loses the keyboard focus

To handle focus events, you must create a class that implements FocusListener, and then define the focusGained and focusLost methods in that class.

The event sent to the `focusGained` and `focusLost` methods is an instance of the `FocusEvent` event, described in Table 6.15.

Table 6.15   `FocusEvent` **Class**

Return	Method	Description
boolean	isTemporary()	Identifies the focus change event as temporary or permanent
String	paramString()	Returns a parameter string identifying this event

To add a focus event to a component, you can call the `addFocusListener` method for all items that derive from `Component`, hence all the AWT and Swing components.

The `addFocusListener` method is defined as follows:

```
public void addFocusListener(FocusListener l)
```

Let's take a look at an example of the `FocusListener` interface by creating two buttons and two labels. Each label gives the current focus state (gained or lost) of its respective button. Try selecting each button in turn and watch the input focus messages change. Refer to Listing 6.3.

Type the code from Listing 6.3, excluding line numbers, into your favorite text editor and save it as `FocusExample.java`, or copy it from the CD. Build it as follows:

```
javac FocusExample.java
java FocusExample
```

The code specific to the `FocusEvent` and `FocusListener` classes is boldface for your convenience and is explained following the source code.

Listing 6.3   `FocusExample.java`

```
 1: // Import the packages used by this class
 2: import javax.swing.*;
 3: import javax.swing.event.*;
 4:
 5: import java.awt.*;
 6: import java.awt.event.*;
 7:
 8: // FocusExample Class
 9: public class FocusExample extends JPanel
                         implements FocusListener
10: {
11:     // Create our output labels
12:     JLabel lblFocusOne = new JLabel( "Button One Focus" );
13:     JLabel lblFocusTwo = new JLabel( "Button Two Focus" );
14:
```

continues

Listing 6.3 continued

```
15:        // Create a label panel
16:        JPanel panelLabel = new JPanel( new GridLayout( 2, 1 ) );
17:
18:        // Create a scroll bar
19:        JButton btnOne = new JButton( "One" );
20:        JButton btnTwo = new JButton( "Two" );
21:
22:        // Create a button Panel
23:        JPanel panelButton = new JPanel( new GridLayout( 1, 2 ) );
24:
25:        // Constructor
26:        public FocusExample()
27:        {
28:            // Set the layout manager
29:            setLayout( new BorderLayout() );
30:
31:            // Center the labels on their panel
32:            lblFocusOne.setHorizontalAlignment( JLabel.CENTER );
33:            lblFocusTwo.setHorizontalAlignment( JLabel.CENTER );
34:
35:            // Add the labels to the label panel
36:            panelLabel.add( lblFocusOne );
37:            panelLabel.add( lblFocusTwo );
38:
39:            // Add the label panel to the JPanel
40:            add( panelLabel );
41:
42:            // Add the buttons to the button panel
43:            panelButton.add( btnOne );
44:            panelButton.add( btnTwo );
45:
46:            // Add the button panel to the JPanel
47:            add( panelButton, BorderLayout.SOUTH );
48:
49:            // Add ourself as a focus listener for the buttons
50:            btnOne.addFocusListener( this );
51:            btnTwo.addFocusListener( this );
52:        }
53:
54:        // Action Event Handler: focusGained
55:        public void focusGained( FocusEvent e )
56:        {
57:            // See which button generated the event
58:            if( e.getSource() == btnOne )
59:            {
60:                lblFocusOne.setText( "Button One gained the focus" );
61:            }
62:            else if( e.getSource() == btnTwo )
63:            {
64:                lblFocusTwo.setText( "Button Two gained the focus" );
```

```
65:          }
66:      }
67:
68:      // Action Event Handler: focusLost
69:      public void focusLost( FocusEvent e )
70:      {
71:          // See which button generated the event
72:          if( e.getSource() == btnOne )
73:          {
74:              lblFocusOne.setText( "Button One lost the focus" );
75:          }
76:          else if( e.getSource() == btnTwo )
77:          {
78:              lblFocusTwo.setText( "Button Two lost the focus" );
79:          }
80:      }
81:
82:      // Main application entry point into this class
83:      public static void main( String[] args )
84:      {
85:          // Create a JFrame object
86:          JFrame frame = new JFrame( "Focus Example!" );
87:
88:          // Create an FocusExample Object
89:          FocusExample example = new FocusExample();
90:
91:          // Add our FocusExample Object to the JFrame
92:          frame.getContentPane().add( example, BorderLayout.CENTER );
93:
94:          // Resize our JFrame
95:          frame.setSize( 340, 180 );
96:
97:          // Make our JFrame visible
98:          frame.setVisible( true );
99:
100:         // Create a window listener to close our application when we
101:         // close our application
102:         frame.addWindowListener
103:         (
104:             new WindowAdapter()
105:             {
106:                 public void windowClosing( WindowEvent e )
107:                 {
108:                     System.exit( 0 );
109:                 }
110:             }
111:         );
112:     }
113:}
```

Figure 6.4 shows the FocusExample application after clicking button Two.

Figure 6.4

The FocusExample
application.

```
9:  public class FocusExample extends JPanel
                        implements FocusListener
```

Line 9 declares our FocusExample class as extending JPanel and implementing FocusListener. Through the FocusListener interface, we can be notified of focus changes by any components we register through the focusGained and focusLost methods.

```
50:        btnOne.addFocusListener( this );
51:        btnTwo.addFocusListener( this );
```

Lines 50 and 51 add our FocusExample class as a focus listener for both buttons.

```
55:    public void focusGained( FocusEvent e )
56:    {
57:        // See which button generated the event
58:        if( e.getSource() == btnOne )
59:        {
60:            lblFocusOne.setText( "Button One gained the focus" );
61:        }
62:        else if( e.getSource() == btnTwo )
63:        {
64:            lblFocusTwo.setText( "Button Two gained the focus" );
65:        }
66:    }
```

Lines 55–66 implement the focusGained method. This method retrieves the object that generated the FocusEvent and compares that to the two buttons. It updates the label that represents the button that generated the event.

```
69:    public void focusLost( FocusEvent e )
70:    {
71:        // See which button generated the event
72:        if( e.getSource() == btnOne )
73:        {
74:            lblFocusOne.setText ( "Button One lost the focus" );
75:        }
76:        else if( e.getSource() == btnTwo )
77:        {
78:            lblFocusTwo.setText( "Button Two lost the focus" );
79:        }
80:    }
```

Lines 69–80 implement the focusList method. This method retrieves the object that generated the FocusEvent and compares that to our two buttons. It updates the label that represents the button that generated the event.

Notice as you run this application that when a button changes focus, both labels change at the same time. Actually the changes happen a fraction of a second apart; one item loses the focus and then the other item gains the focus. So when the first button has the focus and you click on the second button, the first button generates a focusLost event and then the second button generates a focusGained event.

Item Events

Item events indicate that an item was selected or deselected. The ItemListener interface listens for item events and is defined in Table 6.16.

Table 6.16 ItemListener **Interface**

Return	Method	Description
void	itemStateChanged(ItemEvent e)	Invoked when an item has been selected or deselected

To handle item events, you must create a class that implements ItemListener, and then define the itemStateChanged method in that class.

The event sent to the itemStateChanged method is the ItemEvent event, described in Table 6.17.

Table 6.17 ItemEvent **Class**

Return	Method	Description
Object	getItem()	Returns the item affected by the event
ItemSelectable	getItemSelectable()	Returns the originator of the event
int	getStateChange()	Returns the type of state change (selected or deselected)
String	paramString()	Returns a parameter string identifying this item event

You can obtain the object that caused the event, the originator of the event, and the type of event.

To add an item event listener to a component, you can call the `addItemListener` method of the following Swing button components:

- `JButton`
- `JCheckBox`
- `JComboBox`
- `JRadioButton`

The `addItemListener` method is defined in the `AbstractButton` class and is proto-typed as follows:

```
public void addItemListener(ItemListener l)
```

Let's take a look at an example of the `ItemListener` by creating a check box and a label. The label will tell the current state of the check box whenever an item event occurs. Try selecting and deselecting the check box and watch the `JLabel` change.

Type the code from Listing 6.4, excluding line numbers, into your favorite text editor and save it as `ItemExample.java`, or copy it from the CD. Build it as follows:

```
javac ItemExample.java
java ItemExample
```

The code specific to the `ItemEvent` and `ItemListener` classes is boldface for your convenience and is explained following the source code.

Listing 6.4 `ItemExample.java`

```
1:  // Import the packages used by this class
2:  import javax.swing.*;
3:  import javax.swing.event.*;
4:
5:  import java.awt.*;
6:  import java.awt.event.*;
7:
8:  // ItemExample Class
9:  public class ItemExample extends JPanel implements ItemListener
10: {
11:     // Create our output labels
12:     JLabel lblStatus = new JLabel( "JCheckBox Status" );
13:
14:     // Create a button
15:     JCheckBox cbxItem = new JCheckBox( "Item" );
16:
17:     // Constructor
18:     public ItemExample()
19:     {
20:         // Set the layout manager
21:         setLayout( new BorderLayout() );
22:
```

```
23:          // Center the label and the checkbox
24:          lblStatus.setHorizontalAlignment( JLabel.CENTER );
25:          cbxItem.setHorizontalAlignment( JCheckBox.CENTER );
26:
27:          // Add the label to the JPanel
28:          add( lblStatus );
29:
30:          // Add the button to the JPanel
31:          add( cbxItem, BorderLayout.SOUTH );
32:
33:          // Add ourself as a focus listener for the buttons
34:          cbxItem.addItemListener( this );
35:      }
36:
37:      // Item Event Handler: itemStateChanged
38:      public void itemStateChanged(ItemEvent e)
39:      {
40:          // See if the event is ours
41:          if( e.getSource() == cbxItem )
42:          {
43:              // See if the item is selected
44:              if( e.getStateChange() == ItemEvent.SELECTED )
45:              {
46:                  lblStatus.setText( "Item Checkbox Selected" );
47:              }
48:              else if( e.getStateChange() == ItemEvent.DESELECTED )
49:              {
50:                  lblStatus.setText( "Item Checkbox Deselected" );
51:              }
52:          }
53:      }
54:
55:      // Main application entry point into this class
56:      public static void main( String[] args )
57:      {
58:          // Create a JFrame object
59:          JFrame frame = new JFrame( "Item Example!" );
60:
61:          // Create an ItemExample Object
62:          ItemExample example = new ItemExample();
63:
64:          // Add our ItemExample Object to the JFrame
65:          frame.getContentPane().add( example, BorderLayout.CENTER );
66:
67:          // Resize our JFrame
68:          frame.setSize( 340, 180 );
69:
70:          // Make our JFrame visible
71:          frame.setVisible( true );
72:
73:          // Create a window listener to close our application when we
```

continues

Listing 6.4   continued

```
74:          // close our application
75:          frame.addWindowListener
76:          (
77:             new WindowAdapter()
78:             {
79:                public void windowClosing( WindowEvent e )
80:                {
81:                   System.exit( 0 );
82:                }
83:             }
84:          );
85:       }
86: }
```

Figure 6.5 shows the ItemExample application after clicking the Item check box.

Figure 6.5

The ItemExample application.

9: `public class ItemExample extends JPanel implements ItemListener`

Line 9 declares our ItemExample class that extends JPanel and implements ItemListener. Through the ItemListener interface, we can be notified of item changes by any components we register through the itemStateChanged method.

34:       `cbxItem.addItemListener( this );`

Line 34 adds our ItemExample class as an item listener for the JCheckBox object cbxItem.

```
38:    public void itemStateChanged(ItemEvent e)
39:    {
40:       // See if the event is ours
41:       if( e.getSource() == cbxItem )
42:       {
43:          // See if the item is selected
44:          if( e.getStateChange() == ItemEvent.SELECTED )
45:          {
46:             lblStatus.setText( "Item Checkbox Selected" );
47:          }
48:          else if( e.getStateChange() == ItemEvent.DESELECTED )
49:          {
50:             lblStatus.setText( "Item Checkbox Deselected" );
51:          }
```

```
52:        }
53:    }
```

Lines 38–53 define our `ItemListener` interface `itemStateChanged` method. This method simply checks to see if the item that changed is our check box in line 41 and then gets the status through the `ItemEvent` method `getStateChange`. The `getStateChange` method can return one of two values: `ItemEvent.SELECTED` or `ItemEvent.DESELECTED`. The status label is updated appropriately.

Keyboard Events

Keyboard events indicate that a keystroke occurred in some component. The `KeyListener` interface listens for keyboard events and is defined in Table 6.18.

Table 6.18 `KeyListener` Interface

Return	*Method*	*Description*
void	keyPressed(KeyEvent e)	Invoked when a key has been pressed
void	keyReleased(KeyEvent e)	Invoked when a key has been released
void	keyTyped(KeyEvent e)	Invoked when a key has been typed

To handle keyboard events, you must create a class that implements `KeyListener`, and then define the `keyPressed`, `keyReleased`, or `keyTyped` methods in that class, or you can create a new `KeyAdapter` object and just override the methods you want.

The event sent to the `keyPressed`, `keyReleased`, and `keyTyped` methods is the `KeyEvent` event, described in Table 6.19.

Table 6.19 `KeyEvent` Class

Return	*Method*	*Description*
char	getKeyChar()	Returns the character associated with the key in this event
int	getKeyCode()	Returns the integer key-code associated with the key in this event
String	getKeyModifiersText (int modifiers)	Returns a `String` describing the modifier keys, such as "Shift", or "Ctrl+Shift"
String	getKeyText(int keyCode)	Returns a `String` describing the keyCode, such as "HOME", "F1", or "A"
Boolean	isActionKey()	Returns whether or not the key in this event is an "action" key, as defined in `Event.java`

continues

Table 6.19   KeyEvent Class

Return	Method	Description
String	paramString()	Returns a parameter string identifying this event
void	setKeyChar(char keyChar)	Sets the keyChar value to indicate a logical character
void	setKeyCode(int keyCode)	Sets the keyCode value to indicate a physical key
void	setModifiers(int modifiers)	Sets the modifiers to indicate additional keys that were held down (Shift, Ctrl, Alt, Meta) defined as part of InputEvent

With this event, you can obtain the object that caused the event, the integer and string representations of the key that was pressed, and the state of the modifier keys. The set keys are used by classes that are generating the keyboard events and don't concern us when handling events.

To add a keyboard event listener to a component, you can call the addKeyListener method defined in the Component class, and thus available to all components derived from Component, which includes all AWT and Swing components.

The addKeyListener method is defined as follows:

```
public void addKeyListener(KeyListener l)
```

Let's take a look at an example of the KeyListener interface by creating two labels and a text field. One label will show the key typed, and the other will show the key presses and releases for the text field. Note that the text field class reports the key presses and releases very well, but the "keys typed" are reported only when an illegal key has been pressed (just to warn you!). An illegal key is simply one that the keyTyped() method does not recognize, such as the escape key (Esc).

Type the code from Listing 6.5 excluding line numbers, into your favorite text editor and save it as KeyExample.java, or copy it from the CD. Build it as follows:

```
javac KeyExample.java
java KeyExample
```

The code specific to the KeyEvent and KeyListener classes is boldface for your convenience and is explained following the source code.

Listing 6.5   KeyExample.java

```
1:  // Import the packages used by this class
2:  import javax.swing.*;
3:  import javax.swing.event.*;
```

```
4:
5:   import java.awt.*;
6:   import java.awt.event.*;
7:
8:   // KeyExample Class
9:   public class KeyExample extends JPanel implements KeyListener
10:  {
11:      // Create our output labels
12:      JLabel lblStatus = new JLabel( "Keyboard Events" );
13:      JLabel lblTyped  = new JLabel( "Key Typed" );
14:
15:      // Create a label panel
16:      JPanel panelLabel = new JPanel( new GridLayout( 2, 1 ) );
17:
18:      // Create a button
19:      JTextField textField = new JTextField();
20:
21:      // Constructor
22:      public KeyExample()
23:      {
24:          // Set the layout manager
25:          setLayout( new BorderLayout() );
26:
27:          // Center the labels
28:          lblStatus.setHorizontalAlignment( JLabel.CENTER );
29:          lblTyped.setHorizontalAlignment( JLabel.CENTER );
30:
31:          // Add the labels to their panel
32:          panelLabel.add( lblTyped );
33:          panelLabel.add( lblStatus );
34:
35:          // Add the label panel to the JPanel
36:          add( panelLabel );
37:
38:          // Add the text field to the JPanel
39:          add( textField, BorderLayout.SOUTH );
40:
41:          // Add ourself as a keyboard listener for the text field
42:          textField.addKeyListener( this );
43:      }
44:
45:      // Key Event Handler: keyPressed
46:      public void keyPressed(KeyEvent e)
47:      {
48:          if( e.getSource() == textField)
49:          {
50:              int nKeyCode = e.getKeyCode();
51:                  lblStatus.setText( "Key Pressed: " +
                                        e.getKeyText( nKeyCode ) );
52:          }
53:      }
```

continues

Listing 6.5   continued

```
54:
55:     // Key Event Handler: keyReleased
56:     public void keyReleased(KeyEvent e)
57:     {
58:         if( e.getSource() == textField)
59:         {
60:             int nKeyCode = e.getKeyCode();
61:             lblStatus.setText( "Key Released: " +
                                        e.getKeyText( nKeyCode ) );
62:         }
63:     }
64:
65:     // Key Event Handler:  keyTyped
66:     public void keyTyped(KeyEvent e)
67:     {
68:         if( e.getSource() == textField)
69:         {
70:             int nKeyCode = e.getKeyCode();
71:             lblTyped.setText( "Key Typed: " +
                                        e.getKeyText( nKeyCode ) );
72:         }
73:     }
74:
75:     // Main application entry point into this class
76:     public static void main( String[] args )
77:     {
78:         // Create a JFrame object
79:         JFrame frame = new JFrame( "Key Example!" );
80:
81:         // Create an KeyExample Object
82:         KeyExample example = new KeyExample();
83:
84:         // Add our KeyExample Object to the JFrame
85:         frame.getContentPane().add( example, BorderLayout.CENTER );
86:
87:         // Resize our JFrame
88:         frame.setSize( 340, 180 );
89:
90:         // Make our JFrame visible
91:         frame.setVisible( true );
92:
93:         // Create a window listener to close our application when we
94:         // close our application
95:         frame.addWindowListener
96:         (
97:             new WindowAdapter()
98:             {
99:                 public void windowClosing( WindowEvent e )
100:                {
```

```
101: System.exit( 0 );
102:                }
103:           }
104:       );
105:   }
106:}
```

Figure 6.6 shows the KeyExample application after typing Disneyland.

Figure 6.6

The KeyExample application.

```
9:  public class KeyExample extends JPanel implements KeyListener
```

Line 9 declares our KeyExample class as extending JPanel and implementing KeyListener. Through the KeyListener interface, we can be notified of keyboard events by any components we register with through the keyPressed, keyReleased, and keyTyped methods.

```
42:         textField.addKeyListener( this );
```

Line 42 adds our KeyExample class as a key listener for the JTextField.

```
46:     public void keyPressed(KeyEvent e)
47:     {
48:         if( e.getSource() == textField)
49:         {
50:             int nKeyCode = e.getKeyCode();
51:                 lblStatus.setText( "Key Pressed: " +
                                        e.getKeyText( nKeyCode ) );
52:         }
53:     }
```

Lines 46–53 define the KeyListener interface's keyPressed method. Again this method is called when the user presses a key. The method checks to see if our text field generated the event, and if so, it updates the status label by noting what key was pressed.

```
56:     public void keyReleased(KeyEvent e)
57:     {
58:         if( e.getSource() == textField)
59:         {
60:             int nKeyCode = e.getKeyCode();
61:                 lblStatus.setText( "Key Released: " +
                                    e.getKeyText( nKeyCode ) );
62:         }
63:     }
```

Lines 56–63 define the `KeyListener` interface's `keyReleased` method. Again this method is called when the user releases a key after pressing it. The method checks to see if our text field generated the event, and if so, it updates the status label by noting what key was released.

```
66:    public void keyTyped(KeyEvent e)
67:    {
68:        if( e.getSource() == textField)
69:        {
70:            int nKeyCode = e.getKeyCode();
71:            lblTyped.setText( "Key Typed: " +
                                      e.getKeyText( nKeyCode ) );
72:        }
73:    }
```

Lines 66–73 define the `KeyListener` interface's `keyTyped` method. Again this method is called when the user types a key (press then release). The method checks to see if our text field generated the event, and if so, it updates the status label by noting what key was typed.

Mouse Events

Mouse events indicate that a mouse action occurred in some component. The `MouseListener` interface listens for mouse events and is defined in Table 6.20.

Table 6.20 `MouseListener` **Interface**

Return	Method	Description
void	mouseClicked(MouseEvent e)	Invoked when the mouse has been clicked on a component
void	mouseEntered(MouseEvent e)	Invoked when the mouse enters a component
void	mouseExited(MouseEvent e)	Invoked when the mouse exits a component
void	mousePressed(MouseEvent e)	Invoked when a mouse button has been pressed on a component
void	mouseReleased(MouseEvent e)	Invoked when a mouse button has been released on a component

To handle mouse events, you must create a class that implements `MouseListener`, and then define the `mouseClicked`, `mouseEntered`, `mouseExited`, `mousePressed`, and `mouseReleased` methods in that class. Alternatively, you can create an instance of the `MouseAdapter` class that provides default implementations for these methods and override only those that you are interested in handling.

The event sent to the mouse listener methods is the `MouseEvent` event, described in Table 6.21.

Table 6.21   `MouseEvent` **Class**

Return	Method	Description
int	getClickCount()	Returns the number of mouse clicks associated with this event
Point	getPoint()	Returns the x,y position of the event relative to the source component
int	getX()	Returns the horizontal x position of the event relative to the source component
int	getY()	Returns the vertical y position of the event relative to the source component
Boolean	isPopupTrigger()	Returns whether this mouse event is the pop-up menu trigger event for the platform
String	paramString()	Returns a parameter string identifying this event
void	translatePoint(int x, int y)	Translates the event's coordinates to a new position by adding specified x (horizontal) and y (vertical) offsets

You can obtain the object that caused the event, the location of the point where the mouse was located when the event occurred, and the number of mouse clicks that caused the event.

To add an action event listener to a component, you can call the `addMouseListener` method of any component derived from `Component`, hence all the AWT and Swing components.

The `addMouseListener` method is defined as follows:

```
public void addMouseListener(MouseListener l)
```

Let's take a look at an example of the `MouseListener` interface by creating a frame with three labels and one button. The labels will show the following:

- Mouse click status
- Mouse pressed/released status
- Mouse enter/edit status

Each label will show the (x, y) location of the mouse when the mouse event occurs. Try clicking on the button and moving the mouse over different parts of the button and see how it responds. See how and when the events are fired.

Type the code from Listing 6.6, excluding line numbers, into your favorite text editor and save it as `MouseExample.java`, or copy it from the CD. Build it as follows:

```
javac MouseExample.java
java MouseExample
```

The code specific to the `MouseEvent` and `MouseListener` classes is boldface for your convenience and is explained following the source code.

Listing 6.6 MouseExample.java

```
1:   // Import the packages used by this class
2:   import javax.swing.*;
3:   import javax.swing.event.*;
4:
5:   import java.awt.*;
6:   import java.awt.event.*;
7:
8:   // MouseExample Class
9:   public class MouseExample extends JPanel
                             implements MouseListener
10:  {
11:      // Create our output labels
12:      JLabel lblStatus = new JLabel( "Mouse Status" );
13:      JLabel lblClickStatus = new JLabel( "Mouse Click Status" );
14:      JLabel lblPressedStatus = new JLabel( "Mouse Pressed Status" );
15:
16:      // Create a label panel
17:      JPanel panelLabel = new JPanel( new GridLayout( 3, 1 ) );
18:
19:
20:      // Create a scroll bar
21:      JButton btnOne = new JButton( "One" );
22:
23:      // Constructor
24:      public MouseExample()
25:      {
26:          // Set the layout manager
27:          setLayout( new BorderLayout() );
28:
29:          // Center the labels on their panel
30:          lblStatus.setHorizontalAlignment( JLabel.CENTER );
31:          lblClickStatus.setHorizontalAlignment( JLabel.CENTER );
32:          lblPressedStatus.setHorizontalAlignment( JLabel.CENTER );
33:
34:          // Add the labels to the label panel
35:          panelLabel.add( lblClickStatus );
36:          panelLabel.add( lblPressedStatus );
```

```
37:            panelLabel.add( lblStatus );
38:
39:            // Add the label panel to the JPanel
40:            add( panelLabel );
41:
42:            // Add the button panel to the JPanel
43:            add( btnOne, BorderLayout.SOUTH );
44:
45:            // Add ourself as a focus listener for the buttons
46:            btnOne.addMouseListener( this );
47:        }
48:
49:        // Mouse Event Handler: mouseClicked
50:        public void mouseClicked(MouseEvent e)
51:        {
52:            // See if our button generated the event
53:            if( e.getSource() == btnOne )
54:            {
55:                lblClickStatus.setText( "Mouse clicked at: " +
56:                                     e.getX() + ", " + e.getY() );
57:            }
58:        }
59:
60:        // Mouse Event Handler: mousePressed
61:        public void mousePressed(MouseEvent e)
62:        {
63:            // See if our button generated the event
64:            if( e.getSource() == btnOne )
65:            {
66:                lblPressedStatus.setText( "Mouse pressed at: " +
67:                                     e.getX() + ", " + e.getY() );
68:            }
69:        }
70:
71:        // Mouse Event Handler: mouseReleased
72:        public void mouseReleased(MouseEvent e)
73:        {
74:            // See if our button generated the event
75:            if( e.getSource() == btnOne )
76:            {
77:                lblPressedStatus.setText( "Mouse released at: " +
78:                                     e.getX() + ", " + e.getY() );
79:            }
80:        }
81:
82:        // Mouse Event Handler: mouseEntered
83:        public void mouseEntered(MouseEvent e)
84:        {
85:            // See if our button generated the event
86:            if( e.getSource() == btnOne )
87:            {
```

6

continues

Listing 6.6   continued

```
 88:                    lblStatus.setText( "Mouse entered at: " +
 89:                                       e.getX() + ", " + e.getY() );
 90:             }
 91:        }
 92:
 93:        // Mouse Event Handler: mouseExited
 94:        public void mouseExited(MouseEvent e)
 95:        {
 96:            // See if our button generated the event
 97:            if( e.getSource() == btnOne )
 98:            {
 99:                lblStatus.setText( "Mouse exited at: " +
100:                                   e.getX() + ", " + e.getY() );
101:            }
102:        }
103:
104:        // Main application entry point into this class
105:        public static void main( String[] args )
106:        {
107:            // Create a JFrame object
108:            JFrame frame = new JFrame( "Mouse Example!" );
109:
110:            // Create an MouseExample Object
111:            MouseExample example = new MouseExample();
112:
113:            // Add our MouseExample Object to the JFrame
114:            frame.getContentPane().add( example,  BorderLayout.CENTER );
115:
116:            // Resize our JFrame
117:            frame.setSize( 340, 180 );
118:
119:            // Make our JFrame visible
120:            frame.setVisible( true );
121:
122:            // Create a window listener to close our application when we
123:            // close our application
124:            frame.addWindowListener
125:            (
126:                new WindowAdapter()
127:                {
128:                    public void windowClosing( WindowEvent e )
139:                    {
130:                        System.exit( 0 );
131:                    }
132:                }
133:            );
134:        }
135:}
```

Figure 6.7 shows the MouseExample application after moving the mouse over the One button.

Figure 6.7

The MouseExample
application.

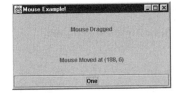

```
9:  public class MouseExample extends JPanel
                              implements MouseListener
```

Line 9 declares our MouseExample class as extending JPanel and implementing
MouseListener. By implementing MouseListener, we can be notified of mouse events
by any components we register through the mouseClicked, mouseEntered,
mouseExited, mousePressed, and mouseReleased methods.

```
46:         btnOne.addMouseListener( this );
```

Line 46 adds our MouseExample class as a mouse listener for the btnOne JButton.

```
50:     public void mouseClicked(MouseEvent e)
51:     {
52:         // See if our button generated the event
53:         if( e.getSource() == btnOne )
54:         {
55:             lblClickStatus.setText( "Mouse clicked at: " +
56:                                 e.getX() + ", " + e.getY() );
57:         }
58:     }
```

Lines 50–58 define the MouseListener interface's mouseClicked method. Again this
method is called when the user clicks the mouse on a component. The method
checks to see whether our button generated the event, and if so, it updates the click
status label by noting the location of the mouse at the time of the event by calling
the MouseEvent methods getX and getY.

```
61:     public void mousePressed(MouseEvent e)
62:     {
63:         // See if our button generated the event
64:         if( e.getSource() == btnOne )
65:         {
66:             lblPressedStatus.setText( "Mouse pressed at: " +
67:                                 e.getX() + ", " + e.getY() );
68:         }
69:     }
```

Lines 61–69 define the MouseListener interface's mousePressed method. Again this
method is called when the user presses a mouse button while over a component. The
method checks to see if our button generated the event, and if so, it updates the
pressed status label by noting the location of the mouse at the time of the event by
calling the MouseEvent methods getX and getY.

```
72:      public void mouseReleased(MouseEvent e)
73:      {
74:          // See if our button generated the event
75:          if( e.getSource() == btnOne )
76:          {
77:              lblPressedStatus.setText( "Mouse released at: " +
78:                                  e.getX() + ", " + e.getY() );
79:          }
80:      }
```

Lines 72–80 define the MouseListener interface's mouseReleased method. Again this method is called when the user releases the mouse button after pressing a mouse button while over a component. The method checks to see whether our button generated the event, and if so, it updates the pressed status label by noting the location of the mouse at the time of the event by calling the MouseEvent methods getX and getY.

```
83:      public void mouseEntered(MouseEvent e)
84:      {
85:          // See if our button generated the event
86:          if( e.getSource() == btnOne )
87:          {
88:              lblStatus.setText( "Mouse entered at: " +
89:                                  e.getX() + ", " + e.getY() );
90:          }
91:      }
```

Lines 83–91 define the MouseListener interface's mouseEntered method. Again this method is called when the mouse enters the screen area occupied by a component. The method checks to see whether our button generated the event, and if so, it updates the status label by noting the location of the mouse at the time of the event by calling the MouseEvent methods getX and getY.

```
94:      public void mouseExited(MouseEvent e)
95:      {
96:          // See if our button generated the event
97:          if( e.getSource() == btnOne )
98:          {
99:              lblStatus.setText( "Mouse exited at: " +
100:                                 e.getX() + ", " + e.getY() );
101:          }
102:      }
```

Lines 94–102 define the MouseListener interface's mouseExited method. Again this method is called when the mouse leaves the screen area occupied by a component. The method checks to see whether our button generated the event, and if so, it updates the status label by noting the location of the mouse at the time of the event by calling the MouseEvent methods getX and getY.

Mouse Motion Events

Mouse motion events indicate that the mouse moved over some component. The `MouseMotionListener` interface listens for mouse motion events and is defined in Table 6.22.

Table 6.22 `MouseMotionListener` **Interface**

Return	Method	Description
void	mouseDragged(MouseEvent e)	Invoked when a mouse button is pressed on a component and then dragged
void	mouseMoved(MouseEvent e)	Invoked when the mouse button has been moved on a component (with no buttons pressed)

To handle mouse motion events, you must create a class that implements `MouseMotionListener`, and then define the `mouseDragged` and `mouseMoved` methods in that class.

The event sent to the `mouseDragged` and `mouseMoved` methods is the `MouseEvent` event, described in the last section in Table 6.21.

To add a mouse motion event listener to a component, you can call the `addMouseMotionListener` method for all components derived from `Component`, which includes all AWT and Swing components.

The `addMouseListener` method is defined as follows:

```
public void addMouseMotionListener(MouseMotionListener l)
```

Let's take a look at an example of the `MouseMotionListener` interface by creating a frame with two labels and a button. The two labels will show the drag status and movement of the mouse, respectively. To initiate the drag status, hold the mouse button down over the button and move the mouse around the screen with the button depressed. All you have to do to see the mouse movement update is move the mouse over the button.

Although you used the mouse listener to listen for mouse clicks, you would use the mouse motion listener to track the mouse position, as in a painting application.

Type the code from Listing 6.7, excluding line numbers, into your favorite text editor and save it as `MouseMotionExample.java`, or copy it from the CD. Build it as follows:

```
javac MouseMotionExample.java
java MouseMotionExample
```

6

The code specific to the MouseEvent and MouseMotionListener classes is boldface for your convenience and is explained following the source code.

Listing 6.7 `MouseMotionExample.java`

```
 1:   // Import the packages used by this class
 2:   import javax.swing.*;
 3:   import javax.swing.event.*;
 4:
 5:   import java.awt.*;
 6:   import java.awt.event.*;
 7:
 8:   // MouseMotionExample Class
 9:   public class MouseMotionExample extends JPanel
                                  implements MouseMotionListener
10:   {
11:        // Create our output labels
12:        JLabel lblDragged = new JLabel( "Mouse Dragged" );
13:        JLabel lblMoved = new JLabel( "Mouse Moved" );
14:
15:        // Create a label panel
16:        JPanel panelLabel = new JPanel( new GridLayout( 2, 1 ) );
17:
18:
19:        // Create a scroll bar
20:        JButton btnOne = new JButton( "One" );
21:
22:        // Constructor
23:        public MouseMotionExample()
24:        {
25:             // Set the layout manager
26:             setLayout( new BorderLayout() );
27:
28:             // Center the labels on their panel
29:             lblDragged.setHorizontalAlignment( JLabel.CENTER );
30:             lblMoved.setHorizontalAlignment( JLabel.CENTER );
31:
32:             // Add the labels to the label panel
33:             panelLabel.add( lblDragged );
34:             panelLabel.add( lblMoved );
35:
36:             // Add the label panel to the JPanel
37:             add( panelLabel );
38:
39:             // Add the button panel to the JPanel
40:             add( btnOne, BorderLayout.SOUTH );
41:
42:             // Add ourself as a focus listener for the buttons
43:             btnOne.addMouseMotionListener( this );
44:        }
45:
46:        // Mouse Motion Event Handler: mouseDragged
47:        public void mouseDragged(MouseEvent e)
```

```
48:     {
49:         // See if the event is ours
50:         if( e.getSource() == btnOne )
51:         {
52:             lblDragged.setText( "Mouse Dragged at (" +
53:                         e.getX() + ", " + e.getY() + ")" );
54:         }
55:     }
56:
57:     // Mouse Motion Event Handler: mouseMOved
58:     public void mouseMoved(MouseEvent e)
59:     {
60:         // See if the event is ours
61:         if( e.getSource() == btnOne )
62:         {
63:             lblMoved.setText( "Mouse Moved at (" +
64:                         e.getX() + ", " + e.getY() + ")" );
65:         }
66:     }
67:
68:     // Main application entry point into this class
69:     public static void main( String[] args )
70:     {
71:         // Create a JFrame object
72:         JFrame frame = new JFrame( "Mouse Example!" );
73:
74:         // Create an MouseMotionExample Object
75:         MouseMotionExample example = new MouseMotionExample();
76:
77:         // Add our MouseMotionExample Object to the JFrame
78:         frame.getContentPane().add( example, BorderLayout.CENTER );
79:
80:         // Resize our JFrame
81:         frame.setSize( 340, 180 );
82:
83:         // Make our JFrame visible
84:         frame.setVisible( true );
85:
86:         // Create a window listener to close our application when we
87:         // close our application
88:         frame.addWindowListener
89:         (
90:             new WindowAdapter()
91:             {
92:                 public void windowClosing( WindowEvent e )
93:                 {
94:                     System.exit( 0 );
95:                 }
96:             }
97:         );
98:     }
99: }
```

6

Figure 6.8 shows an example of the MouseMotionExample application.

Figure 6.8

The MouseMotionExample application.

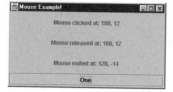

```
 9:    public class MouseMotionExample extends JPanel
                              implements MouseMotionListener
```

Line 9 declares our MouseMotionExample class as extending JPanel and implementing MouseMotionListener. By implementing MouseMotionListener, we can be notified of mouse events by any components we register through the mouseDragged and mouseMoved methods.

```
43:            btnOne.addMouseMotionListener( this );
```

Line 43 adds our MouseMotionExample class as a mouse motion listener for the btnOne JButton.

```
47:    public void mouseDragged(MouseEvent e)
48:    {
49:        // See if the event is ours
50:        if( e.getSource() == btnOne )
51:        {
52:            lblDragged.setText( "Mouse Dragged at (" +
53:                    e.getX() + ", " + e.getY() + ")" );
54:        }
55:    }
```

Lines 47–55 define the MouseMotionListener interface's mouseDragged method. Again this method is called when the user holds down the mouse button over a component and drags the mouse. The method checks to see if our button generated the event, and if so, it updates the dragged status label by noting the location of the mouse at the time of the event by calling the MouseEvent methods getX and getY.

```
58:    public void mouseMoved(MouseEvent e)
59:    {
60:        // See if the event is ours
61:        if( e.getSource() == btnOne )
62:        {
63:            lblMoved.setText( "Mouse Moved at (" +
64:                    e.getX() + ", " + e.getY() + ")" );
65:        }
66:    }
```

Lines 58–66 define the `MouseMotionListener` interface's `mouseMoved` method. Again this method is called when the mouse moves over a component. The method checks to see if our button generated the event, and if so, it updates the moved status label by noting the location of the mouse at the time of the event by calling the `MouseEvent` methods `getX` and `getY`.

Window Events

Window events are low-level events that indicate that a window has changed its status. The `WindowListener` interface listens for window events and is defined in Table 6.23.

Table 6.23 `WindowListener` **Interface**

Return	Method	Description
void	windowActivated(WindowEvent e)	Invoked when the window is set to be the user's active window, which means the window (or one of its subcomponents) will receive keyboard events
void	windowClosed(WindowEvent e)	Invoked when a window has been closed as the result of calling dispose on the window
void	windowClosing(WindowEvent e)	Invoked when the user attempts to close the window from the window's system menu
void	windowDeactivated(WindowEvent e)	Invoked when a window is no longer the user's active window, which means that keyboard events will no longer be delivered to the window or its subcomponents
void	windowDeiconified(WindowEvent e)	Invoked when a window is changed from a minimized to a normal state
void	windowIconified(WindowEvent e)	Invoked when a window is changed from a normal to a minimized state
void	windowOpened(WindowEvent e)	Invoked the first time a window is made visible

To handle window events, you must create a class that implements `WindowListener`, and then define the `windowActivated`, `windowClosed`, `windowClosing`, `windowDeactivated`, `windowDeiconified`, `windowIconified`, and `windowOpened` methods in that class. Alternatively, you can create an instance of `WindowAdapter`, which provides default implementations of these functions, and override only the methods you are interested in.

The event sent to the aforementioned methods is the `WindowEvent` event, described in Table 6.24.

Table 6.24 `WindowEvent` **Class**

Return	Method	Description
Window	getWindow()	Returns the originator of the event
String	paramString()	Returns a parameter string identifying this event

To add a window event listener to a component, you can call the `addWindowListener` method for all classes that are derived from `Window`, such as the following classes:

- `Frame`
- `JFrame`
- `Dialog`
- `JDialog`
- `FileDialog`
- `JWindow`

The `addWindowListener` method is defined as follows:

```
public void addWindowListener(WindowListener l)
```

We have been working with the `windowClosing` event from the beginning of our graphical user interface discussions in Chapter 4, "User Interface Design with AWT," so you should be very familiar with the `WindowAdapter` class, `windowClosing` method, and `addWindowListener` method.

The remaining methods are useful, but I am not going to provide you with an example because displaying events on a window as the window is closing or is minimized isn't all that interesting. Most of the time we will only be interested in the `windowClosing` event because the other events result in actions that should be handled by the framework and passed to us through constructors and other events.

Look through Table 6.23 and familiarize yourself with the types of events you can handle if someday you need them.

Summary

As usual, we covered quite a bit of material in this chapter! We started out talking about events in general and the various types of actions that can cause events. We then discussed how events are implemented in Java; we defined the notions of events, event listeners, and registering classes for event notifications. Finally, we talked in detail about all the standard events found in the JFC and saw examples of how to handle them.

Although you now know how to handle general events, many other events are specific to components, such as the JTable and JList. We will talk more about these custom events as we use them in the next chapter, but rest assured that they operate in a similar manner: You implement a listener, register yourself as a listener with the components you are interested in, and check the event class to see what type of information is available to you.

What's Next

After six chapters, you are finally ready to build a user interface for the Stock Tracker application! I am proud of you; you have come a long way. The one difference between this *From Scratch* book and some of the others is that you need to have a solid understanding of the Java user interface elements before we can build a meaningful application. From this point on, we are in the Stock Tracker application 100%.

In the next chapter we start building the Stock Tracker application user interface. Get ready for a long, but very satisfying, chapter!

Chapter 7

Building the Stock Tracker User Interface

In this chapter, we'll build the user interface for the Stock Tracker application (the user interface you first saw in Figures 1.1 and 1.2 in Chapter 1). We'll start by discussing the design of the user interface on paper and then determine the Java components we want to use to realize the design. We'll spend a little time talking about how to lay out the user interface, and then we'll move right into building it.

Designing the Stock Tracker User Interface

Before we jump into the physical design of the user interface, we must recall all those pesky use cases we defined in Chapter 3, "Designing the Stock Tracker Application," and ensure that our design adheres to them. Back in Chapter 3, we came up with 27 use cases that might or might not be applicable to our user interface. Table 7.1 shows all 27 of the use cases and shows whether the use case reflects a direct function that must be added to the user interface.

Table 7.1   Use Cases

No.	Description	GUI?
1	Add a new stock symbol to a portfolio	Yes
2	Delete a stock symbol from a portfolio	Yes
3	Enable historical tracking for a stock symbol	Yes
4	Calculate the total dollar gain/loss from a portfolio's stocks	No
5	Calculate the total percentage gain/loss from a portfolio's stocks	No
6	Download a Web page for a stock symbol from the Internet	No
7	Download a stock quote for a time other than today	No
8	Persist historical information to/from a data file	Yes
9	Retrieve stock prices from an HTML page	No
10	Set a timer to retrieve stock quotes at a specific interval	Yes
11	Retrieve stock quotes at the set interval	No
12	Add a portfolio	Yes
13	Delete a portfolio	Yes
14	Save a portfolio	Yes
15	Load a portfolio	Yes
16	Set graphing time scale	Yes
17	Graph stock performance points	Yes
18	Import historical data from a CSV file	Yes
19	Export historical data to a CSV file	Yes
20	Import a portfolio from a CSV file	Yes
21	Export a portfolio to a CSV file	Yes
22	Load all portfolios	No
23	Get stock quotes for portfolios	No
24	Save portfolios	Yes
25	Save current stock prices	No
26	Save historical information	No
27	Close active Internet connections	No

Most of these use cases will simply turn into menu items in the user interface, but we must remember to add them.

What flexibility do we have in the user interface given such an extensive set of use cases? Well, the use cases tell us what our application must do (that is, which features must be present in order to say the application is complete), but they do not tell us how to implement them. So we have all the freedom in the world when it comes to designing our user interface, just as long as we satisfy those use cases.

Let's get started with our design!

Paper Design

The first step in designing a user interface is to simply sit down and draw it. A dozen or more different drawings might be required before you get what you like, but keep going until you have something you are happy with. My vision for the Stock Tracker application is shown in Figures 7.1 and 7.2.

Figure 7.1

Stock Tracker drawing one.

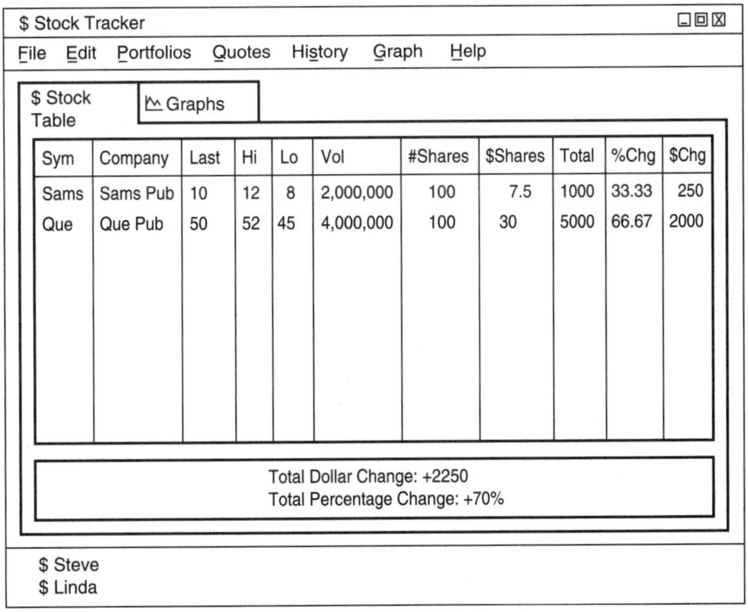
$ Stock Tracker
File Edit Portfolios Quotes History Graph Help
$ Stock Table
Graphs
Sym Company Last Hi Lo Vol #Shares $Shares Total %Chg $Chg
Sams Sams Pub 10 12 8 2,000,000 100 7.5 1000 33.33 250
Que Que Pub 50 52 45 4,000,000 100 30 5000 66.67 2000
Total Dollar Change: +2250
Total Percentage Change: +70%
$ Steve
$ Linda

Figure 7.2

Stock Tracker drawing two.

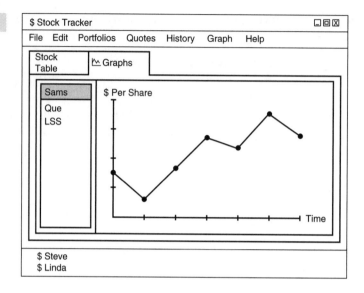

The way I envision the Stock Tracker application is a display consisting of two different tabs: one for stock quotes and information and one to display historical graphs. The portfolio list is separate from the tab control altogether because both the stock table as well as the graph will display information that is read from different portfolios.

Figure 7.1 shows the stock table view of the application. It has two components to it: the stock table and the totals panel. With whatever input methods we implement, the user will enter the following information:

- Stock ticker symbol
- Number of shares owned
- Price paid per share

The application will get the following information from the Internet:

- Company name
- Last price
- Daily high
- Daily low
- Daily volume

And the application will compute the following table fields:

- Total dollar value of investment

- Percentage change
- Dollar amount change

The stock table displays all this information.

The totals panel displays two fields:

- Total dollar change (for all stocks in the portfolio)
- Total percentage change (for all stocks in the portfolio)

Figure 7.2 shows the graphing view of the application. It too is composed of two components: the stock symbol selection list and the graph itself.

The stock symbol selection list displays all the stock symbols in the current portfolio, and the graph shows the selected stock symbol's performance over the time period set in the graphing options menu.

This brings us to the menu. If you go through the use cases, you will find they spell out many menu options. (For example, use case #2 states that the user deletes a stock by selecting Delete from the Edit menu). Table 7.2 tracks the menu items defined in the use cases with their use case numbers.

Table 7.2   Use Case Menu Derivation

Menu	Menu Item	Use Case Number
Edit	Delete	2
Portfolios	Add	13
	Delete	14
	Save	15
	Load	16
	Import	21
	Export	22
Quotes	Update	6
	Timer Options	11
History	Enable Tracking	3
	Get Historical Quote	7
	Import	19
	Export	20
Graph	Options	17

7

You will undoubtedly want to add a File menu with at least an Exit command and a Help menu with an About command (and maybe even a meaningful Help Contentscommand that calls up online help).

Java Components

Let's go ahead and break these drawings down into the components available in the Java Swing packages.

JFrame—StockApplication

Because our Java program is an application and not an applet, the application class is going to be a `JFrame`. The application class is a container that is going to hold the following components:

- Main menu
- Tab control
- Portfolio list

Figure 7.3 shows a drawing of the `StockApplication` class.

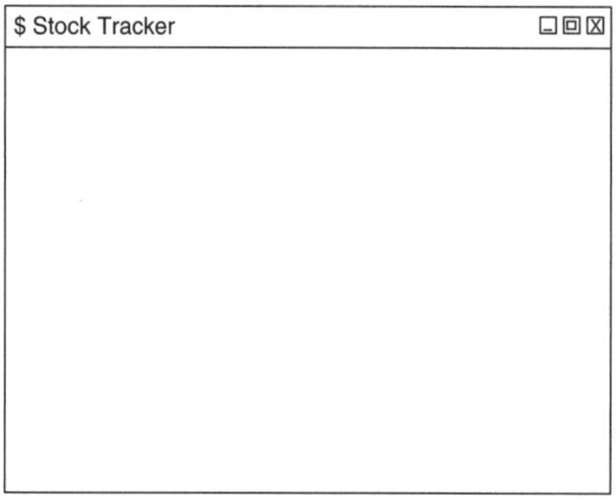

Figure 7.3

The `StockApplication` drawing.

JMenuBar, JMenu, JMenuItem—MainMenu

The main menu is going to be contained by the `StockApplication` class and is composed of `JMenuBar`, `JMenu`, and `JMenuItems` classes. It will look like any standard menu. Take a look at Figure 7.4 for a drawing of the `MainMenu` class.

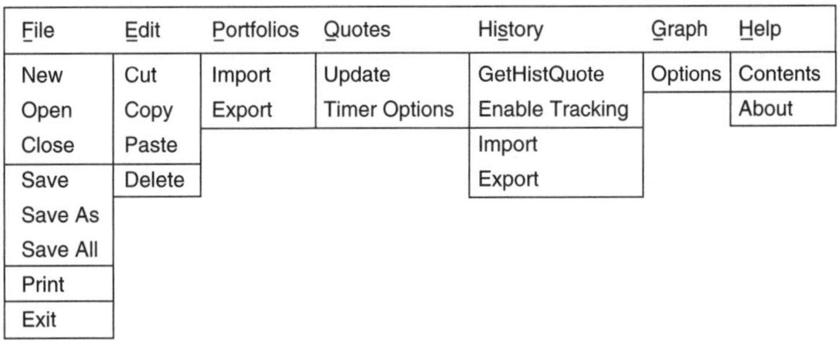

Figure 7.4

The MainMenu *drawing.*

File	Edit	Portfolios	Quotes	History	Graph	Help
New	Cut	Import	Update	GetHistQuote	Options	Contents
Open	Copy	Export	Timer Options	Enable Tracking		About
Close	Paste			Import		
Save	Delete			Export		
Save As						
Save All						
Print						
Exit						

You might notice that I did some work on the layout of the menu that differs from the use cases. I added quite a few entries, and I removed a few that were listed in the use cases. The primary menu I attacked was the Portfolio menu. The use cases showed it as follows:

```
Portfolio
      Add
      Delete
      Save
      Load
      Import
      Export
```

And the new one is as follows:

```
Portfolios
      Import
      Export
```

So what happened to all the other entries? Are we allowed to change them? The answer to the first question is that the File and Edit menus consumed them, according to the following mapping:

```
Portfolios
      Add        ->      File->New
      Delete     ->      Edit->Delete
      Save       ->      File->Save
      Load       ->      File->Open
```

Why did I rearrange them? The changes follow the Microsoft Windows standards. Whether or not you are a fan of the Microsoft way of doing things, most people understand their user interfaces (or at least are used to them). Remember that our primary goal, when defining a user interface, is ease of use.

The answer to the second question is yes, we are allowed to change our minds at this point. Remember that the design process is iterative—we take what we learn at every stage and reapply that to earlier stages. Normally at this point we would go back and update our use cases (#13, #14, #15, and #16), but rather than write those down here, let's keep them in the back of our minds and change them when we get there (if you want, you can flip back to Chapter 3 and change those).

JTabbedPane—StockTabPanel

The next component contained by the StockApplication class is the tab control. A tab control, which we discussed in the last chapter, gives you the ability to show two or more different panels that consume the entire area of the tab control by selecting the tab you want. In this case, we want two tabs:

- Stock Table
- Graphs

Figure 7.5 shows a drawing of the StockTabPanel class.

Figure 7.5

The StockTabPanel drawing.

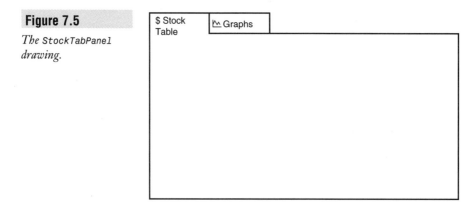

JList, JScrollPane, JLabel, ListCellRenderer— PortfolioListPanel

The final component contained by the StockApplication class is the portfolio list panel. This panel contains all the available portfolios with icons in a scrollable list. Figure 7.6 shows a drawing of the PortfolioListPanel class.

JPanel—StockTableTabPanel

Let's start looking at our Stock Table tab components. There are two components in this tab:

- Stock Table
- Portfolio Totals

Figure 7.6

The
PortfolioListPanel
drawing.

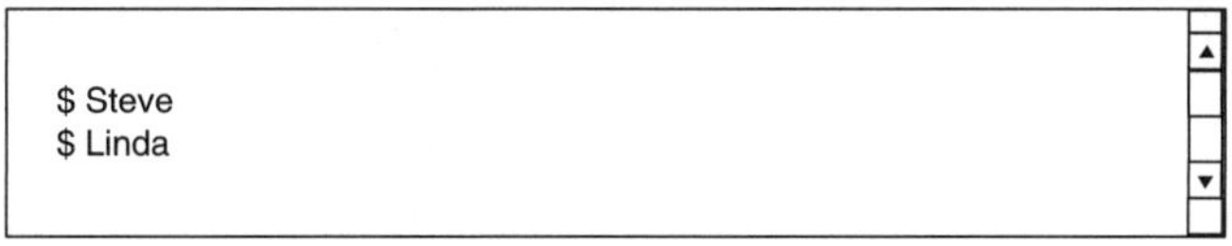

$ Steve
$ Linda

The first thing we need is a `JPanel` that will hold these two components. We will create `StockTableTabPanel`, which will be nothing more than a `JPanel` with a layout manager that supports aligning components one above each other (with the bottom one being very small).

JTable—StockTablePanel

Okay, now we have some meat to the application: the stock table! The stock table will display all the stock information for a portfolio and includes the following columns:

- Symbol
- Company Name
- Last Price
- Daily High
- Daily Low
- Daily Volume
- Number of Shares Owned
- Price Paid per Share
- Total Dollar Value of Investment
- Percentage Change
- Dollar Amount Change

Figure 7.7 shows a drawing of the `StockTablePanel` class.

JLabel—PortfolioTotalsPanel

The second component in the Stock Table tab is the portfolio totals. This component will be composed of just two `JLabels` positioned one above each other. Take a look at Figure 7.8 for a drawing of the `PortfolioTotalsPanel`.

Figure 7.7

The StockTablePanel drawing.

Sym	Company	Last	Hi	Lo	Vol	#Shares	$Shares	Total	%Chg	$Chg
Que	Que Pub	50	52	45	4,000	100	30	5,000	66.67	2000

Figure 7.8

The PortfolioTotalsPanel drawing.

Total Dollar Change: +2000
Total Percentage Change: +66.7%

JSplitPane—GraphTabPanel

Now we're ready for the Graph tab. The Graph tab consists of two components:

- Stock Ticker List
- Graph

The panel that will host these two components is named GraphTabPanel and is derived from the JSplitPane; it will be split using a horizontal split so the user can resize the graphing area. Look at Figure 7.9 for a drawing of the GraphTabPanel.

Figure 7.9

The GraphTabPanel drawing.

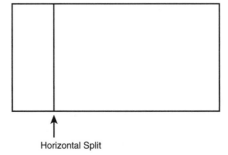

Horizontal Split

JList—TickerListPanel

The first component in the GraphTabPanel is the ticker list; it contains all the stock symbols for the selected portfolio in the PortfolioListPanel. It will be a JList derivative that supports only single selection. Figure 7.10 shows a drawing of the TickerListPanel.

Figure 7.10

The `TickerListPanel`
drawing.

Graphics2D, Line2D—StockGraphPanel

The final component in the `GraphTabPanel` (and our application user interface) is the graphing component. We will use some of the rudimentary Java 2 SDK 2D API (Application Programming Interface) to construct a grid and plot and connect points. We'll call this component `StockGraphPanel`; it is shown in Figure 7.11.

Figure 7.11

The `StockGraphPanel`
drawing.

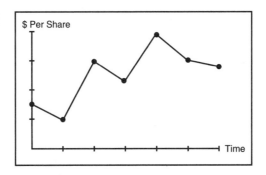

Nested Layout Managers

You might have noticed that almost all the aforementioned class names end with the word `Panel`; this is no coincidence. When you look at the layout of the Stock Tracker application, shown in Figures 7.1 and 7.2, it would certainly be difficult to find one layout manager to build that user interface. I would venture to say that it could be done, with a gridbag layout and many painful constraints, but I know I wouldn't want to try!

Although a clever programmer could build this user interface with a single layout manager, an even more clever programmer might start looking at lightweight containers and their derivation trees. Let's look at `JPanel` for a second. What does its derivation tree look like? Take a look at Figure 7.12.

Figure 7.12

The JPanel derivation tree.

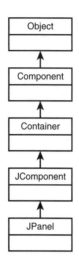

Now let's look at how components are added to containers: through their add methods. There are many add methods, each taking different parameters, but what do they all have in common? Although they have different parameters, the common denominator for all the add methods is the component that is being added: a Component derivative.

But wait a minute: The JPanel is a Component derivative. Does that mean that we can add a JPanel to a container the same way we add a JButton? Yes! We can add JPanels to containers the exact same way we add any other components! Furthermore, we can specify a layout manager inside our JPanel class.

All of a sudden, this looks easy. Adding components to a JPanel with a specified layout manager and then adding JPanels to an application container with its own layout manager is called *nesting layout managers*. Let's take a look at some examples from the Stock Tracker application to see how this is done.

Let's take a look at the Stock Tracker application itself (see Figure 7.13).

The Stock Tracker application layout, shown in Figure 7.13, is a simple example of this idea. The JFrame that parents the application has a BorderLayout layout manager with the StockTabPanel at the top (NORTH) and the PortfolioListPanel occupying the bottom (SOUTH). Each of these components has its own layout manager; both happen to be border layouts as well. Inside the tab control are both the stock table and the portfolio totals; the stock table is another border layout, and the portfolio totals panel is a grid layout.

Figure 7.13

The Stock Tracker application layout.

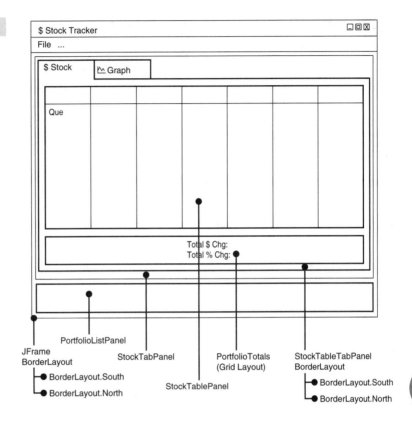

When you break these components down into their own layouts, they are all incredibly simple to classify. When you understand that Figure 7.13 (which is incredibly complicated from a single layout manager perspective) is merely a combination of one meaningful border layout, three border layouts that occupy the entire area of the container, and one grid layout with two rows and one column, it makes things easy.

This technique can help you easily generate complicated-looking applications.

Panels

One last note on panels before we start building the application. Each of the components is derived from `JPanel`, and each component has a `main` method in it so that we can create each component and test it without needing the entire application. This modular design makes it easy to pick up a component and drop it into another application.

Now I think we are ready to create the components. Let's go!

Implementing the Stock Tracker User Interface

When we were deriving the components for this application, we started with the containers and worked our way down to the components. In this section, when we are building our components, we are going to do the opposite: We are going to start with the components and then build the containers around them. This way, we can see our components before the entire application is built. Here is the order in which we are going to approach these components:

- Stock Table tab:
  - StockTablePanel
  - PortfolioTotalsPanel
  - StockTableTabPanel
- Graph tab:
  - TickerListPanel
  - StockGraphPanel
  - GraphTabPanel
- Parent application:
  - StockTabPanel
  - PortfolioListPanel
  - MainMenu
  - StockApplication

One last note: We are going to build all our components in separate Java files and then put them all together in the end to build our application. This makes the components easier to modify and maintain.

StockTablePanel

The first component we are going to talk about is the StockTablePanel. This component is a JTable that is not all that different from the JTable we used in the JTableExample application back in Chapter 5, "User Interface Design with Swing." The structure of the application is the same as in that example. The part that distinguishes this application from the other is the table model.

Think back to Chapter 5 when we were talking about table models. A JTable gets all its column information and table cell values from the table model. Our table model in the Chapter 5 example was very simplistic. Moreover, we did not persist any data in the table at all. We simply computed each table cell value on-the-fly as the row number multiplied by the column number. Although this demonstrated how to use tables and table models, we need something more substantial in our table: enter the StockTableModel.

The StockTableModel is not the final one we are going to be using; as a matter of fact we are going to change the internal data represented in it in Chapter 8, "Implementing Portfolios," when we start talking about portfolios. But for now, we need something meaningful to store in the table model. We are going to need to persist the information shown in Table 7.3.

Table 7.3   Stock Table Fields

Field	Data Type
Ticker Symbol	String
Company Name	String
Last Sale	Float
High	Float
Low	Float
Volume	Double
Number of Shares Owned	Float
Purchase Price per Share	Float
Total Holdings	Float
Percent Change	Float
Dollar Change	Float

Therefore, in the stock table we want to store String, Float, and Double values. Probably the simplest way to do this is to create an array of Objects because these classes are all derived from Object. We are creating an array because we are just going to display a fixed number of values to the user, and we will not permit updates yet. Another point to consider before we start is that the table is a two-dimensional representation of data, so in other words, we must represent two dimensions—we need a two-dimensional array.

A two-dimensional array can be thought of as a table. Take a look at Figure 7.14 for an example of a two-dimensional array.

Figure 7.14

A two-dimensional array.

	Col 0	Col 1	Col 2	Col 3
Row 0	(0, 0)	(0, 1)	(0, 2)	(0, 3)
Row 1	(1, 0)	(1, 1)	(1, 2)	(1, 3)
Row 2	(2, 0)	(2, 1)	(2, 2)	(2, 3)
Row 3	(3, 0)	(3, 1)	(3, 2)	(3, 3)
Row 4	(4, 0)	(4, 1)	(4, 2)	(4, 3)

This two-dimensional array is a 5-row by 4-column array (hence a 5×4 array.) So to create an uninitialized 5×4 array of objects, you would do the following:

```
Object[][] objectArray = new Object[5][4];
```

To create an initialized array, you would just explicitly list the values when creating the array. For example, you might do the following to create a 3×2 array of `int`s:

```
int[][] intArray = {
                          {0, 1},
                          {2, 3},
                          {4, 5},
                  };
```

And then to access one of these values, you would do the following:

```
// Format: intArray[row][col]
int value1 = intArray[0][0];      // = 0
int value2 = intArray[1][0];      // = 2
int value3 = intArray[2][1];      // = 5
```

Aside from the two-dimensional array of table data, we need a one-dimensional `String` array of column names.

Table 7.4 displays all the methods we are going to implement in the `StockTableModel` class.

Table 7.4 `StockTableModel` Methods

Method	*Description*
`getColumnCount`	Returns the number of columns—the length of the string array.
`getRowCount`	Returns the number of rows—the length of the two-dimensional data array.
`getColumnName(col)`	Returns the name of the specified column.
`getValueAt(row,col)`	Returns the data `Object` in the two-dimensional array at (row, col).

Method	Description
getColumnClass(col)	Returns the class type of the Object in the two-dimensional array at (row, col).
isCellEditable(row,col)	Returns true if the cell is editable, false otherwise.
setValueAt(value,row,col)	Sets the cell at (row, col) to value.
getColumnWidth(col)	Our own method to determine column widths for the specified column.
getNumberString(str)	This method is used to validate input for a number field (ensures it is a number).

Okay, so we know how we are going to store data in the table model and what methods we are going to implement. Let's go ahead and take a look at the source code, and then we can go over it when we are finished. Take a look at Listing 7.1.

Type the code from Listing 7.1, excluding line numbers, into your favorite text editor and save it as StockTablePanel.java, or copy it from the CD. Build it as follows:

```
javac StockTablePanel.java
java StockTablePanel
```

Listing 7.1 `StockTablePanel.java`

```
1:  // Import the libraries this application will use
2:  import javax.swing.JTable;
3:  import javax.swing.table.*;
4:  import javax.swing.JScrollPane;
5:  import javax.swing.JFrame;
6:  import javax.swing.SwingUtilities;
7:  import javax.swing.JOptionPane;
8:  import javax.swing.JPanel;
9:  import java.awt.*;
10: import java.awt.event.*;
11:
12: // Main application class:  StockTablePanel
13: public class StockTablePanel extends JPanel
14: {
15:     // Constructor
16:     public StockTablePanel()
17:     {
18:         // Create a new Stock Table Model object
19:         StockTableModel stockTableModel = new StockTableModel();
20:
21:         // Create a new JTable and associate it with the StockTableModel
22:         JTable stockTable = new JTable( stockTableModel );
23:
24:         // Set the size of the table
```

continues

7

Listing 7.1   continued

```
25:              stockTable.setPreferredScrollableViewportSize(
                                          new Dimension(620, 350) );
26:
27:              // Set the column widths for the table
28:              TableColumn column = null;
29:
30:              for (int i = 0; i < 11; i++)
31:              {
32:                  column = stockTable.getColumnModel().getColumn( i );
33:                column.setPreferredWidth( stockTableModel.getColumnWidth( i ) );
34:              }
35:
36:              // Create a scroll pane and add the stock table to it
37:              JScrollPane scrollPane = new JScrollPane( stockTable );
38:
39:              // Add the scroll pane to our panel
40:              add( scrollPane, BorderLayout.CENTER );
41:
42:      }
43:
44:      // Main entry point into the StockTableApplication class
45:      public static void main( String[] args )
46:      {
47:          // Create a frame to hold us and set its title
48:          JFrame frame = new JFrame( "StockTablePanel Application" );
49:
50:          // Create an instance of our stock table panel
51:          StockTablePanel stockTablePanel = new StockTablePanel();
52:
53:          // Add our tab panel to the frame
54:          frame.getContentPane().add( stockTablePanel, BorderLayout.CENTER );
55:
56:          // Resize the frame
57:          frame.setSize(640, 480);
58:
59:          // Make the windows visible
60:          frame.setVisible( true );
61:
62:          // Set up a window listener to close the application window as soon
63:          // as the application window closes
64:          frame.addWindowListener
65:          (
66:              new WindowAdapter()
67:              {
68:                  public void windowClosing( WindowEvent e )
69:                  {
70:                      System.exit( 0 );
71:                  }
72:              }
73:          );
```

```
74:
75:     }
76:
77:     // Table Model Class - holds all of our row and column information
78:     class StockTableModel extends AbstractTableModel
79:     {
80:         // Create the columns for the table
81:         final String[] strArrayColumnNames =
82:         {
83:             "Sym",
84:             "Company Name",
85:             "Last",
86:             "Hi",
87:             "Lo",
88:             "Vol",
89:             "#Shares",
90:             "$Shares",
91:             "Total",
92:             "%Change",
93:             "$Change"
94:         };
95:
96:         // Create the rows for the table - hard coded for now!!
97:         final Object[][] obArrayData =
98:         {
99:             // Row One
100:            {
101:                "QUE",                      // Symbol
102:                "QUE Publishing",           // Company Name
103:                new Float( 10 ),            // Last Sale
104:                new Float( 12 ),            // High
105:                new Float( 8 ),             // Low
106:                new Double( 2000000 ),      // Volume
107:                new Float( 100 ),           // Number of Shares Owned
108:                new Float( 7.5 ),           // Purchase price per share
109:                new Float( 1000 ),          // Total Holdings
110:                new Float( 33 ),            // Percent change (increase!)
111:                new Float( 250 )            // Dollar change
112:            },
113:
114:            // Row Two
115:            {
116:                "Good",                     // Symbol
117:                "Good Company",             // Company Name
118:                new Float( 50 ),            // Last Sale
119:                new Float( 52 ),            // High
120:                new Float( 45 ),            // Low
121:                new Double( 4000000 ),      // Volume
122:                new Float( 100 ),           // Number of Shares Owned
123:                new Float( 30 ),            // Purchase price per share
```

continues

Listing 7.1 continued

```
124:                        new Float( 5000 ),      // Total Holdings
125:                        new Float( 33 ),        // Percent change (increase!)
126:                        new Float( 250 )        // Dollar change
127:                    },
128:
139:                    // Row Three
130:                    {
131:                        "BAD",                  // Symbol
132:                        "Bad Company",          // Company Name
133:                        new Float( 20 ),        // Last Sale
134:                        new Float( 22 ),        // High
135:                        new Float( 18 ),        // Low
136:                        new Double( 2000000 ),  // Volume
137:                        new Float( 500 ),       // Number of Shares Owned
138:                        new Float( 50 ),        // Purchase price per share
139:                        new Float( 10000 ),     // Total Holdings
140:                        new Float( -60 ),       // Percent change (increase!)
141:                        new Float( -25000 )     // Dollar change
142:                    }
143:                };
144:
145:            // Return the number of columns in the table
146:            public int getColumnCount()
147:                {
148:                    return strArrayColumnNames.length;
149:                }
150:
151:            // Return the number of rows in the table
152:            public int getRowCount()
153:                {
154:                    return obArrayData.length;
155:                }
156:
157:            // Get the column name from the strArrayColumnNames array
158:            // for the "col"-th item
159:            public String getColumnName( int col )
160:                    {
161:                    return strArrayColumnNames[col];
162:                }
163:
164:            // Return the value, in the form of an Object, from the
165:            // obArrayData objectarray at position (row, col)
166:            public Object getValueAt( int row, int col )
167:                {
168:                    // We will compute columns 8, 9, and 10, so if the column
169:                    // number is below eight, we can just return it without
170:                    // computing or retrieving anything.
171:                    if( col < 8 )
172:                    {
173:                        return obArrayData[row][col];
```

```
174:                }
175:
176:                // Retrieve the necessary values from the object array to
177:                // compute all the remaining columns
178:                Float fLastSale = ( Float )obArrayData[row][2];
179:                Float fNumberOfShares = ( Float )obArrayData[row][6];
180:                Float fPurchasePrice = ( Float )obArrayData[row][7];
181:
182:                switch( col )
183:                {
184:                 // Total Holdings = Last Sale(2) * Number of Shares Owned(6)
185:                    case 8:
186:
187:                        // Build a new Float object with the product of the two
188:                        Float fTotal = new  Float
189:                    (
190:                        // Note, these have to be converted to type "float" to
191:                        // perform the multiplication
192:                        fLastSale.floatValue() * fNumberOfShares.floatValue()
193:                            );
194:
195:                        // Return the result
196:                        return( fTotal );
197:
198:                // Percent change =
199:                //  (Last Sale Price (2) / Purchase Price (7)) * 100%  - 100 %
200:                        case 9:
201:
202:                        Float fPercentChange = new  Float
203:                        (
204:     ((fLastSale.floatValue() / fPurchasePrice.floatValue  ()) * 100) - 100
205:                        );
206:
207:                        return fPercentChange;
208:
209:                    // Dollar Change =
210:                //   LastSale*NumberOfShares - PurchasePrice * NumberOfShares
211:                        case 10:
212:
213:                        Float fDollarChange = new Float
214:                    (
215:         ( fLastSale.floatValue() * fNumberOfShares.floatValue() )
216:                        -
217:         ( fPurchasePrice.floatValue() * fNumberOfShares.floatValue() )
218:                            );
219:
220:                        return fDollarChange;
221:
222:                // We have included every case so far, but in case we add another
223:                // column and forget about it, let's just return its value
```

continues

Listing 7.1   continued

```
224:                default:
225:                    return obArrayData[row][col];
226:            }
227:        }
228:
229:        // Return the class type, in the form of a Class, for the c-th
                    column in
230:        // the first (0-th indexed) element of the obArrayData object
                    array
231:        public Class getColumnClass( int c )
232:          {
233:            return getValueAt(0, c).getClass();
234:        }
235:
236:        // Return true if the "col"-th column of the table is editable,
237:        // false otherwise.  The following columns are editable:
238:        //
239:        //      Cell        Description
240:        //      ----        -----------
241:        //       0          Symbol
242:        //       6          Number of Shares Owned
243:        //       7          Purchase Price per Share
244:        public boolean isCellEditable(int row,  int col)
245:          {
246:            // Check the column number
247:            if( col == 0 || col == 6 || col == 7 )
248:            {
249:                return true;
250:            }
251:            else
252:            {
253:                return false;
254:            }
255:        }
256:
257:    // Set the value of the (row, col) element of the obArrayData to value
258:        public void setValueAt(Object value, int row, int col)
259:          {
260:            // Symbol
261:            if( col == 0 )
262:            {
263:                // We need a string value - we can convert any
264:                // value to a string, so just assign it
265:                obArrayData[row][col] = value;
266:            }
267:
268:            // Number of Shares owned
269:            else if( col == 6 )
270:            {
271:                // We need a number - either float or int
```

```
272:                        obArrayData[row][col] = new Float( getNumberString(
                                              value.toString() ) );
273:                }
274:
275:                // Purchase Price per share
276:                else if( col == 7 )
277:                {
278:                    // We need a float
279:                    obArrayData[row][col] = new Float( getNumberString(
                                              value.toString() ) );
280:                }
281:
282:                // Cell is not editable
283:                else
284:                {
285:                    return;
286:                }
287:
288:                // Notify our parent of the change
289:                fireTableCellUpdated(row, col);
290:        }
291:
292:        // String getNumberString( String str )
293:        //
294:        // Read through str and return a new string with the numbers and
295:        // decimal points contained in str
296:        public String getNumberString( String str )
297:        {
298:            // Get str as a character array
299:            char[] strSource = str.toCharArray();
300:
301:            // Create a buffer to copy the results into
302:            char[] strNumbers = new char[strSource.length];
303:            int nNumbersIndex = 0;
304:
305:            // Boolean to ensure we only have one decimal value
306:            // in our number
307:            boolean bFoundDecimal = false;
308:
309:            // Loop through all values of str
310:            for( int i=0; i<strSource.length; i++ )
311:            {
312:                // Check for a digit or decimal point
313:                if( Character.isDigit( strSource[i] ) )
314:                {
315:                    strNumbers[nNumbersIndex++] = strSource[i];
316:                }
317:                else if( strSource[i] == '.' && !bFoundDecimal )
318:                {
319:                    // Append the character to the String
```

continues

Listing 7.1   continued

```
320:                        strNumbers[nNumbersIndex++] = strSource[i];
321:
322:                        // Note that we found the decimal value
323:                        bFoundDecimal = true;
324:                    }
325:                }
326:
327:                // Build a new string to return to our caller
328:                String strReturn = new String(strNumbers, 0, nNumbersIndex);
329:
330:                // Return our string
331:                return strReturn;
332:            }
333:
334:            // Return the column width of the column at index nCol
335:            public int getColumnWidth( int nCol )
336:            {
337:                switch( nCol )
338:                {
339:                    case 0:
340:                    case 2:
341:                    case 3:
342:                    case 4:
343:                    case 6:
344:                    case 7:
345:                    case 9:
346:                        return 50;
347:                    case 1:
348:                        return 125;
349:                    default:
350:    return 75;
351:                }
352:            }
353:        }
354:}
```

Figure 7.15 shows the StockTablePanel application. You might need to adjust the width of the columns to display properly on your computer.

First, take a look at the import lines (2–10). Notice how we import only the classes we need instead of importing all of them as we did in the past. This reduces compile time but doesn't have an effect on file size—it's just a programmer decision.

The main method in the StockTablePanel is identical to the ones we had earlier: Create a JFrame, create an instance of the StockTablePanel class, add the StockTablePanel to the JFrame, resize it, and make it visible. Simple stuff now, eh?

Figure 7.15

The StockTablePanel
application.

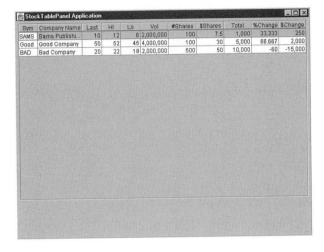

The constructor is more of the same old stuff too!

```
19:        StockTableModel stockTableModel = new StockTableModel();
```

Line 19 creates an instance of the StockTableModel, which I'll describe a little later.

```
22:        JTable stockTable = new JTable( stockTableModel );
```

Line 22 creates a new JTable object with the StockTableModel instance that we just created as the table's model.

```
28:        TableColumn column = null;
30:        for (int i = 0; i < 11; i++)
31:        {
32:            column = stockTable.getColumnModel().getColumn( i );
33:                column.setPreferredWidth(
                        stockTableModel.getColumnWidth( i ) );
34:        }
```

Lines 28–34 loop through all the columns in the table and set the preferred size for each (obtained from the table model).

```
37:        JScrollPane scrollPane = new JScrollPane( stockTable );
```

Line 37 creates a new JScrollPane and adds the stockTable JTable to it. Because of this, if the table is too large to display, scrollbars will appear and allow the user to scroll through the nonvisible regions of the table.

```
40:        add( scrollPane, BorderLayout.CENTER );
```

Finally, line 40 adds the JScrollPane to the JPanel.

7

Okay, on to the more complicated part: the StockTableModel. First let's look at our StockTableModel attributes:

```
final String[] strArrayColumnNames = ...
                 {
                            "Sym",
                       "Company Name",
                       "Last",
                       "Hi",
                       "Lo",
                       "Vol",
                       "#Shares",
                       "$Shares",
                       "Total",
                       "%Change",
                       "$Change"
                 }
```

strArrayColumnNames is a String array that contains the 11 fields we mentioned earlier.

```
final Object[][] obArrayData = ...
```

obArrayData is the two-dimensional array of Objects that we talked about earlier. In lines 97–143, we define three rows of 11 columns. Note that all the nonstring values are newly created class types (Float instead of float and Double instead of double). The reason for this is that our data structure (array) that is holding our data holds objects derived from Object. A float is not derived from Object, but a Float is; see the difference?

Now, let's take the StockTableModel apart method by method.

getColumnCount

The getColumnCount method returns the number of columns in the table by returning the length of the column name array. The length field of a one-dimensional array represents the number of elements in the array.

```
148:              return strArrayColumnNames.length;
```

getRowCount

The getRowCount method returns the number of rows in the table by returning the length of the object data array. The length field of a two-dimensional array returns the number of items in the first dimension. Our array has three rows of 11 items, or is a 3×11 array. The length of this array is 3.

```
154:              return obArrayData.length;
```

getColumnName

The `getColumnName` method returns the name of the specified column by returning the specified array element from the column name array:

```
161:            return strArrayColumnNames[col];
```

getValueAt

Now the `getValueAt` method is a little more complicated, but just a little. For our first eight columns, our model simply holds values that it passes back to the `JTable` when it wants them. So line 173 simply returns the specified array element:

```
173:                return obArrayData[row][col];
```

The last three columns in the table are computed, however. Here are the formulas used for each column:

```
Total Holdings = Last Sale * Number of Shares Owned

Percent change =  (Last Sale Price / Purchase Price) * 100%  - 100 %

Dollar Change = LastSale*NumberOfShares - PurchasePrice*NumberOfShares
```

The rest of the method simply computes and returns the specified value. One thing of interest in this method is the `switch` statement. This method determines what value to return based on the column number, which is determined using a `switch` statement. The `switch` statement is really only a glorified `if` statement. It is prototyped as follows:

```
switch( intValue )
{
    case valueOne:
        // do valueOne stuff
        statement;
        break;

    case valueTwo:
        // do valueTwo stuff
        statement;
        break;

    default:
        // do default stuff
        statement;
}
```

The way this statement works is that the `intValue`, which can be a variable of type `int` or any expression that evaluates to an `int`, is compared to `valueOne` and `valueTwo`. Both `valueOne` and `valueTwo` are called cases and are prefaced with the keyword case (there is no limit to the number of cases you can have). If `intValue` is equal to `valueOne`, the statements associated with `valueOne` are processed. If `intValue` is equal to `valueTwo`, the statements associated with `valueTwo` are processed. If `intValue` is not equal to any of the `cases` presented, the default statements are processed; the `default` keyword denotes the starting point of the default statements.

You might be wondering what that `break` statement is for in there. Well, the `switch` statement does not have the logic to process only the statements for a given case; it simply starts execution at the location of the `case`. So if the `break` statement were not present after the `valueOne` statements, the `valueTwo` statements would also be processed. The `break` statement tells the compiler to break out of the `switch` statement and continue at the line just following it.

To help you understand what this is doing in familiar terms, let me rewrite this `switch-case` statement as an `if-then-else` statement:

```
if( intValue == valueOne )
{
     // do valueOne stuff
     statement;
}
else if( intValue == valueTwo )
{
     // do valueTwo stuff
     statement;
}
else
{
     // do default stuff
     statement;
}
```

In this small example, it might have been easier to write the `if` equivalent, but if you were comparing all 11 columns, 11 `if` statements would be much uglier than one `case` statement.

getColumnClass

The `getColumnClass` method returns the class type of the specified column. This is accomplished by retrieving the first element in the column with a call to `getValueAt` (which we just talked about) and then calling that `Object`'s `getClass` method:

```
233:              return getValueAt(0, c).getClass();
```

The class of the column is used by the table to know what values are possible to include in the column.

isCellEditable

The isCellEditable methodreturns true if the specified cell is editable, false otherwise. Our implementation of this method returns true for columns 0, 6, and 7: ticker symbol, number of shares owned, and price paid per share, respectively. All the rest of the columns are either retrieved from the Internet or computed.

setValueAt

The setValueAt method is an interesting one. When the user double-clicks a cell, that cell's isEditable method is called. If the cell is editable, a cursor appears in the cell and the user can modify its value. When the user finishes editing the cell, the table model's setValueAt method is called with the modified object and cell location. Now it is the responsibility of the table model to validate the modified object and update its internal data structures.

Our implementation of the setValueAt method simply updates the String value in our object array if the update is to a cell in the first column (ticker symbol). But if the cell being edited is from either column 6 or 7, we must validate the object to ensure that it is a float value.

Note The object array does not care whatsoever if you put a text String in a Float field. They are both derived from Object, but the JTable is not so forgiving. Remember our getColumnClass method? The JTable displays the value of a cell based on its class type, and if you try to display a Float as String, you are going to have some problems.

The value of the object passed to the setValueAt method is not really validated as either being a float or not. Instead, we extract only the numbers and first decimal point from whatever input the user entered. You might recall this exact sequence of steps from our JTextField example in Chapter 5 when we created our NumberDocument that accepted only numbers (actually I took the code straight from there). Anyway, we have another method that does this extraction for us: getNumberString.

What our setValueAt method does is convert the object value to a String using its toString method; pass that value to our getNumberString method, which returns a string of numbers; create a new Float value from that String; and then add that value to our data array.

When the setValueAt method is complete, it tells the table that the data in the cell we just edited changed by calling the fireTableCellUpdated() method.

getNumberString

The getNumberString, as I already mentioned, is taken directly from the JTextFieldExample in Chapter 5, but here is a quick summary:

1. Convert the string to an array of characters.
2. Create another array of characters to hold the output.
3. Loop through all the characters in the source string and copy all digits and the first decimal point to the output string.
4. Convert the output character array to a String value and return that to the caller.

getColumnWidth

Finally, the getColumnWidth method is a method of our own creation that tells the JTable how wide we would like our columns to be. If you read through that method, you will notice another switch statement, but this time there seem to be quite a few empty statements and some missing break statements. Well, remember when we were talking about switch statements and mentioned that if the break statement was not present, the compiler would continue processing statements for the next case. This can be done on purpose and is called *falling through*.

What we are doing is saying for cases 0, 2, 3, 4, 6, 7, and 9, return 50. Isn't that neat? We have to write only one return statement instead of seven! A last note about switch statements is that break statements are never required, but for most of your functionality you will need them. Our example returns from inside the cases, so there is no need for any break statements.

And that is all this method does: It returns the column width for the requested column.

PortfolioTotalsPanel

The portfolio totals panel is probably our most simple component. It is a JPanel with two JLabels on it: the dollar amount change for the portfolio and the percentage change for the portfolio. We are going to add to this class later in the chapter, but for now take a look at Listing 7.2.

Type the code from Listing 7.2, excluding line numbers, into your favorite text editor and save it as PortfolioTotalsPanel.java, or copy it from the CD. Build it as follows:

```
javac PortfolioTotalsPanel.java
java PortfolioTotalsPanel
```

Listing 7.2 `PortfolioTotalsPanel.java`

```
1:   // Import the packages used by this class
2:   import javax.swing.*;
3:   import javax.swing.event.*;
4:
5:   import java.awt.*;
6:   import java.awt.event.*;
7:
8:   // PortfolioTotalsPanel Class
9:   public class PortfolioTotalsPanel extends JPanel
10:  {
11:      // Create our labels
12:      JLabel lblDollarChange =
                    new JLabel( "Dollar Change: $1000", JLabel.CENTER );
13:      JLabel lblPercentChange =
                    new JLabel( "Percent Change: 50%", JLabel.CENTER );
14:
15:      // Constructor
16:      public PortfolioTotalsPanel()
17:      {
18:          // Set the layout manager
19:          setLayout( new GridLayout( 2, 1 ) );
20:
21:          // Add the labels to the JPanel
22:          add( lblDollarChange );
23:          add( lblPercentChange );
24:      }
25:
26:      // Main application entry point into this class
27:      public static void main( String[] args )
28:      {
29:          // Create a JFrame object
30:          JFrame frame = new JFrame( "Portfolio Totals" );
31:
32:          // Create a PortfolioTotalsPanel Object
33:          PortfolioTotalsPanel app = new PortfolioTotalsPanel();
34:
35:          // Add our PortfolioTotalsPanel Object to the JFrame
36:          frame.getContentPane().add( app, BorderLayout.CENTER );
37:
38:          // Resize our JFrame
39:          frame.setSize( 600, 100 );
40:
41:          // Make our JFrame visible
42:          frame.setVisible( true );
43:
44:          // Create a window listener to close our application when we
45:          // close our application
46:          frame.addWindowListener
```

7

continues

Listing 7.2   continued

```
47:        (
48:               new WindowAdapter()
49:             {
50:                public void windowClosing( WindowEvent e )
51:                  {
52:  System.exit( 0 );
53:                  }
54:             }
55:         );
56:     }
57: }
```

Figure 7.16 shows the `PortfolioTotalsPanel` application.

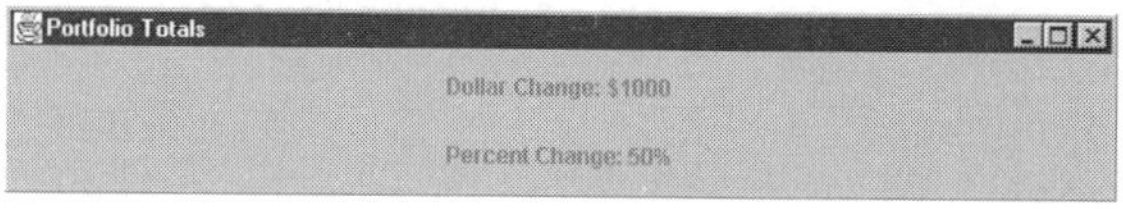

Figure 7.16

The
`PortfolioTotalsPanel`
application.

This component should be very familiar—it looks similar to all the examples in the last chapter, only simpler!

```
12:     JLabel lblDollarChange =
                        new JLabel( "Dollar Change:", JLabel.CENTER );
13:     JLabel lblPercentChange =
                        new JLabel("Percent Change:", JLabel.CENTER );
```

Lines 12 and 13 create two text labels that are center aligned. Recall from that last chapter that we explicitly called the `JLabel` method `setHorizontalAlignment` to set the horizontal alignment, but now we are just setting it in the constructor. The other method was more explicit, but this is shorter and cleaner.

```
22:         add( lblDollarChange );
23:         add( lblPercentChange );
```

Lines 22 and 23 add our labels to our `JPanel`.

See, I told you that one was simple!

StockTableTabPanel

The `StockTableTabPanel` is more than a panel that puts together the `StockTablePanel` and `PortfolioTotalsPanel`; it coordinates the communication between the two components.

First and foremost, it is a panel that contains the two components, combining the two using a `BorderLayout` with the table at the `NORTH` side and the totals panel at the `SOUTH` side. Both components are imported into the `StockTableTabPanel` using the same `import` directive we have been using to import Java packages, and the source files for those classes are included in the same directory.

Now what communications do we need between the two components and how are those communications realized?

We need three forms of communication:

- The `StockTableTabPanel` needs an interface to ask the `StockTablePanel` to compute its total dollar and percentage changes.
- The `StockTableTabPanel` needs an interface to tell the `PortfolioTotalsPanel` to update its labels.
- The `StockTablePanel` needs an interface to inform the `StockTableTabPanel` when its table model data has changed.

An interface in the previous context does not refer to the Java interface, but is similar in concept. When you're defining an object (or class, if you prefer) that is going to be used by other objects, it must specify a *public interface*, or *interface* for short, that other objects will use to manipulate that object. In programming terms, all public methods and public properties (member variables) comprise the public interface.

To facilitate the communication between the `StockTableTabPanel` and the `StockTablePanel`, we are going to add two public methods to the `StockTablePanel` that, when invoked, will return the respective dollar and percent changes for the data in the stock table. Here are the prototypes for these methods:

```
public float getDollarChange()
public float getPercentChange()
```

The `getDollarChange` method returns a `float` value representing the dollar amount change in the user's portfolio, and the `getPercentChange` method returns the percentage change in the user's portfolio.

The `getDollarChange` method is implemented as follows:

```
1:    public float getDollarChange()
2:    {
3:        // Create a variable to hold the total change for all stocks
4:        float fTotal = 0;
5:
6:        // Loop through all rows in the table
7:        for( int i=0; i<stockTable.getRowCount(); i++ )
8:        {
9:            // Retrieve the dollar change for this stock
10:           Float f = ( Float )stockTable.getValueAt( i, 10 );
11:
12:           // Add that value to our total
13:           fTotal = fTotal + f.floatValue();
```

7

```
14:      }
15:
16:      // Return the total change
17:      return fTotal;
18:  }
```

To summarize, this methodmaintains a variable, fTotal, that holds the total dollar amount change in the user's portfolio. The method loops through each row of the table and extracts the dollar change field (column 10) using the JTable method getValueAt. It then adds that change to the total change amount and finally returns that value to the caller.

The getPercentChange method does the functional equivalent for the percentage change. It is implemented as follows:

```
1:  public float getPercentChange()
2:  {
3:      // Create a couple variables to hold the total the user spent
4:      // on the stocks and the current value of those stocks
5:      float fMoneySpent = 0;
6:      float fMoneyWorth = 0;
7:
8:      // Loop through all rows in the table
9:      for( int i=0; i<stockTable.getRowCount(); i++ )
10:     {
11:         // Extract some pertinent information for the computations
12:         Float fLastSale = ( Float )stockTable.getValueAt( i, 2 );
13:         Float fNumberOfShares = ( Float )stockTable.getValueAt( i, 6 );
14:         Float fPricePaidPerShare = ( Float )stockTable.getValueAt( i, 7 );
15:
16:         // Add the amount of money the user spent on this stock
17:         // to the total spent
18:         fMoneySpent += fNumberOfShares.floatValue() *
                                    fPricePaidPerShare.floatValue();
19:
20:         // Add the value of this stock to the total value of the
21:         // stock
22:         fMoneyWorth += fNumberOfShares.floatValue() *
                                    fLastSale.floatValue();
23:     }
24:
25:     // Compute the percentage change:
26:     // TotalValue/TotalSpent * 100% - 100%
27:     float fPercentChange = ( (fMoneyWorth / fMoneySpent) * 100 ) - 100;
28:
29:     // Return the percentage change
30:     return fPercentChange;
31: }
```

Now the only thing complicated in this method is that we have to compute the percentage changes as follows:

```
Value of the portfolio

--------------------    *  100%  -  100%

Amount Spent on portfolio
```

So, the getPercentChange method loops through all rows in the table and computes the total value of the portfolio and the dollar amount spent on the portfolio. It then computes the change based on this formula and returns that amount to the caller.

The next form of communication, between the StockTableTabPanel and the PortfolioTotalsPanel, is facilitated similarly by adding two public methods to the PortfolioTotalsPanel: setDollarChange and setPercentChange. These methods both accept a floating-point value and set the text of their corresponding labels to include the specified value. Furthermore, the methods change the color of the label to a dark green if the portfolio is positive, black if it is neutral, and red if it is negative. Take a look at the following code, extracted from the new PortfolioTotalsPanel:

```
 1: public final static Color darkGreen = new Color( 0, 150, 40 );
 2:
 3: public void setDollarChange( Float fDollarChange )
 4: {
 5:     // Set color based on value
 6:     if( fDollarChange.floatValue() > 0 )
 7:     {
 8:         // Green for positive
 9:         lblDollarChange.setForeground( darkGreen );
10:     }
11:     else if( fDollarChange.floatValue() < 0 )
12:     {
13:         // Red for negative
14:         lblDollarChange.setForeground( Color.red );
15:     }
16:     else
17:     {
18:         // Black for no change
19:         lblDollarChange.setForeground( Color.black );
20:     }
21:
22:     // Set the label text
23:     lblDollarChange.setText( "Dollar Change: $" +
                                     fDollarChange.toString() );
24: }
25:
26: public void setPercentChange( Float fPercentChange )
27: {
```

7

```
28:     // Set color based on value
29:     if( fPercentChange.floatValue() > 0 )
30:     {
31:         // Green for positive
32:         lblPercentChange.setForeground( darkGreen );
33:     }
34:     else if( fPercentChange.floatValue() < 0 )
35:     {
36:         // Red for negative
37:         lblPercentChange.setForeground( Color.red );
38:     }
39:     else
40:     {
41:         // Black for no change
42:         lblPercentChange.setForeground( Color.black );
43:     }
44:
45:     // Set the label text
46:     lblPercentChange.setText( "Percent Change: " +
                                    fPercentChange.toString() + "%" );
47: }
```

First, line 1 creates a new Color object that represents dark green (the standard green was too bright and unreadable). These methods simply test the values passed to them to set the color and then call setText on the JLabels to read "Dollar Change: $..." and "Percent Change: ... %", respectively.

The final form of communication is between the StockTablePanel and the StockTableTabPanel. In this case we must be notified of changes in the table.

Hmm, changes in a table. That sounds a lot like event handling, doesn't it?

It sure does! We can listen for changes in the TableModel by using the TableModelListener interface. The TableModelListener interface is defined in Table 7.5.

Table 7.5 TableModelListener **Interface**

Method	Description
tableChanged(TableModelEvent e)	This fine-grain notification tells listeners the exact range of cells, rows, or columns that changed.

The tableChanged method accepts a TableModelEvent object, defined in Table 7.6.

Table 7.6 `TableModelEvent` **Object**

Method	Description
`int getColumn()`	Returns the column for the event
`int getFirstRow()`	Returns the first row that changed
`int getLastRow()`	Returns the last row that changed
`int getType()`	Returns the type of event—one of `INSERT`, `UPDATE`, and `DELETE`

These methods, combined with the standard methods inherited from `EventObject` (from the last chapter), enable us to find out which table model generated the event, the type of the event, and the exact cell that changed.

The final thing we need is a way to register ourselves as a listener for table model events. This is accomplished through the `TableModel` interface method `addTableModelListener`.

Here are the steps we must take to handle table model change events:

1. Create a class that implements `TableModelListener`.
2. Call the `TableModel` class's `addTableModelListener` method with our `TableModelListener` implementing class as its argument.
3. Implement the `TableModelListener`'s `tableChanged` method.

Let's take a look at the code for the `StockTableTabPanel` and see how it is implemented here. Take a look at Listing 7.3.

Type the code from Listing 7.3, excluding line numbers, into your favorite text editor and save it as `StockTableTabPanel.java`, or copy it from the CD. You will need to either copy the new `StockTablePanel.java` and `PortfolioTotalsPanel.java` files from the CD or add the aforementioned methods to your previous files (it is just too big to print the entire source code). Build it as follows:

```
javac StockTableTabPanel.java
java StockTableTabPanel
```

Listing 7.3 `StockTableTabPanel.java`

```
1:  // Import the packages used by this class
2:  import javax.swing.*;
3:  import javax.swing.event.*;
4:
5:  import java.awt.*;
6:  import java.awt.event.*;
7:
8:  // Import our other components
```

continues

Listing 7.3   continued

```
 9:  import StockTablePanel;
10:  import PortfolioTotalsPanel;
11:
12:  // StockTableTabPanel
13:  public class StockTableTabPanel extends JPanel
14:                                  implements TableModelListener
15:  {
16:      // Create our panels
17:      StockTablePanel stockTablePanel = new StockTablePanel();
18:      PortfolioTotalsPanel portfolioTotalsPanel =
19:                                  new PortfolioTotalsPanel();
20:
21:      // Constructor
22:      public StockTableTabPanel()
23:      {
24:          // Set our layout
25:          setLayout( new BorderLayout() );
26:
27:          // Initialize the portfolio panel
28:          updatePortfolioTotals();
29:
30:          // Add the child panels to our JPanel
31:          add( stockTablePanel );
32:          add( portfolioTotalsPanel, BorderLayout.SOUTH );
33:
34:          // Add our class as a table model listener for the stock table
35:          // model so that we can update the portfolio totals panel
36:          // whenever the table changes.
37:          stockTablePanel.stockTableModel.addTableModelListener(
                                                              this );
38:      }
39:
40:      // TableModelListener: tableChanged
41:      public void tableChanged(TableModelEvent e)
42:      {
43:          // Make sure it is our table that changed
44:          if( e.getSource() == stockTablePanel.stockTableModel )
45:          {
46:              // Call our method to update the portfolio totals
47:              updatePortfolioTotals();
48:          }
49:      }
50:
51:      // public updatePortfolioTotals
52:      //
53:      // Updates the portfolio totals panel labels based on the values
54:      // in the stockTablePanel
55:      public void updatePortfolioTotals()
56:      {
57:          // Get the values from the stockTablePanel and send them
```

```
58:          // to the portfolioTotalsPanel
59:          portfolioTotalsPanel.setDollarChange(
60:              new Float( stockTablePanel.getDollarChange() ) );
61:          portfolioTotalsPanel.setPercentChange(
62:              new Float( stockTablePanel.getPercentChange() ) );
63:      }
64:
65:      // Main application entry point into this class
66:      public static void main( String[] args )
67:      {
68:          // Create a JFrame object
69:          JFrame frame = new JFrame( "Stock Table Tab" );
70:
71:          // Create a StockTableTabPanel Object
72:          StockTableTabPanel app = new StockTableTabPanel();
73:
74:          // Add our StockTableTabPanel Object to the JFrame
75:          frame.getContentPane().add( app, BorderLayout.CENTER );
76:
77:          // Resize our JFrame
78:          frame.setSize( 640, 440 );
79:
80:          // Make our JFrame visible
81:          frame.setVisible( true );
82:
83:          // Create a window listener to close our application when we
84:          // close our application
85:          frame.addWindowListener
86:          (
87:              new WindowAdapter()
88:              {
89:                  public void windowClosing( WindowEvent e )
90:                  {
91:                      System.exit( 0 );
92:                  }
93:              }
94:          );
95:      }
96: }
```

Figure 7.17 shows the StockTableTabPanel application.

Figure 7.17

The
StockTableTabPanel
application.

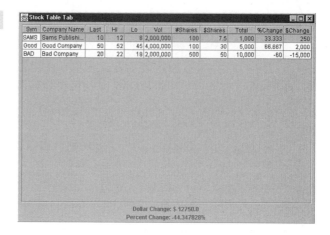

```
 9:  import StockTablePanel;
10:  import PortfolioTotalsPanel;
```

First, lines 9 and 10 import our two other classes. Make sure that you have the .java files in the same directory as this file, and the compiler will not have any problems. This is functionally equivalent to having all your code in one source file, but we really don't want to have all our source code in one file—it would get to be a bit large!

Java allows only one public class per file and the file must be named the same name as the public class with a .java extension. Because of this restriction, you cannot combine multiple public classes into a single file.

```
13: public class StockTableTabPanel extends JPanel
14:                            implements TableModelListener
```

Lines 13 and 14 create our StockTableTabPanel so that it extends JPanel and implements the TableModelListener interface that we discussed earlier.

```
17:     StockTablePanel stockTablePanel = new StockTablePanel();
18:     PortfolioTotalsPanel portfolioTotalsPanel =
19:                          new PortfolioTotalsPanel();
```

Lines 17–19 create the two components that the StockTableTabPanel is going to manage.

```
28:         updatePortfolioTotals();
```

Line 28 calls a method that we are implementing in our `StockTableTabPanel` class called `updatePortfolioTotals`. We will be talking more about it in a minute.

```
37:     stockTablePanel.stockTableModel.addTableModelListener
                                              (this);
```

Line 37 adds our `StockTableTabPanel` as a table model listener for the `StockTablePanel`'s `stockTableModel`. This might look a little tricky, but what we did was to make the `stockTableModel` a public attribute (member variable) of the `StockTablePanel` class so that we could access it at will. We could have put in an access method, such as `getStockTableModel`, to retrieve it for us, but this was the most direct route and we are the only ones using this class for now, so security is not an issue.

```
41:     public void tableChanged(TableModelEvent e)
42:     {
43:         // Make sure it is our table that changed
44:         if( e.getSource() == stockTablePanel.stockTableModel )
45:         {
46:             // Call our method to update the portfolio totals
47:             updatePortfolioTotals();
48:         }
49:     }
```

Lines 41–49 implement the `TableModelListener` class's `tableChanged` method. In this method we verify that our table model generated the event and then call the `updatePortfolioTotals` method to reflect the current values in the `PortfolioTotalsPanel`.

> **Note**
>
> By now, you are used to using `getSource` inside event handlers to get the object that generated the event and comparing the values to ensure that our object generated the event. I'd like to let you in on a little secret: Because we are registering the `StockTableTabPanel` class instance with only one table model, only one can generate the event. This is true of all the event handlers we implemented in the last chapter, so you don't really have to add this comparison.
>
> Why is it there then? I wanted you to get used to doing this so that when you register multiple components (two tables, for example), you will instantly think to find out which one generated the event before responding.

```
55:     public void updatePortfolioTotals()
56:     {
57:         // Get the values from the stockTablePanel and send them
58:         // to the portfolioTotalsPanel
59:         portfolioTotalsPanel.setDollarChange(
60:             new Float( stockTablePanel.getDollarChange() ) );
```

```
61:        portfolioTotalsPanel.setPercentChange(
62:            new Float( stockTablePanel.getPercentChange() ) );
63:    }
```

Okay, here it is: Lines 55–63 define the updatePortfolioTotals method. This method asks the StockTablePanel for its change amounts using the getDollarChange and getPercentChange methods and turns around and sends those values to the PortfolioTotalsPanel using setDollarChange and setPercentChange, respectively.

This method is called initially to put data in the portfolio totals panel and then whenever a tableChanged event is generated. Try changing some of the values in the table, such as purchase price or number of shares owned, and watch the portfolio totals change.

TickerListPanel

The TickerListPanel is also a very simple component: It contains a JList object hosted in a JScrollPane. We are eventually going to add methods to dynamically add items to the list and notification code when the user chooses a new selection, but more on that a little later. You have already seen JLists back in Chapter 5, so for now let's just look at the code and we'll go over it (see Listing 7.4).

Type the code from Listing 7.4, excluding line numbers, into your favorite text editor and save it as TickerListPanel.java, or copy it from the CD. Build it as follows:

```
javac TickerListPanel.java
java TickerListPanel
```

Listing 7.4 `TickerListPanel.java`

```
1:  // Import the packages used by this class
2:  import javax.swing.*;
3:  import javax.swing.event.*;
4:
5:  import java.awt.*;
6:  import java.awt.event.*;
7:
8:  // TickerListPanel
9:  public class TickerListPanel extends JPanel
10: {
11:     // List Model that will hold the data for the list control
12:     DefaultListModel listModelTickers = new DefaultListModel();
13:
14:     // List control
15:     JList listTickers = new JList( listModelTickers );
16:
17:     // Constructor
18:     public TickerListPanel()
19:         {
```

```
20:         // Build our list of symbols (eventually we will look these up!)
21:         listModelTickers.addElement( "SAMS" );
22:         listModelTickers.addElement( "QUE" );
23:         listModelTickers.addElement( "BAD" );
24:
25:         // Set the selection info: single selection, and select the first
                        item
26:         listTickers.setSelectionMode(
                        ListSelectionModel.SINGLE_SELECTION );
27:         listTickers.setSelectedIndex( 0 );
28:
29:         // Create a scroll panel to hold the TickerListPanel JPanel
30:         JScrollPane scrollPaneList = new JScrollPane( listTickers );
31:
32:         // Set our preferred size
33:         scrollPaneList.setPreferredSize( new Dimension(120, 350) );
34:
35:         //Add the scroll pane to this panel.
36:         add( scrollPaneList, BorderLayout.CENTER );
37:     }
38:
39:     // Main application entry point into this class
40:     public static void main( String[] args )
41:     {
42:         // Create a JFrame object
43:         JFrame frame = new JFrame( "Ticker List Panel" );
44:
45:         // Create a TickerListPanel Object
46:         TickerListPanel app = new TickerListPanel();
47:
48:         // Add our TickerListPanel Object to the JFrame
49:         frame.getContentPane().add( app, BorderLayout.CENTER );
50:
51:         // Resize our JFrame
52:         frame.setSize( 200, 400 );
53:
54:         // Make our JFrame visible
55:         frame.setVisible( true );
56:
57:         // Create a window listener to close our application when we
58:         // close our application
59:         frame.addWindowListener
60:         (
61:             new WindowAdapter()
62:             {
63:                 public void windowClosing( WindowEvent e )
64:                 {
65:   System.exit( 0 );
66:                 }
67:             }
68:         );
69:     }
70: }
```

Figure 7.18 shows the `TickerListPanel` application.

Figure 7.18

The `TickerListPanel`
application.

```
12:        DefaultListModel listModelTickers = new DefaultListModel();
```

Line 12 creates a `DefaultListModel` (supplied with the `java.swing` package) for our table to use. We are not going to need to create a custom list model because we are only going to be adding strings to the table and tracking selection changes.

```
15:        JList listTickers = new JList( listModelTickers );
```

Line 15 creates our `JList` object with the `listModelTickers` as our list model.

```
21:            listModelTickers.addElement( "SAMS" );
22:            listModelTickers.addElement( "QUE" );
23:            listModelTickers.addElement( "BAD" );
```

Lines 21–23 add three string elements to our `JList` using the `DefaultListModel` class's `addElement` method.

```
26:            listTickers.setSelectionMode(
                    ListSelectionModel.SINGLE_SELECTION );
```

Line 26 makes this `JList` a single selection list, meaning that only one item in the list can be selected, by calling the `setSelectionMode` method. This makes sense because this list represents the stock our graph will display, and our graph will be able to display only one stock at a time.

```
27:            listTickers.setSelectedIndex( 0 );
```

Line 27 selects the first item in the list, or the zeroth indexed item.

StockGraphPanel

At this point the StockGraphPanel is going to be pretty plain. We will get into our graphing scheme in Chapter 12, "Graphing Historical Data," when we have the data we want to plot, but for now we are just going to instantiate a new Graphics2D object and simply draw the name of our stock symbol in the center of the screen. Sounds easy enough.

The Graphics2D class is quite involved and has many advanced features that I will not have time to cover in this book. I recommend that you read through the Java 2 SDK documentation both on the Graphics2D class as well as the 2D API in general. You can now do some pretty amazing things with Java.

In our example we are going to get into drawing axes and plotting graphs, perfect topics for a business application!

EXCURSION

Constructing a Graphics2D object

One thing of interest to examine before we start is the way a Graphics2D object is constructed. First, all drawing occurs in your **paint** method, which is prototyped as follows:

```
public void paint( Graphics g )
```

The **paint** method is called every time the application must redraw itself for any reason. It is passed a Graphics object; the Graphics object is the drawing surface for the AWT classes. For our application we could use this, but I want to introduce you to the 2D API. Anyway, the Graphics2D class is abstract, so there is no way to construct it directly. Instead, you must cast the Graphics object to the Graphics2D object, as follows:

```
public void paint( Graphics g )
{
        Graphics2D g2d = ( Graphics2D )g;
}
```

At that point you can use the **g2d** object to perform all your painting and drawing using the Graphics2D methods; coincidentally the Graphics2D class is derived from the Graphics class, so you get all that functionality as well.

We are going to talk about graphing in length in Chapter 12, but we need a placeholder right now, so let's look at the code in Listing 7.5.

Type the code from Listing 7.5, excluding line numbers, into your favorite text editor and save it as StockGraphPanel.java, or copy it from the CD. Build it as follows:

```
javac StockGraphPanel.java
java StockGraphPanel
```

Listing 7.5 `StockGraphPanel.java`

```
1:   // Import the packages used by this class
2:   import javax.swing.*;
3:   import javax.swing.event.*;
4:
5:   import java.awt.*;
6:   import java.awt.event.*;
7:
8:   // StockGraphPanel
9:   public class StockGraphPanel extends JPanel
10:  {
11:      // String that will hold our stock ticker symbol
12:      String strSymbol = new String( "QUE" );
13:
14:      // Constructor
15:      public StockGraphPanel()
16:      {
17:          // Set our preferred size
18:          setPreferredSize( new Dimension( 500, 400 ) );
19:      }
20:
21:      // Draw the graph
22:      public void paint(Graphics g)
23:      {
24:          // Get a Graphics2D object
25:          Graphics2D g2 = (Graphics2D) g;
26:
27:          // Get the Dimensions of this JPanel
28:          Dimension d = new Dimension();
29:          getSize(d);
30:
31:          // Set the background to black
32:          g2.setBackground( Color.black );
33:          g2.clearRect( 0, 0, (int)d.getWidth(),
                                            (int)d.getHeight() );
34:
35:          // Write the stock symbol in about the middle of the
                             screen
36:          g2.setColor( Color.cyan );
37:          g2.drawString( strSymbol,
38:                          (int)d.getWidth() / 2,
39:                          (int)d.getHeight() / 2 );
40:
41:      }
42:
43:      // Main application entry point into this class
44:      public static void main( String[] args )
45:      {
46:          // Create a JFrame object
47:          JFrame frame = new JFrame( "Stock Graph Panel" );
48:
```

```
49:          // Create a StockGraphPanel Object
50:          StockGraphPanel app = new StockGraphPanel();
51:
52:          // Add our StockGraphPanel Object to the JFrame
53:          frame.getContentPane().add( app, BorderLayout.CENTER );
54:
55:          // Resize our JFrame
56:          frame.setSize( 640, 440 );
57:
58:          // Make our JFrame visible
59:          frame.setVisible( true );
60:
61:          // Create a window listener to close our application when we
62:          // close our application
63:          frame.addWindowListener
64:          (
65:              new WindowAdapter()
66:              {
67:                  public void windowClosing( WindowEvent e )
68:                  {
69:   System.exit( 0 );
70:                  }
71:              }
72:          );
73:      }
74: }
```

Figure 7.19 shows the StockGraphPanel application.

Figure 7.19

The StockGraphPanel *application.*

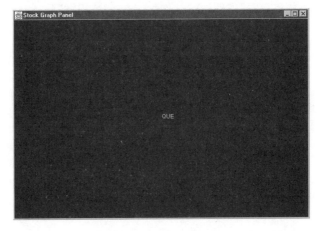

```
12:      String strSymbol = new String( "QUE" );
```

Line 12 defines a String object that will hold the stock ticker symbol. This will come in handy in the next section.

```
18:            setPreferredSize( new Dimension( 500, 400 ) );
```

Line 18 sets the preferred size of the JPanel. This does not do much for us when we own the entire contents of a window, but when we get added to a larger container and have limited space, it will help us fight for our space.

```
22:      public void paint(Graphics g)
23:      {
24:          // Get a Graphics2D object
25:          Graphics2D g2 = (Graphics2D) g;
26:
27:          // Get the Dimensions of this JPanel
28:          Dimension d = new Dimension();
29:          getSize(d);
30:
31:          // Set the background to black
32:          g2.setBackground( Color.black );
33:          g2.clearRect( 0, 0, (int)d.getWidth(),
                                            (int)d.getHeight() );
34:
35:          // Write the stock symbol in about the middle of the
                        screen
36:          g2.setColor( Color.cyan );
37:          g2.drawString( strSymbol,
38:                          (int)d.getWidth() / 2,
39:                          (int)d.getHeight() / 2 );
40:
41:      }
```

Lines 22–41 define the paint method. The first thing we do, in line 25, is get a Graphics2D object from the Graphics object. Next, we retrieve the dimensions of the JPanel by calling the JPanel's getSize method (lines 28 and 29). In line 32 we set the background color to use during fills to black by calling the Graphics2D method setBackground. We then fill the background color by clearing a rectangle that represents the entire JPanel by calling clearRect and specifying the dimensions of the JPanel. Next, in line 36 we set the foreground color of the Graphics2D surface with a call to setColor. Finally, we draw the stock symbol string to the screen with a call to drawString. The string is positioned in the middle of the screen (almost) by starting the drawing at the coordinates that correspond to the center of the screen: (screen width/2, screen height/2).

We are skipping over a lot of details here, but just hold your questions until Chapter 12 when all shall be revealed!

GraphTabPanel

The GraphTabPanel is similar to the StockTableTabPanel class in that it

- Is a panel that contains two components
- Manages the communication mechanism between those two components

First, it is a JPanel that hosts the TickerListPanel and the StockGraphPanel through the use of a JScrollPane.

The communication layer that the GraphTabPanel must implement consists of two scenarios:

- Notification from the TickerListPanel of JList selection updates.
- Notification of the TickerListPanel from the GraphTabPanel to the StockGraphPanel.

The first communication is facilitated through the use of event handling. As you might have guessed, the JList class has its own event listener called ListSelectionListener, which is defined in Table 7.7.

Table 7.7 **ListSelectionListener Object**

Method	Description
void valueChanged(ListSelectionEvent e)	Called whenever the value of the selection changes

Whenever a value changes in a JList component, the valueChanged method is called and sent a ListSelectionEvent, defined in Table 7.8.

Table 7.8 **ListSelectionEvent Object**

Method	Description
int getFirstIndex()	Returns the index of the first row whose selection might have changed
int getLastIndex()	Returns the index of the last row whose selection might have changed
boolean getValueIsAdjusting()	Returns true if this is one of multiple change events
String toString()	Returns a string that displays and identifies this object's properties

This event enables you to retrieve all the row indices for changing values and offers a method, getValueIsAdjusting, that is fired during a change: You will typically want to ignore getValueIsAdjusting events.

Finally, listeners can be registered by calling the JList class's addListSelectionListener method.

The other form of communication we are interested in is informing the StockGraphPanel that the stock ticker symbol has changed. We accomplish this by adding the following method to the StockGraphPanel:

```
void setSymbol( String str )
```

This method updates the string that the StockGraphPanel draws and then forces it to repaint its display area. It is defined as follows:

```
public void setSymbol( String str )
{
    // Save the new value of the symbol
    strSymbol = str;

    // Force the screen to repaint
    repaint();
}
```

And there you have it. Take a look at Listing 7.6 for the GraphTabPanel class.

Type the code from Listing 7.6, excluding line numbers, into your favorite text editor and save it as GraphTabPanel.java, or copy it from the CD. You will need to either copy the new TickerListPanel.java and StockGraphPanel.java files from the CD or add the aforementioned method to the StockGraphPanel file (it is just too big to print the entire source code). Build it as follows:

```
javac GraphTabPanel.java
java GraphTabPanel
```

Listing 7.6 GraphTabPanel.java

```
1:  // Import the packages used by this class
2:  import javax.swing.*;
3:  import javax.swing.event.*;
4:
5:  import java.awt.*;
6:  import java.awt.event.*;
7:
8:  // Import our other components
9:  import TickerListPanel;
10: import StockGraphPanel;
11:
12: // GraphTabPanel
13: public class GraphTabPanel extends JPanel
                                implements ListSelectionListener
14: {
15:     // Declare our panels
16:     TickerListPanel tickerListPanel = new TickerListPanel();
```

```
17:     StockGraphPanel stockGraphPanel = new StockGraphPanel();
18:
19:     // Create a new split pane
20:     JSplitPane splitPane;
21:
22:     // Constructor
23:     public GraphTabPanel()
24:     {
25:         // Create our split panel with our two panels
26:         splitPane = new JSplitPane(
27:                         JSplitPane.HORIZONTAL_SPLIT,
28:                         tickerListPanel,
29:                         stockGraphPanel);
30:
31:         splitPane.setOneTouchExpandable(true);
32:         splitPane.setDividerLocation(150);
33:
34:         //Provide minimum sizes for the two components in the split pane
35:         tickerListPanel.setMinimumSize(new Dimension(120, 350));
36:         stockGraphPanel.setMinimumSize(new Dimension(480, 280));
37:
38:         // Make this class a list selection listener so we know when
39:         // the user selects   something
40:       tickerListPanel.listTickers.addListSelectionListener(this);
41:
42:         // Initialize the controls by selecting the first item in the
43:         // listbox and setting that text as the text for the graph panel
44:         tickerListPanel.listTickers.setSelectedIndex( 0 );
45:         stockGraphPanel.setSymbol(
46: (String)tickerListPanel.listTickers.getModel().getElementAt(0));
47:
48:         //Add the split panel to this panel.
49:         add( splitPane, BorderLayout.CENTER );
50:     }
51:
52:     // ListSelectionListener::valueChanged( e )
53:     public void valueChanged( ListSelectionEvent e )
54:     {
55:         // Ignore adjustment events
56:         if (e.getValueIsAdjusting())
57:         {
58:             return;
59:         }
60:
61:         // Get the list from the event
62:         JList theList = (JList)e.getSource();
63:
64:         // Get the index of the selected item
65:         int index = theList.getSelectedIndex();
66:
```

continues

Listing 7.6 continued

```
67:            // Send the text of the selected item to the graph panel
68:            stockGraphPanel.setSymbol(
                  ( String )theList.getModel().getElementAt( index ) );
69:        }
70:
71:    // Main application entry point into this class
72:    public static void main( String[] args )
73:    {
74:        // Create a JFrame object
75:        JFrame frame = new JFrame( "Graph Tab Panel" );
76:
77:        // Create a GraphTabPanel Object
78:        GraphTabPanel app = new GraphTabPanel();
79:
80:        // Add our GraphTabPanel Object to the JFrame
81:        frame.getContentPane().add( app, BorderLayout.CENTER );
82:
83:        // Resize our JFrame
84:        frame.setSize( 660, 450 );
85:
86:        // Make our JFrame visible
87:        frame.setVisible( true );
88:
89:        // Create a window listener to close our application when we
90:        // close our application
91:        frame.addWindowListener
92:        (
93:            new WindowAdapter()
94:            {
95:                public void windowClosing( WindowEvent e )
96:                {
97:                    System.exit( 0 );
98:                }
99:            }
100:       );
101:   }
102:}
```

Figure 7.20 shows the GraphTabPanel application.

```
9:  import TickerListPanel;
10: import StockGraphPanel;
```

Lines 9 and 10 import the TickerListPanel and StockGraphPanel classes. Be sure that the corresponding .java files are in the same directory.

```
13: public class GraphTabPanel extends JPanel
                        implements ListSelectionListener
```

Figure 7.20

The GraphTabPanel application.

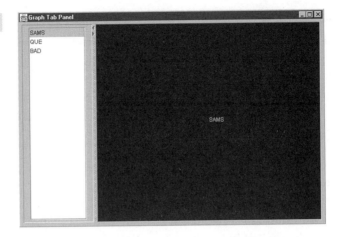

Line 13 declares our GraphTabPanel that extends JPanel and implements ListSelectionListener so that we will be notified of list box selection changes.

```
16:     TickerListPanel tickerListPanel = new TickerListPanel();
17:     StockGraphPanel stockGraphPanel = new StockGraphPanel();
```

Lines 16 and 17 create our instances of the TickerListPanel and StockGraphPanel classes.

```
26:         splitPane = new JSplitPane(
27:                         JSplitPane.HORIZONTAL_SPLIT,
28:                         tickerListPanel,
29:                         stockGraphPanel);
```

Lines 26–29 create a new JSplitPane, which we discussed in Chapter 5, that is split horizontally and has both of our imported panels. The order of the panels is important as the TickerListPanel is on the left and the StockGraphPanel is on the left.

```
31:         splitPane.setOneTouchExpandable(true);
```

Line 31 makes the split pane fully expandable by clicking one button. It creates two buttons that look like arrows on the split pane that expand one of the panels to fill the entire screen.

```
32:         splitPane.setDividerLocation(150);
```

Line 32 positions the divider at the physical location 150.

```
35:         tickerListPanel.setMinimumSize(new Dimension(120, 350));
36:         stockGraphPanel.setMinimumSize(new Dimension(480, 280));
```

Lines 35 and 36 set the minimum sizes that the components can be in the split pane. It will not allow the split pane to be positioned in a manner that makes either panel smaller than this.

```
40:         tickerListPanel.listTickers.addListSelectionListener(this);
```

Line 40 adds our GraphTabPanel as a list selection listener for the TickerListPanel's listTickers list box. Remember that we made the listTickers object public just for this reason. This way we will be notified whenever the current selection in the list box is changed.

```
44:         tickerListPanel.listTickers.setSelectedIndex( 0 );
45:         stockGraphPanel.setSymbol(
46: (String)tickerListPanel.listTickers.getModel().getElementAt(0));
```

Lines 44–46 select the first item in the list and then set the symbol in the StockGraphPanel by asking the TickerListPanel's listTickers list box for the String that represents the first element in its list. The getModel method returns the ListModel for the JList, and getElementAt returns the Object stored at the specified index, which happens to be a String in our application.

```
53:     public void valueChanged( ListSelectionEvent e )
54:     {
55:         // Ignore adjustment events
56:         if (e.getValueIsAdjusting())
57:         {
58:             return;
59:         }
60:
61:         // Get the list from the event
62:         JList theList = (JList)e.getSource();
63:
64:         // Get the index of the selected item
65:         int index = theList.getSelectedIndex();
66:
67:         // Send the text of the selected item to the graph panel
68:         stockGraphPanel.setSymbol(
                ( String )theList.getModel().getElementAt( index ) );
69:     }
```

Lines 53–69 implement the ListSelectionListener's valueChanged method. The first thing this method does is check to see whether the event is an adjustment event by calling getValueIsAdjusting. This method is called multiple times during a list selection change, so we just ignore that. Then in line 62 we extract the JList from the event, and in line 65 we retrieve the currently selected item in the list by calling getSelectedIndex. Now in line 68 we ask the list for its ListModel; then we ask the ListModel for the Object at the selected item's index. We cast this value to a String and send that string to the public StockGraphPanel method setSymbol, which updates the display of the graph panel.

StockTabPanel

The StockTabPanel hosts a JTabbedPane that holds both the SstockTableTabPanel and the GraphTabPanel. We add a few icons and names to it, but that's it! Take a look at Listing 7.7.

Type the code from Listing 7.7, excluding line numbers, into your favorite text editor and save it as StockTabPanel.java, or copy it from the CD. You will need the following files in the same directory:

- StockTableTabPanel.java
- StockTablePanel.java
- PortfolioTotalsPanel.java
- GraphTabPanel.java
- StockGraphPanel.java
- TickerListPanel.java
- iconMoney.gif
- iconGraph.gif

Copy these files from the CD or use the latest ones we have developed thus far in the chapter. Build it as follows:

```
javac StockTabPanel.java
java StockTabPanel
```

Listing 7.7 **StockTabPanel.java**

```
 1:  // Import the packages used by this class
 2:  import javax.swing.*;
 3:  import javax.swing.event.*;
 4:
 5:  import java.awt.*;
 6:  import java.awt.event.*;
 7:
 8:  // Import our other components
 9:  import StockTableTabPanel;
10:  import GraphTabPanel;
11:
12:  // StockTabPanel
13:  public class StockTabPanel extends JPanel
14:  {
15:      // Create a new tabbed pane
16:      JTabbedPane tabbedPane = new JTabbedPane( JTabbedPane.TOP );
17:
18:      // Create icons for the tabs
19:      ImageIcon iconMoney = new ImageIcon( "iconMoney.gif" );
```

continues

Listing 7.7   continued

```
20:      ImageIcon iconGraph = new ImageIcon( "iconGraph.gif" );
21:
22:      // Create our panels
23:      StockTableTabPanel stockTableTabPanel =
                                           new StockTableTabPanel();
24:      GraphTabPanel graphTabPanel = new GraphTabPanel();
25:
26:      // Constructor
27:      public StockTabPanel()
28:      {
29:          // Add the StockTableTabPanel to the tab control and select it
30:          tabbedPane.addTab( "Stock Table", iconMoney,
                      stockTableTabPanel, "Stock Positions");
31:          tabbedPane.setSelectedIndex(0);
32:
33:          // Add the GraphTabPanel to the tab control
34:          tabbedPane.addTab( "Graphs", iconGraph,
                              graphTabPanel, "Stock Graphs");
35:
36:          //Add the tabbed pane to this panel.
37:          add( tabbedPane, BorderLayout.CENTER );
38:      }
39:
40:      // Main application entry point into this class
41:      public static void main( String[] args )
42:      {
43:          // Create a JFrame object
44:          JFrame frame = new JFrame( "Graph Tab Panel" );
45:
46:          // Create a StockTabPanel Object
47:          StockTabPanel app = new StockTabPanel();
48:
49:          // Add our StockTabPanel Object to the JFrame
50:          frame.getContentPane().add( app, BorderLayout.CENTER );
51:
52:          // Resize our JFrame
53:          frame.setSize( 680, 490 );
54:
55:          // Make our JFrame visible
56:          frame.setVisible( true );
57:
58:          // Create a window listener to close our application when we
59:          // close our application
60:          frame.addWindowListener
61:          (
62:              new WindowAdapter()
63:              {
64:                  public void windowClosing( WindowEvent e )
65:                  {
66:                      System.exit( 0 );
```

```
67:                    }
68:                }
69:          );
70:     }
71: }
```

Figure 7.21 shows the StockTabPanel application.

Figure 7.21

The StockTabPanel application.

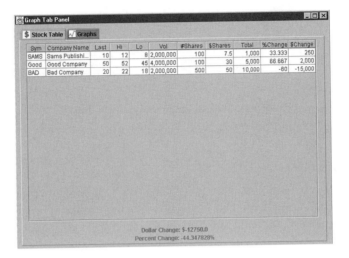

```
9:  import StockTableTabPanel;
10: import GraphTabPanel;
```

Lines 9 and 10 import the two source files that we are going to add to our tab control: StockTableTabPanel and GraphTabPanel. Note that these source files will import the ones that it needs, so there is no need to import all the files used in the application.

```
16:      JTabbedPane tabbedPane = new JTabbedPane( JTabbedPane.TOP );
```

Line 16 creates a JTabbedPane object with the tabs positioned on the top of the component. Refer to Chapter 5 if you have any questions.

```
19:      ImageIcon iconMoney = new ImageIcon( "iconMoney.gif" );
20:      ImageIcon iconGraph = new ImageIcon( "iconGraph.gif" );
```

Lines 19 and 20 create icons that we'll add to the tab control.

```
23:      StockTableTabPanel stockTableTabPanel =
                                        new StockTableTabPanel();
24:      GraphTabPanel graphTabPanel = new GraphTabPanel();
```

Lines 23 and 24 create our StockTableTabPanel and GraphTabPanel classes, respectively.

```
30:              tabbedPane.addTab( "Stock Table", iconMoney,
                              stockTableTabPanel, "Stock Positions");
```

Line 30 adds the `StockTableTabPanel` to the tab control with the tab name Stock Table, the icon `iconMoney`, and the tooltip text Stock Positions.

```
31:              tabbedPane.setSelectedIndex(0);
```

Line 31 selects the first tab in the tab control: the tab at index 0.

```
34:              tabbedPane.addTab( "Graphs", iconGraph,
                              graphTabPanel, "Stock Graphs");
```

Line 34 adds the `GraphTabPanel` to the tab control with the tab name Graphs, the icon `iconGraph`, and the tooltip text Stock Graphs.

```
37:              add( tabbedPane, BorderLayout.CENTER );
```

Finally, line 37 adds our tab control to our `JPanel`.

PortfolioListPanel

The `PortfolioListPanel` is a scrollable `JList` holding items with both text and an icon. We create our `JList` object, create a `DefaultListModel` to use with it, and create a custom cell renderer. This class is similar to our `JListExample` back in Chapter 5, so refer back if some of these terms seem foreign.

Anyway, let's take a look at the code. See Listing 7.8.

Type the code from Listing 7.8, excluding line numbers, into your favorite text editor and save it as `PortfolioListPanel.java`, or copy it from the CD. Build it as follows:

```
javac PortfolioListPanel.java
java PortfolioListPanel
```

Listing 7.8 `PortfolioListPanel.java`

```
1:  // Import the packages used by this class
2:  import javax.swing.*;
3:  import javax.swing.event.*;
4:
5:  import java.awt.*;
6:  import java.awt.event.*;
7:
8:  // PortfolioListPanel
9:  public class PortfolioListPanel extends JPanel
10: {
11:     // List Model that will hold the data for the list control
12:     DefaultListModel listModelPortfolios =
                                      new DefaultListModel();
13:
14:     // Create our JList
```

```
15:     JList listPortfolios = new JList( listModelPortfolios );
16:
17:     // Create a cell renderer
18:     IconCellRenderer cellRenderer = new IconCellRenderer();
19:
20:     // Constructor
21:     public PortfolioListPanel()
22:     {
23:         // Add our list items to the list model
24:         listModelPortfolios.addElement( "Steve" );
25:         listModelPortfolios.addElement( "Linda" );
26:         listModelPortfolios.addElement( "Skie" );
27:         listModelPortfolios.addElement( "Nikko" );
28:
29:         // Set the list component's cell renderer
30:         listPortfolios.setCellRenderer( cellRenderer );
31:
32:         // Set the selection info: single selection,
                    and select the first item
33:         listPortfolios.setSelectionMode(
                            ListSelectionModel.SINGLE_SELECTION );
34:         listPortfolios.setSelectedIndex( 0 );
35:
36:         // Create a scroll panel to hold our JList
37:         JScrollPane scrollPaneList =
                            new JScrollPane( listPortfolios );
38:
39:         // Set our preferred size
40:         scrollPaneList.setPreferredSize( new Dimension(100, 400) );
41:
42:         //Add the scroll pane to this panel.
43:         add( scrollPaneList, BorderLayout.CENTER );
44:     }
45:
46:     // Main application entry point into this class
47:     public static void main( String[] args )
48:     {
49:         // Create a JFrame object
50:         JFrame frame = new JFrame( "Portfolio Panel" );
51:
52:         // Create a PortfolioListPanel Object
53:         PortfolioListPanel app = new PortfolioListPanel();
54:
55:         // Add our PortfolioListPanel Object to the JFrame
56:         frame.getContentPane().add( app, BorderLayout.CENTER );
57:
58:         // Resize our JFrame
59:         frame.setSize( 120, 440 );
60:
61:         // Make our JFrame visible
```

continues

Listing 7.8 continued

```
62:            frame.setVisible( true );
63:
64:            // Create a window listener to close our application when we
65:            // close our application
66:            frame.addWindowListener
67:            (
68:                new WindowAdapter()
69:                {
70:                    public void windowClosing( WindowEvent e )
71:                    {
72:                        System.exit( 0 );
73:                    }
74:                }
75:            );
76:        }
77:
78:        // IconCellRenderer - Draws each cell as it is requested
79:        class IconCellRenderer extends JLabel
                                  implements ListCellRenderer
80:        {
81:            // Define the icons to diplay, one for selected and
                            one for not selected
82:            ImageIcon iconMoney = new ImageIcon("MoneyIcon.gif");
83:            ImageIcon iconMoneySelected =
                            new ImageIcon("MoneyIconSelected.gif");
84:
85:            // Constructor
86:            public IconCellRenderer()
87:            {
88:                // Allow the background color to change
89:                setOpaque(true);
90:            }
91:
92:            // getListCellRendererComponent
93:            //
94:            // Reconfigure the JLabel every time this function is
95:            // called - this is where we set the drawing attributes
                            for the cell
96:            public Component getListCellRendererComponent(
97:                JList list,
98:                Object value,              // value to display
99:                int index,                 // cell index
100:                boolean isSelected,       // is the cell selected
101:                boolean cellHasFocus)     // the list and the cell
                                              have the focus
102:            {
103:                // If this item is selected, set the correct
104:                // background and foreground colors and choose which
                                icon we want to paint
105:                if (isSelected)
```

```
106:            {
107:                setBackground(list.getSelectionBackground());
108:                setForeground(list.getSelectionForeground());
109:                setIcon(iconMoneySelected);
110:            }
111:            else
112:            {
113:                setBackground(list.getBackground());
114:                setForeground(list.getForeground());
115:                setIcon(iconMoney);
116:            }
117:
118:            // Set the text of the field to the value of this
                            cell
119:            String s = value.toString();
120:            setText(s);
121:
122:            // Return  a reference to this IconCellRenderer
123:    return this;
124:        }
125:    }
126:}
```

Figure 7.22 shows the `PortfolioListPanel` application.

Figure 7.22

The
PortfolioListPanel
application.

```
12:    DefaultListModel listModelPortfolios =
                                    new DefaultListModel();
```

Line 12 creates a `DefaultListModel` for us to store our list data in.

```
15:    JList listPortfolios = new JList( listModelPortfolios );
```

Line 15 creates our `JList` and tells it to use the new `DefaultListModel` we just created in line 12 as its list model.

```
18:      IconCellRenderer cellRenderer = new IconCellRenderer();
```

Line 18 creates an instance of our custom cell renderer `IconCellRenderer`. We'll talk more about this in a minute.

```
24:         listModelPortfolios.addElement( "Steve" );
25:         listModelPortfolios.addElement( "Linda" );
26:         listModelPortfolios.addElement( "Skie" );
27:         listModelPortfolios.addElement( "Nikko" );
```

Lines 24–27 add four `String` elements to the list model.

```
30:         listPortfolios.setCellRenderer( cellRenderer );
```

Line 30 sets our custom cell renderer as the cell renderer for this `JList`.

```
33:         listPortfolios.setSelectionMode(
                          ListSelectionModel.SINGLE_SELECTION );
```

Line 33 sets the selection mode of the `JList` to single selection so that only one item in the list can be selected at any given time.

```
34:         listPortfolios.setSelectedIndex( 0 );
```

Line 34 selects the first item in the list, the item at index 0.

```
37:         JScrollPane scrollPaneList =
                                   new JScrollPane( listPortfolios );
```

Line 37 creates a new `JScrollPane` and adds our `JList` to it.

Now lines 79–125 implement our `IconCellRenderer` class.

This class implements `ListCellRenderer`. If you recall from Chapter 5, we said that a `ListCellRenderer` tells the `JList` how to draw every individual item in the list. The only method that the `ListCellRenderer` interface supports is `getListCellRendererComponent`. We use this method to construct a label with both an icon and text.

First, let's talk about the icon we are going to draw and the background and foreground coloring:

```
105:          if (isSelected)
106:          {
107:              setBackground(list.getSelectionBackground());
108:              setForeground(list.getSelectionForeground());
109:              setIcon(iconMoneySelected);
110:          }
111:          else
112:          {
113:              setBackground(list.getBackground());
114:              setForeground(list.getForeground());
115:              setIcon(iconMoney);
116:          }
```

Line 105 checks to see if the item we are asked to draw is currently selected by using the `isSelected` Boolean value passed to the `getListCellRendererComponent` method. If the item is selected, we set the background and foreground colors to the default selected colors in the `JList` by calling `getSelectionBackground` and `getSelectionForeground`, respectively. Finally, we set the icon to the selected icon we loaded earlier in the class. We do just the opposite if the item is not selected: We load the standard colors using `getBackground` and `getForeground` and set the icon to the unselected icon.

```
119:            String s = value.toString();
120:            setText(s);
```

Then we retrieve the text of the list item in line 119 and set it as our `JLabel`'s text in line 120.

This panel is actually a little simpler than the example in Chapter 5. When you have all the primers out of the way and understand how the language works "under the hood," this stuff is easy.

MainMenu

The `MainMenu` class is the traditional menu bar that sits at the top of a `JFrame` displaying the standard File, Edit, Help, and a collection of custom drop-down menus; basically it is exactly what we designed earlier, shown back in Figure 7.4.

Let's talk a little bit about menus in the Java context. Menus are comprised of `JMenuBar`, `JMenu`, and `JMenuItem` objects. Take a look at Figure 7.23 for this relationship.

Figure 7.23

Java menu structure.

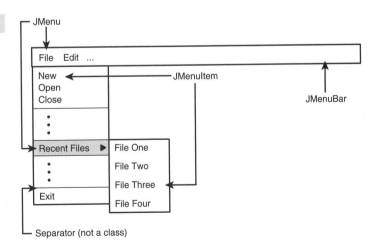

In Figure 7.23, the bar that is holding the File and Edit menus is a JMenuBar. File and Edit, as well as Recent Files, are JMenus. The JMenu class is used to represent drop-down menus as well as submenus (like Recent Files). Finally, all the selectable items in the menu—New, Open, Close, File One, File Two, File Three, File Four, and Exit—are instances of the JMenuItem class.

JMenuBar objects are parents to JMenu objects, and JMenu objects are parents to JMenuItem objects as well as other JMenu objects. So how do you construct a Java menu? Follow these steps:

1. Construct a JMenuBar object.

2. Construct the top-level menu options as JMenu objects.

3. Add the JMenu objects to the JMenuBar object using the JMenuBar class's add method.

4. Construct the selectable menu items as JMenuItem objects.

5. Add the JMenuItem objects to their respective JMenus using the JMenu class's add method.

6. Add the JMenuBar object to its heavyweight container using the heavyweight container class's setJMenuBar.

You can construct submenus by constructing a JMenu object full of JMenuItems and adding that JMenu object to another JMenu object using the add method.

You can add separators to a JMenu by calling the JMenu class's addSeparator method. Tables 7.9, 7.10, and 7.11 show the various constructors for the JMenuBar, JMenu, and JMenuItem, respectively.

Table 7.9 JMenuBar **Constructor**

Constructor	Description
JMenuBar()	Creates a new menu bar

Table 7.10 JMenu **Constructors**

Constructor	Description
JMenu()	Creates a new JMenu with no text
JMenu(String s)	Creates a new JMenu with the supplied string as its text
JMenu(String s, boolean b)	Creates a new JMenu with the supplied string as its text and specified as a tear-off menu or not

Table 7.11   **JMenuItem Constructors**

Constructor	Description
JMenuItem()	Creates a menuItem with no set text or icon
JMenuItem(Icon icon)	Creates a menuItem with an icon
JMenuItem(String text)	Creates a menuItem with text
JMenuItem(String text, Icon icon)	Creates a menuItem with the supplied text and icon
JMenuItem(String text, int mnemonic)	Creates a menuItem with the specified text and keyboard mnemonic

From these constructors, you can see that you can create menu items with or without icons and with or without keyboard mnemonics (hot keys).

Now that you have created this pretty menu, how do you handle its events?

Although you might be expecting some new profound event listener paradigm, you might be a little disappointed to learn that we have done all this before. Several events are actually generated during menu operations, but the ones that we will be concerned with are menu item selections. Who is better equipped to handle menu item selections than the JMenuItem class? Let's take a quick look at the derivation tree of the JMenuItem class (see Figure 7.24).

Figure 7.24

JMenuItem derivation tree.

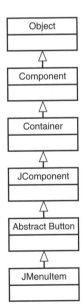

That AbstractButton class that JMenuItem is derived from should look familiar; it was the parent of JButton and JToggleButton (which was the parent to JRadioButton and JCheckBox). How does that help us?

Well, the neat thing about the JMenuItem class is that you handle events the exact same way you handle them with buttons: through ActionEvents. As a refresher from Chapter 6, make your main class implement ActionListener, add your class as an action listener for the AbstractButton by calling addActionListener, and implement an actionPerformed method.

Therefore, it is simple to create a menu and listen for menu item selections. The only difficulty is when your menus start getting so large that they become difficult to maintain. Most of the examples you will find in your searches simply implement menus as I have described, but from a practical perspective it just isn't feasible. Also it does not follow in an object-oriented world.

Now don't get me wrong, you still must do the same amount of work, but I have found it to be the most manageable method to separate out a menu from its application. The way to do this is to create a public class derived from JMenuBar that publicly creates all its menu items and adds them to the JMenuBar in its constructor. Event handling is performed by implementing an addActionListener method in the derived class and forwarding that to all the JMenuItems. Don't worry, it will all make sense in the source code. Take a look at Listing 7.9.

Type the code from Listing 7.9, excluding line numbers, into your favorite text editor and save it as MainMenu.java, or copy it from the CD. Build it as follows:

```
javac MainMenu.java
java MainMenu
```

Listing 7.9 `MainMenu.java`

```
1:  // Import the packages used by this class
2:  import javax.swing.*;
3:  import javax.swing.event.*;
4:
5:  import java.awt.*;
6:  import java.awt.event.*;
7:
8:  // MainMenu
9:  public class MainMenu extends JMenuBar
10: {
11:     // "File" Menu
12:     public JMenu menuFile = new JMenu( "File" );
13:         public JMenuItem fileNew = new JMenuItem( "New" );
14:         public JMenuItem fileOpen = new JMenuItem( "Open" );
15:         public JMenuItem fileClose = new JMenuItem( "Close" );
16:         public JMenuItem fileSave = new JMenuItem( "Save" );
```

```
17:        public JMenuItem fileSaveAs = new JMenuItem( "Save As" );
18:        public JMenuItem fileSaveAll = new JMenuItem( "Save All" );
19:        public JMenuItem filePrint = new JMenuItem( "Print" );
20:        public JMenuItem fileExit = new JMenuItem( "Exit" );
21:
22:    // "Edit" Menu
23:    public JMenu menuEdit = new JMenu( "Edit" );
24:        public JMenuItem editCut = new JMenuItem( "Cut" );
25:        public JMenuItem editCopy = new JMenuItem( "Copy" );
26:        public JMenuItem editPaste = new JMenuItem( "Paste" );
27:        public JMenuItem editDelete = new JMenuItem( "Delete" );
28:
29:    // "Portfolios" Menu
30:    public JMenu menuPortfolios = new JMenu( "Portfolios" );
31:        public JMenuItem portfoliosImport = new JMenuItem( "Import" );
32:        public JMenuItem portfoliosExport = new JMenuItem( "Export" );
33:
34:    // "Quotes" Menu
35:    public JMenu menuQuotes = new JMenu( "Quotes" );
36:        public JMenuItem quotesUpdate = new JMenuItem( "Update" );
37:        public JMenuItem quotesTimerOptions =
                                        new JMenuItem( "Timer Options" );
38:
39:    // "History" Menu
40:    public JMenu menuHistory = new JMenu( "History" );
41:        public JMenuItem historyGetQuote = new JMenuItem( "" );
42:        public JCheckBoxMenuItem historyEnableTracking =
                            new JCheckBoxMenuItem( "Enable Tracking" );
43:        public JMenuItem historyImport = new JMenuItem( "Import" );
44:        public JMenuItem historyExport = new JMenuItem( "Export" );
45:
46:    // "Graph" Menu
47:    public JMenu menuGraph = new JMenu( "Graph" );
48:        public JMenuItem graphOptions = new JMenuItem( "Options" );
49:
50:    // "Help" Menu
51:    public JMenu menuHelp = new JMenu( "Help" );
52:        public JMenuItem helpContents = new JMenuItem( "Contents" );
53:        public JMenuItem helpAbout = new JMenuItem( "About" );
54:
55:    // Constructor
56:    public MainMenu()
57:    {
58:        // "File" Menu
59:
60:        // Add our "File" menu
61:        add( menuFile );
62:
63:        // Add our items to the "File" menu
64:        menuFile.add( fileNew );
```

continues

Listing 7.9 continued

```
65:        menuFile.add( fileOpen );
66:        menuFile.add( fileClose );
67:        menuFile.addSeparator();
68:        menuFile.add( fileSave );
69:        menuFile.add( fileSaveAs );
70:        menuFile. add( fileSaveAll);
71:        menuFile.addSeparator();
72:        menuFile.add( filePrint );
73:        menuFile.addSeparator();
74:        menuFile.add( fileExit );
75:
76:      // "Edit" Menu
77:
78:      // Add our "Edit" menu
79:      add( menuEdit );
80:
81:      // Add our items to the "Edit" menu
82:      menuEdit.add( editCut );
83:      menuEdit.add( editCopy );
84:      menuEdit.add( editPaste );
85:      menuEdit.addSeparator();
86:      menuEdit.add( editDelete );
87:
88:      // "Portfolios" Menu
89:
90:      // Add our "Portfolios" menu
91:      add( menuPortfolios );
92:
93:      // Add our items to the "Portfolios" menu
94:      menuPortfolios.add( portfoliosImport );
95:      menuPortfolios.add( portfoliosExport );
96:
97:      // "Quotes" Menu
98:
99:      // Add our "Quotes" menu
100:     add( menuQuotes );
101:
102:     // Add our items to the "Quotes" menu
103:     menuQuotes.add( quotesUpdate );
104:     menuQuotes.add( quotesTimerOptions );
105:
106:     // "History" Menu
107:
108:     // Add our "History" menu
109:     add( menuHistory );
110:
111:     // Add our items to the "History" menu
112:     menuHistory.add( historyGetQuote );
113:     menuHistory.add( historyEnableTracking );
114:     menuHistory.addSeparator();
```

```
115:        menuHistory.add( historyImport );
116:        menuHistory.add( historyExport );
117:
118:        // "Graph" Menu
119:
120:        // Add our "Graph" menu
121:        add( menuGraph );
122:
123:        // Add our items to the "Graph" menu
124:        menuGraph.add( graphOptions );
125:
126:        // "Help" Menu
127:
128:        // Add our "Help" menu
139:        add( menuHelp );
130:
131:        // Add our items to the "Help" menu
132:        menuHelp.add( helpContents );
133:        menuHelp.add( helpAbout );
134:
135:    }
136:
137:    // addActionListener( listener )
138:    //
139:    // Forwards the listener to all menu items
140:    public void addActionListener( ActionListener listener )
141:    {
142:        // Add listener as the action listener for the "File" menu items
143:        fileNew.addActionListener( listener );
144:        fileOpen.addActionListener( listener );
145:        fileClose.addActionListener( listener );
146:        fileSave.addActionListener( listener );
147:        fileSaveAs.addActionListener( listener );
148:        fileSaveAll.addActionListener( listener );
149:        filePrint.addActionListener( listener );
150:        fileExit.addActionListener( listener );
151:
152:        // Add listener as the action listener for the "Edit" menu items
153:        editCut.addActionListener( listener );
154:        editCopy.addActionListener( listener );
155:        editPaste.addActionListener( listener );
156:        editDelete.addActionListener( listener );
157:
158:        // Add listener as the action listener for the "Portfolios" menu
159:        portfoliosImport.addActionListener( listener );
160:        portfoliosExport.addActionListener( listener );
161:
162:        // Add listener as the action listener for the "Quotes" menu
163:        quotesUpdate.addActionListener( listener );
164:        quotesTimerOptions.addActionListener( listener );
165:
```

continues

Listing 7.9 continued

```
166:         // Add listener as the action listener for the "History" menu
167:         historyGetQuote.addActionListener( listener );
168:         historyEnableTracking.addActionListener( listener );
169:         historyImport.addActionListener( listener );
170:         historyExport.addActionListener( listener );
171:
172:         // Add listener as the action listener for the "Graph" menu items
173:         graphOptions.addActionListener( listener );
174:
175:         // Add listener as the action listener for the "Help" menu items
176:         helpContents.addActionListener( listener );
177:         helpAbout.addActionListener( listener );
178:     }
179:
180:     // Main application entry point into this class
181:     public static void main( String[] args )
182:     {
183:         // Create a JFrame object
184:         JFrame frame = new JFrame( "MainMenu" );
185:
186:         // Create a MainMenu Object
187:         MainMenu mainMenu = new MainMenu();
188:
189:         // Add our MainMenu Object to the JFrame
190:         frame.setJMenuBar( mainMenu );
191:
192:         // Resize our JFrame
193:         frame.setSize( 660, 450 );
194:
195:         // Make our JFrame visible
196:         frame.setVisible( true );
197:
198:         // Create a window listener to close our application when we
199:         // close our application
200:         frame.addWindowListener
201:         (
202:             new WindowAdapter()
203:             {
204:                 public void windowClosing( WindowEvent e )
205:                 {
206:     System.exit( 0 );
207:                 }
208:             }
209:         );
210:     }
211:}
```

Figure 7.25 shows the MainMenu application after I selected the File menu. Try clicking on the various menu headings and see what the menus we just created look like.

Figure 7.25

The MainMenu *application.*

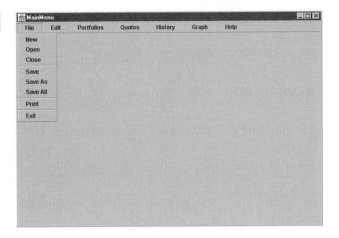

```
9:  public class MainMenu extends JMenuBar
```

Line 9 creates our MainMenu class as derived from JMenuBar.

```
12:     public JMenu menuFile = new JMenu( "File" );
13:         public JMenuItem fileNew = new JMenuItem( "New" );
14:         public JMenuItem fileOpen = new JMenuItem( "Open" );
```

Line 12 creates the File menu and lines 13 and 14 create the File, New and File, Open menu items. I omitted all the others because they are identical, but for different menus.

```
61:     add( menuFile );
```

Line 61 adds the File menu that we created in line 12 to our MainMenu JMenuBar derived class. (Again the rest of the menus have been omitted from this discussion as they are identical to this one.)

```
64:     menuFile.add( fileNew );
65:     menuFile.add( fileOpen );
```

Lines 64 and 65 add the New and Open menu items to the File menu.

```
140:   public void addActionListener( ActionListener listener )
```

Don't get this method confused with the JMenuItem class's addActionListener—it is completely of our own creation. The naming convention is retained to help the readability of the application that is eventually going to implement our MainMenu.

```
143:   fileNew.addActionListener( listener );
144:   fileOpen.addActionListener( listener );
```

Lines 143 and 144 take the action listener passed to our addActionListener method and pass that to each of the menu items; only File, New and File, Open are shown, but the rest are added similarly.

```
187:          MainMenu mainMenu = new MainMenu();
```

Line 187 creates an instance of our MainMenu object.

```
190:          frame.setJMenuBar( mainMenu );
```

Finally, line 190 adds our MainMenu to our JFrame using the setJMenuBar method.

We will handle the menu events in the next section when we implement the StockApplication class.

StockApplication

You've made it this far—only one lap left! The StockApplication class is the class that brings everything together and delivers the user interface for the Stock Tracker application.

The StockApplication class imports the StockTabPanel, PortfolioListPanel, and MainMenu classes. It creates a BorderLayout and adds the StockTabPanel to the north side and the PortfolioListPanel to the south side. The MainMenu is added by calling the JFrame class's setJMenuBar method.

The StockApplication class implements the ActionListener interface so that it can receive action events from the MainMenu class and handles those events in the actionPerformed method.

As you can see, this is all the standard stuff we have been talking about in this chapter. We are just bringing it all together. Take a look at Listing 7.10.

Type the code from Listing 7.10, excluding line numbers, into your favorite text editor and save it as StockApplication.java, or copy it from the CD. You will need the following files in the same directory:

- StockTableTabPanel.java
- StockTablePanel.java
- PortfolioTotalsPanel.java
- GraphTabPanel.java
- StockGraphPanel.java
- TickerListPanel.java
- iconMoney.gif
- iconGraph.gif

- PortfolioListPanel.java

- MoneyIcon.gif

- MoneyIconSelected.gif

- MainMenu.java

Build it as follows:

```
javac StockApplication.java
java StockApplication
```

Listing 7.10   StockApplication.java

```
1:  // Import the packages used by this class
2:  import javax.swing.*;
3:  import javax.swing.event.*;
4:
5:  import java.awt.*;
6:  import java.awt.event.*;
7:
8:  // Import our other components
9:  import StockTabPanel;
10: import PortfolioListPanel;
11: import MainMenu;
12:
13: // StockApplication
14: public class StockApplication extends JFrame
                                       implements ActionListener
15: {
16:     // Create our MainMenu
17:     MainMenu mainMenu = new MainMenu();
18:
19:     // Create our panels
20:     StockTabPanel stockTabPanel = new StockTabPanel();
21:     PortfolioListPanel portfolioListPanel =
                                   new PortfolioListPanel();
22:
23:     // Constructor
24:     public StockApplication()
25:     {
26:         // Set up our title
27:         super( "Stock Tracker Application" );
28:
29:         // Add our main menu
30:         setJMenuBar( mainMenu );
31:
32:         // Add the StockApplication as a listener to the menu
33:         mainMenu.addActionListener( this );
34:
35:         // Add our components
```

continues

Listing 7.10   continued

```
36:            stockTabPanel = new StockTabPanel();
37:            portfolioListPanel = new PortfolioListPanel();
38:
39:            getContentPane().add( stockTabPanel, BorderLayout.NORTH );
40:            getContentPane().add( portfolioListPanel, BorderLayout.SOUTH );
41:
42:            // Set our size
43:            setSize( 680, 600 );
44:
45:            // Make the StockApplication visible
46:            setVisible( true );
47:
48:            // Add a window listener to list for our window closing
49:            addWindowListener
50:            (
51:                new WindowAdapter()
52:                {
53:                    public void windowClosing( WindowEvent e )
54:                    {
55:                        System.exit( 0 );
56:                    }
57:                }
58:            );
59:        }
60:
61:        // Action Event Handler: actionPerformed
62:        public void actionPerformed(ActionEvent e)
63:        {
64:            // Extract the JMenuItem that generated this event
65:            JMenuItem item = ( JMenuItem )e.getSource();
66:
67:            // Find our which JMenuItem generated this event
68:            if( item == mainMenu.fileNew )
69:            {
70:                System.out.println( "File->New" );
71:            }
72:            else if( item == mainMenu.fileOpen )
73:            {
74:                System.out.println( "File->Open" );
75:            }
76:            else if ( item == mainMenu.fileClose )
77:            {
78:                System.out.println( "File->Close" );
79:            }
80:            else if ( item == mainMenu.fileSave )
81:            {
82:                System.out.println( "File->Save" );
83:            }
84:            else if ( item == mainMenu.fileSaveAs )
85:            {
```

```
86:                    System.out.println( "File->Save As" );
87:            }
88:            else if ( item == mainMenu.fileSaveAll )
89:            {
90:                    System.out.println( "File->Save All" );
91:            }
92:            else if ( item == mainMenu.filePrint )
93:            {
94:                    System.out.println( "File->Print" );
95:            }
96:            else if ( item == mainMenu.fileExit )
97:            {
98:                    System.out.println( "File->Exit" );
99:            }
100:           else if ( item == mainMenu.editCut )
101:           {
102:                   System.out.println( "Edit->Cut" );
103:           }
104:           else if ( item == mainMenu.editCopy )
105:           {
106:                   System.out.println( "Edit->Copy" );
107:           }
108:           else if ( item == mainMenu.editPaste )
109:           {
110:                   System.out.println( "Edit->Paste" );
111:           }
112:           else if ( item == mainMenu.editDelete )
113:           {
114:                   System.out.println( "Edit->Delete" );
115:           }
116:           else if ( item == mainMenu.portfoliosImport )
117:           {
118:                   System.out.println( "Portfolios->Import" );
119:           }
120:           else if ( item == mainMenu.portfoliosExport )
121:           {
122:                   System.out.println( "Portfolios->Export" );
123:           }
124:           else if ( item == mainMenu.quotesUpdate )
125:           {
126:                   System.out.println( "Quotes->Update" );
127:           }
128:           else if ( item == mainMenu.quotesTimerOptions )
139:           {
130:                   System.out.println( "Quotes->Timer Options" );
131:           }
132:           else if ( item == mainMenu.historyGetQuote )
133:           {
134:                   System.out.println( "History->Get Quote" );
135:           }
```

continues

Listing 7.10   continued

```
136:            else if ( item == mainMenu.historyEnableTracking )
137:            {
138:                System.out.println( "History->Enable Tracking" );
139:            }
140:            else if ( item == mainMenu.historyImport )
141:            {
142:                System.out.println( "History->Import" );
143:            }
144:            else if ( item == mainMenu.historyExport )
145:            {
146:                System.out.println( "History->Export" );
147:            }
148:            else if ( item == mainMenu.graphOptions )
149:            {
150:                System.out.println( "Graph->Options" );
151:            }
152:            else if ( item == mainMenu.helpContents )
153:            {
154:                System.out.println( "Help->Contents" );
155:            }
156:            else if ( item == mainMenu.helpAbout )
157:            {
158:                System.out.println( "Help->About" );
159:            }
160:        }
161:
162:        // Main entry point into the TickerListPanel class
163:        public static void main( String[] args )
164:        {
165:            StockApplication app = new StockApplication();
166:        }
167:}
```

Figure 7.26 shows the StockApplication application.

```
9:  import StockTabPanel;
10: import PortfolioListPanel;
11: import MainMenu;
```

Lines 9–11 import our StockTabPanel, PortfolioListPanel, and MainMenu classes, respectively.

```
14: public class StockApplication extends JFrame
                                    implements ActionListener
```

Lines 14 creates our StockApplication class that is derived from JFrame and implements the ActionListener interface to listen to menu item selections.

```
17:     MainMenu mainMenu = new MainMenu();
```

Line 17 creates an instance of our MainMenu class.

Figure 7.26

The StockApplication application.

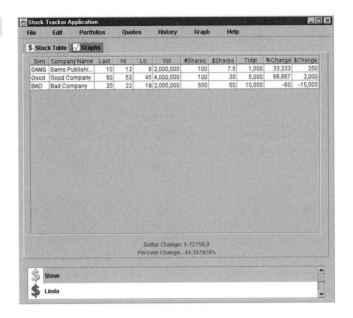

```
20:       StockTabPanel stockTabPanel = new StockTabPanel();
21:       PortfolioListPanel portfolioListPanel =
                                          new PortfolioListPanel();
```

Lines 20 and 21 create instances of our StockTabPanel and PortfolioListPanel classes, respectively.

```
30:          setJMenuBar( mainMenu );
```

Line 30 sets our MainMenu instance to be the menu bar for our JFrame.

```
33:          mainMenu.addActionListener( this );
```

Line 33 calls the MainMenu class's addActionListener method that we implemented in the last section that adds our ActionListener class as an action listener for all the JMenuItems in the MainMenu.

```
62:      public void actionPerformed(ActionEvent e)
```

Line 62 declares the ActionListener interface actionPerformed method, which is called whenever a menu selection occurs.

```
65:          JMenuItem item = ( JMenuItem )e.getSource();
```

Line 65 extracts the JMenuItem that caused the event from the ActionEvent through its getSource method.

```
68:          if( item == mainMenu.fileNew )
69:          {
70:              System.out.println( "File->New" );
71:          }
```

Lines 68–71 are characteristic of the entire `actionPerformed` event handler. Line 68 compares the `JMenuItem` that generated the event with the `MainMenu` object's menu items (`fileNew`) and if the items match, line 70 outputs the item to the standard output device.

Try launching the application and clicking the menu items to see the responses go to your output window (in Windows, this will be the command prompt that you launched the application from). Outputting the menu item that generated the event to the screen doesn't do much for us, but when we hook this up to the classes that will do actual work for us, these are the places where those classes will be invoked.

Summary

In this chapter, we started out looking at the use cases we derived back in Chapter 3 and determining which ones we would need to address in the user interface. Most of the items in the use cases were related to the user interface through menu options, which we graciously included. Next we moved into the paper design of the user interface and sketched out how everything was going to look. We took our sketches and determined what Java components we could use to implement our design.

Then it was time for the implementation of the user interface. We broke the user interface down into self-reliant components and slowly fit them together to eventually build our entire user interface by the end of the chapter. Throughout our journey we encountered some old Swing friends, such as `JList` and `JTable`, and made some new ones: `Graphics2D` (briefly) and the `JMenuBar` family. We also learned how to implement some specific event handlers for some of the more complicated Swing components (`JList` and `JTable` again).

What's Next?

We have a nice-looking user interface, but we are far from done with this application. We are now going to start adding some of the meat of the application—the components and classes that are going to do the actual work. Throughout the rest of the book, we will address major components of the application, implement those components, and then tie them back into the user interface so that we can see our hard work in action.

And now the fun begins!

In this chapter

- *Component Relationships*
- *Implementation Decisions*
- *Data Structures Provided with Java*
- *Our Strategy*
- *StockData*
- *Portfolio*
- *PortfolioManager*
- *Integrating Classes into the User Interface*

Chapter 8

Implementing Portfolios

Now that we have built an attractive user interface, it's time to make it work with real live data. This and most of the remaining chapters will be devoted to implementing different facets of the Stock Tracker application.

I will begin with portfolios. What is a portfolio? Well, if you remember from Chapter 3, "Designing the Stock Tracker Application," when we designed our application, a portfolio is a collection of stock symbols and a user's personal stake (that is, number of shares) in those stocks. Referring to the classes we generated in Chapter 3, portfolios encompass the following three classes:

- StockData—The StockData class holds all the data for one stock:
  - Stock symbol
  - Company name
  - Last sale
  - Day's high
  - Day's low
  - Day's volume
  - Number of shares the user owns
  - Price paid per share class
- Portfolio—The Portfolio class maintains a collection of StockData objects and the name of the owner of the portfolio (or whatever name the user wants to assign to the portfolio).
- PortfolioManager—The PortfolioManager class maintains a collection of Portfolios.

We are going to start this chapter implementing these components and then finish up the chapter integrating them into the user interface.

Component Relationships

Back in Chapter 3, I defined the class diagrams for the `StockData`, `Portfolio`, and `PortfolioManager` classes. The next thing I would like to do in the Unified Modeling Language (UML) design is to define the relationships between these classes and the application. Take a look at Figure 8.1.

Figure 8.1

Portfolio class relationships.

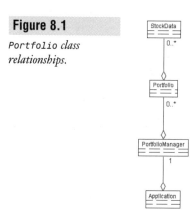

Figure 8.1 shows the relationship between the `Application`, `PortfolioManager`, `Portfolio`, and `StockData` classes. The way to read this diagram is as follows:

- An application contains one `PortfolioManager`.
- A `PortfolioManager` contains zero or more `Portfolio` objects.
- A `Portfolio` contains zero or more `StockData` objects.

The line with a small diamond on the end connecting the classes in the diagram shown in Figure 8.1 represents a special type of aggregation between the two components. An *aggregation* represents a form of "asymmetrical association" between two classes where one class plays a more important role than the other does. This is represented by the more important class having a hollow diamond on its end of the association. A special type of aggregation is composition; a *composition* states that one class is completely contained by the other class. A composition is represented in UML by a solid diamond next to the containing class.

The multiplicity, or the number of objects that may participate in a relationship, is read backward from the way you might think of it. The way to read the relationship between the `StockData` class and the `Portfolio` class is as follows: A `Portfolio` contains zero or more `StockData` objects and any given `StockData` object can be contained by only one `Portfolio`; if there is not a number next to the class, a one is assumed.

Implementation Decisions

The classes that make up the portfolio collection are fairly straightforward, but there are a few implementation decisions we have to make before we start. We will address the following points:

- File Strategy
- Data Structures
- Package Strategy

File Strategy

We are going to implement our data storage in flat text files, just as you would create with Windows Notepad. Chapter 15 talks about how you might store this information in a database using the Java Database Connectivity API (JDBC), but for the rest of this book I am going to stick to flat files.

 The term *flat* file refers to an unstructured file, like a text file, where the user defines the structure of data in the file. A *structured* file, on the other hand, usually represents a database and is organized by the database management system; typically a database file contains tables, search indexes, and other database elements.

Java provides support for text file manipulation through two classes: `FileReader` and `FileWriter`. Before I get into the intricacies of these classes, let me give you a bit of theory.

Data can be obtained from many sources—the file system, Internet, computer memory, and so on—and Java provides a common mechanism to obtain this information: streams. A *stream* is really only a path data travels in your application. An *input stream* represents data sent to your application, and an *output stream* represents data sent from your application to some other destination. Java provides different types of *streams* to facilitate this data exchange; one special type of stream that handles textual data is referred to as a *character stream*. The two base classes that Java provides for character streams are the `Reader` class and the `Writer` class. These classes are both abstract and thus you cannot directly create an instance of either of them, but specialized classes are derived from them that provide streaming functionality for individual data sources.

The `FileReader` and `FileWriter` classes are specialized classes that provide streaming functionality with respect to text files. Take a look at Figure 8.2 to see the derivation tree for both classes.

Figure 8.2

FileReader and FileWriter derivation tree.

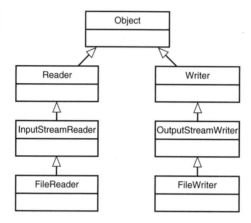

I'll start with the `FileReader` class. The `FileReader` class, as its name implies, is used to read files, text files specifically. Take a look at Table 8.1 to see its constructors.

Table 8.1   `FileReader` Constructors

Constructor	Description
FileReader(File file)	Creates a new `FileReader` from the specified file
FileReader(FileDescriptor fd)	Creates a new `FileReader` from the specified `FileDescriptor` object
FileReader(String fileName)	Creates a new `FileReader` from the specified filename

A `File` object represents file and directory pathnames; when you create a `FileReader` by specifying a filename, a `File` object is implicitly created. In this chapter I am going to use the third constructor to specify a filename for the files we are going to work with. When you create a `FileReader` object, the file is implicitly opened for you.

```
FileReader file = new FileReader( "Portfolios.txt" );
```

If the specified file does not exist, the `FileReader` constructor throws a `java.io.FileNotFoundException` exception.

You will need a set of methods to use the `FileReader` class, and they are shown in Table 8.2.

Table 8.2   `FileReader` Methods

Methods	Description
`int read()`	Reads a single character
`int read(char[] cbuf, int off, int len)`	Reads characters into a portion of an array
`void close()`	Closes the stream

The first `read()` method reads a single character from the file stream and returns it as an int; you can manually cast that to a char by prefacing the return value with "`(char)`":

```
char ch = ( char )file.read();
```

The `read()` method returns an integer instead of a character because of the way the `InputStreamReader` class (the `FileReader` class extends the `InputStreamReader` class) retrieves data. The `InputStreamReader` class's `read()` method returns the next character (as a 32-bit byte) from the file or -1 if it found the end of the file. A 32-bit integer represents more data than a 16-bit character and provides the caller with more information (such as the end of file marker).

The second `read()` method specifies a character array to read a specific number of characters into. This is beneficial if you are reading a large amount of data because you can make one method call instead of potentially thousands of method calls.

Finally, the `close()` method closes the file stream. Be sure to close the file when you are finished reading it:

```
file.close();
```

The next class I want to talk about is the `FileWriter` class. The `FileWriter` class, as its name implies, writes text to files. Table 8.3 shows its constructors.

Table 8.3   `FileWriter` Constructors

Constructor	Description
`FileWriter(File file)`	Creates a new `FileWriter` object from the specified `File` object. If the file already exists, overwrite it.
`FileWriter(FileDescriptor fd)`	Creates a new `FileWriter` object from the specified `FileDescriptor` object. If the file already exists, overwrite it.
`FileWriter(String fileName)`	Creates a new `FileWriter` object from the specified file-name. If the file already exists, overwrite it.
`FileWriter(String fileName, boolean append)`	Opens an existing file with the specified filename and append mode: `true` = append data to the end of this file, `false` = write data to the beginning of the file.

The constructors for the `FileWriter` class are similar to those of the `FileReader` class, but the one difference is the append mode. Using the fourth constructor and setting append to `true` causes an existing file to be opened for writing at the end of the file. This type of constructor would be good for a log file, for example, where you want to add a statement to a file leaving all the existing data intact. Using the fourth constructor and setting the append mode to `false` causes data to be written to the beginning of the file.

```
FileWriter file = new FileWriter( "Portfolios.txt" );
```

There is a set of methods you will need to use with this class, and they are shown in Table 8.4.

Table 8.4 `FileWriter` **Methods**

Methods	Description
void close()	Closes the stream
void flush()	Flushes the stream
void write(char[] cbuf, int off, int len)	Writes a portion of an array of characters
void write(int c)	Writes a single character
void write(String str, int off, int len)	Writes a portion of a string

The `FileWriter` class provides three `write` methods: one to write a single character to a file, one to write a specified number of characters from a character array to the file, and one to write a portion of a string to the file:

```
// Write a character to the file
file.write( 'a' );

// Write the entire character array to the file
char[] ca = { 'a', 'b', 'c' };
file.write( ca, 0, 2 );
```

Similar to the `read()` method, the `write()` method accepts an integer instead of a character.

Much of the data you send to the `FileWriter` is buffered (stored in memory) before it is written out to the file system. This is why calling the `write(char)` method 10 times may be similar in performance to calling the `write(char[])` method with an array of 10 characters: The `FileWriter` class may make only one call to write them to the file. This is a benefit to performance, but may not necessarily be what you want to happen.

If it is important that your data is written to the file immediately, you can call the `flush()` method that "flushes the stream," or in other words forces all the buffered data in the file stream to be written out to the file:

```
file.flush();
```

Finally, when you are finished with a file, you call the `FileWriter`'s `close()` method, similar to the `FileReader close()` method:

```
file.close();
```

Portfolio File Management

Now that you understand how files work, we can talk about our file strategy. The portfolios are going to require two file types:

- Portfolio Index—The portfolio index file will be used by the `PortfolioManager` class and includes the names of all portfolios for the application.
- Portfolio File—A portfolio file represents an individual portfolio. It is a collection of all the stock symbols and data for each stock in the portfolio. The name of the file will match the name listed in the portfolio index file.

Three classes make up the portfolio. Here are their roles with respect to files:

- `PortfolioManager`—Manages the portfolio index file.
- `Portfolio`—Manages a portfolio by opening the file, asking its `StockData` objects to read from and write to the file, and closing the file. The `Portfolio` file does not ever read from or write to the file directly.
- `StockData`—The `StockData` class does not open or close files, but it does know how to read from and write to files. The `Portfolio` class creates `FileReader` and `FileWriter` objects and passes those objects to the `StockData` class to be written to.

The reason for the separation of file operations between the `Portfolio` and `StockData` classes is that the `Portfolio` object logically represents a collection of `StockData`, and it naturally follows that it should maintain the file that holds their information. The `StockData` class does not know about a `Portfolio` class nor does it care; it knows how to represent its data, read its data from a file, and write its data to a file. The `Portfolio` class needs intimate knowledge of the file that is representing its `StockData`.

8

What Is a Data Structure?

Before we talk about what data structures are provided in Java, let me tell you a little bit about the purpose of data structures. A *data structure* is a container that holds data objects with the following properties:

- There is a way to add data to the data structure.
- There is a way to retrieve data from the data structure.
- There is a way to search for data in the data structure.
- There is a way to delete data from a data structure
- There is a way to update data in a data structure

The data structure that I have already exposed you to is a simple array. An array is a fixed-size (usually) indexed collection of like data types, for example we had arrays of String classes in our table model class in Chapter 7 representing column names. Let me show you how it works with the aforementioned criteria. The following paragraphs describe these operations on an array data structure.

Creation

You create an array in the standard way we have been using thus far in the book:

```
String[] stringArray = new String[10];
int nIndex = 0;
```

Add

You add a new string to the array at the next available index:

```
// Add an item to the next available index
StringArray[nIndex] = "My String";

// Increment the count of elements in the array
nIndex = nIndex + 1;
```

Retrieve

You retrieve an element from an array by specifying the index of the array item you want, for example:

```
// Print the first element of our string array to the standard output
System.out.println( stringArray[0] );
```

Search

You can search an array using a `for` loop and comparing the array values, for example if you were searching for the string "Linda", you would do the following:

```
for( int i=0; i<nIndex; i++ )
{
    if( stringArray[i] == "Linda" )
    {
        System.out.println( "Found Linda!" );
    }
}
```

Delete

Deleting an item from an array is more specific to the data type of the elements in the array. For a string array, you might set the value to an empty string:

```
// Set the first element of the array to an empty string
stringArray[0] = "";
```

Update

Finally, you can update an array by referencing the index of the value you want to update:

```
// Retrieve the first element in the array
String str = stringArray[0];

// Modify the contents of the string
str = str + "Modified";

// Set the first element of the array to the modified string
stringArray[0] = str;
```

This is all pretty simple stuff. But you might be thinking that there must be a better way to represent data, a better way to access data, a better way to search for a data item, and so on. Luckily, the software development community has several different data structures all designed for specific purposes.

Java is laden with a plethora of useful data structures. There are so many, however, that we cannot discuss all of them in depth. So what I am going to do is give you a little description of each, a scenario or two when each would be useful, and point you to the classes you will want to look at for more information.

Data Structures Provided with Java

Java maintains a set of interfaces that define data structure concepts. Java also provides implementations of those interfaces that represent specific data structures. These interfaces basically break down to three types:

- List—A List is an ordered collection or sequence. It usually permits duplicate elements and supports positional access (access to individual data elements at a specified location in the data structure). Java List types include AbstractList, AbstractSequentialList, LinkedList, Vector, Stack, and ArrayList. All the aforementioned classes are derived either directly or indirectly from the AbstractList class. Figure 8.3 shows the class hierarchy for these classes.

Figure 8.3

List hierarchy.

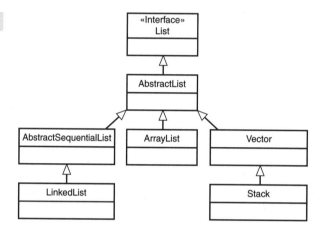

- Set—A Set is a collection of elements in which no duplicate elements are permitted and there is at most one null element. A special type of set, known as a SortedSet, provides sorting of the set elements in "natural order." Java Set types include AbstractSet, TreeSet and HashSet. All sets are derived directly from AbstractSet. Figure 8.4 shows the class hierarchy for these classes.

Figure 8.4

Set hierarchy.

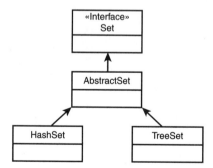

- Map—A Map is a collection of key and value pairs in which a key is mapped to a value. No duplicate keys are permitted, and each key can map to at most one value. A special type of map, known as a SortedMap, provides sorting of the map keys in natural order. Java Map types include AbstractMap, HashMap, Hashtable, WeakHashMap, and TreeMap. Figure 8.5 shows the class hierarchy for these classes.

Figure 8.5

Map hierarchy.

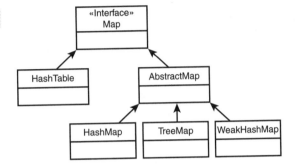

Array

I have already talked about arrays, but let me give you a more formal definition. An array is a fixed-size data structure that holds like elements and facilitates random access of those elements.

Random access means that you can access any element in the array at any time, without having to traverse through any other elements to get the one you want. In some data structures that I will show you in a minute, if you want the 15th element in the data structure, you must go through several elements, and sometimes all 14 preceding elements, to get to it. But with *random access*, you can extract the 15th element directly.

Arrays are very tight data structures that are well suited to cases where you will always have a fixed number of elements. A good example of where to use an array is a mathematical vector used in computer graphics to represent a two- or three-dimensional point; a vector is either a three-number or four-number array of integers or floats by definition. If you have a vector that is a three-integer array, you can perform all kinds of operations on it, but you will always have a three-integer array, no matter what.

The drawback of an array is that you must know the number of elements you want to store in the array at compile time (when you are writing the program). If you create an array of 15 elements and you want to add a 16th element, you are out of luck. One way to work around this problem is to create an array that is larger than you need, but this can be a waste of memory.

Arrays are created as part of the language, using brackets ([ ]), so there is not a class provided by the Java language for arrays. There is, however, a class that can help you manipulate arrays: `java.lang.reflect.Array`.

Vector

A *vector* is similar to an array in that it holds multiple elements and supports random access through indexed values. The main difference between arrays and vectors is that vectors automatically grow when they run out of room. Furthermore, they provide methods to add and remove elements from a vector that you would normally have to do manually with arrays.

With a vector, you specify an initial capacity and a growth rate, and it will take care of its expansion and compression as needed. Vectors are more versatile than arrays but also add a little more overhead by bringing in an additional class. Vectors are supported in Java through the `Vector` class. You can probably think of half a dozen cases where you could use a vector, and it will be a good fit wherever you want to store an unknown number of elements in a data structure. Take, for example, a collection of stock symbols in a portfolio: You do not know the number of symbols that will be in the portfolio, and you do not want to necessarily limit the number of symbols in the portfolio.

Vectors are not the "be all and end all" of data structures, however. Searching for an element in a vector is slow and, in the worst case, you might have to compare all the elements in the vector before you find your match. Furthermore, insertions in a vector are time-consuming because of the nature of the structure; a vector, in actuality, is a refined representation of an array.

Stack

A `Stack` is a special type of `Vector` that specifies the order in which elements are added and removed from the stack. A stack follows the paradigm of last-in-first-out (or LIFO for short). This works like a stack of books. If you have 10 books and stack them one on top of the other, when you want to get a book out you will need to take the top book off, then the next book, and so on, until you get to the book you want. This type of data structure is very useful when creating text parsing classes (classes that extract specific tokens from a text stream). The `Stack` class represents stacks.

Linked List

A *linked list* is an ordered collection of data elements. It supports inserting elements at any position and has no size limit; furthermore, it uses only the exact amount of memory that it needs, so there is no growth rate. Linked lists can be singly linked, meaning that to traverse a list you must start at the beginning and go through the list one element at a time only moving forward through the list, or doubly linked, meaning that you can go forward and backward through the list.

Storage space is optimal for a linked list, and insertions and deletions are great, but searches are slow if the list is large.

You could use linked lists in the same scenarios as vectors. Linked lists are represented in Java through the `LinkedList` class.

Set

As I said earlier, a *set* is a collection of data elements in which there are no duplicate elements and at most one null value. A set is a general concept represented by the `Set` interface and can be implemented in different ways: You can derive a class from `AbstractSet` or you can use the `HashSet` and `TreeSet` classes. A set data structure is similar to a mathematical set that is a collection of non-duplicate numbers.

Map

As I mentioned earlier, a map is a data structure that maps keys to values; no duplicate keys are allowed and each key can map to at most one value. You search for an object by specifying its key. A map can be viewed as either a set of keys, a collection of values, or a set of key-value mappings. You can use maps by deriving a class from `AbstractMap`, or you can use the `HashMap`, `HashTable`, and `WeakHashMap` classes. A map is useful to represent pairs of elements, such as a collection of people's names and their favorite food: Steve—Mee Krob, Linda—Papaya Salad (both fine Thai dishes).

8

Hashtable

A *hashtable*, again, is a collection of key and value pairs. A hash table works in the following way: An algorithm is applied to the key to determine the location in the table to store the value. If two keys map to the same table location, a collision occurs and a collision resolution algorithm is used to determine the next location. The details of implementing a hashtable are beyond the scope of this book, but the important things you should know about them are:

- Keys are mapped to values
- Duplicate keys are not permitted
- Adding elements is simple and fast
- Deleting elements is simple and fast
- Searching for elements is difficult and slow
- Sorting elements is not supported
- Displaying all elements is difficult

`Hashtables` can be used directly but are most commonly used with maps and sets through the `HashMap` and `HashSet` classes.

Trees

Trees are powerful data structures that are used in Java to implement maps and sets that are ordered. Trees are much more difficult to implement than the other data structures, but have some great benefits with respect to sorting and data retrieval. If you have a large amount of data, searches are incredibly simple and very fast. Displaying an ordered set of elements is also very simple. The tradeoff is that adding and deleting elements from a tree are difficult and slow operations. You would use a tree data structure when you know that you are not going to be adding and removing elements frequently, but you are going to be searching for elements very frequently.

I do not have time to go too deeply into trees, but I do think they deserve a little explanation. First, take a look at Figure 8.6 to see a visual representation of a tree.

Figure 8.6

A sample tree.

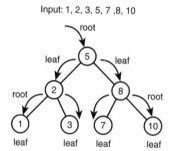

A tree is composed of *nodes* and there are two types: *root nodes* and *leaf nodes*. These terms are relative to their position. For example, in Figure 8.6, 5 is the *root node* and 2 and 8 are its *leaf nodes*, whereas 2 is a *root node* with 1 and 3 being its *leaf nodes*. There are different types of trees, but the tree shown in Figure 8.6 is the most common. The order of this type of tree is defined such that lower values are to the left of the tree and higher values are to the right. Every *root node* maintains this relationship.

Why is this important? Consider the example of a tree set where you have these integers in the tree: 1, 2, 3, 5, 7, 8, 10, and you are trying to find out if 7 is in the tree. Here are the steps you would perform:

1. Look at the root: 5.

2. Is 7 greater than 5?

3. Yes, move right.

4. Look at the node: 8.

5. Is 7 greater than 8?

6. No, move left.

7. Look at the node: 7

8. Done!

The point is that you have seven items in the list and you had to do only three comparisons. In an array, for example, you might have to look at all seven items before you find the one you are looking for. Furthermore, look at this tree: You will never have to make more than three comparisons before you find the node you are looking for. That might not sound that impressive now, but build a tree of 1000 elements and you will only have to look at seven nodes at most (ln 1000—natural log of 1000) to find your element. Comparing three to seven items isn't that impressive, but comparing seven to 1000 is! I am not going to derive any of this for you; if you are interested, you can look at a wide assortment of books on algorithms and data structures. The point here is that trees are good for a lot of elements that you are going to have to either sort or search frequently.

Our Strategy

Our `Portfolio` and `PortfolioManager` classes are going to need to maintain collections of elements: A `Portfolio` will maintain a collection of `StockData` objects and a `PortfolioManager` will maintain a collection of `Portfolio` objects. First let's discuss the `Portfolio` object. It has the following operations:

- Additions: Add a stock to the portfolio (infrequent).
- Deletions: Remove a stock from the portfolio (infrequent).
- Search: List all elements at startup (infrequent).
- Number of elements: Not too many, maybe a maximum of 20 or 30 (small).

Because a `Portfolio` contains only a small number of elements and there is no real search involved and we do not want to specify a maximum number of elements, I would recommend a list. What type of list do I like? How about a vector? It is small, maintains low overhead, grows dynamically, and supports all the options we are looking for.

Now, let's examine `PortfolioManager`. It has the following operations:

- Additions: Add a portfolio to its collection (infrequent).
- Deletions: Delete a portfolio from its collection (infrequent).
- Search: List all elements at startup (infrequent).
- Number of elements: Smaller than the `Portfolio` class, maybe five (small).

8

The `PortfolioManager` is small and not very demanding on the system, so I am going to recommend a `Vector` for this class as well.

I know that these examples are boring compared to the data structures we discussed earlier, but I do not want to use them for the sake of using them; the application should be functional and perform well! Don't worry too much, we will revisit our data structures in Chapter 12, "Graphing Historical Data," when we need to maintain a list of points. Think about what type of data structure you would use to represent a collection of data points and the reasons you would choose that data structure. If you are really curious, peek ahead to Chapter 12 or if you want to be surprised, you will get there soon!

Package Strategy

We have been importing packages and using them in our applications all throughout this book, but what exactly is a package and how do you implement one? A *package* is a collection of related classes and denoted by the `package` reserved word. The `package` reserved word is used to denote a class's membership in a defined group.

Creating a package is fairly simple; there are four steps.

Define a Package Name

A package name is a unique name that identifies your package. The recommended way for a company with Internet presence to define its package name is to use its World Wide Web domain name in reverse order. For example, consider Macmillan Computer Publishing:

```
mcp.com
```

The name of the package would be

```
com.mcp
```

Furthermore, you might want to specify some descriptive information to the package name, for example, suppose you are creating a stock package:

```
com.mcp.stock
```

Typically, package names all start with lowercase letters and classes start with uppercase letters, so a `Portfolio` class in this package would be referenced as follows:

```
com.mcp.stock.Portfolio
```

The reason for using your company's World Wide Web domain name is to maintain uniqueness in your package names. This is important because you do not want to have a name clash with someone else's class; if you create a `stock` package with a `Stock` class and another person creates a different `stock` package with a `Stock` class,

Java will not know which one to use. A World Wide Web domain name is unique to a company, so you should not have any problems with external vendors.

Create a Folder Structure for the Package

The organization of packages on your computer is implemented through folders. You must create a folder for each element separated by a period in the package name and add your classes to that folder. Consider the `Portfolio` example we just talked about.

In Figure 8.7, you can see that there is a `com` folder with an `mcp` folder in it. The `mcp` folder has a `stock` folder that contains the `Portfolio.java`, `PortfolioManager.java`, and `StockData.java` files.

Figure 8.7

Stock package directory structure.

Add Classes to the Package

Finally, you add classes to your package by using the `package` reserved word at the very beginning of the file and specifying the desired package name. So in the `Portfolio.java` file, the first noncomment line in the file would be

```
package com.mcp.stock;
```

Update the CLASSPATH Environment Variable

When you import classes from your packages into your other programs, you import it the same way you do the standard Java packages:

```
import com.mcp.stock.*;
```

For this import to work, you must update your CLASSPATH environment variable to include the folder that contains the `com` folder; the `import` statement knows that when it sees `com` that it must go all the way down `mcp` and `stock` to find your classes. Take a look at Appendix A, "Setting Up the Java 2 SDK," to find out how to set this variable on your operating system.

Our package strategy is going to follow this same Macmillan example, but I am going to categorize the classes even further than just packaging them all into the stock package. Under the *stock* package, I am going to add a `portfolios` package that is going to host our three classes. Thus at the beginning of the `Portfolio.java`,

8

PortfolioManager.java, and StockData.java files, I will add the following:

package com.mcp.stock.portfolios;

Our directory structure is going to look like Figure 8.8.

Figure 8.8

Stock package strategy.

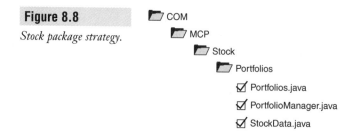

I will continue with this strategy as we develop the other classes in this book; the other classes will be grouped in like packages and added to the com.mcp.stock package.

Now that we have our foundation established, it is time to implement these classes!

StockData

Refer to the class diagram that we derived for the StockData class in Chapter 3; see Figure 8.9.

Figure 8.9

StockData class diagram.

From Figure 8.9, you can see that you must represent all the attributes for a stock, each attribute's get/set methods, a method to persist stock data from disk, a method to persist stock data to disk, and a method to update the stock information from the Internet. The neat thing about defining your class diagrams before you start coding is that the code almost writes itself. You know what attributes and methods you need in your class—all you have to do is implement them! It is really not all that difficult to implement an application after you have designed it—it might take more time to implement an application, but the design is the hard part.

Figure 8.10 shows a new class diagram for the implementation of the StockData class. Its attributes and methods are shown in Tables 8.5 and 8.6, respectively.

Figure 8.10

Revised StockData class diagram.

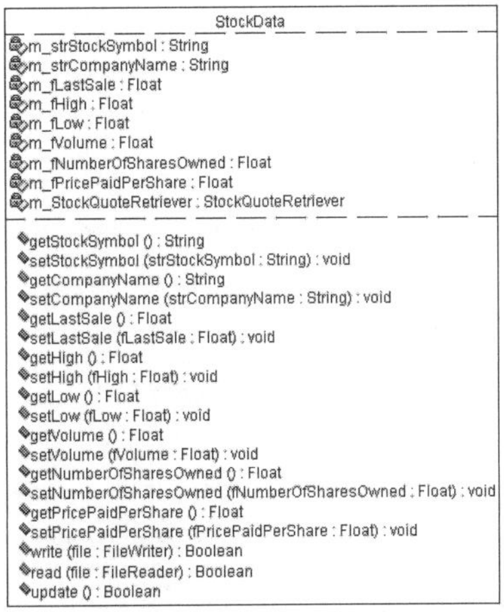

8

Table 8.5   StockData **Attributes**

Type	Name	Description
String	m_strStockSymbol	The stock ticker symbol.
String	m_strCompanyName	The full name of the company whose stock symbol is m_strStockSymbol.
Float	m_fLastSale	The price of the last recorded sale.
Float	m_fHigh	The highest sale price of the day thus far.
Float	m_fLow	The lowest sale price of the day thus far.
Float	m_fVolume	The number of shares of this stock that have been bought/sold for the day thus far.
Float	m_fNumberOfSharesOwned	The number of shares of this stock that the user owns.
Float	m_fPricePaidPerShare	The price per share paid for this stock.
StockQuoteRetriever m_StockQuoteRetriever		Not implemented in this chapter; see Chapter 9.

Table 8.6 **StockData Methods**

Method	Description
String getStockSymbol()	Gets the stock symbol
void setStockSymbol(String strStockSymbol)	Sets the stock symbol
String getCompanyName()	Gets the company name
void setCompanyName(String strCompanyName)	Sets the company name
Float getLastSale()	Gets the last sale
void setLastSale(Float fLastSale)	Sets the last sale
Float getHigh()	Gets the high of the day
void setHigh(Float fHigh)	Sets the high of the day
Float getLow()	Gets the low of the day
void setLow(Float fLow)	Sets the low of the day
Float getVolume()	Gets the volume of the day
void setVolume(Float fVolume)	Sets the volume of the day
Float getNumberOfSharesOwned()	Gets the number of shares owned
void setNumberOfSharesOwned(Float fNumberOfSharesOwned)	Sets the number of shares owned
Float getPricePaidPerShare()	Gets the price paid per share
void setPricePaidPerShare(Float fPricePaidPerShare)	Sets the price paid per share
Boolean read(FileReader file)	Reads a record from the specified FileReader and fills this StockData's fields with the record
Boolean write(FileWriter file)	Writes the data stored in the StockData to the specified FileWriter
Boolean update()	Updates our stock data from the Internet.

The only methods of consequence in this list are read, write, and update. The write method writes all the StockData's attributes to the FileWriter separated by commas and ending with a newline character. The read method reads in one entire line from the FileReader and then fills all its fields from that line; this line was previously written by the write method, so all the fields it reads are comma-separated and terminated by a newline. Finally, the update method is not implemented in the class yet; I will talk about that in Chapter 9, "Implementing the Stock Quote Retriever."

Take a look at Listing 8.1 for the complete source code for the StockData class, and I will discuss it afterward.

Type the code from Listing 8.1, excluding line numbers, into your favorite text editor and save it as StockData.java, or copy it from the CD. Build it as follows:

```
javac StockData.java
```

Listing 8.1 StockData.java

```java
1:  // Define the package we belong to
2:  package com.mcp.stock.portfolios;
3:
4:  // Import the Java Packages we are going to need
5:  import java.io.*;
6:  import java.util.*;
7:
8:  // public class: StockData
9:  public class StockData extends Object
10: {
11:     // Attributes
12:     protected String m_strStockSymbol = new String( "None" );
13:     protected String m_strCompanyName = new String( "None" );
14:     protected Float  m_fLastSale = new Float( 0 );
15:     protected Float  m_fHigh = new Float( 0 );
16:     protected Float  m_fLow = new Float( 0 );
17:     protected Float  m_fVolume = new Float( 0 );
18:     protected Float  m_fNumberOfSharesOwned = new Float( 0 );
19:     protected Float  m_fPricePaidPerShare = new Float( 0 );
20:     // protected StockQuoteRetriever m_StockQuoteRetriever;
21:
22:     // Constructor
23:     public StockData()
24:     {
25:     }
26:
27:     public StockData( String strStockSymbol, Float fNumberOfSharesOwned,
                                        Float fPricePaidPerShare )
28:     {
29:         // Copy the values passed in to our member variables
30:         m_strStockSymbol = strStockSymbol;
31:         m_fNumberOfSharesOwned = fNumberOfSharesOwned;
32:         m_fPricePaidPerShare = fPricePaidPerShare;
33:
34:         // Call update to retrieve the rest of the information from
35:         // the Internet
36:         update();
37:     }
38:
39:     public StockData( String strStockSymbol )
```

continues

Listing 8.1 **continued**

```
40:     {
41:         // Copy the values passed in to our member variables
42:         m_strStockSymbol = strStockSymbol;
43:     }
44:
45:     // Get / Set attribute methods
46:     public String getStockSymbol()
47:     {
48:         return m_strStockSymbol;
49:     }
50:
51:     public void setStockSymbol( String strStockSymbol )
52:     {
53:         m_strStockSymbol = strStockSymbol;
54:     }
55:
56:     public String getCompanyName()
57:     {
58:         return m_strCompanyName;
59:     }
60:
61:     public void setCompanyName( String strCompanyName )
62:     {
63:         m_strCompanyName = strCompanyName;
64:     }
65:
66:     public Float getLastSale()
67:     {
68:         return m_fLastSale;
69:     }
70:
71:     public void setLastSale( Float fLastSale )
72:     {
73:         m_fLastSale = fLastSale;
74:     }
75:
76:     public Float getHigh()
77:     {
78:         return m_fHigh;
79:     }
80:
81:     public void setHigh( Float fHigh )
82:     {
83:         m_fHigh = fHigh;
84:     }
85:
86:     public Float getLow()
87:     {
88:         return m_fLow;
89:     }
```

```
 90:
 91:     public void setLow( Float fLow )
 92:     {
 93:         m_fLow = fLow;
 94:     }
 95:
 96:     public Float getVolume()
 97:     {
 98:         return m_fVolume;
 99:     }
100:
101:     public void setVolume( Float fVolume )
102:     {
103:         m_fVolume = fVolume;
104:     }
105:
106:     public Float getNumberOfSharesOwned()
107:     {
108:         return m_fNumberOfSharesOwned;
109:     }
110:
111:     public void setNumberOfSharesOwned( Float fNumberOfSharesOwned )
112:     {
113:         m_fNumberOfSharesOwned = fNumberOfSharesOwned;
114:     }
115:
116:     public Float getPricePaidPerShare()
117:     {
118:         return m_fPricePaidPerShare;
119:     }
120:
121:     public void setPricePaidPerShare( Float fPricePaidPerShare )
122:     {
123:         m_fPricePaidPerShare = fPricePaidPerShare;
124:     }
125:
126:     // public Boolean read( file )
127:     //
128:     //  Reads the next line from "file" and extracts all of the
139:     //  StockData fields from it.
130:     //
131:     //  Returns true    on success
132:     //          false   on failure
133:     public Boolean read( FileReader file )
134:     {
135:         // Create a String to hold an entire line from the file
136:         String strLine = new String();
137:
138:         try
139:         {
140:             // Read the first character
```

continues

Listing 8.1 **continued**

```
141:            int nChar = file.read();
142:
143:            // Clear out any carriage returns or linefeeds:
144:            //   (1) Carriage Return = '\r'
145:            //   (2) Newline = '\n'
146:            while( nChar == '\n' || nChar == '\r' )
147:            {
148:                nChar = file.read();
149:            }
150:
151:            // Loop through all of the characters until we hit
152:            //   (1) The end of the line = -1
153:            //   (2) Newline = '\n'
154:            //   (3) Carriage Return = '\r'
155:            while( nChar != -1 && nChar != '\n' && nChar != '\r' )
156:            {
157:                // Copy the character to the line string
158:                strLine = strLine + ( char )nChar;
159:
160:                // Get the next character
161:                nChar = file.read();
162:            }
163:        }
164:        catch( IOException e )
165:        {
166:            // An error occurred during FileReader.read(). Display
167:            // the error and return false.
168:            System.out.println("StockData.read Error: " + e.toString() );
169:            return new Boolean( false );
170:        }
171:
172:        // See if the line  has anything in it
173:        if( strLine.length() == 0 )
174:        {
175:            return new Boolean( false );
176:        }
177:
178:        // Create a string tokenizer to parse the our line into
179:        // tokens with the following delimiters:
180:        //   (1) Tab             =   '\t'
181:        //   (2) Newline         =   '\n'
182:        //   (3) Carriage Return =   '\r'
183:        //   (4) Form Feed       =   '\f'
184:        //   (5) Comma           =   ','
185:        StringTokenizer st = new StringTokenizer( strLine, "\t\n\r\f," );
186:
187:
188:        // Get the count of the number of tokens in the line
189:        if( st.countTokens() != 8 )
190:        {
```

```
191:            // Error, not the correct number of tokens!
192:            System.out.println(
193:                "StockData.read Error: Expected 8 tokens, but received "
194:                + st.countTokens() );
195:
196:            // Return false
197:            return new Boolean( false );
198:        }
199:
200:        try
201:        {
202:            // Set our properties by extracing our 8 tokens
203:            m_strStockSymbol = st.nextToken();
204:            m_strCompanyName = st.nextToken();
205:            m_fLastSale = new Float( st.nextToken() );
206:            m_fHigh = new Float( st.nextToken() );
207:            m_fLow = new Float( st.nextToken() );
208:            m_fVolume = new Float( st.nextToken() );
209:            m_fNumberOfSharesOwned = new Float( st.nextToken() );
210:            m_fPricePaidPerShare = new Float( st.nextToken() );
211:        }
212:        catch( NoSuchElementException e )
213:        {
214:            // An error occurred during StringTokenizer.nextToken()
215:            // Log the error and return false
216:            System.out.println("StockData.read Error: " + e.toString() );
217:            return new Boolean( false );
218:        }
219:
220:        // Success! Return true
221:        return new Boolean( true );
222:    }
223:
224:    // public Boolean write( file )
225:    //
226:    //  Write all of our StockData fields to the FileWriter: file.
227:    //
228:    //  Returns true    on success
229:    //          false   on failure
230:    public Boolean write( FileWriter file )
231:    {
232:        try
233:        {
234:            // Write our fields to the FileWriter
235:            file.write( m_strStockSymbol + ","  );
236:            file.write( m_strCompanyName + "," );
237:            file.write( m_fLastSale.toString() + "," );
238:            file.write( m_fHigh.toString() + "," );
239:            file.write( m_fLow.toString() + "," );
240:            file.write( m_fVolume.toString() + "," );
241:            file.write( m_fNumberOfSharesOwned.toString() + "," );
```

continues

Listing 8.1 continued

```
242:              file.write( m_fPricePaidPerShare.toString() + "\r\n" );
243:          }
244:          catch( IOException e )
245:          {
246:              // An error occurred during FileWriter.read(). Display
247:              // the error and return false.
248:              System.out.println("StockData.write Error: "+e.toString() );
249:              return new Boolean( false );
250:          }
251:
252:          // Success! Return true
253:          return new Boolean( true );
254:
255:      }
256:
257:      // public Boolean update()
258:      //
259:      //   Not implemented yet.
260:      public Boolean update()
261:      {
262:          // Not implemented
263:          return new Boolean( false );
264:      }
265:}
```

Now let me go through some of the key areas of the class.

Line 2 defines the package that this file is part of: com.mcp.stock.portfolios. This statement defines this file and all the classes in it as being part of this package.

Line 9 is the declaration of the StockData class. The important thing to note in this declaration is that the StockData class is derived from the Object class. We did this because a Vector can only hold items in it that are derived from Object, and we are going to be storing StockData objects in a Vector within the Portfolio class.

Lines 12–20 define the attributes for the class. Note that the StockQuoteRetriever class instance is commented out; I will be uncommenting that in Chapter 9. All the Float variables are initialized to zero and all String variables are initialized to empty strings. Note that all these member variables are declared as protected, so that classes outside our package cannot access them; other classes must use the get and set methods to access these variables.

Line 23 defines an empty constructor that will be used later to create an instance of the StockData class without any values. Line 27 defines a constructor for the StockData class with the stock symbol, number of shares owned, and price paid per share defined. And finally, line 39 defines a constructor with just a stock symbol defined.

Lines 45–124 define `get` and `set` methods for all the `StockData` attributes. All the `get` methods simply return their respective attributes, whereas the `set` methods set their attributes. Pretty simple stuff!

Lines 133–222 define the `read` method. The `read` method accepts a `FileReader` object and reads one line from it. It then parses out its attributes from the line. Sounds easy, but now let's go through it.

First, lines 138–163 are enclosed in a `try-catch` block. A `try-catch` block is used to catch exceptions.

An *exception* is an error that occurs somewhere in a method. From an implementation perspective, when an error occurs, instead of returning an error code to the calling method, the method *throws* an *exception*. This has two benefits: You can send a very detailed description of an error to the caller, passing him as much information as you want, and you can still return meaningful variable types (for example a `String`) from your methods and not status or error codes. What do you do to use a method that throws exceptions? You enclose them in a `try-catch` block.

EXCURSION
Exception Handling

What you are saying is "Try the code in the `try` block and if any errors occur, notify me in the `catch` block." You use the reserved word `try` followed by the code that can throw exceptions enclosed in braces (`{}`). Immediately following the `try` block you use the reserved word `catch`. Now `catch` acts like a method that accepts a parameter of a specific type: a specific exception type. Methods will throw specific exception types, so you must have one `catch` statement for each type of exception you want to handle; this is accomplished by adding `catch` block after `catch` block until you are done. I will show you a little later where we implement multiple `catch` blocks. Anyway, an exception type is just a class that is derived from the `java.lang.Exception` class. The Java 2 SDK documentation will show you all the possible exceptions that a method can call; the compiler will also return an error if you do not try to catch an exception that can be thrown by a method.

Exception handling is a powerful development tool that allows you to gracefully recover from error conditions. Whether this recovery is logging an error message to the standard error (`System.err`) or displaying a message box, or simply ignoring it and continuing the application in a limited capacity is up to you—the user will be shielded from errors!

If you use a class's method that throws an exception, Java will make you put the method call in a try block and force you to catch the exception that it throws. This way, it ensures that the error will never reach the user directly without your code knowing about it.

The `FileReader` class's `read()` method can throw an `IOException` exception, so in line 164 the `catch` statement handles the `IOException`. Line 141 reads one character from the `FileReader`. Next, in lines 146–149, a `while` loop is used to clear out any carriage returns or new lines that are at the beginning of the file stream. A carriage return is represented by the character combination `'\r'` and a new line is represented by the character combination `'\n'`.

A `while` loop simply says "While the condition is `true`, process the statements in the `while` loop and then check the condition again." The form of a `while` loop is

```
while( condition )
{
    statement;
}
```

The condition is checked before the statements are processed and immediately after the statement block is processed.

In this `while` loop, I just read characters from the `FileReader` by calling `read()` (line 148).

After we have all the carriage returns and linefeeds from the input stream, it is time to read a line from the `FileReader`. We accomplish this with another `while` loop that adds a new character to the string line variable we defined (`strLine`) and reads a character from the `FileReader` (lines 158 and 161). The `while` loop in line 155 terminates when a carriage return, a linefeed, or the end of file is reached. The end of file is reported by a value of -1.

When we have an entire line stored in `strLine`, we check to see if the line truly has any data in it by comparing its length to zero. The `String` class has a method, `length()`, that returns the number of characters in the string. If this value is zero, there are no characters in the string—it is empty. We just return `false` if this occurs.

Line 185 is an interesting one. We define a new `StringTokenizer` object; the `StringTokenizer` class is used to break a string down into its parts delimited by specific criteria. In our case we use all the standard delimiters the `StringTokenizer` supports: tab, newline, carriage return, and form feed (`\t`, `\n`, `\r`, and `\f`) and our important one, a comma. It is important to visualize what the string we read in will look like when we are writing this. Consider the following:

```
QUE,Que Publishing,50.0,52.0,48.0,4000000.0,100.0,30.0
```

So all the values are separated by commas and terminated at the end by a carriage return and newline (note this may be different on your platform, but we handle everything).

The `StringTokenizer` constructors are shown in Table 8.7.

Table 8.7 `StringTokenizer` **Constructors**

Constructor	Description
`StringTokenizer(String str)`	Constructs a string tokenizer for the specified string
`StringTokenizer(String str, String delim)`	Constructs a string tokenizer for the specified string
`StringTokenizer(String str, String delim, boolean returnTokens)`	Constructs a string tokenizer for the specified string

In these constructors, `str` is the input string to tokenize, `delim` is a string with all the delimiters, and `returnTokens` is a Boolean that, if `true`, returns the delimiters as tokens. In our case, we pass the line we constructed earlier as the `str` parameter, and we build a string of delimiters and pass that as the `delim` parameter.

The first thing we do with the `StringTokenizer` is to count the tokens in it; this is accomplished by calling the `StringTokenizer` class's `countTokens()` method. We are expecting eight tokens: symbol, company name, last sale, high, low, volume, number of shares owned, and price paid per share. In line 189 we count the tokens and return `false` if we do not have eight tokens.

Lines 200–211 extract the tokens, in order, from the `StringTokenizer` to the class's attributes using the `StringTokenizer` class's `nextToken()` method. The `nextToken()` method, as its name implies, returns the next token from the string passed to the `StringTokenizer` as the `str` parameter. The `nextToken()` method throws a `NoSuchElementException` exception if there are no more tokens available. We handle that exception in line 212 and then subsequently return `false`, denoting that the read method failed.

Finally, in line 221 we are done, so we return `true`.

The `write()` method is much simpler. It is defined in lines 230–255. The `write()` method accepts a `FileWriter` as a parameter and simply calls its `write()` method passing the `StockData` attributes in the same order we will read it back in the `read()` method later, delimited by commas. At the end of the line we add a carriage return and newline. The only caveat here is that the `FileWriter` class's `write()` method can throw an `IOException` exception if an error occurs while writing. We catch that exception in line 244, output the error and then return `false` denoting that the `StockData` `write()` method failed.

Now for the easiest method in the class, the `update()` method. The `update()` method is not implemented yet, so it just returns `false`.

8

The StockData class is done for this chapter. We will revisit it in the next chapter to add a meaningful update() method and a StockQuoteRetriever attribute.

Portfolio

The Portfolio class does not do too much more than maintain a Vector of StockData objects. The class diagram we derived in Chapter 3 is shown again in Figure 8.11.

Figure 8.11

Portfolio class diagram.

Figure 8.12 shows a new class diagram for the implementation of the Portfolio class. Its attributes and methods are shown in Tables 8.8 and 8.9, respectively.

Figure 8.12

Revised Portfolio class diagram.

Table 8.8   Portfolio **Attributes**

Attributes	Description
Vector m_vectorStockData	Vector collection of StockData objects
String m_strPortfolioName	The name of the Portfolio

Table 8.9   Portfolio **Methods**

Methods	Description
String getName()	Returns the name of the portfolio
void setName(String strPortfolioName)	Sets the name of the portfolio
StockData getStockDataObject(int nIndex)	Returns the StockData object stored at the specified position
Boolean savePortfolio()	Saves the Portfolio to disk

Methods	Description
`Boolean loadPortfolio()`	Loads the Portfolio from a disk file
`int getNumberOfStockDataObjects()`	Returns the number of StockData objects in the Portfolio
`Boolean updateStockPrices()`	Tells all the `StockData` objects to update their stock prices and statistics
`void addStock(StockData stockData)`	Adds a StockData object to the Portfolio
`void removeStock(int nIndex)`	Removes the `StockData` object at the specified position in the `Portfolio`

You might notice that we changed a few things. First, we removed the variable that maintains the number of StockData items in our collection. By implementing our StockData collection object as a Vector, it takes care of that for us. We also added two methods: addStock() and removeStock() to help streamline some of the Portfolio options. Take a look at Listing 8.2 and then I will go over it.

Type the code from Listing 8.2, excluding line numbers, into your favorite text editor and save it as Portfolio.java, or copy it from the CD. Build it as follows:

```
javac Portfolio.java
```

Listing 8.2 `Portfolio.java`

```
1:  // Define the package we belong to
2:  package com.mcp.stock.portfolios;
3:
4:
5:  // Import the Java Packages we are going to need
6:  import java.io.*;
7:  import java.util.*;
8:
9:  // public class: Portfolio
10: public class Portfolio extends Object
11: {
12:      // Variable to hold our StockData objects
13:      protected Vector m_vectorStockData = new Vector();
14:
15:      // The name of this portfolio object
16:      protected String m_strPortfolioName = new String();
17:
18:      // Constructor
19:      public Portfolio()
20:      {
21:      }
22:
23:      public Portfolio( String strName )
```

continues

Listing 8.2 continued

```
24:     {
25:         // Save our name
26:         m_strPortfolioName = strName;
27:     }
28:
29:     // public String getName()
30:     //
31:     //  Returns the name of the portfolio
32:     public String getName()
33:     {
34:         return m_strPortfolioName;
35:     }
36:
37:     // public void setName( strPortfolioName )
38:     //
39:     //  Set the name of the portfolio
40:     public void setName( String strPortfolioName )
41:     {
42:         m_strPortfolioName = strPortfolioName;
43:     }
44:
45:     // public StockData getStockDataObject( nIndex )
46:     //
47:     //  Retrieve the StockData object in the vector at index nIndex
48:     //  Throws ArrayIndexOutOfBoundsException on error!
49:     public StockData getStockDataObject( int nIndex )
50:     {
51:         // See if the index the user is requesting is valid
52:         if( nIndex >= m_vectorStockData.size() )
53:         {
54:             // Index is not valid, generate an
55:             // ArrayIndexOutOfBoundsException
56:             ArrayIndexOutOfBoundsException e =
57:                 new ArrayIndexOutOfBoundsException
58:                 (
59:                     "Requested Index: " +
60:                     Integer.toString( nIndex ) +
61:                     " of a vector with " +
62:                     Integer.toString( m_vectorStockData.size() ) +
63:                     " elements"
64:                 );
65:
66:             throw e;
67:         }
68:
69:         // Return the StockData Object at the given index
70:         return ( StockData )m_vectorStockData.elementAt( nIndex );
71:     }
72:
73:     // public Boolean savePortfolio()
```

```
74:      //
75:      //  Save the portfolio to the filename m_strPortfolioName.txt by
76:      //  creating a FileWriter object and calling each element's write
77:      //  method.
78:      //
79:      //  Returns true    on success
80:      //           false   on failure
81:      public Boolean savePortfolio()
82:      {
83:          try
84:          {
85:              // Create a new FileWriter with the filename being the
86:              // portfolio name.txt
87:              FileWriter file = new FileWriter(m_strPortfolioName+".txt");
88:
89:              // Loop through all elements in the vector
90:              for( int i=0; i<m_vectorStockData.size(); i++ )
91:              {
92:                  // Retrieve the element at index i
93:                  StockData data =
                          (StockData)m_vectorStockData.elementAt(i);
94:
95:                  // Tell it to write its data to our file writer
96:                  data.write( file );
97:              }
98:
99:              // Close the FileWriter object
100:             file.close();
101:         }
102:         catch( IOException e )
103:         {
104:             // An error occurred during one of the file operations
105:             System.out.println( "Portfolios.savePortfolio Error: " +
                                                  e.toString() );
106:             return new Boolean( false );
107:         }
108:
109:         // Success
110:         return new Boolean( true );
111:     }
112:
113:     // public Boolean loadPortfolio()
114:     //
115:     //  Load the portfolio from the file "m_strPortfolioName.txt" by:
116:     //      (1) Create a FileReader object
117:     //      (2) Create a new StockData object
118:     //      (3) Call the StockData object's read method on the FileReader
119:     //      (4) If successful, add the element to our vector
120:     public Boolean loadPortfolio()
121:     {
```

8

continues

Listing 8.2 continued

```
122:        try
123:        {
124:            // Create a new FileWriter with the filename being the
125:            // portfolio name.txt
126:            FileReader file = new FileReader(m_strPortfolioName+".txt");
127:
128:            // Create a Boolean Object to tell us when we hit the
139:            // end of file marker
130:            Boolean bEndOfFile = new Boolean( true );
131:
132:            // While we haven't reached the end of the file
133:            while( bEndOfFile.booleanValue() )
134:            {
135:                // Create a new StockData object
136:                StockData data = new StockData();
137:
138:                // Read in data for this StockData
139:                bEndOfFile = data.read( file );
140:
141:                // If we were successful, add this element to our vector
142:                if( b.booleanValue() )
143:                {
144:                    m_vectorStockData.addElement( data );
145:                }
146:            }
147:
148:            // Close the FileReader object
149:            file.close();
150:        }
151:        catch( FileNotFoundException e )
152:        {
153:            // File does not exist. This is not necessarily an error, the
154:            // Portfolio will just be empty. Return false nonetheless.
155:            return new Boolean( false );
156:        }
157:        catch( IOException e )
158:        {
159:            System.out.println
160:            (
161:                "Portfolio.loadPortfolio Error: " +
162:                e.toString()
163:            );
164:        }
165:
166:        // Success! Return true
167:        return new Boolean( true );
168:    }
169:
170:    // public int getNumberOfStockDataObjects()
171:    //
172:    //  Return the number of items in the stock data vector.
173:    public int getNumberOfStockDataObjects()
```

```
174:    {
175:        return m_vectorStockData.size();
176:    }
177:
178:    // public Boolean updateStockPrices()
179:    //
180:    //  Call each vector element's update method.
181:    //  Return true     on success
182:    //        false     on failure
183:    public Boolean updateStockPrices()
184:    {
185:        // Loop through all of the elements in the vector
186:        for( int i=0 ; i<m_vectorStockData.size(); i++ )
187:        {
188:            // Retrieve the StockData object at index i
189:            StockData data = (StockData)m_vectorStockData.elementAt(i);
190:
191:            // Call its update method
192:            if( data.update().booleanValue() == false )
193:            {
194:                // Update method failed, return False
195:                return new Boolean( false );
196:            }
197:        }
198:
199:        // Success! Return true
200:        return new Boolean( true );
201:    }
202:
203:    // public void addStock( StockData stockData )
204:    //
205:    //  Add stockData to our StockData vector.
206:    public void addStock( StockData stockData )
207:    {
208:        m_vectorStockData.addElement( stockData );
209:    }
210:
211:    // public void removeStock( int nIndex )
212:    //
213:    //  Removed the StockData object at the specified position.
214:    public void removeStock( int nIndex )
215:    {
216:        try
217:        {
218:            m_vectorStockData.removeElementAt( nIndex );
219:        }
220:        catch( ArrayIndexOutOfBoundsException e )
221:        {
222:            throw e;
223:        }
224:    }
225:}
```

8

Line 2 defines the package that the Portfolio class is part of:

com.mcp.stock.portfolios

Line 10 declares our Portfolio class. Note that it extends Object similar to the StockData class because the Portfolio class is eventually going to be contained in a Vector, which as we learned earlier can only hold objects derived from Object.

Line 13 declares a new Vector, which at this point does not have anything in it. Line 16 declares the String that will hold the name of the Portfolio. Both of these attributes are declared as protected so that other classes outside of the package will not be able to access them.

Lines 18–27 define two constructors for the Portfolio class, one that is empty and one that accepts the name to assign to the Portfolio. Speaking of the name of the Portfolio, lines 32–43 define the get and set name methods.

Lines 49–71 define the getStockDataObject() method that returns a StockData class instance that is stored at the specified index of the StockData vector. In line 52 it verifies that the requested index is valid and throws an ArrayIndexOutOfBoundsException exception if it is not (lines 56–66).

This is our first example of throwing an exception ourselves. To throw an exception, you construct a new exception object (in this case an ArrayIndexOutOfBoundsException object) and then use the reserved word throw to throw the actual exception. The ArrayIndexOutOfBoundsException constructor accepts a string describing the exception, so we give it the requested index number and the total number of elements in the Vector (lines 59–63).

Finally, if the index is valid, it extracts the specified element from the vector using the elementAt() method, casts it to a StockData class instance, and returns it to the caller (line 70).

Lines 81–111 define the savePortfolio() method. This method declares a new FileWriter object in line 87 with the name of the portfolio with .txt appended to it. Line 90 declares a for loop that loops through all the elements in the StockData Vector. It extracts the StockData element at the current index in line 93 and then tells that StockData object to write() its data to the FileWriter object. Finally, in line 100, it closes the FileWriter object.

The FileWriter object can throw an IOException during its constructor and during its close() method, so all the aforementioned statements are enclosed in a try-catch block that handles the IOException in line 102. Finally, the method returns true in line 110.

Lines 120–168 define the `loadPortfolio()` method. The `loadPortfolio()` method creates a new `FileReader` object in line 126 and declares a `Boolean` value to note when we reach the end of the file in line 130. This time we use a `while` loop to loop until our end-of-file Boolean notification is `false` in line 133. We create a new empty `StockData` object and tell it to read its data from the `FileReader` object. If the `StockData` `read()` method returns `false`, we have reached the end of the file and we can stop. If the value is `true`, we add this `StockData` object to our `Vector` by calling the `Vector` class's `addElement()` method. Finally, we close the `FileReader` object in line 149.

The `FileReader` constructor can throw a `FileNotFoundException` exception and its `read()` and `close()` methods can throw an `IOException` exception, so we handle both of those exceptions in lines 151–164. This shows an example of what we talked about earlier—handling multiple exceptions by adding multiple `catch` statements. Finally, in line 167 we return `true`.

Lines 173–176 define the `getNumberOfStockDataObjects()` method by returning the number of elements in the `StockData` `Vector`. This is accomplished by calling the `Vector` class's `size()` method.

Lines 183–201 define the `updateStockPrices()` method, and although this functionality is not implemented in the `StockData` class, this method is completely implemented. It loops through all the `StockData` elements in its `Vector`, retrieves each `StockData` (line 189) object and then calls its `update()` method (line 192). If the `update()` method returns `false`, the `updateStockPrices()` method returns `false`.

Lines 206–209 define the `addStock()` method by adding the specified `StockData` object to the `Vector` by calling its `addElement()` method.

Finally, lines 214–224 define the `removeStock()` method. This method calls the `Vector` class's `removeElementAt()` method passing it the index of the item to remove. This method can throw an `ArrayIndexOutOfBoundsException` exception if the index passed to it is invalid. Because we are simply passing this call on to the `Vector`, we will just catch the exception and re-throw it to the method that called us.

That is the `Portfolio` class in its entirety!

PortfolioManager

The `PortfolioManager` class is probably the simplest of the bunch in the sense that it does not have any knowledge about any real data. It is responsible for maintaining a collection of `Portfolio` objects and managing the communication between the user interface and the `Portfolios`. Take a look at Figure 8.13 to see the class diagram we derived for the `PortfolioManager` back in Chapter 3.

8

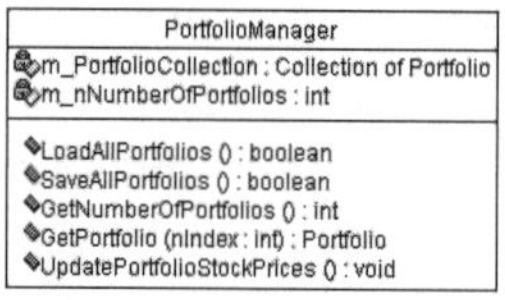

Figure 8.13

PortfolioManager class diagram.

```
              PortfolioManager
m_PortfolioCollection : Collection of Portfolio
m_nNumberOfPortfolios : int

LoadAllPortfolios () : boolean
SaveAllPortfolios () : boolean
GetNumberOfPortfolios () : int
GetPortfolio (nIndex : int) : Portfolio
UpdatePortfolioStockPrices () : void
```

Figure 8.14 shows a new class diagram for the implementation of the PortfolioManager class. Its attributes and methods are shown in Tables 8.10 and 8.11, respectively.

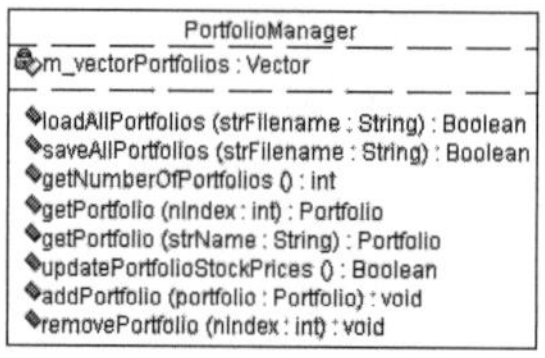

Figure 8.14

Revised PortfolioManager class diagram.

```
              PortfolioManager
m_vectorPortfolios : Vector

loadAllPortfolios (strFilename : String) : Boolean
saveAllPortfolios (strFilename : String) : Boolean
getNumberOfPortfolios () : int
getPortfolio (nIndex : int) : Portfolio
getPortfolio (strName : String) : Portfolio
updatePortfolioStockPrices () : Boolean
addPortfolio (portfolio : Portfolio) : void
removePortfolio (nIndex : int) : void
```

Table 8.10 `PortfolioManager` **Attributes**

Attributes	Description
Vector m_vectorPortfolios	Vector of Portfolio objects

Table 8.11 `PortfolioManager` **Methods**

Methods	Description
Boolean loadAllPortfolios (String strFilename)	Loads all the Portfolios listed in the specified filename
Boolean saveAllPortfolios (String strFilename)	Saves all the Portfolios listed in the specified filename
int getNumberOfPortfolios()	Returns the number of Portfolios in the Portfolio Vector
Portfolio getPortfolio(int nIndex)	Gets the specified Portfolio object by position
Portfolio getPortfolio (String strName)	Gets the specified Portfolio by Portfolio name
Boolean updatePortfolioStockPrices()	Tells all Portfolio objects to update all their stock prices
void addPortfolio(Portfolio portfolio)	Adds a Portfolio to the Vector of Portfolios
void removePortfolio(int nIndex)	Removes the specified Portfolio from the Portfolio Vector

The only real changes we made to this class implementation from the class diagram were the removal of the number of portfolios attribute (we will use a vector that will maintain that information for us), and we added two management methods: addPortfolio() and removePortfolio(). Furthermore, we added two variations of the getPortfolio() method to get a Portfolio object by position or by name; this was done for easier integration with the user interface.

Anyway, take a look at Listing 8.3, and then I will go over it.

Type the code from Listing 8.3, excluding line numbers, into your favorite text editor and save it as PortfolioManager.java, or copy it from the CD. Build it as follows:

```
javac PortfolioManager.java
```

Listing 8.3   `PortfolioManager.java`

```
1:  // Define the package we belong to
2:  package com.mcp.stock.portfolios;
3:
4:  // Import the Java Packages we are going to need
5:  import java.io.*;
6:  import java.util.*;
7:
8:  // public class: PortfolioManager
9:  public class PortfolioManager
10: {
11:     // Create a vector of portfolios
12:     Vector m_vectorPortfolios = new Vector();
13:
14:     // Constructor
15:     public PortfolioManager()
16:     {
17:     }
18:
19:     // public Boolean loadAllPortfolios( strFilename )
20:     //
21:     //   Loads a vector of Portfolios from their names, which are listed
22:     //   in strFilename.
23:     public Boolean loadAllPortfolios( String strFilename )
24:     {
25:         try
26:         {
27:             // Create a FileReader to read the portfolio manager file
28:             FileReader file = new FileReader( strFilename );
29:
30:             // Get the first character from the file
31:             int nChar = file.read();
32:
```

continues

8

Listing 8.3 continued

```
33:              // Loop through the file until we get an end of file
34:              // marker (-1)
35:              while( nChar != -1 )
36:              {
37:                  // String to hold the portfolio names
38:                  String strPortfolio = new String();
39:
40:                  // Clear out any carriage returns or linefeeds:
41:                  //  (1) Carriage Return = '\r'
42:                  //  (2) Newline = '\n'
43:                  while( nChar == '\n' || nChar == '\r' )
44:                  {
45:                      nChar = file.read();
46:                  }
47:
48:
49:                  // Read a line from the file
50:                  while( nChar != '\r' && nChar != '\n' && nChar != -1 )
51:                  {
52:                      // Append this character to our string
53:                      strPortfolio = strPortfolio + ( char )nChar;
54:
55:                      // Get the next character
56:                      nChar = file.read();
57:                  }
58:
59:                  // Make sure we read something!
60:                  if( strPortfolio.length() != 0 )
61:                  {
62:                      // Create a new Portfolio Object
63:                      Portfolio portfolio = new Portfolio( strPortfolio );
64:
65:                      // Tell the Portfolio to load itself
66:                      portfolio.loadPortfolio();
67:
68:                      // Add this portfolio to the Portfolio vector
69:                      m_vectorPortfolios.addElement( portfolio );
70:                  }
71:              }
72:
73:          }
74:      catch( FileNotFoundException e )
75:      {
76:          // Not necessarily an error, this just means that there
77:          // are no portfolios yet — could be the first time the
78:          // user ran the application
79:          return new Boolean( false );
80:      }
81:      catch( IOException e )
82:      {
```

```
83:                // A FileReader.read method call failed!
84:                System.out.println
85:                (
86:                    "PortfolioManager.loadAllPortfolios Error: " +
87:                     e.toString()
88:                );
89:
90:                return new Boolean( false );
91:            }
92:
93:            // Success! Return true
94:            return new Boolean( true );
95:        }
96:
97:        // public Boolean saveAllPortfolios( strFilename )
98:        //
99:        //  Save the list of portfolio names to strFilename and tell all
100:       //  portfolios to save themselves.
101:       public Boolean saveAllPortfolios( String strFilename )
102:       {
103:           try
104:           {
105:               // Create a file that we are going to write to
106:               FileWriter file = new FileWriter( strFilename );
107:
108:               for( int i=0; i<m_vectorPortfolios.size(); i++ )
109:               {
110:                   // Get the i-th portfolio from our vector
111:                   Portfolio portfolio =
                           (Portfolio)m_vectorPortfolios.elementAt(i);
112:
113:                   // Tell the portfolio to save itself
114:                   portfolio.savePortfolio();
115:
116:                   // Save the portfolio name in our portfolio
117:                   // manager file
118:                   file.write( portfolio.getName() );
119:
120:                   // append a carriage return and line feed to the end
121:                   // of this line
122:                   file.write( "\r\n" );
123:               }
124:
125:
126:               // Close the FileWriter object
127:               file.close();
128:           }
129:           catch( IOException e )
130:           {
131:               System.out.println
```

8

continues

Listing 8.3 **continued**

```
132:            (
133:                "PortfolioManager.saveAllPortfolio Error: " +
134:                e.toString()
135:            );
136:        }
137:
138:        // Success! Return true
139:        return new Boolean( true );
140:    }
141:
142:    // public int getNumberOfPortfolios()
143:    //
144:    //  Return the number of portfolios in the portfolio manager
145:    public int getNumberOfPortfolios()
146:    {
147:        return m_vectorPortfolios.size();
148:    }
149:
150:    // public Portfolio getPortfolio( nIndex )
151:    //
152:    //  Retrieves the nIndex-th portfolio from the portfolio manager.
153:    //  Throws ArrayIndexOutOfBoundsException on error!
154:    public Portfolio getPortfolio( int nIndex )
155:    {
156:        // See if the index the user is requesting is valid
157:        if( nIndex >= m_vectorPortfolios.size() )
158:        {
159:            // Index is not valid, generate an
160:            // ArrayIndexOutOfBoundsException
161:            ArrayIndexOutOfBoundsException e =
162:                new ArrayIndexOutOfBoundsException
163:                (
164:                    "Requested Index: " +
165:                    Integer.toString( nIndex ) +
166:                    " of a vector with " +
167:                    Integer.toString( m_vectorPortfolios.size() ) +
168:                    " elements"
169:                );
170:
171:            throw e;
172:        }
173:
174:        // Return the StockData Object at the given index
175:        return ( Portfolio )m_vectorPortfolios.elementAt( nIndex );
176:    }
177:
178:    // public Portfolio getPortfolio( strName )
179:    //
180:    //  Retrieve the portfolio by name.
181:    //  Throws NoSuchElementException on error
```

```
182:    public Portfolio getPortfolio( String strName )
183:    {
184:        try
185:        {
186:            // Loop through the portfolio vector
187:            for( int i=0; i<m_vectorPortfolios.size(); i++ )
188:            {
189:                // Get the Portfolio object form the vector at i
190:                Portfolio p = (Portfolio)m_vectorPortfolios.elementAt(i);
191:
192:                // Do we have a match?
193:                if( p.getName() == strName )
194:                {
195:                    // Match! Return this object
196:                    return p;
197:                }
198:            }
199:        }
200:        catch( ArrayIndexOutOfBoundsException e )
201:        {
202:            // Should never get here!
203:            System.out.println( "PortfolioManager.getPortfolio Error: " +
                                                        e.toString() );
204:        }
205:
206:        // Create a NoSuchElementException - we do not have this
207:        // element in our vector
208:        NoSuchElementException e =
209:            new NoSuchElementException( "Could not find " + strName   +
                                                    in portfolio " );

210:
211:        // Throw our exception
212:        throw e;
213:    }
214:
215:    // public Boolean updatePortfolioStockPrices()
216:    //
217:    //  Tell all of the portfolios in the portfolio manager to update
218:    //  their stock prices
219:    public Boolean updatePortfolioStockPrices()
220:    {
221:        // Loop through all of the portfolios in the vector
222:        for( int i=0; i<m_vectorPortfolios.size(); i++ )
223:        {
224:            // Retrieve the i-th portfolio
225:            Portfolio portfolio =
                    (Portfolio)m_vectorPortfolios.elementAt(i);
226:
227:            // Tell it to update its stock price
228:            if( portfolio.updateStockPrices().booleanValue() == false )
229:            {
```

continues

Listing 8.3 continued

```
230:                    // An error occurred! Return false
231:                    return new Boolean( false );
232:            }
233:        }
234:
235:        // Success! Return true
236:        return new Boolean( true );
237:    }
238:
239:    // public void addPortfolio( portfolio )
240:    //
241:    //   Add a portfolio to our vector
242:    public void addPortfolio( Portfolio portfolio )
243:    {
244:        m_vectorPortfolios.addElement( portfolio );
245:    }
246:
247:    // public void removePortfolio( nIndex )
248:    //
249:    //   Remove the portfolio at index nIndex from the vector.
250:    //   Throws ArrayIndexOutOfBoundsExceptions on error.
251:    public void removePortfolio( int nIndex )
252:    {
253:        try
254:        {
255:            m_vectorPortfolios.removeElementAt( nIndex );
256:        }
257:        catch( ArrayIndexOutOfBoundsException e )
258:        {
259:            throw e;
260:        }
261:    }
262:}
```

Line 2 defines the package that the PortfolioManager belongs to:

```
com.mcp.stock.portfolios
```

Line 9 declares our class. This is the first class in the package that is not derived from Object; we do not need this derivation because there is only one instance of this class per application and we are not going to add it to any generic container (like a Vector).

Line 12 declares a Vector that we are going to add our Portfolio objects to.

Line 14 defines an empty constructor for the PortfolioManager.

Lines 23–95 define the `loadAllPortfolios()` method. This method reads the file passed to it as the `strFilename` parameter to determine the portfolios that it must load. It then creates a new `Portfolio` object and tells it to load its information from disk. This portfolio index file is going to look similar to the following:

```
Steve
Linda
Nikko
Skie
DeeDee
```

It is simply a collection of names of portfolios.

The first thing we do is create a new `FileReader` object in line 28. We then construct a `while` loop in line 35 that will read to the very end of the file (until the character read is -1). First, we skip over all new lines and carriage returns in lines 43–46 (read a character and compare it to `'\n'` and `'\r'`). We then add characters to a portfolio `String` object repeatedly until we read a newline, carriage return, or end-of-file marker (lines 50–57).

Next we make sure that the portfolio name has data in it (compare its length to 0, as we did in the `StockData read()` method) and then we construct a new `Portfolio` object with this name (line 63). We tell the `Portfolio` object to load its portfolio information (line 66), and then we add it to our `Vector` using the `Vector` class's `addElement()` method (line 69).

You might recall that the `FileReader` class can throw a `FileNotFoundException` exception if the specified file does not exist, and the `FileReader` class's `read()` method can throw an `IOException` exception. We handle both of these exceptions in lines 74–91.

Finally, we return `true` in line 94 if the method has succeeded.

Lines 101–140 define the `saveAllPortfolios()` method. This method is much simpler than the `loadAllPortfolios()` method. It creates a new `FileWriter` object in line 106 with the specified filename for the portfolio index file. It then loops through all `Portfolios` in its `Portfolio Vector` in the `for` loop in line 108. For each `Portfolio` in the `Vector`, it extracts the `Portfolio` (line 111), tells it to save its portfolio (line 114), writes the name of the portfolio to the portfolio index file (line 118) and then appends a carriage return and newline to the portfolio index file. Finally, it closes the portfolio index file in line 127. It handles the `IOException` that `write()` and `close()` can throw in lines 129–136 and finally returns `true` in line 139.

Lines 145–148 define the `getNumberOfPortfolios()` method by asking the `Vector` for its size to get the number of elements in the vector and then returning that value.

8

Lines 154–176 define the getPortfolio() by position method. This method first checks to see if the requested index is too high (line 157), and if it is, it throws an ArrayIndexOutOfBoundsException (lines 161–171).

If the requested index is valid, we get the Portfolio object at the specified index and return it to the caller (line 175).

Lines 182–213 define the getPortfolio() by name method. This method loops through all elements in the Portfolio Vector using a for loop (line 187). It extracts the Portfolio object from the Vector (line 190) and compares it to the requested portfolio name (line 193). If successful, it returns the Portfolio. If it is not successful, this method creates a new NoSuchElementException exception object (line 208) and throws that to the caller (line 212). Remember that the Vector class's elementAt() method can throw an ArrayIndexOutOfBoundsException exception, so lines 200–204 catch it.

Lines 219–237 define the updatePortfolioStockPrices() method. This method loops through all the Portfolios in the Portfolio Vector using a for loop (line 222). For each Portfolio, it extracts the Portfolio from the Vector (line 225) and then tells the Portfolio to update its stocks' prices by calling its updateStockPrices() method (line 228). If an error occurs, it returns false; otherwise, it returns true.

Lines 242–245 define the addPortfolio() method by calling the Vector class's addElement() method.

Lines 251–261 define the removePortfolio() method by calling the Vector class's removeElementAt() method, passing the specified index. If the removeElementAt() method throws an ArrayIndexOutOfBoundsException exception, this method re-throws it to the caller.

There you have it: all three classes!

Integrating Classes into the User Interface

Now that we have these classes written, we have to implement them into our user interface so that they are of some value to us! There are quite a few changes that we have to make to the Stock Tracker user interface to implement these classes. I am going to give you a summary of the changes, and you are going to have to refer to the source code on the CD-ROM to see the final implementations (there is not enough room in the book to reprint the entire last chapter).

PortfolioListPanel

The PortfolioListPanel displays the list of Portfolios that are active in the Stock Tracker application. We are going to need to add four methods to this class, as shown in Table 8.12.

Table 8.12   New PortfolioListPanel Methods

Methods	Description
void addPortfolio(String strName)	Adds the specified text string to the list box
void removeAllPortfolios()	Clears all items from the list box
void addListSelectionListener (ListSelectionListener listener)	Adds the specified ListSelectionListener to the Portfolio list box
void setSelectedIndex(int nIndex)	Selects the specified item in the list box

Here is the implementation of the addPortfolio() method:

```
// public void addPortfolio( strName )
//
//   Adds strName to our list box
public void addPortfolio( String strName )
{
    listModelPortfolios.addElement( strName );
}
```

The addPortfolio() method simply calls the DefaultListModel class's addElement() method with the specified string. Recall that the DefaultListModel holds all the data contained in the JList.

```
// public void removeAllPortfolios()
//
//   Removes all portfolios from the listbox
public void removeAllPortfolios()
{
    listModelPortfolios.removeAllElements();
}
```

This method calls the DefaultListModel class's removeAllElements() method. This method, as its name implies, removes all elements from the DefaultListModel.

```
// public void addListSelectionListener( listener )
//
//   Adds listener as a ListSelctionListener for the ListModel
public void addListSelectionListener( ListSelectionListener listener )
{
    listPortfolios.addListSelectionListener( listener );
}
```

8

The addListSelectionListener() method calls the JList class's addListSelectionListener() method. We added this method so that the parent class (StockApplication) can listen to list box selection changes.

```
// public void setSelectedIndex( nIndex )
//
//  Forwards this call to the JList
public void setSelectedIndex( int nIndex )
{
   listPortfolios.setSelectedIndex( nIndex );
}
```

The setSelectedIndex() method simply forwards the setSelectedIndex() method request to the JList object.

StockTablePanel

Recall that the StockTablePanel displays all the stock information for a given portfolio in a tabular form. We have to make a few changes to the StockTablePanel class to implement our portfolio suite. The main change we have to make is with respect to the table data and more specifically the table model. The table model currently used in the StockTablePanel holds a set of "dummy," or fake, values in an array. Luckily for us, the Portfolio class represents all the data we want to display in the table, thus we are going to modify the table model such that it has a Portfolio object it gets its data from. We are going to add setPortfolio() and getPortfolio() methods to update the portfolio for the table and then get all our information from that portfolio.

Because the changes to the StockTableModel are so extensive, Listing 8.4 shows the new StockTableModel class.

Listing 8.4 StockTableModel

```
 1:  class StockTableModel extends AbstractTableModel
 2:  {
 3:      // Create the columns for the table
 4:      final String[] strArrayColumnNames =
 5:      {
 6:          "Sym",
 7:          "Company Name",
 8:          "Last",
 9:          "Hi",
10:          "Lo",
11:          "Vol",
12:          "#Shares",
13:          "$Shares",
14:          "Total",
15:          "%Change",
16:          "$Change"
17:      };
```

```
18:
19:     // Declare the Portfolio that this table will be representing
20:     Portfolio m_portfolio = new Portfolio();
21:
22:     public StockTableModel()
23:     {
24:     }
25:
26:     // public void setPortfolio( portfolio )
27:     //
28:     //  Set the portfolio that this table will represent
29:     public void setPortfolio( Portfolio portfolio )
30:     {
31:         m_portfolio = portfolio;
32:         fireTableDataChanged();
33:     }
34:
35:     // public Portfolio getPortfolio()
36:     //
37:     //  Retrieve the portfolio that this table is representing
38:     public Portfolio getPortfolio()
39:     {
40:         return m_portfolio;
41:     }
42:
43:     // Return the number of columns in the table
44:     public int getColumnCount()
45:       {
46:         return strArrayColumnNames.length;
47:       }
48:
49:     // Return the number of rows in the table
50:     public int getRowCount()
51:       {
52:          return m_portfolio.getNumberOfStockDataObjects();
53:       }
54:
55:     // Get the column name from the strArrayColumnNames array for the
56:     // "col-th item
57:     public String getColumnName( int col )
58:       {
59:         return strArrayColumnNames[col];
60:       }
61:
62:     // Return the value, in the form of an Object, from the obArrayData
63:     // object array at position (row, col)
64:     public Object getValueAt( int row, int col )
65:       {
66:           // Get the StockData item for this row
67:           StockData data = m_portfolio.getStockDataObject( row );
68:
```

continues

Listing 8.4 **continued**

```
69:        // We will compute columns 8, 9, and 10, so if the column number
70:        // is below eight, we can just return it without computing or
71:        // retrieving anything.
72:        if( col < 8 )
73:        {
74:            switch( col )
75:            {
76:                case 0:
77:                    return data.getStockSymbol();
78:                case 1:
79:                    return data.getCompanyName();
80:                case 2:
81:                    return data.getLastSale();
82:                case 3:
83:                    return data.getHigh();
84:                case 4:
85:                    return data.getLow();
86:                case 5:
87:                    return data.getVolume();
88:                case 6:
89:                    return data.getNumberOfSharesOwned();
90:                case 7:
91:                    return data.getPricePaidPerShare();
92:            }
93:        }
94:
95:        // Retrieve the necessary values from the object array to compute
96:        // all of the remaining columns
97:        Float fLastSale = data.getLastSale();
98:        Float fNumberOfShares = data.getNumberOfSharesOwned();
99:        Float fPurchasePrice = data.getPricePaidPerShare();
100:
101:        switch( col )
102:        {
103:            // Total Holdings = Last Sale(2) * Number of Shares Owned(6)
104:            case 8:
105:
106:                // See whether we own any of this stock
107:                if( fNumberOfShares.floatValue() == 0 )
108:                {
109:                    return new Float( 0 );
110:                }
111:
112:                // Build a new Float object with the product of the two
113:                Float fTotal = new  Float
114:                (
115:                    // Note, these must be converted to type "float" to
116:                    // perform the multiplication
117:                    fLastSale.floatValue() * fNumberOfShares.floatValue()
118:                );
```

```
119:
120:                    // Return the result
121:                    return( fTotal );
122:
123:              // Percent change =
124:              //   (Last Sale Price (2) / Purchase Price (7)) * 100%   - 100 %
125:              case 9:
126:
127:                    // See whether we own any of this stock
128:                    if( fNumberOfShares.floatValue() == 0 )
129:                    {
130:                        return new Float( 0 );
131:                    }
132:
133:                    Float fPercentChange = new  Float
134:                    (
135:                        ((fLastSale.floatValue() /
136:                                fPurchasePrice.floatValue ()) * 100) - 100
                        );
137:
138:                    return fPercentChange;
139:
140:              // Dollar Change =
141:              //   LastSale*NumberOfShares - PurchasePrice * NumberOfShares
142:              case 10:
143:
144:                    // See whether we own any of this stock
145:                    if( fNumberOfShares.floatValue() == 0 )
146:                    {
147:                        return new Float( 0 );
148:                    }
149:
150:                    Float fDollarChange = new Float
151:                    (
152:                        (fLastSale.floatValue()*fNumberOfShares.floatValue())
153:                        -
154:                        (fPurchasePrice.floatValue()*fNumberOfShares.floatValue())
155:                    );
156:
157:                    return fDollarChange;
158:
159:       } //End of switch on col
160:
161:    // A column was requested that this class does not support so
162:    // create a NoSuchElementException exception specifying the invalid
163:    // row and column numbers
164:    NoSuchElementException e =
165:        new NoSuchElementException( "Row, column: (" +
166:        Integer.toString( row) +
167:        ", " +
```

continues

Listing 8.4   continued

```
168:                Integer.toString(col) +
169:                ") not found!");
170:
171:         // Throw our exception
172:         throw e;
173:     }
174:
175:     // Return the class type, in the form of a Class, for the c-th column
176:     // in the first (0-th indexed) element of the obArrayData object array
177:     public Class getColumnClass( int c )
178:         {
179:         return getValueAt(0, c).getClass();
180:     }
181:
182:     // Return true if the "col"-th column of the table is editable, false
183:     // otherwise.  The following columns are editable:
184:     //
185:     //     Cell        Description
186:     //     ----        -----------
187:     //      0          Symbol
188:     //      6          Number of Shares Owned
189:     //      7          Purchase Price per Share
190:     //
191:     public boolean isCellEditable(int row, int col)
192:         {
193:         // Check the column number
194:         if( col == 0 || col == 6 || col == 7 )
195:             {
196:             return true;
197:             }
198:         else
199:             {
200:             return false;
201:             }
202:     }
203:
204:     // Set the value of the (row, col) element of the obArrayData to value
205:     public void setValueAt(Object value, int row, int col)
206:         {
207:         // Get the StockData object for this row
208:         StockData data = m_portfolio.getStockDataObject( row );
209:
210:         // Symbol
211:         if( col == 0 )
212:             {
213:             // We need a string value - we can convert any
214:             // value to a string, so just assign it
215:             data.setStockSymbol( ( String )value );
216:             }
217:
```

```
218:         // Number of Shares owned
219:         else if( col == 6 )
220:         {
221:             // We need a number - either float or int
222:             data.setNumberOfSharesOwned(
                     new Float( getNumberString( value.toString() ) ) );
223:         }
224:
225:         // Purchase Price per share
226:         else if( col == 7 )
227:         {
228:             // We need a float
229:             data.setPricePaidPerShare(
                     new Float( getNumberString( value.toString() ) ) );
230:         }
231:
232:         // Cell is not editable
233:         else
234:         {
235:             return;
236:         }
237:
238:         // Notify our parent of the change
239:         fireTableCellUpdated(row, col);
240:     }
241:
242:     // String getNumberString( String str )
243:     //
244:     // Read through str and return a new string with the numbers and
245:     // decimal points contained in str
246:     public String getNumberString( String str )
247:     {
248:         // Get str as a character array
249:         char[] strSource = str.toCharArray();
250:
251:         // Create a buffer to copy the results into
252:         char[] strNumbers = new char[strSource.length];
253:         int nNumbersIndex = 0;
254:
255:         // Boolean to ensure we only have one decimal point in the number
256:         // in our number
257:         boolean bFoundDecimal = false;
258:
259:         // Loop through all values of str
260:         for( int i=0; i<strSource.length; i++ )
261:         {
262:             // Check for a digit or decimal point
263:             if( Character.isDigit( strSource[i] ) )
264:             {
265:                 strNumbers[nNumbersIndex++] = strSource[i];
266:             }
```

continues

Listing 8.4   continued

```
267:                else if( strSource[i] == '.' && !bFoundDecimal )
268:                {
269:                    // Append the character to the String
270:                    strNumbers[nNumbersIndex++] = strSource[i];
271:
272:                    // Note that we found the decimal value
273:                    bFoundDecimal = true;
274:                }
275:        }
276:
277:        // Build a new string to return to our caller
278:        String strReturn = new String( strNumbers, 0, nNumbersIndex );
279:
280:        // Return our string
281:        return strReturn;
282:    }
283:
284:    // Return the column width of the column at index nCol
285:    public int getColumnWidth( int nCol )
286:    {
287:        switch( nCol )
288:        {
289:            case 0:
290:            case 2:
291:            case 3:
292:            case 4:
293:            case 6:
294:            case 7:
295:            case 9:
296:                return 50;
297:            case 1:
298:                return 125;
299:            default:
300:                return 75;
301:        }
302:    }
303:}
```

Line 20 creates a new empty `Portfolio` object that the `StockTableModel` is going to use for its data.

Lines 29–33 define the `setPortfolio()` method that sets the `Portfolio` object and tell the table to update itself by calling the `firstTableDataChanged()` method.

Lines 38–41 define the `getPortfolio()` method by returning the saved `Portfolio` object.

Lines 50–53 modify the getRowCount() method to return the number of StockData objects in its Vector by calling its getNumberOfStockDataObjects() method.

Lines 64–173 define the getValueAt() method. We left most of the information of this method intact, but we changed its source. It now retrieves all of its information from the StockData item for the specified row. The other change to this method are that it now throws a NoSuchElementException exception if a value is requested that is not in the Portfolio; this should not happen because the JTable is the only one calling this method, but if it is not defined properly, it could happen.

Lines 205–240 define the setValueAt() method. The only additions we made to this method is to get the corresponding StockData item for the row (line 208) and call its set methods for the attributes that changed (lines 215, 222, and 229).

The only other change we made to the StockTablePanel was to import our Portfolio class by adding the following import statement to the top of the StockTablePanel source file:

```
import com.mcp.stock.portfolios.*;
```

TickerListPanel

Recall that the TickerListPanel is responsible for displaying the stock ticker symbols in the current Portfolio for graphing purposes. In this class we are going to add a new ListModel class to hold a Portfolio object it will get its information from. Listing 8.5 shows the implementation of the TickerListModel class.

Listing 8.5   **TickerListModel**

```
 1:  // TickerListModel
 2:  public class TickerListModel extends AbstractListModel
 3:  {
 4:      // Portfolio that holds all of our stock symbols
 5:      Portfolio m_portfolio = new Portfolio();
 6:
 7:      // Constructor
 8:      public TickerListModel()
 9:      {
10:      }
11:
12:      // public void setPortfolio( portfolio )
13:      //
14:      //   Save the new portfolio and tell the list control to update its
15:      //   display.
16:      public void setPortfolio( Portfolio portfolio )
17:      {
18:          m_portfolio = portfolio;
```

continues

Listing 8.5   continued

```
19:            this.fireContentsChanged( this, 0 ,
                       m_portfolio.getNumberOfStockDataObjects() );
20:        }
21:
22:    // public int getSize()
23:    //
24:    //  Return the size of the list model (number of
25:    //  items in the list)
26:    public int getSize()
27:    {
28:        return m_portfolio.getNumberOfStockDataObjects();
29:    }
30:
31:    // public Object getElementAt( index )
32:    //
33:    //  Return the element at position index
34:    public Object getElementAt( int index )
35:    {
36:        if( m_portfolio.getNumberOfStockDataObjects() == 0 )
37:        {
38:            return( new String() );
39:        }
40:        StockData data = m_portfolio.getStockDataObject( index );
41:        return data.getStockSymbol();
42:    }
43: }
```

Line 5 creates a new `Portfolio` object.

Lines 16–20 define a new `setPortfolio()` method that saves the `Portfolio` sent to it and tells the `ListModel` that its contents have changed by calling `fireContentsChanged()` so that it will update its display.

Lines 26–29 define the `getSize()` method that returns the number of elements in the `Portfolio`.

Finally, lines 24–42 define the `getElementAt()` method, which gets the `StockData` object at the specified index and then returns its stock symbol by calling the `StockData` class's `getStockSymbol()` method. Note that if there are no `StockData` objects in the `Portfolio`, this method returns an empty string; the `JList` may ask for an initial element even though there may not be any, so this protects us.

The only other change we made to the `TickerListPanel` was to import our `Portfolio` class by adding the following `import` statement to the top of the `TickerListPanel` source file:

```
import com.mcp.stock.portfolios.*;
```

GraphTabPanel

Recall that the GraphTabPanel class facilitates the communication between the TickerListPanel and the StockGraphPanel classes. The changes we have to make to this class are minimal. We have to add a setPortfolio() method that sends the Portfolio object to both the TickerListPanel and StockGraphPanel classes. Here is the new setPortfolio() method:

```
// public void setPortfolio( portfolio )
//
//  Set the portfolio on the ticker list panel and tell the
//  graph which symbol to display
public void setPortfolio( Portfolio portfolio )
{
    // Set the ticker list portfolio
    tickerListPanel.setPortfolio( portfolio );

    // Update the graph
    stockGraphPanel.setSymbol(
    ( String )tickerListPanel.listTickers.getModel().getElementAt( 0 ) );
}
```

The only other change we made to the GraphTabPanel was to import our Portfolio class by adding the following import statement to the top of the GraphTabPanel source file:

```
import com.mcp.stock.portfolios.*;
```

MainMenu

The MainMenu class really does not have to change for the portfolio updates we are making, but I opted to modify the File, New method to have three options:

- Portfolio Manager—Create a new PortfolioManager object. This will not be implemented at this time.
- Portfolio—Create a new Portfolio object and add it to the PortfolioManager.
- Stock—Create a new StockData object and add it to the currently selected Portfolio object.

Originally, I suggested one File, New menu option, and we would check for component input focus to determine what type of item to create, but after reconsidering the usability, I decided it will be easier for a user to specify explicitly what he/she wants to create.

Here are the changes made to the MainMenu class:

```
// Make fileNew a JMenu instead of a JMenuItem
public JMenu fileNew = new JMenu( "New" );
```

8

```
      // Create our three new JMenuItems
         public JMenuItem fileNewPortfolioManager =
                 new JMenuItem("Portfolio Manager");
         public JMenuItem fileNewPortfolio = new JMenuItem( "Portfolio" );
         public JMenuItem fileNewStock = new JMenuItem( "Stock" );
...

public MainMenu()
{
       // Add our "File" menu
      add( menuFile );

      // Add our items to the "File" menu
      fileNew.add( fileNewPortfolioManager );
      fileNew.add( fileNewPortfolio );
      fileNew.add( fileNewStock );

      ...
}

...

public void addActionListener( ActionListener listener )
{
       // Add listener as the action listener for the "File" menu items
      fileNewPortfolioManager.addActionListener( listener );
      fileNewPortfolio.addActionListener( listener );
      fileNewStock.addActionListener( listener );
}
```

There you have it. We have already talked about all these commands in the last chapter, so this should all be familiar to you. If not, thumb back to the last chapter and look up the `MainMenu` class.

StockApplication

The modifications to the `StockApplication` are by far the most significant. Let me go through the changes one by one.

First, we have to import the portfolio package:

```
import com.mcp.stock.portfolios.*;
```

Next, in order to know when a user changes the selection of a `Portfolio` in the `PortfolioListPanel`, we have to add the `StockApplication` as a `ListSelectionListener` for it, thus our class declaration changes to implement `ListSelectionListener`:

```
public class StockApplication extends JFrame
                    implements ActionListener, ListSelectionListener
```

If you recall our implementation of PortfolioManager, you will know that we specify the filename of the portfolio index file that we want to use. We need to decide on a filename; the best implementation for this file is to define a constant variable with the filename:

```
public final static String portfolioFile = new String( "Portfolios.txt" );
```

I am calling the file Portfolios.txt; it is easy and descriptive. In the future, we could create a configuration file for the application that specifies where to look for this file or we could store all the data in a database, but for now this file will suffice.

Now we have to create a new instance of our PortfolioManager class:

```
protected PortfolioManager portfolioManager = new PortfolioManager();
```

Next we have to make some major modifications to the constructor. The main problem at this point is that we do not have a "Portfolios.txt" file and do not have any mechanism to create one. Let me show you the code for the constructor and then I will go over it; this discussion will make more sense afterward. See Listing 8.6.

Listing 8.6 **StockApplication Constructor**

```
1:  public StockApplication()
2:  {
3:      // Set up our title
4:      super( "Stock Tracker Application" );
5:
6:      // Add our main menu
7:      setJMenuBar( mainMenu );
8:
9:      // Add the StockApplication as a listener to the menu
10:     mainMenu.addActionListener( this );
11:
12:     // Add our components
13:     stockTabPanel = new StockTabPanel();
14:     portfolioListPanel = new PortfolioListPanel();
15:
16:     getContentPane().add( stockTabPanel, BorderLayout.NORTH );
17:     getContentPane().add( portfolioListPanel, BorderLayout.SOUTH );
18:
19:     // Set our size
20:     setSize( 680, 600 );
21:
22:     // Load our portfolio manager
23:     if( portfolioManager.loadAllPortfolios(portfolioFile ).booleanValue()
                    == false )
24:     {
25:         // We don't have any portfolios yet so prompt the user for one
26:         Object obResult = new Object();
```

continues

Listing 8.6   continued

```
27:            String strNewPortfolio = new String();
28:            obResult = null;
29:
30:            // Loop until we get a good value
31:            while( (obResult == null) || (strNewPortfolio.length() == 0) )
32:            {
33:                // Prompt the user
34:                obResult = JOptionPane.showInputDialog(
35:                    this,
36:                    "Welcome to QStock! Please enter a new portfolio name",
37:                    "QStock Startup",
38:                    JOptionPane.INFORMATION_MESSAGE);
39:
40:                // See if the user pressed OK or CANCEL
41:                if( obResult != null )
42:                {
43:                    // User pressed OK, get the string return value
44:                    strNewPortfolio = ( String )obResult;
45:                }
46:            }
47:
48:            // Add the new portfolio to the portfolio manager
49:            portfolioManager.addPortfolio( new Portfolio( strNewPortfolio) );
50:        }
51:
52:        // Initialize our portfolio list panel with all of the
53:        // portfolios in our portfolio manager
54:        for( int i=0; i<portfolioManager.getNumberOfPortfolios(); i++ )
55:        {
56:            portfolioListPanel.addPortfolio(
57:                    portfolioManager.getPortfolio( i ).getName() );
58:        }
59:
60:        // Select the first item in the portfolio list
61:        portfolioListPanel.setSelectedIndex( 0 );
62:
63:        // Add the StockApplication as a listener to the PortfolioListPanel
64:        portfolioListPanel.addListSelectionListener( this );
65:
66:        // Set the stock table's portfolio
67:        stockTabPanel.stockTableTabPanel.stockTablePanel.stockTableModel.
68:                setPortfolio(
                    portfolioManager.getPortfolio( 0 ) );
69:
70:        // Set the graph panel's portfolio
71:        stockTabPanel.graphTabPanel.setPortfolio(
                                portfolioManager.getPortfolio( 0 ) );
72:
73:        // Make the StockApplication visible
74:        setVisible( true );
```

```
75:
76:     // Add a window listener to list for our window closing
77:     addWindowListener
78:     (
79:         new WindowAdapter()
80:         {
81:             public void windowClosing( WindowEvent e )
82:             {
83:                 exitApp();
84:             }
85:         }
86:     );
87: }
```

It all starts on line 22 when we call the PortfolioManager class's loadAllPortfolios() method. If this method returns true, we already have a portfolio index file created and we are ready to go. If not, we have to create a portfolio. Instead of randomly creating one, we are going to prompt the user to create one.

We can prompt the user for information using a modal dialog box by using the JOptionPane class. This class has a plethora of different uses, but we are only going to be concerned with one right now, its input dialog. This dialog box will present the user with a string, usually a question; a text input field that the user can type something in, usually a response to the question; and two buttons: OK and Cancel. This input dialog returns an object representing the value entered in the text input field or null if the user clicked Cancel. Line 31 defines a while loop that will repeatedly show the input dialog box until the user enters something in the text input box and clicks OK. Line 34 displays the input dialog by explicitly calling the JOptionPane class's showInputDialog() method:

```
34:             obResult = JOptionPane.showInputDialog(
35:                 this,
36:                 "Welcome to QStock! Please enter a new portfolio name",
37:                 "QStock Startup",
38:                 JOptionPane.INFORMATION_MESSAGE);
```

If the user entered something in the text input field and clicked OK, a String is extracted from the Object that the JOptionPane returned (line 44). In line 49 a new Portfolio object is created and added to the PortfolioManager.

Lines 54–58 loops through all the portfolios in the PortfolioManager and adds the portfolio names to the PortfolioListPanel class by calling the addPortfolio() method. We then select the first Portfolio object in line 61 and then add the StockApplication class as a list selection listener to it in line 64.

Lines 67 and 68 set the `Portfolio` of the `StockTableModel` class in a rather lengthy way:

```
66:     // Set the stock table's portfolio
67:     stockTabPanel.stockTableTabPanel.stockTablePanel.stockTableModel.
           setPortfolio(
68:         portfolioManager.getPortfolio( 0 ) );
```

We use the `StockTabPanel` object that we created in the `StockApplication` class to get its `StockTableTabPanel` object. We then get its `StockTablePanel` object and then finally get its `StockTableModel` object. Finally, we set the first `Portfolio` from the `PortfolioManager` and set it to the `StockTableModel`.

Is all this legal? Yes! Is this neat? No, not really. We may clean this up later, and as an exercise I challenge you to add some nice interfaces in here to facilitate this cleanup. The point is, if you make all your attributes public, someone may have the nerve to do what I have just done!

In line 71 sets the `GraphTabPanel` class's portfolio to the first `Portfolio` in the `PortfolioManager`. This time it does it cleanly though, using a `setPortfolio()` method.

Finally, in line 83 we close the application by calling the `exitApp()` method. This method is our own implementation and performs one additional step before closing the application: It tells the `PortfolioManager` to save all its `Portfolios`. Here is the implementation of that method:

```
protected void exitApp()
    {
        // Save our portfolios
        portfolioManager.saveAllPortfolios( portfolioFile );

        // Close our application
        System.exit( 0 );
    }
```

The next thing we have to implement is the `valueChanged()` method. This method is called when the `PortfolioListPanel` class's `JList` selection changes. Listing 8.7 shows the implementation of the `valueChanged()` method.

Listing 8.7 `StockApplication valueChanged` **Implementation**

```
1:  public void valueChanged(ListSelectionEvent e)
2:  {
3:      // Ignore adjustment events
4:      if (e.getValueIsAdjusting())
5:      {
6:          return;
7:      }
8:
9:      // Get the list from the event
```

```
10:     JList theList = (JList)e.getSource();
11:
12:     // Get the index of the selected item
13:     int index = theList.getSelectedIndex();
14:
15:     // Get the name of the item in the list box
16:     String strName = ( String )theList.getModel().getElementAt( index );
17:
18:     // This is the portfolio we are going to abstract for
19:     // this event
20:     Portfolio p = new Portfolio();
21:
22:     // Retrieve the portfolio for this item
23:     try
24:     {
25:         p = portfolioManager.getPortfolio( strName );
26:     }
27:     catch( NoSuchElementException ex )
28:     {
29:         System.out.println(
30:             "Cannot find " +
31:             strName +
32:             " in this portfolio! " +
33:             ex.toString() );
34:
35:         return;
36:     }
37:
38:     // Set this portfolio on the table
39:     stockTabPanel.stockTableTabPanel.stockTablePanel.
40:                     stockTableModel.setPortfolio( p );
41:     // Set this portfolio on the graph
42:     stockTabPanel.graphTabPanel.setPortfolio( p );
43: }
```

In line 10 we get the JList that generated the event, which should be the
PortfolioListPanel list.

In line 13 we extract the index of the item in the list that is currently selected; this
will be the item that generated the event.

Next in line 16 we use that index to get the element from the ListModel associated with
the JList. This element will be a String as we have only been adding strings to list.

We have the name of the Portfolio. Now we need to get the entire Portfolio
object from the PortfolioManager, so in line 25 we call the PortfolioManager class's
getPortfolio() method. Remember that we added a NoSuchElementException
exception to this method, so we are going to have to catch it (lines 27–36).

Lines 39 and 42 set this `Portfolio` object on the `StockTableModel` and the `TickerListPanel`, respectively.

Our next change shows up in the `actionPerformed()` method. This is our `MainMenu` menu item selection event handler. We have to add handlers for the "File->New->Portfolio" and "File->New->Stock" items. Listing 8.8 shows the modifications made to the `actionPerformed()` method.

Listing 8.8 `StockApplication actionPerformed` **Modifications**

```
1:  // Find out which JMenuItem generated this event
2:  if( item == mainMenu.fileNewPortfolioManager )
3:  {
4:      System.out.println( "File->New->Portfolio Manager" );
5:  }
6:
7:  // File -> New -> Portfolio
8:  else if( item == mainMenu.fileNewPortfolio )
9:  {
10:     // Debug output
11:     System.out.println( "File->New->Portfolio" );
12:
13:     // Prompt the user
14:     Object obResult = JOptionPane.showInputDialog(
15:         this,
16:         "Please enter a new portfolio name",
17:         "QStock Startup",
18:         JOptionPane.INFORMATION_MESSAGE);
19:
20:     // See if the user pressed OK or CANCEL
21:     if( obResult == null )
22:     {
23:         return;
24:     }
25:
26:     // Cast the Object to a String
27:     String strNewPortfolio = ( String )obResult;
28:
29:     // Add the new portfolio to the portfolio manager
30:     portfolioManager.addPortfolio( new Portfolio( strNewPortfolio) );
31:
32:     // Add the portfolio to the portfolio list
33:     portfolioListPanel.addPortfolio( strNewPortfolio );
34:
35: }
36:
37: // File -> New ->Stock
38: else if( item == mainMenu.fileNewStock )
39: {
40:     // Debug Output
41:     System.out.println( "File->New->Stock" );
```

```
42:
43:        // Prompt the user
44:        Object obResult = JOptionPane.showInputDialog(
45:            this,
46:            "Please enter a new stock symbol",
47:            "New Stock",
48:            JOptionPane.INFORMATION_MESSAGE );
49:
50:        // See if the user pressed OK or CANCEL
51:        if( obResult == null )
52:        {
53:            // User pressed CANCEL
54:            return;
55:        }
56:
57:        // Cast the Object to a String
58:        String strNewStock = ( String )obResult;
59:
60:        if( strNewStock.length() == 0 )
61:        {
62:            // User didn't enter anything
63:            return;
64:        }
65:
66:        // Find out which portfolio to add this stock to
67:        int nSelectedIndex =
                        portfolioListPanel.listPortfolios.getSelectedIndex();
68:        String strPortfolioName = ( String )
69:            portfolioListPanel.listPortfolios.getModel().getElementAt
70:            (
71:                nSelectedIndex
72:            );
73:
74:        // Get the portfolio
75:        Portfolio portfolio =
                        portfolioManager.getPortfolio(strPortfolioName);
76:
77:        // Add the new element to the portfolio
78:        portfolio.addStock( new StockData( strNewStock ) );
79:
80:        // Tell the table to update itself
81:        stockTabPanel.stockTableTabPanel.stockTablePanel.
                        stockTableModel.fireTableDataChanged();
82: }
```

Lines 8–35 define our implementation of the File, New, Portfolio menu item selection event. We simply use another JOptionPane showInputDialog() method to prompt the user for a Portfolio name (lines 14–18), extract the text the user entered (line 27), create a new Portfolio and add it to the PortfolioManager (line 30), and finally add it to the PortfolioListPanel (line 33).

Lines 38–82 define our implementation of the File, New, Stock menu item selection event. We prompt the user for the stock symbol to add using a JOptionPane showInputDialog(), shown in lines 44–48. If the user clicked Cancel, we return; otherwise, we extract the String object from the Object returned by the showInputDialog() method (line 58). We verify that the user entered something in lines 60–64.

Next we ask the PortfolioListPanel for the currently selected Portfolio and extract the String name (lines 67–72). We call the PortfolioManager class's getPortfolio() by name method to get the Portfolio object (line 75) to add a new StockData object to (line 78). Finally, in line 81 we send a notification to the StockTableModel that the table data has changed.

Take a look at the CD for complete versions of all these classes, but if you have been adventurous and added all these changes yourself, you should have a functional Stock Tracker application!

Summary

This chapter covered a great deal of material. You started out learning some Java programming concepts:

- Files—You learned how to use the FileReader and FileWriter classes to read from and write to text files.

- Data structures—You learned about the three different types of data structures Java supports—lists, sets, and maps—and then you learned about several individual data structure implementations—vectors, stacks, linked lists, set variations, map variations, hashtables, and trees.

- Packages—You learned how to implement packages, name packages, and add classes to packages.

Next, we implemented the three classes that make up the "portfolio suite": StockData, Portfolio, and PortfolioManager.

And finally, we integrated these three classes into the user interface.

What's Next?

By this point you should be very proficient at Java and have a lot of your own ideas about how to implement the rest of the Stock Tracker application—but if there wasn't anything else interesting to learn, why would you need me? Anyway, you should find the next chapter interesting. We are going to set up the `StockQuoteRetriever` class. For this we are going to use an Internet connection to download live stock quotes from a chosen Web site. This is where the fun really begins!

8

Chapter 9

Implementing the Stock Quote Retriever

This chapter uncovers some of the Java technologies that I as a programmer find to be the most exciting and fulfilling. I enjoy communications programming and the idea of gathering information from some other source and using it in my application. That is the focus of this chapter: gathering information from the Internet and presenting it in the Stock Tracker application. The chapter is laid out as follows:

- First, I will review the three classes that make up the Stock Quote Retriever, InternetManager, HTMLParser, and StockQuoteRetriever, and how they fit into the Stock Tracker application.

- Then I will discuss the Java technologies you will use to implement these classes.

- Next, I will show you how to implement the Stock Quote Retriever classes.

- Finally, I will show you how to integrate these classes into the Stock Tracker application.

In the last chapter we added the functionality to create portfolios and add stock symbols to them. In this chapter we will add the ability to retrieve information about those stocks from the Internet and display those changes in the user interface. By the end of this chapter, you will have a very useful and functional application!

Component Relationships

Recall our discussions in Chapter 3, "Designing the Stock Tracker Application," when we designed the Internet aspect of the Stock Tracker application. We said that we were going to have three classes that performed our Internet-related functionality:

- InternetManager—This class is responsible for downloading HTML Web pages from the Internet.

- HTMLParser—This class is responsible for interpreting the HTML Web pages and extracting the desired stock information from them.

- StockQuoteRetriever—This is the primary interface that the Stock Tracker application has with the other two; the Stock Tracker application just gives the StockQuoteRetriever a stock symbol and asks it for the information it wants to display (such as the last sale, high, low, and so on).

How are these classes related to each other? They are related through containment, which if you recall from the last chapter is an aggregate relationship in which one class completely contains another. Take a look at Figure 9.1 to see this relationship expressed in UML.

Figure 9.1

Stock Quote Retriever internal relationship class diagram.

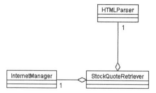

Figure 9.1 is read as follows:

- The StockQuoteRetriever class contains one InternetManager class.

- The StockQuoteRetriever class contains one HTMLParser class.

How do these classes fit into the Stock Tracker application? If you recall from Chapter 3, we said that the StockData class was going to perform its own stock communications with the Internet through the StockQuoteRetriever class. This relationship is expressed in Figure 9.2.

Figure 9.2 shows that every StockData class contains one StockQuoteRetriever class. So with respect to our complete design, the Application class (StockApplication) contains one PortfolioManager that contains zero or more Portfolio classes that contain zero or more StockData classes that all contain one StockQuoteRetriever class.

Figure 9.2

Stock Quote Retriever system relationship class diagram.

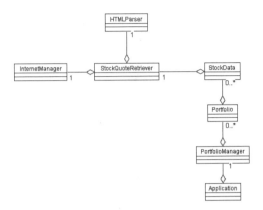

Implementation Decisions

Before we start implementing our classes, I want to discuss how we are going to approach the following challenges:

- How to download an HTML Web page from the Internet in Java
- How to extract meaningful information from an HTML page using Java classes
- How to use threads to improve the performance of retrieving stock quotes
- How to notify the StockApplication when the stock quote retrieval is complete
- How to package these classes together

Internet Strategy

Downloading HTML pages from the Internet in Java is actually very simple. There are really only three steps:

1. Create a URL object that represents the Web address you want to download.
2. Open a connection to the URL.
3. Use some form of stream reader to read the data from the URL.

First, you must create a URL object. You might be asking yourself what is a URL? A *uniform resource locator* (URL), for the purpose of this discussion, is the fully qualified address of a Web page. In actuality a URL can represent more than just Web addresses (such as File Transfer Protocol [FTP] addresses, Gopher addresses, and so on) and you should remember this, but the important address type for this discussion is a Web address. A typical URL looks like the following:

```
http://www.mcp.com/publishers/que/series/from_scratch/
```

I do not want to spend too much time talking about URLs, but to understand how a URL is constructed you will need a little background. In general, URLs are written as follows:

```
<scheme>://<user>:<password>@<host>:<port>/<url-path>
```

Table 9.1 defines the URL fields.

Table 9.1   URL Definition

Field	Description
`<scheme>`	The scheme, or protocol, being used by the URL, such as http, ftp, gopher, telnet, news, and so on.
`<user>`	An optional user name to connect to the URL
`<password>`	An optional password for the specified user name
`<host>`	The fully qualified domain name of a network host or its IP address, such as `www.mcp.com` or `198.70.146.70`
`<port>`	An optional port you specify to connect to on the host, defaults to 80 for the HTTP protocol
`<url-path>`	The rest of the locator, such as `/publishers/que/series/from_scratch`

To simplify this definition, the World Wide Web uses the HTTP protocol, so the URL takes the following form:

```
http://<host>:<port>/<path>?<searchpart>
```

Table 9.2 describes the HTTP URL fields.

Table 9.2   HTTP URL definition

Field	Description
`<host>`	Same as in Table 9.1
`<port>`	Same as in Table 9.1
`<path>`	An optional path that specifies the location of the requested object
`<searchpart>`	An optional search part that specifies additional data sent to the specified URL

Referring back to the Macmillan Computer Publishing Web site example:

```
http://www.mcp.com/publishers/que/series/from_scratch/
```

The `<scheme>` is `http`, the `<host>` is `www.mcp.com`, the `<port>` is 80 (default), and the `<path>` is `/publisher/que/series/from_scratch`. The only change in Java's terminology for a URL is that it refers to the `<host>` as the protocol.

Uniform resource locators are represented in Java by the `java.net.URL` class. The `java.net.URL` constructors are shown in Table 9.3.

Table 9.3   `java.net.URL` Constructors

Constructor	Description
`URL(String spec)`	Creates a URL object from the `String` representation
`URL(String protocol, String file)`	Creates a URL object from `String host`, `int port`, the specified protocol,host, port number, and file
`URL(String protocol, String host, int port, String file, java.net.URLStreamHandler handler)`	Creates a URL object from the specified protocol, host, port number, file, and handler
`URL(String protocol, String host, String file)`	Creates an absolute URL from the specified protocol name, host name, and filename
`URL(URL context, String spec)`	Creates a URL by parsing the specification spec within a specified context
`URL(URL context, String spec, java.net.URLStreamHandler handler)`	Creates a URL by parsing the specification spec within a specified context

From these constructors, you can see the now-familiar protocol, host, and port items. The "file" attribute specifies the file on the host you are requesting, and the "handler" specifies a protocol-specific stream handler that will manage communications between the Java application and the Web host. The "context" is a reference URL used to fill in any gaps left in the "spec." For example, if you have already built a URL for Macmillan Computer Publishing, to download a specific file from it you only need to specify the path and file you want and use the Macmillan Computer Publishing context URL to get the rest of the information. All these constructors will throw a `MalformedURLException` exception if your URL specification is not valid.

In the Stock Tracker application, I am going to build the URL by specifying a complete HTTP URL string using the first constructor in Table 9.2. For example:

```
URL urlMacmillan = new URL( "http://www.mcp.com" );
```

Now that we have created a `java.net.URL` object, we need to open a connection to that URL. Luckily, this functionality is provided for us by the `java.net.URL` class through the `openStream()` method. The `openStream()` method is defined as follows:

```
public final InputStream openStream() throws IOException
```

`openStream()` opens a connection to the URL specified in the `java.net.URL` constructor and returns a `java.io.InputStream` object. The `openStream()` method is actually shorthand for another URL method:

```
public URLConnection openConnection() throws IOException
```

This method opens a connection to the URL. Then the following `URLConnection` class method is called:

```
public InputStream getInputStream() throws IOException
```

Because we are only interested in retrieving an `InputStream`, the `openStream()` method fits perfectly for us.

Finally, we need a stream reader that can read data from an `InputStream`. In the last chapter we talked a little bit about streams and discussed the `FileReader` and `FileWriter` classes. You can read Internet files in the same way you can read text from the keyboard and from files; Java is so consistent it is great! I want to talk about a few classes that we will use to read from an `InputStream`: `InputStreamReader` and `BufferedReader`. An `InputStreamReader` is responsible for reading bytes from an `InputStream` and translating them into characters. Table 9.4 shows the constructors for the `InputStreamReader`.

Table 9.4   `BufferedReader` **Constructors**

Constructor	*Description*
`InputStreamReader(InputStream in)`	Creates an `InputStreamReader` that uses the default character encoding
`InputStreamReader(InputStream in, String encoding)`	Creates an `InputStreamReader` that uses the named character

The "encoding" parameter refers to the internal encoding used by the `InputStream` that is being read; this is used primarily for internationalization purposes. An `InputStreamReader` is therefore constructed from the URL input stream as follows:

```
URL url = new URL( "http://www.mcp.com" );
InputStreamReader in = new InputStreamReader( url.openStream() );
```

For maximum efficiency, it is recommended that `InputStreamReader` instances be wrapped by a `BufferedReader`. The `BufferedReader` class is actually very interesting. It reads text from a character input stream (such as `InputStreamReader`) and buffers the characters (stores them internally to the `BufferedReader`) for later retrieval. This optimizes read requests, which is something very important when downloading data over the Internet. A `BufferedReader` is constructed as shown in Table 9.5.

Table 9.5   `BufferedReader` **Constructors**

Constructor	*Description*
`BufferedReader(Reader in)`	Creates a buffering character-input stream that uses a default-size input buffer
`BufferedReader(Reader in, int sz)`	Creates a buffering character-input stream that uses an input buffer of the specified size

A `Reader` class is the base class for both `BufferedReader` as well as `InputStreamReader`, so you can simply construct your `BufferedReader` from your `InputStreamReader`. The `BufferedReader` for a URL input stream is constructed as follows:

```
URL url = new URL( "http://www.mcp.com" );
InputStreamReader in = new InputStreamReader( url.openStream() );
BufferedReader reader = new BufferedReader( in );
```

Or for short:

```
URL url = new URL( "http://www.mcp.com" );
BufferedReader reader = new BufferedReader(
        new InputStreamReader( url.openStream() ) );
```

When you have a `BufferedReader`, you can read data from the stream using one of the `BufferedReader`'s read methods, shown in Table 9.6.

Table 9.6   `BufferedReader` read **Methods**

Method	Description
`int read()`	Reads a single character
`int read(char[] cbuf)`	Reads characters into an array
`int read(char[] cbuf, int off, int len)`	Reads characters into a portion of an array
`String readLine()`	Reads a line of text

Each of these methods throws an `IOException` exception if an error occurs during the read.

Because of Internet reliability issues, I recommend reading one character at a time from the URL input stream using the first `read()` method, remembering that the `BufferedReader` will take care of buffering and optimizing your request for you. The reason for this is that trying to read data all at once from a source that is not 100 percent reliable and can suffer from timeouts could result in some loss of data.

Before I leave this section, I want to mention that you can actually wrap a `FileReader` class object with a `BufferedReader` class in the same way I just wrapped the `InputStreamReader`. Therefore, the interface for reading a file from the Internet is the same as the interface for reading a file from the local file system.

Stock Quote Server

Now that you know how to build a URL, what URL can you connect to for stock information? If you are building an application for your own noncommercial use, the World Wide Web is full of sites that offer 20-minute delayed stock prices for free, for example `www.yahoo.com`, `www.quote.com`, and `www.pcquote.com`. If you are developing commercial software that you plan to sell at a profit, you must obtain permission to use any of the information presented on any Web site.

The main thing that you will notice about the World Wide Web is that sites are constantly changing their appearance, which modifies the HTML you must parse to get your information. So our goal here is to locate a site that is going to change minimally or not at all. One such stock quote site is provided for Microsoft Excel's use through www.pcquote.com:

```
http://webservices.pcquote.com/cgi-bin/excelget.exe?TICKER=SYMBOL
```

In this example, SYMBOL is the stock ticker symbol for the desired stock.

Being a frequent Microsoft Excel user, I noticed that this is the URL it retrieves its stock quotes from if you specify "Detailed Stock Quote by PC Quote, Inc." Because Microsoft Excel is a popular commercial application, this site should stay fairly constant. Figure 9.3 shows a sample screenshot of the PC Quote Web site.

Figure 9.3

PC Quote stock quote example.

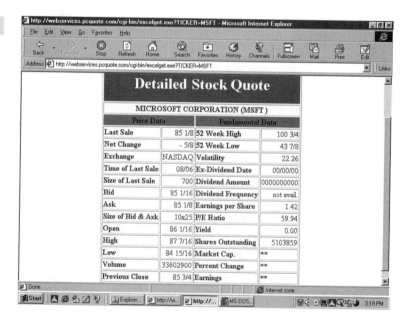

As you can see, this site lists all the information you need for the Stock Tracker application: Last Sale, High, Low, Volume, as well as some other information you might be interested in retrieving: open, previous close, 52-week high, 52-week low, P/E ratio, and so on.

HTML Parsing Strategy

Before I can talk about HTML parsing, I need to tell you a little about HTML. Web pages are currently all written in Hypertext Markup Language (HTML), which is similar to a text formatting language; it also been extended to embed different objects such as pictures, videos, Java applets, and a plethora of other things. One thing that is nice about HTML is that there is a set of raw text in the document, and all the formatting information is contained in tags. A *tag* is delimited by less than and greater than signs "<" ">" and specifies a specific command for the Web page or for the formatting for the page's raw text. For example, consider the following:

```
1: <HTML>
2: <HEAD>
3: <TITLE> My Web Page </TITLE>
4: </HEAD>
5: <BODY>
6: Welcome to my <B>Web Site!</B>
7: </BODY>
8: </HTML>
```

Each of these tags has a special meaning. For example, lines 1 and 8 denote the beginning and ending of the Web page, respectively: <HTML> and </HTML>. Lines 2 and 4 delimit the head of the page (top part): <HEAD> and </HEAD>. Lines 5 and 7 denote the body of the page: <BODY> and </BODY>. The title of the page as it appears on the title bar of your Web browser is delimited by the <TITLE> and </TITLE> tags. Finally, the words "Web Site!" in line 6 are bold, as noted by the <B> and </B> pairs.

As you might have surmised, all formatting commands begin with a tag, such as <B>, and end with the same tag name prepended with a forward slash '/', such as </B>. HTML supports a great number of tags and is growing almost daily; I would suggest picking up a book on HTML if you are interested in learning more. What does all this mean to you in the context of parsing HTML text?

Well, the presence of these formatting tags obscures our view of the raw data in the Web page. If we want to get to the actual text of the page, we are going to have to strip out these tags! Consider the following excerpt of the HTML text taken from the PC Quote Web site shown in Figure 9.3:

```
<td><b>Last Sale</b></td>
<td align=right
style="vnd.ms-excel.numberformat:# ??/??">  85  1/8</td><td>
<b>52 Week High</b></td>
<td align=right style="vnd.ms-excel.numberformat:# ??/??"> 100  3/4</td>
```

Now I know that this looks like a mess, but let me strip out the tags and group the remaining text as individual strings. We are left with the following strings:

```
1: "Last Sale"
2: "85 1/8"
3: "52 Week High"
4: "100 3/4"
```

This looks a little better now. Note that after the tags are removed, the last sale amount immediate follows the string "Last Sale" and the 52-week high amount immediately follows the string "52 Week High". We are going to use the relative position of the numeric values to specific strings in the HTML page to extract our data.

So our HTML parsing strategy is going to look as follows:

1. From a given HTML page of text, strip out all tags.
2. Build a collection of tokens where a token is anything outside of an HTML tag and is delimited by HTML tags.
3. Find the location of specific strings in our collection.
4. Retrieve values at locations relative to the strings located in step 3.

You will find this a worthwhile strategy to use in all HTML parsing routines you write in the future. I have been doing this for years, and although you can never guarantee that the Web site owner will not change his site, it is usually not difficult to adapt to minor changes and in most cases it still works seamlessly!

Threading Strategy

Retrieving information from the Internet is a great feature you can add to your applications, but there is one drawback to the Internet that everyone from 14.4Kbps modem users to T3 users complains about: It is too slow! You click on a URL and wait, and wait, and wait. Now think about our Stock Tracker application: If the end user selects Update from the Quotes menu, how long is it going to take before the application returns to the user? Let's see: The application must download a Web page from the Internet and extract information from it for every stock symbol in every portfolio in the application. That could take a while!

What are our options? How can we speed this process up? Or how can we let the application continue running while all this is going on in the background?

First, we cannot considerably speed up this process; if we could, there would be great jobs waiting for us at every Internet service provider in the country! However, we can run code in the background while the application continues running. The answer lies in threads!

So what is a thread? A *thread* is a path of execution in a program. Programs are composed of one or more threads of execution that run concurrently. The Java Virtual Machine supports running multiple threads in one program at the same time. This means that you can design your application such that multiple things are happening at the same time.

For example, Microsoft Word has one thread that manages the user interface that allows you to type your document and a second thread that is always running that checks your spelling; this is why you see misspelled words appear underlined with red as soon as you press the spacebar.

This is exactly the type of technology we should implement in the Stock Tracker application: We should have one thread that controls the user interface and one thread that connects to the Internet, downloads a Web page, and extracts the information from it.

Java supports threads through the `java.lang.Thread` class. The `Thread` class constructors are shown in Table 9.7.

Table 9.7   Thread Constructors

Constructor	*Description*
`Thread()`	Allocates a new `Thread` object
`Thread(Runnable target)`	Allocates a new `Thread` object for the specified target
`Thread(Runnable target, String name)`	Allocates a new `Thread` object for the specified `target` with the given `name`
`Thread(String name)`	Allocates a new `Thread` object with the given `name`
`Thread(ThreadGroup group, Runnable target)`	Allocates a new `Thread` object for the specified `target` that belongs to the specified `group`
`Thread(ThreadGroup group, Runnable target, String name)`	Allocates a new `Thread` object so that it has `target` as its run object, has the specified name as its name, and belongs to the thread group referred to by `group`
`Thread(ThreadGroup group, String name)`	Allocates a new `Thread` object with the specified name and group

9

The fields of interest in the thread constructors are

- `Runnable target`—A class that implements the `Runnable` interface that supports threading operations
- `String name`—A name that represents the thread
- `ThreadGroup group`—The group that the thread belongs to; good for grouping similar threads

There are two ways to use a thread:

- Declare a class to be a subclass of the `Thread` class.
- Declare a class that implements the `Runnable` interface and pass an instance of that class to a newly constructed `Thread` class.

With all this talk of the `Runnable` interface and the `Thread` class, let me tell you what you need to do to use both. To start with, the `Thread` class itself implements `Runnable`, which is defined as follows:

```
public interface Runnable
{
    public abstract void run();
}
```

There is one method, `run()`, that holds the body of code that will be executed by the `Thread` class when the thread starts. The `Thread` class has a large set of methods for thread maintenance but has two methods of importance: `start()` and `run()`. The `run()` method is derived from the `Runnable` interface, and the `start()` method starts the thread and calls the `run()` method.

The steps to creating a new thread are as follows:

1. Derive a class from `Thread`.
2. Implement the `run()` method to do everything you want to do inside the thread.
3. Create an instance of your class.
4. Call your class instance's `start()` method.

And that is it! Here is an example:

```
class MyThread extends Thread
{
    public void run()
    {
        System.out.println( "Welcome to my thread" );
    }
}
...
```

```
MyThread thread = new MyThread();
thread.start()
```

Here is an example of creating a class that implements the `Runnable` interface and passing it to a `Thread` instance:

```
class MyRunnableClass implements Runnable
{
    public void run()
    {
        System.out.println( "Welcome to my runnable class" );
    }
}
...
MyRunnableClass runnableClass = new MyRunnableClass();
new Thread( runnableClass ).start();
```

Or:

```
Thread thread = new Thread( runnableClass );
thread.start();
```

Event Notification Strategy

Making the Stock Tracker application multithreaded adds great value, but it creates another problem: Now that the stock update call is asynchronous, how does the application know the operation is complete so that it can update the user interface? It does this by using synchronous event notification method calls.

 A *synchronous* method call completes all its operations before returning. An *asynchronous* method call returns immediately after it is called and then continues processing in the background.

I spent some time talking about using handling events in Chapter 6, "Handling Events in Your User Interface." However, in this chapter I am going to show you how to implement custom events modeling the standard Java event paradigm.

What are the components of an event? An event in Java is composed of four components:

- Event object—This is the object that is passed to all classes that are registered as event listeners when an event occurs.
- Event listener interface—This is the interface that all classes that want to be event listeners must implement.
- Optional event adapter class—This is a helper class that implements the event listener interface with all empty methods so that the user can choose to implement only a subset of the event methods.
- Object that generates the event—This is the object that classes will register as listeners to that generates events.

In the Stock Tracker application, we are going to add event-generating support to the PortfolioManager class: It is going to fire an event when it has completed updating each Portfolio and when it has completed the entire PortfolioManager. Let's take a look at each event object in the context of the PortfolioManager.

Event Object

In Chapter 6, "Handling Events in Your User Interface," we listened to Java events as they were fired by implementing an event listener, such as ActionEventListener, that delivered events to us, such as ActionEvent. Now in this chapter we are turning that scenario around and creating our own custom event listeners and object. The Event object identifies the object that generated the event. Event objects are derived from the from the java.util.EventObject class and can contain any additional information specific to the event. Examples of Java Event objects are ActionEvent, AdjustmentEvent, MenuEvent, TextEvent, and so on.

Let's take a quick look at the ActionEvent. This class is derived from AWTEvent, which is derived from EventObject. It adds a few methods above and beyond the EventObject: getActionCommand(), getModifiers(), and paramString(). It inherits the getSource() method from EventObject, which identifies the object that generated the event.

So what do you have to do to create your own event?

1. Create a new class that is derived from java.util.EventObject that follows the naming convention of [YourEventType]Event.

2. Add a constructor that accepts the event-generating object and pass that object to the EventObject constructor using the super reserved word.

3. Add any event-specific methods and attributes to the class.

Let's create a StockUpdateEvent that the PortfolioManager can fire when it is done downloading information from the Internet. See Listing 9.1.

Listing 9.1 `StockUpdateEvent.java`

```
1:  // Import the Java Packages we are going to need
2:  import java.util.*;
3:
4:  // StockUpdateEvent
5:  public class StockUpdateEvent extends EventObject
6:  {
7:      public StockUpdateEvent( PortfolioManager source )
8:      {
9:          super( source );
10:     }
11: }
```

In line 5 we created a class named `StockUpdateEvent` that is derived from `EventObject`.

Line 7 defines the constructor of the `StockUpdateEvent` that accepts a `PortfolioManager` that generated the event as an argument. In line 9, it passes the source of the event to the `EventObject` class using the `super` reserved word. `super` simply calls the superclass, or base class, implementation of the constructor.

Because we are interested only when events occur, we are not adding any other event-specific information to the class.

Event Listener Interface

Event listeners are all derived from `java.util.EventListener`, which as you might recall is an abstract tagging interface; it does not provide any methods and is used solely to identify an interface as an event listener. This interface must include the method prototypes for each event that the event-generating object can fire.

Here are the steps to create an event listener:

1. Create a new interface that is derived from `java.util.EventListener` that follows the naming convention of `[YourEventType]Listener`.

2. Add method prototypes for every event that the event generator can fire: Each must be public, return void, and have as its sole argument the event object (defined in the last section).

In the stock update event we are going to create the `StockUpdateListener` interface that defines two methods: `portfolioComplete()` and `portfolioManagerComplete()`. Take a look at Listing 9.2.

Listing 9.2   StockUpdateListener.java

```
1:  // Import the Java Packages we are going to need
2:  import java.util.*;
3:
4:  // StockUpdateListener
5:  public interface StockUpdateListener extends EventListener
6:  {
7:      // A portfolio has completed its update
8:      public void portfolioComplete( StockUpdateEvent e );
9:
10:     // The portfolio manager has completed its update
12:     public void portfolioManagerComplete( StockUpdateEvent e );
13: }
```

In line 5 we create a new interface that is derived from `EventListener`.

Line 8 defines the prototype for the `portfolioComplete()` method.

Line 12 defines the prototype for the `portfolioManagerComplete()` method.

You can see that both methods are public, return void, and pass the `StockUpdateEvent` that we created in the last section.

Event Adapter Class

Event adapters are an optional component to the Java event paradigm, but they can be helpful if your objects generate multiple events. Event adapters are simple to implement. You must perform the following steps:

1. Create a class that implements the corresponding event listener that follows the naming convention of [YourEventType]Adapter.

2. Define every method in the event listener with an empty method (begin and end curly braces: {}).

In the case of the `PortfolioManager`, we are going to create a `StockUpdateAdapter` class. Take a look at Listing 9.3.

Listing 9.3 `StockUpdateAdapter.java`

```
1:  // Import the Java Packages we are going to need
2:  import java.util.*;
3:
4:  // StockUpdateAdapter
5:  public class StockUpdateAdapter implements StockUpdateListener
6:  {
7:      // A portfolio has completed its update
8:      public void portfolioComplete( StockUpdateEvent e )
9:      {
10:     }
11:
12:     // The portfolio manager has completed its update
13:     public void portfolioManagerComplete( StockUpdateEvent e )
14:     {
15:     }
16: }
```

In line 5 we create the `StockUpdateAdapter` class that implements the `StockUpdateListener` interface.

Lines 8–10 define an empty method for `portfolioComplete()`.

Lines 13–15 define an empty method for `portfolioManagerComplete()`.

Event-Generating Object

Now that you have an event, an event listener, and an event adapter, it is time to create an object that can generate events. This class is the most complicated of the four and has the most overhead but can still be implemented without too many headaches. Here are the steps involved:

1. Add a `Vector` to your class to hold a list of event listeners.

2. Add a public method to your class that adds an event listener to the `Vector`, follows the naming convention add[MyEventListener], and accepts the specific event listener type.

3. Add a method for each event that the class fires that iterates through the `Vector` and calls the corresponding event method. Follow the naming convention fire[MyEventName].

4. And, obviously, fire a few events every now and then.

Let's talk about this in the context of the `PortfolioManager` class and `StockUpdateEvent` event class. We are going to add a method to register an event listener: addStockUpdateListener(). And we are going to set up two event notification methods: firePortfolioComplete() and firePortfolioManagerComplete(). Take a look at Listing 9.4.

Listing 9.4   `PortfolioManager.java` Excerpts

```
1:   // Import the Java Packages we are going to need
2:   import java.io.*;
3:   import java.util.*;
4:   import java.util.EventObject.*;
5:
6:   // public class: PortfolioManager
7:   public class PortfolioManager
8:   {
9:   ...
10:      // Vector of StockUpdateListener Objects
11:      private Vector m_vStockUpdateListeners = new Vector();
12:
13:      // addStockUpdateListener( StockUpdateListener l )
14:      public void addStockUpdateListener( StockUpdateListener l )
15:      {
16:          // See if this listener is already in our Vector
17:          if( m_vStockUpdateListeners.contains( l ) )
18:          {
19:              return;
20:          }
21:
22:          // Add this listener to our Vector
```

continues

9

Listing 9.4   continued

```
23:            m_vStockUpdateListeners. add( l );
24:    }
25:
26:    public void removeStockUpdateListener( StockUpdateListener l )
27:    {
28:        // Remove this listener from our Vector
29:        m_vStockUpdateListeners.removeElement( l );
30:    }
31:
32:    private void firePortfolioComplete()
33:    {
34:        // Build a StockUpdateEvent Object
35:        StockUpdateEvent event = new StockUpdateEvent( this );
36:
37:        // Notify all of our Listeners
38:        for( int i=0; i<m_vStockUpdateListeners.size(); i++ )
39:        {
40:            StockUpdateListener listener =
41:                (StockUpdateListener)m_vStockUpdateListeners.elementAt(i);
42:            listener.portfolioComplete( event );
43:        }
44:    }
45:
46:    private void firePortfolioManagerComplete()
47:    {
48:        // Build a StockUpdateEvent Object
49:        StockUpdateEvent event = new StockUpdateEvent( this );
50:
51:        // Notify all of our Listeners
52:        for( int i=0; i<m_vStockUpdateListeners.size(); i++ )
53:        {
54:            StockUpdateListener listener =
55:                (StockUpdateListener)m_vStockUpdateListeners.elementAt(i);
56:            listener.portfolioManagerComplete( event );
57:        }
58:    }
59: ...
60:    public voidsomeMethod()
61:    {
62:        firePortfolioComplete();
63:    }
64: }
```

Line 11 creates a private Vector for the PortfolioManager class's
StockUpdateListener objects.

Lines 14–24 define the addStockUpdateListener() method. This method first checks
to see if the listener is already in the Vector (line 17) and then adds the
StockUpdateListener to the Vector in line 23.

Lines 26–30 define the `removeStockUpdateListener()` method. This method simply removes the `StockUpdateListener` from the `Vector`.

Lines 32–44 define the `firePortfolioComplete()` method. This method creates a new `StockUpdateEvent` event object, in line 35, passing it the `this` reserved word (which refers to this instance of the `PortfolioManager`). Next, it loops through all `StockUpdateListener` objects in the `Vector` (line 38), extracts the `StockUpdateListener` (line 41), and calls the listener's `portfolioComplete()` method (line 42).

Lines 46–58 define the `firePortfolioManagerComplete()` method. As you can see, this is implemented in the same way as the `firePortfolioComplete()` method, except that it calls the listener's `portfolioManagerComplete()` method (line 56).

Finally, in some method in the `PortfolioManager` class it calls `firePortfolioComplete()` (line 62). We will implement this later in the chapter in the "PortfolioManager Updates" section.

So here are the final classes and interfaces we have for the `PortfolioManager` `StockUpdate` event:

- `StockUpdateEvent`
- `StockUpdateListener`
- `StockUpdateAdapter`
- `PortfolioManager`

Package Strategy

This chapter is going to follow a similar package strategy to the last chapter. In the last chapter we put all our specialty classes into the `com.mcp.stock.portfolios` package. This time we are going to create a new package for our Internet classes, `com.mcp.stock.internet`, and a new package for our event classes, `com.mcp.stock.portfolios.event`. Take a look at Figure 9.4 to see the layout of the classes in the new packages.

The `com.mcp.stock.internet` package will contain the `InternetManager`, `HTMLParser`, and `StockQuoteRetriever` classes. The `com.mcp.stock.portfolios.event` package will contain the `StockUpdateEvent` and `StockUpdateAdapter` classes and the `StockUpdateListener` interface.

9

Figure 9.4

Portfolio events and Internet package strategies.

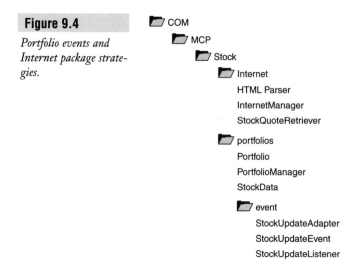

Internet Manager

Refer to the class diagram we derived in Chapter 3 for the InternetManager class, shown in Figure 9.5.

Figure 9.5

InternetManager class diagram.

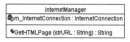

From Figure 9.5 you can see that the InternetManager class maintains an Internet connection attribute and has one method:

```
public String getHTMLPage( String strURL )
```

In the actual implementation of the InternetManager class, we are going to bypass the Internet connection attribute because it is not really necessary in Java, but we are still going to implement the getHTMLPage() method. The InternetManager class had only one public method, getHTMLPage(), that is implemented in the same manner discussed in the "Internet Strategy" section of this chapter. Take a look at Listing 9.5 for the complete listing of the InternetManager class.

Listing 9.5 `InternetManager.java`

```
1:  // Define the package we belong to
2:  package com.mcp.stock.internet;
3:
4:  // Import the packages used by this class
5:  import java.util.*;
6:  import java.io.*;
```

```
 7:  import java.net.*;
 8:
 9:  // InternetManager
10:  public class InternetManager
11:  {
12:      // Constructor
13:      public InternetManager()
14:      {
15:      }
16:
17:      // public String getHTMLPage( String strURL )
18:      //
19:      //   Retrieves the HTML text for the specified URL, the URL
20:      //   must include a valid URL-able String (see URL constructor).
21:      //
22:      //   Returns the HTML text on success
23:      //   Throws MalformedURLException if the URL is not valid
24:      //   Throws IOException if there is an error reading the page
25:      public String getHTMLPage( String strURL )
26:              throws MalformedURLException, IOException
27:      {
28:          // Construct a URL object for the specified URL
29:          URL url;
30:
31:          try
32:          {
33:              // Build a URL object from the query string
34:              url = new URL( strURL );
35:          }
36:          catch( MalformedURLException e )
37:          {
38:              System.out.println
39:              (
40:                  "InternetManager.getHTMLPage() - Bad URL: " +
41:                  strURL +
42:                  " Error Message: " +
43:                  e.toString()
44:              );
45:              throw e;
46:          }
47:
48:          // Read the HTML text from the URL
49:
50:          // Create a character array to hold the contents of the URL
51:          // and a Vector to hold the tokens from the URL text
52:          char[] caInput = new char[16384];
53:          int nCount = 0;
54:
55:          try
56:          {
57:              // Create a BufferReader to read the URL
```

continues

Listing 9.5 continued

```
58:                BufferedReader in = new BufferedReader(
59:                      new InputStreamReader( url.openStream() ) );
60:
61:                // Read in all of the data from the URL
62:                int ch = in.read();
63:                while( (ch != -1) && nCount<16384 )
64:                {
65:                    caInput[nCount++] = ( char ) ch;
66:                    ch = in.read();
67:                }
68:            }
69:            catch( IOException e )
70:            {
71:                System.out.println
72:                (
73:                    "InternetManager.getHTMLPage() BufferReader Error: " +
74:                    e.toString()
75:                );
76:                throw e;
77:            }
78:
79:            // Return the HTML text of the URL
80:
81:            // Build a String object with the contents of the URL
82:            String strURLText = new String( caInput, 0, nCount );
83:
84:            // Return a String representing the HTML text of the
85:            // specified URL
86:            return strURLText;
87:        }
88: }
```

Line 2 includes the InternetManager class as a member of the com.mcp.stock. internet package.

Lines 25–87 define the getHTMLPage() method. It accepts the String representation of a URL as its only parameter and can throw two exceptions: MalformedURLException denoting that the String URL is not valid and IOException denoting that there was an error reading data from the Internet.

Line 34 constructs a new java.net.URL from the String URL method parameter. The java.net.URL class constructor will throw the MalformedURLException exception if the String URL is not correct. This class simply catches it, outputs it to the screen, and then rethrows it.

Line 52 creates a character array that can hold 16,384 characters that will hold the raw text of the Web page we are retrieving. The choice of 16,384 is special in that it is 2^{14}; you will notice that programmers typically do things in powers of 2 because of the low-level implementation of variable types. You could just as easily use 16,000, and for the creation of an array it would be perfectly fine (old habits are hard to break).

Lines 58 and 59 construct a new `BufferedReader` object from an `InputStreamReader` object from the `java.net.URL` instance's `InputStream` (refer to the "Internet Strategy" section for more information).

Line 62 reads one character from the `BufferedReader`. Then line 63 compares the character to `-1` (denoting the end of the stream).

Although the character read from the `BufferedReader` class is not the end of the stream marker and the character array is not full (16,384 characters), line 65 adds the character read to the character array and line 66 reads the next character.

The `BufferedReader` class `read()` can throw `IOException` exceptions, which are caught in line 69. The `InternetManager` class outputs the exception to the screen and rethrows it.

Finally, line 82 creates a new `String` object from the character array spanning the number of characters in the character array. If we create a new `String` from the character array without specifying the number of characters to copy, we will get 16,384 characters in our `String`, even if there are only two characters in the array! So we use the following `String` constructor:

```
String(char[] value, int offset, int count)
```

So in line 82 we are creating a new `String` object from the character array, starting at the character array element 0 and copying nCount characters.

Finally, we return this `String` in line 86.

HTML Parser

Refer to the class diagram we derived in Chapter 3 for the `HTMLParser` class, shown in Figure 9.6.

Figure 9.6

HTMLParser class diagram.

From Figure 9.6, you can see that the `HTMLParser` class has HTML page as a `String` and maintains a collection of tokens. In our implementation of the `HTMLParser` class, we are going to let the `InternetManager` class maintain the text of the HTML page and we are only going to maintain a `Vector` of tokens. We are, however, going to implement all the methods in the class diagram with one additional method, which I will discuss shortly. Table 9.8 shows the methods supported by the `HTMLParser` class.

Table 9.8 `HTMLParser` **Methods**

Method	Description
Boolean parsePage(String strHTMLText)	Parses the specified HTML text into tokens to be searched for and retrieved using getToken() and findToken()
String getToken(int nIndex)	Retrieves the token at the specified index
String getToken(String strSearchString, int nOffset)	Retrieves the token that is nOffset (positive or negative) tokens away from the specified string
int getNumberOfTokens()	Returns the number of tokens in the HTML page
int findToken(String strToken)	Finds the specified token in the HTML page, returns the index of the entry or -1 if the specified token does not exist

From Table 9.8 you can see that we implemented all the methods in the `HTMLParser` class diagram we designed in Chapter 3 with the additional `getToken()` method that retrieves tokens relative to other tokens. This additional functionality is added to support the HTML parsing strategy we discussed earlier in this chapter. Take a look at Listing 9.6 for the complete source code for the `HTMLParser` class, and I will discuss it afterward.

Listing 9.6 `HTMLParser.java`

```
1:  // Define the package we belong to
2:  package com.mcp.stock.internet;
3:
4:  // Import the packages used by this class
5:  import java.util.*;
6:  import java.io.*;
7:  import java.net.*;
8:
9:  // HTMLParser
10: public class HTMLParser
11: {
12:     // Define a Vector to hold tokens
13:     Vector m_vTokens = new Vector();
```

```
14:
15:     // Empty Constructor
16:     public HTMLParser()
17:     {
18:     }
19:
20:     // Constructor( strHTMLText )
21:     //
22:     //   Send strHTMLText to parsePage
23:     public HTMLParser( String strHTMLText )
24:     {
25:         parsePage( strHTMLText );
26:     }
27:
28:     // public boolean parsePage( String strHTMLText )
29:     public Boolean parsePage( String strHTMLText )
30:     {
31:         // Initialize our token Vector
32:         m_vTokens.removeAllElements();
33:
34:         // Set the tokens that we are going to use as delimiters:
35:         // \r      =   Carriage Return
36:         // \n      =   New line
37:         // <       =   Less than (HTML tag prefix)
38:         // >       =   Greater than (HTML tag postfix)
39:         String strTokens = "\r\n<>";
40:
41:         // Create a StringTokenizer object - note we are leaving in all
42:         // delimiter tokens!
43:         StringTokenizer st =
                    new StringTokenizer(strHTMLText, strTokens,true );
44:
45:         // Loop through all tokens in our token vector
46:         while (st.hasMoreTokens())
47:         {
48:             // Extract a string token
49:             String tok = st.nextToken();
50:
51:             // See if we have an HTML tag prefix
52:             if( tok.equals( "<" ) )
53:             {
54:                 // We don't want any HTML tags, so keep reading tokens
55:                 // until we get to an HTML tag postfix
56:                 while( !tok.equals( ">" ) && st.hasMoreTokens() )
57:                 {
58:                     tok = st.nextToken();
59:                 }
60:             }
61:
62:             // See if we have a valid token
63:             if( !tok.equals( "\n" ) &&
```

continues

Listing 9.6   continued

```
64:                    !tok.equals( "\r" ) &&
65:                    !tok.equals( "<" ) &&
66:                    !tok.equals( ">" ) &&
67:                    tok.length() != 0 )
68:            {
69:                    // Remove all leading and trailing whitespace
70:                    tok = tok.trim();
71:
72:                    // Add this token to our vector of tokens
73:                    m_vTokens.add( tok );
74:            }
75:        }
76:
77:        // Success - Return true
78:        return new Boolean( true );
79:    }
80:
81:    // public String getToken( int nIndex )
82:    //
83:    //  Retrieve the String token at position nIndex.
84:    public String getToken( int nIndex )
th                                     rows ArrayIndexOutOfBoundsException
85:    {
86:        // Verify that the requested index is valid
87:        if( nIndex >= m_vTokens.size() )
88:        {
89:            ArrayIndexOutOfBoundsException e =
90:                new ArrayIndexOutOfBoundsException
91:                (
92: "Requested Index: " +
93:                    Integer.toString( nIndex ) +
94:                    " of a vector with " +
95:                    Integer.toString( m_vTokens.size() ) +
96:                    " elements"
97:                );
98:
99:            throw e;
100:        }
101:
102:        // Return the requested token
103:        return ( String )m_vTokens.elementAt( nIndex );
104:    }
105:
106:    // public String getToken( String strSearchString, int nOffset )
107:    //
108:    //  Retrieve the token that is nOffset (positive or negative)
109:    //  units away from strSearchString.
110:    public String getToken( String strSearchString, int nOffset )
111:    {
112:        // Search for the relative token
113:        int nIndex = findToken( strSearchString );
```

```
114:
115:        // See if we found the relative token
116:        if( nIndex == -1 )
117:        {
118:            NoSuchElementException e =
119:                new NoSuchElementException
120:                (
121:                    "HTMLParser.getToken() Error: " +
122:                    strSearchString +
123:                    " does not exist in the Token list"
124:                );
125:
126:            throw e;
127:        }
128:
139:        // Ensure that the offset is legal
130:        if( nIndex + nOffset >= m_vTokens.size() )
131:        {
132:            ArrayIndexOutOfBoundsException e =
133:                new ArrayIndexOutOfBoundsException
134:                (
135:                    "Requested Index: " +
136:                    Integer.toString( nIndex ) +
137:                    " of a vector with " +
138:                    Integer.toString( m_vTokens.size() ) +
139:                    " elements"
140:                );
141:
142:            throw e;
143:        }
144:
145:        // Return the requested token
146:        return getToken( nIndex + nOffset );
147:    }
148:
149:    // public int getNumberOfTokens()
150:    //
151:    //  Returns the number of tokens in the page
152:    public int getNumberOfTokens()
153:    {
154:        return m_vTokens.size();
155:    }
156:
157:    // public int findToken( String strToken )
158:    //
159:    //  Returns the index of strToken in the token vector
160:    //  Returns -1 if strToken is not in the vector
161:    public int findToken( String strToken )
162:    {
163:        // Loop through all tokens in the vector
164:        for( int i=0; i < m_vTokens.size(); i++ )
```

continues

Listing 9.6 continued

```
165:        {
166:            // Extract a String token from the vector
167:            String tok = ( String )m_vTokens.elementAt( i );
168:
169:            if( tok.equalsIgnoreCase( strToken ) )
170:            {
171:                return i;
172:            }
173:        }
174:
175:        // Could not find the requested token
176:        return -1;
177:    }
178:}
```

Line 2 defines this file as belonging to the com.mcp.stock.internet package.

Line 13 creates a Vector that will be used to hold all the tokens in the page. I chose to use a Vector here over the more sophisticated searchable data structures, such as hashtable- and tree-based data structures, because the order of these tokens is paramount to the design. Remember that we are extracting tokens that are relative to other tokens, and a data structure that sorts the tokens would defeat that!

Lines 16–18 define an empty constructor for the HTMLParser class. To use the class with the empty constructor, just create an instance of the class and call its parsePage() method, passing it the HTML String to parse.

Lines 23–26 define a constructor that accepts an HTML String that it passes to the parsePage() method.

Lines 29–79 define the parsePage() method. This method removes all HTML tags and places the remaining text as tokens into the token Vector. It starts by deleting everything from the token Vector in line 32. Next, it builds a String with the token delimiters: carriage return, newline, less than sign, and greater than sign. Line 43 creates a new StringTokenizer class; we discussed this class in the last chapter, but to refresh your memory, it accepts a String and divides it up into tokens with the specified delimiters. We are using the most complicated constructor for the StringTokenizer class:

StringTokenizer(String str, String delim, boolean returnTokens)

It accepts as its first parameter the string to tokenize, the delimiters as its second parameter, and finally a Boolean denoting whether or not to return the delimiters as tokens. In this case we want the delimiters as tokens so that when we find a less than sign (<), we can skip all tokens until we get a greater than sign (>). This is the way we will remove all the <>-delimited HTML tags!

Line 36 loops through all tokens in the StringTokenizer by calling its hasMoreTokens() method that returns true until it has no more tokens.

In line 49 we extract a token and then compare it to "<" in line 52. If we find a "<" token, we loop through all tokens until we find its ">" end delimiter (lines 56–59). In lines 63–67 we compare the token we have to our delimiters (remember that we do not want to add our tokens to the Vector) and ensure that the token has something in it.

If the token is valid, we strip off all leading and trailing white space (spaces, tabs, and basically anything you cannot see) in line 70. Finally, in line 73, we add the token to the token Vector.

Lines 84–104 define the getToken() method that retrieves a token by index. It starts off in lines 87–100 checking to make sure that the requested index is valid. If it is not, lines 89–97 construct a new ArrayIndexOutOfBoundsException exception and then line 99 throws it. Finally line 103 extracts the specified object from the Vector, casts it to a String and returns it.

Lines 110–147 define the getToken() method that retrieves a token that is a specified offset in index away from an existing token. This method would be used as follows if we wanted the token exactly two tokens after the "Last Sale" token:

```
String strLastSale = getToken( "Last Sale", 2 );
```

This method starts by calling the findToken() method (which I will describe shortly) that returns the index of a String token or -1 if the token does not exist in the Vector (line 113). If the token is not in the Vector, the method constructs and throws a NoSuchElementException (lines 116–127). Next, it validates that the located token index added with the offset is a valid index into the Vector (line 130). If it is not valid, an ArrayIndexOutOfBoundsException exception is constructed and thrown (lines 132–142).

Finally, in line 146, getToken() returns the requested method by calling the previous getToken() method with the index as the index of the specified token added to the offset. All along we have been implementing quite a bit of error checking, and this method in particular has a lot of error checking. If we did not want this level of error checking, we could write the entire method as:

```
public String getToken( String strSearchString, int nOffset )
{
    return getToken( findToken( strSearchString ) + nOffset );
}
```

Sure looks easier, right? But what happens if the search token is not valid or if the offset is too large? The application will crash.

Anyway, lines 152–155 implement the `getNumberOfTokens()` method that simply returns the size of the token `Vector`.

The last method in the class is the `findToken()` method, defined in lines 161–177. This method loops through all elements in the token `Vector` (lines 164–173), searching for the specified token. It extracts the `String` token from the `Vector` in line 167 and then compares it to the specified token in line 169. As soon as the token is found, its index is returned (line 171). If the `Vector` does not contain the token, `-1` is returned (line 176).

Stock Quote Retriever

Refer to the class diagram we derived in Chapter 3 for the `StockQuoteRetriever` class, shown in Figure 9.7.

Figure 9.7

StockQuoteRetriever class diagram.

From Figure 9.7, you can see that the `StockQuoteRetriever` class is fairly simple: It contains an `InternetManager` object and an `HTMLParser` object and supports some kind of "get" method for stock information. In this implementation I kept both the `InternetManager` and `HTMLParser` objects and added a set of "get" methods and an explicit `update()` method to retrieve the stock information. Tables 9.9 and 9.10 show the `StockQuoteRetriever` attributes and methods, respectively.

Table 9.9   `StockQuoteRetriever` Attributes

Attribute	Description
`InternetManager m_internetManager`	`InternetManager` object that downloads Web pages from the Internet
`HTMLParser m_htmlParser`	`HTMLParser` object that extracts information from an HTML page

Table 9.10   `HTMLParser` Methods

Method	Description
`StockQuoteRetriever()`	Empty constructor.
`StockQuoteRetriever(String strSymbol)`	Constructor that sets the class's stock symbol.
`void setSymbol(String strSymbol)`	Sets the symbol that the class will download stock information for.

Method	Description
`String getSymbol()`	Returns the stock symbol for this stock.
`String getCompanyName()`	Returns the company name for this stock.
`Float getLastSale()`	Returns the last sale for this stock.
`Float getHigh()`	Returns the daily high value for this stock.
`Float getLow()`	Returns the daily low value for this stock.
`Float getVolume()`	Returns the daily volume for this stock.
`Float getOpen()`	Returns the opening price for this stock.
`Float getClose()`	Returns the previous day's closing price for this stock.
`Float get52WeekHigh()`	Returns the 52-week high for this stock.
`Float get52WeekLow()`	Returns the 52-week low for this stock.
`Boolean update()`	Updates the stock information from the Internet. You must call this method before any of the "get" methods.
`Float makeFloat(String strNumber)`	Internal helped method to convert string numbers to Float values.
`void dumpTokens()`	Debug method to display all tokens and their indexes to the standard output device.

Now for the issue of determining the relative positions of token values. Suppose you want to get the last sale price of a stock; how would you do that? The answer lies in the `dumpTokens()` method. You could very easily write a test application that downloads a Web page from the Internet using the `InternetManager` class, tokenize it with the `HTMLParser`, and then display all the tokens. However, because this is already done for you with the `StockQuoteRetriever` class, I wrote a small utility that uses the `StockQuoteRetriever` class to do just that. I know that it might sound weird to use the class before we actually write it, but this utility does not use any of the token placement methods; it just piggybacks on the `StockQuoteRetriever` for its Internet knowledge. Anyway, this application, `DisplayWebTokens`, is very simple: It creates a `StockQuoteRetriever` object, asks it to update a stock's information, and then calls `dumpTokens()`. Take a look at Listing 9.7.

Listing 9.7 `DisplayWebTokens.java`

```
1:  // Import the Internet package
2:  import com.mcp.stock.internet.*;
3:
4:  // public class DisplayWebTokens
5:  public class DisplayWebTokens
6:  {
```

continues

Listing 9.7   continued

```
 7:     // public static void main( String[] args )
 8:     //  Main entry point into the application
 9:     public static void main( String[] args )
10:     {
11:         try
12:         {
13:             // Create a StockQuoteRetriever object with the given
14:             // argument
15:             StockQuoteRetriever sqr = new StockQuoteRetriever( args[0] );
16:
17:             // Tell it to update its stock information
18:             sqr.update();
19:
20:             // Tell it to display its tokens to the screen
21:             sqr.dumpTokens();
22:         }
23:         catch( ArrayIndexOutOfBoundsException e )
24:         {
25:             // If the user did not enter a stock symbol, display the
26:             // usage
27:             System.out.println("Usage: DisplayWebTokens [Stock Symbol]");
28:         }
29:     }
30: }
```

Listing 9.7 shows the source code for the DisplayWebTokens application.

In line 2 it imports the com.mcp.stock.internet package that holds the StockQuoteRetriever class.

In line 15 it creates a StockQuoteRetriever object, calls its update() method in line 18, and finally calls its dumpTokens() in line 21. All this is in a try-catch block that catches ArrayIndexOutOfBoundsException. This is because if the user does not enter a stock symbol when he launches the application, referencing arg[0] will throw this exception. This exception tells us that the user did not enter a stock symbol and hence we can display the usage of the tool (line 27).

To use this tool to display Microsoft's page, enter the following:

```
java DisplayWebTokens MSFT
```

Your output should look something like this:

```
0: Enter a new Symbol:
1:
2: Symbol Guide
3: Detailed Stock Quote
4: MICROSOFT CORPORATION                    (MSFT   )
5: Price Data
6: Fundamental Data
```

```
 7: Last Sale
 8: 82 15/16
 9: 52 Week High
10: 100  3/4
11: Net Change
12: -      7/8
13: 52 Week Low
14: 43  7/8
15: Exchange
16: NASDAQ
17: Volatility
18: 22.26
19: Time of Last Sale
20: 08/10
21: Ex-Dividend Date
22: 00/00/00
23: Size of Last Sale
24: 300
25: Dividend Amount
26: 0000000000
27: Bid
28: 82  7/8
29: Dividend Frequency
30: not avail.
31: Ask
32: 82 15/16
33: Earnings per Share
34: 1.42
35: Size of Bid & Ask
36: 13x46
37: P/E Ratio
38: 58.40
39: Open
40: 83  9/16
41: Yield
42: 0.00
43: High
44: 85  3/4
45: Shares Outstanding
46: 5103859
47: Low
48: 81  5/8
49: Market Cap.
50: **
51: Volume
52: 31371500
53: Percent Change
54: **
55: Previous Close
56: 83 13/16
57: Earnings
58: **
```

You can see the fields we are interested in displayed in Table 9.11.

Table 9.11 Token Positions

Token	Index	Value	Index
Detailed Stock Quote	3	MICROSOFT CORPORATION	4
Last Sale	7	82 15/16	8
52 Week High	9	100 3/4	10
52 Week Low	13	43 7/8	14
Open	39	83 9/16	40
High	43	85 3/4	44
Low	47	81 5/8	48
Volume	51	31371500	52
Previous Close	55	83 13/16	56

From this table you can see that all the tokens we are interested in have their values in the very next token. Take a look at Listing 9.8 for the complete source code for the StockQuoteRetriever class.

Listing 9.8 StockQuoteRetriever.java

```
 1: // Define the package we belong to
 2: package com.mcp.stock.internet;
 3:
 4: // Import the packages used by this class
 5: import java.util.*;
 6: import java.io.*;
 7: import java.net.*;
 8:
 9: // StockQuoteRetriever
10: public class StockQuoteRetriever
11: {
12:     // Variables for this stock symbol
13:     protected String m_strSymbol = new String();
14:     protected String m_strCompanyName = new String();
15:     protected String m_strLastSale = new String();
16:     protected String m_strHigh = new String();
17:     protected String m_strLow = new String();
18:     protected String m_strVolume = new String();
19:     protected String m_strOpen = new String();
20:     protected String m_strClose = new String();
21:     protected String m_str52WeekHigh = new String();
22:     protected String m_str52WeekLow = new String();
23:
24:     // Define an Internet Manager
25:     InternetManager m_internetManager = new InternetManager();
26:
```

```
27:     // Define an HTML Parser
28:     HTMLParser m_htmlParser = new HTMLParser();
29:
30:     // Empty Constructor
31:     public StockQuoteRetriever()
32:     {
33:     }
34:
35:     // Constructor( strSymbol )
36:     public StockQuoteRetriever( String strSymbol )
37:     {
38:         setSymbol( strSymbol );
39:     }
40:
41:     public void setSymbol( String strSymbol )
42:     {
43:         m_strSymbol = strSymbol;
44:     }
45:
46:     public String getSymbol()
47:     {
48:         return m_strSymbol;
49:     }
50:
51:     public String getCompanyName()
52:     {
53:         return m_strCompanyName;
54:     }
55:
56:     public Float getLastSale()
57:     {
58:         return makeFloat( m_strLastSale );
59:     }
60:
61:     public Float getHigh()
62:     {
63:         return makeFloat( m_strHigh );
64:     }
65:
66:     public Float getLow()
67:     {
68:         return makeFloat( m_strLow );
69:     }
70:
71:     public Float getVolume()
72:     {
73:         return makeFloat( m_strVolume );
74:     }
75:
76:     public Float getOpen()
77:     {
```

continues

Listing 9.8   continued

```
78:             return makeFloat( m_strOpen );
79:         }
80:
81:     public Float getClose()
82:     {
83:             return makeFloat( m_strClose );
84:     }
85:
86:     public Float get52WeekHigh()
87:     {
88:             return makeFloat( m_str52WeekHigh );
89:     }
90:
91:     public Float get52WeekLow()
92:     {
93:             return makeFloat( m_str52WeekLow );
94:     }
95:
96:
97:     // public Boolean update()
98:     //
99:     // Downloads the class's stock symbol information from the
100:    // Internet, parses out its pertinent information and makes
101:    // that information available through the various get methods
102:    public Boolean update()
103:    {
104:        // Make sure we have a stock symbol
105:        if( m_strSymbol.length() == 0 )
106:        {
107:            return new Boolean( false );
108:        }
109:
110:        // Build our URL
111:        String strURL = new String
112:        (
113:            "http://webservices.pcquote.com/cgi-bin/excelget.exe?TICKER="
114:            + m_strSymbol
115:        );
116:
117:        // Get the HTML for this stock symbol
118:        String strHTML = new String();
119:        try
120:        {
121:            strHTML = m_internetManager.getHTMLPage( strURL );
122:        }
123:        catch( MalformedURLException e )
124:        {
125:            System.out.println( "URL Error: " +
126:                                    e.toString() );
127:
128:            return new Boolean( false );
```

```
129:        }
130:        catch( IOException e )
131:        {
132:            System.out.println( "IO Error: " +
133:                                   e.toString() );
134:
135:            return new Boolean( false );
136:        }
137:
138:        // Parse the HTML
139:        if( m_htmlParser.parsePage( strHTML ).booleanValue() == false )
140:        {
141:            return new Boolean( false );
142:        }
143:
144:        // Extract our fields from the HTML Parser
145:
146:        // Company Name
147:        m_strCompanyName =
             m_htmlParser.getToken( "Detailed Stock Quote", 1 );
148:
149:        // Last Sale
150:        m_strLastSale = m_htmlParser.getToken( "Last Sale", 1 );
151:
152:        // High
153:        m_strHigh = m_htmlParser.getToken( "High", 1 );
154:
155:        // Low
156:        m_strLow = m_htmlParser.getToken( "Low", 1 );
157:
158:        // Volume
159:        m_strVolume = m_htmlParser.getToken( "Volume", 1 );
160:
161:        // Open
162:        m_strOpen = m_htmlParser.getToken( "Open", 1 );
163:
164:        // Close
165:        m_strClose = m_htmlParser.getToken( "Previous Close", 1 );
166:
167:        // 52 Week High
168:        m_str52WeekHigh = m_htmlParser.getToken( "52 Week High", 1 );
169:
170:        // 52 Week Low
171:        m_str52WeekLow = m_htmlParser.getToken( "52 Week Low", 1 );
172:
173:        // Success - return true
174:        return new Boolean( true );
175:    }
176:
177: // public Float makeFloat( String strNumber )
178: //
```

9

continues

Listing 9.8 **continued**

```
179:    //  This method accepts a String version of a number with an
180:    //  optional fractional percentage expressed as x/y and builds
181:    //  a Float object out of it
182:    public Float makeFloat( String strNumber )
183:    {
184:        int nIndex = 0;
185:
186:        // Skip any leading whitespace
187:        while( nIndex<strNumber.length() &&
                            strNumber.charAt(nIndex) == ' ' )
188:        {
189:            nIndex++;
190:        }
191:
192:        // Get the whole part of the number
193:        String strWholeNumber = new String();
194:        while( nIndex<strNumber.length() &&
                            strNumber.charAt(nIndex) != ' ' )
195:        {
196:            strWholeNumber = strWholeNumber + strNumber.charAt(nIndex);
197:            nIndex++;
198:        }
199:
200:        // Get the fraction part of the number
201:        String strNumerator = new String();
202:        String strDenominator = new String();
203:        if( nIndex != strNumber.length() )
204:        {
205:            // Skip any whitespace
206:            while( nIndex<strNumber.length() &&
                                strNumber.charAt(nIndex) == ' ' )
207:            {
208:                nIndex++;
209:            }
210:
211:            // Get the fraction numerator
212:            while( nIndex<strNumber.length() &&
                                strNumber.charAt(nIndex) != '/' )
213:            {
214:                strNumerator = strNumerator + strNumber.charAt(nIndex);
215:                nIndex++;
216:            }
217:
218:            // Skip passed the '/'
219:            if( nIndex<strNumber.length() &&
                            strNumber.charAt(nIndex) == '/' )
220:            {
221:                nIndex++;
222:            }
223:
224:            // Get the fraction denominator
```

```
225:                while( nIndex<strNumber.length() &&
                                strNumber.charAt(nIndex) != ' '  )
226:            {
227:                strDenominator = strDenominator +
                                    strNumber.charAt(nIndex);
228:                nIndex++;
229:            }
230:
231:        }
232:
233:        // Convert the parts of the number to floats
234:        Float fWholeNumber = new Float( strWholeNumber );
235:
236:        Float fNumerator;
237:        if( strNumerator. length() == 0 )
238:        {
239:            fNumerator = new Float( 0 );
240:        }
241:        else
242:        {
243:            fNumerator = new Float( strNumerator );
244:        }
245:
246:        Float fDenominator;
247:        if( strDenominator.length() == 0 )
248:        {
249:            fDenominator = new Float( 1 );
250:        }
251:        else
252:        {
253:            fDenominator = new Float( strDenominator );
254:        }
255:
256:        // Build the number
257:        Float fResult = new Float
258:                            (
259:                                fWholeNumber.floatValue() +
260:                                ( fNumerator.floatValue() /
261:                                  fDenominator.floatValue() )
262:                            );
263:
264:        // Return the result
265:        return fResult;
266:    }
267:
268:    // public void dumpTokens()
269:    //
270:    //  Displays all of the tokens in downloaded web page to the
271:    //  standard output (System.out)
272:    public void dumpTokens()
273:    {
```

continues

Listing 9.8 continued

```
274:            for( int i=0; i<m_htmlParser.getNumberOfTokens(); i++ )
275:            {
276:                System.out.println( i + ": " + m_htmlParser.getToken( i ) );
277:            }
278:    }
279:}
```

Line 2 defines this file as belonging to the com.mcp.stock.internet package.

Lines 13–22 declare protected String objects that represent all the stock information fields.

Line 24 creates an instance of the InternetManager, and line 28 creates an instance of the HTMLParser.

Lines 31–33 define an empty constructor for the StockQuoteRetriever class, and lines 36–39 define a constructor that accepts a stock symbol and passes it to the setSymbol() method.

Lines 41–44 define the setSymbol() method. If the empty constructor is used, the setSymbol() method must be called before calling update() to get the stock information (the class must know what stock you want information about).

Lines 46–94 define the following "get" methods for the various stock information fields: getSymbol(), getCompanyName(), getLastSale(), getHigh(), getLow(), getVolume(), getOpen(), getClose(), get52WeekHigh(), and get52WeekLow().

Lines 102–175 define the update() method that uses the InternetManager to download a specific Web page from the Internet, uses the HTMLParser to tokenize the page and extract all the stock quote information, and then stores it all in class variables. The first thing the update() method does is verify that a stock symbol is set for the class (line 105), and then it returns false if there is not one.

Next, it builds the URL we talked about in the "Stock Quote Server" section earlier in this chapter:

http://webservices.pcquote.com/cgi-bin/excelget.exe?TICKER=SYMBOL

In this case, we build a String in this format with the stock symbol class member variable as the stock symbol (lines 113 and 114). In line 121, it asks the InternetManager to download the Web page by calling its getHTMLPage() method. All the code is added there to catch both exceptions that the getHTMLPage() can throw: MalformedURLException and IOException; for both exceptions it outputs an error to the standard output device and returns false.

In line 139 the update() method sends the HTML page to the HTMLParser and asks it to parse the information into tokens by calling its parsePage() method. If this call fails, the update() method returns false.

Lines 147–171 extract the stock quote information from the HTMLParser by calling its getToken() relative token method. In this page, all the stock information is the next token after the value label.

And finally in line 174, the update() method returns true.

One thing that you might have noticed is that all the "get" methods that return a Float described earlier first converted the number to a Float using the makeFloat() method. Lines 182–266 define the makeFloat() method.

The reason for this method is that the stock information numbers that have a fractional part are of the type:

98 1/2

Where 98 is the whole number and 1/2 is the fractional part. To store this in Java, we need this to appear as 98.5. Also the number can have leading and trailing white space that we need to remove.

We use an index variable to step through the stock information string, so in line 187 the makeFloat() method removes the leading white space by comparing the character at the index value to a space ' '. Now that the leading white space is removed, lines 193–198 construct a new String to hold the whole number part of the number (for example "98").

The next thing to do is get the numerator and denominator of the fraction part if it exists; its existence is checked in line 203 by comparing the index location with the length of the String.

Lines 206–209 remove any white space between the whole number and numerator. Lines 212–216 extract the numerator by looking for the forward slash '/'.

Lines 218–222 skip over the forward slash to get to the denominator.

Lines 225–231 extract the denominator.

Now that we have the whole number, the numerator, and the denominator, it is time to convert these to Float objects and build one number. We do this by using the Float constructor that accepts a String object—it does the conversion for us. Line 234 converts the whole number part, and lines 236–254 convert the numerator and denominator to their respective parts or if not present to 0 and 1, respectively. We set the numerator to 0 and the denominator to 1 if they do not exist because we want the fraction part to be 0 and not to generate any errors (like trying to divide by zero!).

Finally, in lines 257–262, we build the whole number as follows:

```
fWholeNumber + ( fNumerator / fDenominator )
```

And we return this value in line 265.

The last method in the class is the `dumpTokens()` method defined in lines 272–279. It simply iterates through all the elements in the `HTMLParser` and displays them with their respective indexes.

Integrating the New Classes into the User Interface

The things we have to do to implement the Internet functionality into the Stock Tracker application include the following:

- Update the `StockData` class's `update()` method so that it retrieves meaningful data from the Internet
- Enable the `StockApplication` class's Quotes, Update menu item to initiate an update
- Add in the event code to the `PortfolioManager` to notify the `StockApplication` when the update is complete
- Add the multithreaded support to the `PortfolioManager` to perform its `updatePortfolioStockPrices()` in the background

Let's go through each in turn.

StockData Updates

The updates to the `StockData` class are relatively straightforward. We have to do the following:

- Add a `StockQuoteRetriever` object to the class
- Update the `update()` method to use the `StockQuoteRetriever` class to download stock information from the Internet

Here are the updates to `StockData.java`:

```
1:      protected StockQuoteRetriever m_StockQuoteRetriever =
2:              new StockQuoteRetriever();
3:  ...
4:      // public Boolean update()
5:      //
6:      //  Asks the StockQuoteRetriever class to download stock
7:      //  information for us.
8:      public Boolean update()
9:      {
10:         // Set our StockQuoteRetriever stock symbol
```

```
11:            m_StockQuoteRetriever.setSymbol( m_strStockSymbol );
12:
13:            // Get the stock quotes from the Internet
14:            if( m_StockQuoteRetriever.update().booleanValue() == false )
15:            {
16:                return new Boolean( false );
17:            }
18:
19:            // Update our fields
20:            m_strCompanyName = m_StockQuoteRetriever.getCompanyName();
21:            m_fLastSale = m_StockQuoteRetriever.getLastSale();
22:            m_fHigh = m_StockQuoteRetriever.getHigh();
23:            m_fLow = m_StockQuoteRetriever.getLow();
24:            m_fVolume = m_StockQuoteRetriever.getVolume();
25:
26:            // Success
27:            return new Boolean( true );
28:    }
```

Lines 1 and 2 construct a new StockQuoteRetriever object.

Lines 8–28 define the update() method. To begin with, the update() method, in line 11, sets the stock symbol about which to download information. Then it calls the StockQuoteRetriever method update(), in line 14, to download the information. Finally, in lines 20–24 it extracts the company name, last sale, high, low, and volume. In line 27 it returns true.

PortfolioManager Updates

In the last chapter, we set up the PortfolioManager class's udpatePortfolioStockPrices() method to synchronously tell each Portfolio to update its stock prices, but after our "Threading Strategy" discussion earlier, we are going to modify that code to start a thread and handle it for us. We must make the following changes to the PortfolioManager class:

- Add a thread to the PortfolioManager class to perform the updatePortfolioStockPrices() functionality
- Modify the updatePortfolioStockPrices() method to start that thread
- Set up the event notification we talked about in the "Event Notification Strategy" section, including all the Event classes

The next two sections will show the modifications made directly to the PortfolioManager class and then the new event classes and interfaces.

PortfolioManager Class Modifications

Listing 9.9 shows the modifications made to the PortfolioManager class.

Listing 9.9 `PortfolioManager.java` **(Modifications Only)**

```
 1:  // Define the package we belong to
 2:  package com.mcp.stock.portfolios;
 3:
 4:  // Import the Java Packages we are going to need
 5:  import java.io.*;
 6:  import java.util.*;
 7:  import java.util.EventObject.*;
 8:
 9:  // public class: PortfolioManager
10:  public class PortfolioManager
11:  {
12:      // Create our thread that is going to do all of our stock updates
13:      StockUpdateThread m_threadStockUpdate = new StockUpdateThread(this);
14:
15:      // public Boolean updatePortfolioStockPrices()
16:      //
17:      //  Tell all of the portfolios in the portfolio manager to update
18:      //  their stock prices
19:      public Boolean updatePortfolioStockPrices()
20:      {
21:          // Start our update thread
22:          m_threadStockUpdate.start();
23:
24:          // Success! Return true
25:          return new Boolean( true );
26:      }
27:
28:      // addStockUpdateListener( StockUpdateListener l )
29:      //
30:      //  Add l to the list of listeners for this object
31:      public void addStockUpdateListener( StockUpdateListener l )
32:      {
33:          m_threadStockUpdate.addStockUpdateListener( l );
34:      }
35:
36:      // removeStockUpdateListener( StockUpdateListener l )
37:      //
38:      //  Remove l from the list of listeners for this object
39:      public void removeStockUpdateListener( StockUpdateListener l )
40:      {
41:          m_threadStockUpdate.removeStockUpdateListener( l );
42:      }
43:
44:      // StockUpdateThread
45:      //
46:      //  Used to update all stock prices for all of the portfolios in
47:      //  the portfolio manager
48:      protected class StockUpdateThread extends Thread
49:      {
50:          // Reference to our parent
51:          private PortfolioManager m_portfolioManager;
```

```
52:
53:            // Vector of StockUpdateListener Objects
54:            private Vector m_vStockUpdateListeners = new Vector();
55:
56:            // Constructor
57:            public StockUpdateThread( PortfolioManager portfolioManager )
58:            {
59:                m_portfolioManager - portfolioManager;
60:            }
61:
62:            // addStockUpdateListener( StockUpdateListener l )
63:            //
64:            //   Add a StockUpdateListener to this object
65:            public void addStockUpdateListener( StockUpdateListener l )
66:            {
67:                // See if this listener is already in our Vector
68:                if( m_vStockUpdateListeners.contains( l ) )
69:                {
70:                    return;
71:                }
72:
73:                // Add this listener to our Vector
74:                m_vStockUpdateListeners.add( l );
75:            }
76:
77:            // removeStockUpdateListener( StockUpdateListener l )
78:            //
79:            //   Remove a StockUpdateListener from this object
80:            public void removeStockUpdateListener( StockUpdateListener l )
81:            {
82:                // Remove this listener from our Vector
83:                m_vStockUpdateListeners.removeElement( l );
84:            }
85:
86:            // firePortfolioComplete()
87:            //
88:            //   Notify our listeners that a portfolio is complete
89:            private void firePortfolioComplete()
90:            {
91:                // Build a StockUpdateEvent Object
92:                StockUpdateEvent event =
                                new StockUpdateEvent( m_portfolioManager );
93:
94:                // Notify all of our Listeners
95:                for( int i=0; i<m_vStockUpdateListeners.size(); i++ )
96:                {
97:                    StockUpdateListener listener =
                      ( StockUpdateListener )m_vStockUpdateListeners.elementAt( i );
98:                    listener.portfolioComplete( event );
99:                }
100:           }
```

9

continues

Listing 9.9   continued

```
101:
102:        // firePortfolioManagerComplete()
103:        //
104:        //   Notify our listeners that the portfolio manager is complete
105:        private void firePortfolioManagerComplete()
106:        {
107:            // Build a StockUpdateEvent Object
108:            StockUpdateEvent event =
                    new StockUpdateEvent( m_portfolioManager );
109:
110:            // Notify all of our Listeners
111:            for( int i=0; i<m_vStockUpdateListeners.size(); i++ )
112:            {
113:                StockUpdateListener listener =
                ( StockUpdateListener )m_vStockUpdateListeners.elementAt( i );
114:                listener.portfolioManagerComplete( event );
115:            }
116:        }
117:
118:        // public void run()
119:        //
120:        //   Main body of the thread that is called when this thread
121:        //   is started
122:        public void run()
123:        {
124:            // Loop through all of the portfolios in the vector
125:            for( int i=0; i<m_vectorPortfolios.size(); i++ )
126:            {
127:                // Retrieve the i-th portfolio
128:                Portfolio portfolio =
                    ( Portfolio )m_vectorPortfolios.elementAt( i );
139:
130:                // Tell it to update its stock price
131:                if(portfolio.updateStockPrices().booleanValue()==false)
132:                {
133:                    // An error occurred!
134:                    return;
135:                }
136:
137:                // Notify our listeners that a portfolio has completed
138:                firePortfolioComplete();
139:            }
140:
141:          // Notify our action listener that the stock update is complete
142:            firePortfolioManagerComplete();
143:        }
144:    }
145:}
```

Line 13 creates a new `StockUpdateThread` object that will be discussed a little later in the code and passes a reference to this `PortfolioManager` class as its event generator (explained later).

Lines 19–26 define the `updatePortfolioStockPrices()` method to just start the `StockUpdateThread` object (line 22) and return `true` (line 25).

Because the `StockUpdateThread` is going to handle all the event notifications itself, we add `addStockUpdateListener()` and `removeStockUpdateListener()` methods that the `PortfolioManager` simply passes to the thread in lines 31–34 and lines 39–42, respectively.

Finally, we are up to the `StockUpdateThread`. This class is derived from `java.lang.Thread`. It maintains a `PortfolioManager` object (line 51) that it will build into `StockUpdateEvent` objects when firing events. Next, it maintains a `Vector` of `StockUpdateListener` objects (line 54), as described earlier in the "Event Notification Strategy" section.

Its constructor saves a copy of the `PortfolioManager` that created it in lines 57–60.

Lines 65–75 define the `addStockUpdateListener()` method in the same manner as discussed in the "Event Notification Strategy" section. The `removeStockUpdateListener()` method is similarly defined in lines 80–84.

Lines 89–100 and lines 105–116 define the `firePortfolioComplete()` and `firePortfolioManagerComplete()` methods, again implemented as discussed in the "Event Notification Strategy" section.

Finally, lines 122–144 define the body of the `run()` method. This method is similar to our old `updatePortfolioStockPrices()` method with the addition of lines 138 and 142. Line 138 calls the `firePortfolioComplete()` method to notify its listeners that a `Portfolio` has completed and line 142 calls the `firePortfolioManagerComplete()` method to notify its listeners that the entire `PortfolioManager` has completed its update.

If any of this seems foreign to you, review the "Event Notification Strategy" section earlier in this chapter.

Event Classes and Interfaces

I described the event notification strategy earlier in the chapter in some detail, but I wanted to give you the final source code for these classes and interfaces. Listings 9.10, 9.11, and 9.12 show the complete source code for `StockUpdateEvent`, `StockUpdateListener`, and `StockUpdateAdapter`, respectively.

Listing 9.10 `StockUpdateEvent.java`

```
1:   // Define the package we belong to
2:   package com.mcp.stock.portfolios.event;
3:
4:   // Import the Java Packages we are going to need
5:   import com.mcp.stock.portfolios.*;
6:   import java.util.*;
7:
8:   // StockUpdateEvent
9:   public class StockUpdateEvent extends EventObject
10:  {
11:      public StockUpdateEvent( PortfolioManager source )
12:      {
13:   super( source );
14:      }
15:  }
```

Listing 9.11 `StockUpdateListener.java`

```
1:   // Define the package we belong to
2:   package com.mcp.stock.portfolios.event;
3:
4:   // Import the Java Packages we are going to need
5:   import java.util.*;
6:
7:   // StockUpdateListener
8:   public interface StockUpdateListener extends EventListener
9:   {
10:      // A portfolio has completed its update
11:      public void portfolioComplete( StockUpdateEvent e );
12:
13:      // The portfolio manager has completed its update
14:      public void portfolioManagerComplete( StockUpdateEvent e );
15:  }
```

Listing 9.12 `StockUpdateAdapter.java`

```
1:   // Define the package we belong to
2:   package com.mcp.stock.portfolios.event;
3:
4:   // Import the Java Packages we are going to need
5:   import java.util.*;
6:
7:   // StockUpdateAdapter
8:   public class StockUpdateAdapter implements StockUpdateListener
9:   {
10:      // A portfolio has completed its update
11:      public void portfolioComplete( StockUpdateEvent e )
12:      {
13:      }
14:
```

```
15:     // The portfolio manager has completed its update
16:     public void portfolioManagerComplete( StockUpdateEvent e )
17:     {
18:     }
19: }
```

StockApplication Updates

The updates to the StockApplication class are simple, so I will go over them as you look at modifications to the StockApplication class in Listing 9.13.

Listing 9.13 **StockApplication.java (Modifications Only)**

```
1:  // Import our custom package
2:  import com.mcp.stock.portfolios.*;
3:  import com.mcp.stock.internet.*;
4:
5:  // StockApplication
6:  public class StockApplication extends JFrame
7:      implements ActionListener, ListSelectionListener, StockUpdateListener
8:  {
9:      // Constructor
10:     public StockApplication()
11:     {
12:         // Add ourself as a StockUpdateListener
13:         portfolioManager.addStockUpdateListener( this );
14:     }
15:
16:     public void portfolioComplete( StockUpdateEvent e )
17:     {
18:     }
19:
20:     public void portfolioManagerComplete( StockUpdateEvent e )
21:     {
22:         stockTabPanel.stockTableTabPanel.stockTablePanel.
23:                     stockTableModel.fireTableDataChanged();
23:     }
24:
25:     // Action Event Handler: actionPerformed
26:     public void actionPerformed(ActionEvent e)
27:     {
28:         // Extract the JMenuItem that generated this event
29:         JMenuItem item = ( JMenuItem )e.getSource();
30:
31:         // Find out which JMenuItem generated this event
32:         if( item == mainMenu.fileNewPortfolioManager )
33:         {
34:             System.out.println( "File->New->Portfolio Manager" );
35:         }
36:         ...
```

continues

Listing 9.13   continued

```
37:          else if ( item == mainMenu.quotesUpdate )
38:          {
39:              // Tell the PortfolioManager to update its stock prices
40:              portfolioManager. updatePortfolioStockPrices();
41:          }
42:      }
43: }
```

Lines 6 and 7 create the StockApplication class, but note the additional StockUpdateListener interface that it implements.

In the constructor in line 13, this StockApplication class is added as a StockUpdateListener by calling the PortfolioManager class's addStockUpdateListener(). Remember that this call is sent to the PortfolioManager class's StockUpdateThread to be added to its Vector of listeners.

Lines 16–18 provide the definition of the StockUpdateListener class's portfolioComplete() method. In this case we are not doing anything with it, but we must implement it because we implemented the StockUpdateListener interface.

Lines 20–23 implement the StockUpdateListener class's portfolioManagerComplete() method. Recall that this event is fired when the entire PortfolioManager is complete. When this happens, we want to update the table display, so we call the stock table's table model's fireTableDataChanged() method in line 22.

Lines 26–42 implement the actionPerformed() method, which, as you might recall, handles menu commands. In this case we are interested in handling the Quotes, Update menu item (lines 37–41). In line 40 we simply call the PortfolioManager class's updatePortfolioStockPrices() method to update all the portfolio manager's portfolios. This starts the PortfolioManager class's StockUpdateThread thread to initiate the download procedure.

And there you go: all the updates to all the Stock Tracker application's classes. Try compiling and running the Stock Tracker application. If you have any questions about where to place the code in the updates I have shown in this chapter, copy the code from the CD and try running that. Two warnings:

1. You must have an active Internet connection for this application to run—Windows will prompt you to establish the connection if you have Dial-Up Networking configured.

2. If you are trying to connect to the Web through a proxy (like at work, shh!), you will need to tell Java to use your proxy by invoking the application as follows:

```
java -Dhttp.proxyHost=proxyhost applicationname
```

where the `proxyhost` is the name of your proxy host (ask your system administrator). For the Stock Tracker application, you would use

```
java -Dhttp.proxyHost=proxyhost StockApplication
```

Summary

In this chapter we added Internet support to our Stock Tracker application through the `InternetManager`, `HTMLParser`, and `StockQuoteRetriever` classes. We covered the following Java concepts and technology:

- Downloading data from the Internet using Java classes
- Parsing HTML data using the Java `StringTokenizer` class
- Adding multiple threads to your applications using the `Thread` class
- Defining custom events that follow the Java event paradigm

Most important, after reading this chapter, you should be able to download a Web page from the Internet and extract whatever information you want from it. Don't worry if you didn't completely get it; we will talk about it again in Chapter 11, "Implementing the Historical Data Manager," when we go after another Web page and extract more information.

What's Next?

Now that you have the Stock Tracker application connected to the Internet, with updates available through the Quotes, Update menu command, it is time to automate the quote updates. In the next chapter we are going to set up a timer that lets the user specify how often to automatically go out to the Internet and update its stock data. This is a simple feature, but something that any stock tracking application must support.

9

Chapter 10

Retrieving Stock Quotes on a Fixed Time Interval

In the last chapter, we added the ability to download stock quotes over the Internet, but with the limitation that the user must specifically choose to perform the update manually every time. In this chapter, we are going to automate this process by enabling the user to configure a time interval in which the Stock Tracker application updates its stock quotes on its own.

In this chapter, I will talk about the following topics:

- Using the Swing timer
- Implementing a custom dialog box to configure the timer
- Integrating the timer with the user interface

Use Cases

Before we look at the timer itself, let's look at the use cases that the timer will satisfy. From Chapter 3, "Designing the Stock Tracker Application," we derived two use cases related to the timer: 10 and 11.

UC10: Set a Timer to Retrieve Stock Quotes at a Specific Interval

Use case:

Set a timer to retrieve stock quotes at a specific interval.

Scenario(s):

1. A timer is set that will initiate a retrieval of all supported stock quotes.

Preconditions:

1. The user has launched the Stock Tracker application.

Triggers:

1. The user chooses Timer Options from the Quotes menu.

Description:

1. The user chooses Timer Options from the Quotes menu.
2. A dialog box is displayed showing the user the current stock settings.
3. The user enables stock retrieval on a timer.
4. The user closes the dialog box.

Post Conditions:

The timer is set to the user's preference.

UC11: Retrieve Stock Quotes at the Set Interval

Use case:

Retrieve stock quotes at the set interval.

Scenario(s):

1. The system updates all stock quotes at the specified timer interval.
2. The system fails to update its stock quotes.

Preconditions:

1. The user has launched the Stock Tracker application.
2. The user has entered one or more stocks into one or more portfolios. (Use Case #1)
3. The user has set a timer interval. (Use Case #11)

Triggers:

1. The timer goes off and starts the update.

Description:

Scenario 1:

1. The timer goes off and starts the update.
2. The component initiates a stock quote retrieval for each stock in each portfolio (excluding duplicates).
3. The component receives the stock quotes and updates the tables.

Scenario 2:

1. The timer goes off and starts the update.
2. The component initiates a stock quote retrieval for each stock in each portfolio (excluding duplicates).
3. An error occurs, such as an invalid Internet connection.
4. The user is notified.

Post Conditions:

The table displays the updated stock quote prices.

Timer Responsibilities

You can see from these two use cases that we have the following tasks to perform:

1. Implement the Quotes, Update menu item.
2. Display a dialog to set the timer configuration.
3. Start the timer.
4. On a timer message, update the stock prices.

Component Relationships

Now that we know what the timer must do, take a look at Figure 10.1 to see how it interacts with the other components.

Figure 10.1

Timer class relationships.

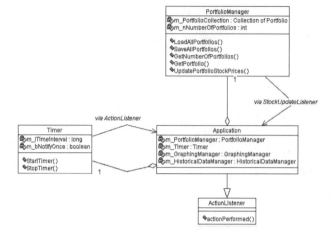

Figure 10.1 is a little complicated, but let me explain it:

- The `Application` object (`StockApplication`) contains one `Timer` object.
- The `Application` object contains one `PortfolioManager` object.
- The `Application` object implements the `ActionListener` interface.
- The `Timer` communicates with the Application using the `ActionListener` interface.

I will talk more about the internal workings of the `Timer` later in the chapter, but as you can see, the `Application` object contains the `Timer`, and there is some form of communication between the two.

Implementation Decisions

Implementing a timer object could be a challenging task, but luckily, Java provides this functionality through the `Timer` class.

Swing Timer

The `javax.swing.Timer` class provides the functionality we are looking for:

- You can set a time interval in milliseconds.
- You can start and stop the timer.
- The timer will notify you when the time interval expires.

Take a look at Table 10.1 to see how the `javax.swing.Timer` class is constructed.

Table 10.1   Timer Constructors

Constructor	Description
Timer(int delay, ActionListener listener)	Creates a Timer that will notify its listeners every delay milliseconds

From Table 10.1 you can see that there is only one Timer constructor; it accepts the timer delay in milliseconds and an ActionListener to notify when the specified time interval has expired. The Timer class notifies its listeners of timer events through the ActionListener interface, similar to the JButton class; your class must implement the ActionListener interface and provide a definition of the actionPerformed() method.

Table 10.2 shows some of the more useful methods that can be performed on a Timer.

Table 10.2   Timer Methods

Method	Description
addActionListener (ActionListener listener)	Adds an actionListener to the Timer
int getDelay()	Returns the Timer's delay
int getInitialDelay()	Returns the Timer's initial delay
boolean isRepeats()	Returns true if the Timer will send an actionPerformed() message to its listeners multiple times
setDelay(int delay)	Sets the Timer's delay, the number of milliseconds between successive actionPerformed() messages to its listeners
setInitialDelay(int initialDelay)	Sets the Timer's initial delay
setRepeats(boolean flag)	If flag is false, instructs the Timer to send actionPerformed() to its listeners only once, and then stop
start()	Starts the Timer, causing it to send actionPerformed() messages to its listeners
stop()	Stops a Timer, causing it to stop sending actionPerformed() messages to its target
restart()	Restarts a Timer, canceling any pending firings and causing it to fire with its initial delay

10

The Timer class has the notion of an initial delay and a delay: An *initial delay* is the amount of time the Timer will wait the first time it starts, and the *delay* is the amount of time the Timer will wait subsequent times. Also, the Timer class can be used for single events (fires once) or for recurring events (fires at a specified interval until stopped). You start a Timer by calling its start() method (or restart() if it is already running), and you stop a Timer by calling its stop() method. For example:

```
public class MyClass implements ActionListener
{
    // Create a timer
    Timer timer = new Timer( 5000, this );

    public MyClass()
    {
        timer.start();
    }

    actionPerformed( ActionEvent e )
    {
        if( e.getSource() == timer )
        {
            System.out.println( "Timer Message!" );
        }
    }

    ...
}
```

This example creates a Timer that goes off every 5000 milliseconds, or 5 seconds, when it writes "Timer Message!" to the screen.

Configuring the Timer

From Use Case 10, you can see that you must provide a custom dialog box that enables the user to configure the timer. This dialog box will be created when the user selects Timer Options from the Quotes menu. So how do you create a custom dialog box?

You are already familiar with the JOptionPane and several of its variations: display a message to the user and prompt the user for a String. However, we are going to need more in this case. We need the following components:

- A label that prompts the user for the interval
- A text entry field
- A check box that enables and disables the timer
- OK button
- Cancel button

Creating a custom dialog box is actually a pretty simple process. There are three steps:

1. Derive a class from `javax.swing.JDialog`.
2. Create an instance of that class in the "parent" class.
3. Call the dialog's `show()` method.

First take a look at Table 10.3 to see how to construct a `javax.swing.JDialog` object.

Table 10.3   `JDialog` **Constructors**

Constructor	Description
JDialog()	Creates a non-modal dialog without a title and without a specified frame owner
JDialog(Dialog owner)	Creates a non-modal dialog without a title with the specified dialog as its owner
JDialog(Dialog owner, boolean modal)	Creates a modal or non-modal dialog without a title and with the specified owner dialog
JDialog(Dialog owner, String title)	Creates a non-modal dialog with the specified title and with the specified owner dialog
JDialog(Dialog owner, String title, boolean modal)	Creates a modal or non-modal dialog with the specified title and the specified owner frame
JDialog(Frame owner)	Creates a non-modal dialog without a title with the specified frame as its owner
JDialog(Frame owner, boolean modal)	Creates a modal or non-modal dialog without a title and with the specified owner frame
JDialog(Frame owner, String title)	Creates a non-modal dialog with the specified title and with the specified owner frame
JDialog(Frame owner, String title, boolean modal)	Creates a modal or non-modal dialog with the specified title and the specified owner frame

There are two points of interest in these constructors:

- A `JDialog` should be owned by a class derived from `java.awt.Frame`, such as `javax.swing.JFrame` or `java.awt.Dialog`.
- The dialog can be modal or non-modal (modeless).

A *modal* dialog box is displayed above the application frame and receives the input focus. You cannot perform any action in the application until the modal dialog box is closed.

A *modeless* dialog box is displayed at the same level as the application; you can actively switch back and forth between the two—one does not monopolize the input focus over the other.

In our application, we are going to want our dialog box to be modal so that we can suspend the application activity until the user finishes his selection. Classes derived from JDialog are similar to those derived from JFrame in their construction; when we get to the code later in the chapter, you will see that it has a RootPane that we use to get the content pane to add panels and components to. Most of what you learned about building applications is directly applicable to the JDialog class as well.

Table 10.4 shows the JDialog methods specific to showing and hiding the dialog.

Table 10.4   JDialog Methods

Method	Description
show()	Makes the dialog visible. If the dialog is modal, this call will block until the dialog is hidden by calling setVisible (false) or dispose().
dispose()	Releases all the native screen resources used by this window and its subcomponents.
setVisible(boolean b)	Shows or hides this component depending on the value of parameter b.

Building the Timer Configuration Dialog Box

We will implement the Timer Configuration dialog box through the TimerOptionsDialog class. Table 10.5 shows its public methods.

Table 10.5   TimerOptionsDialog Methods

Method	Description
TimerOptionsDialog(Frame owner)	Creates a new TimerOptionsDialog that is owned by the specified Frame
void setTimerEnabled(Boolean b)	Sets the state of the timer: true = enabled, false = disabled

Method	Description
Boolean getTimerEnabled()	Returns true if the timer is enabled, false if it is disabled
void setTimerInterval (int nInterval)	Sets the timer interval
Integer getTimerInterval()	Returns the timer interval
Boolean isOK()	Returns true if the user closed the dialog box by clicking OK, false if the user selected Cancel

The TimerInterval is displayed on the dialog box in the text field, and the TimerEnabled Boolean value is reflected through the aforementioned check box. You might be questioning the isOK() method. This method is required because the show() method that shows the dialog box does not return a value when the dialog is closed, so there must be some way to determine how the user closed the dialog.

Take a look at Listing 10.1 for the complete source code for the TimerOptionsDialog class. Note that this class is not compilable in its current state; we will actually add the completed class to the StockApplication source file later in the chapter.

Listing 10.1 `TimerOptionsDialog` **Class**

```
1:  class TimerOptionsDialog extends JDialog implements ActionListener
2:  {
3:      // Timer Interval Prompt Panel
4:      JLabel lblIntervalPrompt = new JLabel( "Update Interval (min):" );
5:      JTextField txtInterval = new JTextField( "5", 20 );
6:      JPanel panelInterval = new JPanel( new FlowLayout() );
7:
8:      // Timer Enabled CheckBox
9:      JCheckBox chkEnableTimer = new JCheckBox( "Enable Timer" );
10:
11:     // OK / Cancel buttons and panel
12:     JButton btnOK = new JButton( "OK" );
13:     JButton btnCancel = new JButton( "Cancel" );
14:     JPanel panelButtons = new JPanel( new GridLayout( 1, 2 ) );
15:
16:     // Close Status
17:     Boolean bOK = new Boolean( true );
18:     Boolean bTimerEnabled = new Boolean( false );
19:
20:     // Constructor
21:     public TimerOptionsDialog( Frame owner )
22:     {
23:         // Initialize the JDialog
```

10

continues

Listing 10.1   continued

```
24:            super( owner, "Timer Options", true );
25:
26:            // Set the dialog layout
27:            getContentPane().setLayout( new GridLayout( 3, 1 ) );
28:
29:            // Build the Interval panel
30:            panelInterval.add( lblIntervalPrompt );
31:            panelInterval.add( txtInterval );
32:
33:            // Add the Interval panel to the dialog (0, 0)
34:            getContentPane().add( panelInterval );
35:
36:            // Add the JCheckBox to the dialog (0, 1)
37:            chkEnableTimer.setVerticalAlignment( JCheckBox.CENTER );
38:            chkEnableTimer.setHorizontalAlignment( JCheckBox.CENTER );
39:            getContentPane().add( chkEnableTimer );
40:
41:            // Set our dialog class as an action listener for the
42:            // buttons
43:            btnOK.addActionListener( this );
44:            btnCancel.addActionListener( this );
45:
46:            // Build the Button Panel
47:            panelButtons.add( btnOK );
48:            panelButtons.add( btnCancel );
49:
50:            // Add the Button Panel to the dialog (0, 2)
51:            getContentPane().add( panelButtons );
52:
53:            // Resize the dialog box
54:            setSize( 300, 200 );
55:        }
56:
57:    public void actionPerformed( ActionEvent e )
58:    {
59:        if( e.getSource() == btnOK )
60:        {
61:            bOK = new Boolean( true );
62:        }
63:        else
64:        {
65:            bOK = new Boolean( false );
66:        }
67:
68:        // Hide the window
69:        setVisible( false );
70:    }
71:
72:    public void setTimerEnabled( Boolean b )
73:    {
```

```
74:              chkEnableTimer.setSelected ( b.booleanValue() );
75:          }
76:
77:      public Boolean getTimerEnabled()
78:      {
79:          return new Boolean(chkEnableTimer.getSelectedObjects() != null);
80:      }
81:
82:      public void setTimerInterval( int nInterval )
83:      {
84:          txtInterval.setText( Integer.toString( nInterval ) );
85:      }
86:
87:      public Integer getTimerInterval()
88:      {
89:          return new Integer( txtInterval.getText() );
90:      }
91:
92:      public Boolean isOK()
93:      {
94:          return bOK;
95:      }
96: }
```

Line 1 shows that the TimerOptionsDialog class is derived from JDialog and implements ActionListener. The ActionListener is used to listen for the JButton clicks of the OK and Cancel buttons.

Lines 4–6 create the top panel of our dialog box: a JLabel that prompts for the time interval in minutes, a 20-column JTextField to hold the user's entry, and a FlowLayout JPanel to hold the components.

Line 9 creates a JCheckBox that displays whether the timer is enabled or disabled.

Lines 12–14 create the button panel: two JButton instances for OK and Cancel and a JPanel to hold them.

Line 17 creates a Boolean that records the state of the OK button when the dialog closes.

Line 18 creates a Boolean that maintains whether the timer is enabled or disabled.

Lines 21–55 define the constructor for the TimerOptionsDialog class. It accepts a Frame or Frame derivation object as its parameter that it passes to the JDialog constructor through the super reserved word in line 24. Line 24 creates the dialog with the title Timer Options and specifies that it is a modal dialog box.

Line 27 sets the layout manager of the dialog to be a GridLayout with three rows and one column.

10

Lines 30–34 construct the interval panel and add it to the dialog.

Lines 37–39 tell the JCheckBox to center itself in its allocated area and then add it to the dialog.

Lines 43 and 44 add this instance of the TimerOptionsDialog class as an ActionListener for the OK and Cancel buttons.

Lines 47 and 48 build the button panel and line 51 adds the button panel to the dialog.

Finally, line 54 ends the constructor by resizing it to 300×200.

Lines 57–70 defined the ActionListener actionPerformed() method by setting the OK button clicked status based on the button that fired the event and then hiding the dialog box by calling setVisible(false) in line 68.

Lines 72–75 define the setTimerEnabled() method by setting the selection state of the Enable Timer check box.

Lines 77–80 define the getTimerEnabled() method by asking the Enable Timer check box if it has any items selected in it. getSelectedObjects() returns an array of Object objects or null if nothing is selected, so by checking for null we can determine if the check box is checked.

Lines 82–85 define the setTimerInterval() method that converts the integer value to a String and sets the JTextField to that value.

Lines 87–90 define the getTimerInterval() method by converting the JTextField component to an Integer and returning it.

Finally, lines 92–95 define the isOK() method that returns true if the OK button was used to close the dialog or false if the Cancel button was used to close the dialog.

Integrating the Timer with the User Interface

Now that we know how to create a dialog box to prompt the user for timer options and how to create a timer, it is time to add this functionality to the Stock Tracker application. All the changes in this chapter are made to the StockApplication class source file.

Listing 10.2 shows the modifications made to the StockApplication class source file.

Listing 10.2 `StockApplication.java` **(Modifications Only)**

```
 1:   // StockApplication
 2:   public class StockApplication extends JFrame
 3:    implements ActionListener, ListSelectionListener, StockUpdateListener
 4:   {
 5:       // Create a timer for updating stock quote prices - default to
 6:       // 300,000ms (5 minutes)
 7:       Timer m_timerUpdateQuotes = new Timer( 300000, this );
 8:       Boolean m_bTimerEnabled = new Boolean( false );
 9:       Integer m_nTimerInterval = new Integer( 5 );
10:
11:       // Constructor
12:       public StockApplication()
13:       {
14:           // Add the StockApplication as a listener to the update
15:           // quotes timer
16:           m_timerUpdateQuotes.addActionListener( this );
17:
18:       }
19:
20:       // Action Event Handler: actionPerformed
21:       public void actionPerformed(ActionEvent e)
22:       {
23:           // Check for a timer event
24:           if( e.getSource() == m_timerUpdateQuotes )
25:           {
26:               System.out.println( "Received a timer event" );
27:
28:               // Tell the PortfolioManager to update its stock prices
29:               portfolioManager.updatePortfolioStockPrices();
30:
31:               return;
32:           }
33:
34:           ...
35:
36:           else if ( item == mainMenu.quotesTimerOptions )
37:           {
38:               System.out.println( "Quotes->Timer Options" );
39:
40:               // Create a new TimerOptionsDialog dialog box
41:               TimerOptionsDialog dlg = new TimerOptionsDialog( this );
42:               dlg.setTimerEnabled( m_bTimerEnabled );
43:               dlg.setTimerInterval ( m_nTimerInterval.intValue() );
44:
45:               // Display the dialog (modal)
46:               dlg.show();
47:
48:               // If the user pressed OK, update the results
```

10

continues

Listing 10.2 continued

```
49:                 if( dlg.isOK().booleanValue() )
50:                 {
51:                     // If the timer is already running, stop it
52:                     if( m_bTimerEnabled.booleanValue() )
53:                     {
54:                         m_timerUpdateQuotes.stop();
55:                     }
56:
57:                     // Get the new timer enabled value
58:                     m_bTimerEnabled = dlg.getTimerEnabled();
59:
60:
61:                     // If the timer is enabled, start it
62:                     if( m_bTimerEnabled.booleanValue() )
63:                     {
64:                         m_nTimerInterval = dlg.getTimerInterval();
65:                         m_timerUpdateQuotes.setInitialDelay( 1000 * 60 *
                                        m_nTimerInterval.intValue() );
66:                         m_timerUpdateQuotes.setDelay( 1000 * 60 *
                                        m_nTimerInterval.intValue() );
67:                         m_timerUpdateQuotes.start();
68:                     }
69:                 }
70:             }
71:         }
72:
73:     class TimerOptionsDialog extends JDialog implements ActionListener
74:     {
75:         ...
76:     }
77: }
```

Line 7 creates a new `Timer` object that is initially set to go off every 300,000ms (5 minutes) and notify the `StockApplication` class.

Line 8 creates a new `Boolean` object that represents whether or not the timer is enabled—it defaults to `false` or disabled.

Line 9 creates a new `Integer` object that represents the timer interval in minutes—it defaults to 5 minutes.

In the `StockApplication` constructor, we add the `StockApplication` as an `ActionListener` to the `Timer` (line 16).

Lines 21–71 define the `actionPerformed()` method that handles menu item selections and timer events. Line 24 checks to see whether this event is a timer event by comparing the source of the event to the `StockApplication` class's timer. If it is the timer that generated the message, line 26 outputs the message to the standard output device, and then line 29 asks the `PortfolioManager` to update its portfolio stock prices.

Later in the `actionPerformed()` method during the menu item handlers, lines 36–70 handle the Quotes, Timer Options. This handler starts off by displaying a message to the standard output (line 38), and then it creates a new `TimerOptionsDialog` object in line 41. Lines 42 and 43 set the timer enabled status and timer interval, respectively. Line 46 shows the `TimerOptionsDialog` dialog box. This call blocks until the user closes the dialog box.

After the dialog box is closed, line 49 checks to see whether the user closed it by clicking OK. If the user selected Cancel, the changes are ignored; otherwise, the handler continues in line 52 by stopping the timer if it is already running. Line 58 gets the enabled state of the timer, and then line 62 checks its value. If the timer is enabled, line 64 gets the timer interval and lines 65 and 66 set the initial delay and delay values in milliseconds, respectively. Finally, line 67 starts the timer by calling the `Timer` class's `start()` method.

After the `StockApplication` class's definition, line 73 starts the `TimerOptionsDialog` class. This class is exactly the class that we created in Listing 10.1, so the code is not reprinted here.

Figure 10.2 shows the Timer Options dialog box, shown by selecting Timer Options from the Quotes menu.

Figure 10.2

The Timer Options dialog box.

10

You can either copy the source code for Chapter 10 from the CD-ROM and compile and run it, or if you are working along with me, go ahead and make the aforementioned changes to the `StockApplication.java` source file and use that. When you launch the application, the timer is disabled by default, so you must turn it on by selecting Quotes, Timer Options and configuring the timer. As an exercise, try enabling the timer by default: You will have to set the timer enabled `Boolean` value to `true` and then start the timer yourself in the constructor.

Summary

This chapter covered two major Java concepts by adding timer-based stock updates to the Stock Tracker application:

- Using the Java Timer class
- Creating a custom dialog box

You were also exposed to a little refresher in Swing component development and layout managers through the construction of the Timer Options custom dialog box.

What's Next?

At this point we have pretty much completed our work on the stock table and the information in it; we have live data downloaded from the Internet in the table, and we now have the ability to automatically retrieve that data at any specified interval. In the next two chapters we are going to switch gears and start looking at the graphing capabilities of the Stock Tracker application. In Chapter 11, "Implementing the Historical Data Manager," we are going to implement our historical data manager class that will download historical data from the Internet. Then in Chapter 12, "Graphing Historical Data," we are going to take that historical data and display it in a graph.

Chapter 11

Implementing the Historical Data Manager

Now it is time to change gears a bit and start looking into historical data. The focus of this chapter is downloading stock prices from the Internet over a specified time interval and saving it to the local file system. In the next chapter, we will take that historical data and graph it.

In this chapter I will talk about the following topics:

- Using the Internet package
- General text parsing
- Writing a small test application

Use Cases

Two use cases are related to historical data persistence in the Stock Tracker application:

- Use Case #8: Persist historical information to and from a data file
- Use Case #26: Save historical information

Use Case 8 refers to loading and saving historical data in its entirety, whereas Use Case 26 refers to it more in the context of adding the current day's data to the historical data for a stock that has historical tracking enabled. The point is that we need the facility to load and save historical data.

Two use cases are related to graphing historical data:

- Use Case #17: Set graphing time scale
- Use Case #18: Graph stock performance points

Use Case 17 is related to the time interval that the application must graph, and Use Case 18 is the actual graphing of data. We must provide the capability to retrieve stock data for the time interval specified in Use Case 17.

Finally, two use cases are related to importing and exporting historical data:

- Use Case #19: Import historical data from a CSV file
- Use Case #20: Export historical data to a CSV file

These use cases will be addressed in Chapter 13, "Implementing the CSV Importer/Exporter," but we can plan for them here in the way we treat the historical data and design the final implementation of the HistoricalDataManager class.

Implementation Decisions

Initially the task of implementing a historical data manager might appear overwhelming, but compared to the other classes you wrote, this task is relatively simple. You have several decisions to make:

- Where do you obtain your historical data?
- How do you want to represent this data on the local file system?
- What components can you reuse to make your job easier?

Data Source

As discussed in Chapter 9, "Implementing the Stock Quote Retriever," selecting a reliable server is important. This server can change at any time because you do not run it. Furthermore, you must look at how the data is presented and whether it is easy enough for you to extract information from.

For this chapter, I went to my favorite search engine and searched on "Free Historical Stock Quotes" and found quite a few sites. One site in particular has a page that accepts a stock symbol and number of business days to display. It then simply outputs the data in comma-separated form. I thought this was quite convenient, so I opted to use it. It is a little different to parse than the ones you have been using thus far, but it will greatly help in Chapter 13 when we start talking about Comma Separated Variable (CSV) files. The query is of the following form:

```
http://www.tradepbs.com/cgi-bin/hstpdwn?Symbol=SYM&Period=DAYS
```

SYM is the stock symbol and DAYS is the number of days to retrieve. For example, suppose you downloaded the following URL to download data on the last 10 days of Microsoft's stock:

```
http://www.tradepbs.com/cgi-bin/hstpdwn?Symbol=MSFT&Period=10
```

You would get the following results:

```
" 8/13/1999"," 84.688 "," 82.938 "," 85.625 "," 82.750 "," 32,549,900"
" 8/12/1999"," 81.750 "," 83.938 "," 84.188 "," 81.625 "," 30,531,000"
" 8/11/1999"," 84.188 "," 84.000 "," 84.688 "," 82.313 "," 33,052,600"
" 8/10/1999"," 82.938 "," 83.563 "," 84.063 "," 81.625 "," 31,371,500"
" 8/09/1999"," 84.000 "," 85.625 "," 85.813 "," 83.938 "," 17,467,000"
" 8/06/1999"," 85.125 "," 86.063 "," 86.438 "," 84.938 "," 33,602,900"
" 8/05/1999"," 85.750 "," 85.375 "," 86.375 "," 84.750 "," 38,317,000"
" 8/04/1999"," 84.938 "," 85.125 "," 87.188 "," 84.750 "," 37,786,700"
" 8/03/1999"," 84.750 "," 85.875 "," 86.063 "," 84.375 "," 27,521,500"
" 8/02/1999"," 84.813 "," 85.688 "," 86.938 "," 84.375 "," 24,018,800"
```

Here are the columns that are represented by this table, in order:

- Date
- Close
- Open
- High
- Low
- Volume

There are two problems with this table:

- There are no markers in the table that the HTMLParser class can use.
- All the entries are in quotes.

What this results in is the fact that (1) we will have to implement a new parsing algorithm to read the data and (2) the parsing will be more difficult with the quotation marks. But do not fret! When you have this information, Java's support classes make this parsing a cakewalk!

Modified CSV Parsing

I would have named this section "CSV Parsing" except for those pesky quotation marks you have to deal with! I will talk more about true CSV parsing in Chapter 13, but for now let's determine how we are going to solve the problem at hand. Take a look at the following line from the Web page:

```
" 8/13/1999"," 84.688 "," 82.938 "," 85.625 "," 82.750 "," 32,549,900"
```

11

Think of this in terms of the tokens you can break it into. With a standard CSV file, you would break it into tokens by commas, which would give you the following tokens:

```
" 8/13/1999"
" 84.688 "
" 82.938 "
" 85.625 "
" 82.750 "
" 32
549
900"
```

This looks fine until you get to the volume. That isn't going to work. Now you could break it up by quotation marks, which would give you the following tokens:

```
8/13/1999
,
 84.688
,
 82.938
,
 85.625
,
 82.750
,
 32,549,900
```

This looks a little better, but you still have all those commas in there! There is a more difficult implementation that would handle both cases, which would involve tokenizing by commas and counting quotation marks, but for now it is easy enough just to tokenize by quotation marks and throw out all tokens that are just commas. Take a look at Listing 11.1 for this algorithm.

Listing 11.1 **Quotation Tokenizing Algorithm**

```
1: StringTokenizer stLine =
2:        new StringTokenizer( strLine, "\"\r\n", false );
3:
4:  // Loop through each token in the line
5:  while( stLine.hasMoreTokens())
6:  {
7:      // Get the next token
8:      String str = stLine.nextToken();
9:      System.out.println( "Token: " + str );
10:
11:     // See if the token is a comma
12:     if( str.compareToIgnoreCase( "," ) != 0 )
13:     {
14:         // Not a token, trim it and add it to the Vector
```

```
15:          str = str.trim();
16:          vTokens.add( str );
17:      }
18: }
```

Lines 1 and 2 create a new StringTokenizer class instance that tokenizes the String strLine into tokens by three criteria:

- Quotation mark
- Carriage return
- Newline

Line 5 loops through all the tokens in the StringTokenizer.

Line 8 extracts a String token, and line 9 displays it to the standard output device (for debugging purposes).

Line 12 performs the test to remove commas; it will skip all commas.

Line 15 removes the leading and trailing white space from the token. You might have noticed from the data provided that there was a little white space in there.

Finally, line 16 adds the token to a Vector of tokens named vTokens (defined in the full listing later).

One last note before we leave this topic: This algorithm works great on a single line of information, but we must get the data parsed into lines for this to work. This is an even easier task using the StringTokenizer class, as shown in Listing 11.2.

Listing 11.2 Tokenizing a String into Lines

```
1:  // Tokenize the page into lines
2:  StringTokenizer stDoc = new StringTokenizer( strSource, "\r\n", false );
3:
4:  // Read each line
5:  while( stDoc.hasMoreTokens() )
6:  {
7:      strLine = stDoc.nextToken();
8:
9:      // Insert the code for listing 11.1 here ...
10: }
```

Line 2 creates a new StringTokenizer that works exclusively on carriage returns and newlines.

Lines 5 and 7 loop through all the lines in the String page.

11

Persistence Strategy

As I said earlier, we are responsible for persisting this stock information to and from the local file system. We need a convention for the data files that meets two criteria:

- Consistent and intuitive naming
- Reusable with the later CSV file support (as much as possible!)

My proposal for the persistence strategy for the historical data manager is to name the data files SYMBOL.txt and leverage the StockData class's built-in persistence support. I am suggesting that the HistoricalDataManager class represent its data as a Vector of StockData objects, open a file using a FileReader as the Portfolio class did earlier, and ask each StockData object to read() or write() from or to that file.

Modifications must be made to the StockData class to facilitate the data, open, and close fields, but that work is insignificant. We must add three new variables to the StockData class: the date that the stock data represents, the closing price for that date, and the opening price for that date. These are declared as follows:

```
protected String m_strDate = new String( "None" );
protected Float m_fClose = new Float( 0 );
protected Float m_fOpen = new Float( 0 );
```

Then we have to add the respective get and set methods for these variables:

```
public String getDate()
{
    return m_strDate;
}

public void setDate( String strDate )
{
    m_strDate = strDate;
}

public Float getClose()
{
    return m_fClose;
}

public void setClose( Float fClose )
{
    m_fClose = fClose;
}

public Float getOpen()
{
    return m_fOpen;
}
```

```
public void setOpen( Float fOpen )
{
    m_fOpen = fOpen;
}
```

Next, we must add support for these fields to be persisted in the StockData class's read() and write() methods. Listings 11.3 and 11.4 show the StockData read() and write() methods, respectively.

Listing 11.3 StockData read() Method

```
 1:  public Boolean read( FileReader file )
 2:  {
 3:      // Create a String to hold an entire line from the file
 4:      String strLine = new String();
 5:
 6:      try
 7:      {
 8:          // Read the first character
 9:          int nChar = file.read();
10:
11:          // Clear out any carriage returns or linefeeds:
12:          //   (1) Carriage Return = '\r'
13:          //   (2) Newline = '\n'
14:          while( nChar == '\n' || nChar == '\r' )
15:          {
16:              nChar = file.read();
17:          }
18:
19:          // Loop through all of the characters until we hit
20:          //   (1) The end of the line = -1
21:          //   (2) Newline = '\n'
22:          //   (3) Carriage Return = '\r'
23:          while( nChar != -1 && nChar != '\n' && nChar != '\r' )
24:          {
25:              // Copy the character to the line string
26:              strLine = strLine + ( char )nChar;
27:
28:              // Get the next character
29:              nChar = file.read();
30:          }
31:      }
32:      catch( IOException e )
33:      {
34:          // An error occurred during FileReader.read(). Display
35:          // the error and return false.
36:          System.out.println( "StockData.read Error: " + e.toString() );
37:          return new Boolean( false );
38:      }
39:
40:      // See if we successfully read a line from the file
```

continues

Listing 11.3 continued

```
41:    if( strLine.length() == 0 )
42:    {
43:        return new Boolean( false );
44:    }
45:
46:    // Create a string tokenizer to parse the line into
47:    // tokens with the following delimiters:
48:    //   (1) Tab              =  '\t'
49:    //   (2) Newline          =  '\n'
50:    //   (3) Carriage Return  =  '\r'
51:    //   (4) Form Feed        =  '\f'
52:    //   (5) Comma            =  ','
53:    StringTokenizer st = new StringTokenizer( strLine, "\t\n\r\f," );
54:
55:
56:    // Get the count of the number of tokens in the line
57:    if( st.countTokens() != 11 )
58:    {
59:        // Error, not the correct number of tokens!
60:        System.out.println(
61:            "StockData.read Error: Expected 11 tokens, but received "
62:            + st.countTokens() );
63:
64:        // An error occurred, so return false
65:        return new Boolean( false );
66:    }
67:
68:    try
69:    {
70:        // Set our properties by extracting our 11 tokens
71:        m_strStockSymbol = st.nextToken();
72:        m_strCompanyName = st.nextToken();
73:        m_fLastSale = new Float( st.nextToken() );
74:        m_fHigh = new Float( st.nextToken() );
75:        m_fLow = new Float( st.nextToken() );
76:        m_fVolume = new Float( st.nextToken() );
77:        m_fNumberOfSharesOwned = new Float( st.nextToken() );
78:        m_fPricePaidPerShare = new Float( st.nextToken() );
79:        m_strDate = new String( st.nextToken() );
80:        m_fClose = new Float( st.nextToken() );
81:        m_fOpen = new Float( st.nextToken() );
82:    }
83:    catch( NoSuchElementException e )
84:    {
85:        // An error occurred during StringTokenizer.nextToken()
86:        // Log the error and return false
87:        System.out.println( "StockData.read Error: " + e.toString() );
88:        return new Boolean( false );
```

```
89:     }
90:
91:     // Success! Return true
92:     return new Boolean( true );
93: }
```

Line 57 updates our token comparison from 8 to 11 to add the three new tokens.

Lines 79–81 retrieve the date, close, and open fields from the StringTokenizer, respectively.

Listing 11.4   `StockData write()` **Method**

```
1:  public Boolean write( FileWriter file )
2:  {
3:      try
4:      {
5:          // Write our fields to the FileWriter
6:          file.write( m_strStockSymbol + ","  );
7:          file.write( m_strCompanyName + "," );
8:          file.write( m_fLastSale.toString() + "," );
9:          file.write( m_fHigh.toString() + "," );
10:         file.write( m_fLow.toString() + "," );
11:         file.write( m_fVolume.toString() + "," );
12:         file.write( m_fNumberOfSharesOwned.toString() + "," );
13:         file.write( m_fPricePaidPerShare.toString() + "," );
14:         file.write( m_strDate + "," );
15:         file.write( m_fClose + "," );
16:         file.write( m_fOpen + "\r\n" );
17:     }
18:     catch( IOException e )
19:     {
20:         // An error occurred during FileWriter.read(). Display
21:         // the error and return false.
22:         System.out.println( "StockData.write Error: " + e.toString() );
23:         return new Boolean( false );
24:     }
25:
26:     // Success! Return true
27:     return new Boolean( true );
28: }
```

Lines 14–16 write the date, close, and open values to the FileWriter, respectively.

Existing Components

I have already talked about using the StockData class to represent the historical data, but there is one other class that you can use: InternetManager. As a matter of fact, you can use this class in your future products because it provides a simple interface to retrieve Web pages from the Internet.

11

Anyway, we will use the InternetManager class to download all our data from the Internet for us.

HistoricalDataManager

Refer to the class diagram for the HistoricalDataManager that we designed in Chapter 3, shown in Figure 11.1.

Figure 11.1

HistoricalData Manager *class diagram.*

This class diagram was pretty vague when it was designed because at that point we had not chosen the Web server from which we were downloading the historical data and the form of that data. From what you have learned earlier in this chapter, you will not need the HTMLParser object, but you will still need the InternetManager. Figure 11.2 shows an updated class diagram for the HistoricalDataManager class, and Tables 11.1 and 11.2 show the attributes and methods of the HistoricalDataManager class, respectively.

Figure 11.2

HistoricalData Manager *revised class diagram.*

```
          HistoricalDataManagerImplementation
m_internetManager : InternetManager
m_vStockData : Vector
m_strStockSymbol : String

getHistoricalData (strStockSymbol : String, nNumberOfDays : int) : Boolean
buildHistoricalData (strSource : String) : Boolean
loadHistoricalData (strStockSymbol : String) : Boolean
saveHistoricalData () : Boolean
stripCommas (strSource : String) : String
getNumberOfHistoricalRecords () : int
getStockDataElement (nIndex : int) : StockData
```

Table 11.1 HistoricalDataManager **Attributes**

Attribute	Description
m_internetManager	InternetManager that this class uses to obtain information from the Internet
m_vStockData	Vector of StockData objects for each of the dates the HistoricalDataManager is maintaining
m_strStockSymbol	Stock symbol of the stock the HistoricalDataManager is maintaining

Table 11.2 `HistoricalDataManager` **Methods**

Method	Description
`HistoricalDataManager()`	Empty constructor used for creating an instance of this class.
`Boolean getHistoricalData(String strStockSymbol, int nNumberOfDays)`	Retrieves the stock information for the specified information for the stock symbol and number of days—note that this is the number of days the stock was traded, not calendar days.
`Boolean buildHistoricalData (String strSource)`	Extracts historical data from a CSV string with all data elements delimited by quotation marks.
`Boolean loadHistoricalData (String strStockSymbol)`	Loads the historical data for the specified stock symbol from the local file system.
`Boolean saveHistoricalData()`	Saves the historical data in the `HistorialDataManager` to the local file system.
`String stripCommas(String strSource)`	Utility method that returns the specified string without commas.
`int getNumberOfHistoricalRecords()`	Returns the number of historical records stored in the `HistoricalDataManager`.
`StockData getStockDataElement (int nIndex)`	Returns the `StockData` element stored at the specified position in the `Vector`.

We expanded the `HistoricalDataManager` class's method list quite a bit from the class diagram in Figure 11.1, but it was required to fulfill the use cases for our implementation. Take a look at Listing 11.5 for the complete listing for the `HistoricalDataManager` class.

Listing 11.5 `HistoricalDataManager.java`

```
 1: // Define the package we belong to
 2: package com.mcp.stock.internet;
 3:
 4: // Import the packages used by this class
 5: import java.util.*;
 6: import java.io.*;
 7: import java.net.*;
 8: import com.mcp.stock.portfolios.*;
 9:
10:
```

11

continues

Listing 11.5   continued

```
11: public class HistoricalDataManager
12: {
13:     // InternetManager to perform our Internet functionality
14:     protected InternetManager m_internetManager = new InternetManager();
15:
16:     // Vector of StockData objects representing the stock for
17:     // information for each day requested
18:     protected Vector m_vStockData = new Vector();
19:
20:     // The Stock Symbol that this HistoricalDataManager is holding
21:     protected String m_strStockSymbol = new String();
22:
23:     // Constructors
24:     public HistoricalDataManager()
25:     {
26:     }
27:
28:     // getHistoricalData( strStockSymbol, nNumberOfDays )
29:     //
30:     //   Retrieves the historical stock data for the specified symbol
31:     //   and for the specified number of days from the Internet
32:     public Boolean getHistoricalData( String strStockSymbol,
33:                                       int nNumberOfDays )
34:     {
35:         // Save the Stock Symbol
36:         m_strStockSymbol = strStockSymbol;
37:
38:         // Build the URL
39:         String strURL = new String
40:         (
41:             "http://www.tradepbs.com/cgi-bin/hstpdwn?Symbol=" +
42:             strStockSymbol +
43:             "&Period=" +
44:             nNumberOfDays
45:         );
46:
47:         // Retrieve the URL from the Internet
48:         String strHTML = new String();
49:
50:         try
51:         {
52:             strHTML = m_internetManager.getHTMLPage( strURL );
53:         }
54:         catch( MalformedURLException e )
55:         {
56:             System.out.println( e.toString() );
57:             return new Boolean( false );
```

```
58:            }
59:            catch( IOException e )
60:            {
61:                System.out.println( e.toString() );
62:                return new Boolean( false );
63:            }
64:
65:            // Take the historical data from its comma separated values
66:            // and build our historical data Vector
67:            return buildHistoricalData( strHTML );
68:        }
69:
70:        // buildHistoricalData( String strSource )
71:        //
72:        // Builds the historical data Vector with entries extracted
73:        // from strSource.
74:        //
75:        // strSource must be in the form:
76:        //      "Date","Close","Open","High","Low","Volume"
77:        public Boolean buildHistoricalData( String strSource )
78:        {
79:            // Create a Vector to hold tokens
80:            Vector vTokens = new Vector();
81:
82:            // Tokenize the HTML page into lines
83:            StringTokenizer stDoc =
84:                    new StringTokenizer( strSource, "\r\n", false );
85:
86:            // Read each line
87:            while( stDoc.hasMoreTokens() )
88:            {
89:                // Tokenize the line by quotes '"'
90:                StringTokenizer stLine =
91:                 new StringTokenizer( stDoc.nextToken(), "\"\r\n", false );
92:
93:                // Loop through each token in the line
94:                while( stLine.hasMoreTokens())
95:                {
96:                    // Get the next token
97:                    String str = stLine.nextToken();
98:                    System.out.println( "Token: " + str );
99:
100:                    // See if the token is a comma
101:                    if( str.compareToIgnoreCase( "," ) != 0 )
102:                    {
103:                        // Not a token, trim it and add it to the Vector
104:                        str = str.trim();
105:                        vTokens.add( str );
106:                    }
107:                }
108:            }
```

continues

Listing 11.5 continued

```
109:
110:            // Loop through each token in the Vector
111:            for( int i=0; i<vTokens.size(); i++ )
112:            {
113:                // Create a new StockData object
114:                StockData data = new StockData();
115:
116:                // Set its attributes
117:                data.setStockSymbol( m_strStockSymbol );
118:                data.setDate( ( String )vTokens.elementAt( i++ ) );
119:                data.setClose(new Float((String)vTokens.elementAt(i++)));
120:                data.setOpen(new Float((String)vTokens.elementAt(i++)));
121:                data.setHigh(new Float((String)vTokens.elementAt(i++)));
122:                data.setLow(new Float((String)vTokens.elementAt(i++)));
123:                String strVolume = ( String )vTokens.elementAt( i++ );
124:                data.setVolume( new Float( stripCommas( strVolume ) ) );
125:
126:                // Add it to our StockData Vector
127:                m_vStockData.add( data );
128:            }
139:
130:            // Success - return true!
131:            return new Boolean( true );
132:    }
133:
134:    // loadHistoricalData( strStockSymbol )
135:    //
136:    // Attempts to load the historical data for the specified stock
137:    // from the local file system.
138:    //
139:    // Returns true if it succeeds or false if the file does not
140:    // exist or an error occurred.
141:    public Boolean loadHistoricalData( String strStockSymbol )
142:    {
143:        // Save the stock symbol
144:        m_strStockSymbol = strStockSymbol;
145:
146:        // Clear any existing data from the StockData Vector
147:        m_vStockData.removeAllElements();
148:
149:        try
150:        {
151:            // Create a new FileWriter with the filename being the
152:            // symbol.txt
153:            FileReader file = new FileReader( strStockSymbol + ".txt" );
154:
155:            // Create a Boolean Object to tell us when we hit the
```

```
156:                // end of file marker
157:                Boolean bEndOfFile = new Boolean( true );
158:
159:                // While we haven't reached the end of the file
160:                while( bEndOfFile.booleanValue() )
161:                {
162:                    // Create a new StockData object
163:                    StockData data = new StockData();
164:
165:                    // Read in data for this StockData
166:                    bEndOfFile = data.read( file );
167:
168:                    // If we were successful, add this element to our vector
169:                    if( bEndOfFile.booleanValue() )
170:                    {
171:                        m_vStockData.addElement( data );
172:                    }
173:                }
174:
175:                // Close the FileReader object
176:                file.close();
177:            }
178:            catch( FileNotFoundException e )
179:            {
180:                // File does not exist. This is not necessarily an error, we
181:                // may not have downloaded its information yet.
182:                // Return false nonetheless.
183:                return new Boolean( false );
184:            }
185:            catch( IOException e )
186:            {
187:                System.out.println
188:                (
189:                    "HistoricalDataManager.loadHistoricalData Error: " +
190:                    e.toString()
191:                );
192:            }
193:
194:            // Success! Return true
195:            return new Boolean( true );
196:        }
197:
198:        // saveHistoricalData()
199:        //
200:        // Saves the historical data in this class to the local file
201:        // system.
202:        public Boolean saveHistoricalData()
203:        {
204:            try
205:            {
206:                // Create a new FileWriter with the filename being the
```

continues

Listing 11.5 continued

```
207:                    // portfolio name.txt
208:                    FileWriter file = new FileWriter(m_strStockSymbol + ".txt");
209:
210:                    // Loop through all elements in the vector
211:                    for( int i=0; i<m_vStockData.size(); i++ )
212:                    {
213:                        // Retrieve the element at index i
214:                        StockData data = (StockData)m_vStockData.elementAt(i);
215:
216:                        // Tell it to write its data to our file writer
217:                        data.write( file );
218:                    }
219:
220:                    // Close the FileWriter object
221:                    file.close();
222:                }
223:            catch( IOException e )
224:            {
225:                // An error occurred trying to create our file
226:                System.out.println(
227:                    "HistoricalDataManager.saveHistoricalData Error: " +
228:                    e.toString() );
229:                return new Boolean( false );
230:            }
231:
232:            // Success
233:            return new Boolean( true );
234:
235:    }
236:
237:    // String stripCommas( strSource )
238:    //
239:    //  Utility method used to remove commas from a String.
240:    protected String stripCommas( String strSource )
241:    {
242:        // Create a destination string
243:        String strDestination = new String();
244:
245:        // Loop through all characters in the source string
246:        for( int i=0; i<strSource.length(); i++ )
247:        {
248:            // If the character is not a comma
249:            if( strSource.charAt( i ) != ',' )
250:            {
251:                // Add the character to the destination string
252:                strDestination = strDestination + strSource.charAt( i );
253:            }
254:        }
255:
256:        return strDestination;
```

```
257:    }
258:
259:    // int getNumberOfHistoricalRecords()
260:    //
261:    //  Returns the number of historical records are in the
262:    //  HistoricalDataManager.
263:    public int getNumberOfHistoricalRecords()
264:    {
265:        return m_vStockData.size();
266:    }
267:
268:    // StockData getStockDataElement( int nIndex )
269:    //
270:    // Returns the StockData element at the given position in the Vector.
271:    public StockData getStockDataElement( int nIndex )
272:    {
273:
274:        // Verify that the specified index is valid
275:        if( nIndex >= m_vStockData.size() )
276:        {
277:
278:            // Create and throw an ArrayOutOfBoundsException exception
279:            ArrayIndexOutOfBoundsException e =
280:                new ArrayIndexOutOfBoundsException
281:                (
282:                    "HistoricalDataManager.getStockData Error: " +
283:                    "Requested element: " +
284:                    nIndex +
285:                    " of a " +
286:                    m_vStockData.size() +
287:                    " element Vector"
288:                );
289:
290:            throw e;
291:        }
292:
293:        // Return the specified StockData element
294:        return ( StockData )m_vStockData.elementAt( nIndex );
295:    }
296:}
```

Line 2 declares that we are adding this class to the com.mcp.stock.internet package.

Line 8 imports the com.mcp.stock.portfolios package so that we have access to the StockData class.

Line 14 creates our InternetManager class variable to facilitate Internet communications.

Line 18 creates a Vector that will hold StockData items.

11

Line 21 declares a variable to hold the stock symbol that this HistoricalDataManager is maintaining.

Lines 24–26 define an empty constructor.

Lines 32–68 define the getHistoricalData() method, which downloads the historical data for the specified stock symbol and number of days from the Internet. First, in line 36 it saves the requested symbol, and then it moves on to building the URL String in lines 39–45. Remember that the format of the URL is

```
http://www.tradepbs.com/cgi-bin/hstpdwn?Symbol=SYMBOL&Period=DAYS
```

SYMBOL is the stock symbol and DAYS is the number of days requested.

Line 48 builds a String object to hold the historical data that line 52 returns. Line 52 sends our request to the Internet through the InternetManager class's getHTMLPage() method. Finally, line 67 initializes the StockData Vector by calling the buildHistoricalData() method.

Lines 77–132 define the buildHistoricalData() method. This method is separate from getHistoricalData() simply for the preparation of the CSV functionality. It functions in the following steps:

1. It tokenizes the source string (page) into lines.
2. It loops through all these tokens, tokenizing them by quotation mark delimiters.
3. It builds a Vector of every token from every line, preserving the order.
4. It loops through this Vector and creates a new StockData object from its data and adds that to the StockData Vector.

Line 80 creates the Vector that the method will store all its tokens in.

Line 83 tokenizes the source String into lines by creating a new StringTokenizer instance with carriage return and newline as delimiters.

Line 86 loops through all lines in the page.

Lines 90 and 91 create another StringTokenizer from the line, this time tokenized by quotation marks.

Line 94 loops through each quotation mark delimited token comparing it to a comma (line 101). If it is not a comma, it is added to the Vector. All this was described earlier in the chapter.

Line 111 loops through all tokens in the Vector. Line 114 creates a new StockData object and fills its attributes in lines 117–124. The volume attribute may have commas in it, as you might recall, so they are extracted in line 123 and added to the StockData object in its comma-stripped form in line 124. Finally, it is added to the historical data Vector in line 127. You might notice that the loop control variable i is incremented multiple times throughout the loop; this is because each iteration of the loop extracts six different tokens that comprise a StockData object.

Lines 141–196 define the loadHistoricalData() method. This method should look incredibly similar to the Portfolio class's loadPortfolio() method—I used most of the same code. First, it saves the stock symbol it is working with in line 144, and then it removes all items from the current StockData Vector.

It creates a FileReader in line 153 and loops through the file until it reaches the end (line 160). It creates a new StockData object and tells it to read a set of data from the FileReader and adds it to the StockData Vector in line 171. And finally in line 176, it closes the FileReader.

Lines 202–235 define the saveHistoricalData() method, which should look surprisingly like the Portfolio class's savePortfolio() method (or maybe not). It creates a FileWriter object in line 208, loops through all the StockData objects in the Vector in line 211, and asks them to write their data to the FileReader (line 217). Then in line 221 it closes the FileWriter.

Lines 240–254 implement the stripCommas() utility method I spoke of earlier. It simply loops through the source String (line 246) and copies each character that is not a comma (line 249) to the destination string (line 252). Then it returns the destination String.

Lines 263–266 define the getNumberOfHistoricalRecords() method, which returns the number of elements in the StockData Vector (line 265).

Finally, lines 271–295 define the getStockDataElement() method. This method verifies that the index is valid (lines 275–291) and then returns the requested element (line 294).

HistoricalDataTester

11

Now that the HistoricalDataManager is complete, it would be a good idea to test its functionality before using it with the GraphingManager in the next chapter. One important thing to learn as a software developer is to perform unit testing.

Unit testing is the act of testing components that will work together separately so that bugs can be isolated in an individual component.

Unit testing helps diagnose problems in your components before you integrate them. For example, if you built this HistoricalDataManager class, built the GraphingManager class, and then tested them when they were integrated, tracking bugs would be difficult. If the GraphingManager simply did not draw anything, the problem could be in the GraphingManager or maybe the HistoricalDataManager is not downloading its data properly. If we test as many of the methods in the HistoricalDataManager now as we can and verify that they work, we will have more confidence that the problem most likely exists in the GraphingManager.

I will not have time in this book to perform extensive unit testing of all the components, but I thought this would be a good place to introduce you to the concept and write a small class that exercises some of the HistoricalDataManager methods. The HistoricalDataTester class is small and simple. It performs the following steps:

1. Creates an instance of the HistoricalDataManager
2. Retrieves the historical stock data for a particular stock symbol for a particular number of days
3. Displays that data to the standard output device
4. Saves that data to the local file system
5. Loads the data back from the local file system
6. Displays the data back to the standard output device

It exercises the following HistoricalDataManager methods:

- Constructor
- getHistoricalData
    - buildHistoricalData
        - stripCommas
- getNumberOfHistoricalRecords
- getStockDataElement
- saveHistoricalData
- loadHistoricalData

This test suite exercises all the methods in the class. It is a simple test; a full-blown test would incorporate testing the limits of each method and purposely creating error conditions, but I am going to keep this simple for you right now. Take a look at Listing 11.6 for the complete source code for the HistoricalDataTester.

Listing 11.6   `HistoricalDataManager.java`

```
 1:  // Import the packages used by this class
 2:  import com.mcp.stock.internet.*;
 3:
 4:  // public class HistoricalDataTester
 5:  public class HistoricalDataTester
 6:  {
 7:      public static void main( String[] args )
 8:      {
 9:          try
10:          {
11:              // Create an HistoricalDataManager object
12:              HistoricalDataManager app = new HistoricalDataManager();
13:
14:              // Extract the number of days to retrieve from the command
15:              // line argument
16:              Integer nNumberOfDays = new Integer( args[1] );
17:
18:              // Get the information from the Internet
19:              System.out.println( "Downloading the last " +
20:                                  nNumberOfDays +
21:                                  " days of the stock: "  +
22:                                  args[0] +
23:                                  " from the Internet"
24:                                  );
25:              app.getHistoricalData( args[0], nNumberOfDays.intValue() );
26:
27:              // Output the data to the screen
28:              System.out.println
29:              (
30:                  "\nSymbol\tDate\t\tOpen\tClose\tHigh\tLow\tVolume"
31:              );
32:              for( int i=0; i<app.getNumberOfHistoricalRecords(); i++ )
33:              {
34:                  System.out.println
35:                  (
36:                      app.getStockDataElement( i ).getStockSymbol() +"\t" +
37:                      app.getStockDataElement( i ).getDate() + "\t" +
38:                      app.getStockDataElement( i ).getOpen() + "\t" +
39:                      app.getStockDataElement( i ).getClose() + "\t" +
40:                      app.getStockDataElement( i ).getHigh() + "\t" +
41:                      app.getStockDataElement( i ).getLow() + "\t" +
42:                      app.getStockDataElement( i ).getVolume()
43:                  );
44:              }
45:
46:              // Save the data to a file
47:              System.out.println( "\nSaving: " + args[0] );
48:              app.saveHistoricalData();
```

11

continues

Listing 11.6   continued

```
49:
50:                     // Load the data back from the file
51:                     System.out.println( "\nLoading: " + args[0] );
52:                     app.loadHistoricalData( args[0] );
53:
54:                     // Display the data to the screen again
55:                     System.out.println
56:                     (
57:                         "\nSymbol\tDate\t\tOpen\tClose\tHigh\tLow\tVolume"
58:                     );
59:                     for( int i=0; i<app.getNumberOfHistoricalRecords(); i++ )
60:                     {
61:                         System.out.println
62:                         (
63:                             app.getStockDataElement( i ).getStockSymbol() +"\t" +
64:                             app.getStockDataElement( i ).getDate() + "\t" +
65:                             app.getStockDataElement( i ).getOpen() + "\t" +
66:                             app.getStockDataElement( i ).getClose() + "\t" +
67:                             app.getStockDataElement( i ).getHigh() + "\t" +
68:                             app.getStockDataElement( i ).getLow() + "\t" +
69:                             app.getStockDataElement( i ).getVolume()
70:                         );
71:                     }
72:
73:                 }
74:                 catch( ArrayIndexOutOfBoundsException e )
75:                 {
76:                     // The user did not specify the right number of arguments,
77:                     // so display the usage
78:                     System.out.println(
79:                             "Usage: java HistoricalDataManager [SYM] [PERIOD]" );
79:                     System.out.println( "    [SYM] = Stock Symbol, e.g. MSFT" );
80:                     System.out.println( "    [PERIOD] = Number of Days, e.g. 10");
81:                 }
82:         }
83: }
```

The HistoricalDataTester class functions as follows:

```
java HistoricalDataTester SYMBOL DAYS
```

For example:

```
java HistoricalDataTester MSFT 10
```

It accepts a stock symbol and the number of days to download.

Line 2 imports the com.mcp.stock.internet package so that it can use the
HistoricalDataManager class.

Lines 7–82 define the main() method. This class consists only of a main() method and performs all its tests in the main() method itself.

Line 12 creates a HistoricalDataManager object.

Line 16 extracts the second item in the command line as the number of days to retrieve.

Line 25 calls the HistoricalDataManager class's getHistoricaData() method with the two arguments passed in the command line.

Line 32 loops through all the items in the HistoricalDataManager class (getNumberOfHistoricalRecords()) and outputs all the fields of the StockData class. It obtains the StockData item by calling getStockDataElement(), and then it calls the StockData respective methods for the desired fields.

Line 48 saves the historical data by calling the HistoricalDataManager class's saveHistoricalData() method.

Line 52 reloads that information from the local file system by calling the loadHistoricalData() method.

Lines 55–73 repeat earlier code to output the data in the HistoricalDataManager to the standard output device.

Lines 74–81 implement the ArrayIndexOutOfBoundsException exception catch block for all the rest of the code in this method. This is the method we use to check for an empty command line (a user executes the application without a command line or one that is too short). Back in lines 16, 25, 47, 51, and 52, we access the command-line arguments in their String array by index. If an item is not present in the command line, the String class will throw an ArrayIndexOutOfBoundsException exception and signal us that the command line was missing. In this case we simply display the usage to the standard output device (lines 78–80).

Go ahead and compile and run this code. Remember to add the location of your com directory to your CLASSPATH variable so that the Java compiler can build the HistoricalDataTester class. Try downloading a variety of stock information; use a small number of days and a large number of days (you can go up to 500 or more if you want!). Experiment and have fun.

11

Summary

In this chapter we talked more about downloading data from the Internet, namely historical stock data. This time the data was not in a familiar form, so we were forced to manually parse the data without using the classes that you were already familiar with. Text parsing is made simple using the `StringTokenizer` class, and you saw an instance where we used it to break a page up into lines. We used it again to break a line up into tokens.

Then we changed gears and talked a little bit about unit testing and wrote a command-line test class to test the `HistoricalDataManager`. It was simple, but we used it to exercise all the methods in the `HistoricalDataManager` class.

What's Next?

Now that we have all our historical data in a nice and easy-to-use format, we will display it in a graphical format in the next chapter. We will implement the `GraphingManager` class to add graphing support to the Stock Tracker application.

Chapter 12

Graphing Historical Data

In the last chapter, I showed you how to retrieve historical stock data from the Internet. In this chapter, I am going to show you how to take that stock information and display it in a graph. When you are finished with this chapter, the Stock Tracker application will be able to display graphs of the opening or closing prices of a stock for the last week, month, three months, or six months. The Java graphics classes will help us out a little, but we still have the bulk of the work to do ourselves.

In this chapter I will talk about the following topics:

- Drawing in Java
- Drawing concepts: coordinate systems, scaling points, and coordinate transformations
- Dates
- Review of multithreading

Use Cases

The graphing aspect of the Stock Tracker application involves three use cases:

- Use Case #3: Enable historical tracking for a stock symbol
- Use Case #17: Set graphing time scale
- Use Case #18: Graph stock performance points

From what you learned in the last chapter about downloading historical stock information from the Internet, the concept of enabling historical tracking for a stock does not seem necessary; downloading data from the Internet when it is needed is sufficient. Furthermore, the process of enabling the historical tracking before historical data can be displayed is not friendly. Thus I suggest that we throw out Use Case #3. All those in favor say "Aye."

 Note

Always remember that we are following an iterative design process, so things you learn in one section can be reapplied to our design at any time. When writing this book, I took the approach of developing the application with you in each chapter. This way you can see how the development process actually works. Something that sounds good on paper might not be the best solution in practical application, so you learn about your application as you are developing it.

This is how iterative development works in practice, especially in large-scale projects. Large-scale projects are usually broken into vertical slices, or small sets of functionality, and the design is re-evaluated at the end of each slice (or in the middle if a major flaw is found). The point is that things can change as you are developing a project.

For Use Case #17 we are going to support the following time intervals: one week, one month, three months, and six months.

Because Use Case #18 did not specify which data points to graph, we are going to expand it to include both opening prices and closing prices. I will spend the bulk of the time in this chapter talking about graphing because it is the difficult part!

Component Relationships

Figure 12.1 shows the relationships between the StockApplication (Application), the GraphingManager, and the HistoricalDataManager. From this class diagram you can see that the StockApplication contains one GraphingManager and the GraphingManager contains one HistoricalDataManager. Recall that the GraphingManager is responsible for graphing historical data, and the HistoricalDataManager is responsible for downloading historical data from the Internet.

Figure 12.1

GraphingManager rela-
tionships.

In our implementation we are going to take the functionality of the GraphingManager and integrate it into the StockGraphPanel class (the StockGraphPanel is already responsible for drawing graphs, so it is a logical fit). But more on that later.

Painting Primer

Before we start implementing the graphing functionality, let me give you a little background on general painting and graphing fundamentals. Start by taking a look at Figure 12.2, which shows a typical two-dimensional graphing coordinate system.

Figure 12.2

*A typical two-
dimensional graphing
coordinate system.*

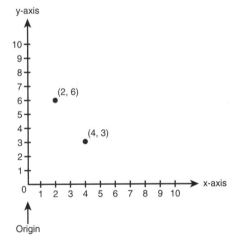

From Figure 12.2, you can see that there are two axes: the *x-axis* runs horizontally across the bottom of the graph, and the *y-axis* runs vertically down the left side of the graph. The point where they meet in the lower left corner is known as the *origin*. Point coordinates are listed in x and y coordinate pairs, displayed as (x, y). Figure 12.2 has two points to illustrate this naming convention: (4, 3) and (2, 6).

Take a look at Figure 12.3 to see a sample graph.

Figure 12.3

A sample graph.

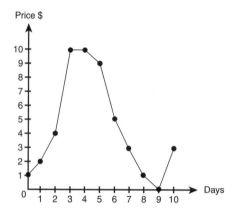

Points: (0, 1)
(1, 2)
(2, 4)
(3, 10)
(4, 10)
(5, 9)
(6, 5)
(7, 3)
(8, 1)
(9, 0)
(10, 3)

To plot a graph, first you label the axes according to what they represent (for example, price over a period of days—the y-axis represents the price and the x-axis represents the days). Next, you plot each point in the point line on the graph and connect the points with lines.

A graph is just one type of painting application, but the theory is the same for all painting. A painting surface is nothing more than a collection of rows and columns of points. In graphics terms, these points are called *pixels*. Figure 12.4 shows what this looks like graphically.

Figure 12.4

A sample painting surface.

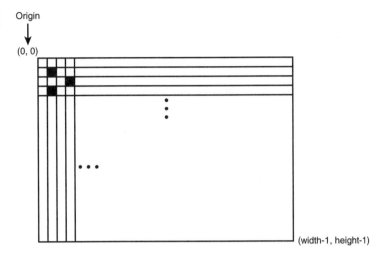

Painting surfaces are similar to two-dimensional arrays in that their origin starts at (0, 0) and their bounds are the number of elements per dimension (width or height) minus 1. To paint an image, you simply specify the color to display in any one of the given pixels. A painting surface can be any size, and its size is specified by its (width, height) pair, for example, your screen may be set to (800, 600) where it is 800 pixels wide and 600 pixels high.

From this rudimentary explanation, you can probably already surmise that we are going to have a bit of a problem graphing because of the placement of the origin, but I will explain that shortly.

Implementation Decisions

Before you can implement the graphing functionality into the Stock Tracker application, we need to address a few issues:

- How do you draw in Java and what classes should you use?
- How do you scale points in a specified range to fit your graph, for both price and time?
- How do you translate the scaled points to device points to be graphed?
- How can you use threads to optimize the historical data retrieval from the Internet?
- How can you optimize Internet downloads by persisting data to the local file system?

12

Painting in Java

Painting in Java with Swing is accomplished by creating a class that is derived from JComponent and overriding its paint() method (with AWT, you must derive a class from Container and override its paint() method). In our case we are going to create a class derived from JPanel and override its paint() method.

The paint() method is prototyped as follows:

```
public void paint(Graphics g)
```

It provides a Graphics instance that represents a surface to paint on. As we mentioned back in Chapter 7, "Building the Stock Tracker User Interface," the Swing classes provide an enhanced version of the Graphics class called Graphics2D. The Graphics2D class is very advanced and provides features such as rendering, translation, rotation, and scaling, but we are only going to touch upon a few of its simple features: drawing lines, drawing text, drawing rectangles, and changing the color; for a statistical graph, these features are all that is necessary. You can extract a Graphics2D object from a Graphics object by casting the Graphics object to a Graphics2D object:

```
public void paint( Graphics g )
{
    Graphics2D g2 = ( Graphics2D )g;
}
```

Table 12.1 shows some of the Graphics2D methods we will make use of in this chapter.

Table 12.1 Graphics2D **Basic Methods**

Method	Description
setBackground(Color color)	Sets the background color for the Graphics2D context
setColor(Color c)	Sets this graphics context's current color to the specified color
setFont(Font font)	Sets this graphics context's font to the specified font
drawString(String s, float x, float y)	Renders the text specified by the specified String, using the current Font and Paint attributes in the Graphics2D context
drawString(String str, int x, int y)	Renders the text of the specified String, using the current Font and Paint attributes in the Graphics2D context
drawLine(int x1, int y1, int x2, int y2)	Draws a line, using the current color, between the points (x1, y1) and (x2, y2) in this graphics context's coordinate system

Method	Description
clearRect(int x, int y, int width, int height)	Clears the specified rectangle by filling it with the background color of the current drawing surface
drawRect(int x, int y, int width, int height)	Draws the outline of the specified rectangle
fillRect(int x, int y, int width, int height)	Fills the specified rectangle

Let me reiterate that these are some of the most basic drawing features of the `Graphics2D` class. If Java graphing programming interests you, I would highly recommend that you look through the Java 2 SDK documentation and pick up a book on the Java 2D API and the Java 3D API (Application Programmer's Interface); the information is great but would take far more room than I have here (and it wouldn't do much for the Stock Tracker graphs).

As I mentioned earlier, painting in Java is really only plotting pixels relative to the origin in the upper left corner of the surface. Therefore all the aforementioned coordinates are relative to the upper left corner of the surface. For example, consider the following code segment:

```
public class GraphClass extends JPanel
{
    public void paint( Graphics g )
    {
        // Get a Graphics2D object
        Graphics2D g2 = ( Graphics2D )g;

        // Draw the words "Hello, world" at position (0, 30)
        g2.drawString( new String( "Hello, world" ), 0, 30 );

        // Draw a diagonal line down the screen
        g2.drawLine( 0, 0, 100, 100 );

        // Draw a rectangle connected to the line
        g2.drawRect( 100, 100, 200, 100 );
    }
}
```

12

Figure 12.5

*Sample drawing
commands.*

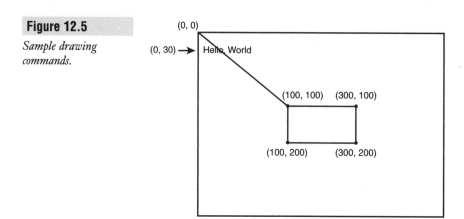

Later when we talk about the code for the `StockGraphPanel` class, I will describe these methods in more detail.

Scaling Points

The stock data points we have to plot are going to be in the range of, for example, 94.8 to 97.3, and remember that we are working with a finite number of pixels when graphing. How do we scale our points that span 2.5 units (dollars) to 100 pixels, for example?

If we have a point at 96.8, we can compute the relative percentage it is occupying in the range and apply that percentage to the number of pixels. For example, consider the following formula:

```
Given:
x   = 96.8
priceRange = 2.5
highPrice = 97.3
lowPrice = 94.8
pixelHeight = 100

xPixels = ( (x - lowPrice) / priceRange ) * pixelHeight
```

So we take the difference between actual value and the lowest value:

```
96.8 - 94.8 = 2.0
```

Divide that by the range:

```
2.0 / 2.5 = 0.8   (80%)
```

And multiply that by the number of pixels:

```
0.8 * 100 = 80 pixels
```

Now we know that 96.8 takes 80 pixels in the range 94.8–97.3 when there are 100 pixels to work with!

Prices

To represent prices we are going to do exactly what I just mentioned:

1. Build a collection of stock points
2. Bind the highest and lowest prices
3. Compute the range of prices
4. Ask the JPanel class for the number of pixels we can use
5. Apply the aforementioned formula to all points before we plot them

Date Strategy

Floating-point numbers easily represent price data, but dates are a different story. Java provides default implementation for dates through the java.util.Date class, which represents a specific instance of time accurate to the millisecond. The java.util.Date class, along with its partner, the java.util.Calendar class, also offers internationalization support: The dates can be localized to a specific region. They are very powerful classes, and I would highly recommend using them if you need a calendar in your applications. But for our case all the data will be accurate only to the day, not the millisecond, and we are not interested in localization: We are interested only in computing the relative position of a date to the range of dates.

Our date strategy for this chapter is going to include the implementation of a SimpleDate class that will be accurate only to the day and will provide us with a numerical representation of the date for comparisons. Take a look at Listing 12.1 to see this class.

Listing 12.1   SimpleDate **Class**

```
1:  // class SimpleDate
2:  class SimpleDate
3:  {
4:      // Date attributes
5:      protected int m_nMonth;
6:      protected int m_nDay;
7:      protected int m_nYear;
8:
9:      // Constructors
10:     public SimpleDate()
11:     {
12:     }
13:
```

continues

Listing 12.1   **continued**

```
14:     public SimpleDate( int nMonth, int nDay, int nYear )
15:     {
16:         m_nMonth = nMonth;
17:         m_nDay = nDay;
18:         m_nYear = nYear;
19:     }
20:
21:     public SimpleDate( String strDate )
22:     {
23:         // Create a new / delimited StringTokenizer that does not
24:         // return the slash
25:         StringTokenizer st =
26:                 new StringTokenizer( strDate.trim(), "/", false );
27:
28:         // Extract the date information
29:         m_nMonth = Integer.valueOf( st.nextToken() ).intValue();
30:         m_nDay = Integer.valueOf( st.nextToken() ).intValue();
31:         m_nYear = Integer.valueOf( st.nextToken() ).intValue();
32:     }
33:
34:     public SimpleDate( Calendar date )
35:     {
36:         m_nYear = date.get( Calendar.YEAR );
37:         m_nMonth = date.get( Calendar.MONTH );
38:         m_nDay = date.get( Calendar.DAY_OF_WEEK );
39:     }
40:
41:
42:     // Attribute Retrieval
43:     public int getMonth()
44:     {
45:         return m_nMonth;
46:     }
47:
48:     public int getDay()
49:     {
50:         return m_nDay;
51:     }
52:
53:     public int getYear()
54:     {
55:         return m_nYear;
56:     }
57:
58:     // public int compare( SimpleDate date )
59:     //
60:     //  Returns:
61:     //      0 = equal
62:     //      -1 = this < date
63:     //      1 = this > date
```

```
64:     public int compare( SimpleDate date )
65:     {
66:         // Compare years
67:         if( m_nYear > date.getYear() )
68:         {
69:             return 1;
70:         }
71:         else if( m_nYear < date.getYear() )
72:         {
73:             return -1;
74:         }
75:
76:         // Same year, compare months
77:         if( m_nMonth > date.getMonth() )
78:         {
79:             return 1;
80:         }
81:         else if( m_nMonth < date.getMonth() )
82:         {
83:             return -1;
84:         }
85:
86:         // Same month, compare days
87:         if( m_nDay > date.getDay() )
88:         {
89:             return 1;
90:         }
91:         else if( m_nDay < date.getDay() )
92:         {
93:             return -1;
94:         }
95:
96:         // Equal dates
97:         return 0;
98:
99:     }
100:
101:    // public long getLongValue()
102:    //
103:    //  Converts the date to a long value representing the number
104:    //  of days since 1/1/0000
105:    public long getLongValue()
106:    {
107:        long lYearDays = m_nYear * 365;
108:
109:        long lMonthDays = 0;
110:
111:        if( m_nMonth > 1 )
112:        {
113:            lMonthDays += 31;
```

continues

Listing 12.1   continued

```
114:          }
115:          if( m_nMonth > 2 )
116:          {
117:              if( m_nYear%4 == 0 )
118:              {
119:                  lMonthDays += 29;
120:              }
121:              else
122:              {
123:                  lMonthDays += 28;
124:              }
125:          }
126:
127:          if( m_nMonth > 3 ) lMonthDays += 31;
128:          if( m_nMonth > 4 ) lMonthDays += 30;
139:          if( m_nMonth > 5 ) lMonthDays += 31;
130:          if( m_nMonth > 6 ) lMonthDays += 30;
131:          if( m_nMonth > 7 ) lMonthDays += 31;
132:          if( m_nMonth > 8 ) lMonthDays += 31;
133:          if( m_nMonth > 9 ) lMonthDays += 30;
134:          if( m_nMonth > 10 ) lMonthDays += 31;
135:          if( m_nMonth > 11 ) lMonthDays += 30;
136:
137:          return lYearDays + lMonthDays + m_nDay;
138:      }
139:
140:  // public String displayMonthDay()
141:  //
142:  //  Returns a string with only the month and day: MM/DD
143:  public String displayMonthDay()
144:  {
145:      return new String( "" + m_nMonth + "/" + m_nDay );
146:  }
147:}
```

Lines 4–7 declare our month, day, and year variables, respectively.

There are four constructors for this class: SimpleDate(), SimpleDate(nMonth, nDay, nYear), SimpleDate(strDate), and SimpleDate(Calendar date). The first two are fairly basic, but the latter two are a little more interesting.

Lines 21–32 define the SimpleDate(strDate) method. It accepts a date of the form "MM/DD/YYYY", tokenizes the string by forward slashes "/", and then converts the values to integers.

Lines 34–39 accept a Calendar object as a parameter and simply call its get() method, specifying the YEAR, MONTH, and DAY_OF_WEEK, to extract the date.

Lines 64–99 define the `compare()` method that compares this `SimpleDate` object with another `SimpleDate` object, returning `-1` if this date is before the specified date, `0` if the dates are equal, and `1` if this date is later than the specified date. It performs its comparisons by checking the year, then the month, and then the day.

Lines 105–138 compute a `long` value representing the date as the number of days that have passed since 1/1/0000. It docs this by adding the number of days in each month for the year (including leap year) to 365 × the year to the number of days.

Finally, lines 143–146 return a `String` representing the date in its simple month and day form: "MM/DD". This will be used later by the `StockGraphPanel`.

We will do the same thing with dates as we did with prices:

1. Build a collection of dates
2. Bind the highest and lowest dates
3. Compute the range of dates
4. Ask the `JPanel` class for the number of pixels we can use
5. Apply the following formula to all points before we plot them:

```
yPixels = ( (y - lowDate) / dateRange ) * pixelWidth
```

There is one more issue surrounding the date: The number of dates might actually exceed the number of available pixel columns in our painting surface. If this occurs, we will start skipping dates to plot: Plot every other or every third date to get it to fit. The point is that we must take this into account.

Drawing Strategy

We have already talked about translating a point from its actual value to its logical point, and we came up with the following formulas:

```
xPixels = ( (x - lowPrice) / priceRange ) * pixelHeight
yPixels = ( (y - lowDate) / dateRange ) * pixelWidth
```

The next translation we need to make is to take these points and map them to screen coordinates. Remember that the origin of our graphing axes is at the lower left corner of the graph and the origin of the Java painting surface is at the upper left corner of the painting surface. We need some mechanism to translate each point accordingly.

Before we start, let me suggest that we leave a border, or inset, around the graphing area. This way we will have room to write our labels, and the graph will stand out in the center of the display. The arbitrary value that I chose was 40 pixels. You are free to choose any value you want, but 40 looked nice on my display.

12

Figure 12.6 labels all the major pieces we are going to need to do our conversion:

- Base
- Drawing height
- Drawing width
- Arbitrary point on the y-axis
- Arbitrary point on the x-axis

Figure 12.6

Device point metrics.

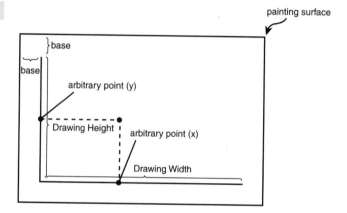

We are starting with a point as a number of pixels from the graphing origin (lower-left corner), say point (x, y) (or (100, 200) if you like. Figure 12.7 shows the start of this conversion.

Let's break this into two parts: x-axis and y-axis.

Starting with the y-axis (or the height), use the following formula to translate that point:

```
yDevice = base + drawingHeight - y

yDevice = 40 + 300 - 200

yDevice = 140
```

And then use the following formula for the x-axis:

```
xDevice = base + x

xDevice = 40 + 100

xDevice = 140
```

Figure 12.7

Logical point -> device point conversion.

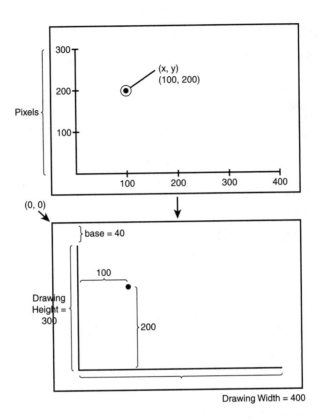

Although it seemed intimidating, it is really a very simple conversion. The difficult part is the y-axis where we find the origin position (base + drawingHeight = 40 + 300 = 340) and then subtract the point's y-coordinate (200) from the origin to count the number of pixels up (negative number).

So the point (100, 200) translates to (140, 140) on a graphing system with a height of 300 pixels and a width of 400 pixels and a base of 40 pixels.

Multithreading

Just as we did with the PortfolioManager when we told it to download Internet data using a separate thread, we are again going to create a thread to perform the historical data download. It is probably more important here because there is potentially so much more data!

12

Internet Strategy

We could make the decision to download a stock's data every time the user selects a new stock to graph, but that would not be optimal; if the user switched back and forth between two stocks 100 times, that would result in 100 downloads. Instead what we are going to do is persist the data to the local file system and attempt to load the data before we ever go to the Internet. We check the date and number of items in the file to verify that it has the most recent data and enough data to perform the graphing. If it does not, it makes the decision to download the data from the Internet.

I will talk more about this in the code explanation coming up later in the chapter.

StockGraphPanel

Originally we had a `GraphingManager` object defined in our design, but I have opted to add its functionality directly to the `StockGraphPanel` class.

The `StockGraphPanel` is composed of two other classes: `UpdateHistoricalDataThread`, used to get the historical data either from the local file system or from the Internet, and `SimpleDate`, which we discussed earlier. Tables 12.2 and 12.3 show the attributes and methods of the `StockGraphPanel` class, Tables 12.4 and 12.5 show the attributes and methods of the `UpdateHistoricalDataThread` class, and Tables 12.6 and 12.7 show the attributes and methods of the `SimpleDate` class.

Table 12.2 `StockGraphPanel` **Attributes**

Attribute	Description
`String m_strSymbol`	Current stock symbol
`HistoricalDataManager m_historicalDataManager`	`HistoricalDataManager` representing its data
`Integer m_nNumberOfDays`	Number of days to graph
`UpdateHistoricalDataThread m_historicalDataThread`	Thread runnable class that will update the graphing information
`static final int m_nBase = 40`	Base insets to limit the graph's drawing area
`float m_fLowPrice`	The lowest price in the graph
`float m_fHighPrice`	The highest price in the graph
`long m_lStartTime`	The starting time for the graph
`long m_lEndTime`	The ending time for the graph
`int m_nGraphingMode`	The current graphing mode; valid values are `GRAPHOPENPRICES` and `GRAPHCLOSEPRICES`

public static final int GRAPHOPENPRICES = 1	Constant graphing mode variable
public static final int GRAPHCLOSEPRICES = 2	Constant graphing mode variable
public static final int GRAPHDAILYRANGES = 3	Constant graphing mode variable

Table 12.3 `StockGraphPanel` **Methods**

Method	Description
StockGraphPanel()	Constructor
void setGraphMode(int nGraphingMode)	Sets the graphing mode; valid values are GRAPHOPEN PRICES and GRAPHCLOSEPRICES
void updateGraph(String strSymbol, Integer nNumberOfDays)	Updates the graph data and repaints the graph
void updateGraph(String strSymbol)	Updates the graph data by symbol with the existing number of days
void updateGraph(Integer nDays)	Updates the graph data for the specified number of days and the existing symbol
void paint(Graphics g)	Draws the display
long getLongDate(String strDate)	Returns a String date object as a long value

Table 12.4 `UpdateHistoricalDataThread` **Attributes**

Attribute	Description
StockGraphPanel m_stockGraphPanel	Parent StockGraphPanel object

Table 12.5 `UpdateHistoricalDataThread` **Methods**

Method	Description
UpdateHistoricalDataThread (StockGraphPanel stockGraphPanel)	Constructor
void run()	Body that the thread processes on start; updates the historical data

12

Table 12.6 `SimpleDate` Attributes

Method	Description
`protected int m_nMonth`	Date's month
`protected int m_nDay`	Date's day
`protected int m_nYear`	Date's year

Table 12.7 `SimpleDate` Methods

Method	Description
`SimpleDate()`	Default constructor
`SimpleDate(int nMonth, int nDay, int nYear)`	Builds a `SimpleDate` from the month, day, and year
`SimpleDate(String strDate)`	Builds a date from a `String` of the form: "MM/DD/YYYY"
`SimpleDate(Calendar date)`	Builds a date from a `Calendar` object
`int getMonth()`	Returns the month of the date
`int getDay()`	Returns the day of the date
`int getYear()`	Returns the year of the date
`int compare(SimpleDate date)`	Compares this date with the specified date; if this date is before `date`, it returns `-1`; if it is later, it returns `+1`; and if they are equal, it returns `0`
`long getLongValue()`	Returns the date as a `long` integer value
`String displayMonthDay()`	Returns a `String` of the form "MM/DD"

Listing 12.2 shows the complete source code for the `StockGraphPanel` class, which I will discuss following the listing.

Listing 12.2 `StockGraphPanel.java`

```
1:  // Import the packages used by this class
2:  import javax.swing.*;
3:  import javax.swing.event.*;
4:
5:  import java.awt.*;
6:  import java.awt.event.*;
7:
8:  import java.lang.*;
9:  import java.util.*;
10:
11: // Import our custom packages
12: import com.mcp.stock.portfolios.*;
13: import com.mcp.stock.internet.*;
14:
```

```
15: // StockGraphPanel
16: public class StockGraphPanel extends JPanel
17: {
18:     // String that will hold our stock ticker symbol
19:     String m_strSymbol = new String();
20:
21:     // Create a HistoricalDataManager that will give us the points to
22:     // plot
23:     HistoricalDataManager m_historicalDataManager =
24:                             new HistoricalDataManager();
25:
26:     // Integer representing the number of days to display in the graph
27:     Integer m_nNumberOfDays = new Integer( 20 );
28:
29:     // Create our Runnable class that will perform the updates for us
30:     UpdateHistoricalDataThread m_historicalDataThread =
31:                         new UpdateHistoricalDataThread( this );
32:
33:     // Define the Base number of pixels to set the graph
34:     public static final int m_nBase = 40;
35:
36:     // Graphing Variables
37:     public float m_fLowPrice = 0;
38:     public float m_fHighPrice = 0;
39:
40:     public long m_lStartTime = 0;
41:     public long m_lEndTime = 0;
42:
43:     protected int m_nGraphingMode = GRAPHOPENPRICES;
44:
45:     // Define the graphing mode constants
46:     public static final int GRAPHOPENPRICES = 1;
47:     public static final int GRAPHCLOSEPRICES = 2;
48:     public static final int GRAPHDAILYRANGES = 3;
49:
50:     // Constructor
51:     public StockGraphPanel()
52:     {
53:         // Set our preferred size
54:         setPreferredSize( new Dimension( 500, 400 ) );
55:     }
56:
57:     // public void setGraphMode( int nGraphingMode )
58:     //
59:     //   Sets the graph mode:
60:     //       GRAPHOPENPRICES - Opening prices
61:     //       GRAPHCLOSEPRICES - Closing prices
62:     //       GRAPHDAILYRANGES (Not Implemented)
63:     public void setGraphMode( int nGraphingMode )
64:     {
```

12

continues

Listing 12.2   continued

```
65:           m_nGraphingMode = nGraphingMode;
66:           repaint();
67:       }
68:
69:   // public void updateGraph( String strSymbol, Integer nNumberOfDays )
70:   //
71:   //   Loads the historical data for the specified symbol and
72:   //   number of days and updates the graph to reflect this value
73:   public void updateGraph( String strSymbol, Integer nNumberOfDays )
74:   {
75:       // Save the new value of the symbol
76:       m_strSymbol = strSymbol;
77:
78:       // Save the number of days to display
79:       m_nNumberOfDays = nNumberOfDays;
80:
81:       // Save the current data that is in the list
82:       if( m_historicalDataManager.getNumberOfHistoricalRecords() > 0 )
83:       {
84:           m_historicalDataManager.saveHistoricalData();
85:       }
86:
87:       // Clean up the HistoricalDataManager
88:       m_historicalDataManager.removeAllElements();
89:
90:       // Create a thread to update our stock information
91:       Thread thread = new Thread( m_historicalDataThread );
92:
93:       // Start the thread
94:       thread.start();
95:   }
96:
97:   // public void updateGraph( String strSymbol )
98:   //
99:   //   Calls updateGraph() with the specified symbol and a default
100:  //   of 1 month (20 Days) time frame.
101:  public void updateGraph( String strSymbol )
102:  {
103:      // Call updateGraph() for the existing number of days
104:      updateGraph( strSymbol, new Integer( 20 ) );
105:  }
106:
107:  // public void updateGraph( Integer nDays )
108:  //
109:  //   Updates the current stock's number of days to graph
110:  public void updateGraph( Integer nDays )
111:  {
112:      // Call the updateGraph for the current symbol and the
113:      // specified number of days
114:      updateGraph( m_strSymbol, nDays );
```

```
115:    }
116:
117:    // Draw the graph
118:    public void paint(Graphics g)
119:    {
120:        // Get a Graphics2D object
121:        Graphics2D g2 = (Graphics2D) g;
122:
123:        // Get the Dimensions of this JPanel
124:        Dimension d = new Dimension();
125:        getSize(d);
126:
127:        // Set the background to black
128:        g2.setBackground( Color.black );
129:        g2.clearRect( 0, 0, (int)d.getWidth(), (int)d.getHeight() );
130:
131:
132:        // Get the pixel width and heights for the drawing area
133:        int nDrawingHeight = d.height - ( 2 * m_nBase );
134:        int nDrawingWidth = d.width - ( 2 * m_nBase );
135:
136:        // Compute our logical ranges
137:        float fPriceRange = m_fHighPrice - m_fLowPrice;
138:        long lTimeRange = m_lEndTime - m_lStartTime;
139:
140:
141:        if( m_historicalDataManager.getNumberOfHistoricalRecords() <
               m_nNumberOfDays.intValue() )
142:        {
143:            // Write the stock symbol in about the middle of the screen
144:            g2.setColor( Color.cyan );
145:            g2.drawString( "Processing: " + m_strSymbol,
146:                            (int)d.getWidth() / 2,
147:                            (int)d.getHeight() / 2 );
148:        }
149:        else
150:        {
151:            // Set the color to draw the axes
152:            g2.setColor( Color.lightGray );
153:
154:            // Draw y-axis
155:            g2.drawLine( m_nBase, m_nBase, m_nBase, d.height - m_nBase );
156:            // Draw x-axis
157:            g2.drawLine( m_nBase, d.height - m_nBase,
                   d.width - m_nBase, d.height - m_nBase );
158:            // Draw tick marks...
159:            g2.drawLine( m_nBase - 2,
160:                            m_nBase,
161:                            m_nBase + 2,
162:                            m_nBase );
```

continues

Listing 12.2   continued

```
163:            g2.drawLine( m_nBase - 2,
164:                         m_nBase + nDrawingHeight/2,
165:                         m_nBase + 2,
166:                         m_nBase + nDrawingHeight/2 );
167:            g2.drawLine( m_nBase + nDrawingWidth/2,
168:                         m_nBase + nDrawingHeight - 2,
169:                         m_nBase + nDrawingWidth/2,
170:                         m_nBase + nDrawingHeight + 2 );
171:            g2.drawLine( m_nBase + nDrawingWidth,
172:                         m_nBase + nDrawingHeight - 2,
173:                         m_nBase + nDrawingWidth,
174:                         m_nBase + nDrawingHeight + 2 );
175:
176:         // Draw our price labels
177:         g2.drawString( "$ Price", 0, 15 );
178:         g2.drawString( "" + m_fHighPrice, 0, m_nBase - 5 );
179:         g2.drawString( "" + m_fLowPrice, 0,
                 m_nBase + nDrawingHeight + 5 );
180:         float fMiddlePrice = (m_fLowPrice + m_fHighPrice) / 2;
181:         g2.drawString( "" + fMiddlePrice, 0,
                m_nBase + nDrawingHeight / 2 );
182:
183:         // Draw our date labels
184:         SimpleDate dateStart = new SimpleDate
185:                 (
186:                     m_historicalDataManager.getStockDataElement
187:                     (
188:         m_historicalDataManager.getNumberOfHistoricalRecords() - 1
189:                     ).getDate()
190:                 );
191:
192:         g2.drawString( dateStart.displayMonthDay(),
193:                        m_nBase,
194:                        m_nBase + nDrawingHeight + 15 );
195:
196:         SimpleDate dateEnd = new SimpleDate
197:         ( m_historicalDataManager.getStockDataElement(0).getDate() );
198:
199:         g2.drawString( dateEnd.displayMonthDay(),
200:                        m_nBase + nDrawingWidth - 10,
201:                        m_nBase + nDrawingHeight + 15 );
202:
203:
204:         SimpleDate dateMiddle = new SimpleDate
205:                 (
206:                     m_historicalDataManager.getStockDataElement
207:                     (
208:         ( m_historicalDataManager.getNumberOfHistoricalRecords() ) / 2
209:                     ).getDate()
210:                 );
```

```
211:
212:                g2.drawString( dateMiddle.displayMonthDay(),
213:                               m_nBase + nDrawingWidth/2 - 10,
214:                               m_nBase + nDrawingHeight + 15 );
215:
216:
217:                // Create a Vector to hold the points
218:                Vector vPoints = new Vector();
219:
220:                // Build the Vector of points
221:                for( int i=m_nNumberOfDays.intValue()-1; i>=0; i-- )
222:                {
223:                    // Retrieve the StockData object
224:                    StockData stockData =
                        m_historicalDataManager.getStockDataElement( i );
225:
226:                    // x and y coordinates to plot
227:                    float x=0;
228:                    float y=0;
229:
230:                    // Set the x and y coordinate based off the graphing mode
231:                    switch( m_nGraphingMode )
232:                    {
233:                    case GRAPHOPENPRICES:
234:                        x = getLongDate( stockData.getDate() );
235:                        y = stockData.getOpen().floatValue();
236:                        g2.setColor( Color.green );
237:                        g2.drawString( "Opening Prices",
                              m_nBase + nDrawingWidth - 50, 15 );
238:                        break;
239:
240:                    case GRAPHCLOSEPRICES:
241:                        x = getLongDate( stockData.getDate() );
242:                        y = stockData.getClose().floatValue();
243:                        g2.setColor( Color.yellow );
244:                        g2.drawString( "Closing Prices",
                                  m_nBase + nDrawingWidth - 50, 15 );
245:                        break;
246:                    }
247:
248:
249:                    // Compute the y-coordinate
250:                    float yLogical = ( (y - m_fLowPrice) / fPriceRange ) *
                                  nDrawingHeight;
251:                    int yDevice = ( nDrawingHeight + m_nBase ) -
                                  ( int )yLogical;
252:
253:                    // Compute the x-coordinate
254:                    float xLogical = ( ( float )(x - m_lStartTime) /
                                  ( float )lTimeRange ) * nDrawingWidth;
```

12

continues

Listing 12.2 continued

```
255:                    int xDevice = m_nBase + ( int )xLogical;
256:
257:                    // Create a new Point from these values
258:                    Point pt = new Point( xDevice, yDevice );
259:
260:                    // Add the points to the Vector
261:                    vPoints.add( pt );
262:                }
263:
264:
265:                // Compute the increment value = number of points to
266:                // skip to fit it in the drawing area
267:                int nIncrement = 1;
268:                for( int i=10; i>0; i-=2 )
269:                {
270:                    if( vPoints.size() >= (nDrawingWidth*i) )
271:                    {
272:                        nIncrement = i;
273:                        break;
274:                    }
275:                }
276:
277:                // Loop through all the points in the Vector and plot them
278:                Point ptStart = ( Point )vPoints.elementAt( 0 );
279:                for( int i=1; i<vPoints.size(); i+=nIncrement )
280:                {
281:                    // Extract the next point from the Vector
282:                    Point ptEnd = ( Point )vPoints.elementAt( i );
283:
284:                    // Draw a line from the first point to the second point
285:                    g2.drawLine( ptStart.x, ptStart.y, ptEnd.x, ptEnd.y );
286:
287:                    // Set the new start point
288:                    ptStart = ptEnd;
289:                }
290:        }
291:    }
292:
293:    // public long getLongDate( strDate )
294:    //
295:    // Converts the string date to a long - representing the number
296:    // of milliseconds that have passed since the epoch (1/1/70)
297:    public long getLongDate( String strDate )
298:    {
299:        SimpleDate date = new SimpleDate( strDate );
300:        return date.getLongValue();
301:    }
302:
303:    // Main application entry point into this class
304:    public static void main( String[] args )
```

```
305:    {
306:        // Create a JFrame object
307:        JFrame frame = new JFrame( "Stock Graph Panel" );
308:
309:        // Create a StockGraphPanel Object
310:        StockGraphPanel app = new StockGraphPanel();
311:
312:        // Add our StockGraphPanel Object to the JFrame
313:        frame.getContentPane().add( app, BorderLayout.CENTER );
314:
315:        // Resize our JFrame
316:        frame.setSize( 640, 440 );
317:
318:        // Make our JFrame visible
319:        frame.setVisible( true );
320:
321:        // Create a window listener to close our application when we
322:        // close our application
323:        frame.addWindowListener
324:        (
325:            new WindowAdapter()
326:            {
327:                public void windowClosing( WindowEvent e )
328:                {
329:                    System.exit( 0 );
330:                }
331:            }
332:        );
333:    }
334:
335:    // class UpdateHistoricalDataThread
336:    class UpdateHistoricalDataThread implements Runnable
337:    {
338:        // Our parent StockGraphPanel object
339:        StockGraphPanel m_stockGraphPanel;
340:
341:        // Constructor
342:        public UpdateHistoricalDataThread(StockGraphPanel stockGraphPanel)
343:        {
344:            m_stockGraphPanel = stockGraphPanel;
345:        }
346:
347:        // public void run()
348:        //
349:        //   Method thread executes.
350:        public void run()
351:        {
352:
353:            // Try to load the data from disk first
354:            if(
```

continues

Listing 12.2   continued

```
                  m_stockGraphPanel.m_historicalDataManager.loadHistoricalData
355:                  ( m_stockGraphPanel.m_strSymbol ).booleanValue()
356:                  )
357:              {
358:                  if(
         m_stockGraphPanel.m_historicalDataManager.getNumberOfHistoricalRecords()
         >=
359:                      m_stockGraphPanel.m_nNumberOfDays.intValue() )
360:                  {
361:                      // Get today's date
362:                      SimpleDate dateToday = new SimpleDate(
                          Calendar.getInstance() );
363:
364:                      // Get the latest date from the historical data manager
365:                      SimpleDate dateLatest = new SimpleDate
366:                          (
367:    m_stockGraphPanel.m_historicalDataManager.getStockDataElement(0).getDate()
368:                          );
369:
370:                      // Compare the two dates
371:                      if( dateLatest.compare( dateToday ) < 0 )
372:                      {
373:                          // The data is not recent enough, get it from
374:                          // the Internet
375:          m_stockGraphPanel.m_historicalDataManager.getHistoricalData
376:                          (
377:                              m_stockGraphPanel.m_strSymbol,
378:                              m_stockGraphPanel.m_nNumberOfDays.intValue()
379:                          );
380:                      }
381:                  }
382:                  else
383:                  {
384:                      // Clear all entries in the historical data manager
385:          m_stockGraphPanel.m_historicalDataManager.removeAllElements();
386:
387:                      // Load the data from the Internet
388:          m_stockGraphPanel.m_historicalDataManager.getHistoricalData
389:                          (
390:                              m_stockGraphPanel.m_strSymbol,
391:                              m_stockGraphPanel.m_nNumberOfDays.intValue()
392:                          );
393:                  }
394:
395:              }
396:              else
397:              {
398:                  // Load the data from the Internet
399:          m_stockGraphPanel.m_historicalDataManager.getHistoricalData
400:                  (
401:                      m_stockGraphPanel.m_strSymbol,
```

```
402:                        m_stockGraphPanel.m_nNumberOfDays.intValue()
403:                    );
404:                }
405:
406:
407:
408:            // Find the highest and lowest dates and prices
409:
410:            float fLowPrice = 0;
411:            float fHighPrice = 0;
412:            long lStartDate = 0;
413:            long lEndDate = 0;
414:
415:            // Initialize the values
416:            if(
     m_stockGraphPanel.m_historicalDataManager.getNumberOfHistoricalRecords()
                            == 0 )
417:            {
418:                return;
419:            }
420:
421:            StockData sd =
     m_stockGraphPanel.m_historicalDataManager.getStockDataElement(0);
422:            if( m_nGraphingMode == GRAPHOPENPRICES )
423:            {
424:                fLowPrice = sd.getOpen().floatValue();
425:                fHighPrice = sd.getOpen().floatValue();
426:            }
427:            else if( m_nGraphingMode == GRAPHCLOSEPRICES )
428:            {
429:                fLowPrice = sd.getClose().floatValue();
430:                fHighPrice = sd.getClose().floatValue();
431:            }
432:
433:            lStartDate = getLongDate( sd.getDate() );
434:            lEndDate = getLongDate( sd.getDate() );
435:
436:            // Loop through all of the StockData in the
437:            // HistoricalDataManager
438:        for( int i=1; i<m_stockGraphPanel.m_nNumberOfDays.intValue(); i++)
439:            {
440:                // Extract the StockData object
441:                StockData stockData =
             m_stockGraphPanel.m_historicalDataManager.getStockDataElement(i);
442:
443:                // Get the price for this stock
444:                float fPriceOpen = stockData.getOpen().floatValue();
445:                float fPriceClose = stockData.getClose().floatValue();
446:
447:                // Compare the open price to the low price
```

12

continues

Listing 12.2   continued

```
448:                    if( fPriceOpen < fLowPrice )
449:                    {
450:                        fLowPrice = fPriceOpen;
451:                    }
452:
453:                    // Compare the open price to the high price
454:                    if( fPriceOpen > fHighPrice )
455:                    {
456:                        fHighPrice = fPriceOpen;
457:                    }
458:
459:                    // Compare the close price to the low price
460:                    if( fPriceClose < fLowPrice )
461:                    {
462:                        fLowPrice = fPriceClose;
463:                    }
464:
465:                    // Compare the close price to the high price
466:                    if( fPriceClose > fHighPrice )
467:                    {
468:                        fHighPrice = fPriceClose;
469:                    }
470:
471:                    // Get the date
472:                    long lDate = getLongDate( stockData.getDate() );
473:
474:                    // Compare the date to the start date
475:                    if( lDate < lStartDate )
476:                    {
477:                        lStartDate = lDate;
478:                    }
479:
480:                    // Compare the date to end date
481:                    if( lDate > lEndDate )
482:                    {
483:                        lEndDate = lDate;
484:                    }
485:                }
486:
487:            // Set the StockGraphPanel values
488:            m_stockGraphPanel.m_fLowPrice = fLowPrice;
489:            m_stockGraphPanel.m_fHighPrice = fHighPrice;
490:            m_stockGraphPanel.m_lStartTime = lStartDate;
491:            m_stockGraphPanel.m_lEndTime = lEndDate;
492:
493:            // Tell the StockGraphPanel to repaint itself
494:            m_stockGraphPanel.repaint();
495:        }
496:    }
497:
498:    // class SimpleDate
```

```
499:    class SimpleDate
500:    {
501:        // Date attributes
502:        protected int m_nMonth;
503:        protected int m_nDay;
504:        protected int m_nYear;
505:
506:        // Constructors
507:        public SimpleDate()
508:        {
509:        }
510:
511:        public SimpleDate( int nMonth, int nDay, int nYear )
512:        {
513:            m_nMonth = nMonth;
514:            m_nDay = nDay;
515:            m_nYear = nYear;
516:        }
517:
518:        public SimpleDate( String strDate )
519:        {
520:            // Create a new / delimited StringTokenizer that does not
521:            // return the slash
522:            StringTokenizer st =
                  new StringTokenizer( strDate.trim(), "/", false );
523:
524:            // Extract the date information
525:            m_nMonth = Integer.valueOf( st.nextToken() ).intValue();
526:            m_nDay = Integer.valueOf( st.nextToken() ).intValue();
527:            m_nYear = Integer.valueOf( st.nextToken() ).intValue();
528:        }
529:
530:        public SimpleDate( Calendar date )
531:        {
532:            //m_nYear = date.getYear() + 1900;
533:            //m_nMonth = date.getMonth();
534:            //m_nDay = date.getDay();
535:
536:            m_nYear = date.get( Calendar.YEAR );
537:            m_nMonth = date.get( Calendar.MONTH );
538:            m_nDay = date.get( Calendar.DAY_OF_WEEK );
539:        }
540:
541:
542:        // Attribute Retrieval
543:        public int getMonth()
544:        {
545:            return m_nMonth;
546:        }
547:
```

12

continues

Listing 12.2   continued

```
548:         public int getDay()
549:         {
550:             return m_nDay;
551:         }
552:
553:         public int getYear()
554:         {
555:             return m_nYear;
556:         }
557:
558:         // public int compare( SimpleDate date )
559:         //
560:         //  Returns:
561:         //       0 = equal
562:         //      -1 = this < date
563:         //       1 = this > date
564:         public int compare( SimpleDate date )
565:         {
566:             // Compare years
567:             if( m_nYear > date.getYear() )
568:             {
569:                 return 1;
570:             }
571:             else if( m_nYear < date.getYear() )
572:             {
573:                 return -1;
574:             }
575:
576:             // Same year, compare months
577:             if( m_nMonth > date.getMonth() )
578:             {
579:                 return 1;
580:             }
581:             else if( m_nMonth < date.getMonth() )
582:             {
583:                 return -1;
584:             }
585:
586:             // Same month, compare days
587:             if( m_nDay > date.getDay() )
588:             {
589:                 return 1;
590:             }
591:             else if( m_nDay < date.getDay() )
592:             {
593:                 return -1;
594:             }
595:
596:             // Equal dates
597:             return 0;
```

```
598:
599:        }
600:
601:        // public long getLongValue()
602:        //
603:        //   Converts the date to a long value representing the number
604:        //   of days since 1/1/0000
605:        public long getLongValue()
606:        {
607:            long lYearDays = m_nYear * 365;
608:
609:            long lMonthDays = 0;
610:
611:            if( m_nMonth > 1 )
612:            {
613:                lMonthDays += 31;
614:            }
615:            if( m_nMonth > 2 )
616:            {
617:                if( m_nYear%4 == 0 )
618:                {
619:                    lMonthDays += 29;
620:                }
621:                else
622:                {
623:                    lMonthDays += 28;
624:                }
625:            }
626:
627:            if( m_nMonth > 3 ) lMonthDays += 31;
628:            if( m_nMonth > 4 ) lMonthDays += 30;
629:            if( m_nMonth > 5 ) lMonthDays += 31;
630:            if( m_nMonth > 6 ) lMonthDays += 30;
631:            if( m_nMonth > 7 ) lMonthDays += 31;
632:            if( m_nMonth > 8 ) lMonthDays += 31;
633:            if( m_nMonth > 9 ) lMonthDays += 30;
634:            if( m_nMonth > 10 ) lMonthDays += 31;
635:            if( m_nMonth > 11 ) lMonthDays += 30;
636:
637:            return lYearDays + lMonthDays + m_nDay;
638:        }
639:
640:        // public String displayMonthDay()
641:        //
642:        //   Returns a string with only the month and day: MM/DD
643:        public String displayMonthDay()
644:        {
645:            return new String( "" + m_nMonth + "/" + m_nDay );
646:        }
647:    }
648:}
```

12

I know that this is a huge file, but I will break it down so that it is easy to understand the pieces.

Lines 23–24 create the `HistoricalDataManager` instance that we are going to use to manage our historical data.

Line 27 creates an `Integer` that holds the number of days we are going to display in the graph.

Lines 30 and 31 create a new `UpdateHistoricalDataThread` object that we will define later. In a nutshell, its responsibility is to obtain the historical data, either from the local file system or from the Internet; compute the upper and lower limits; and then tell the graph to update itself.

Line 34 defines the base that I was talking about earlier; this represents the number of pixels to inset the graph's drawing area.

Lines 37–41 define variables that will hold the low and high prices and the start time (date) and end time (date), respectively.

Line 43 defines the graphing mode: It tells the `StockGraphPanel` class's paint method what points to plot: open, close, or both.

Lines 46–48 define constants that are used for the graphing mode. The `GRAPHDAILYRANGES` option is not implemented here, and I challenge you as an exercise after going through this chapter to add this functionality. There are a few changes you will have to make to the other components to enable this option (update the main menu and the handler). After that you will have to do some work on the `paint()` method to draw a vertical line between the opening and closing prices—it is a relatively challenging task, but one that will help you better understand the Java 2D API and all this coordinate business!

Lines 63–67 define the `setGraphMode()` method to simply change the graphing mode variable and call `repaint()` to cause the `JPanel` to repaint itself.

Lines 73–95 define the `updateGraph()` method. This version of the `updateGraph()` method is the ultimate destination of all `updateGraph()` methods. It saves the stock symbol and the number of days in class variables (lines 76 and 79), saves the current data in the historical data manager (lines 82–85), and then removes all elements from the historical data manager (line 88).

Next it creates a new `Thread` instance from the `UpdateHistoricalDataThread` class variable that implements `Runnable` (line 91) and then starts the thread (line 94). I will talk more about the `UpdateHistoricalDataThread` in a minute.

Lines 101–105 define the updateGraph() method that accepts only a symbol to call the previous updateGraph() method with the current specified number of days.

Lines 110–115 define the updateGraph() method that accepts only the number of days to graph to call the first updateGraph() method with the current stock symbol.

Lines 118–291 define the paint() method. It is huge, but not too difficult to understand from our previous discussions.

First, it converts the Graphics object to a Graphics2D object in line 121. Next in lines 124 and 125 it gets the size of the display in a java.awt.Dimension class instance. The java.awt.Dimension class is a simple class that maintains width and height integers. The JPanel getSize() method fills in the Dimension class attributes with the size of its panel.

Line 128 sets the Graphics2D instance's background color to the constant color: Color.black, using the Graphics2D class's setBackground() method.

Line 129 calls the Graphics2D class's clearRect() method to erase the background. The clearRect() method simply fills the specified rectangle (in our case the width and height of the panel) with the current background color.

Lines 133 and 134 compute the drawing area height and width, respectively, as the size of the JPanel excluding the base area (it is double the base area because there is area on each of the sides).

Lines 137 and 138 compute the price range (high–low) and the time range (end time–start time), respectively.

If we do not have enough data to display yet, we are simply going to display "Processing: SYMBOL" in the center of the panel, so line 141 makes this comparison for us. Line 144 sets the color of the Graphics2D object to cyan, and then lines 145–147 call the Graphics2D class's drawString() method to draw it on the screen.

Line 152 sets the Graphics2D class's color to light gray to draw our axes and labels. Lines 155 and 156 draw the y-axis and x-axis, respectively. Remember that we are simply drawing the left and bottom sides of a rectangle for the whole JPanel excluding our base.

Lines 159–174 draw tick marks on the graph axes. These are just 5-pixel-long lines to note the ends of the axes and one middle point on each axis.

Lines 177–181 draw the price labels. These are drawn next to the price tick marks. One shortcut that I took when drawing the prices was to build a String from a floating-point variable by writing

```
"" + m_fVariableName.
```

12

Prefacing the float variable with `" "` + tells the compiler to treat the rest of this value as a `String` and not a float—an interesting shortcut to calling

```
Float.toString(m_fVariableName)
```

Lines 184–214 draw the dates by creating a `SimpleDate` object and calling its `displayMonthDay()` method. The dates are retrieved from the `HistoricalDataManager` using the fact that the dates are arranged from most recent at the beginning to oldest at the end.

Line 218 creates a new `Vector` that we are going to fill with `java.awt.geom.Point` objects that represent the device points for each data point we have. The `java.awt.geom.Point` class maintains an x and y pair of integers.

Line 221 is a `for` loop that starts at the earliest date and loops through to the most recent date in the `HistoricalDataManager` values. Remember that the `HistoricalDataManager` maintains its data from latest to oldest, so we must go through its values backwards.

Line 224 extracts the specified `StockData` object from the `HistoricalDataManager`.

Lines 227 and 228 create two float values to hold the values we want to plot.

Lines 231–246 define a `switch` statement that determines the graphing mode we are in. This is one of those places in the code that I talked about earlier where you will want to make modifications to enable `GRAPHDAILYRANGES`. If the graphing mode is `GRAPHOPENPRICES`, the y variable is set to the open value of the `StockData` object, the color is set to green, and the label "Opening Prices" is painted in the upper right corner of the graph. If the graphing mode is `GRAPHCLOSEPRICES`, the y variable is set to the close value of the `StockData` object, the color is set to yellow, and "Closing Prices" is painted in the upper right corner of the graph. Either way the x coordinate is the long value of the `StockData` object—retrieved from the `getLongDate()` method, which I will discuss later.

Line 250 computes the y logical coordinate from the formula I discussed earlier, and then line 251 computes the y device coordinate. Lines 254 and 255 compute the x logical and x device coordinates, respectively. You must be saying to yourself, "That long discussion for a measly four lines of code?" But that is how it goes with graphics—determining the formulas may take pages (as it does with most 3D algorithms), but implementing them involves just a handful of lines.

Line 258 creates a new `Point` object, and then line 261 adds it to the `Vector` of points.

Remember our discussion about how we were going to draw dates when there were too many dates to display compared to the number of columns in the painting surface? Lines 267–275 implement this functionality. Basically they check the number of points we have through the `Vector.size()` method and compare that to the width of the drawing area. If the number of points is greater than or equal to two times the drawing width, we only want to graph every second point. The `for` loop determines when we reach the point when we have more points than a multiple of the drawing width. After we reach this point, we plot every i-th point.

Line 278 retrieves the first point from the `Vector`, and then the `for` loop in lines 279–289 retrieves the next point (line 282), draws a line from the first to the second (line 285), and then resets the start point for the next line (line 288).

Lines 297–301 accept a `String` date, build a `SimpleDate` from it, and call the `SimpleDate` class's `getLongValue()` method. This method is not needed but is a convenience for other methods.

Lines 336–496 define the `UpdateHistoricalDataThread` class. This class implements `Runnable` so that a `Thread` can run it. Recall that the `Runnable` interface has only one method, `run()`, which the `Thread` class calls when its `start()` method is called.

The `UpdateHistoricalDataThread` class has one constructor that accepts the `StockGraphPanel` that acts as its parent.

The `run()` method is where the fun starts! It is implemented in lines 350–495.

The first thing the `run()` method does is try to load the historical data from the local file system (lines 354–356). If this succeeds, it compares the number of items in the `HistoricalDataManager` it just loaded to the number of items we need to retrieve. If it has enough data, the `run()` method gets today's date (line 362) and gets the latest date from the `HistoricalDataManager` object (lines 365–368), and compares the two to ensure that we have recent data. If any of the aforementioned comparisons fail, the `run()` method downloads the information from the Internet.

Next we spend some time finding the high and low prices and dates to set the limits on the graph. Line 421–434 extract the first `StockData` object and set the initial high and low prices and dates. Line 438 starts a `for` loop that loops through each subsequent `StockData` object.

Line 441 extracts a `StockData` object and lines 444 and 445 get the open and close prices. Lines 448–469 compare the two values with the current lowest and highest prices and set them if they find a higher or lower value.

Line 472 retrieves the date from the `StockData` class and compares it to the start and end dates.

12

Lines 488–491 set the `UpdateHistoricalDataThread` class's parent's attributes.

Finally, line 494 tells the parent `StockGraphPanel` to repaint itself.

The remainder of the file is the `SimpleDate` class that we discussed in depth earlier.

Integrating with the User Interface

Now that we have the `StockGraphPanel` complete, it is time to integrate it back in with the Stock Tracker application. Several classes need to be updated, but the nature of the updates is not that severe. The major updates are made to the `MainMenu` class to add support for the new graphing options and the `StockApplication` class to handle those options and forward them to the `StockGraphPanel`. Nonetheless, the following classes need to be modified:

- `InternetManager`
- `GraphTabPanel`
- `HistoricalDataManager`
- `MainMenu`
- `StockApplication`

InternetManager

The `InternetManager` class currently supports downloading only 16 kilobytes worth of text from the Internet, which is far more than we will ever need to download information on one stock, but with the introduction of historical data, we can easily exceed that limit. For this chapter I increased this limit from 16 kilobytes to 32 kilobytes, which will cover historical date for more than a year.

I made the changes shown in Listing 12.3.

Listing 12.3 `InternetManager.java` **(Modifications Only)**

```
 1:  public class InternetManager
 2:  {
 3:      public String getHTMLPage( String strURL )
                        throws MalformedURLException, IOException
 4:      {
 5:          ...
 6:          char[] caInput = new char[32768];
 7:
 8:          try
 9:          {
10:              ...
11:              // Read in all of the data from the URL
12:              int ch = in.read();
```

```
13:                    while( (ch != -1) && nCount<32768 )
14:                    {
15:                        ...
16:                    }
17:            }
18:        ...
19:    }
20: }
```

The changes consisted solely of changing lines 6 and 13 from 16384 to 32768.

GraphTabPanel

The GraphTabPanel has the responsibility of forwarding the stock symbol from callers to the StockGraphPanel through both its setPortfolio() method and valueChanged() method from the ListSelectionListener it has registered with the TickerListPanel. Anyway, in the past it called the StockGraphPanel class's setSymbol() method to set the stock symbol, but that method has been removed in favor of the new updateGraph() method. So these two methods have to reflect those changes. Take a look at Listing 12.4.

Listing 12.4 **GraphTabPanel.java (Modifications Only)**

```
1:  public class GraphTabPanel extends JPanel
                    implements ListSelectionListener
2:  {
3:      public void setPortfolio( Portfolio portfolio )
4:      {
5:          // Set the ticker list portfolio
6:          tickerListPanel.setPortfolio( portfolio );
7:
8:          // Update the graph
9:          stockGraphPanel.updateGraph(
10:         (String)tickerListPanel.listTickers.getModel().getElementAt(0));
11:     }
12:
13:     public void valueChanged( ListSelectionEvent e )
14:     {
15:         // Ignore adjustment events
16:         if (e.getValueIsAdjusting())
17:         {
18:             return;
19:         }
20:
21:         // Get the list from the event
22:         JList theList = (JList)e.getSource();
23:
24:         // Get the index of the selected item
25:         int index = theList.getSelectedIndex();
```

12

continues

Listing 12.4 continued

```
26:
27:          // Send the text of the selected item to the graph panel
28:          stockGraphPanel.updateGraph(
                          (String)theList.getModel().getElementAt(index));
29:     }
30: }
```

The changes are shown in lines 9 and 28.

HistoricalDataManager

I added two methods to the HistoricalDataManager class: getStockSymbol(), which returns the stock symbol it is representing, and removeAllElements(), which removes all elements from the StockData Vector. Listing 12.5 shows the implementation of these methods.

Listing 12.5 HistoricalDataManager.java (Modifications Only)

```
1:  public class HistoricalDataManager
2:  {
3:      public String getStockSymbol()
4:      {
5:          return m_strStockSymbol;
6:      }
7:
8:      public void removeAllElements()
9:      {
10:          m_vStockData.removeAllElements();
11:     }
12: }
```

MainMenu

In the MainMenu class I removed the Graph, Options menu item and added in its place two groups of JRadioButtonMenuItem items, one for the time frame—one week, one month, three months, and six months—and one to determine what prices to plot—opening or closing.

Listing 12.6 shows the modifications to the MainMenu class.

Listing 12.6 MainMenu.java (Modifications Only)

```
1:  public class MainMenu extends JMenuBar
2:  {
3:      // "Graph" Menu
4:      public JMenu menuGraph = new JMenu( "Graph" );
```

```
5:            public JRadioButtonMenuItem graph1Week =
6:                    new JRadioButtonMenuItem( "One Week" );
7:            public JRadioButtonMenuItem graph1Month =
8:                    new JRadioButtonMenuItem( "One Month", true );
9:            public JRadioButtonMenuItem graph3Months =
10:                   new JRadioButtonMenuItem( "Three Months" );
11:           public JRadioButtonMenuItem graph6Months =
12:                   new JRadioButtonMenuItem( "Six Months" );
13:           public ButtonGroup timeGroup = new ButtonGroup();
14:           public JRadioButtonMenuItem graphOpen =
15:                   new JRadioButtonMenuItem( "Opening Prices", true );
16:           public JRadioButtonMenuItem graphClose =
17:                   new JRadioButtonMenuItem( "Closing Prices" );
18:           public ButtonGroup openCloseGroup = new ButtonGroup();
19:
20:     public MainMenu()
21:     {
22:         // "Graph" Menu
23:
24:         // Add our "Graph" menu
25:         add( menuGraph );
26:
27:         // Add our items to the "Graph" menu
28:         menuGraph.add( graph1Week );
29:         menuGraph.add( graph1Month );
30:         menuGraph.add( graph3Months );
31:         menuGraph.add( graph6Months );
32:         timeGroup.add( graph1Week );
33:         timeGroup.add( graph1Month );
34:         timeGroup.add( graph3Months );
35:         timeGroup.add( graph6Months );
36:         menuGraph.addSeparator();
37:         menuGraph.add( graphOpen );
38:         menuGraph.add( graphClose );
39:         openCloseGroup.add( graphOpen );
40:         openCloseGroup.add( graphClose );
41:     }
42:
43:     public void addActionListener( ActionListener listener )
44:     {
45:         // Add listener as the action listener for the "Graph" menu items
46:         graph1Week.addActionListener( listener );
47:         graph1Month.addActionListener( listener );
48:         graph3Months.addActionListener( listener );
49:         graph6Months.addActionListener( listener );
50:         graphOpen.addActionListener( listener );
51:         graphClose.addActionListener( listener );
52:     }
53: }
```

12

StockApplication

In the StockApplication we have to add menu item event handlers for the new menu items that we added to the MainMenu class. Listing 12.7 shows these modifications to the StockApplication class.

Listing 12.7 `StockApplication.java` **(Modifications Only)**

```
 1:  public class StockApplication extends JFrame
 2:      implements ActionListener, ListSelectionListener, StockUpdateListener
 3:  {
 4:      public void actionPerformed(ActionEvent e)
 5:      {
 6:          // Extract the JMenuItem that generated this event
 7:          JMenuItem item = ( JMenuItem )e.getSource();
 8:
 9:          ...
10:
11:          else if ( item == mainMenu.graph1Week )
12:          {
13:              System.out.println( "Graph->One Week" );
14:              stockTabPanel.graphTabPanel.stockGraphPanel.updateGraph(
15:                                              new Integer( 5 ) );
16:
17:          }
18:          else if ( item == mainMenu.graph1Month )
19:          {
20:              System.out.println( "Graph->One Month" );
21:              stockTabPanel.graphTabPanel.stockGraphPanel.updateGraph(
22:                                              new Integer( 20 ) );
23:          }
24:          else if ( item == mainMenu.graph3Months )
25:          {
26:              System.out.println( "Graph->Three Months" );
27:              stockTabPanel.graphTabPanel.stockGraphPanel.updateGraph(
28:                                              new Integer( 60 ) );
29:          }
30:          else if ( item == mainMenu.graph6Months )
31:          {
32:              System.out.println( "Graph->Six Months" );
33:              stockTabPanel.graphTabPanel.stockGraphPanel.updateGraph(
34:                                              new Integer( 120 ) );
35:          }
36:          else if ( item == mainMenu.graphOpen )
37:          {
38:              System.out.println( "Graph->Opening Prices" );
39:              stockTabPanel.graphTabPanel.stockGraphPanel.setGraphMode(
40:                                      StockGraphPanel.GRAPHOPENPRICES );
41:          }
42:          else if ( item == mainMenu.graphClose )
43:          {
44:              System.out.println( "Graph->Closing Prices" );
```

```
45:                stockTabPanel.graphTabPanel.stockGraphPanel.setGraphMode(
46:                         StockGraphPanel.GRAPHCLOSEPRICES );
47:        }
48:    }
49: }
```

Line 7 extracts the JMenuItem instance that generated the event, and lines 11–47 compare that item to the graph options.

Lines 11–17 handle the selection of Graph, One Week by telling the StockGraphPanel to update its graph to plot the data for five days or one week (in business days).

Lines 18–33 handle the selection of Graph, One Month by telling the StockGraphPanel to update its graph to plot the data for 20 days, which is four weeks or one month (in business days).

Lines 24–29 handle the selection of Graph, Three Months by telling the StockGraphPanel to update its graph to plot the data for 60 days, which is 12 weeks or three months (in business days).

Lines 30–35 handle the selection of Graph, Six Months by telling the StockGraphPanel to update its graph to plot the data for 120 days, which is 24 weeks or six months (in business days).

Lines 36–41 handle the selection of Graph, Opening Prices by setting the graph mode of the StockGraphPanel to StockGraphPanel.GRAPHOPENPRICES.

Lines 42–47 handle the selection of Graph, Closing Prices by setting the graph mode of the StockGraphPanel to StockGraphPanel.GRAPHCLOSEPRICES.

Summary

In this chapter we added graphing capabilities to the Stock Tracker application, and through that experience you learned a lot about graphing and about Java's painting support.

I spent quite a bit of time talking about how to take a two-dimensional graph that is in the standard Cartesian coordinate system and translate that to the two-dimensional paint surface coordinate system that Java provides. The good news is that this information is also applicable to other programming languages. Computers like to think about drawing surfaces from left to right and top to bottom, and the language just gives different ways of handling it.

12

Then I talked about the Java classes and methods that can be used to paint on the screen. I talked primarily about the Graphics2D class and noted that we only touched the surface of its capabilities.

Next I took you though the implementation of the StockGraphPanel class as we implemented all the graphing functionality of the Stock Tracker application.

We ended the chapter making some minor changes to the existing classes to integrate our new StockGraphPanel with the Stock Tracker application.

What's Next?

After completing this chapter, you have a fully functional application: You can get live stock updates from the Internet at random or on a timer, you can download historical stock data from the Internet, and you can display graphs of historical stock performance.

In the next chapter we are going to talk about Comma Separated Variable (CSV) files and how we can import and export data into the Stock Tracker application. This way we can export historical data to a CSV file and import it into a spreadsheet for more sophisticated analysis than the Stock Tracker application is providing.

Implementing the CSV Manager

The Stock Tracker application's graphing capability provides a nice feature and is very useful for analyzing quick trends, but I don't think it is going to win any awards. Don't get me wrong; I do feel this functionality is essential to the Stock Tracker application and is very valuable, but for detailed analysis and extended trend analysis, there are other applications that are far more suited to this task (such as spreadsheets and databases).

If other applications already have this functionality, what can we offer?

Well, the Stock Tracker application has two things to offer:

1. It knows how to download historical data from the Internet.
2. In situations when a user does not need to perform extensive analysis, it provides a very readable and friendly graphical display.

How can we leverage our Internet functionality to enhance other applications that can analyze data?

The answer lies in exporting that data from our Stock Tracker application into a form that these other applications can read. You could learn every proprietary spreadsheet and database format and implement them, but luckily there is a universal format that all spreadsheets and databases know how to read: comma-separated variable files. To review, a comma-separated variable file format consists of groups of data fields separated by commas delimited by newline characters.

Comma-separated variable (CSV) files are the focus of this chapter. I will talk about the following topics:

- Importing and exporting portfolios from and to comma-separated variable files
- Importing and exporting historical data from and to comma-separated variable files
- Prompting users to locate or specify files in Java

Use Cases

The Comma Separated Variable functionality for the Stock Application is defined in the following four use cases:

- Use Case #19: Import historical data from a CSV file
- Use Case #20: Export historical data to a CSV file
- Use Case #21: Import a portfolio from a CSV file
- Use Case #22: Export a portfolio to a CSV file

Each of these use cases is driven by menu options that prompt the user for a file-name and then perform their respective functionality.

Implementation Decisions

In this chapter we must consider three strategies:

- How do you allow the user to select a file on the local file system?
- How is the output of the comma-separated variable files going to be formatted?
- Where are you going to package the CSV Manager?

Selecting Files

Selecting files from the local file system is a relatively simple task in Java because of the javax.swing.JFileChooser class; it provides a standard file open/file save dialog box that allows the user to navigate the file system and select or specify a file. The appearance and navigation of the JFileChooser dialog box should look very familiar to you.

Table 13.1 shows the javax.swing.JFileChooser constructors.

13

Table 13.1 `JFileChooser` **Constructors**

Constructor	Description
`JFileChooser()`	Creates a `JFileChooser` pointing to the user's home directory
`JFileChooser(File currentDirectory)`	Creates a `JFileChooser` using the given `File` as the path
`JFileChooser(File currentDirectory, FileSystemView fsv)`	Creates a `JFileChooser` using the given current directory and `FileSystemView`
`JFileChooser(FileSystemView fsv)`	Creates a `JFileChooser` using the given `FileSystemView`
`JFileChooser(String currentDirectoryPath)`	Creates a `JFileChooser` using the given path
`JFileChooser(String currentDirectoryPath, FileSystemView fsv)`	Creates a `JFileChooser` using the given current directory path and `FileSystemView`

The basic construction of a `JFileChooser` is basically a determination of the starting path you want the dialog to display. The `javax.swing.filechooser.FileSystemView` class is the `JFileChooser` class's gateway to the file system and provides it with functionality to retrieve file system information. For our uses, we will want to create a default `JFileChooser` object pointing to the user's home directory:

```
JFileChooser fileChooser = new JFileChooser();
```

The `JFileChooser` class has two methods used display a dialog box, as shown in Table 13.2.

Table 13.2 `JFileChooser` **Methods to Display Dialogs**

Method	Description
`int showOpenDialog(Component parent)`	Pops up an Open File file selection dialog
`int showSaveDialog(Component parent)`	Pops up a Save File file selection dialog

These two methods return the value of the button that was selected: `JFileChooser.CANCEL_OPTION` denotes the Cancel button, and `JFileChooser.APPROVE_OPTION` denotes the Open button for the Open dialog and the Save button for the Save dialog. You can then retrieve the name of the file or files that were selected by calling the `JFileChooser` class's methods shown in Table 13.3.

Table 13.3 `JFileChooser` **Methods to Retrieve File Information**

Method	Description
`File getSelectedFile()`	Returns the selected file
`File[] getSelectedFiles()`	Returns a list of selected files if the `JFileChooser` is set to allow multiselection

The rest of the action takes place in the `java.io.File` class that these methods return. The `java.io.File` class provides an abstract representation of file and directory path names as well as options to interact with the directory or path name. Some of the important methods that are relative to our discussion are shown in Table 13.4.

Table 13.4 `java.io.File` **Methods**

Method	Description
`boolean createNewFile()`	Creates a new, empty file named by this abstract pathname if and only if a file with this name does not yet exist
`File createTempFile(String prefix, String suffix)`	Creates an empty file in the default temporary-file directory, using the given prefix and suffix to generate its name
`File createTempFile(String prefix, String suffix, File directory)`	Creates a new empty file in the specified directory, using the given prefix and suffix strings to generate its name
`boolean delete()`	Deletes the file or directory denoted by this abstract pathname
`File getAbsoluteFile()`	Returns the absolute form of this abstract pathname
`String getAbsolutePath()`	Returns the absolute pathname string of this abstract pathname
`String getName()`	Returns the name of the file or directory denoted by this abstract pathname

Method	Description
`String getPath()`	Converts this abstract pathname into a pathname string
`boolean isDirectory()`	Tests whether the file denoted by this abstract pathname is a directory
`boolean isFile()`	Tests whether the file denoted by this abstract pathname is a normal file
`boolean isHidden()`	Tests whether the file named by this abstract pathname is a hidden file
`long lastModified()`	Returns the time that the file denoted by this abstract pathname was last modified
`long length()`	Returns the length of the file denoted by this abstract pathname
`boolean renameTo(File dest)`	Renames the file denoted by this abstract pathname
`boolean setReadOnly()`	Marks the file or directory named by this abstract pathname so that only read operations are allowed
`String toString()`	Returns the pathname string of this abstract pathname

The `java.io.File` class has quite a bit of functionality, but we are really only going to be concerned with retrieving the file name and path. Listing 13.1 shows sample code to display a file open dialog using the `JFileChooser` class and then displays the complete file path to the standard output.

Listing 13.1 `JFileChooser` Example

```
1:  // Create a new JFileChooser object
2:  JFileChooser fileChooser = new JFileChooser();
3:
4:  // Show the "Open" file dialog box
5:  int returnVal = fileChooser.showOpenDialog( this );
6:
7:  // If the user chose "Open"
8:  if (returnVal == JFileChooser.APPROVE_OPTION)
9:  {
10:     // Extract the File object from the file chooser
11:     File file = fileChooser.getSelectedFile();
12:
13:     // Display full file name to the standard output
14:     System.out.println( "File: " + file.getPath() );
15: }
16: else
17: {
18:     // The user pressed cancel
19:     System.out.println( "User pressed Cancel" );
20: }
```

File Output Strategy

Now that we know how to prompt the user for a filename, we have to decide how to format the file and what data to include in it. The StockData class that we have been using for the last several chapters contains all the information we could want:

- Stock Symbol
- Company Name
- Last Sale
- High
- Low
- Volume
- Number Of Shares Owned
- Price Paid Per Share
- Date
- Close
- Open

And the beauty of our earlier design is that the StockData class already knows how to persist its data to and from the local file system in comma-separated variable file format! You read correctly—we have already done all the work for this chapter! Back in chapters 8 and 11 when we had to decide a format to persist our data, I made the decision to use the CSV format to satisfy this requirement.

The Portfolio and HistoricalDataManager classes are responsible for opening a file and passing the StockData object a FileReader or FileWriter object to persist its data to. We have to make a few modifications to the Portfolio and HistoricalDataManager classes so that a specific filename can be used, but that is fairly trivial.

Package Strategy

The CSVManager class is going to exist in the com.mcp.stock.csv package because its functionality differs significantly from the com.mcp.stock.internet and com.mcp.stock.portfolios packages.

Implementing the `CSVManager` Class

Figure 13.1 shows the `CSVManager` class diagram that we derived back in Chapter 3.

Figure 13.1

CSVManager class diagram.

From Figure 13.1 you can see that there are four methods that the `CSVManager` class exposes, as shown in Table 13.5.

Table 13.5   `java.io.File` Methods

Method	Description
`Portfolio importPortfolio()`	Prompts the user for a filename to import a `Portfolio` from, imports the `Portfolio` data, and returns the `Portfolio` to the caller
`Boolean exportPortfolio(Portfolio portfolio)`	Prompts the user for a filename to export the `Portfolio` to and exports the `Portfolio` to that filename; returns `true` on success, `false` on failure
`HistoricalDataManager importHistoricalData()`	Prompts the user for a filename to import historical data from, imports the historical data, and returns the data in a `HistoricalDataManager` object
`Boolean exportHistoricalData (HistoricalDataManager historicalDataManager)`	Prompts the user for a filename to export the specified `HistoricalDataManager` data to and exports the data to that file; returns `true` on success and `false` on failure

All four of these methods can throw the `java.io.IOException` exception, which can occur when reading from or writing to a file. Take a look at Listing 13.2 for the complete source code for the `CSVManager` class, and I will talk about it afterwards.

Listing 13.2 CSVManager.java

```
 1: // Define the package this file belongs to
 2: package com.mcp.stock.csv;
 3:
 4: // Import the packages we need
 5: import java.awt.*;
 6: import java.awt.event.*;
 7:
 8: import javax.swing.*;
 9: import javax.swing.filechooser.*;
10: import java.util.*;
11: import java.io.*;
12:
13: // Import our custom packages
14: import com.mcp.stock.portfolios.*;
15: import com.mcp.stock.internet.*;
16:
17: // public class CSVManager
18: public class CSVManager extends JComponent
19: {
20:     // Constructor
21:     public CSVManager()
22:     {
23:     }
24:
25:     // public Portfolio importPortfolio()
26:     //
27:     //   Prompts the user for the file to import the data from,
28:     //   imports the data into a Portfolio object and returns it
29:     //   to the caller.
30:     //
31:     //   Throws IOException on a read error
32:     //   Returns null on any other error
33:     public Portfolio importPortfolio() throws IOException
34:     {
35:         // Create a new JFileChooser object to search the local file
36:         // system
37:         JFileChooser fileChooser = new JFileChooser();
38:
39:         // Show the "Open" file dialog box
40:         int returnVal = fileChooser.showOpenDialog( this );
41:
42:         // If the user chose "Open"
43:         if (returnVal == JFileChooser.APPROVE_OPTION)
44:         {
45:             // Extract the File object from the file chooser
46:             File file = fileChooser.getSelectedFile();
47:
48:             // Get the portfolio name
49:             String strPortfolioName = new String();
50:             StringTokenizer st =
```

```
51:                   new StringTokenizer( file.getName(), "." );
52:              if( st.hasMoreTokens() )
53:              {
54:                  strPortfolioName = st.nextToken();
55:              }
56:              else
57:              {
58:                  strPortfolioName = file.getName();
59:              }
60:
61:              // Set the portfolio name
62:              Portfolio portfolio = new Portfolio( strPortfolioName );
63:
64:              // Load the portfolio
65:              if( portfolio.loadPortfolio
66:                  ( file.getPath() ).booleanValue() == true )
69:              {
70:                  return portfolio;
71:              }
72:              else
73:              {
74:                  // An error occurred, throw an exception
75:                  IOException e =
76:                      new IOException(
77:                          "Could not load the portfolio: " +
78:                          file.getPath() );
79:
80:                  throw e;
81:              }
82:          }
83:
84:          // Return null, the user chose Cancel
85:          return null;
86:      }
87:
88:      // public Boolean exportPortfolio( Portfolio portfolio )
89:      //
90:      // Exports the specified Portfolio object to a user
91:      // specified file (through the JFileChooser dialog)
92:      //
93:      // Throws IOException on a write error
94:      public Boolean exportPortfolio( Portfolio portfolio )
95:                                            throws IOException
96:      {
97:          // Create a new JFileChooser object to search the local file
98:          // system
99:          JFileChooser fileChooser = new JFileChooser();
100:
101:          // Show the "Save" file dialog box
102:          int returnVal = fileChooser.showSaveDialog( this );
```

continues

Listing 13.2   continued

```
103:
104:          // If the user chose "Open"
105:          if (returnVal == JFileChooser.APPROVE_OPTION)
106:          {
107:              // Extract the File object from the file chooser
108:              File file = fileChooser.getSelectedFile();
109:
110:              // Tell the Portfolio to save itself to the specified file
111:              if( portfolio.savePortfolio
112:                  ( file.getPath() ).booleanValue() == false )
113:              {
114:                  // An error occurred, throw an exception
115:                  IOException e =
116:                      new IOException(
117:                          "Could not save the portfolio: " +
118:                          portfolio.getName() +
119:                          " to the file: " +
120:                          file.getPath() );
121:
122:                  throw e;
123:              }
124:          }
125:          else
126:          {
127:              // The user chose "Cancel", return false
128:              return new Boolean( false );
129:          }
130:
131:          // Success, return true!
132:          return new Boolean( true );
133:      }
134:
135:  // public HistoricalDataManager importHistoricalData()
136:  //
137:  //   Prompts the user for the file to import the data from,
138:  //   imports the data into a HistoricalDataManager object and
139:  //   returns it to the caller.
140:  //
141:  //   Throws IOException on a read error
142:  //   Returns null on any other error
143:  public HistoricalDataManager importHistoricalData()
144:                                          throws IOException
145:  {
146:      // Create a new JFileChooser object to search the local file
147:      // system
148:      JFileChooser fileChooser = new JFileChooser();
149:
150:      // Show the "Open" file dialog box
151:      int returnVal = fileChooser.showOpenDialog( this );
152:
```

```
153:        // If the user chose "Open"
154:        if (returnVal == JFileChooser.APPROVE_OPTION)
155:        {
156:            // Extract the File object from the file chooser
157:            File file = fileChooser.getSelectedFile();
158:
159:            // Build a HistoricalDataManager
160:            HistoricalDataManager historicalDataManager =
161:                    new HistoricalDataManager();
162:
163:            // Load the historical data
164:            if( historicalDataManager.loadHistoricalData
165:                (
166:                    file
167:                ).booleanValue() == true )
168:            {
169:                return historicalDataManager;
170:            }
171:            else
172:            {
173:                // An error occurred, throw an exception
174:                IOException e =
175:                    new IOException(
176:                        "Could not load the historical data: " +
177:                        file.getPath() );
178:
179:                throw e;
180:            }
181:        }
182:
183:        // Return null, the user chose Cancel
184:        return null;
185:    }
186:
187: // public Boolean exportHistoricalData(
188: //                  HistoricalDataManager historicalDataManager )
189: //
190: //  Exports the specified HistoricalDataManager object to a user
191: //  specified file (through the JFileChooser dialog)
192: //
193: //  Throws IOException on a write error
194: public Boolean exportHistoricalData(
195:                  HistoricalDataManager historicalDataManager )
196:                  throws IOException
197: {
198:     // Create a new JFileChooser object to search the local file
199:     // system
200:     JFileChooser fileChooser = new JFileChooser();
201:
202:     // Show the "Save" file dialog box
```

continues

Listing 13.2　continued

```
203:          int returnVal = fileChooser.showSaveDialog( this );
204:
205:          // If the user chose "Save"
206:          if( returnVal == JFileChooser.APPROVE_OPTION )
207:          {
208:              // Extract the File object from the file chooser
209:              File file = fileChooser.getSelectedFile();
210:
211:              // Tell the HistoricalDataManager to save itself to the
212:              // specified file
213:              if( historicalDataManager.saveHistoricalData
214:                  (
215:                      file.getPath()
216:                  ).booleanValue() == false )
217:              {
218:                  // An error occurred, throw an exception
219:                  IOException e =
220:                      new IOException(
221:                          "Could not save the Historical Data for: " +
222:                          historicalDataManager.getStockSymbol() +
223:                          " to the file: " +
224:                          file.getPath() );
225:
226:                  throw e;
227:              }
228:          }
229:
230:          // Success, return true!
231:          return new Boolean( true );
232:      }
233:}
```

Line 2 declares that this file and its contents are going to be part of the com.mcp.stock.csv package.

Lines 14 and 15 import our com.mcp.stock.portfolios and com.mcp.stock.internet packages so that we can gain access to the Portfolio and HistoricalDataManager classes.

Line 18 declares the CSVManager class as a javax.swing.JComponent derivative. This is required because the JFileChooser class's showOpenDialog() and showSaveDialog() methods require a class that is derived from java.awt.Component as its parent; it extracts its look-and-feel information from this class.

Lines 21–23 define an empty constructor. This constructor exists only so that an instance of the CSVManager can be constructed (and saved for later reuse).

Lines 33–86 define the importPortfolio() method. This method first creates a new javax.swing.JFileChooser object in line 37 and then calls its showOpenDialog() method to prompt for the Portfolio file the user wants to import. If the user chooses Cancel, the importPortfolio() method returns null in line 85; otherwise, it does the following:

1. Gets the selected file using the JFileChooser class's getSelectedFile() method (line 46).

2. Extracts the Portfolio name by retrieving the selected files name using the java.io.File class's getName() method and removing its extension. This is accomplished by creating a StringTokenizer class that parses for a period and extracting the first token (filename without extension). If the filename does not have an extension, the entire filename is used as the Portfolio name (lines 49–59).

3. It creates a new Portfolio object in line 62.

4. In lines 65–68 it asks the Portfolio object to load a Portfolio from the specified filename by passing it the complete filename—the call to getPath() returns the absolute filename.

5. Finally, in line 70 it returns the Portfolio it just created.

If an error occurs during the file loading, the importPortfolio() method throws an IOException exception.

Lines 94–133 define the exportPortfolio() method. This method accepts a Portfolio object, prompts the user for a filename and path to write it to, and then exports the data to that file.

It starts off in line 99 creating a new JFileChooser object and then displaying its Save dialog box by calling the JFileChooser class's showSaveDialog() method. If the user canceled the operation, the method returns false; otherwise, it does the following:

1. Gets the selected file using the JFileChooser class's getSelectedFile() method (line 108).

2. Retrieves the absolute path of the selected file by calling the File class's getPath() method and asks the specified Portfolio object to save its portfolio data to that file by calling its savePortfolio() method (lines 111–114).

If an error occurs while writing the file, the exportPortfolio() method throws an IOException exception; otherwise, it returns true (line 132).

Lines 143–185 define the importHistoricalData() method. It begins by creating a new JFileChooser object (line 148) and calling its showOpenDialog() method. If the user cancels the operation, the method returns null (line 184); otherwise, it does the following:

1. Gets the selected file using the JFileChooser class's getSelectedFile() method (line 157).

2. Builds a new HistoricalDataManager (lines 162–162).

3. Asks the HistoricalDataManager to load the historical data in the specified File object (lines 164–167).

If an error occurs during the read operation, the importHistoricalData() method throws an IOException exception; otherwise, it returns the new HistoricalDataManager object.

Lines 194–232 define the exportHistoricalData() method, which accepts a HistoricalDataManager object to export. It starts in line 200 by creating a new JFileChooser object and displaying its Save dialog box by calling its showSaveDialog() method (line 203). If the user selects the Save button, it does the following:

1. Gets the selected file using the JFileChooser class's getSelectedFile() method (line 209).

2. Retrieves the absolute path of the selected file and asks the HistoricalDataManager object to save its data to that file (lines 213–216).

If an error occurs while saving the file, the exportHistoricalData() method throws an IOException exception; otherwise, it returns true in line 231.

Integrating with the User Interface

Three components in the Stock Tracker application are affected by the CSVManager class:

- Portfolio
- HistoricalDataManager
- StockApplication

Portfolio

We must make four changes to the Portfolio class to make it work with the CSVManager (and not break any of the existing classes):

- Create a new `savePortfolio()` method that accepts a filename to write the portfolio to
- Create a `savePortfolio()` method that accepts no parameters and saves the file to PORTFOLIO_NAME.txt
- Create a new `loadPortfolio()` method that accepts a filename to read the portfolio from
- Create a `loadPortfolio()` method that does not accept any parameters and opens the file PORTFOLIO_NAME.txt

Listing 13.3 shows the modified source code for the `Portfolio` class.

Listing 13.3 `Portfolio.java` **(Modified)**

```
1:  public Boolean savePortfolio()
2:  {
3:      return savePortfolio( m_strPortfolioName + ".txt" );
4:  }
5:
6:  public Boolean savePortfolio( String strFilename )
7:  {
8:      try
9:      {
10:         // Create a new FileWriter with the specified filename
11:
12:         FileWriter file = new FileWriter( strFilename );
13:
14:         // Loop through all elements in the vector
15:         for( int i=0; i<m_vectorStockData.size(); i++ )
16:         {
17:             // Retrieve the element at index i
18:             StockData data =
19:                 (StockData)m_vectorStockData.elementAt( i );
20:
21:             // Tell it to write its data to our file writer
22:             data.write( file );
23:         }
24:
25:         // Close the FileWriter object
26:         file.close();
27:     }
28:     catch( IOException e )
29:     {
30:         // An error occurred
31:         System.out.println( "Portfolios.savePortfolio Error: " +
32:                             e.toString() );
33:         return new Boolean( false );
34:     }
35:
```

continues

Listing 13.3 continued

```
36:     // Success
37:     return new Boolean( true );
38: }
39:
40: public Boolean loadPortfolio()
41: {
42:     return loadPortfolio( m_strPortfolioName + ".txt" );
43: }
44:
45: public Boolean loadPortfolio( String strFilename )
46: {
47:     try
48:     {
49:         // Create a new FileWriter with the specified filename
50:
51:         FileReader file = new FileReader( strFilename );
52:
53:         // Create a Boolean Object to tell us when we hit the
54:         // end of file marker
55:         Boolean bEndOfFile = new Boolean( true );
56:
57:         // While we haven't reached the end of the file
58:         while( bEndOfFile.booleanValue() )
59:         {
60:             // Create a new StockData object
61:             StockData data = new StockData();
62:
63:             // Read in data for this StockData
64:             bEndOfFile = data.read( file );
65:
66:             // If we were successful, add this element to our vector
67:             if( bEndOfFile.booleanValue() )
68:             {
69:                 m_vectorStockData.addElement( data );
70:             }
71:         }
72:
73:         // Close the FileReader object
74:         file.close();
75:     }
76:     catch( FileNotFoundException e )
77:     {
78:         // File does not exist. This is not necessarily an error, the
79:         // Portfolio will just be empty. Return false nonetheless.
80:         return new Boolean( false );
81:     }
82:     catch( IOException e )
83:     {
84:         System.out.println
85:         (
```

```
86:                "Portfolio.loadPortfolio Error: " +
87:                e.toString()
88:          );
89:    }
90:
91:    // Success! Return true
92:    return new Boolean( true );
93: }
```

Lines 1–4 define the empty savePortfolio() method to call the other version of the savePortfolio() method with the filename PORTFOLIO_NAME.txt in line 3.

Lines 6–38 define the savePortfolio() method that accepts a filename to write the Portfolio to. It is identical to the savePortfolio() method we implemented back in Chapter 8 except that in line 12 the FileWriter class is constructed with a specified filename and not with the hard-coded string that we have been using.

Lines 40–43 define the empty loadPortfolio() method to call the other version of the loadPortfolio() method with the filename PORTFOLIO_NAME.txt.

Lines 45–93 define the loadPortfolio() method that accepts a filename. It is identical to the loadPortfolio() method we implemented back in Chapter 8, "Implementing Portfolios," except that in line 51 the FileReader class is constructed with the specified filename and not with the hard-coded string that we have been using.

With this strategy we have preserved the interface that the existing classes will use and have added the functionality to load and save the data from and to a specified file.

HistoricalDataManager

The modifications to the HistoricalDataManager are very similar to those we just made to the Portfolio class:

- Create a new saveHistoricalData() method that accepts a filename to write the historical data to
- Create a saveHistoricalData() method that accepts no parameters and saves the file to SYMBOL.txt
- Create a new loadHistoricalData() method that accepts a File object to read the historical data from
- Create a loadHistoricalData() method that accepts the stock symbol as a parameter and opens the file SYMBOL.txt

We cannot simply add a `load` method that specifies a filename for the historical data because the existing `loadHistoricalData()` method already specifies a name string. So we need to find a way to preserve the interface and still allow for a new method to specify the method of our choosing. I opted to use a `java.io.File` object to accomplish this because our `CSVManager` class already has one, and it resolves the ambiguity of specifying a filename `String`.

Listing 13.4 shows the modified source code for the `HistoricalDataManager` class.

Listing 13.4   `HistoricalDataManager.java` (Modified)

```
1:  public Boolean loadHistoricalData( String strStockSymbol )
2:  {
3:      // Save the stock symbol
4:      m_strStockSymbol = strStockSymbol;
5:
6:      // Create a File object with the name stock's Symbol + ".txt"
7:      File fileData = new File( strStockSymbol + ".txt" );
8:
9:      // Call the meaningful loadHistoricalData method
10:     return loadHistoricalData( fileData );
11: }
12:
13: // loadHistoricalData( strStockSymbol )
14: //
15: //  Attempts to load the historical data for the specified stock
16: //  from the local file system.
17: //
18: //  Returns true if it succeeds or false if the file does not
19: //  exist or an error occurred.
20: public Boolean loadHistoricalData( File fileData )
21: {
22:     // Get the HistoricalDataManager name
23:     StringTokenizer st =
24:         new StringTokenizer( fileData.getName(), "." );
25:     if( st.hasMoreTokens() )
26:     {
27:         m_strStockSymbol = st.nextToken();
28:     }
29:     else
30:     {
31:         m_strStockSymbol = fileData.getName();
32:     }
33:
34:     // Clear any existing data from the StockData Vector
35:     m_vStockData.removeAllElements();
36:
37:     try
38:     {
39:         // Create a new FileWriter with the specified filename
40:         FileReader file = new FileReader( fileData.getPath() );
```

```
41:
42:          // Create a Boolean Object to tell us when we hit the
43:          // end of file marker
44:          Boolean bEndOfFile = new Boolean( true );
45:
46:          // While we haven't reached the end of the file
47:          while( bEndOfFile.booleanValue() )
48:          {
49:              // Create a new StockData object
50:              StockData data = new StockData();
51:
52:              // Read in data for this StockData
53:              bEndOfFile = data.read( file );
54:
55:              // If we were successful, add this element to
56:              // our vector
57:              if( bEndOfFile.booleanValue() )
58:              {
59:                  m_vStockData.addElement( data );
60:              }
61:          }
62:
63:          // Close the FileReader object
64:          file.close();
65:      }
66:      catch( FileNotFoundException e )
67:      {
68:          // File does not exist. This is not necessarily an error,
69:          // we may not have downloaded its information yet.
70:          // Return false nonetheless.
71:          return new Boolean( false );
72:      }
73:      catch( IOException e )
74:      {
75:          System.out.println
76:          (
77:              "HistoricalDataManager.loadHistoricalData Error: " +
78:              e.toString()
79:          );
80:      }
81:
82:      // Success! Return true
83:      return new Boolean( true );
84: }
85:
86: public Boolean saveHistoricalData()
87: {
88:      return saveHistoricalData( m_strStockSymbol + ".txt" );
89: }
90:
```

continues

Listing 13.4   continued

```
91: // saveHistoricalData()
92: //
93: //  Saves the historical data in this class to the local file
94: //  system.
95: public Boolean saveHistoricalData( String strFilename )
96: {
97:     try
98:     {
99:         // Create a new FileWriter with the specified filename
100:
101:         FileWriter file = new FileWriter( strFilename );
102:
103:         // Loop through all elements in the vector
104:         for( int i=0; i<m_vStockData.size(); i++ )
105:         {
106:             // Retrieve the element at index i
107:             StockData data =
108:                 (StockData)m_vStockData.elementAt( i );
109:
110:             // Tell it to write its data to our file writer
111:             data.write( file );
112:         }
113:
114:         // Close the FileWriter object
115:         file.close();
116:     }
117:     catch( IOException e )
118:     {
119:         // An error occurred
120:         System.out.println
121:         (
122:             "HistoricalDataManager.saveHistoricalData Error: " +
123:             e.toString()
124:         );
125:         return new Boolean( false );
126:     }
127:
128:     // Success
139:     return new Boolean( true );
130:}
```

Lines 1–11 define the loadHistoricalData() method that specifies the stock symbol as a String. It begins by saving the stock symbol in line 4, and then creating a new File object with the filename "SYMBOL.txt" in line 7, and finally calling the other version of the loadHistoricalData() method in line 10.

Lines 20–84 define the `loadHistoricalData()` method that accepts a `java.io.File` parameter to load its historical data from. This method first extracts the name of the stock symbol the same way we did back in the `CSVManager` discussion (using a `StringTokenizer` with a period delimiter in lines 23–32). Then it functions identically to the version we created in Chapter 11, "Implementing the Historical Data Manager," except that in line 40 it creates its `FileReader` object with the specified `File` class's absolute path (through `getPath()`) and not with the name "STOCK.txt".

Lines 86–89 define the empty `saveHistoricalData()` method to call the other version of the `saveHistoricalData()` method with the filename "STOCK.txt".

Lines 95–130 define the `saveHistoricalData()` method that accepts a filename to save the historical data to. This method is identical to the one we created in Chapter 11 except that in line 101 we create the `FileWriter` object with the specified filename and not with the name "STOCK.txt".

Again with this class we were able to preserve the `HistoricalDatManager` existing interfaces so that we do not break any of our existing code and still provide support for the `CSVManager`.

StockApplication

To integrate the `CSVManager` class with the Stock Tracker application, the `StockApplication` class requires two updates:

- Import the new `com.mcp.stock.csv` package
- Add menu message handlers for Portfolios, Import; Portfolios, Export; History, Import; and History, Export

Listing 13.5 shows the modified source code for the `StockApplication` class.

Listing 13.5 `StockApplication.java` **(Modified)**

```
 1:  import com.mcp.stock.csv.*;
 2:
 3:  public void actionPerformed(ActionEvent e)
 4:  {
 5:      // Extract the JMenuItem that generated this event
 6:      JMenuItem item = ( JMenuItem )e.getSource();
 7:
 8:      ...
 9:
10:      // Portfolios -> Import
11:      else if ( item == mainMenu.portfoliosImport )
12:      {
13:          System.out.println( "Portfolios->Import" );
```

continues

Listing 13.5   continued

```
14:
15:        try
16:        {
17:            // Create a CSVManager object
18:            CSVManager csv = new CSVManager();
19:
20:            // Import a portfolio
21:            Portfolio portfolio = csv.importPortfolio();
22:
23:            // Make sure that the portfolio is valid
24:            if( portfolio != null )
25:            {
26:                // Add that portfolio to our PortfolioManager
27:                portfolioManager.addPortfolio( portfolio );
28:
29:                // Add the portfolio name to the PortfolioListPanel
30:                portfolioListPanel.addPortfolio( portfolio.getName() );
31:
32:                // Notify the user
33:                JOptionPane.showMessageDialog
34:                (
35:                    this,
36:                    "Portfolio Successfully Imported",
37:                    "Portfolio",
38:                    JOptionPane.INFORMATION_MESSAGE
39:                );
40:
41:            }
42:            else
43:            {
44:                // Import failed
45:                JOptionPane.showMessageDialog
46:                (
47:                    this,
48:                    "Could not import the specfied portfolio",
49:                    "Portfolio Import Failure",
50:                    JOptionPane.ERROR_MESSAGE
51:                );
52:            }
53:        }
54:        catch( IOException ioException )
55:        {
56:            // An error occurred reading the file
57:            System.out.println( "Error importing a portfolio: " +
58:                                ioException.toString() );
59:
60:            // Import failed
61:            JOptionPane.showMessageDialog
62:            (
63:                this,
```

```
64:                    "An error occurred reading the portfolio file",
65:                    "Portfolio Import Failure",
66:                    JOptionPane.ERROR_MESSAGE
67:                );
68:            }
69:        }
70:
71:        // Portfolios -> Export
72:        else if ( item == mainMenu.portfoliosExport )
73:        {
74:            System.out.println( "Portfolios->Export" );
75:
76:            // Extract the Portfolio name from the PortfolioListPanel
77:            String strPortfolio =
78:                portfolioListPanel.getSelectedPortfolio();
79:
80:            // Build a new Portfolio from the name
81:            Portfolio portfolio = new Portfolio( strPortfolio );
82:
83:            // Load the portfolio
84:            if( portfolio.loadPortfolio().booleanValue() == true )
85:            {
86:                try
87:                {
88:                    // Construct a new CSVManager object
89:                    CSVManager csv = new CSVManager();
90:
91:                    // Export the portfolio
92:                    if( csv.exportPortfolio
93:                        (portfolio).booleanValue() == true )
94:                    {
95:                        // Success! Notify the user.
96:                        JOptionPane.showMessageDialog
97:                        (
98:                            this,
99:                            "Portfolio Successfully Exported",
100:                            "Portfolio",
101:                            JOptionPane.INFORMATION_MESSAGE
102:                        );
103:                    }
104:
105:                    // false means that the user cancelled the operation
106:                }
107:                catch( IOException ioException )
108:                {
109:                    // An error occurred writing to the file
110:                    System.out.println( "Error importing a portfolio: " +
111:                                        ioException.toString() );
112:
113:                    // Export failed
114:                    JOptionPane.showMessageDialog
```

continues

Listing 13.5 continued

```
115:                    (
116:                        this,
117:                        "An error occurred writing the portfolio file",
118:                        "Portfolio Export Failure",
119:                        JOptionPane.ERROR_MESSAGE
120:                    );
121:                }
122:            }
123:            else
124:            {
125:                System.out.println(
126:                    "Error loading the current portfolio" );
127:            }
128:        }
139:
130:        // History -> Import
131:        else if ( item == mainMenu.historyImport )
132:        {
133:            System.out.println( "History->Import" );
134:
135:            try
136:            {
137:                // Create a CSVManager object
138:                CSVManager csv = new CSVManager();
139:
140:                // Import a portfolio
141:                HistoricalDataManager history =
142:                        csv.importHistoricalData();
143:
144:                // Make sure that the portfolio is valid
145:                if( history != null )
146:                {
147:                    // Save the historical data in the current folder
148:                    // so that the HistoricalDataManager can load it
149:                    // when it needs to
150:                    history.saveHistoricalData();
151:
152:                    // Notify the user
153:                    JOptionPane.showMessageDialog
154:                    (
155:                        this,
156:                        "Historical Data Successfully Imported",
157:                        "Historical Data",
158:                        JOptionPane.INFORMATION_MESSAGE
159:                    );
160:
161:                }
162:                else
163:                {
164:                    // Import failed
```

```
165:                    JOptionPane.showMessageDialog
166:                    (
167:                        this,
168:                        "Could not import the specfied historical data",
169:                        "Historical Data Import Failure",
170:                        JOptionPane.ERROR_MESSAGE
171:                    );
172:                }
173:            }
174:        catch( IOException ioException )
175:        {
176:            // An error occurred reading the file
177:            System.out.println( "Error importing historical data: " +
178:                                ioException.toString() );
179:
180:            // Import failed
181:            JOptionPane.showMessageDialog
182:            (
183:                this,
184:                "An error occurred reading the historical data file",
185:                "Historical Import Failure",
186:                JOptionPane.ERROR_MESSAGE
187:            );
188:        }
189:    }
190:
191:    // History -> Export
192:    else if ( item == mainMenu.historyExport )
193:    {
194:        System.out.println( "History->Export" );
195:
196:        // Extract the HistoricalDataManager name from the
197:        String strHistory = (String)
198: stockTabPanel.graphTabPanel.tickerListPanel.listTickers.
     ➥getSelectedValue();
199:
200:        // Build a new HistoricalDataManager
201:        HistoricalDataManager history = new HistoricalDataManager();
202:
203:        // Load the historical data
204:        if( history.loadHistoricalData
205:            ( strHistory ).booleanValue() == true )
206:        {
207:            try
208:            {
209:                // Construct a new CSVManager object
210:                CSVManager csv = new CSVManager();
211:
212:                // Export the portfolio
213:                if( csv.exportHistoricalData
```

continues

Listing 13.5   continued

```
214:                         ( history ).booleanValue() == true )
215:                    {
216:                        // Success! Notify the user.
217:                        JOptionPane.showMessageDialog
218:                        (
219:                            this,
220:                            "Historical Data Successfully Exported",
221:                            "Historical Data",
222:                            JOptionPane.INFORMATION_MESSAGE
223:                        );
224:                    }
225:
226:                    // false means that the user cancelled the operation
227:                }
228:                catch( IOException ioException )
229:                {
230:                    // An error occurred writing to the file
231:                    System.out.println(
232:                        "Error exporting the historical data: " +
233:                        ioException.toString() );
234:
235:                    // Export failed
236:                    JOptionPane.showMessageDialog
237:                    (
238:                        this,
239:                        "An error occurred writing the historical data file",
240:                        "Historical Data Export Failure",
241:                        JOptionPane.ERROR_MESSAGE
242:                    );
243:                }
244:            }
245:            else
246:            {
247:                System.out.println(
248:                    "Error loading the current historical data" );
249:            }
250:        }
251:        ...
252:}
```

Line 1 imports the new com.mcp.stock.csv package.

Lines 3–252 display a snippet from the actionPerformed() method that handles menu items.

Lines 10–72 define the Portfolios, Import menu option. This handler creates a new CSVManager object in line 18 and immediately asks it to import a portfolio by calling its importPortfolio() method in line 21. If the import succeeded and a valid Portfolio was created, this handler adds the Portfolio to the PortfolioManager (line 27), adds the Portfolio name to the PortfolioListPanel, and notifies the user by displaying a JOptionPane message box (lines 33–39). Refer to Chapter 8 for more information about the JOptionPane class. If the import failed, signified by a null Portfolio, the user is notified with an error message box (lines 45–51). Finally, if there was a read error, the user is notified with a different error message box (lines 61–67).

Lines 71–128 define the Portfolios, Export menu item handler. It first extracts the Portfolio name of the currently selected Portfolio from the PortfolioListPanel by calling its getSelectedPortfolio() method (lines 77 and 78). Next, it constructs a new Portfolio object from that name in line 81 and then loads the Portfolio data in line 84. If the load succeeds, it creates a new CSVManager object (line 89) and then asks it to export the Portfolio by calling its exportPortolio() method in lines 92 and 93. Results of each operation are displayed to the user via JOptionPane message boxes. If an error occurs, an exception is thrown and the error is presented to the user via a JOptionPane message box.

Lines 131–189 define the History, Import menu item handler. It first creates a new CSVManager object in line 138 and then asks it to import historical data by calling the importHistoricalData() method in lines 141 and 142. If the import succeeds, it simply saves the historical data to the Stock Tracker application's location so that it can be retrieved as needed (line 150). All actions are displayed to the user via JOptionPane message boxes. If an error occurs, an exception is thrown and the error is presented to the user via a JOptionPane message box.

Finally, lines 192–250 define the History, Export menu item handler. It first extracts the currently selected stock symbol from the TickerListPanel (this controls which stock is being shown in the graph) in lines 197 and 198. Next it builds a new HistoricalDataManager object in line 201 and loads the historical data for that stock symbol in lines 204 and 205.It then constructs a new CSVManager object in line 210 and asks it to export the HistoricalDataManager we just created (lines 213 and 214). If it succeeds, the user is notified via a JOptionPane information message; otherwise, error messages are displayed.

Try running the Stock Tracker application and select some of the import and export options. Take a look at the files you have exported and see if they make sense. Finally, take one or more of your historical data files and import it into your favorite spreadsheet and see how it looks. You might need to spend some time learning about your spreadsheet before you can build nice pie charts or 3D graphs, but if you are interested in analyzing stocks, the time will be well spent.

Summary

In this chapter, we talked about comma-separated variable files in general, and then we talked more specifically about how our Stock Tracker application storage strategy already supported them. I showed you how to use the JFileChooser to allow users to browse their local file systems and how to extract information from them. We finished the chapter by writing the CSVManager class to provide an interface to import and export CSV files using our existing persistence methods and then integrated it with the Stock Tracker application.

After completing this chapter, you should have a solid understanding of the JFileChooser class, and you should be a whiz at handling menu items and displaying message boxes.

What's Next?

You now have a stock tracking application that is fully functional:

- It can persist multiple stocks in multiple portfolios.
- It can download live stock quotes from the Internet on demand or at a fixed time interval.
- It can download historical data from the Internet.
- It can graph historical data from within the application.
- It can import and export both portfolios as well as historical data from and to comma-separated variable files.

What else is left to do?

In the next chapter I am going to show you ways you can use the standard Java classes to enhance your application. Then we will finish up the book talking briefly about other Java technologies that you could apply to this and future applications.

Chapter 14

Enhancing the Stock Tracker User Interface

In the last 13 chapters, you have constructed a fully functional Stock Tracker application. You have accomplished the following tasks:

- Designed an application
- Designed the user interface using Swing objects
- Downloaded live stock information from the Internet
- Set up a timer
- Downloaded historical data from the Internet
- Graphed the historical data
- Exported portfolio and historical data to comma-separated variable files for use with databases and spreadsheets

After spending time concentrating on the functionality of the application, it is time to address some of its aesthetic aspects. In this chapter we are going to spend some time making the application look more professional by adding some of the features you would normally find in commercial applications. I am going to discuss several topics, including the following:

- Adding a splash screen to the application during startup
- Adding a toolbar with popular functionality
- Adding keyboard mnemonics for popular menu options

Centering a Frame Onscreen

One thing that is very simple but has a good effect on your application's presentation is positioning the application in the center of the screen. You do not often see applications that position themselves in the upper left corner as our application does. Instead, most professional applications initialize in the center of the screen. The code that does this is also very simple. All we have to do is

1. Get the dimensions of the screen
2. Get the dimensions of the application's frame
3. Move the upper-left corner of the frame to the following position:

```
x = (screenSize.width - windowSize.width) / 2
y = (screenSize.height - windowSize.height) / 2
```

To begin with, you can get the dimensions of the screen using the `java.awt.Toolkit` class and its `getScreenSize()` method. The `java.awt.Toolkit` class is an abstract class that binds the Abstract Window Toolkit (AWT) with its platform-specific toolkit. You can ask the `java.awt.Toolkit` to provide you with the default toolkit for the current platform by calling its `getDefaultToolkit()` method. From this default toolkit, you can query it for its screen size:

```
Dimension screenSize = Toolkit.getDefaultToolkit().getScreenSize();
```

This method returns a `java.awt.Dimension` object that has two attributes: width and height. There are two methods used to access these attributes: `getWidth()` and `getHeight()`. After making the previous call to `getScreenSize()`, you can access the width and height of the screen as follows:

```
int width = screenSize.getWidth();
int height = screenSize.getHeight();
```

Next, to get the dimensions of the application's frame, you simply have to make a call to the frame's `getSize()` method. This method also returns a `java.awt.Dimension` object.

You can change the position of any object derived from `java.awt.Component`, including windows and frames, by using the `java.awt.Component` class's `setBounds()` method, defined as follows:

```
setBounds(int x, int y, int width, int height)
```

The `setBounds()` method moves and resizes this component. The new location of the top-left corner is specified by x and y, and the new size is specified by `width` and `height`.

To put it all together in a small example, look at Listing 14.1.

Listing 14.1   Centering a Frame

```
 1:  public class MyFrame extends JFrame
 2:  {
 3:      public MyFrame()
 4:      {
 5:          ...
 6:          // Center our window
 7:          Dimension screenSize = Toolkit.getDefaultToolkit().getScreenSize();
 8:          Dimension windowSize = getSize();
 9:          setBounds( (screenSize.width - windowSize.width) / 2,
10:                     (screenSize.height - windowSize.height) / 2,
11:                     windowSize.width,
12:                     windowSize.height);
13:
14:      }
15:  }
```

Splash Screens

Splash screens are those nice-looking displays you see while your applications are loading; they do not have a window title bar, but they do usually have a nice graphic, and many contain a status bar displaying the loading status. The windows entertain the user while the application is loading and provide some visual feedback that the application is doing something. This is a nice feature to add to your application to make it look professional.

Let's take a look at how we might implement a splash screen in the Stock Tracker application. Speaking of which, "Stock Tracker application" doesn't sound very exciting. Now that we are going to create a nice graphic title for the application, it is a good time to pick a name for it. In honor of Que Publishing, I am going to title my application "Que Stock"; feel free to customize yours to the name of your choice.

Figure 14.1 shows a sample screen shot of the Que Stock splash screen.

As you look at Figure 14.1, notice the following elements:

- Graphic
- Status bar along the bottom
- No title bar (or minimize/maximize)
- Raised bevel border

Figure 14.1

The Que Stock splash screen.

What do we need to do to provide this functionality?

First, we must find a Java window that does not have a title bar. Luckily, the `java.awt.Window` class is exactly that: A `Window` is a top-level window with no borders and no menu bar. Table 14.1 shows the constructors for the `Window` class.

Table 14.1 **Window Constructors**

Constructor	Description
Window(Frame owner)	Constructs a new invisible window with the specified frame as its owner
Window(Window owner)	Constructs a new invisible window with the specified window as its owner

Basically all that is required to create a `Window` is either a `Frame` or another `Window` to act as its parent.

Next, we need a way to display the graphic. If you recall from Chapter 5, "User Interface Design with Swing," we talked about the `javax.swing.JLabel` class and its ability to display a graphic. There is no size constraint on the image it can display, and it does not have to display text (as it usually does). We already talked about its constructors, but Table 14.2 shows the two constructors we can use to display images only.

Table 14.2   JLabel **Constructors**

Constructor	*Description*
JLabel(Icon image)	Creates a JLabel instance with the specified image
JLabel(Icon image, int horizontalAlignment)	Creates a JLabel instance with the specified image and horizontal alignment

The JLabel class constructors accept an image class that supports the Icon interface. Throughout this book we have been using the ImageIcon class for this functionality as it supports loading GIF and JPEG image file formats. The Chapter 14 CD contents have the image file shown in Figure 14.1, but feel free to construct or customize this image file for your application—remember to save it as either a GIF or JPEG file!

Next, we need a status label for the bottom of the splash screen. A natural choice for this object is another instance of the JLabel class.

We are almost ready to go: We have our image file, our JLabel built from an ImageIcon that can display the image file, and a Window that can host both of them. The final step is to create the raised bevel border.

Java supports borders through the javax.swing.border.AbstractBorder base class. Several different types of borders are derived from this class:

- BevelBorder
- CompoundBorder
- EmptyBorder
- EtchedBorder
- LineBorder
- TitledBorder

Because most splash screen borders are bevel borders, I want to focus on that, but I urge you to look through the Java 2 SDK documentation under "AbstractBorder" and follow the links to the other border types.

The javax.swing.border.BevelBorder class constructors are shown in Table 14.3.

Table 14.3   `javax.swing.border.BevelBorder` **Constructors**

Constructor	Description
`BevelBorder(int bevelType)`	Creates a bevel border with the specified type whose colors will be derived from the background color of the component passed into the `paintBorder` method
`BevelBorder(int bevelType,` `Color highlight, Color shadow)`	Creates a bevel border with the specified type, highlight, and shadow colors

`BevelBorder(int bevelType,`
`Color highlightOuter, Color`
`highlightInner, Color shadowOuter,`
`Color shadowInner)`
	Creates a bevel border with the specified type, highlight, and shadow colors

You can specify a bevel type, which can be either `BevelBorder.RAISED` or `BevelBorder.LOWERED`. In addition, you can specify the colors of the border.

SplashScreen Class

I took the liberty of implementing this functionality into a class of its own: `SplashScreen`. Its constructor is shown in Table 14.4 and its methods are shown in Table 14.5.

Table 14.4   `SplashScreen` **Constructor**

Constructor	Description
`SplashScreen(String strImageFilename)`	Creates a new invisible SplashScreen object with image from the specified image filename

Table 14.5   `SplashScreen` **Methods**

Methods	Description
`void updateStatus(String strStatus)`	Updates the status message on the status bar below the image and makes the `SplashScreen` visible
`void openWindow()`	Makes the `SplashScreen` visible
`void closeWindow()`	Hides the `SplashScreen`

Take a look at Listing 14.2, which shows the complete implementation of the `SplashScreen` class.

Listing 14.2 `SplashScreen.java`

```
1:   package com.mcp.stock.tools;
2:
3:   import java.awt.*;
4:   import javax.swing.*;
5:   import javax.swing.border.*;
6:
7:   public class SplashScreen extends Window
8:   {
9:       // Create the status label
10:      protected JLabel labelStatus =
11:          new JLabel( "Hello, world!", JLabel.CENTER );
12:
13:      public SplashScreen( String strImageFilename )
14:      {
15:          super( new Frame() );
16:
17:          // Create our ImageIcon
18:          ImageIcon imageScreen = new ImageIcon( strImageFilename );
19:
20:          // Create a JLabel to hold the image
21:          JLabel labelImage = new JLabel( imageScreen, JLabel.CENTER );
22:
23:          // Create a JPanel to hold our JLabels
24:          JPanel panelImage = new JPanel( new BorderLayout() );
25:
26:          // Add the Image Icon JLabel to the image panel
27:          panelImage.add( labelImage, BorderLayout.CENTER );
28:
29:          // Add the status label to the panel
30:          panelImage.add( labelStatus, BorderLayout.SOUTH );
31:
32:          // Set the border type to be a BevelBorder
33:          panelImage.setBorder( new BevelBorder( BevelBorder.RAISED ) );
34:
35:          // Add the image panel to the Window
36:          add( panelImage );
37:
38:          // Compress the window to fit the size of the components
39:          pack();
40:
41:          // Center our window
42:          Dimension screenSize =
43:              Toolkit.getDefaultToolkit().getScreenSize();
44:          Dimension windowSize = getSize();
45:          this.setBounds( (screenSize.width - windowSize.width) / 2,
46:                          (screenSize.height - windowSize.height) / 2,
47:                          windowSize.width,
48:                          windowSize.height);
```

continues

Listing 14.2 continued

```
49:
50:          // Hide our Window
51:          setVisible( false );
52:      }
53:
54:      public void updateStatus( String strStatus )
55:      {
56:          labelStatus.setText( strStatus );
57:          setVisible( true );
58:      }
59:
60:      public void openWindow()
61:      {
62:          setVisible( true );
63:      }
64:
65:      public void closeWindow()
66:      {
67:          setVisible( false );
68:      }
69: }
```

In line 1 you can see that I created a new package added to the com.mcp.stock set of packages, com.mcp.stock.tools, and added the SplashScreen class to it.

Line 5 shows that we are importing the javax.swing.border package that contains the BevelBorder class that we will use later.

Line 7 shows the declaration of the SplashScreen class as a derivative of the java.awt.Window class; again, the Window class gives us a window with no border or menu bar.

Lines 10 and 11 create a new JLabel object to hold the status message for the status bar on the bottom of the SplashScreen.

Lines 13–52 define the constructor of the SplashScreen class. In line 13 you can see that it accepts a filename of an image in String format.

The first thing that the SplashScreen class does is call its superclass's constructor (java.awt.Window). If you recall, that constructor requires either a Window or Frame derivative. In line 15 we construct a new Frame object to be the parent of the SplashScreen window.

Next, in line 18 we construct an ImageIcon from the specified filename and pass that to the JLabel constructed in line 21.

14

Next we construct a new JPanel object with a BorderLayout layout manager to hold our image and status. It is important that we construct a JPanel for this task because when we get to adding a border, only the Swing classes support borders.

Line 27 adds the image JLabel to the center of the JPanel and line 30 adds the status JLabel to the bottom (BorderLayout.SOUTH) of the JPanel.

Line 33 constructs a new BevelBorder class with the raised bevel type (BevelBorder.RAISED) and sets it as the border for the JPanel using the setBorder() method.

Line 36 adds the JPanel to the Window and then line 39 compresses the window to fit the size of the components. The pack() method is responsible for just that—it computes the minimum size of the window that holds all its components.

Lines 41–48 center the Window on the screen as described earlier, and line 51 hides the Window for later use.

Lines 54–58 define the updateStatus() method. This method sets the text of the status JLabel by calling its setText() method (line 56), and then it makes the Window visible.

Lines 60–63 define the openWindow() method that actually only makes the window visible (line 62).

Finally, lines 65–68 define the closeWindow() method that makes the window invisible. You could modify this method to dispose of the window and free up memory by calling the Window class's dispose() method, but then it would need to be reconstructed if you wanted to show it again.

I will show you how to use this class later when we integrate it into the Stock Tracker application.

Toolbars

You should already be familiar with the concepts and uses of toolbars, but (to reiterate), a traditional toolbar is a collection of graphical buttons that perform some functionality (usually available through an additional menu item). In Java, a toolbar is not limited to simple graphical buttons; you can add anything to a toolbar that generates Action events.

Toolbars are constructed in Java using the JToolBar class. The JToolBar constructors are shown in Table 14.6.

Table 14.6   JToolBar **Constructors**

Constructor	Description
JToolBar()	Creates a new toolbar
JToolBar(int orientation)	Creates a new toolbar with the specified orientation (HORIZONTAL/VERTICAL)

A JToolBar can be constructed with a horizontal (default) or vertical orientation using the two constructors shown in Table 14.6. The JToolBar class also provides a set of methods to add items to the toolbar, modify its orientation, and control its floating property (whether the toolbar has to be docked on a side of the frame or is free to exist in a floating window). Take a look at Table 14.7 for some of the more popular JToolBar methods.

Table 14.7   JToolBar **Methods**

Method	Description
JButton add(Action a)	Adds a new JButton that dispatches the action
void addSeparator()	Appends a toolbar separator of default size to the end of the toolbar
void addSeparator(Dimension size)	Appends a toolbar separator to the end of the toolbar
int getOrientation()	Returns the current orientation of the toolbar
boolean isFloatable()	Returns true if the toolbar can be dragged out by the user
void remove(Component comp)	Removes the Component from the toolbar
void setFloatable(boolean b)	Sets whether the toolbar can be made to float
void setOrientation(int o)	Sets the orientation of the toolbar (HORIZONTAL/VERTICAL)

The basic usage of the JToolBar is as follows:

1. Create a JToolBar object.
2. Create one or more objects that generate action events (JButton for example).
3. Register an ActionListener directly to the buttons.
4. Add the buttons to the JToolBar using the add() and addSeparator() methods.
5. Set the JToolBar class's floatable property.
6. Add the JToolBar to the frame like any other component.

Listing 14.3 shows a code snippet of the basic implementation of a JToolBar.

Listing 14.3 `JToolBar` **Basic Example**

```
1:  public class MyClass extends JFrame implements ActionListener
2:  {
3:      // Create a new JToolBar
4:      JToolBar toolBar = new JToolBar();
5:
6:      // Create a couple JButtons
7:      JButton fileNew = new JButton( new ImageIcon( "fileNew.jpg" ) );
8:      JButton fileOpen = new JButton( new ImageIcon( "fileOpen.jpg" ) );
9:
10:      public MyClass()
11:      {
12:          ...
13:
14:          // Add MyClass as an ActionListener for these buttons
15:          fileNew.addActionListener( this );
16:          fileOpen.addActionListner( this );
17:
18:          // Add our buttons to the JToolBar
19:          toolBar.add( fileNew );
20:          toolBar.addSeparator();
21:          toolBar.add( fileOpen );
22:
23:          // Add the JToolBar to the JFrame
24:          getContentPane().setLayoutManager( new BorderLayout() );
25:          getContentPane().add( toolBar, BorderLayout.NORTH );
26:
27:          ...
28:      }
29:
30:      public void actionPerformed(ActionEvent e)
31:      {
32:          if( e.getSource() == fileNew )
33:          {
34:              ...
35:          }
36:          else if( e.getSource == fileOpen )
37:          {
38:              ...
39:          }
40:      }
41: }
```

StockToolBar

Listing 14.3 shows the basic implementation of a JToolBar, but I would like to have a class similar to the MainMenu class that takes care of all the details for the StockApplication. I want to create a class that I can create an instance of, add the StockApplication as a listener for, and then simply have to worry about handling messages. Enter the StockToolBar class.

First, what options do we want to have in our toolbar? Given that we do not have that many options implemented, I suggest the following six:

- New Portfolio
- New Stock
- Import Portfolio
- Export Portfolio
- Import Historical Data
- Export Historical Data

After we go through this example, I urge you to add toolbar options for whatever other functionality you want. I do not claim to be an artist (and as a matter of fact I claim to be less than an artist), so how can I be assured that my icons are understood by users? One basic premise in user interface design is that you can never anticipate how all users are going to interpret anything; a picture of a trashcan may look like a cookie jar to a person who saves money in cookie jars, and he may interpret it as meaning "Save" instead of "Delete."

At any point there is a reasonable solution to this problem: tooltips. The StockToolBar buttons will all have tooltips assigned to them to avoid confusion.

 A tooltip is a floating message that appears above a component. It provides additional information, such as a text description of a potentially ambiguous icon.

The StockToolBar is relatively simple; it has six public JButton objects as attributes that a parent class can compare in ActionListener events. Take a look at Table 14.8 for the StockToolBar attributes.

Table 14.8 **StockToolBar Attributes**

Attribute	Description
btnNewStock	New Stock button
btnNewPortfolio	New Portfolio button
btnImportPortfolio	Import Portfolio button
btnExportPortfolio	Export Portfolio button
btnImportHistory	Import Historical Data button
btnExportHistory	Export Historical Data button

The StockToolBar has only one empty constructor and a method to add an action listener to all the buttons in the class. Take a look at Table 14.9 for the StockToolBar methods.

14

Table 14.9 StockToolBar Methods

Method	Description
StockToolBar()	Constructs a new StockToolBar
void addActionListener (ActionListener listener)	Adds the specified listener as an ActionListener to all the JButtons defined in Table 14.8

Listing 14.4 shows the complete implementation of the StockToolBar class.

Listing 14.4 StockToolBar.java

```
1:  // Import the packages this class will use
2:  import java.awt.*;
3:  import java.awt.event.*;
4:
5:  import javax.swing.*;
6:  import javax.swing.event.*;
7:
8:  // public class StockToolBar
9:  public class StockToolBar extends JToolBar
10: {
11:     // Create the ToolBar buttons
12:     public JButton btnNewStock =
13:             new JButton( new ImageIcon( "newStock.jpg" ) );
14:     public JButton btnNewPortfolio =
15:             new JButton( new ImageIcon( "newPortfolio.jpg" ) );
16:     public JButton btnImportPortfolio =
17:             new JButton( new ImageIcon( "importPortfolio.jpg" ) );
18:     public JButton btnExportPortfolio =
19:             new JButton( new ImageIcon( "exportPortfolio.jpg" ) );
20:     public JButton btnImportHistory =
21:             new JButton( new ImageIcon( "importHistory.jpg" ) );
22:     public JButton btnExportHistory =
23:             new JButton( new ImageIcon( "exportHistory.jpg" ) );
24:
25:     // Constructor
26:     public StockToolBar()
27:     {
28:         // Add tooltips to qualify the button images
29:         btnNewStock.setToolTipText( "New Stock" );
30:         btnNewPortfolio.setToolTipText( "New Portfolio" );
31:         btnImportPortfolio.setToolTipText( "Import Portfolio" );
32:         btnExportPortfolio.setToolTipText( "Export Portfolio" );
33:         btnImportHistory.setToolTipText( "Import History" );
34:         btnExportHistory.setToolTipText( "Export History" );
```

continues

Listing 14.4   continued

```
35:
36:              // Add New Item buttons
37:              add( btnNewStock );
38:              add( btnNewPortfolio );
39:
40:              addSeparator();
41:
42:              // Add Import/Export Portfolio buttons
43:              add( btnImportPortfolio );
44:              add( btnExportPortfolio );
45:
46:              addSeparator();
47:
48:              // Add the Import/Export Historical Data buttons
49:              add( btnImportHistory );
50:              add( btnExportHistory );
51:      }
52:
53:      // public void addActionListener( ActionListener listener )
54:      public void addActionListener( ActionListener listener )
55:      {
56:          btnNewStock.addActionListener( listener );
57:          btnNewPortfolio.addActionListener( listener );
58:          btnImportPortfolio.addActionListener( listener );
59:          btnExportPortfolio.addActionListener( listener );
60:          btnImportHistory.addActionListener( listener );
61:          btnExportHistory.addActionListener( listener );
62:      }
63:
64:      // Main application entry point into this class
65:      public static void main( String[] args )
66:      {
67:          // Create a JFrame object
68:          JFrame frame = new JFrame( "Toolbar Example" );
69:
70:          StockToolBar toolBar = new StockToolBar();
71:
72:          frame.getContentPane().setLayout( new BorderLayout() );
73:          frame.getContentPane().add( toolBar, BorderLayout.NORTH );
74:
75:          // Resize our JFrame
76:          frame.setSize( 660, 450 );
77:
78:          // Make our JFrame visible
79:          frame.setVisible( true );
80:
81:          // Create a window listener to close our application when we
82:          // close our application
83:          frame.addWindowListener
84:              (
```

```
85:                  new WindowAdapter()
86:               {
87:                   public void windowClosing( WindowEvent e )
88:                   {
89:                       System.exit( 0 );
90:                   }
91:               }
92:           );
93:       }
94: }
```

Figure 14.2 shows the StockToolBar in its own sample application.

Figure 14.2

The StockToolBar in a
sample application.

Line 9 declares the StockToolBar class as a direct derivative of JToolBar.

Lines 12–23 create the set of JButton objects for the following functionality:

- New Stock
- New Portfolio
- Import Portfolio
- Export Portfolio
- Import Historical Data
- Export Historical Data

Each of these buttons has an associated JPEG image that is included on the CD.

Lines 26–51 define the StockToolBar constructor.

Lines 29–34 add tooltips to each of the JButton objects by calling the setToolTipText() method. This method is inherited from the javax.swing.JComponent class, so you can use it with any of the components derived from JComponent (which pretty much includes all the Swing components).

Lines 37 and 38 add the "New Stock" and "New Portfolio" JButton objects to the JToolBar.

Line 40 adds a separator after the "New Portfolio" JButton by calling the JToolBar class's addSeparator() method.

Lines 43 and 44 add the "Import Portfolio" and "Export Portfolio" JButton objects to the JToolBar and then another separator in line 46.

Lines 49 and 50 finish off the constructor by adding the "Import Historical Data" and "Export Historical Data" JButton objects to the JToolBar.

Lines 54–62 define the addActionListener() method that simply calls each of the JButton object's addActionListener() method.

Lines 65–94 define a main() method that can be used to test the StockToolBar class. It creates a new JFrame in line 68.

Then it creates a new StockToolBar object in line 70.

In line 72 it sets the layout manager to a BorderLayout and then adds the StockToolBar to the top of it in line 73.

The rest of the code brings up the application and ends it when the window closes.

So if you want to extend this class to add more functionality, here is what you have to do:

1. Create a fine-looking icon (as I did).
2. Create a new public JButton object (around line 24).
3. Add tooltip text to the JButton using the setToolTipText() method (line 35).
4. Add the JButton to the JToolBar somewhere in the constructor.
5. Add the new JButton to the addActionListner() method and tell it to add the specified action listener by calling the JButton object's addActionListener() method (as in lines 56–61).

Keyboard Mnemonics

One characteristic of professional applications is the ability to use keyboard mnemonics, or hot keys, as shortcuts to perform actions. For example, in Microsoft Word pressing Ctrl+S saves the current file (the same as choosing Save from the File menu or clicking the disk icon on the toolbar).

Keyboard mnemonics are available to all classes that are derived from javax.swing.AbstractButton characteristic through the setMnemonic() method. It has the prototypes shown in Table 14.10.

Table 14.10 `javax.swing.AbstractButton setMnemonic()` **Methods**

Method	Description
void setMnemonic(char mnemonic)	Specifies the mnemonic value
void setMnemonic(int mnemonic)	Sets the keyboard mnemonic on the current model

You can call setMnemonic() to add an ActionListener event for an individual key, for example "A" or "4", but it does not support key combinations such as Ctrl+S.

Luckily most of the keyboard combinations we want to use are shortcuts to menu items. The JMenuItem class offers an alternative to setMnemonic() that handles actual keystrokes, which can be a combination of keys. The setAccelerator() method provides this functionality and is prototyped as follows:

```
void setAccelerator(KeyStroke keyStroke)
```

The javax.swing.KeyStroke class represents a key being typed on the keyboard—it contains both a character code for the key and a modifier (Alt, Shift, Ctrl, Meta, or a combination). You can use the KeyStroke class to build a key combination and send it to the JMenuItem class's setAccelerator() method using the KeyStroke class's getKeyStroke() method (see Table 14.11).

Table 14.11   `javax.swing.KeyStroke getKeyStroke()` **Methods**

Method	Description
KeyStroke getKeyStroke(char keyChar)	Returns a shared instance of a keystroke that is activated when the key is pressed (that is, a KeyStroke for the KeyEvent.KEY_TYPED event).
KeyStroke getKeyStroke(int keyCode, int modifiers)	Returns a shared instance of a keystroke given a char code and a set of modifiers—the key is activated when it is pressed.
KeyStroke getKeyStroke(int keyCode,int modifiers, boolean onKeyRelease)	Returns a shared instance of a keystroke given a numeric keycode and a set of modifiers, specifying whether the key is activated when it is pressed or released.
KeyStroke getKeyStroke(String representation)	Returns a shared instance of a keystroke matching a string representation.

We are going to use the second getKeyStroke() method in Table 14.11 to build a KeyStroke with a key and a modifier. So how do you specify keys?

Well, the KeyEvent class has constants defined for every key imaginable, so I recommend that you peruse the KeyEvent class for more information. The basics that I want to mention here are the constants for letters and numbers:

- Numbers are represented by the constants VK_0 to VK_9
- Characters are represented by the constants VK_A through VK_Z

Recall that JMenuItem objects generate ActionEvent events. Thus, the modifier keys specified in the ActionEvent class are used in the KeyStroke getKeyStroke() methods. These are defined in Table 14.12.

Table 14.12 ActionEvent **Modifier Key Constants**

Key Code	Description
ALT_MASK	The Alt key modifier
CTRL_MASK	The Control key modifier
META_MASK	The Meta key modifier
SHIFT_MASK	The Shift key modifier

Now when we put this all together, we have the following code to add a keystroke to a menu item:

```
JMenuItem item = new JMenuItem( "My Menu Item" );

item.setAccelerator
    (
        KeyStroke.getKeyStroke( KeyEvent.VK_I,
                                ActionEvent.CTRL_MASK )
    );
```

This code snippet adds the accelerator key combination Ctrl+I to the item JMenuItem.

MainMenu Accelerators

Let's go ahead and add some accelerator keys to our MainMenu class for the following menu options:

- New, Portfolio (Alt+P)
- New, Stock (Alt+S)
- Quotes, Update (Alt+U)
- Graph, One Month (Alt+1)
- Graph, Three Months (Alt+3)
- Graph, Six Months (Alt+6)

When we have the accelerator keys in place, how does the user learn of them? Luckily for us, when you add an accelerator key to a menu item, the key combination appears in the menu next to the item. Take a look at Figure 14.3 to see a screen shot of the MainMenu File, New menu with accelerator keys active.

Figure 14.3

MainMenu File, New menu showing the accelerator keys.

Again you are free and encouraged to add more accelerator keys for the other menu options or change the ones for this example to suit your own needs. Take a look at Listing 14.5 for the updated source code to the MainMenu class.

Listing 14.5   MainMenu.java (Modified)

```
 1:     ...
 2:
 3:     public JMenuItem fileNewPortfolio =
 4:             new JMenuItem( "Portfolio" );
 5:     public JMenuItem fileNewStock =
 6:             new JMenuItem( "Stock" );
 7:     public JMenuItem quotesUpdate =
 8:             new JMenuItem( "Update" );
 9:     public JRadioButtonMenuItem graph1Month =
10:             new JRadioButtonMenuItem( "One Month", true );
11:     public JRadioButtonMenuItem graph3Months =
12:             new JRadioButtonMenuItem( "Three Months" );
13:     public JRadioButtonMenuItem graph6Months =
14:             new JRadioButtonMenuItem( "Six Months" );
15:
16:     ...
17:
18:     public MainMenu()
19:     {
20:         // Add some keyboard accelerators
21:         fileNewPortfolio.setAccelerator
22:         (
23:             KeyStroke.getKeyStroke( KeyEvent.VK_P,
24:                                     ActionEvent.ALT_MASK )
25:         );
26:
27:         fileNewStock.setAccelerator
28:         (
29:             KeyStroke.getKeyStroke( KeyEvent.VK_S,
```

continues

Listing 14.5   continued

```
30:                                        ActionEvent.ALT_MASK )
31:          );
32:
33:          quotesUpdate.setAccelerator
34:          (
35:              KeyStroke.getKeyStroke( KeyEvent.VK_U,
36:                                      ActionEvent.ALT_MASK )
37:          );
38:
39:          graph1Month.setAccelerator
40:          (
41:              KeyStroke.getKeyStroke( KeyEvent.VK_1,
42:                                      ActionEvent.ALT_MASK )
43:          );
44:
45:          graph3Months.setAccelerator
46:          (
47:              KeyStroke.getKeyStroke( KeyEvent.VK_3,
48:                                      ActionEvent.ALT_MASK )
49:          );
50:
51:          graph6Months.setAccelerator
52:          (
53:              KeyStroke.getKeyStroke( KeyEvent.VK_6,
54:                                      ActionEvent.ALT_MASK )
55:          );
56:          ...
57:      }
58:  ...
```

Lines 3–14 create the various JMenuItem objects and derivatives
(JradioButtonMenuItem).

Lines 18–57 define the MainMenu constructor.

Lines 21–25 set the accelerator Alt+P to the File, New, Portfolio menu option.

Lines 27–31 set the accelerator Alt+S to the File, New, Stock menu option.

Lines 33–37 set the accelerator Alt+U to the Quotes, Update menu option.

Lines 39–43 set the accelerator Alt+1 to the Graph, One Month menu option.

Lines 45–49 set the accelerator Alt+3 to the Graph, Three Months menu option.

Lines 51–55 set the accelerator Alt+6 to the Graph, Six Months menu option.

Integrating with the Stock Application

I have already shown you the new `StockToolBar` class and the modifications made to the `MainMenu` class, but now let me show you what is left to integrate these classes as well as our window centering code into the Stock Tracker application.

StockApplication

We have to make four changes to the `StockApplication` class:

- Add the `StockToolBar` to the `StockApplication` class
- Modify the `ActionListener` `actionPerformed()` method to respond to the `StockToolBar` commands
- Add our `SplashScreen` object
- Center the `StockApplication` on the screen at startup

Adding the `StockToolBar` to the `StockApplication`

First, we need to add the `StockToolBar` to the `StockApplication`. This is accomplished through the modifications shown in Listing 14.6.

Listing 14.6 `StockApplication.java` **(Modified to Add `StockToolBar`)**

```
 1:  public class StockApplication extends JFrame
 2:                          implements ActionListener,
 3:                                      ListSelectionListener,
 4:                                      StockUpdateListener
 5:  {
 6:      // Create our ToolBar
 7:      StockToolBar stockToolBar = new StockToolBar();
 8:
 9:      // Constructor
10:      public StockApplication()
11:      {
12:          // Add ourself as a listener to the ToolBar
13:          stockToolBar.addActionListener( this );
14:
15:          // Build a panel to hold the tab panel and portfolio
16:          // list panel
17:          JPanel panel = new JPanel( new BorderLayout() );
18:          panel.add( stockTabPanel, BorderLayout.NORTH );
19:          panel.add( portfolioListPanel, BorderLayout.SOUTH );
20:
21:          // Add the StockToolBar to the top of the display
22:          getContentPane().add( stockToolBar, BorderLayout.NORTH );
23:
24:          // Add our StockTabPanel and PortoflioListPanel
25:          getContentPane().add( panel, BorderLayout.SOUTH );
26:
27:          ...
28:      }
29:  }
```

In Listing 14.6 we create a new StockToolBar in line 7. Then we add the StockApplication as an ActionListener for the StockToolBar in line 13. To place the StockToolBar on the StockApplication, we have to create an auxiliary panel that holds the previous contents of the JFrame—the StockTabPanel and the PortfolioListPanel (lines 17–19)—add the StockToolBar to the top of the JFrame (line 22), and add this new JPanel to the bottom of the JFrame (line 25).

Modifying the actionPerformed() Method

The largest amount of work is with the actionPerformed() method. I am changing the way this method works slightly. Originally we extracted the Object that generated the event, cast it to a JMenuItem, and then compared it to the existing JMenuItem objects. Now we are going to skip the whole casting operation and just do the actual comparisons with the result of the ActionEvent.getSource() calls. This enables us to compare the Object to a JMenuItem and to a JButton without performing any casting or runtime type identification (determining the class of the item while the application is running).

Take a look at Listing 14.7 for the StockApplication class's modifications to the actionPerformed() method.

Listing 14.7 **StockApplication.java actionPerformed() Method (Modified)**

```
 1:  public void actionPerformed(ActionEvent e)
 2:  {
 3:      // Check for a timer event
 4:      if( e.getSource() == m_timerUpdateQuotes )
 5:      {
 6:          ...
 7:      }
 8:
 9:      // Find out which JMenuItem generated this event
10:      if( e.getSource() == mainMenu.fileNewPortfolioManager )
11:      {
12:          ...
13:      }
14:
15:      // File -> New -> Portfolio
16:      else if( e.getSource() == mainMenu.fileNewPortfolio ||
17:               e.getSource() == stockToolBar.btnNewPortfolio )
18:      {
19:          ...
20:      }
21:
22:      // File -> New ->Stock
23:      else if( e.getSource() == mainMenu.fileNewStock ||
24:               e.getSource() == stockToolBar.btnNewStock )
25:      {
26:          ...
```

14

```
27:        }
28:        else if( e.getSource() == mainMenu.fileOpen )
29:        {
30:            ...
31:        }
32:        else if ( e.getSource() == mainMenu.fileClose )
33:        {
34:            ...
35:        }
36:        else if ( e.getSource() == mainMenu.fileSave )
37:        {
38:            ...
39:        }
40:        else if ( e.getSource() == mainMenu.fileSaveAs )
41:        {
42:            ...
43:        }
44:        else if ( e.getSource() == mainMenu.fileSaveAll )
45:        {
46:            ...
47:        }
48:        else if ( e.getSource() == mainMenu.filePrint )
49:        {
50:            ...
51:        }
52:        else if ( e.getSource() == mainMenu.fileExit )
53:        {
54:            ...
55:        }
56:        else if ( e.getSource() == mainMenu.editCut )
57:        {
58:            ...
59:        }
60:        else if ( e.getSource() == mainMenu.editCopy )
61:        {
62:            ...
63:        }
64:        else if ( e.getSource() == mainMenu.editPaste )
65:        {
66:            ...
67:        }
68:        else if ( e.getSource() == mainMenu.editDelete )
69:        {
70:            ...
71:        }
72:
73:        // Portfolios -> Import
74:        else if ( e.getSource() == mainMenu.portfoliosImport ¦¦
75:                  e.getSource() == stockToolBar.btnImportPortfolio )
76:        {
```

continues

Listing 14.7 continued

```
77:        ...
78:      }
79:
80:      // Portfolios -> Export
81:      else if ( e.getSource() == mainMenu.portfoliosExport ¦¦
82:                   e.getSource() == stockToolBar.btnExportPortfolio )
83:      {
84:         ...
85:      }
86:
87:      else if ( e.getSource() == mainMenu.quotesUpdate )
88:      {
89:         ...
90:      }
91:      else if ( e.getSource() == mainMenu.quotesTimerOptions )
92:      {
93:         ...
94:      }
95:      else if ( e.getSource() == mainMenu.historyGetQuote )
96:      {
97:         ...
98:      }
99:      else if ( e.getSource() == mainMenu.historyEnableTracking )
100:     {
101:        ...
102:     }
103:
104:     // History -> Import
105:     else if ( e.getSource() == mainMenu.historyImport ¦¦
106:                  e.getSource() == stockToolBar.btnImportHistory )
107:     {
108:        ...
109:     }
110:
111:     // History -> Export
112:     else if ( e.getSource() == mainMenu.historyExport ¦¦
113:                  e.getSource() == stockToolBar.btnExportHistory )
114:     {
115:        ...
116:     }
117:     else if ( e.getSource() == mainMenu.graph1Week )
118:     {
119:        ...
120:     }
121:     else if ( e.getSource() == mainMenu.graph1Month )
122:     {
123:        ...
124:     }
125:     else if ( e.getSource() == mainMenu.graph3Months )
126:     {
```

```
127:        ...
128:    }
139:    else if ( e.getSource() == mainMenu.graph6Months )
130:    {
131:        ...
132:    }
133:    else if ( e.getSource() == mainMenu.graphOpen )
134:    {
135:        ...
136:    }
137:    else if ( e.getSource() == mainMenu.graphClose )
138:    {
139:        ...
140:    }
141:    else if ( e.getSource() == mainMenu.helpContents )
142:    {
143:        ...
144:    }
145:    else if ( e.getSource() == mainMenu.helpAbout )
146:    {
147:        ...
148:    }
149:}
```

You can see that all the comparisons in the `actionPerformed()` method are now made directly with the result of the `ActionEvent.getSource()` method call. The `StockToolBar` specific event handlers are found in lines 16 and 17 when a comparison is made for the File, New, Portfolio menu option. In this case it compares the object that generated the event with the `MainMenu.fileNewPortfolio` option and the `StockToolBar.btnNewPortfolio` object. This statement is read as follows: If the item that generated the event is either the File, New, Portfolio menu option or the toolbar's New Portfolio button, then perform the following actions. The logical OR operator "¦¦" returns `true` if either of the two conditions are `true`.

Lines 23 and 24 compare the File, New, Stock menu option and the New Stock toolbar button.

Lines 73 and 74 compare the Portfolios, Import menu option and the Import Portfolio toolbar button.

Lines 81 and 82 compare the Portfolios, Export menu option and the Export Portfolio toolbar button.

Lines 105 and 106 compare the History, Import menu option and the Import Historical Data toolbar button.

Lines 112 and 113 compare the History, Export menu option and the Export
Historical Data toolbar button.

Adding a Splash Screen

The next change to the StockApplication class is to add the SplashScreen object we
created earlier. I made a modification to the StockApplication constructor so that it
creates a new SplashScreen object when it starts up and then closes it when the constructor ends. Because this is such a short time frame, I added a 5-second delay at the
end of the constructor so that users can see the SplashScreen we spent so much time
working on earlier in the chapter (not to mention my excursion into building the
image for the SplashScreen!).

Listing 14.8 shows the modifications made to the StockApplication constructor.

Listing 14.8   **StockApplication.java SplashScreen Modifications**

```
 1: // Constructor
 2: public StockApplication()
 3: {
 4:     ...
 5:
 6:     // Create a SplashScreen
 7:     SplashScreen splash = new SplashScreen( "QStock.jpg" );
 8:     splash.updateStatus( "Loading QStock v1.0..." );
 9:
10:     ...
11:
12:     // Sleep for 5 seconds to show the SplashScreen
13:     try
14:     {
15:         String strUpdate = new String( "Loading QStock v1.0" );
16:         for( int i=0; i<5; i++ )
17:         {
18:             strUpdate = strUpdate + ".";
19:             splash.updateStatus( strUpdate );
20:             Thread.sleep( 1000 );
21:         }
22:     }
23:     catch( InterruptedException e )
24:     {
25:         // Just continue
26:     }
27:
28:     // Close the SplashScreen
29:     splash.closeWindow();
30:
31:     ...
32:}
```

Line 7 creates a new SplashScreen object with the image in the file "Qstock.jpg," and line 8 displays it with the status message "Loading Qstock v1.0..." by calling its updateStatus() method.

The constructor loads all its components and then right before it makes itself visible, Lines 12–26 start modifying the SplashScreen. It creates a new String in line 15 and then sets up a for loop in line 16 that will run five times. The first thing it does is append a period to the end of the update string (line 18), and then it calls the SplashScreen class's updateStatus() method with the new String. Finally it sleeps for 1000 milliseconds (1 second) by calling Thread.sleep(1000) in line 20. If the sleep is interrupted for any reason, an InterruptedException occurs and the constructor continues.

Finally, in line 29 the constructor closes the SplashScreen by calling its closeWindow() method.

Centering the StockApplication Onscreen

The last thing we said we wanted to do with the StockApplication was to center it on the screen. You already saw the code to do this earlier in the chapter, so you simply have to add it to the StockApplication constructor. Take a look at Listing 14.9 for a review of this code.

Listing 14.9   StockApplication.java **Centering Modifications**

```
 1: // Constructor
 2: public StockApplication()
 3: {
 4:     ...
 5:     // Center our window
 6:     Dimension screenSize = Toolkit.getDefaultToolkit().getScreenSize();
 7:     Dimension windowSize = getSize();
 8:     setBounds( (screenSize.width - windowSize.width) / 2,
 9:                (screenSize.height - windowSize.height) / 2,
10:                windowSize.width,
11:                windowSize.height);
12:
13:     // Make the StockApplication JFrame visible
14:     setVisible( true );
15:     ...
16: }
```

Resizing

One thing that I started to notice when we added the toolbar was that the height of the Stock Tracker application is starting to exceed the height of a standard 800×600 display. As a matter of fact, before you can launch the StockApplication class, you must resize it to larger than 600 pixels high to see both the toolbar and the tabs of the StockTabPanel. All the sizing information occurs inside the constructor of the individual classes, and Table 14.13 shows the new sizes of the various classes.

Table 14.13 `StockApplication` **Component Sizes**

Component	New Size
GraphTabPanel	Set `tickerListPanel` to 120×200 and `stockGraphPanel` to 480×200
StockTablePanel	Set the size to 620×240
StockApplication	Set the size to 680×560

Summary

We covered some pretty interesting aesthetic elements to user interfaces in this chapter. We talked about the following topics:

- Centering an application on the screen
- Adding a splash screen to the startup of a Java application
- Adding a toolbar to an application
- Adding keyboard mnemonics and accelerators to an application

We finished the chapter by taking the time to add this functionality to the Stock Tracker application.

What's Next?

The next chapter is going to expose you to two of the more advanced and evolving Java technologies: JavaBeans and the Java Database Connectivity API (JDBC), and show you where you could apply them to the Stock Tracker application.

Chapter 15

JavaBeans and JDBC

Up to this point in the book, we have talked extensively about individual topics and technologies that we implemented directly into the Stock Tracker application. Now I want to introduce you to two more advanced technologies that we do not have room in this book to implement, but that you might consider exploring on your own. The goal for this chapter is to introduce you to these two technologies, explain a little about how you use them, and provide suggestions about where you would implement them in the Stock Tracker application.

I am going to talk about the following two technologies:

- JavaBeans
- The Java Database Connectivity (JDBC) API

JavaBeans

The current paradigm companies are using when developing software is known as *software component modeling*. The premise is to break an application down into individual reusable components and build the application from these components. These components live as separate entities within a container and provide interfaces to facilitate communications both between the container and component as well as between individual components. This method of application development lends itself nicely to software reuse and supports true object orientation.

Two popular component modeling implementations are Microsoft's Component Object Model (COM) and the Common Object Request Broker Architecture (CORBA). These models are responsible for defining the communication mechanism between components. Furthermore, these object models support the distribution of components across machine boundaries throughout a network, thus creating an application that lives on up to hundreds of computers.

JavaBeans are Java's answer to a software component model. They can be used for two purposes:

- A bean can be used as a building block in composing applications; for example, an AWT button may be built as a bean for use as part of an application.
- A bean can be an entire application that could be presented on a Web page.

The JavaBeans Specification defines a Java bean as "a reusable software component that can be manipulated visually in a builder tool" (builder tools may include Web page builders, visual application builders, GUI layout builders, or server application builders). The purpose of a builder tool is to provide a simple platform to integrate components and construct an application (or applet).

JavaBeans offer support for the following functionality:

- Introspection—So that a builder tool can analyze how a bean works
- Customization—So that the user of a builder tool can customize the appearance and behavior of a bean
- Events—A communication mechanism between a bean and its host
- Properties—For both customization and programmatic use
- Persistence—So that a bean can save and reload its state

JavaBeans are composed of three important features: properties, events, and methods.

 Properties are named attributes of a bean that can be accessed via get and set methods. Properties in beans are functionally similar to the class properties we have been discussing thus far in this book: The StockData class has a property representing its stock symbol and is accessed through the getStockSymbol() and setStockSymbol() methods. This paradigm holds true with JavaBeans.

 Methods are standard Java class methods that you are used to using. All public methods of a bean are exposed by default by a mechanism that is provided to export only a subset of these methods.

Events provide a mechanism for a bean to notify its host that something interesting has happened. The implementation of bean events follows the standard event model where a component can register as an event listener with an event source.

As you can see, JavaBeans are functionally equivalent to standard Java classes with respect to their properties, events, and methods, but they provide much more. They define the interface components use to communicate through, and they provide both a design-time and runtime aspect. The design-time aspect is the visual configuration provided when working from within one of the aforementioned builder tools. The runtime aspect is displayed in the container application while it is running (if it has a visual runtime display).

JavaBeans can have a visible runtime display or can be invisible; invisible beans have no graphical user interface but can still possess properties, methods, and events, and they can persist. Typically, invisible beans are used to assist applications at runtime or are used in server components where there is no graphical user interface to speak of. Invisible beans do, however, usually provide a visual design-time interface to use for configuration from within a builder tool.

Speaking of this runtime versus design-time representation, what do these actually look like? Well, the runtime representation of a bean is usually the functional aspect that you are using the bean for. For example, if you were using a bean that displays a calendar in your application, the calendar would be the runtime representation of the bean. The design-time aspect is typically represented by a property sheet, which is nothing more than a list of the configurable properties displayed in a data entry type fashion, usually set within multiple property tabs. Beans can, however, implement more custom design-time representations, such as a wizard configuration, through what the JavaBeans specification calls customizers.

The JavaBeans API

Java provides a JavaBeans API that consists of a collection of smaller APIs dedicated to specific JavaBean functionality. The main functionality provided in these APIs is represented by the following categories:

- Merging user interface elements
- Persistence
- Event handling
- Introspection
- Builder tool support

The API that provides user interface merging support allows a component to merge its configuration elements with its container. If a container supports menus and toolbars, the user interface merging APIs provide a mechanism for the JavaBean to merge its own menus and toolbars with existing ones in the container.

Persistence is a mechanism by which a component can store and retrieve its configuration from within the context of an individual container application. Java itself provides a default mechanism for persistence, but the persistence APIs allow developers to build more elaborate persistence solutions.

Event handling follows the standard Java event model; JavaBeans use the same interfaces and thus ensure consistency with other language elements.

Introspection is an interesting topic as it defines the mechanism through which components make their internal structure available to a developer at design time. It is through the introspection APIs that builder tools can query the internal state of a component and gain access to the interfaces, methods, and properties that compose the component. There are two types of introspection APIs: low-level APIs and high-level APIs. The low-level APIs give builder tools direct access to the component's internal structures, which is something you would really want to hide from a developer constructing an application from within a builder tool. The high-level APIs, however, use the low-level APIs to determine the aspects of the component that are exported for manipulation by the component user. Thus, although the builder tools use both APIs, all information provided to the user from a builder tool is gathered from the high-level APIs.

Finally, there are APIs that provide support for builder tools; these provide the overhead necessary for editing and configuring components at design time. Builder tools use these APIs to allow users to visually lay out and configure beans in design time while building an application. Now the visual editing functionality provided by components is purposely removed from the context of the component itself and exists solely for use during design time. JavaBeans are very advanced in the context that after their design-time configuration, their runtime component can be compacted by including only the functionality selected during the design time; other functionality can be omitted from the component, which can reduce its size significantly.

The JavaBeans API is a topic that warrants a book of its own, and if you look hard enough, you will have no problem finding one. At the time this book was printed, Sun Microsystems does provide a 114-page specification document on its World Wide Web site free of charge that is very useful. Furthermore, it is very readable, so if JavaBeans intrigues you, I would highly recommend reading it!

See the JavaBeans Web site at the following URL:

`http://java.sun.com/beans`

JavaBeans could be used all throughout the Stock Tracker application: Each component—the stock table, the graph, the portfolio list, and so on—could be designed as JavaBeans. Furthermore, you could have used a builder tool to construct the Stock Tracker application and insert each of the components as JavaBeans. This would be an interesting way to implement the Stock Tracker application, but it would have required too much Java knowledge before you could do anything meaningful with it. I challenge you to try to implement the Stock Tracker application as a JavaBeans-based application if you are interested. It would teach you all about JavaBeans and component software development!

JDBC

The Java Database Connectivity (JDBC) API provides an interface to access a wide range of data sources, including Structured Query Language (SQL)-based databases all the way down to flat files (text files). Because of its popular acceptance throughout the Java industry, the JDBC API has become part of the core Java API and is now at version 2.0.0.

Microsoft provided a standard known as the Open Database Connectivity (ODBC) interface several years back that provided an invaluable service to application developers wanting to programmatically access a relational database using a vendor-neutral API. Before an open standard was developed, an application developer had to either obtain source code libraries used to talk to specific database systems or write source code that knew how to talk to each and every database the application could support. With the advent of the Open Database Connectivity interface, database developers provided generic ODBC drivers used to talk to their respective databases, and then application developers talked to ODBC, which routed the request. Developing a database-aware application and configuring it to work with a database was simple: The user installs a database and sets up a data source (a name that ODBC uses to find the database) and then points the database application to that data source.

Java extends the Open Database Connectivity model through its own Java Database Connectivity (JDBC) model, which not only supports ODBC-based databases but provides a truly platform-independent model for all operating systems and databases that want to develop their own JDBC interface.

Let me give you a little background on JDBC and programmatic database access in general. JDBC provides four primary classes that are used for each phase of database access:

- DriverManager
- Connection
- PreparedStatement
- ResultSet allows

The DriverManager class loads and configures a database driver on your client.

The Connection class performs connection and authentication to a database server.

The PreparedStatement class sends SQL statements to the database engine for pre-processing and eventually execution.

The ResultSet class allows for the inspection of results from SELECT statements.

EXCURSION

Structured Query Language (SQL)

Structured Query Language, or SQL, is the standard language used to talk to databases. Sometimes database documentation will refer to SELECT statements, which map to a query statement on a database.

Let me first give you a little database primer. A database is a collection of tables (among other things) built with rows of data. A table looks quite similar to the JTable that we used in the StockTablePanel earlier: It has a set of columns with each one having a specific data type, and the visual representation would appear much like a JTable. Internally a table is defined simply as a set of columns where one (or a combination of one or more) is considered a "primary key." A primary key is the distinguishing element that makes each row in a given table unique.

These tables can be created, modified, deleted, or queried using a language known as Structured Query Language, or SQL. A query statement is sometimes referred to as a SELECT statement due to its SQL representation. The SELECT statement in SQL is used to select one or more rows from one or more tables with specified criteria. The format for a simple SELECT statement is as follows:

```
SELECT [COLUMNS] FROM [TABLE] WHERE [CRITERIA]
```

Where [COLUMNS] represents the columns you want displayed in your result set (the result of the query), [TABLE] represents the table you want to gather the columns from, and [CRITERIA] represents the specific criteria each row in the table is evaluated by before displaying it in the result set.

Let me set up an example for you here. Consider a phone book database that has a table called HomePhoneNumbers that has two fields: Name and PhoneNumber. The primary key is the person's name. The simplest query statement is to retrieve all data from the HomePhoneNumbers table as follows:

```
SELECT * FROM HomePhoneNumbers
```

The asterisk is used as a wild card and tells the database to return all columns. The output of this statement might look something like the following:

Name	PhoneNumber
Linda Haines	(999-555-9998
Steve Haines	(999)555-9999

Now suppose you wanted to find the row in the table for me, Steve Haines. You could accomplish that with the following query statement:

```
SELECT * FROM HomePhoneNumbers WHERE Name='Steve Haines'
```

This would have output that looked something like the following:

Name	PhoneNumber
Steve Haines	(999)555-9999

Finally, consider the fact that we know who we want and just want to retrieve Linda's phone number. That query would look like the following:

```
SELECT PhoneNumber FROM HomePhoneNumbers WHERE Name='Linda Haines'
```

And the result of that query might look like the following:

PhoneNumber
(999)555-9998

SQL provides similar statements to insert new records into a table (`INSERT INTO`), to update a table (`UPDATE`), to delete rows from a table (`DELETE`), and to create new tables (`CREATE TABLE`). Structured Query Language is very powerful, and you would be surprised as to how involved `SELECT` statements can get when you start combining data from multiple tables (`JOIN`) and embedding `SELECT` statements. If you are interested in databases, I would highly recommend picking up a book on SQL and on relational database design.

To summarize, the `DriverManager` class is used to find a database, the `Connection` class is used to connect to a database, the `PreparedStatement` class is used to send SQL statements to the database, and the `ResultSet` class is used to browse the results of your query.

To begin using JDBC, you are going to need a driver for your database. Your database should come with a JDBC driver or an ODBC driver. If it already has its JDBC driver, you are set; otherwise, you can use an ODBC-JDBC bridge to make use of the ODBC drivers. Furthermore, you may be able to use a third-party JDBC driver written specifically for your database. You can find links to JDBC drivers at Sun Microsystems' Web site at the following URL:

```
http://java.sun.com/products/jdbc/drivers.html
```

When you have this `DriverManager`, you must load its class in your class by using the following statement:

```
Class.forName( "driverclassname" );
```

Or if you were using the i-net Software driver to connect to a SQL Server 7.0 database, the statement would appear as follows:

```
Class.forName( "com.inet.tds.TdsDriver" );
```

Furthermore, if you already have an ODBC data source configured on your computer, you can use the JDBC-ODBC bridge driver provided by Java; that class is loaded as follows:

```
Class.forName( "sun.jdbc.odbc.JdbcOdbcDriver" );
```

Then you use the `DriverManager` class to establish a connection with the database through its `getConnection()` method. The `getConnection()` method prototypes are specified in Table 15.1.

Table 15.1   `DriverManager getConnection()` **Methods**

Method	Description
getConnection(String url)	Attempts to establish a connection to the given database URL
getConnection(String url, Properties info)	Attempts to establish a connection to the given database URL
getConnection(String url, String user, String password)	Attempts to establish a connection to the given database URL

The database is specified by a `String` object in URL format, and an optional username and password can be combined with the connection request. The `getConnection()` method returns a `Connection` object. For example, if you were using the i-net Software's SQL Server 7.0 database driver, the connection would look something like the following:

```
Connection conn = DriverManager.getConnection
(
    "jdbc:inetdae:localhost:8889?database=dbname&language=us_english",
    "sa",
    ""
);
```

The URL is composed of the main protocol `jdbc`, the subprotocol `inetdae`, the host name `localhost`, the port `8889`, and the database name `dbname`. The connection is made as user name "sa" and password "". Again, all this information is specific to the driver you decide to use.

If you already have a database set up using ODBC, you have the option of using the JDBC-ODBC bridge driver provided by Java to connect to an existing data source. When the ODBC data source is configured, connecting to it is performed as follows:

```
Connection conn = DriverManager.getConnection
(
    "jdbc:odbc:datasourcename"
    "user"
    "password"
}
```

The getConnection() method throws an SQLException exception if an error occurs trying to connect to the database, so you are responsible to catch that exception.

Connection is actually an interface that the JDBC specific driver implements. The main method you invoke on it is the prepareStatement() method. This method creates a PreparedStatement object that can be sent to the database. The prepareStatement() method prototypes are shown in Table 15.2.

Table 15.2   `Connection prepareStatement()` **Methods**

Method	*Description*
prepareStatement(String sql)	Creates a PreparedStatement object for sending parameterized SQL statements to the database
prepareStatement(String sql, int resultSetType, int resultSetConcurrency)	For version 2.0; creates a PreparedStatement object that will generate ResultSet objects with the given type and concurrency

The following is a sample prepareStatement() call to retrieve all records in the HomePhoneNumbers table:

```
try
{
    PreparedStatement preparedStatement = conn.prepareStatement
            (
                "SELECT * FROM HomePhoneNumbers"
            );
}
catch ( SQLException e )
{
    System.out.println ( e.messageString() );
}
```

Again PreparedStatement is an interface that the JDBC specific driver will implement. When you have the PreparedStatement built, you can execute the query using one of its execute methods, shown in Table 15.3.

15

Table 15.3   `PreparedStatement execute` **Methods**

Method	Description
`boolean execute()`	Executes any kind of SQL statement
`ResultSet executeQuery()`	Executes the SQL query in this `PreparedStatement` object and returns the result set generated by the query
`int executeUpdate()`	Executes the SQL INSERT, UPDATE, or DELETE statement in this `PreparedStatement` object

To query a database, you would call the `executeQuery()` method, which returns an object that implements the `ResultSet` interface. The following shows how you would execute the aforementioned query:

```
ResultSet rs = preparedStatement.executeQuery();
```

Again the `ResultSet` interface will be implemented by one of the JDBC specific driver classes. The `ResultSet` interface is quite large, but the navigation through rows in the table is straightforward. Take a look at Table 15.4 for the list of `ResultSet` navigation methods.

Table 15.4   `ResultSet` **Navigation Methods**

Method	Description
`boolean first()`	JDBC 2.0 Moves the cursor to the first row in the result set
`boolean isFirst()`	JDBC 2.0 Indicates whether the cursor is on the first row of the result set
`boolean isLast()`	JDBC 2.0 Indicates whether the cursor is on the last row of the result set
`boolean last()`	JDBC 2.0 Moves the cursor to the last row in the result set
`void moveToCurrentRow()`	JDBC 2.0 Moves the cursor to the remembered cursor position, usually the current row
`void moveToInsertRow()`	JDBC 2.0 Moves the cursor to the insert row
`boolean next()`	Moves the cursor down one row from its current position
`boolean previous()`	JDBC 2.0 Moves the cursor to the previous row in the result set

When you have the `ResultSet` object initialized, you can traverse the list using the following syntax:

```
rs.first();
while( rs.isLast() == false )
{
    // Do stuff with the data
```

```
    // Move to the next row in the table
    rs.next();
}
```

The `ResultSet` interface defines a set of methods referred to as the `getXXX` methods by the JDBC community. These methods are used for retrieving specified datatypes from either a named or indexed column in the current row. You can retrieve data of various types from integers to arrays to strings. Peruse Table 15.5 for the various `getXXX` methods.

15

Table 15.5 `ResultSet getXXX` **Methods**

Method	*Description*
`Array getArray(int i)`	JDBC 2.0 Gets a SQL ARRAY value from the current row of this `ResultSet` object
`Array getArray(String colName)`	JDBC 2.0 Gets a SQL ARRAY value in the current row of this `ResultSet` object
`InputStream getAsciiStream(int columnIndex)`	Gets the value of a column in the current row as a stream of ASCII characters
`InputStream getAsciiStream(String columnName)`	Gets the value of a column in the current row as a stream of ASCII characters
`BigDecimal getBigDecimal(int columnIndex)`	JDBC 2.0 Gets the value of a column in the current row as a `java.math.BigDecimal` object with full precision
`BigDecimal getBigDecimal(String columnName)`	JDBC 2.0 Gets the value of a column in the current row as a `java.math.BigDecimal` object with full precision
`InputStream getBinaryStream(int columnIndex)`	Gets the value of a column in the current row as a stream of uninterpreted bytes
`InputStream getBinaryStream (String columnName)`	Gets the value of a column in the current row as a stream of uninterpreted bytes
`Blob getBlob(int i)`	JDBC 2.0 Gets a BLOB value in the current row of this `ResultSet` object

continues

Table 15.5   continued

Method	Description
Blob getBlob(String colName)	JDBC 2.0 Gets a BLOB value in the current row of this ResultSet object
boolean getBoolean(int columnIndex)	Gets the value of a column in the current row as a Java boolean
boolean getBoolean(String columnName)	Gets the value of a column in the current row as a Java boolean
byte getByte(int columnIndex)	Gets the value of a column in the current row as a Java byte
byte getByte(String columnName)	Gets the value of a column in the current row as a Java byte
byte[] getBytes(int columnIndex)	Gets the value of a column in the current row as a Java byte array
byte[] getBytes(String columnName)	Gets the value of a column in the current row as a Java byte array
Reader getCharacterStream(int columnIndex)	JDBC 2.0 Gets the value of a column in the current row as a java.io.Reader
Reader getCharacterStream(String columnName)	JDBC 2.0 Gets the value of a column in the current row as a java.io.Reader
Clob getClob(int i)	JDBC 2.0 Gets a CLOB value in the current row of this ResultSet object
Clob getClob(String colName)	JDBC 2.0 Gets a CLOB value in the current row of this ResultSet object
int getConcurrency()	JDBC 2.0 Returns the concurrency mode of this result set
String getCursorName()	Gets the name of the SQL cursor used by this ResultSet
Date getDate(int columnIndex)	Gets the value of a column in the current row as a java.sql.Date object
Date getDate(int columnIndex, Calendar cal)	JDBC 2.0 Gets the value of a column in the current row as a java.sql.Date object
Date getDate(String columnName)	Gets the value of a column in the current row as a java.sql.Date object

Method	Description
`Date getDate(String columnName, Calendar cal)`	Gets the value of a column in the current row as a `java.sql.Date` object
`double getDouble(int columnIndex)`	Gets the value of a column in the current row as a Java `double`
`double getDouble(String columnName)`	Gets the value of a column in the current row as a Java `double`
`int getFetchDirection()`	JDBC 2.0 Returns the fetch direction for this result set
`int getFetchSize()`	JDBC 2.0 Returns the fetch size for this result set
`float getFloat(int columnIndex)`	Gets the value of a column in the current row as a Java `float`
`float getFloat(String columnName)`	Gets the value of a column in the current row as a Java `float`
`int getInt(int columnIndex)`	Gets the value of a column in the current row as a Java `int`
`int getInt(String columnName)`	Gets the value of a column in the current row as a Java `int`
`long getLong(int columnIndex)`	Gets the value of a column in the current row as a Java `long`
`long getLong(String columnName)`	Gets the value of a column in the current row as a Java `long`
`ResultSetMetaData getMetaData()`	Retrieves the number, types, and properties of a `ResultSet`'s columns
`Object getObject(int columnIndex)`	Gets the value of a column in the current row as a Java object
`Object getObject(int i, Map map)`	JDBC 2.0 Returns the value of a column in the current row as a Java object
`Object getObject(String columnName)`	Gets the value of a column in the current row as a Java object
`Object getObject(String colName, Map map)`	JDBC 2.0 Returns the value in the specified column as a Java object

continues

15

Table 15.5 continued

Method	Description
Ref getRef(int i)	JDBC 2.0 Gets a REF(<structured-type>) column value from the current row
Ref getRef(String colName)	JDBC 2.0 Gets a REF(<structured-type>) column value from the current row
int getRow()	JDBC 2.0 Retrieves the current row number
short getShort(int columnIndex)	Gets the value of a column in the current row as a Java short
short getShort(String columnName)	Gets the value of a column in the current row as a Java short
Statement getStatement()	JDBC 2.0 Returns the Statement that produced this ResultSet object
String getString(int columnIndex)	Gets the value of a column in the current row as a Java String
String getString(String columnName)	Gets the value of a column in the current row as a Java String
Time getTime(int columnIndex)	Gets the value of a column in the current row as a java.sql.Time object
Time getTime(int columnIndex, Calendar cal)	Gets the value of a column in the current row as a java.sql.Time object
Time getTime(String columnName)	Gets the value of a column in the current row as a java.sql.Time object
Time getTime(String columnName, Calendar cal)	Gets the value of a column in the current row as a java.sql.Time object
Timestamp getTimestamp(int columnIndex)	Gets the value of a column in the current row as a java.sql.Timestamp object
Timestamp getTimestamp(int columnIndex, Calendar cal)	Gets the value of a column in the current row as a java.sql.Timestamp object

Method	Description
`Timestamp getTimestamp(String columnName)`	Gets the value of a column in the current row as a `java.sql.Timestamp` object
`Timestamp getTimestamp(String columnName, Calendar cal)`	Gets the value of a column in the current row as a java.sql.Timestamp object

From our previous example, we could retrieve the name of the person in our HomePhoneNumber table with the following statement:

```
String strName = rs.getString( "Name" );
```

Finally, when you are done with a `ResultSet`, you call its `close()` method:

```
void close()
```

The `close()` method releases the `ResultSet` object's database and JDBC resources immediately instead of waiting for this to happen when it is automatically closed.

The JDBC API is very large and there are complete books on the subject, along with the Java 2 SDK documentation, which I recommend you read.

You might wonder how this is applicable to the Stock Tracker application. There are many uses for database interactivity with a stock application, but the best use I can find for it (and something that I am going to add into my copy of the Stock Tracker application later) is to retrieve detailed stock information from the Internet and populate that into a database. Then you can use database queries to analyze the data and search for specific criteria.

Summary

We covered an incredible amount of material in this book in a relatively short number of pages. To close out this chapter (and this book), I want to give you a quick review of the technologies this book has exposed you to.

We first started talking about user interface elements found in the Abstract Window Toolkit (AWT) in Chapter 4, "User Interface Design with AWT." Specifically we talked about the following components:

- Labels
- Buttons
- Text fields

- Text areas
- Check boxes
- Choice lists

Then we moved through a discussion on layout managers and how they are used to build user interfaces and arrange AWT components:

- Flow layout
- Grid layout
- Border layout
- Card layout
- Grid bag layout

In Chapter 5, "User Interface Design with Swing," we moved into more advanced user interfaces and talked about the Swing components. We spent some time talking about the internal structure of a Swing application and then specifically we talked about the following components:

- `JLabel`
- `JTextField`
- `JTextArea`
- `JButton`
- `JRadioButton`
- `JCheckBox`
- `JList`
- `JTable`
- `JTabbedPane`
- `JScrollPane`
- `JSplitPane`

In Chapter 6, "Handling Events in Your User Interface," we moved into the Swing event model where I talked about the internal structure of Swing events and event listeners. Then you learned about the following general event categories:

- Action events
- Adjustment events
- Focus events
- Item events
- Keyboard events

- Mouse events
- Mouse motion events
- Window events

Then, in Chapter 7, "Building the Stock Tracker User Interface," we built the entire Stock Tracker user interface where you used all that you learned in Chapters 5 and 6 and you were exposed to several more Swing components, specifically the following:

- `JMenuBar`
- `JMenu`
- `JMenuItem`
- `Graphics2D`

Furthermore, you learned how to handle component-specific events that extend beyond the general event categories.

In Chapter 8, "Implementing Portfolios," we implemented the portfolio aspect of the Stock Tracker application through which you learned about data structures and file manipulation using the following two classes:

- `FileReader`
- `FileWriter`

In Chapter 9, "Implementing the Stock Quote Retriever," we implemented the stock quote retriever, which introduced you to downloading data from the Internet using the following classes:

- `URL`
- `URLConnection`
- `BufferedReader`

Then we talked about parsing HTML text, and you were introduced to the power of the `StringTokenizer` class.

Chapter 10, "Retrieving Stock Quotes on a Fixed Time Interval," talked about using a timer in your application and the Java `Timer` class. Furthermore we implemented a custom dialog box derived straight from `JDialog` to prompt the user for timer options.

Chapter 11, "Implementing the Historical Data Manager," sent you back to the Internet to download historical stock data. Through this chapter you learned more about data parsing and again more about the `StringTokenizer` class; but by this point, you should have grown very attached to the power Java has to offer.

In Chapter 12, "Graphing Historical Data," we started graphing the historical data and you were introduced both to graphing and painting concepts as well as to the basic uses of the Java 2D API.

Next, in Chapter 13, "Implementing the CSV Manager," we talked about comma-separated variable (CSV) files and how to import and export data. We talked at length about the JFileChooser class and its uses.

In Chapter 14, "Enhancing the Stock Tracker User Interface," we broke away from key functionality and talked about some of the things that make an application aesthetically pleasing: a splash screen, toolbars, and accelerator keys. Through this we talked about the following classes:

- Window
- Thread
- JToolBar

In this chapter, I introduced you to JavaBeans and the JDBC API. The JavaBeans technology is constantly evolving and will help you design highly scalable and very object-oriented applications. The future of JavaBeans has already evolved into what are known as Enterprise JavaBeans, which are JavaBeans that are fully distributed across a network. We talked about component models and why this technology is paramount to the future of application development.

I took you through an example using JDBC and (I hope) gave you enough information to inspire you to pursue this technology more on your own. Read through the Java 2 SDK documentation along with all the resources provided by the Sun Microsystems Web site—you will find this a great reference for the latest white papers and specifications.

You have a fully functional Stock Tracker application, but there are many things that you can still add to make it better. I suggest you play around more with the code and the Java 2 SDK documentation and see if you can implement those features we left placeholders for. A stock tracking application was quite an endeavor, and we completed enough for our first release! Good luck and happy programming!

Appendix A

Setting Up the Java 2 SDK

This appendix gives the procedures for setting up the Java 2 Development Kit (SDK) in either the Windows or Solaris operating systems.

Setting Up the SDK in Microsoft Windows

The following installation instructions are posted on the Sun Microsystems Web site at http://java.sun.com.

In this procedure, you will run the self-installing executable to unpack and install the Java Development Kit (SDK) software bundle on a Windows system. After that, you can install the SDK documentation bundle, or you can start using the newly installed SDK software.

The installation procedure has the following steps:

1. Run the SDK software installer.
2. Update the PATH variable.
3. Check the CLASSPATH variable (if upgrading).
4. Start using the SDK tools.

If you have any difficulties, see the "Troubleshooting the Installation" section at the end of this section.

Run the SDK Software Installer

The file jdk1_2_1-win.exe is the SDK software installer for the Windows platform. Double-click on the installer's icon in your CD-ROM root directory. Then follow the instructions the installer provides.

Note

If you already installed the documentation bundle, the docs directory was created in a location similar to c:\jdk1.2.1\docs. In that case, make sure you install the SDK software at c:\jdk1.2.1 to create the directory structure shown in Figure A.1. This step ensures that all the SDK software's HTML links work properly.

Windows 98

The installer will sometimes hang in Windows 98 if you choose a location to install the Runtime Environment that is different from the default directory suggested by the installer. If this happens to you, rerun the installer and accept the default installation location that it suggests.

Installed Directory Tree

After you install both the SDK software and documentation, the SDK directory will have the structure shown in Figure A.1. The docs directory is created when you install the SDK documentation bundle.

Figure A.1

The SDK installed directory tree for Windows.

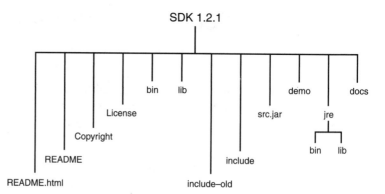

Update the PATH Variable

You can run the SDK software just fine without setting the PATH variable, or you can optionally set it as a convenience.

Should I Set the PATH Variable?

Set the PATH variable if you want to be able to conveniently run the SDK executables (javac.exe, java.exe, javadoc.exe, and so on) from any directory without having to type the full path of the command. If you don't set the PATH variable, you need to specify the full path to the executable every time you run it, as follows:

```
C:> \jdk1.2.1\bin\javac MyClass.java
```

It's useful to set the PATH permanently so it will persist after rebooting.

Setting the PATH Variable

To set the PATH permanently, add the full path of the jdk1.2.1\bin directory to the PATH variable. Typically, this full path looks something like C:\jdk1.2.1\bin. Set the PATH as shown in the following two sections, according to whether you are on Windows NT or Windows 95/98.

Windows NT: Setting the PATH Permanently

1. Start the Control Panel, select System, select Environment, and look for Path in the User Variables and System Variables. If you're not sure where to add the path, add it to the right end of the Path in the User Variables. A typical value for PATH is

   C:\jdk1.2.1\bin

 Note

> Capitalization doesn't matter. Click Set, OK, or Apply.
>
> The PATH can be a series of directories separated by semicolons (;). Microsoft Windows looks for programs in the PATH directories in order, from left to right. You should only have one bin directory for the SDK software in the path at a time (those following the first are ignored), so if one is already present, you can update it to 1.2.1.

2. The new path takes effect in each new command prompt window you open after setting the PATH variable.

Windows 98 and Windows 95: Setting the PATH Permanently

To set the PATH permanently, open the AUTOEXEC.BAT file and add or change the PATH statement as follows:

1. Start the system editor: Choose Start, Run, and enter sysedit, and then click OK. The system editor starts up with several windows showing. Go to the window that is displaying AUTOEXEC.BAT.

2. Look for the PATH statement. (If you don't have one, add one.) If you're not sure where to add the path, add it to the right end of the PATH. For example, in the following PATH statement, we have added the bin directory at the right end:

   PATH C:\WINDOWS;C:\WINDOWS\COMMAND;**C:\JDK1.2.1\BIN**

Capitalization doesn't matter. The PATH can be a series of directories separated by semicolons (;). Microsoft Windows searches for programs in the PATH directories in order, from left to right. You should only have one bin directory for the SDK software in the path at a time (those following the first are ignored), so if one is already present, you can update it to 1.2.1.

3. To make the path take effect in the current Command Prompt window, execute the following:

```
C:> c:\autoexec.bat
```

To find out the current value of your PATH in order to see if it took effect, at the command prompt type

```
C:> path
```

Check the CLASSPATH Variable (If Upgrading)

The CLASSPATH variable is one way to tell applications written in the Java programming language (including the SDK tools) where to look for user classes. (The -classpath command-line switch is the preferred way.) If you never set up the CLASSPATH variable for an earlier version of the SDK software, you can ignore this step. Otherwise, you might want to clean up your CLASSPATH settings, so read on.

Should I Modify the CLASSPATH Variable?

The way Java 2 SDK software works, you don't need to worry about the settings of the CLASSPATH variable. The SDK 1.2.1 release will work fine even if CLASSPATH is set for an earlier version of the SDK software. However, if your CLASSPATH contains classes.zip for an earlier SDK version, and you don't plan to continue using that version, you can remove that setting from the CLASSPATH now.

How Do I Modify the CLASSPATH?

Use the same procedure you used for the PATH variable in the previous step and do either of the following:

- Remove classes.zip from the CLASSPATH. (Leave any application-specific settings and the current directory, ".")

- Remove the CLASSPATH environment variable entirely. (With SDK 1.2.1, the default value is "." which is the current directory. For specific applications, you can use the -classpath command-line switch.)

Setting the CLASSPATH Variable

The classpath can be set using either the `-classpath` option when calling an SDK tool (the preferred method) or by setting the CLASSPATH environment variable. The `-classpath` option is preferred because you can set it individually for each application without affecting other applications and without other applications modifying its value; for example:

```
C:> sdkTool -classpath path1;path2...
```

or

```
C:> set CLASSPATH=path1;path2...
```

where `sdkTool` is a command-line tool, such as java, javac, or javadoc, and `path1;path2` are paths to the .jar, .zip, or .class files. Each path should end with a filename or directory depending on what you are setting the classpath to:

- For a .jar or .zip file that contains .class files, the path ends with the name of the .zip or .jar file.
- For .class files in an unnamed package, the path ends with the directory that contains the .class files.
- For .class files in a named package, the path ends with the directory that contains the root package (the first package in the full package name).

Multiple path entries are separated by semicolons. With the set command, it's important to omit spaces from around the equals sign (=).

The default classpath is the current directory. Setting the CLASSPATH variable or using the `-classpath` command-line option overrides that default, so if you want to include the current directory in the search path, you must include dot (.) in the new settings.

Classpath entries that are neither a directory nor an archive (.zip or .jar file) are ignored.

Description

The classpath tells Java tools and applications where to find third-party and user-defined classes; that is, classes that are not Java extensions or part of the Java platform. The classpath must find any classes you've compiled with the javac compiler—its default is the current directory to conveniently enable those classes to be found.

Java 2 SDK, the JVM, and other SDK tools find classes by searching the Java platform (bootstrap) classes, any extension classes, and the classpath, in that order. Class libraries for most applications will want to take advantage of the extensions mechanism. You must set the classpath only when you want to load a class that is not in the current directory or in any of its subdirectories and not in a location specified by the extensions mechanism.

If you are upgrading from an older version of the SDK, your startup settings might include CLASSPATH settings that are no longer needed. You should remove any settings that are not application-specific, such as classes.zip. Some third-party applications that use the Java Virtual Machine might modify your CLASSPATH environment variable to include the libraries they use. Such settings can remain.

You can change the classpath by using the Java tools' -classpath option when you invoke the JVM or other SDK tools or by using the CLASSPATH environment variable. Using the -classpath option is preferred over setting CLASSPATH environment variable because you can set it individually for each application without affecting other applications and without other applications modifying its value.

Classes can be stored either in directories (folders) or in archive files. The Java platform classes are stored in rt.jar.

Note

Older versions of the SDK included a `<sdk-dir>/classes` entry in the default classpath. That directory exists for use by the SDK and should not be used for application classes. Application classes should be placed in a directory outside the SDK. That way, installing a new SDK does not force you to reinstall application classes. For compatibility with older versions, applications that use the `<sdk-dir>/classes` directory as a class library will run in the current version, but there is no guarantee that they will run in future versions.

Using the Java Tools' `-classpath` Option

The Java tools java, jdb, javac, and javah have a -classpath option that replaces the path or paths specified by the CLASSPATH environment variable while the tool runs. This is the recommended option for changing classpath settings because each application can have the classpath it needs without interfering with any other application.

The runtime tools java and jdb have a -cp option, as well. This option is an abbreviation for -classpath.

For very special cases, both java and javac have options that let you change the path they use to find their own class libraries. The vast majority of users will never to need to use those options, however.

Using the CLASSPATH Environment Variable

In general, you will want to use the -classpath command-line option, as explained in the previous section. This section shows you how to set the CLASSPATH environment variable if you want to do that, or clear settings left over from a previous installation.

Setting CLASSPATH

The CLASSPATH environment variable is modified with the set command. The format is

```
set CLASSPATH=path1;path2 ...
```

The paths should begin with the letter specifying the drive; for example, C:\. That way, the classes will still be found if you happen to switch to a different drive. (If the path entries start with backslash (\) and you are on drive D:, for example, the classes will be expected on D: rather than C:.)

Clearing CLASSPATH

If your CLASSPATH environment variable has been set to a value that is not correct, or if your startup file or script is setting an incorrect path, you can unset CLASSPATH by using

```
C:> set CLASSPATH=
```

This command unsets CLASSPATH for the current command prompt window only. You should also delete or modify your startup settings to ensure that you have the right CLASSPATH settings in future sessions.

Changing Startup Settings

If the CLASSPATH variable is set at system startup, the place to look for it depends on your operating system:

Operating System	Method
Windows 95 and 98	Examine autoexec.bat for the set command.
Windows NT	Start the Control Panel, select System, click the Environment tab and, in the User Variables section, examine the CLASSPATH variable.

Understanding the Classpath and Package Names

Java classes are organized into packages that are mapped to directories in the file system. However, unlike the file system, whenever you specify a package name, you specify the whole package name—never part of it. For example, the package name for java.awt.Button is always specified as java.awt.

For example, suppose you want the Java runtime to find a class named `Cool.class` in the package `utility.myapp`. If the path to that directory is `C:\java\MyClasses\utility\myapp`, you would set the classpath so it contains `C:\java\MyClasses`. To run that application, you could use the following JVM command:

```
C:> java -classpath C:\java\MyClasses utility.myapp.Cool
```

When the application runs, the JVM uses the classpath settings to find any other classes defined in the `utility.myapp` package that are used by the `Cool` class.

Note that the entire package name is specified in the command. It is not possible, for example, to set the classpath so it contains `C:\java\MyClasses\utility` and use the command `java myapp.Cool` because the class would not be found. (You might be wondering what defines the package name for a class. The answer is that the package name is part of the class and cannot be modified, except by recompiling the class.)

 Note   An interesting consequence of the package specification mechanism is that files that are part of the same package might actually exist in different directories. The package name will be the same for each class, but the path to each file might start from a different directory in the classpath.

Folders and Archive Files

When classes are stored in a directory (folder), such as `c:\java\MyClasses\utility\myapp`, the classpath entry points to the directory that contains the first element of the package name (in this case, `C:\java\MyClasses` because the package name is `utility.myapp`). However, when classes are stored in an archive file (a .zip or .jar file) the classpath entry is the path to and including the .zip or .jar file. For example, to use a class library that is in a .jar file, the command would look something like this:

```
C:> java -classpath C:\java\MyClasses\myclasses.jar utility.myapp.Cool
```

Multiple Specifications

To find class files in the directory `C:\java\MyClasses` as well as classes in `C:\java\OtherClasses`, you would set the classpath to

```
C:> java -classpath C:\java\MyClasses;C:\java\OtherClasses ...
```

Note that the two paths are separated by a semicolon.

Specification Order

The order in which you specify multiple classpath entries is important. The Java interpreter will look for classes in the directories in the order they appear in the classpath variable. In the preceding example, the Java interpreter will first look for a needed class in the directory C:\java\MyClasses. Only if it doesn't find a class with the proper name in that directory will the interpreter look in the C:\java\OtherClasses directory.

Start Using the SDK Tools

Your Windows computer system should now be ready to use the Java Development Kit. In this step, you'll run some simple commands to make sure it is working properly.

You start the compiler, interpreter, or other tool by typing its name into the Command Prompt window, generally with a filename as an argument. The SDK development tools need to be run from the command line and have no GUI interfaces (except AppletViewer). Double-clicking a tool's file icon, such as java.exe, will not do anything useful. To get started, open the DOS Prompt window (on 95 or 98) or Command Prompt window (on NT) if you haven't already done so.

You can specify the path to a tool either by typing the path in front of the tool each time, or by adding the path to the system as in the previous step. The following assumes the SDK software is installed at C:\jdk1.2.1 and you have set the path variable. (If you have not, add **C:\jdk1.2.1\bin** ahead of the javac and AppletViewer commands.)

Compiling a Java Class

To run the compiler on a file HelloWorldApp.java, go to the prompt window and execute the following:

```
C:> javac HelloWorldApp.java
```

Running Applets

You can run applets in AppletViewer. Here's an example (you must install the examples with the Java 2 SDK):

- Use cd to change to the TicTacToe directory that contains the html file example1.html that embeds an applet:

  ```
  C:> cd \jdk1.2.1\demo\applets\TicTacToe
  ```

- Run AppletViewer with the following html file:

  ```
  C:> appletviewer example1.html
  ```

  This example lets you interactively play Tic-Tac-Toe.

Refer to the "Troubleshooting" section for this topic if you have problems running the SDK software.

Where Do I Go from Here?

At this point, you will probably want to install the documentation bundle, if you have not already done so. Although you can use the SDK tools without installing the documentation, it makes sense to install it if you are going to do any extensive work. You can find the SDK documentation bundle and complete installation instructions on the CD-ROM in the docs folder.

You can also go to the following sites:

- Documentation for the SDK tools:

    http://java.sun.com/products/jdk/1.2/docs/tooldocs/tools.html

    For descriptions of the SDK tools you used in the previous step to test the installation, as well as the other SDK tools. This version is on the Web site. After you install the documentation bundle, the same document is available at jdk1.2.1\docs\tooldocs\tools.html.

- Java Plug-in Web site:

    http://java.sun.com/products/plugin

    If you installed this plug-in, both Internet Explorer and Netscape Navigator will use this plug-in when encountering HTML pages with special <OBJECT> and <EMBED> tags that invoke it. For details on how to configure your HTML pages, click the Java Plug-in Web site link, and then click Documentation and Java Plug-In HTML Specification.

Troubleshooting the Installation

If you see the following error messages:

```
net.socketException: errno = 10047
```

or

```
Unsupported version of Windows Socket API
```

Check which TCP/IP drivers you have installed. The AppletViewer supports only the Microsoft TCP/IP drivers included with Windows 95. If you are using third-party drivers (for example, Trumpet Winsock), you'll need to change over to the native Microsoft TCP/IP drivers if you want to load applets over the network.

If you see the following error message:

```
System Error during Decompression
```

You might not have enough space on the disk that contains your TEMP directory.

If you see the following error message:

```
This program cannot be run in DOS mode.
```

Do the following:

1. Open the MS-DOS shell (Windows/Start/Programs/MS-DOS Prompt).
2. Right-click on the title bar.
3. Select Properties.
4. Choose the Program tab.
5. Select the Advanced button.
6. Make sure the item Prevent MS-DOS-Based Programs from Detecting Windows is unchecked.
7. Select OK.
8. Select OK again.
9. Exit the MS-DOS shell.
10. Restart your computer.

If the AppletViewer does not load applets, you might try the following:

1. Type the following and restart the AppletViewer (in the same Command Prompt window):

   ```
   set HOMEDRIVE=c:
   set HOMEPATH=\
   ```

2. Type the following and restart the AppletViewer (in the same Command Prompt window):

   ```
   set HOME=c:\
   ```

3. If none of these work, try

   ```
   java -verbose sun.applet.AppletViewer
   ```

   This lists the classes that are being loaded. From this output, you can determine which class the AppletViewer is trying to load and where it's trying to load it from. Check to make sure that the class exists and is not corrupted in some way.

AppletViewer Locks Up

This happens with NT Workstation 4.0, update 3, where the DISPLAY is configured for "true color." The AppletViewer (and perhaps other entities) will lock up and then freeze the system by consuming 100 percent of your CPU.

To test this, type `java -verbose sun.applet.AppletView` and notice that it locks up when it tries to run the `MToolkit.class`.

Winsock Issues

SDK software no longer includes Microsoft Winsock 2.0. It is extremely likely that your system already has Winsock 2.0. Windows NT 4.0 and Windows 98 operating platforms come with Winsock 2.0. The Windows 95 operating platform comes with Winsock 1.1 or 1.2, but most Windows 95 systems have been upgraded to Winsock 2.0 by now.

To check which version of Winsock you have, search for winsock.dll. Then choose Properties from the File menu and click the Version tab.

Microsoft provides a free software bundle, the Microsoft Windows Sockets 2.0 Software Development Kit, that includes Winsock 2.0. Even if you don't need to upgrade your own system, you might want to obtain this kit so you can deploy network applications on Windows 95 systems. For more information, see the JRE README.

Creating Source Files in Notepad

In Windows Notepad, to save a file with the .java extension, you have to type the new file name with the .java extension in the File Name field and choose All Files in the Save as Type pop-up menu. If you specify one but not the other, your file will be saved as filename.java.txt. Each subsequent time you save the file, you must choose All Files in the Save as Type option.

Setting Up the SDK in Solaris

In this procedure, you will run the self-installing executable to unpack and install the SDK software bundle on a Solaris system. After that, you can install the SDK documentation bundle, or you can start using the newly installed SDK.

The installation procedure has the following steps:

1. If necessary, install Solaris patches.
2. Change to the directory you want to install into.
3. Unpack the SDK.
4. Update the `PATH` variable.
5. Check the `CLASSPATH` variable (if upgrading).
6. Start using the SDK.

If you have any difficulties, see the "Troubleshooting the Installation" section at the end of this chapter.

If Necessary, Install Solaris Patches

Go to the following page to determine which patches your system needs and to install them:

```
http://java.sun.com/products/jdk/1.2/install-solaris-patches.html
```

Change to the Directory You Want to Install Into

For example, if you want to install the software in the /usr/local/ directory, execute the following:

```
% cd /usr/local
```

Unbundling the software in the next step automatically creates a directory called jdk1.2.1.

You should unbundle the SDK software bundle and the SDK documentation bundle in the same directory. Unbundling them in the same directory ensures that HTML links between them will work properly. You can download and install the software bundle and the documentation bundle in either order.

Unpack the SDK

If you unpack the software or documentation in a directory that contains a subdirectory named jdk1.2.1, the new software will overwrite files of the same name in that jdk1.2.1 directory. Please be careful to rename the old directory if it contains files you would like to keep.

In a shell window, execute the following commands. Specify <path> to the download bundle, which can be a dot "." if installing into the current directory.

- For SPARC:
  ```
  % chmod a+x jdk1_2_1-solsparc.sh
  % <path>/jdk1_2_1-solsparc.sh
  ```

- For x86:
  ```
  % chmod a+x jdk1_2_1-solx86.sh
  % <path>/jdk1_2_1-solx86.sh
  ```

After you agree to the license, a directory called jdk1.2.1 is created and the software is installed into it.

SDK Directory Tree

After you install both the SDK software and documentation, the SDK directory will have the structure in Figure A.2. The docs directory is created when you install the SDK documentation bundle.

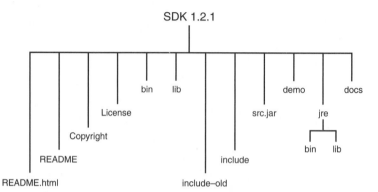

Update the PATH Variable

You can run the SDK just fine without setting the PATH variable, or you can optionally set it as a convenience.

Should I Set the PATH Variable?

Set the path variable if you want to be able to run the executables (javac, java, javadoc, and so on) from any directory without having to type the full path of the command. If you don't set the PATH variable, you need to specify the full path to the executable every time you run it, such as:

```
% /usr/local/jdk1.2.1/bin/javac MyClass.java
```

Is the PATH Already Set?

To find out whether the path is currently set for any java tools, execute the following command:

```
% which java
```

This will print the path to the java tool, if it can find it. If the PATH is not set properly, you will get the following error:

```
% java: Command not found
```

How do I Set the PATH Permanently?

To set the path permanently, set the path in your startup file.

- For C shell (csh), edit the startup file (~/.cshrc):

```
set path=($path /usr/local/jdk1.2.1/bin)
```

- For ksh, bash, or sh, edit the profile file (~/.profile):

```
PATH=$PATH:/usr/local/jdk1.2.1/bin
```

Then load the startup file and verify that the path is set by repeating the which command:

- For C shell (csh):

```
% source ~/.cshrc
% which java
```

- For ksh, bash, or sh:

```
$ . $HOME/.profile
$ which java
```

Check the CLASSPATH Variable (If Upgrading)

The CLASSPATH variable is one way to tell Java applications (including the SDK tools) where to look for user classes. (The -classpath command-line switch is the preferred way.) If you never set up the CLASSPATH variable for an earlier version of the SDK, you can ignore this step. Otherwise, you might want to clean up your CLASSPATH settings, so read on.

Should I Modify the CLASSPATH Variable?

The way the Java 2 SDK, version 1.2.1 works, you don't need to worry about the settings of the CLASSPATH variable. The SDK will work fine even if CLASSPATH is set for an earlier version of the SDK. However, if your CLASSPATH contains classes.zip for an earlier SDK version, and you don't plan to continue using that version, you can remove that setting from the CLASSPATH now.

How do I Modify the CLASSPATH?

Use the same procedure you used for the PATH variable in the previous step and do either of the following:

- Remove classes.zip from the CLASSPATH (leave any application-specific settings and the current directory, ".").

- Remove the CLASSPATH environment variable entirely. (With SDK 1.2.1, the default value is "." [the current directory]. For specific applications, you can use the -classpath command-line switch.)

For more information, see "Setting the Classpath."

Setting the Classpath

The classpath can be set using either the -classpath option when calling an SDK tool (the preferred method) or by setting the CLASSPATH environment variable. The -classpath option is preferred because you can set it individually for each application without affecting other applications and without other applications modifying its value.

```
% jdkTool -classpath path1:path2...
```

or

```
% setenv CLASSPATH path1:path2...
```

where jdkTool is a command-line tool, such as java, javac, or javadoc, and path1:path2 are paths to the .jar, .zip, or .class files. Each path should end with a filename or directory depending on what you are setting the classpath to:

- For a .jar or .zip file that contains .class files, the path ends with the name of the .zip or .jar file.
- For .class files in an unnamed package, the path ends with the directory that contains the .class files.
- For .class files in a named package, the path ends with the directory that contains the "root" package (the first package in the full package name).

Multiple path entries are separated by semicolons. With the set command, it's important to omit spaces from around the equals sign (=) .

The default classpath is the current directory. Setting the CLASSPATH variable or using the -classpath command-line option overrides that default, so if you want to include the current directory in the search path, you must include a dot (.) in the new settings.

Classpath entries that are neither a directory nor an archive (.zip or .jar file) are ignored.

Description

The classpath tells Java tools and applications where to find third-party and user-defined classes; that is, classes that are not Java extensions or part of the Java platform. The classpath must find any classes you've compiled with the javac compiler—its default is the current directory to conveniently enable those classes to be found.

The Java 2 SDK, the JVM, and other SDK tools find classes by searching the Java platform (bootstrap) classes, any extension classes, and the classpath, in that order. Class libraries for most applications will want to take advantage of the extensions mechanism. You must set the classpath only when you want to load a class that's not in the current directory or in any of its subdirectories, and not in a location specified by the extensions mechanism.

If you are upgrading from an older version of the SDK, your startup settings can include CLASSPATH settings that are no longer needed. You should remove any settings that are not application-specific, such as classes.zip. Some third-party applications that use the Java Virtual Machine might modify your CLASSPATH environment variable to include the libraries they use. Such settings can remain.

You can change the classpath by using the Java tools' -classpath option when you invoke the JVM or other SDK tools or by using the CLASSPATH environment variable. Using the -classpath option is preferred over setting CLASSPATH environment variable because you can set it individually for each application without affecting other applications and without other applications modifying its value.

Classes can be stored either in directories (folders) or in archive files. The Java platform classes are stored in rt.jar. For more details on archives and information on how the classpath works, see "Understanding the Classpath and Package Names," later in this chapter.

> **Note** Older versions of the SDK included a <jdk-dir>/classes entry in the default classpath. That directory exists for use by the SDK and should not be used for application classes. Application classes should be placed in a directory outside the SDK. That way, installing a new SDK does not force you to reinstall application classes. For compatibility with older versions, applications that use the <jdk-dir>/classes directory as a class library will run in the current version, but there is no guarantee that they will run in future versions.

Using the Java Tools' -classpath Option

The Java tools java, jdb, javac, and javah have a -classpath option that replaces the path or paths specified by the CLASSPATH environment variable while the tool runs. This is the recommended option for changing classpath settings because each application can have the classpath it needs without interfering with any other application.

The runtime tools java and jdb have a `-cp` option, as well. This option is an abbreviation for `-classpath`.

For very special cases, both java and javac have options that let you change the path they use to find their own class libraries. The vast majority of users will never to need to use those options, however.

Using the CLASSPATH Environment Variable

In general, you will want to use the `-classpath` command-line option, as explained in the previous section. This section shows you how to set the CLASSPATH environment variable if you want to do that, or clear settings left over from a previous installation.

Setting CLASSPATH

In csh, the CLASSPATH environment variable is modified with the `setenv` command. The format is

```
setenv CLASSPATH path1:path2
```

In sh, the CLASSPATH environment variable can be modified with these commands:

```
CLASSPATH = path1:path2:...
export CLASSPATH
```

Clearing CLASSPATH

If your CLASSPATH environment variable has been set to an incorrect value, or if your startup file or script is setting an incorrect path, you can unset CLASSPATH in csh by using

```
unsetenv CLASSPATH
```

In sh, you would use

```
unset CLASSPATH
```

These commands unset CLASSPATH for the current shell only. You should also delete or modify your startup settings to ensure that you have the right CLASSPATH settings in future sessions.

Changing Startup Settings

If the CLASSPATH variable is set at system startup, the place to look for it depends on the shell you are running (see Table A.1).

Table A.1   Shell Startup Scripts

Shell	Startup Script
csh, tcsh	Examine your .cshrc file for the setenv command.
sh, ksh	Examine your .profile file for the export command.

Understanding the Classpath and Package Names

Java classes are organized into packages that are mapped to directories in the file system. However, unlike the file system, whenever you specify a package name, you specify the whole package name—never part of it. For example, the package name for java.awt.Button is always specified as java.awt.

For example, suppose you want the Java runtime to find a class named Cool.class in the package utility.myapp. If the path to that directory is /java/MyClasses/ utility/myapp, you would set the classpath so that it contains /java/MyClasses.

To run that application, you could use the following JVM command:

```
% java -classpath /java/MyClasses utility.myapp.Cool
```

When the app runs, the JVM uses the classpath settings to find any other classes defined in the utility.myapp package that are used by the Cool class.

Note that the entire package name is specified in the command. It is not possible, for example, to set the classpath so it contains /java/MyClasses/utility and use the command java myapp.Cool. The class would not be found. (You might be wondering what defines the package name for a class. The answer is that the package name is part of the class and cannot be modified except by recompiling the class.)

> **Note**   An interesting consequence of the package specification mechanism is that files which are part of the same package can actually exist in different directories. The package name will be the same for each class, but the path to each file might start from a different directory in the classpath.

Folders and Archive Files

When classes are stored in a directory (folder), such as /java/MyClasses/utility/myapp, the classpath entry points to the directory that contains the first element of the package name (in this case, /java/MyClasses because the package name is utility.myapp). However, when classes are stored in an archive file (a .zip or .jar file), the classpath entry is the path to and including the .zip or .jar file. For example, to use a class library that is in a .jar file, the command would look something like this:

```
% java -classpath /java/MyClasses/myclasses.jar utility.myapp.Cool
```

Multiple Specifications

To find class files in the directory /java/MyClasses as well as classes in /java/OtherClasses, you would set the classpath to

```
% java -classpath /java/MyClasses:/java/OtherClasses ...
```

Note that the two paths are separated by a colon.

Specification Order

The order in which you specify multiple classpath entries is important. The Java interpreter will look for classes in the directories in the order they appear in the classpath variable. In the preceding example, the Java interpreter will first look for a needed class in the directory /java/MyClasses. Only if it doesn't find a class with the proper name in that directory will the interpreter look in the /java/OtherClasses directory.

Start Using the SDK

Your Solaris computer system should now be ready to use the Java Development Kit. In this step, you'll run some simple commands to make sure it is working properly.

You start the compiler, interpreter, or other tool by typing its name at the shell window command line, generally with a filename as an argument. The SDK development tools need to be run from the command line and have no GUI interfaces (except AppletViewer). Double-clicking a tool's file icon, such as java, will not do anything useful.

You can specify the path to a tool either by typing the path in front of the tool each time, or by adding the path to the system as in the previous step. The following assumes the SDK is installed at /usr/local/jdk1.2.1, and you have set the path variable. (If you have not, add /usr/local/jdk1.2.1 ahead of the javac and AppletViewer commands.)

Compiling a Java Class

To run the compiler on a file MyClass.java, go to the prompt window and execute this:

```
% javac MyClass.java
```

Running Applets

You can run applets in AppletViewer. Here's an example:

- Use `cd` to change to the TicTacToe directory that contains the html file example1.html that embeds an applet:

  ```
  % cd jdk1.2.1/demo/applets/TicTacToe
  ```

- Run AppletViewer with the HTML file:

  ```
  % appletviewer example1.html
  ```

  This example lets you interactively play Tic-Tac-Toe.

Refer to the Troubleshooting section for this topic if you have problems running the SDK.

Where Do I Go from Here?

At this point, you will probably want to install the documentation bundle, if you have not already done so. Although you can use the SDK tools without installing the documentation, it makes sense to do so if you are going to do any extensive work. You can find the SDK documentation bundle and complete installation instructions on the CD-ROM in the `docs` folder.

You can also go to the following sites:

- Documentation for the SDK tools:

  ```
  http://java.sun.com/products/jdk/1.2/docs/tooldocs/tools.html
  ```

  Descriptions of the SDK tools you used in the previous step to test the installation, as well as the other SDK tools. This version is on the Web site. After you install the documentation bundle, the same document is available at

  ```
  jdk1.2.1\docs\tooldocs\tools.html.
  ```

- Java Plug-in Web site:

  ```
  http://java.sun.com/products/plugin
  ```

  If you installed this plug-in, both Internet Explorer and Netscape Navigator will use this plug-in when encountering HTML pages with special `<OBJECT>` and `<EMBED>` tags that invoke it. For details on how to configure your HTML pages, click the Java Plug-in Web site link, and then click Documentation and Java Plug-In HTML Specification.

Troubleshooting the Installation

If you get the following error message

```
The download file appears to be corrupted.
```

The SDK's installation script does a checksum to ensure that the software bundle was not corrupted during the download. If the checksum indicates that your file is corrupted, delete the file and download a new copy.

Appendix B

Third-Party Development Environments

The Java 2 SDK version 1.2.1, included on this book's CD, provides all the tools you will need to develop Java 2 applications. However, development with the SDK alone can be difficult. The reason for this difficulty is that the SDK consists of only command-line tools; you must choose your own editor. For many of you, that may be as simple as opening Notepad, entering the code, saving the file, going to the command line, and executing the compiler (javac). Then you launch your application with the Java runtime engine (java). Furthermore, if you need to debug an application, you are forced to use a text-based debugger; I don't know if you have ever tried this, but in comparison to today's integrated development environment debuggers, it is a headache!

Because of this, third parties have developed their own integrated set of tools. Using these, you can enter your source code in an environment that will do a lot of formatting for you and highlight keywords. You can compile the application in the same environment, you can launch the application from the same environment, and finally, you have a visual debugger. A visual debugger is simple to use and incredibly effective in finding problems in your code.

A visual debugger lets you set breakpoints at certain lines in your code. You then launch your application through the debugger, and when that line of code is reached, the debugger stops execution and allows you to step through your program, line by line. Furthermore, you can see the values of all of your variables, of the computer's registers, and so on. Basically, I would not recommend trying to debug an application rapidly without a visual debugger.

The following sections list some third-party debuggers that Sun Microsystems has listed as compatible with Java 2. They include the operating systems that the tools support. You can refer to Sun's Web site for an up-to-date list of supported development environments:

```
http://java.sun.com/products/jdk/1.2/index.html
```

Inprise JBuilder

Inprise JBuilder has three JBuilder Products that support Java 2:

- JBuilder 3 Standard
- JBuilder 3 Professional
- JBuilder 3 Enterprise

Each runs on Windows 95/98/NT platforms.

You can find JBuilder at

```
http://www.borland.com/jbuilder
```

Sybase PowerJ

Sybase PowerJ 3.0 runs on Windows 95/98/NT platforms.

You can find PowerJ at

```
http://www.sybase.com/products/powerj
```

Symantec Visual Café

Symantec Visual Café has three products that support Java 2:

- Visual Café Standard Edition 3.0
- Visual Café Professional Edition 3.0
- Visual Café Database Edition 3.0

Each runs on Windows 95/98/NT platforms.

You can find Visual Café at

```
http://www.symantec.com/domain/cafe/vcafe30.html
```

NetBeans Developer

NetBeans Developer X2.2.1 is a Java-based IDE, and is therefore platform-independent. At the time of this writing, they claim it will work on Windows 95/98/NT and Solaris. It requires a platform that supports Java 2, so as Java 2 appears on other operating systems, Developer X2 will run on them.

Furthermore, take a look at NetBeans' non-commercial licensing policy:

```
http://www.netbeans.com/non_commercial.html
```

At the time this book was printed, this policy states that they allow the free use of the software for noncommercial purposes—including educational and evaluation purposes.

Take a look at their forthcoming Gandalf IDE and their NetBeans Enterprise products while you are there.

NetBeans can be found at

```
http://www.netbeans.com
```

B

Oracle JDeveloper

Oracle's JDeveloper Suite 2.0 runs on Windows NT. It is aimed more at enterprise development and includes a suite of powerful tools. JDeveloper actually results from Oracle's licensing of Inprise JBuilder and subsequently adding advanced Oracle database capabilities. Therefore, if you are familiar with JBuilder, your transition to JDeveloper will be virtually automatic.

JDeveloper can be found at

```
http://www.oracle.com/tools/jdeveloper
```

Metrowerks CodeWarrior Professional

Metrowerks has released CodeWarrior Professional for Java. It is a multiplatform development toolset that supports Java 2 for Macintosh, Windows, and Solaris as well as platform-specific versions.

You can find CodeWarrior Professional at

```
http://www.metrowerks.com
```

Java Resources

This book is a great reference to get you started on your Java programming career, but where do you go from here? This appendix lists some of the resources that are at your disposal as a Java developer. Wherever possible, I tried to find you resources that do not have an associated cost with them—the Internet is a beautiful thing!

Web Sites

The following Web sites are great sources for Java information. Each of these sites should lead you to additional information.

Sun Microsystems

Probably the best Web site to look at is Sun Microsystems; they invented Java and set the standard, so they are best suited to give you up-to-date and thorough information.

You can find Sun's Java Web site at

```
http://java.sun.com
```

Java Developer Connection (JDC)

The Java Developer Connection, part of Sun Microsystems, is a great place to go for Java information and discussions. They also publish a newsletter that gives tips and industry information.

You can find the Java Developer Connection at

```
http://developer.java.sun.com/developer/jdchome.html
```

Java Lobby

Join over 38,000 members at the Java Lobby, where you can participate in Java discussions and sign up for email list servers at

`http://www.javalobby.org`

Newsgroups

Check the following Java newsgroups:

- `comp.lang.java.advocacy`
- `comp.lang.java.announce`
- `comp.lang.java.api`
- `comp.lang.java.beans`
- `comp.lang.java.corba`
- `comp.lang.java.databases`
- `comp.lang.java.gui`
- `comp.lang.java.help`
- `comp.lang.java.machine`
- `comp.lang.java.misc`
- `comp.lang.java.programmer`
- `comp.lang.java.security`
- `comp.lang.java.setup`
- `comp.lang.java.softwaretools`
- `comp.lang. java.tech`

Books

The following sections show links to electronic books that you can read online.

Macmillan Computer Publishing

Want a plethora of good material to read? Want a good subset of that material available free over the Internet? Check out the Web site of Macmillan Computer Publishing (the publisher of this fine book). This site enables you to browse through Macmillan's forthcoming and new releases as well as provides you with more than 200 electronic books (at print time).

This site is an invaluable resource that you are wasting if you are not taking advantage of it.

You can find Macmillan Computer Publishing at

`http://www.mcp.com`

The Java Tutorial

The Java Tutorial is well-written and provides a plethora of Java development information—updated to support Java 2. Provided as an online resource by Sun Microsystems, it can be found at

`http://java.sun.com/docs/books/tutorial`

Thinking in Java

Read the Prentice-Hall book that Software Development Magazine gave its productivity award to in 1999. Bruce Eckel is a master developer whose *Thinking in C++* changed the way many C++ developers thought about their language! He has now finished his book *Thinking in Java*, which would be of benefit to any aspiring Java developer.

You can find *Thinking in Java*, in its electronic form, at

`http://www.eckelobjects.com/javabook.html`

Java Look and Feel Design Guidelines

The Java Look and Feel Design Guidelines, straight from Sun Microsystems, are available on the Internet at

`http://java.sun.com/products/jlf`

The *Java Language Specification*

The *Java Language Specification* is an early release from Sun that describes the initial versions of Java. A bit outdated but still a decent Internet reference, it's available free at

`http://java.sun.com/docs/books/jls/html/index.html`

Magazines

The following magazines have good online resources.

Java Developer's Journal

Find out more about this online and printed publication at

```
http://www.sys-con.com/java/index2.html
```

JavaWorld

JavaWorld is IDG's magazine for the Java community:

```
http://wwww.javaworld.com
```

Java Report Online

The *Java Report Online* provides up-to-date product information, the latest in Java techniques, as well as all the listings that appear in the printed version of *Java Report*:

```
http://www.javareport.com
```

Java Pro

Java Pro provides practical Java information and techniques for enterprise developers:

```
http://www.java-pro.com
```

Focus on Java

Compiled Web information and links to great references—some other online books too—can be found at

```
http://java.miningco.com
```

Index

Get **FREE** books and more...when you register this book online for our Personal Bookshelf Program

http://register.quecorp.com/

 Register online and you can sign up for our *FREE Personal Bookshelf Program...*unlimited access to the electronic version of more than 200 complete computer books—immediately! That means you'll have 100,000 pages of valuable information onscreen, at your fingertips!

 Plus, you can access product support, including complimentary downloads, technical support files, book-focused links, companion Web sites, author sites, and more!

 And you'll be automatically registered to receive a *FREE subscription to a weekly email newsletter* to help you stay current with news, announcements, sample book chapters, and special events, including sweepstakes, contests, and various product giveaways!

 We value your comments! Best of all, the entire registration process takes only a few minutes to complete, so go online and get the greatest value going—absolutely FREE!

Don't Miss Out On This Great Opportunity!

QUE® is a brand of Macmillan Computer Publishing USA.

For more information, please visit *www.mcp.com*

What's on the Disc

The companion CD-ROM contains many useful third-party software, plus all the source code from the book.

Windows 95/98 Installation Instructions

1. Insert the CD-ROM disc into your CD-ROM drive.
2. From the Windows 95 desktop, double-click the My Computer icon.
3. Double-click the icon representing your CD-ROM drive.
4. Double-click the icon titled START.EXE to run the program.

Note If Windows 95 is installed on your computer and you have the AutoPlay feature enabled, the START.EXE program starts automatically whenever you insert the disc into your CD-ROM drive.

Windows NT Installation Instructions

1. Insert the CD-ROM disc into your CD-ROM drive.
2. From File Manager or Program Manager, choose Run from the File menu.
3. Type <drive>\START.EXE and press Enter, where <drive> corresponds to the drive letter of your CD-ROM. For example, if your CD-ROM is drive D:, type D:\START.EXE and press Enter.

NetBeans DeveloperX2 2.1 Binary Code License Agreement

PLEASE READ THIS DOCUMENT CAREFULLY. BY INSTALLING THE SOFTWARE, YOU ARE AGREEING TO BECOME BOUND BY THE TERMS OF THIS AGREEMENT. IF YOU DO NOT AGREE TO THE TERMS OF THE AGREEMENT, PLEASE DO NOT INSTALL THE SOFTWARE.

This is a legal agreement between you and NetBeans, Inc. ("NetBeans"). This Agreement states the terms and conditions upon which NetBeans offers to license the software installed from the attached CD together with all related documentation and accompanying items including, but not limited to, the executable programs, drivers, libraries and data files associated with such programs (collectively, the "Software").

1. License. NetBeans grants to you ("Licensee") a nonexclusive, nontransferable, world-wide, royalty-free license to use this version of the Software for non-commercial and educational purposes.

2. Copyright. The Software is owned by NetBeans and is protected by United States copyright laws and international treaty provisions. You may not remove the copyright notice from any copy of the Software or any copy of the written materials, if any, accompanying the Software.

3. One Archival Copy. You may make one (1) archival copy of the machine-readable portion of the Software for backup purposes only in support of your use of the Software on a single computer, provided that you reproduce on the copy all copyright and other proprietary rights notices included on the originals of the Software.

4. Transfer of License. You may not transfer your license of the Software to a third party.

5. Decompiling, Disassembling, or Reverse Engineering. You acknowledge that the Software contains trade secrets and other proprietary information of NetBeans and its licensors. Except to the extent expressly permitted by this Agreement or by the laws of the jurisdiction where you are located, you may not decompile, disassemble or otherwise reverse engineer the Software, or engage in any other activities to obtain underlying information that is not visible to the user in connection with normal use of the Software. In particular, you agree not for any purpose to transmit the Software or display the Software's object code on any computer screen or to make any hard copy memory dumps of the Software's object code. If you believe you require information related to the interoperability of the Software with other programs, you shall not decompile or disassemble the Software to obtain such information, and you agree to request such information from NetBeans. Upon receiving

continues on previous page

continued from next page

such a request, NetBeans shall determine whether you require such information for a legitimate purpose and, if so, NetBeans will provide such information to you within a reasonable time and on reasonable conditions. In any event, you will notify NetBeans of any information derived from reverse engineering or such other activities, and the results thereof will constitute the confidential information of NetBeans that may be used only in connection with the Software.

6. Termination. The license granted to you is effective until terminated. You may terminate it at any time by destroying the Software (including any portions or copies thereof) currently in your possession or control. The license will also terminate automatically without any notice from NetBeans if you fail to comply with any term or condition of this Agreement. You agree upon any such termination to destroy the Software (including any portions or copies thereof). Upon termination, NetBeans may also enforce any and all rights provided by law. The provisions of this Agreement that protect the proprietary rights of NetBeans will continue in force after termination.

7. NO WARRANTY. ANY USE BY YOU OF THE SOFTWARE IS AT YOUR OWN RISK. THE SOFTWARE IS PROVIDED FOR USE "AS IS" WITHOUT WARRANTY OF ANY KIND. TO THE MAXIMUM EXTENT PERMITTED BY LAW, NetBeans DISCLAIMS ALL WARRANTIES OF ANY KIND, EITHER EXPRESS OR IMPLIED, INCLUDING, WITHOUT LIMITATION, IMPLIED WARRANTIES OR CONDITIONS OF MERCHANTABILITY AND FITNESS FOR A PARTICULAR PURPOSE.

NetBeans does not warrant that the functions contained in the Software will meet your requirements or that the operation of the Software will be uninterrupted or error-free. Any representation, other than the warranties set forth in this Agreement, will not bind NetBeans. You assume full responsibility for the selection of the Software to achieve your intended results, and for the downloading, use and results obtained from the Software. You also assume the entire risk as it applies to the quality and performance of the Software.

This warranty gives you specific legal rights, and you may also have other rights which vary from country/state to country/state. Some countries/states do not allow the exclusion of implied warranties, so the above exclusion may not apply to you.

continues on previous page

continued from next page

8. NO LIABILITY FOR DAMAGES, INCLUDING WITHOUT LIMITATION CONSEQUENTIAL DAMAGES. In no event shall NetBeans or its Licensors be liable for any damages whatsoever (including, without limitation, incidental, direct, indirect, special or consequential damages, damages for loss of business profits, business interruption, loss of business information, or other pecuniary loss) arising out of the use or inability to use this Software, even if NetBeans or its Licensors have been advised of the possibility of such damages. Because some states/ countries do not allow the exclusion or limitation of liability for consequential or incidental damages, the above limitation may not apply to you.

9. INDEMNIFICATION BY YOU. If you distribute the Software in violation of this Agreement, you hereby indemnify, hold harmless and defend NetBeans from and against any and all claims or lawsuits, including attorney's fees and costs that arise, result from or are connected with the use or distribution of the Software in violation of this Agreement.

10. GENERAL. This Agreement is binding on you as well as your employees, employers, contractors and agents, and on any successors and assignees. Neither the Software nor any information derived therefrom may be exported except in accordance with the laws of the U.S. or other applicable provisions. This Agreement is governed by the laws of the Czech Republic. This Agreement is the entire agreement between you and NetBeans and you agree that NetBeans will not have any liability for any untrue statement or representation made by its, its agents or anyone else (whether innocently or negligently) upon which you relied upon entering this Agreement, unless such untrue statement or representation was made fraudulently. This Agreement supersedes any other understandings or agreements, including, but not limited to, advertising, with respect to the Software.

If any provision of this Agreement is deemed invalid or unenforceable by any country or government agency having jurisdiction, that particular provision will be deemed modified to the extent necessary to make the provision valid and enforceable, and the remaining provisions will remain in full force and effect.

For questions concerning this Agreement, please contact NetBeans at info@netbeans.com.